UNITED STATES ARMY IN WORLD WAR II

The Technical Services

THE SIGNAL CORPS: THE EMERGENCY

(To December 1941)

by

Dulany Terrett

MILITARY INSTRVCTION

OFFICE OF THE CHIEF OF MILITARY HISTORY

DEPARTMENT OF THE ARMY

WASHINGTON, D. C., 1956

Copyright 1956 by Albert C. Smith

Library of Congress Catalog Card Number: 56–60002

For sale by the Superintendent of Documents, U. S. Government Printing Office
Washington 25, D. C. — Price of this volume $3.50 (Cloth)

UNITED STATES ARMY IN WORLD WAR II

Kent Roberts Greenfield, General Editor*

Advisory Committee
(As of 1 December 1954)

James P. Baxter
President, Williams College

Samuel Flagg Bemis
Yale University

Gordon A. Craig
Princeton University

Elmer Ellis
University of Missouri

William T. Hutchinson
University of Chicago

Brig. Gen. Samuel G. Conley
Army Field Forces

Brig. Gen. Thomas W. Dunn
Army War College

Brig. Gen. Charles E. Beauchamp
Command and General Staff College

Brig. Gen. Urban Niblo
Industrial College of the Armed Forces

Col. Thomas D. Stamps
United States Military Academy

Charles H. Taylor
Harvard University

Office of the Chief of Military History
Maj. Gen. Albert C. Smith, Chief**

Chief Historian

Chief, War Histories Division

Chief, Editorial and Publication Division

Chief, Editorial Branch

Chief, Cartographic Branch

Chief, Photographic Branch

Kent Roberts Greenfield

Col. Ridgway P. Smith, Jr.

Lt. Col. T. E. Bennett

Joseph R. Friedman

Wsevolod Aglaimoff

Maj. Arthur T. Lawry

---

*General Editor of the Technical Service volumes, Lt. Col. Leo J. Meyer, Deputy Chief Historian.

**Maj. Gen. Orlando Ward was succeeded by General Smith on 1 February 1953.

iii

History of

THE SIGNAL CORPS

The Emergency
The Test
The Outcome

This volume, one of the series UNITED STATES ARMY IN WORLD WAR II, is the first to be published in the group of three Signal Corps volumes in the subseries THE TECHNICAL SERV-ICES. All the volumes will be closely related and the series will present a comprehensive account of the activities of the Military Establishment during World War II. A tentative list of subseries is appended at the end of this volume.

...to Those Who Served

Foreword

The more mobile an armed force becomes, the more rugged the terrain it encounters, or the more widely the force is deployed, the greater becomes the difficulty of securing and maintaining rapid, completely linked communications.

In the U.S. Army the Signal Corps is the agency charged with developing, procuring, and furnishing signal equipment to overcome the difficulties mentioned above. In an age of swift and startling progress in electronics, this phase of its mission demands that it keep abreast of scientific advances at home and abroad and maintain close ties with civilian laboratories and industry in order to take advantage of their capabilities.

This volume traces the course which the Signal Corps followed between the first and second world wars, a period of planning and preparation. Others to follow will recount the testing of the Corps' organization and equipment, and the results achieved at home and overseas. The author has dealt with the subject on a chronological basis, instead of following the topical treatment used in other technical service volumes. This broad-front approach has enabled him to weave into one pattern the many activities in which the Signal Corps was simultaneously engaged. The reader can here follow from birth the history of Army radar and mobile radio, the first steps taken in the conversion of the civilian communications industry to war production, the expansion of training facilities, and the beginnings of the far-flung communications network that eventually encircled the globe. He will see the uncertainties of planning and the difficulties of organization incident to rapidly changing conditions, meager appropriations, and the clash of interest within the military household. These and many other matters showing human beings and institutions under pressure are replete with significance to us who must live in a turbulent world where revolution tends to have the upper hand over evolution.

Washington, D. C.
30 January 1953

ORLANDO WARD
Maj. Gen., U.S.A.
Chief of Military History

The Author

Dr. Dulany Terrett was born and reared in Montana and at present lives in Washington, D. C. He holds a Ph.B. in English from the University of Chicago and a Ph.D. in English from Northwestern University, where he served on the faculty from 1936 to 1942.

During World War II he was an Air Corps officer with the Flying Training Command and the Air Transport Command. In the latter capacity, he wrote the history of the Air Transport Command in Brazil and Ascension Island.

Upon his discharge in 1946, he became the Signal Corps chief historian, first in the Office of the Chief Signal Officer and then in the Office of the Chief of Military History. In 1952 he resigned in order to become a consultant.

Preface

The prefacing of his book long after he has written it does not ordinarily come a writer's way. If the present volume be a case in point, history is one form which permits it. At least to the extent that it has happened, history is unchangeable; and to the extent that it is unchangeable it will stand and wait for the attention of those who sooner or later come to it, or of those who, like the present author, return to it after having drawn apart from its details.

This view seems justified in retrospect as well, it appears to me. The history of the realizations, disappointments, mistakes, and successes of the United States Army Signal Corps before and during the war which ended in 1945 was itself undertaken entirely after that period had passed into history, and was planned and written with an eye to chronological and panoramic structure. It was in an effort to capture perspective and proportion, those qualities of necessary removal from the subject which every writer closely attached to his subject will despair of along with me, that I decided to devote the first volume of a history of the Signal Corps in World War II to a period beginning a number of years earlier. The massive gift which the Infantry makes to the national interest is made mostly in the battle itself, wherefore infantry history is combat history above all else. Technical arms and services like the Signal Corps, which must enter a war with technical gear ready to go, exert a large share of their productive effort before it begins. For this reason, this volume surveys *The Emergency* and the years, half lassitude and half desperation, just before the Emperor Hirohito's bombers came in over Kahuku Point.

Opening with the panorama of Signal Corps interests and distinguishing each of the characteristic landmarks of the scene, it develops by moving closer for repeated and prolonged views at most of these dominant features and by returning to the whole view often enough to keep it in mind. As the Signal Corps is an agent of communications, the main theme is the snaillike, lightning-like race toward radar, frequency modulation, and a multitude of electronic devices. Other parts of the narrative illustrate the lesson of the extravagant and enervating results of interservice strife. One can draw it primarily from the long story of unequal rivalry between the Air Corps and the Signal Corps. Yet the alarums and excursions of this melodrama never drowned out the quieter actions. Of these, the quietest was the development of radar, second only to nuclear fission as the greatest scientific advance of the war. *The Emergency* makes modest but firm claims for the Signal Corps' part in this development, at the same time producing evidence against a common notion that radar was the invention of a single scientist or of a single country; as was true of the atomic bomb, its origins were so wide as to be nearly universal. Next to radar and possibly of even greater significance to the average man was the emergence of FM, the frequency modulation system of radio, which all but revolutionized the use of tanks in the war, not to speak of its record afterward. The advance of crystal control, along with the ticklish triumph over the presumed insufficiency of the crystal supply, makes an episode interlinked with the FM story. The influence of the communications industry in the Signal Corps is an important element, showing the close relationship between the two in the selection and manufacturing of equipment and in the selection and training of officers and signalmen. A wider but very much weaker relationship described is that between ourselves and our allies, especially the British. One of the sections in this field recalls the mutually fruitful mission of Sir Henry Tizard and other electronic scientists and physicists to the United States in 1940. Finally, I trust that *The Emergency* demonstrates a discrepancy which later years closed: the gap between the pygmy Army and the jumbo. I hope, in sum, that the Signal Corps history adds its part to the defining and emphasizing of the two broad characteristics which have come to be so dominant in modern war that they will increasingly make up the bulk of military histories: first, the long preparations incident to a war or to any single day of it; and second, the technological aspect which has so transformed conflict that either wars or the men who fight them may consequently disappear.

The writing of this book produced many pleasures, of which the most frequent and most happily remembered were the acts of interest and assistance very gratefully acknowledged here. My colleagues in the writing of this series, all of whom have shared with me the repeated profit of these acts, have for their own part bulwarked me with them to a point I cannot begin to acknowledge in full. Suffice it to say that upon Miss Pauline M. Oakes, Mrs. Dixie R. Harris, and Dr. George Raynor Thompson I urge my devoted thanks for all their intelligent appraisals, unflagging perseverance, and liberal contributions. Miss Helen Kasenchak's expert typing deserves full recognition, as does the research and writing, at an earlier stage, of Miss Ruth E. McKee. I should like to thank individually the hundreds of persons who have found files for me between Washington and Alaska, smoothed my way to interviews, notified me of opportunities I had overlooked, and in general shown an abundance of cares and courtesies which one has no right to expect but welcomes. Since I must content myself with a mass acknowledgment, I want it to be known that in my grateful mind the mass is made up of individuals. Miss Ruth Stout, Mr. Joseph R. Friedman, and Mr. Arthur Henne have shepherded the book editorially. May its appearance in print be at least a token tribute to them.

Washington, D. C.   DULANY TERRETT
May 1954

Contents

Charts

Illustrations

All illustrations are from Department of Defense Files.

PART ONE

BEFORE WORLD WAR II

CHAPTER I

Military Communications

Shortly before World War II was over, the General Assembly of the United Nations met in an auditorium which provided the delegates with five almost simultaneous versions of an address. With a selecting device, they might choose the language they wished to listen to. This gear was welcomed with a casualness which only emphasized the distance an important utilitarian science had come during the half-dozen years when its advances had been obscured by war. In the first postwar years, also, cities commenced to equip their airports with radar systems which regulated an incoming airplane from the ground. Telephones began to be installed in automobiles, and home television sets and frequency-modulated radios to be promised to the general commercial market of the United States, Great Britain, and a few of their allies. In many treason and war-crimes trials of the era, wire and tape recordings formed an important part of the evidence. International allotment of radio frequencies meant as much, in a renewed contest for spheres of influence, as control of mountain passes had in earlier history. Telephotography and a special lens for long-range detail appeared in the news and picture industries. The coaxial cable, radio relay, page teletype, facsimile processes, and a hundred other contrivances stood ready to forward the revival of general communication. Whether these developments would have occurred sooner or later or not at all, if there had been no war, is a point apart from history. They did take place and, with many others in other fields, dispassionately demonstrated that practical advances had been made in response to the destructive demands of battle.

In the advances of this particular realm, the realm of mechanical aids to human communication, the Signal Corps of the U.S. Army had taken some part; for the military services were the greatest users of such devices during that period, and the Signal Corps was the communications corps of the Army. If the Army were one of its own soldiers, the Signal Corps would be his hand in the act of writing, his larynx, palate, and tongue in the act of speaking, the ears hearing, and the surface of the skin registering impressions from external invisible energy. It would signal that he was about to communicate, it would provide the mechanics for him to do so, and it would enable him to receive the messages of others. Thus in communications the Signal Corps had a notably single mission. Yet almost infinite possibility for variety made it also as complex as the processes of hearing and speaking are. Moreover, like those processes, it was vital. To be able to communicate—to *signal*—is to be alive.

Applied through a period when earlier scientific development had seemed to make it quaint, the name *Signal Corps* had reattained exactness as World War II approached. At one time associated with the torch and the square flags, a signal had come to designate a whole scale of ways in which the electromagnetic spectrum could give notice that it was carrying a message. Signals were generated by the human hand and voice, and by electronic impulses as well. Once as rudimentary as a shaking of spears in the sunlight, military signaling now suggested a multitude of devices. Even the basic information which the savage required—"I am a friend" or "I am a foe"—could appear in a dozen forms. Over the wire paths of the telegraph, the cable, and the telephone, over the wireless ones of radio, signal communication filled the ground, water, and air. Photographs conveyed messages in a way everyone was likely to grasp; cryptographic appliances obscured them in the hope that almost nobody could grasp them. Radar was opening a new avenue of communications, the quivering patterns of the oscilloscope being a form as specialized as wigwag had briefly been.

Message sending, which had altered scarcely at all between Pheidippides at Marathon and the Emperor's courier at Ratisbon, had acquired a myriad of devices between the mid-nineteenth and mid-twentieth centuries, and war had altered them in being altered by them. Most of this change had come about in less than a hundred years of supplementing *communication,* a message, with *communications,* apparatus for carrying a message. It had reached such an extent that every margin of efficiency had become a vital prize among armies. Not only did the message have to be spoken, heard, written, or read, but also it had to be received without interference from others; it had to be sent and received over long dis-

tances; it had to arrive on time; it had to be so precisely transmitted that it left no room for doubt, or so deliberately garbled and obscured that only those intended to understand it could do so. Army communications were often less than the ideal—even the most fabulous aid to aerial navigation, artillery spotting, tank command, or long-range detection aroused the abuse of harried operators from time to time; but ideally they were supposed to be swift, rugged, adaptable, simple, and secure beyond any average standard.

The military means of communication used in World War II were often not different from the nonmilitary means: a command teletype paralleled a news or stock exchange ticker; a messenger on a motorcycle was the "hand-carrying" equivalent of a bicycling Western Union boy. Their use was distinctive, however, and attained an importance hard to overstate. Warfare intensified the use of the office telephone, the newspaper teletype, radio broadcasting, control towers, railway semaphores, and the other apparatus of communication in the nonbelligerent pursuits.

Military communications had developed in three main aspects. These were general sensory signaling, likely to be nonelectrical, electrical signaling over wires, and electrical signaling without wires. Although in the growth of modern means of communication these aspects formed early, middle, and recent stages, they did not form a line of succession. Samuel F. B. Morse's telegraph was already in considerable use when Albert J. Myer introduced systematic wigwag, but flag signaling quickly reached its limits, whereas Morse's invention started a development which still had no boundaries a hundred years later. Rather, the three aspects represented degrees in the extension of signaling techniques. Within the Signal Corps of World War II they existed concurrently.

First, there were the primary means of signaling, which are usually visual: the torch and flags, as elemental as pillars of fire by night, cloud by day; the semaphore, which Napoleon developed into a system of 1,200 stations between Paris and Moscow; wigwag; the heliograph, mirrors flashing in the sunlight; Very pistols and other pyrotechnics; panels (signaling to airplanes with arrangements of colored cloth upon the ground); and blinker. Pigeons were also primary means of signaling, and so were sirens, gongs, and whistles. As a class, the primary means of signaling were historically earliest, and, by contrast with World War II's complicated reaches of invisible communication, they seemed primitive; yet they were not outdated. Wigwag could still be useful in the business of sorting out supplies on a beachhead, and blinker was as much a stand-by for the Navy as the automatic semaphore was for rail transportation. The chief difference was a matter not of date but of limitation. The best means of communication was that which could carry the most messages fastest with the fewest mistakes. In this sense, the simple devices for signaling directly to the eye and ear lacked capacity, speed, and precision.

When the art of communications had become electrified, it had suddenly advanced in all of these qualities, and the technical aspects of military communications commanded the field to such an extent that virtually the whole history of World War II communications is theirs. The second form of signaling involved electrical communication over wires: cable, telegraph, telephone, teletype. Throughout World War II, this was the principal form of Signal Corps communications. The third advanced electrical signaling to wireless devices: radio, radiotelegraph, radiotelephone, radioteletype, television, radar; in this field, the most thorough and significant change became evident. The accomplishments of radio in attaining teletypewriter transmission at a hundred words a minute, in reporting the weather locally by radiosonde, in radio control of airways, or in the handie-talkie which pleased Winston Churchill during a visit to Fort Jackson, South Carolina,[1] and with which he pleased the newsreel audience—all of these were part of a story of startling change. Television had not yet come into its own sufficiently to contend for wide interest. Radar was the crown of communications efforts during the war. Radar learned to guide an airplane at a distance, to return it safely and to land it; radar mapped landfalls or storms; matching itself to searchlights and antiaircraft artillery, it gave them unheard-of precision; it twice enabled the British Isles to ward off a nearly supreme German aerial assault, once from the Luftwaffe, once from the V–1; and it looked toward postwar successes which were as gentle as leading the blind and as ungentle as marshaling long-range missiles. GCI, GCA, loran, shoran, racon, IFF, MEW, ASV, BTO, rawin became the new black magic.[2] Resulting from interservice, international, interacting achievement of many minds fully as much as the

[1] Winston S. Churchill, *The Second World War: The Hinge of Fate* (Boston: Houghton Mifflin Co., 1950), p. 386.

[2]
GCI	ground-controlled interception
GCA	ground-controlled approach
loran	long-range navigation
shoran	short-range navigation
racon	radar beacons
IFF	identification, friend or foe
MEW	microwave early warning equipment
ASV	air-to-surface-vessel radar detection
BTO	bombing through overcast
rawin	radio or radar determination of wind velocity

atomic bomb,[3] in no sense was radar thought of as U.S. Army equipment strictly. Nor did it diminish for the Signal Corps the importance of the routine job of signal communications which was on hand at the beginning of the war and still on hand at the close; but as an instrument to open the imagination it took first place.

The span from visual signals to radar was enormous; yet they shared a basic function: passage of information. In the course of the Signal Corps' emergence into the form it possessed in the 1940's, two departures from this essential function made themselves felt. One of these was pictures—still pictures, training films, combat newsreels—undeniably a form of communication but a form at least once removed from the commonly accepted meaning of it. The other stood not for communication, but for countercommunication. It was an interruption, obscuring, or obstruction of communication. "Chaff," "cigar," "carpet," and such devices for jamming enemy radar; speech scrambling and other endeavors to hinder interception of telephone conversations; monitoring and interception of both friendly and enemy radio; and all modes of cryptography came under this classification.

With these two exceptions, however, all of the devices within the field of responsibility of military signaling, whether they used simple or complex, natural or artificial means, had the single function of passing information. In executing it, the Signal Corps had become, at one time or another, either permanently or temporarily, the Army's center of activity for captive balloons, weather observation, codes and ciphers, ocean cables, carrier pigeons, aviation, goniometrics, field telephoning, thermal detection, and many other efforts. By the time of the laboratory

and field experiments of the 1930's, the Signal Corps was long established as a partner in the development of the communications science. Even in the days of equipping Union armies with telegraph wagons, military communications had penetrated, although unknowingly and in a matter-of-fact way, the splendid scale which joins sound, light, and energy. (Chart 1) When electronics emerged eighty years later at the forefront of this scientific research, Signal Corps experimentation contributed to the general advance.

The Place of the Signal Corps

The major mission, however, was pursued not through science but through practical mechanics. For the most part, during World War II, the Signal Corps was described as one of seven technical services. The adjective was significant, because several of these services were essentially applied sciences. Before the war the Signal Corps had been classified as an arm, but during the war it was bracketed with the six other technical services as an agency of the Services of Supply, or Army Service Forces.[4] As a part of the Army Service Forces, it thus took its place in one of three major groupings of resources of men and matériel, the other two being the Army Ground Forces and the Army Air Forces.[5]

---

[3] The fact of radar's international parentage "will surprise only those who cling to a Hero Theory of scientific progress and demand for each discovery a single putative inventor. . . ." Henry Guerlac, "The Radio Background of Radar," *Journal of the Franklin Institute,* CCL, No. 4 (October, 1950), 285.

[4] WD Cirs 59, 2 Mar 42, and 138, 14 May 46, sub: WD Reorganization. The Corps of Engineers also occupied a prewar category as an arm.

[5] The Army Ground Forces drew in the Infantry, Cavalry, Field Artillery, Coast Artillery Corps, Armored Force, Antiaircraft Command, and Tank Destroyer Command.

CHART 1—RADIATION SPECTRUM, WORLD WAR II

Speed constant at 186,000 miles (300,000,000 meters) per second.

Frequency (relative rates of radiation per second) diminishing toward the left, increasing toward the right.
Wave length (relative length of radiated units, i. e., of waves or of rays) diminishing toward the right, increasing toward the left.

Frequency / Wavelength	Radiation	Band info	Wave type	Application
1 quadrillion megacycles	cosmic rays			
	gamma rays			Nuclear radiation — NUCLEAR FISSION
1 trillion megacycles	X-rays			THERAPEUTICS
	ultraviolet rays			
1 billion megacycles (.333 microns)	(0.4 microns) violet			SUNLIGHT, ARTIFICIAL LIGHT
	indigo			
	blue			
	light rays green			Molecular and atomic radiation
	yellow			
	orange			
	(0.7 microns) red			
1 million megacycles (333 microns)	infrared rays			INFRARED PHOTOGRAPHY, THERMAL DEVICES
300,000 megacycles (1 millimeter)				
30,000 megacycles (1 centimeter)	V-band, 50,000 mc extremely high frequencies (EHF) K-band, 30,000 mc X-band, 10,000 mc		Microwaves (above 1,000 megacycles)	RADAR, TELEVISION
3,000 megacycles (10 centimeters)	superhigh frequencies (SHF) S-band, 3,000 mc L-band, 1,000 mc			
300 megacycles (1 meter)	ultrahigh frequencies (UHF) P-band, 200 mc		Sky waves	Radio frequencies — RADIO COMMUNICATION Special channels
30 megacycles (10 meters)	very high frequencies (VHF)			
3,000 kilocycles (3 megacycles) (100 meters)	high frequencies (HF) (short waves)			Commercial channels (550–1600 kilocycles)
300 kilocycles (1,000 meters)	medium frequencies (MF) (medium length waves)		Ground waves	RADIO COMMUNICATION Special channels
30 kilocycles (10,000 meters)	low frequencies (LF) (long waves)			
20 kilocycles	usual high limit of audibility			Audio frequencies
10 kilocycles (30,000 meters)	very low frequencies (VLF) (very long waves)			SPEECH, MUSIC, TELEPHONE COMMUNICATION
256 cycles	middle C			
16 cycles	lowest limit of audibility			

Army Air, Ground, and Service Forces were designed to be interdependent; although administratively the Signal Corps served as a component of the Army Service Forces, Signal Corps equipment, functions, and trained men appeared throughout the Ground and Air Forces and in theaters and defense and base commands as well. The same relationships characterized the other technical services[6] and the administrative services[7] which, with the service commands (erstwhile corps areas, zone of interior administrative divisions), made up the Army Service Forces.

The way to see the Signal Corps of World War II, therefore, is to plot it on a world-wide chart. Such a chart begins with the President, the Secretary of War, and the Chief of Staff, continues with the General and Special Staffs, with theaters, task forces, defense and base commands, and with the Army Ground, Air, and Service Forces, and subdivides again into the big ground and air arms and services. Most of its space must still be devoted to an extraordinary complexity of army groups, armies, corps, divisions, regiments, battalions, companies, and platoons, of air forces and commands, wings, groups, squadrons, and flights, of administrative divisions, branches, sections, subsections, and units. Within this vast wartime framework, the Signal Corps was to be thought of chiefly as a technical service, as the principal communications agency for the whole organization.

It was to be thought of also as an arm. Signaling was indisputably operational, and the signalmen were attendant upon the air force and the infantry closely enough to qualify as combat-zone soldiers. The duality is clearly marked in the common Signal Corps distinction between tactical networks and administrative net-

works. Tactically, all forward communication was the province of the using arm: for example, of the Infantry, the Cavalry, the Armored Force. The crew of a B-17-E or -F, during the first year of the war, used an interphone set, RC-36; a tank or armored car would employ a frequency-modulated radio, SCR-508: this is the way in which the using arms required a fundamental Signal Corps contribution. Each division had a signal company, each army corps a signal battalion, and each field army a signal construction and a signal operations battalion, as well as depot, repair, radio intelligence, photographic, headquarters signal service, and other companies, depending upon the field army table of organization and the tactical situation which was applicable. In the Army Air Forces, a similar pattern was drawn, signal units being assigned at wing, division, command, and air force levels.[8]

The conception of the Signal Corps function both as arm and as service changed, however. During the war, all of the arms and services underwent a meta-

---

[6] The Chemical, Engineer, Quartermaster, and Transportation Corps and the Medical and Ordnance Departments. For the purposes of this history this is a standard list, although Department of the Army Circular 64, 10 March 1948, added to it the Finance Department, and although Circular 59, 2 March 1942, also subordinated to Army Service Forces the supply and procurement functions of the Coast Artillery Corps.

[7] The Adjutant General's, Judge Advocate General's, and Provost Marshal General's Departments and the Offices of the Chiefs of Chaplains, Special Services, and Finance.

[8] FM 1-45, Army Air Forces Field Manual: Signal Communication, 4 Dec 42, par 2b. See also the basic manual on signal communication, FM 24-5, 19 Oct 42, and all of the pertinent manuals in the FM-11, or Signal Corps, series. Sometimes official usage links the terms *signals* and *communication*, as it does in the titles to these field manuals; sometimes it separates them, as in referring to army, corps, and divisional *signal* officers, but to regimental, and lower, *communication* officers.

morphosis, the Cavalry most of all, the Signal Corps not least. Quiet and small in peacetime, characterized by such familiar objects as the telephone,[9] it became a world-wide, strategic service, wielding prodigies like radar. Even some time after the war had begun, the Signal Corps could still be thought of as an organization which devoted itself primarily to message-center work and which, in its tactical duties, rated visual communications high alongside telephone and telegraph.[10] But at the end of the war, the Signal Corps described its mission as "not only [the provision of] communication facilities for the War Department in the zone of the interior and all overseas theaters, but [also] the design, procurement, construction, installation and major maintenance for radar, radio, telephone and telegraph communications for the operations of the U.S. Army throughout the world." [11]

The Early Signal Corps

Among the technical services, the Signal Corps was neither the biggest nor the oldest.[12] Its work was concentrated, and its history covered only eighty years. Historical hindsight, in fact, would suggest that modern military signaling was a conditioned response to Morse's improvement in message sending; that in former days the Army had had no need for a Signal Corps because quick means of communication were unknown, but that a revolutionary invention had had to be met with an arm capable of exercising it. Hindsight falters a little, for under this sort of cause and effect the Army would have produced a Transportation Corps soon after Fulton and certainly after Stephenson. Moreover, the Signal Corps had its recognizable beginnings in a region far from the electric telegraph, along the Rio Grande in Texas,

where Dr. Albert J. Myer, recently commissioned an assistant surgeon and detailed to Fort Duncan, Texas, was carefully altering a system of hand signals which he had developed for deaf mutes into a system of flag signals for use at distances out of earshot altogether.[13] From this start, Myer was to become the first Chief Signal Officer of the Army. He had realized that the same sort of alternation and spacing by which a telegrapher controlled his key

---

[9] "The principal weapon of the Signal Corps man is the telephone with its associated material just as the rifle with its ammunition is the principal weapon of the infantryman." Memo, Lt Col Alvin C. Voris for Maj Gen Charles McK. Saltzman, CSigO, 9 Oct 24. SigC 475.7 Equip.

[10] WD, *Introduction to Employment in the War Department—A Reference Manual for Employees,* Aug 42, p. 21.

The *Annual Report of the Chief Signal Officer, 1942,* listed the following agencies of communication employed in signal systems within Army divisions:

1. Message centers	5. Visual communication
2. Messenger communication	a. Lamps
a. Airplane messenger	b. Flags
b. Motor messenger	c. Panels
c. Motorcycle messenger	d. Pyrotechnics
d. Mounted (horse) messenger	e. Airplanes
e. Dismounted messenger (runner)	6. Sound communication
3. Pigeon communication	7. Wire communication
4. Radio communication	a. Telephone
a. Telegraph	b. Telegraph
b. Telephone	c. Teletypewriter

[11] Info Br OCSigO, The Signal Corps, U.S. Army, 16 Dec 46. SigC Hist Sec File. (See Bibliographical Note.) Formal statement of Signal Corps functions appears in Army regulations. The versions which were in force at various stages from the end of World War I through World War II were: AR 105–5, 14 Jan 22, 15 Dec 26, 15 Mar 33, 10 May 39, and 1 Dec 42; AR 105–15, 12 Nov 21, 1 Aug 25, 17 Apr 40, 1 Aug 42.

[12] The quartermaster, medical, and engineer functions, which were part of the Army during the Revolution, were the oldest, and by most measurements the largest. The Ordnance Department, which dates from the War of 1812, remained small but always had large appropriations. For the sources on the historical origins of the services, as well as those on the beginnings and development of the Signal Corps, see the Bibliographical Note.

[13] (1) Hq of the Army, New York City, SO's 128 and 129, 4 and 6 Oct 1854. National Archives. (2) Albert J. Myer, A New Sign Language for Deaf Mutes, Being a Thesis for the Degree of Doctor of Medicine, 1851, University of Buffalo.

could be applied to flags or torches for visual signaling. He patented his system, got the Army to adopt it, experimented with it just before the Civil War, and then in frustration saw it work for the Confederate forces at the First Battle of Bull Run, while he himself was too late for the battle. Afterward, it proved itself for the Union Army at Gettysburg, for the Union Navy at Mobile Bay, and in a hundred other engagements. Sometimes the armies put up chains of elevated platforms in order to facilitate the flag signaling.[14]

Myer also was attempting to construct the new Signal Service upon long-distance, mechanical signaling as well as upon short-distance, manual methods; but the regular telegraph, which ordinarily followed the tracks of the railroad, was in the hands of the U.S. Military Telegraph. Ostensibly military, but actually a private concession, it controlled the Morse equipment and the teen-aged boys who were skilled at using it. Civilian aeronauts organized a balloon corps for observation and signaling. Myer wanted no part of that, and ultimately deflated it in 1863 when he rejected an opportunity to take it over. Instead, he assembled wagon trains and equipped them with alphabet dials and magnetized pointers which, responding to the electric impulses being transmitted from another part of the train, indicated a message letter by letter. Without effectively challenging the civilian telegraph monopoly, he developed thirty such trains for the Union troops, each extending the tactical situation by wire for six or eight miles. On 3 March 1863 Myer had the satisfaction of seeing Congress create the signals arm,[15] but his continued attempt to draw administrative as well as tactical wire communication into his new organization brought him into conflict with

Secretary of War Edwin M. Stanton, sent him into eclipse, and helped to allow the Signal Service to expire unredeemed at the end of the war. Within a year and a half, his point of view was sufficiently vindicated to restore the organization, with himself at its head. From then on, although with vicissitudes, it survived. In 1875 the Signal Service was given bureau status in the War Department, and on 24 February 1880 it became the Signal Corps, with Myer its general and his *Manual of Signals* its guide.[16]

For a time within its first quarter century, part of the emphasis of its mission shifted from signaling to meteorology. In 1870 it took on responsibility for scientific weather observation, especially in the shipping areas of the Great Lakes and the Atlantic coast. Until this work was transferred in 1891 to the Weather Bureau of the Department of Agriculture,[17] Signal Corpsmen pursued meteorology, especially in two notable expeditions to the north. Famous at the time, these arctic projects made magnetic, pendular, and tidal observations and collected weather and natural

---

[14] At the beginning of the Civil War the Union had few secrets from the Confederacy. J. E. B. Stuart had been a signal officer; and Jefferson Davis and John B. Floyd, both former Secretaries of War, as well as Robert E. Lee, had been acquainted with Myer's work. Lt. E. P. Alexander, who knew about this method of signaling because he had been assigned to work on it with Myer, was present at the First Battle of Bull Run and warned Beauregard of the approach of Mc-Dowell's column. In turn, poetic justice thwarted him at Gettysburg, when signal flags on Little Round Top led him to believe it was better defended than it was.

[15] PL 58, Secs 17–20, 37th Cong. The official birth date of the Signal Corps is 21 June 1860, the date of Myer's appointment as Army Signal Officer. Comment 3, OCMH to OCSigO, 11 Feb 54, sub: Birthday of SigC. SigC Hist Sec File 314.7 General 1954.

[16] This work was published in various editions from the Civil War to the close of the nineteenth century.

[17] Except for gathering marine meteorological data, which the Hydrographic Office took over in 1904.

history information at points then the farthest north reached by white men. The Point Barrow party, led by 1st Lt. P. Henry Ray, left San Francisco in midsummer, 1881, and came safely back two years later. The Ellesmere Island party, leaving from St. John's, Newfoundland, at the same time, was not seen in the United States again until 1884, when the six survivors told bitter tales of hardship and death, including the execution of one man for rifling food supplies.

The commander of this group, Adolphus W. Greely, became Chief Signal Officer in 1887 and remained so into the era of radio and the airplane, twenty years afterward.[18] The fame he won as head of this meteorological expedition led to his appointment as Chief Signal Officer, yet he reflected almost every interest of the Signal Corps, and his career spanned the maturity of the earlier forms of communication and the origins of the later ones. Before his arctic assignment, he had been putting in telegraph lines in the territorial west. More than two thousand miles of such construction took place between 1876 and 1879, and commercial communications and the Signal Corps then began the close relation which continued thereafter. As the railroads consolidated the west and as the number of Army outposts diminished, private interests took over the telegraph lines. Outside Washington, D. C., Fort Whipple, then a Signal Corps post and later named Fort Myer in honor of the general, had installed a practice telephone line in 1878.[19] Also in that year, the Corps had begun its first experiments with pigeons.[20] The last years of Indian fighting advanced the heliograph as a means of military signaling. In 1888 the Corps brought out a new type of heliograph which weighed only fourteen pounds packed and which

had a range of as much as sixty miles in clear atmosphere.[21]

Only visual signaling counted for much in the field. Telegraph trains, increased in size to nine wagons, were still rear-echelon communications, and the telephone gave no promise of sturdy military usefulness. A Signal Corps sergeant combined it in a field kit with a Morse key and battery in 1889, but the device was too expensive to be practical. Military ballooning came in again in 1892, and experiments in air-to-ground telephoning a few years later re-

[18] For an excellent sketch of Greely's life and works, see W. Elmer Ekblaw's account in the *Dictionary of American Biography*, XXI (Supplement One), 352–55.

After General Myer, who died in 1880, the succession of Chief Signal Officers through World War II was as follows:

Brig. Gen. William B. Hazen	1880–1887
Maj. Gen. Adolphus W. Greely	1887–1906
Brig. Gen. James Allen	1906–1913
Brig. Gen. George P. Scriven	1913–1917
Maj. Gen. George O. Squier	1917–1923
Maj. Gen. Charles McK. Saltzman	1924–1928
Maj. Gen. George S. Gibbs	1928–1931
Maj. Gen. Irving J. Carr	1931–1934
Maj. Gen. James B. Allison	1935–1937
Maj. Gen. Joseph O. Mauborgne	1937–1941
Maj. Gen. Dawson Olmstead	1941–1943
Maj. Gen. Harry C. Ingles	1943–1947

The list of Chief Signal Officers might also contain the names of two officers who held the place briefly during the period when Myer was in disfavor. These were Lt. Col. William J. L. Nicodemus, who occupied it from 10 November 1863 to 26 December 1864, and Col. Benjamin F. Fisher, whose tenure, beginning with Nicodemus' departure, ended indeterminately between 28 July 1866, when Myer's administration retroactively recommenced, and 15 November of the same year, when Fisher was formally relieved.

[19] 1st Lt. George I. Back, "The Telephone; Commercial v. Military History and Development," Signal Corps Bulletin, No. 42 (March, 1928), p. 10.

[20] Unsuccessfully, because the hawks of the region preyed upon them. The experiments took place in Dakota Territory with Col. Nelson A. Miles's 5th Infantry. Capt. Evan D. Cameron, "The Development and Use of Homing Pigeons for Military Purposes," Signal Corps Bulletin, No. 24 (February, 1924), p. 26.

[21] Possibly the greatest range achieved by this device (in 1890) was 125 miles. *Historical Sketch of the Signal Corps (1860–1941)*, Eastern SigC Schools Pamphlet 32 (Ft. Monmouth, N. J., 1942), p. 30.

ONE EARLY MEANS OF SIGNAL-
ING *employed flags hoisted by balloon.*

called the air-to-ground telegraph demonstrations of the Civil War. Most Army
posts had a few telephones, some owned
by the Signal Corps, some rented from the
Bell Company. Even so short a conflict as
the Spanish-American War, however, increased the advance of new sciences. The
Army gave its first contract for a powered
airplane in the year of that war, 1898,
allotting the money to Samuel P. Langley.
The laying of submarine cable in the
waters of Cuba and the Philippines extended the scope of signal communications, and in the expansive aftermath of
the war the Signal Corps undertook the
Washington-Alaska Military Cable and
Telegraph System. This became the most
important continuous field operation.[22]
The knowledge of the north obtained in

the Ray-Greely expeditions, the experience gained in building frontier communications systems, the scientific background derived from meteorological duties,
and the exercise provided in establishing
relatively long lines during the war with
Spain all contributed to the formation of a
chain which employed telegraph, cable,
telephone, and even the newest wonder,
wireless communication.

In 1899 the Signal Corps had radioed
experimentally between Fire Island and
the lightship twelve miles away and a year
later installed two stations for New York
Harbor traffic.[23] In 1903 a pair of stations
provided space telegraph—in those days
an excellent description of radio—across
Norton Sound, to and from Nome. By
1908 there were eight stations in Alaska,
six in the United States, five upon Army
transports, three in the Philippines, and
one in Cuba. Their spark-gap sets ranged
in power from 750 watts to 10 kilowatts.
Field tests improving upon Boer War
models meanwhile developed the Army's
first vehicular sets, loaded into wagons or
on pack mules.[24] Cumbersome as these
were, they illustrated the fact that the researches of Maxwell and Hertz[25] were
giving birth to the era of Marconi and

[22] First Draft, Alaska Communication System History, 1944. SigC Hist Sec File. When the predominant
use of radio made the early title inappropriate, the
Washington-Alaska Military Cable and Telegraph
System became the Alaska Communication System.

[23] Capt. Edwin R. Petzing, "Development of Radio
in the United States," Signal Corps Bulletin, No. 42
(March, 1928), p. 34. Mention of this work should
not slight Capt. Leonard H. Wildman, who contributed to the installation of wireless at both Long Island
Sound and Norton Sound.

[24] S. I. Neiman, "Vehicular Radio," *Signals,* I, No.
6 (July–August, 1947), 20–25.

[25] James Clerk Maxwell (1831–1879), British physicist, and Heinrich R. Hertz (1857–1894), German
physicist. The principles of electromagnetic radiation
which Maxwell forecast in 1866 were confirmed in the
experiments of Hertz in the '90's.

De Forest. Military communication was assuming its twentieth-century character.

The emergence of a science of electronics was paralleled by the appearance, after long waiting and frustration, of a science of heavier-than-air flight. On 1 August 1907 the current Chief Signal Officer, Brig. Gen. James Allen, established an Aeronautical Division, to "have charge of all matters pertaining to military ballooning, air machines, and all kindred subjects." [26] A captain, a corporal, and a private staffed the division. Specifications for the Army's first airplane required that it be able to carry the pilot, a passenger, and enough fuel for 125 miles, that its speed average forty miles an hour in a ten-mile test, that it stay aloft for an hour, and that it be capable of being dismounted and loaded into Army wagons. [27] The Wright brothers produced such a plane in 1908 and tested it successfully (despite the fatal accident to 1st Lt. Thomas E. Selfridge), with a series of passengers including Maj. George O. Squier, later the World War I Chief Signal Officer.

For a period, there was a possibility that airplanes and radio, the two inventions which had suddenly opened the element of air as a space for the hitherto grounded army to move within, would develop inside the same organization. Squier, the man who had drawn up the specifications for the military airplane, represents the transition which was then altering the Signal Corps. In 1911 he described experiments covering the use of wires to guide high-frequency oscillations, [28] a process fundamental to the multiplex telegraphy and telephony which made up the largest part of World War II military communications. Joseph O. Mauborgne, a lieutenant who was to be Chief Signal Officer twenty years after Squier,

CIVIL WAR SIGNAL TOWER *on Cobb's Hill, Appomattox, Virginia.*

was beginning to achieve recognition as a contributor both to airborne transmitting, in 1912 and 1913, at Fort Riley, Kansas, and to airborne receiving, over Corregidor in December 1914. [29] These demonstrations, however crude, had opened aerial

[26] OCSigO Office Memo 6, 1 Aug 07. AAF 321.91–A SigC Org.

[27] WDSS, Information and Education Div, "The Army Air Forces—Organization," *Army Talk,* No. 159, 25 January 1947.

[28] George O. Squier, "Multiplex Telephony and Telegraphy by Means of Electric Waves Guided by Wires," *Proceedings of the American Institute of Electrical Engineers,* 1911. Originally called wire wireless, wired wireless, or line radio, the process came to be called wire radio (possibly the most descriptive term), carrier frequency, or the carrier-frequency, carrier-current, or guided-wave method.

[29] (1) The Signal Corps, United States Army: A Popular History, MS, p. 75; (2) Maj Gen Joseph O. Mauborgne, My Early Work in Airplane Radio Development. SigC 342 Gen.

THE WRIGHT BROTHERS' AIRPLANE *during tests at Fort Myer, Virginia.*

communications as a major field of Signal Corps work. Congress recognized military aviation by converting a small office division into an Aviation Section of a top strength of 320.[30] The range of air-to-ground Morse increased to 140 miles, and Signal Corps pilots experimented with air-to-air Morse exchange. The most perplexing problem was noise. Airplane design had substituted tractor for pusher engines, with the result that all the disturbance lay directly in front of the pilot. By 1916 the Aviation Section felt that a different generator and headset had solved the problem; and Michael Pupin and Edwin H. Armstrong, whom Brig. Gen. George O. Squier asked to convert the radio signal into a visual signal which would show up on the instrument panel, agreed that radio reception was preferable and possible even in spite of the roar and static. It is significant that Signal Corps activity of this era, at a time while it was still attached to a rudimentary tactical mission, produced names associated with both of the world wars, when scientific research tended to become as important in the mission as utilitarian skill. An older Signal Corps and a newer one, soon to be old itself, coexisted.

[30] PL 143, 63d Cong, 18 Jul 14. The testimony of Signal Corps officers at the preliminary hearings on this bill a year before had made clear the fact that in early military aviation the most important function was reconnaissance and communication, not bombardment. Capt. William Mitchell, 1st Lt. Benjamin D. Foulois, and 1st Lt. Henry H. Arnold, future Air Corps generals, agreed with Brig. Gen. George P. Scriven, the Chief Signal Officer, that the time was not then ripe for separation from the Signal Corps, "where all aeronautic work has been done for the last 20 years." *Hearings before the Committee on Military Affairs,* HR, 63d Cong, 1st Sess, On HR 5304, 16 May 13, p. 51 and *passim.*

EARLY EXPERIMENTS WITH RADIO *included installation of sets in aircraft (above) and automobiles (below).*

The Signal Corps in World War I

The older was dominant. The United States began and completed its role in the 1917–1918 war without reaching a development in either combat communications or combat aviation comparable to that of France or Great Britain. In both fields the nation's war experience was shorter, its appropriations smaller, and to a considerable degree its industry slow to start and its research too late to be felt. The only battle testing of the Aviation Section had consisted of mail and reconnaissance flights during the Punitive Expedition into Mexico in 1916. None of its fifty-five airplanes carried any kind of weapon; nor had the experiments with aerial wireless communication introduced radio into any cockpit. When, in March 1918, the Signal Corps was faced for the first time with the need to install radio apparatus aboard Spads which the Air Service was flying in France, the French supplied it, having supplied the airplanes also.[31] American air-to-ground radiotelephone, shown the summer before to the Secretary of War, Newton D. Baker, was not ready.

Correspondingly, in ground signaling, the old methods had sufficed before the war for an Army engaged in small-scale maneuvers or patrolling the borders of Mexico. Quenched-spark sets carried by pack or wagon had introduced radio into both the Punitive Expedition and maneuvers, but, in general, buzzers, messengers, and visual signaling answered the need for command communications within infantry brigades; and although the field artillery had telephones for fire control, provided by the Signal Corps since 1905, it also used flags. Tactically, there was little need for, or opportunity to employ, electrical communications. Thus, much of the equip-

ment which the Signal Corps brought over to Europe in 1917 was wholly unsuitable for the character of warfare then existing.[32] In the early stages, the American Expeditionary Forces was obliged to rely solely upon French telephone and telegraph facilities; large purchases, as of poles and crossarms, dry batteries, buzzerphones, switchboards, and radio and earth telegraphy sets, were necessary before the communications mission for the American Expeditionary Forces could be fulfilled. Titles in the procurement list were grouped into but fourteen categories.[33]

In France, wire quickly became the almost exclusive instrument of army communications. It was the best means whether within the regiment or from the division back to corps and army headquarters. Heliographs appeared only far back of the lines, if at all; panels were reserved to signaling to aircraft; the pigeon service, attempted at General Pershing's order, had a limited success, although a bird named Cher Ami proved to be a help to the "Lost Battalion." But wire was paramount; the Meuse-Argonne offensive used it at the rate of 2,500 miles a week.[34]

---

[31] "Report of the Chief Signal Officer," *War Department Annual Reports, 1919*, p. 1190. Also separately published, the *Annual Report of the Chief Signal Officer, 1919*, is by far the most comprehensive source of information on the World War I Signal Corps.

[32] (1) Petzing article cited n. 23, p. 36. (2) Col C. F. Martin, Hist Sec Army War College, Signal Communications in World War I, Aug 42, p. 8. SigC Hist Sec File.

[33] Telephones, telegraphs, radios, line construction materials, batteries, wire and cable, field glasses, chests, kits and tools, mechanical and electrical signals, wire carts, pigeon supplies, meteorological equipment, and watches. James V. Clarke, Contract Adjustment in the Signal Corps, 1 July 1939–15 August 1945, Nov 45, p. 3. SigC Hist Sec File.

[34] By the close of World War I, U.S. production of field wire had reached 8,000 miles a month. After a similar time interval in World War II, the production rate of W-110-B wire was 150,000 miles a month.

SIGNAL CORPS INSTALLATIONS IN FRANCE IN 1918 *included a telephone and telegraph station at Château-Thierry (above) and a goniometric station at Royaumeix (below).*

Multiplex printing telegraph equipment connected Tours, Chaumont, Paris, and London. Transatlantic cable was called into use, at reduced rates, for EFM's (expeditionary force messages) from the troops to their friends and relatives in the United States.[35] Both forward and rear zones depended upon the telephone network, after construction crews had fanned it out from Chaumont and Tours.[36] This was an achievement for the period, admirable for trench warfare. In the mobile situation of World War II it would have been, first of all, nearly impossible to build and, second, not relatively worth building.

Although a transatlantic radio station was built near Bordeaux, the War Department in Washington had no radio contact with its commanders in the field, and these commanders had no very dependable wireless systems among themselves. Radio carried little of the war's communications load. In the first place, the tactical situation again and again brought the Western Front into small areas and mired it there. For another reason, although nearly 10,000 radio sets, chiefly airborne radiotelegraph, were produced for the Signal Corps and Air Service, the conflict was over too soon for the combat signalman or aviator to use them much. Finally, radio was too new to have passed the awkward age. Spark-type equipment did have the advantage of not requiring a skilled man to tune it or mend it, but was so heavy it could scarcely be moved, was often unintelligible, and was frequently out of commission. Tube equipment generally replaced it. Radio's chief use was for intelligence work. At goniometric stations it took what were later called "fixes" upon enemy transmitters and identified their location by the intersection of the angles. It intercepted German ground telegraph,

telephone, aircraft, and artillery signals; and, in a foreshadowing of the succeeding war's signal intelligence and monitoring companies, it policed communications on the Allied side.

The most interesting aspect of Signal Corps radio in World War I was the consolidation of the hitherto scattered efforts in scientific research. The Signal Corps Laboratories had their beginnings in a World War I radio research division which functioned in company with the electric communications industry and with a special wartime Signal Corps laboratory in Paris. This division worked upon aircraft radiotelegraph and radiotelephone sets, aircraft interphone equipment, aircraft direction-finding systems (given first priority),[37] three types of continuous-wave radiotelegraph sets, wavemeters, battery-charging radios, four improved T.P.S. (earth telegraphy) items, radio operating and repair trucks, and a radiotelegraph set for tanks. The prewar invention of vacuum tubes enabled Signal Corps researchers to try them for electric wave detection, amplification of radiofrequency and audiofrequency, continuous wave transmission, voice modulation, regulation

[35] Col Edgar Russel, CSigO AEF, AEF Memo, 17 Jun 17. SigC 676 Wired Wireless and Tree Tel & Tel.

[36] History of the Signal Corps, American Expeditionary Forces. SigC Hist Sec File.
The Signal Corps wire networks for the American Expeditionary Forces, including those leased from France, comprised approximately 50,000 miles of administrative lines and 40,000 of tactical lines. The exact figures are difficult to determine, because the standards for calculation vary. (1) "Signal Corps Work in the A.E.F.," Signal Corps Bulletin, No. 1 (April, 1920), p. 14. (2) Maj. Alfred E. Larabee, "The Signal Corps and Signal Communication," Signal Corps Bulletin, No. 31 (September, 1925), pp. 33–34. (3) Lt. Col. Frank H. Fay, "A.E.F. Telephone and Telegraph System," Signal Corps Bulletin, No. 56 (September–October, 1930), pp. 25–27.

[37] History of Camp Alfred Vail, New Jersey, 1918. SigC Hq Ft. Monmouth File 314.7.

of current and voltage in generators, and other special purposes without which the multiple applications of World War II radio would never have been possible. But despite the fact that an American, Lee De Forest, was the inventor, the United States was behind in the use of vacuum tubes. Industrial production of them started from almost nothing when the nation went into the war.

For the most part, none of the laboratory improvements got into production before the Armistice. Had any been developed before the war, radio history would have been made, for the critical inadequacy of equipment necessitated remarkable advances in the field. For example, a two-way radio loop set was contrived because the enemy shot away the antennas of ordinary radio. The new device laid the receiving antenna on the ground, and for the transmitting antenna substituted a small loop connected with the spark gap. This set had a range of six miles, transmitted on two wavelengths, and could be transported in three sections each weighing less than thirty pounds. Developments in electric communications of the American Expeditionary Forces were in part the contributions of Edwin H. Armstrong, then a Signal Corps captain and a noted radio scientist since 1910. He applied Langmuir's master oscillator-power amplifier circuit to improve tank communication, and he invented the amplifier to facilitate reception of high-frequency signals. The master oscillator-power amplifier became basic in radio design, although the war was over before it could be tried in battle, and high-frequency amplification made possible the superheterodyne receiver and revolutionized wireless communications.[38] Signal Corps and Tank Corps men together devised equipment on the master-

oscillator principle which the signalmen installed after the Armistice to make a radiotelegraph network connecting the Paris headquarters with the Army of Occupation. Of considerable extent and surely one of the earliest successes of the sort, the network engaged stations at Antwerp, Spa, Koblenz, Trier, Toul, and Chaumont at various stages between November 1918 and September 1919. The control was twenty miles outside Paris, at a site in the British zone far enough away to escape the radiodiffusion from the Eiffel Tower spark transmitter. The purpose of the net was to take the place of the telephone and telegraph lines in case they were sabotaged; and on one occasion, when the wire transmission was interrupted for forty-five minutes, it did convey to Paris an address which President Woodrow Wilson was making in Germany. During the time of its operation, the network carried thousands of messages, as only wire networks had done up to that point.[39]

Historically the most interesting of all the experiments was an initial attempt at radar. The only means of being warned of the approach of an airplane was to catch sight of it, which was usually too late, or to hear it, which, even with the aid of sound

---

[38] Armstrong's contributions to radio science, although generally acknowledged, were persistently challenged in court, and the decisions often went against him. "Revolution in Radio," *Fortune,* XX (October, 1939), 86 ff. De Forest was the principal figure to press counterclaims. So far as the superheterodyne discovery is concerned, 1943 adjudication assigned the credit to Lucien Lévy, who like Armstrong was a World War I officer. Henry W. Roberts, *Aviation Radio,* introduction by Lee De Forest (New York: W. Morrow & Company, 1945), p. 90. Nevertheless, and taking account of the fact that the decisions were essentially commercial rather than technical, Armstrong's place in the development of radio is secure.

[39] Ltr, Edwin H. Armstrong to author, 21 May 52, with incls. SigC Hist Sec File.

locators, gave advance notice only as fast as sound travels. During the work which led to his contribution to the superheterodyne receiving circuit, Armstrong considered the possibility of a receiver sensitive enough to pick up the electromagnetic disturbances given off by an airplane's ignition system.[40] Another attempt made in the same period was thermal detection. This, too, was an effort to intercept the electromagnetic radiations from an airplane engine, but to measure its heat as it drew near or receded from range. Thermal detection was a tantalizing field of research. Even with the later successful development of pulse detection, scientists, including those in the Signal Corps Laboratories, never wholly gave it up; but it seemed always to promise better results than it produced, and until the outset of World War II, aural detectors (sound locators), in association with searchlights, marked American aircraft warning sites.

In order to meet its World War I mission, the Signal Corps had to multiply itself by thirty-five. At the time of the 1916 National Defense Act, the Corps was smaller even than when it had taken part in the Spanish-American War. It comprised 42 officers and 1,212 enlisted men, scattered over half the world. The Aviation Section alone had grown as large. At the declaration of war Signal strength was only 371 more. Half were in the Washington-Alaska Military Cable and Telegraph System, half were organized into a pattern of field and telegraph companies.[41] To supplement them, there were 6,000 licensed amateur radio operators. More than 4,000 of these responded to a spirited recruiting campaign which even promised "assignment in a battle plane flying over the front lines," [42] and, under a World War I precursor of World War II's Affiliated Plan,

thousands of men came in from the commercial communications companies. Among the regular Signal Corps troops at the outset of the war, there had been organized two telegraph and two field battalions. The National Guard had ten field signal battalions, no telegraph companies, but sixteen separate companies— all together 163 officers, 3,510 enlisted men. The strength deficiency, then, was in telegraph units, and it was to make up this difference that the Signal Corps had persuaded American Telephone and Telegraph, Postal Telegraph, Western Union, and Western Electric to organize battalions of skilled technicians and to permit many of their engineers to become Signal Corps Reserve officers in 1916.[43]

Training started at Fort Leavenworth,

---

[40] E. H. Armstrong, "Vagaries and Elusiveness of Invention," *Electrical Engineering*, LXII, No. 4 (April, 1943), 149.

[41] The field signal company authorized in 1907 consisted of 4 officers and 100 enlisted men. From 1910, regulations provided for one field signal battalion to each infantry and cavalry division. The field battalion comprised an outpost, a wire and a radio company. (Memo, CSigO for CofS [1 Jan 36], sub: Study of the reorganization of sig coms of div and higher units. SigC OT 322 Gen.) The telegraph company, unlike a field company, did not serve at the front; it had been created by War Department General Order 55 in 1913. Two of them made up a battalion from 1916 on. Until just before the United States entered the war, the signal field and telegraph battalions existed only on paper. The first reference to them in the *Army List and Directory* appeared on 20 December 1916. The issue for that date lists four battalions of each type.

[42] Kenneth B. Warner, "Radio Amateurs in War and Peace," *Signals*, I, No. 2 (November–December, 1946), 38.

[43] For narratives of this expedient, see: (1) Ruth F. Sadler, History of the Signal Corps Affiliated Plan, Aug 44, pp. 1–14. SigC Hist Sec File. (2) Peter L. Schauble, *The First Battalion, the Story of the 406th Telegraph Battalion, Signal Corps, U.S. Army* (Philadelphia, 1921). (3) *313th Field Signal Battalion History* (Des Moines, Iowa, 1939). (4) A. Lincoln Lavine, *Circuits of Victory* (New York: Doubleday Page & Company, 1921).

Kansas, at Camp Meade, Maryland, most particularly at Camp Alfred Vail, New Jersey, and at several other locations; forty-five universities and colleges organized special courses of instruction in telephone and radio engineering, meteorology, and photography; [44] at Vail a camp of 129 buildings arose equipped with every known device used in field signal work, including a divisional wire net with underground stations. In Washington the Office of the Chief Signal Officer moved from building to building as it outgrew itself. Well over 50 percent of the total force of the Signal Corps went into the American Expeditionary Forces, there to become about 4 percent of a much greater total. [45] This is not to count the Aviation Section. In the American Expeditionary Forces at the time of the Armistice, there were 50 field signal battalions, 28 telegraph battalions, 11 depot battalions, and 19 service companies: a sum of 1,462 officers and 33,038 enlisted men.

After demobilization had drained off the wartime strength, after the years intervening between the two world wars had dispelled the full recollection of the earlier, a residue of accomplishment was still to be observed. There was, for one thing, a pictorial record of conflict compiled by the cameras of thirty-eight Signal Corps photographic teams. [46] There had been a practical demonstration of the Affiliated Plan. At General Pershing's demand for weather service in France, military meteorology had come back to the Signal Corps. [47] Electronic knowledge had noticeably widened. And the principal Signal Corps post had come into being in northern New Jersey, with its character permanently established. Not until 1925 did it become a permanent installation and change its

name from Camp Alfred Vail to Fort Monmouth; but almost from the end of the war it was the recognized center for two principal functions, communications training and communications research; it was the site of the Signal School and the Signal Corps Laboratories. With this post, as possibly nowhere else in its range of interest, the Signal Corps assumed the aspect which it held at the outset of the next war twenty years later.

---

[44] (1) Memo, CSigO for CofS, cited n. 41. (2) Courtney R. Hall, The Development of the Office of the Chief Signal Officer, Pt. I: 1917–1943, Sep 44, pp. 17–18. SigC Hist Sec File.

[45] Exec Order 2862, 20 May 18.

[46] At the end of World War I, the Signal Corps had become the repository for almost 7,000,000 feet of historical motion picture film and for about 85,000 still negatives, most of them purchased from outside sources. This material joined the collection of military pictures taken since the days of Mathew B. Brady in the Civil War.

Although the photographic activities of the Signal Corps began in 1881, the primary photographic duty was assigned officially in July 1917. Memo, Brig Gen Joseph E. Kuhn, Chief War College Div WDGS, for CofS, 17 Jul 17, sub: Photography of military operations. PM–10122–1WCD Record Div National Archives. Training films came to be a part of this duty; the Army's first one, Close Order Drill, was photographed at the Military Academy in 1916. Pictures for surveying and ground photomapping were a responsibility reserved to the Corps of Engineers. Memo, CofS for TAG, 19 Jul 17. PM–10122–1WCD Record Div National Archives. The Air Service, after its divorce from the Signal Corps on 20 May 1918, took over aerial photography, along with 2,700 of the 3,000 men engaged in the military pictorial work. M. E. Boswell, Signal Corps Photography in World War I, Apr 46. SigC Hist Sec File.

WPD, Hist Br, Catalogue of Official A.E.F. Photographs Taken by the Signal Corps, U.S.A., WD Doc 903 (Washington, 1919), is an excellent guide to the still pictures of World War I. The motion picture film can be referred to from a title list in the National Archives.

[47] In 1917. Signal Corps weather stations commenced in the United States itself in 1918, and the Meteorological Service was formalized in AR 105–210, 12 November 1921. At its peak, it comprised thirty-nine stations. AG file 665.6, passim, especially Memo, OCSigO for WP&T Div, 30 Oct 31.

CHAPTER II

The Army in Limbo

Postwar Curtailment

The sudden evaporation of a large army, the change from crowded training camps and busy offices to a backwater organization, put a drain on military efficiency and sense of identity. In the confidence bursting forth from a victory and with a natural reluctance to think of wars in the future tense, the nation was glad to revert to its normal civilian status and to put the Army back in perspective. The Army saw its recent strength vanishing, and its brief influence wiped away as it resumed the pleasant life of peacetime service. The abrupt ebbing, followed by gradual stagnation and ultimately a recommencing rise, formed the soil of the next twenty years.

Ten days after the Armistice the remaining allowances for the current fiscal year were almost erased.[1] For industry's sake, Congress continued most of the 1,244 contracts outstanding; they were fulfilled in spite of the fact that the war was over, and Signal Corps war-ordered equipment piled up in the sudden peace with nobody to use it. Civilian employees, drafted soldiers, National Guardsmen, Reservists—all went out along with most of the money. The National Defense Act of 1920 provided a strength of 5,000 men for the Signal Corps. In 1921 the figure was down to 3,000 and in 1922 had fallen to 2,184.[2] The 51st Signal Battalion, stationed at Camp Vail, was the only one authorized for the post-World War I Army. In every way, the dwarfing of the Military Establishment left little opportunity for studying and applying the gigantic lessons of the war. Planning for mobilization of industry in a future war began with a marked lack of encouragement.[3] Many laboratory projects came to a halt. From time to time, enlisted men, confronting frozen promotion lists and meager pay, secured their release by paying to the finance officer a sum proportionate to their unexpired term of service. The Signal Corps continued, proud in its own household but feeling, with the rest of the Army, that at the national dinner table it was sitting below the salt.

Raids and forays from other branches of the service filled the place of the recent war. The Field Artillery, the Air Service, and the Tank Corps asked the Signal Corps to concur in a change in Army regulations which would let them install, maintain, and operate their own signal communications systems. The Adjutant General's Office endeavored, without success, to take over the War Department Message Center. The Coast Artillery Corps expressed a preference for having the Corps of Engineers install its fire-control systems. The Air Corps wanted

---

[1] Memo, SW for Chiefs of Bureaus, 21 Nov 18.

[2] CSigO, *Annual Reports, 1920, 1921, 1922.*

[3] H. D. Hausmann, Signal Corps Activity in Industrial Mobilization and Procurement Planning, 1920–1940, Pt. I. SigC Hist Sec File.

photography, military meteorology, and development, procurement, installation, and maintenance of air navigation equipment.[4]

The hardest blow of all came first. In its capacity as a prominent arm of the Army, the Signal Corps had controlled combat communications, except for the Field Artillery, well down to all but the smallest echelons, or, to put it in another direction, from the rear all the way to the front. During the war just past, some signal units within the infantry brigade had been made up in part of Infantrymen, in part of Signal Corpsmen from the outpost companies of the field signal battalions; but the general fact was that the communications of the great combat organizations had been in sole charge of the Signal Corps. The 1920 Army reorganization carried this responsibility through the divisional level, stopped it there, and from that point on assigned communications to the Infantry, Field Artillery, or Cavalry.[5] In effect, given the postwar Army, in which units greater than a division scarcely existed, the order wiped out most of the tactical interest of the Signal Corps and permanently moved its center of gravity away from classification as an arm and toward classification as a service.

Every Chief Signal Officer protested, beginning with Maj. Gen. George O. Squier, who pointed out the confusion he felt sure would result if several independent radio or wire systems operated in one area, and who declared that signal communication "MUST BE one complete and coordinated system from battalion headquarters of the combat units to the Commander in Chief of the Army."[6] Col. George C. Marshall expressed himself in much the same way, saying that he believed that communication troops should

all be Signal Corps troops. But he had made it clear that the units should be indivisible parts of the combat organizations which they served, not, as had often been the case in the American Expeditionary Forces, to be broken in upon and deprived of this man or that by the signal officer of a higher level. They must "train and serve habitually with the organization to which attached."[7]

Nevertheless, and although there were doubts as to the legality of the shift, the change took place. It had much to recommend it for other arms and services. In many ways, it marked the beginning of an essential Army-wide interest in communications matters.[8] The new arrangement specified that the commander of each unit would establish the unit's communications system, his signal officer being responsible for its efficiency. For the Infantry and

---

[4] (1) Memo, CSigO for CofS, 22 Jan 20, sub: Sig com sv. SigC 676 Gen, 1918–1938. (2) Pauline M. Oakes, The Army Command and Administrative Communications System, Pt. I: War Department Radio Net, 1920–1940, Oct 45, pp. 16–18. SigC Hist Sec File. (3) Memo, Lt Col Consuelo A. Seoane for Col Charles McK. Saltzman, 8 Mar 23. SigC 676 Gen 1918–1938. (4) Summary Report on Photographic Activities of the Signal Corps Since August 4, 1941, in the Fields of Motion Pictures and Visual Aid, 26 Feb 43, pp. 374–76. SigC APS Div File. (5) Courtney R. Hall, The Development of the Office of the Chief Signal Officer, Pt. I: 1917–1943, Sep 44, p. 72. SigC Hist Sec File. (6) M. P. Claussen, The Development of Radio and Radar Equipment for Air Operations, 1939–1944, p. 11. Photostat copy in same file. (7) Ltr, TAG to CSigO, 18 Jul 34, sub: Radio direction compass, and 6th Ind, Chief of AC to TAG, 11 Mar 35. SigC 413.44 Compasses 1, 1919–1934.

[5] WD GO 9, 18 May 20.

[6] Memo, CSigO for CofS, cited n. 4(1).

[7] Memo, CSigO for CofS [1 Jan 36], sub: Study of reorgn of sig coms of div and higher units. SigC OT 322 Gen.

[8] (1) Memo, Maj Gen William G. Haan, WPD, for [TAG?], 4 May 20. SigC 676 Gen, 1918–1938. (2) AR 105–15, 12 Nov 21 and 1 Aug 25. (3) Brig Gen Paul M. Robinett, Ret., Chief Special Studies Div OCMH, comment on MS, 25 Oct 51. Copy in OCMH.

Cavalry, it solved the problem of having signalmen arbitrarily transferred without reference to the tactical problems of the commander. Yet other difficulties arose. Men not trained in communications work contended that the Signal Corps equipment was too delicate or was improperly made. Signal platoons and detachments became indistinct and undependable. The using arms were authorized to train their communications men by whatever methods worked best inside the regiment or battalion or squadron, whereas signal communication takes place much oftener between than within units.

Thus an un-co-ordinated pattern of separate training procedures invited chaos. Six arms—the Infantry, Cavalry, Field Artillery, Coast Artillery, Air Corps, and Signal Corps—began to use diverse methods. "The Signal Corps is making the utmost endeavor to assist in producing standard training for all communications troops of the Army, with a view to doing its part in making the system workable," said Maj. Gen. Charles McK. Saltzman, Squier's successor, "but it is the duty of this office to express the view that the principle is not sound." [9] In 1923 the Cavalry endorsed a resumption of the old system, and the War College commandant suggested that for the Infantry the dividing line could be drawn so that brigade communications returned to the Signal Corps; but the parceling-out of responsibility continued. [10]

Periodically, the Chief Signal Officers denounced it, declaring that it had not been thought suitable for the last war and would not remain long in another one. [11] The opinion was universal in the Signal Corps that communications must operate under single rather than divided control. The greater their complexity—and means of communication were becoming more complex every day—the greater the apparent urgency for having one agency alone develop the signal plans, produce the signal equipment, train the signalmen. Maj. Harry C. Ingles, for instance, said that the principle applied in the Air Corps, too. Ingles became a World War II Chief Signal Officer, and his words therefore pass into and merge with an official position insisted upon for twenty-five years. The Signal Corps ought to have the responsibility for communications all the way to the front in the Infantry and the Cavalry, he asserted, and ought to have it all the way for the Air Corps as well. So far as the Air Corps went, "the original reason for the present arrangement was that it was thought [by the General Staff] that airplanes would be operating from landing fields and airdromes so far in the rear that it would not be practicable" to assign air signal troops anywhere else than at the rear, where they would presumably spend their time putting in wire communications for the big headquarters. Air signal communications, Ingles felt, would certainly entail much more than that, particularly when aviation, having ceased to be subordinate, was no longer attached to the ground arms. In his opinion, "This reason never had very much foundation and now . . . has even less." [12]

Maj. Jerry V. Matejka, also a Signal Corps general of World War II, conceded that a tactical commander must be "solely responsible" for his own communications

[9] Ltr, CSigO to TAG, 2 Apr 24. SigC 300.3 AR 105–15.

[10] SigC 676 Gen, 1918–1938, *passim*.

[11] *Historical Sketch of the Signal Corps (1860–1941)*, p. 95.

[12] Notation by Maj Ingles on Ltr, Capt Fred G. Borden to Ingles, 8 Feb 30. SigC 676 Use of Army Com Systems 3, 1929.

system and "must have absolute military control" of all of the men assigned to it, but contended that there was no reason why the men must belong to the same arm as the commander. Matejka repeated the conviction that standardization of training was vital, because good communications in one regiment must be matched by good communications in another regiment, if there is to be good communication between the two. This training, he argued, is a specialized knowledge, and the men who master it need to know that they will be rewarded for their skill, not held back because, being signalmen, they do not command troops. He recommended, therefore, that Signal Corps units should be reestablished in echelons from which they had disappeared, should be commanded by Signal Corps officers on the commanders' staffs, should be attached to the tactical organization rather than assigned, and, the tactical mission being completed, should once again become part of the parent Signal Corps units from which they had been detached.[13]

Maj. Gen. Joseph O. Mauborgne, likewise, becoming Chief Signal Officer, met the lingering controversy. It came up in 1937 over the question of who was obligated actually to put a radio into a combat vehicle. Did responsibility for signal communications extend to installing signal equipment? The chiefs of the Infantry, Cavalry, and Field Artillery, as well as G-1, G-2, G-4, and Mauborgne, held opinions at variance with each other. The combat arms wanted to have the Signal Corps do the installation of every set in every one of their vehicles. But the lines of authority had been drawn at a point which made this impossible, the Chief Signal Officer objected. His organization, not being provided with the men or the

funds for going throughout the Military Establishment in order to install radios, could only install them at the factory, as part of an assembly-line process. Assembly-line installation could occur only if the Infantry, Cavalry, and others synchronized their procurement of vehicles with the procurement of accessories, yet so far was this from being the case that appropriations for the radio equipment were not even sought in the same fiscal year as appropriations for the vehicles themselves. The combat arms must be prepared to train specialists for handling communications. This was the point of major importance. Installing a radio was not difficult; an untrained infantryman could do it. The Signal Corps would put the pilot model in, and would enclose specific instructions with every set, but the Infantry, Cavalry, Artillery, and other arms must use their own men for the responsibilities which they claimed.[14]

Every year, meanwhile, put all forms of signaling several years ahead of the stages of development reached before the 1920 reorganization. The man who had been expert in 1918 was ignorant in 1928 unless he had kept himself informed of the new devices and methods. Far from being able to be communications mentor to the whole Army, the Signal Corps could barely maintain the pace itself. General Saltzman took note of a growing demand for apparatus of greater capacity and variety, but was unable to do much to supply it.[15] His

[13] Maj J. V. Matejka, "Signal Communication," Signal Corps Bulletin, No. 89 (March–April, 1936), pp. 20–24.

[14] Memo, Actg ACofS G-3 for CofS, 20 Aug 37, sub: Revision of AR 105–15—re responsibility for installation of radio equip in vehicles. AG 676 (3-19-37) (1) Revision of AR 105–15.

[15] Ltr, CSigO to All SigC Officers, 28 Mar 24. SigC 676 Gen, 1918–1938.

organization could afford almost no new equipment for its operating functions in Washington, the corps areas, Alaska and the departments, nor even for its Signal School at Fort Monmouth, where the demands of the future made it particularly important.

Recognizing the necessity for modernizing its curriculum, the school tried to keep its instruction up to date and its enrollment at a high enough level to warrant the instruction. But only a few men could be allotted to training without affecting the efficiency of the Corps' daily responsibility; and there was considerable dissatisfaction, moreover, with the caliber of officers, whether from the Signal Corps or from another branch, who were allotted.[16] Many a field officer was "deplorably ignorant of signal communications."[17] In a few cases, men who could not be spared from their duties in order to go to the school sought further study at local technical schools and universities; and partly for their advantage, partly to maintain interest among Reserve and National Guard officers, the school gave correspondence courses. Even in these, however, students did not always show the reasonable familiarity with their own component of the Army which the printed lessons and monographs took for granted.

Occupied with routine duties, some Signal Corps officers and men vegetated. Routine duties, some essential, some unessential, told particularly upon enlisted men. It became increasingly difficult to maintain morale; the rate of turnover was heavy. The Army Pay Act of 1922 had reduced the grades available to radio operators; as a result, a good operator did not often re-enlist unless he had one of the higher noncommissioned officer ratings. From Monmouth, the 51st Signal Battal-

ion was supplying qualified enlisted instructors and qualified enlisted administrative or technical specialists, but against a steady demand that always exceeded the supply. Of ninety-four men from the battalion who were going to classes in 1928, fifty-one were made available for assignment as a pool of trained specialists. So great was the need for them that the pool was drained within six months.[18] Officers found themselves faced with the requirement that they develop attainments like skill in public speaking and an elementary acquaintance with international affairs, with business administration, or with languages.[19] In another connection but on the same theme, Maj. Spencer B. Akin, later the postwar Chief Signal Officer, suggested that it might be a good thing for a Signal Corps officer to have at least "a general idea of the probable effects on his specialty of the most recently developed agencies of warfare."[20]

The Continuing Technical Tradition

Taking a much firmer view, from time to time members of the Corps offered plans for rebuilding it as a strong technical or-

[16] (1) Ltr, Maj George L. Van Deusen, Sig School, to Maj David McL. Crawford, OCSigO, 27 Mar 29; (2) Ltr, CSigO to Comdt Sig School, 28 Mar 29; (3) Ltr, CSigO to CO Ft. Monmouth, 24 Jul 29, sub: Home study courses for officers. SigC 352.11 Gen Courses of Instruction 1.

[17] Ltr, Maj Ingles, Sig School, to Maj Otis K. Sadtler, OCSigO, 9 Mar 25. SigC 352.11 Gen 1.

[18] S Sgt Leo W. Bundy, History of Fort Monmouth, 1936, pp. 1-8. SigC Hq Ft. Monmouth 322 51st FM 1928.

[19] AG Ltr, 22 Aug 30, sub: Honor courses in sv schools. AG 352.01 (8-18-30) Misc (0).

[20] 2d Wrapper Ind, [Maj Akin, Asst Comdt] Sig School Ft. Monmouth to CSigO, 7 Oct 31, on AG Ltr, AG 352.01 (4-15-31) Misc M, 24 Sep 31. SigC 352.11 Gen 2.

ganization.[21] For steadily the technician claimed a larger part of the soldier. Year by year, it was becoming more necessary for even a basic signalman to know Ohm's law than the manual of arms. In field exercises there was little change; old habits persisted like campaign hats.[22] But many minds in the Corps were conscious of the honorable tradition of scientific interest and contribution which they inherited, as well as alert to the studies and experiments of their own day. The laboratories of the Signal Corps [23] were the centers of this interest. Whatever was amateur became professional there; what was speculative took a position well behind practical military uses but was not cast aside altogether. The growth of the service, such as it was in the stunted years between wars, occurred more in the technical than in the tactical or administrative sides of the Signal Corps.

Research and invention of considerable variety took place. Master Signal Electrician Samuel O. Hoffman led off with an experiment in thermal detection. In January 1919, at Langley Field, Virginia, he endeavored to locate an airplane by intercepting the heat of its engine. He was able to register on a galvanometer the presence of a Jenny which was flying at 3,500 feet just after nightfall in thick, wet weather. Beyond that, he failed, because unluckily "the slightest whiff of cloud gave a warm indication as large as a plane would give." [24] This was an effort in a scarcely opened field of the communications spectrum.

In the better-known yet still sufficiently novel span which ground waves occupy, General Squier's wired wireless came forward to reach a wider public. Squier had his invention demonstrated between the Signal Corps Research Laboratory at the Bureau of Standards (in Washington) and

Baltimore, again between New York and Albany on the telephone lines of the New York Central Railway, and over a Chesapeake Bay cable of the Weather Bureau.[25] Among other things, the tests made clear the feasibility of telephoning from moving trains. Working from the wired wireless principle, R. D. Duncan, Jr., who was the chief engineer of the Signal Corps Research Laboratory, developed an instrument which he named the superphone, because it promised "absolute secrecy of communication without any chance of the conversation being overheard, interrupted or broken into." [26] The promise exceeded the performance.

Experiments in optical signaling made use of polarized light. The physicist Robert A. Millikan, later a Nobel prize winner, had instituted this research when he was a Signal Corps major in 1917. Dr. Louis Cohen and Maj. Joseph O. Mauborgne worked on a new method of eliminating

---

[21] E. g., Ltr, Sig Supply Officer, Sig Sec N.Y. Gen Intermediate Depot, to CSigO, 29 May 24, sub: Sig coms systems, with 2d Ind, CO Camp Alfred Vail, to CSigO, 16 Jun 24, and 3d Ind, Col Voris to O/C Sig Sec N.Y. Gen Intermediate Depot, 20 Jun 24. SigC 352.11 Gen 2.

[22] See, for example, the 1933 training film, Signal Communication Within the Infantry Regiment, TF-13.

[23] Before their consolidation on 12 August 1929 as the Signal Corps Laboratories at Fort Monmouth, these consisted of the Electrical Laboratory and the Research Laboratory in Washington (the latter at the Bureau of Standards) and the Radio Laboratory at Monmouth. In addition, there was the Signal Corps Aircraft Radio Laboratory at Dayton, Ohio.

[24] S. O. Hoffman, "The Detection of Invisible Objects by Heat Radiation," paper read at ninety-seventh meeting of the American Physical Society, 25–26 April 1919, Physical Review, 2d Ser., XIV (August, 1919), 154.

[25] "Recent Experiments in Wire Radio," Signal Corps Bulletin, No. 6 (February, 1921), pp. 4–6.

[26] Maj. Gen. George O. Squier, "A New Telephone Invention, the 'Superphone,'" Signal Corps Bulletin, No. 12 (January, 1922), p. 1.

static. Capt. Fred P. Andrews developed a variable condenser for use on the Alaska cable system. A transmitter-receiver resonance indicator was worked out by 1st Lt. Wesley T. Guest, although after four years' negotiation he was unable to patent it for the government.[27] O. E. Marvel, a radio engineer for the Signal Corps at McCook Field, Dayton, Ohio, contributed to the development of a radio-controlled automobile with which the Engineering Division of the Air Service at that field used to mystify visitors.

The Signal Corps had become responsible for radio research and development in the broadest sense in February 1919, the authorization only confirming what was already the case, because both the American Expeditionary Forces and the Air Service had depended upon it for wireless equipment.[28] After the Armistice, the work which had been carried on in Paris, Washington, and Little Silver, New Jersey, shrank and concentrated. Some of it continued at the Bureau of Standards for a time, along with Navy research. Then it was moved to Little Silver, ultimately to be joined by the Signal Corps electrical and meteorological laboratories in the area to be known as Fort Monmouth.[29] Close confidence surrounded the work, for *radio* was a generic term which covered many technical experiments. To the public, conveniently, it meant little else than broadcasting—just as *aviation* was coming to signify heavier-than-air flight only; and even to uninitiates within the Signal Corps itself, the term raised no notion of anything more than a weak competitor to the standard wire means for communication. However, to the engineers in the Signal Corps Laboratories, as to electrical science and commerce generally, it meant, above all, wireless communication in the established fields of telephone and telegraph.

Loop radio, having reached postwar official status as the SCR-77,[30] made its appearance at Fort Sill, Oklahoma, where Mauborgne showed it to the Field Artillery Board. Airborne radio began to achieve real importance, and a clear distinction grew up between ground and air equipment. There came to be three kinds of air radio equipment, depending upon a primary use for communications, navigation, or meteorology. The Signal Corps Laboratories established a liaison staff at McCook Field, in 1922, in order to supervise the testing of air communication and air navigation sets, but kept meteorological development at Camp Vail. Since the Meteorological Service, which had been revived in 1917 and 1918, was for the Army as a whole, it seemed a good idea to retain meteorological devices, whether for air or ground use, at the New Jersey development agency. McCook Field was incorporated into Wright Field, and Wright Field became the air matériel center. The liaison group there became the Signal Corps Aircraft Radio Laboratory; from 1927 on, it proposed as well as tested the equipment which the Signal Corps developed for the Air Corps.

[27] SigC 072. Patents, assembled alphabetically by name of inventor: Andrews, Guest, *et al.*

[28] For a few months in 1918 the Air Service had attempted both to install radio sets and to train radio operators, but, overreaching itself, had conceded the training to the Signal Corps. Thereafter, the Air Service provided personnel and school facilities for the instruction and airfields and pilots for research experiments and practice trials. WD, *Annual Reports, 1919,* Vol. I, Pt. I, pp. 1189–93.

[29] CSigO, *Annual Report, 1930,* p. 41.

[30] Originally standing for "set, complete, radio," the initials SCR came by general consent to mean "Signal Corps radio" instead. Although to the public, a radio set was likely to mean only a receiver, to a Signal Corpsman a set included, not only the receiver, but also the transmitter, antenna, and power supply.

THE SCR–77 *in use during ROTC training at Camp Vail, New Jersey.*

Meanwhile, Camp Vail became Fort Monmouth, and the main Laboratories there had reached the "130" series of SCR's. These were portable sets which showed the sharp functional distinction of their World War II descendants: the SCR-130, 131, and 132 were ground forces radios (and the 131 continued in use until 1944), whereas the next four in order were made for the air forces. The SCR-133 was for pursuit airplanes; observation planes would employ the 134; night bombers, the 135; and the SCR-136 was a ground-to-air set. The view which prevailed then of the prime function of a military airplane is indicated by the fact that the SCR-134, the observation plane set, received the most attention; comparably, the bombard-ment airplane's SCR-135 was projected as "a set whose range when used as a radio-telephone will be from 80 to 100 miles, and . . . as an undamped wave radiotele-graph . . . from 200 to 250 miles." [31] Armstrong's superheterodyne receiver had vanished into an eddy of patent difficulties before his postwar successors in the Signal Corps could smooth out its performance for military uses. Unable to use the super-heterodyne, and rendered dependent by the Congresses of the 1920's which awarded all government enterprise to pri-vate business, the Signal Corps did what it could with commercial radios of the day. These sets cramped the receiving antenna into a small space in order to achieve a marketable compactness, but had the ad-vantage of the simple tuned frequency.

[31] "New Airplane Radio Set: Experimental Work on SCR–135, Airplane Radio Transmitter," Signal Corps Bulletin, No. 6 (February, 1921), pp. 1–3.

Some of the disputed patents expired in 1931 and, with the commercial companies engaged in rivalry to bring out new superheterodyne sets, the Signal Corps was able to ask them to produce one for the Army. The receiver BC-189, the first superheterodyne receiver standardized for an Army set, was ready by 1934.[32]

In navigational radio, the Bureau of Standards, the Air Service, and the Signal Corps collaborated on the radio beacon, a device which the ever-lengthening range of airplanes was making inevitable. Flight tests had been made with it at Bolling Field, Washington, D. C., in 1921. Shortly afterward, the work was transferred to Ohio. A variety of other flights tested and improved it until, in 1927, it guided Air Corps 1st Lts. Lester J. Maitland and Albert F. Hegenberger to Hawaii, slightly in advance of the late-summer "Dole Derby" over the same route.

In 1935 a noteworthy reorganization collected all development work in air communication and air navigation equipment, whether Signal Corps or Air Corps work, and lodged it in the single agency, the Aircraft Radio Laboratory of Wright Field. Progress in new types resulted. The joint effort produced military versions of the radio range and the radio compass; versions of all of the instruments for blind flying (altimeter, gyrocompass, artificial horizon, airspeed indicator, bank-and-turn indicator, rate-of-climb meter); and the instrument-landing system which developed into ground-controlled approach.[33]

Military airfields throughout the United States and in the Canal Zone and Hawaiian Islands were gradually equipped with homing beacons and radio ranges. The ranges, of a new type advocated by the Department of Commerce, permitted an extra channel for radiotelephony. Thus, the station could broadcast weather information along with the beacon signals (the "A," the "N," and the steady, on-course tone). With the speed of flight increasing, this was a great advantage, because a pilot could lose his course if he had to switch off the range signal in order to get the weather. At that stage of aviation, however, radio aids to flying had by no means established themselves. The least progress made at the Aircraft Radio Laboratory was in the fundamental decision of whether to include radio equipment in the blueprint design of aircraft. The ability to fly by instruments held forth such obvious advantages that it seems astonishing that radio was not integral to all military aircraft from the moment that it was available. Designers and aviators alike, nevertheless, were often reluctant to part with the maneuverability and speed which the weight and bulk of the radio sets would cause them to lose. For some time the airborne equipment developed at the Aircraft Radio Laboratory was merely accessory. In 1936, however, the Signal Corps announced that "the Army's 1,150 war planes at last were equipped fully with radio communication and the utmost in military navigation devices."[34] The communications equipment thus replaced had been in use since 1922.

Meteorological research, at the Fort Monmouth laboratories, acknowledged a debt to Maj. William R. Blair, which was also acknowledged in the Air Service's 1924 round-the-world flight. Blair, who had been head of the Meteorological Section in the American Expeditionary Forces

[32] Signal Corps Information Letter, No. 11 (October 10, 1936), p. 8. (See Bibliographical Note.)

[33] Capt. F. L. Ankenbrandt, "Ceiling Zero—Visibility Zero," Signal Corps Bulletin, No. 109 (July-December, 1940), pp. 10–25.

[34] Kansas City Star, February 13, 1936.

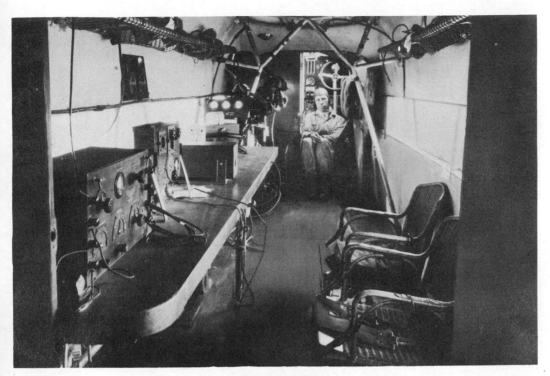

A FLYING RADIO LABORATORY

EXPERIMENTAL ANTENNAS *installed on an airplane.*

and who took a leading part in the work at Fort Monmouth for many years, joined scientists of the Bureau of Standards, especially Harry Diamond, in working out the principles of an audiomodulated radiosonde. It was not called the radiosonde then, but the radiometeorograph. Any weather-station man was practiced in releasing a small pilot balloon and calculating its rise and drift by following it with a theodolite until it disappeared from view. The new meteorograph held out a promise of being useful at night and on cloudy days, when the weather man could not see the balloon, and of providing information regarding temperature, pressure, and humidity as well as wind data above the clouds. It consisted of an automatic, battery-powered, miniature weather station and transmitter, borne by the

pilot balloon. When the expanding balloon burst in increasingly thin air, the instruments would parachute to earth, to be salvaged, if they could be found, for another flight; meanwhile, the meteorologist would track the automatic squeaks of the transmitter with directional receiving antenna on the ground.

In the summer of 1935 the Meteorological Service sent 1st Lt. William H. Wenstrom and three enlisted men to set up a temporary weather station at Rapid City, in the South Dakota Black Hills. There the Air Corps and the National Geographic Society undertook a successful balloon ascension into the stratosphere. Wenstrom and his men gave radiometeorography a series of tests, sending 45-inch and 12-inch pilot balloons aloft and detecting the signals by means of a superheterodyne receiver. By 1938 the Air Corps' Patterson Field, Ohio, and Barksdale Field, California, were using the radiometeorograph, in a form standardized at one and one-half pounds for the device itself, one-half pound for its parachute, and one pound for the balloon; it broadcast its signals on a frequency of 179.6 megacycles.[35]

In addition to all of these tangible evidences of advance, the pages of the Signal Corps Bulletin reflected the possibilities—not yet the actualities, but the possibilities—which excited radio scientists and engineers. William D. Hershberger, associate physicist at the Laboratories, wrote in the Bulletin of experiments in radio optics, a term then used to refer to the area of the spectrum from the P-band to the K-band where radar afterward materialized; it derived from Hertz's demonstration in 1886 of the optical properties of radio waves. Capt. John J. Downing published a theory of radio reflection. Paul E. Watson, for whom the Signal Corps Eatontown Laboratory was renamed after his death in the midst of World War II, explained antenna radiation characteristics and devised a method for computing ground-wave intensities. Capt. K. M. Soukaras analyzed the propagation of radio waves into the ionosphere. In a summary of essential facts known about radio energy, and emphasizing the debt which any item of military equipment owes to the theory that precedes it, Maj. Roger B. Colton offered rules of thumb for the Laboratories in their radio equipment projects:

(1) Frequencies below 100 kc . . . require extensive and expensive antenna systems; (2) frequencies between 100 and 1,500 kc are generally useful . . . (3) frequencies between 1,500 and 2,500 kc are especially good for vehicles, small boats, and airplanes, and for short and medium distances, but in airplanes it is generally preferable to use frequencies from 3,000 to 3,500 kc alternatively with frequencies from 5,000 to 6,000 kc; . . . (5) frequencies above 30,000 kc are very short distance frequencies; (6) frequencies above 300 mc (300,000 kc) behave very much like light and are as yet hard to produce efficiently.[36]

Colton, a graduate of Yale and the Massachusetts Institute of Technology, later became director of the Signal Corps Laboratories during the three years before Pearl Harbor.

Wire projects gradually assembled much of the wire equipment that was to be used in the forthcoming war. There appeared a lightweight field teletype, the first which the Signal Corps had, an adaptation of a commercial teleprinter; another teleprinter, applicable to radio as well, and produced by George A. Graham, who was afterward the chief engineer of the Wire Section at Fort Monmouth; W-110 field wire, for which the Laboratories investigated the possibility of replacing tin and rubber with cellophane and duprene, two Du Pont synthetics; laryngaphones and, later, built-in diaphragms,

[35] (1) Interv, SigC Hist Sec with William R. Blair, SigC Ret., Locust, N. J., 12 Feb 50. (2) Signal Corps Information Letter, No. 6 (July 10, 1935), p. 18, No. 18 (July 1, 1938), p. 16, No. 19 (October 10, 1938), p. 15.

[36] W. D. Hershberger, "A Survey of Radio Optics," No. 79 (July–August, 1934), pp. 15–23; Capt. J. J. Downing, "Reflection of Radio Waves," No. 99 (January–March, 1938), pp. 27–30; Paul E. Watson, "Antenna Radiation Characteristics," No. 99 (January–March, 1938), pp. 65–78; Watson, "A Method of Computing Ground Wave Intensities," No. 103 (January–March, 1939), pp. 48–55; Capt. K. M. Soukaras, "Radio Wave Propagation and the Ionosphere," No. 106 (October–December, 1939), pp. 27–32; Maj. Roger G. Colton, "Radio Energy Radiation and Propagation," No. 86 (September–October, 1935), pp. 18–25. All in Signal Corps Bulletin.

so that gas masks could be used with standard telephones; the EE-8-T2 telephone; and the sound-powered telephone. The last, as its name indicates, was an instrument which dispensed with dry batteries and activated its transmitter merely from the power of the human voice. Dubious about it, the Signal Corps nevertheless bought two sets for testing. These came from the Bell Telephone Laboratories, and were identical with those the Navy used on battleships. In addition, the Signal Corps scrutinized Radio Corporation of America and Control Instrument Company sets, and signed a 1937 contract for a dozen of still another model with the Automatic Electric Company.[37] The sound-powered telephone was never a favorite in those years, however.

The EE-8 telephone, Type 2, became the answer to a general need among all components of the service for a superior military field instrument, light of weight, rugged, easily maintained. First standardized in 1932, although not procurable until 1937, it was one of the items developed well in advance of World War II which proved themselves in that conflict. Outdoing the maximum transmission range of its predecessor, the EE-5, by at least six miles, it was also lighter in weight and "talked up much better." [38] Other items of wire communication equipment which these years brought out included the telegraph set, TG-5, which won the approbation of the Field Artillery; reel units with improved wire-laying and wire-recovering devices; a loading coil for Coast Artillery and Signal Corps long field lines which trebled their range; and W-130 wire, a strand even lighter than the field wire W-110. Assault wire, as it was known, had to be flexible and light of weight, very easy to handle and carry, be-

cause front-line men would use it. If the outer rubber insulation were applied by the usual extrusion process in manufacture, the wire would be too thick and stiff. Drawing it instead through liquid latex seemed to solve the difficulty.[39]

Much of the development work took place without the sympathy of the Army as a whole, which, encased in a skintight budget, was likely to declare that no money should be frittered away on tomorrow-projects when today had to be taken care of first. The nation at large, which as an electorate was responsible for the tight budget, insisted moreover that the Army use up what it had before ever asking for more. Admirable as this sort of thriftiness was in checking wastefulness, it did not help the services to keep up to date. Stocks left over from ten years earlier had to be "consumed" even though from the engineering point of view they were obsolete. Often this meant dismantling models of several types and recombining them, in order to get something as close as possible to what the consumer required without going to any expense except considerable overhead and salaries.

Although in 1927 the Signal Corps Technical Committee endorsed the development of a monocord switchboard, the Chief Signal Officer indicated that neither time nor funds would permit it.[40] The

---

[37] Hist Sec E&T Divs OCSigO, History of Signal Corps Research and Development in World War II, 1945–46, Vol. V, Wire Communication, Pt. 4, Proj 562-B. SigC Hist Sec File.

[38] Memos for Record, Maj Louis Cansler, OCSigO, 25 May and 5 Sep 36. SigC C&E Equip Gen.

[39] Signal Corps Information Letter, No. 18 (July 1, 1938), p. 12.

[40] Capt George I. Back, O/C Wire Equip Projs SCL, History of Wire Communication Development Projects and Certain Miscellaneous Development Projects During the Period 1924 to 1933, 23 Aug 33, p. 9. SigC Hist Sec File.

engineers proposed an improved telegraph set in the same year, but could not order it while numbers of the old sets were on hand. They abandoned an interesting project for a mobile meteorological station for lack of money. There was very little progress until the 1930's in the redesigning of fire-control systems for coastal guns. The Office of the Chief Signal Officer had to cancel an assault-wire project. Poverty seemed pretty constricting. Yet sometimes these cancellations came from decisions which held, not that they cost too much, but that they had no value. In 1928, for instance, the Research and Engineering Division improved a signal lamp, only to find that although the Coast Artillery did want it the Infantry did not, and the Field Artillery was unenthusiastic.[41] A more striking case in point, particularly to those who struggled a decade later with wet, rusted, gritty, or fungus-clogged equipment, is the dropping of a project for shelter for communications in the field, because "no need could be foreseen for equipment of this character." [42]

Usually, though, the fault was not shortsightedness but shortness of means. Considering the whole annual appropriation, research and development got what looked like a generous share, but it was not a relatively predictable, day-by-day activity, and other Signal Corps functions were.[43] The nub of the problem, indeed, was that research and development demanded heavy outlays if there was to be any return at all, yet could not be certain of rewarding every investment.

Defense-Strategy Signaling

The riskiest, the most elusive of all projects now a successful part of past history were the detection projects. Militarily they were of unmistakable significance. They were related to a fundamental rule: know where your enemy is. To the United States of the 1920's and 1930's, which thought solely in terms of defense, detection was associated with the desire for enough warning; and because the airplane was above all others the weapon most likely to appear without warning, detection projects became to an ever greater extent aircraft warning projects. Detection also implied the discovery of targets on land and sea, and the location of objects or persons that were not targets as well as of those that were. In later usages, even, it included finding the fixed as well as the moving—landfalls and mountains, along with mobile objects like approaching bombers, submarines, night scouting parties, birds, rain clouds, and V-2 projectiles.

Some methods of locating used one-way devices; that is to say, they depended upon picking up radiations from the object being detected. Others were two-way, sending out radiant energy and measuring it when the target reflected it. Detection research ranged the known spectrum. It explored visual means, as in bringing an airplane within the beam of an antiaircraft gun battery's searchlights or comput-

---

[41] Capt. Jay D. B. Lattin had noted that the French, in putting down the rebellion of Abd-el-Krim, had used visual signals. He thought that the American Army ought to keep them, too, and develop them "rather than let [them] become discarded because of cumbersome apparatus and insufficiently trained personnel." Ltr, Lattin, Office Mil Attaché, Paris, to CSigO, 4 Nov 25. SigC 676 Sig Coms of the French Army.

[42] Back hist cited n. 40, p. 35.

[43] For example, in one subunit fiscal plan which estimated $1,950,000 for construction of communication systems, the main activity of the Signal Corps, research was budgeted at $480,000. Memo, Fiscal Div for Maj Owen S. Albright, 19 Feb 25. SigC OR 381 Mob Plng.

ing the position of a 16-inch railway-mounted gun by measuring its muzzle flash. It depended upon sound, as in the aural detectors of the nation's 1939 coastal defenses. It produced results by heat, or infrared rays; by ultraviolet rays; by short radio waves; and, most impressively of all, by microwaves. Several of these avenues had opened in World War I. Light was the principal means of detection then, when flares and star shells illuminated no man's land and searchlights attempted to catch zeppelins in their beams. Radio direction finding was a valuable adjunct to ground tactics; and the efforts at detecting airplanes by intercepting the very short waves given off by the ignition systems or by locating their infrared radiations had led to the postwar experiments in thermal detection of aircraft which Signal Corpsmen engaged in at Langley Field and also at Columbia University.

Sound-locating equipment, turned to after the early thermal experiments, absorbed a good deal of both Signal Corps and Ordnance attention. Scientists understood its physical limitation—the basic fact that the objects to be detected were already flying half as fast as sound travels—but had to bring it into being anyway, pending something better. In the equipment which they brought out the Army got its first practical means of detecting airplanes at a distance. Just as searchlights, the first method attempted, extended the sense of sight, and as pulse radar is figuratively an extraordinary heightening of the sense of touch, so the intermediate method sharpened the hearing. Binaural detectors employed large horns in order to track an approaching airplane by the noise of its engines. Originally there were four horns, one pair funneling sound into the ears of the az-

imuth operator, the other pair serving the elevation operator, but the number was reduced to three in the last models just before radar replaced sound location.[44] Binaural equipment controlled 60-inch searchlights, in an association of extra sight with extra sound. Aural detection passed through a series of refinements which kept it a part of the nation's antiaircraft defenses until after World War II had begun. Nonetheless, it was doomed from the outset, because sounds move too slowly to provide much warning.

Sound ranging in another field led to experimentation in hydracoustics or marine aural detection. In July 1922 the Signal Corps fell heir to some of the sound-ranging projects of the Coast Artillery Corps,[45] and in 1930, making the customary arrangement with a using arm, took over all of the laboratory development of the equipment while the Coast Artillery assumed its field testing. Some of the equipment was for ground sound location, but the Coast Artillery Corps had particular interest, next to antiaircraft projects, in detecting water-borne targets. Hydrocoustic ranging, as the words suggest, endeavored to calculate the distance of an object by hearing it through water. Scattered attempts had been made to develop it, as an aid to navigation solely, before World War I. The technique was based upon the fact that surface or underwater craft emit sound waves which delicate underwater microphones can pick up and transmit to instruments on shore. In its simplest terms, such an arrangement

[44] Harry M. Davis, History of the Signal Corps Development of U.S. Army Radar Equipment, Pt. I, 1944, Fig. 1. SigC Hist Sec File.

[45] "Engineering and Research" and "Development Projects of the Signal Corps," Signal Corps Bulletin, No. 18 (February, 1923), pp. 27–28, and No. 21 (August, 1923), p. 7.

EARLY SOUND DETECTION DEVICE

provided a "seeing ear" by which the observer on land could tell what was going
on underneath the water or on its surface,
in spite of distance or poor visibility. During its years of work in subaqueous sound
ranging, the Signal Corps produced several instruments, and had binaural sets
ready for service test by 1935.

Other forms of detection of ships, challenging the aural methods, claimed attention. One means tried by the French liner
Normandie called for the transmission of
ultrahigh-frequency (15-centimeter) radio
waves in a 45° arc in front of the bow.
When the radio waves encountered an
object not more than a dozen miles away,
they were reflected into a sensitive receiver and amplified so as to be made audible
in a telephone receiver. "This was a sort
of ear-radar," and an extraordinary advance.[46] A suggestion closer to Signal
Corps interests, because it came to the
Laboratories from the Hawaiian Department, proposed an adaptation of Millikan's "black light" to alert the coast of
Oahu with a system of ultraviolet beams
impinging upon photoelectric cells. An incoming ship or landing party would her-
ald itself by interrupting the beam. The
Laboratories, however, pointed out the
impracticability of the proposal. Such
rays are tangential to the surface of the
earth; the only way to cover the island approaches would have been with a dense
series of beams, and some of the apparatus
might have had to be placed 250 feet
above the water line.[47]

Infrared methods, both for airplanes
and for ships, were steadily under trial.
When Major Blair was the officer in
charge of the Research and Engineering
Division of the Office of the Chief Signal
Officer in the late '20's, he expressed his
dissatisfaction with sound locators and

recommended that money be allocated
for both high-frequency radio and heat
detection. He was especially interested in
the former, being one of the few men of
that time who saw possibilities in detection by means of having radio waves
"bouncing back like an echo."[48]

Upon becoming director of the Laboratories in 1930, Blair scheduled a project to
inquire into the potentialities of both. Set
up in February 1931, Project 88 had the
title Position Finding by Means of Light,
but what was in mind was more nearly
Detection by Means of Electromagnetic
Radiation—in that part of the spectrum
which spans both microwaves and infrared rays. Scientists referred to it as the
"radio-optic" field because the radiations
are of such high frequency as to have line-
of-sight characteristics. The assignment of
Project 88 to the Sound and Light Section
brought into proximity all of the explora-
tions of means of detection. Blair first put
the emphasis on heat ranging. Year by
year thermal research had reached several
more of its frustrating yet elusively promising climaxes. At the Aberdeen Proving
Ground, in 1926, the Ordnance Department had detected an airplane by reflected
infrared rays and the Naval Research
Laboratory had reported successful experiments. Because Ordnance had just

[46] Orrin E. Dunlap, Jr., *Radar: What Radar Is and
How It Works* (New York: Harper & Brothers, 1946),
p. 117. For a contemporary description of this equip-
ment, see "'Feelers' for Ships: New Micro-Wave
Equipment Described," *Wireless World,* XXXVIII
(June 26, 1936), 623–24.

[47] Ltr, CG Hawaiian Dept to TAG, 30 Mar 34, sub:
Use of ultraviolet-ray projectors, and 2d Wrapper Ind,
Dir SCL to CSigO, 16 May 34. SigC 311.6 Ultra-
violet-Ray Projectors—Defense of Oahu.

[48] "I remember those exact words." Statement by
Brig. Gen. Oliver L. Spiller, Coast Artillery Corps, in
an interview with Capt. Harry M. Davis, 28 June
1945, Washington, D. C. SigC A46-160 Data on Blair
Patent Search.

withdrawn in favor of the Signal Corps, infrared work in the new Project 88 was based upon the Ordnance researches. Signal Corps experience going back to the 1919 tests was added to it in the person of the section chief, Dr. S. H. Anderson, who had been present at Langley Field when Hoffman made them. In 1932 the Laboratories tracked a Navy blimp to 6,300 feet by the reflected infrared means.[49]

In 1934 it became apparent that, although the Ordnance-Signal Corps duplication had been resolved, another had taken its place. The exchange of correspondence over the Hawaiian Department's electric eye suggestion brought to the attention of the General Staff the fact that secret thermal research was in progress in two parts of the Army; for the Signal Corps, in pointing out that its infrared projects were more likely to turn out well than the ultraviolet method, drew an objection from the Corps of Engineers. Charged with the responsibility for developing searchlights, the Engineers had sponsored research in infrared detection after a 1933 Air Corps-Antiaircraft exercise at Fort Knox, Kentucky, had shown how unsatisfactory the accustomed aircraft warning equipment was. Pending a decision on the question of responsibility, both combat services kept their thermal detection projects in force.

Meanwhile, the method inherited from Ordnance, the reflected (two-way) method, proved disappointing and the Signal Corps suspended further work on it; the equipment could not generate enough heat to be detectable after any moderately long round trip. The radiated, or one-way, approach was kept open. With a thermolocator, which they produced for marine detection only, the Fort Monmouth experimenters more or less successfully tracked a series of ocean liners sailing past them from New York Harbor: the *Mauretania* to a distance of 23,000 yards in 1934, the *Normandie* to 30,000 in 1935 and, in the same year, the *Aquitania* to 18,000 through a fog. They were even able to distinguish the *Mauretania's* dummy smokestack from her three real ones.[50] Nevertheless, the Laboratories' detection research was due for a new departure. Radio-wave work was about to take full precedence over heat ranging. Thermal detectors were delivering much better results than radio, but their limit of efficiency persisted in arriving too soon.

The services' study of radiolocation had begun in detail at the Naval Research Laboratory in 1930. On December 10 of that year, Dr. A. Hoyt Taylor and his colleagues there had demonstrated Doppler-method equipment to representatives of the Signal Corps, the Coast Artillery, and the Air Corps. The Doppler method is more commonly referred to as *beat* detection, in distinction to *pulse* detection, the means finally adopted for most of the wartime radar equipment. The principle of beat detection is much the same as that of the superheterodyne receiver, because it depends upon a difference in frequencies. A transmitter sends out high-frequency waves, the waves strike a moving object, and the contact changes their frequency. The interruption has slightly retarded or accelerated them, with the result that they return at a frequency just different enough so that as they beat against the new outgoing waves the difference is perceptible. It is a difference of only a few hundred or a few thousand cycles, and thus can be heard in a re-

[49] Davis hist cited n. 44, p. 20.
[50] (1) SCL, Supplementary Prog Rpt, 1935. (2) Interv with Gen Spiller cited n. 48.

ceiver. It can also be indicated on an
oscillograph, and the speed and direction
of the object which the waves are intercepting can be precisely measured. The
naval laboratory research in the radio-
interference method had not reached this
stage; it was in its beginnings. Indeed,
Blair was unenthusiastic about it because
it seemed to offer no precision at all. It
showed generally that there were airplanes in the vicinity, but not where each
one was.[51]

Here was a case where no one was
wholly wrong or right. In terms of the
interceptor aviation of that day, beat detection promised to permit a squadron to
be warned, get into the air, catch sight
of the enemy, and engage in a dogfight.
From this point of view, both naval aviation and the Army Air Corps would be
interested. But the Signal Corps was developing aircraft warning equipment for
the use of the Coast Artillery primarily,
and, in terms of ground antiaircraft fire,
beat detection sounded unpromising. The
guns would have no exact firing information and the attacking planes would be
past and out of sight before they could get
it. Nevertheless, the Signal Corps Laboratories put William D. Hershberger to
work on radio interference in the Radio
Section.

In 1931 Taylor's tests indicated that the
beat method would require a wide separation of the transmitter from the receiver.
Given a characteristic of that sort, the
equipment would be almost impossible to
install on a ship. The Secretary of the
Navy, forwarding to the Secretary of War
in January 1932 a report on the Naval
Research Laboratory's work, suggested
that the Army might have more use for it.
Actually, the laboratory continued with it,
Taylor, Leo C. Young and Lawrence A.

Hyland taking out a patent on it in 1934.[52]

Hershberger, whose practice at first was
simply to note an increase in the signal
strength at the receiver when the reflections came back, was assigned to the
Sound and Light Section in 1933. As the
work became a segment of the whole program of radio-optic research, it began to
undergo more hopeful exploration.[53] In
1934 a Signal Corps detector of substantially the same type as the *Normandie*
equipment showed itself capable of following a truck which was being driven on
the parade ground, a boat off Sandy
Hook, and so on. It was made with an
RCA-Victor 9-centimeter magnetron and
used a parabolic reflector. Dr. Irving
Wolff of the RCA laboratories conducted
the tests. This may well have been the first
successful use in the United States of
microwave radar, or of what eventually
became microwave radar.[54]

A decade later, the fact that the beat
method readily distinguishes moving objects from a stationary background, such
as a mountain, was to cause a revival of
interest in it, just as, for different reasons,
thermal research again became important.
The radio interference equipment used in
1934, however, was not further developed
by the Signal Corps Laboratories at that
time. Its range was limited, and (this was
the key difficulty, not to be solved until

[51] 1st Ind, Dir SCL to CSigO, 14 Jan 31, on Ltr,
CSigO to Dir SCL, 8 Jan 31, sub: Aircraft detection
by reflected radio waves. SigC 413.44 Detector against
Aircraft (Heat or Radio) 12-F.

[52] U.S. 1981884, System for Detecting Objects by
Radio, issued 27 Nov 34, filed 13 Jun 33.

[53] Interv, SigC Hist Sec with Dr. S. H. Anderson, 20
Nov 44.

[54] (1) Interv, SigC Hist Sec, with Col James D.
O'Connell, CO SCEL, 14 Apr 47, Belmar, N.J. (2)
Ltr, Pres SigC Bd to CSigO, 22 Nov 39, sub: Demon-
stration of SCR-270-T1, Incl 1, draft speech. SigC
CE 334, Case 312, Folder 1.

the fortuitous appearance of the cavity magnetron) the power of the tubes was low. Moreover, the Laboratories' acquaintance with the Navy's work only confirmed the impression that, however well it might do for that service, the different attributes of coastal defense gunfire made another approach necessary. Writing in his annual report for the fiscal year 1934, Blair observed that the new attempt might involve "projecting an interrupted sequence of trains of oscillations against the target and attempting to detect the echoes during the interstices between the projections."[55] This was the principle of pulse radar.

In making such a suggestion, Signal Corps science took a notable step. The suggestion did not immediately alter the program, for further development and repeated testing continued with the equipment which was already in existence; and in any case there was the normal lag between a proposal and the time when it takes effect. Nonetheless, Blair's remark opened to the Laboratories the possibility that light location, sound location, heat location, and radio interference might all retreat before a new method which projected pulses of electromagnetic energy into space and noted the exact time, in millionths of a second, required for them to bounce back from any obstacle in their range.

Radar was not yet named. Its development in military, naval, commercial, and foreign laboratories was then commencing, a world-wide secret of which no one possessed more than a fraction and which none shared with another. From place to place and time to time until publicity and usage standardized the term, it went by such designations as the British *radiolocation* and *RDF* (radio direction finding), or was

described as *RPF* (radio position finding), *microwave,* and *pulse-and-echo.* In preserving its nature from the public, the Signal Corps referred to it merely as radio—as SCR's. U.S. Navy nomenclature resulted in the word *radar: ra* for *radio, d* for *detection* or *direction finding* and *r* for *range.*[56] But in 1934 that name was not known.

The preliminary hints were.[57] As early as 1900 Nikola Tesla had called attention to the phenomenon of electromagnetic wave reflection and had predicted that "we may determine the relative position or course of a moving object, such as a vessel at sea, the distance traversed by the same, or its speed." In 1904 a German, Christian Huelsmeyer, took out patents in both Germany and Great Britain for "a method of detecting and recording distant metallic objects (ships, railway trains, etc.) by means of electromagnetic rays." Although the patent application showed a drawing of "a steamship carrying this equipment, sighting an unidentified vessel by wireless," Huelsmeyer's idea was totally neglected for thirty years; then German, French, British, American, and other radar began to evolve all at once.[58] Marconi had tentatively pointed out the use of short waves for detection in 1922. Observing that short waves had been neglected in radio science since its early days a quarter of a century before, and taking note of the fact that Hertz had shown that metals can reflect electric waves, Marconi

---

[55] Dir SCL, Annual Rpt to CSigO, 1934, Annex.

[56] Ltr, Rear Adm J. A. Furer, Co-ordinate R&D, Navy Dept, to CSigO, 31 Jan 42, sub: Definition of radar. SigC SPSTC 5 Misc.

[57] The antecedents and infancy of radar make a story told in many sources. See the Bibliographical Note.

[58] (1) Nikola Tesla, "The Problem of Increasing Human Energy," *Century Magazine,* LX (June, 1900), 208. (2) L. Brandt, "German Radio-location in Retrospect," *Interavia,* V (1950), English version, 315.

prophesied a development which would automatically warn vessels in fog or darkness of the presence and bearing of other ships.[59] Also in 1922, at the Naval Research Laboratory, Taylor and Young had noticed that a Potomac river boat, passing between a radio transmitter and a receiver, had reflected the transmitted waves. The British scientists, E. V. Appleton and M. A. F. Barrett, had obtained ionospheric reflections in 1924 and 1925. Dr. Gregory Breit and Dr. Merle A. Tuve had demonstrated the principle itself during the course of measurements of the ionosphere taken for the Carnegie Institution in 1925.

But so soon as the startling military value of radio reflection had become evident, secrecy tightened. When governments realized that it was a national instrument of the first magnitude in a world deteriorating into warfare, there was no longer any possibility of exchanging information on it through the periodicals, offices, and market places of scientific research. The secret was to be protected at every point of contact—against possible enemies, against possible allies, against commercial enterprises, particularly those with extranational interests, and even against other services of the inner defense force of the nation. Yet despite all efforts of Germany, Japan, France, Britain, and the United States to cloak and obscure from one another the urgent sense which each one had of being on the verge of a new weapon which none other possessed, from country to country radar developed in many of the same ways, faced many of the same problems, reached many of the same compromises.[60]

In 1934 the Germans had obtained radio reflections at a distance of 20 meters from the hull of a decommissioned battle-ship in Luebeck Bay, then at a distance of 2,000 meters from another target ship at Schilkee. The Reich Navy permitted these experiments to fall into some neglect, from which Reichsmarschall Hermann Goering summarily rescued them for his Luftwaffe, although in a different form which bypassed microwave work.[61] Starting out with radio interference in January 1935, British scientists shifted to the pulse method in May and by the middle of June had tracked an airplane to seventeen miles. Between 1935 and 1939, their CH stations (that is, the *chain* of radars at *home*) took shape in the high-frequency area, the wavelength being 11–13 meters. As the nations lined up for war, Robert Watson-Watt and his colleagues succeeded in stringing a chain of figuratively invisible radio-direction-finding towers along the Channel and North Sea coasts of Britain. They were not invisible to Germany, but presumably the Reich discounted them. Goering's boast that no enemy aircraft could ever get through to Berlin was not so incredibly presumptuous as it sounded; for at the time he made it Germany was developing both of the basic types of radar. When, in 1939, the time seemed ripe for a war, early warning appa-

[59] Guglielmo Marconi, "Radio Telegraphy" (address presented June 20, 1922, New York), *Proceedings of the Institute of Radio Engineers*, X (1922), 215–38. It is interesting to see that an abstract made of Marconi's speech and published at the end of its printed form missed his point and thus stands as evidence of the way in which the principle of radar was generally overlooked, although at hand.

[60] Thus, for example, the Germans attempted to get sharpness of definition for their *Freya* by means of a thermal unit, just as the Americans did with their SCR-268. A. E. Hoffman-Heyden, "German Radio-location in Retrospect, (II) The Anti-Aircraft Artillery's Radar Equipment," *Interavia*, VI (1951), 623.

[61] Curt Bley, *Geheimnis Radar: Eine Geschichte der Wissenschaftlichen Kriegfuehring* (Hamburg: Rowahlt, 1949), *passim*.

ratus, the Freya, scanned the approaches to German defenses from about a hundred stations; and the gun layer, the Wuerzburg, was ready to go onto the production lines. After 1943, Allied aviation over Germany suffered more from antiaircraft fire laid by Wuerzburgs than from anything else.[62]

In 1937 France's 15-centimeter *Normandie* "ear-radar" gave way to a beat system developed by Pierre David, tested in great secrecy at Metz for military engineers and antiaircraft experts, tried out at aerial maneuvers near Reims in 1938, and established at scattered points along all three coasts by 1939. In Japan the pioneer University of Osaka professors, Kinjiro Okabe and Hidetsugu Yagi, worked from 1936 on, but with Doppler apparatus, without an oscilloscope (they used continuous wave) and without the confidence of either their Army or Navy. In the United States, where the length of the coast line made unsuitable any fixed chain of warning radars such as the British had, and where consequently the effort was toward mobile defense positions, secrecy was equally shrouding. It steadily moved Army and Navy detection research farther apart. Although there were occasional contacts, neither knew exactly what the other was doing, and each duplicated some of the brainwork, the tests, the plans and mistakes of the other. The Signal Corps Laboratories were better acquainted with what was being done at the National Bureau of Standards and in the commercial laboratories: Bell, General Electric, Radio Corporation of America, and Westinghouse.

Blair, as director of the Laboratories, and Colton, heading the Research and Engineering Division in the Office of the Chief Signal Officer, had a heavy responsibility to back the right horse. They kept the one-way thermal detection project high on the list; and sound detectors, which were all that the public knew of the development of aircraft warning instruments, received their due in attention to improved models. In the microwave subproject, Hershberger's tests went forward with a succession of tubes then available. Again and again, their inability to generate a strong signal thwarted progress. Acknowledging disappointment in the Signal Corps gear so far, Blair still reiterated his interest in radio-wave detection in his 1935 report. "With improvements in the radiated power of [the] transmitter and sensitivity of the receiver," he noted, "this method of position finding may well reach a stage of usefulness."[63] Late in the year, and at the urging of Colton, Hershberger prepared a memorandum which summarized the advantages of the pulse method. A visit the next month (January 1936) to the Naval Research Laboratory for a demonstration of the Taylor-Young-Hyland beat equipment confirmed Hershberger in the same objections which he and Blair had made before: that it provided no discrimination of the target. The Navy engineers were also, he learned, working on pulse equipment, with a 10-microsecond signal and with the transmitter and receiver close together.

Although Navy and Army research was parallel, there was a noteworthy difference. The Navy laboratory was set up as a research laboratory, specified and supported by Congress in the name of research. It could range farther within the

---

[62] Radio Research Lab, Harvard University [O. G. Villard, Jr.?], Flak Radar Countermeasures in the European Theater of Operations—A Review and Evaluation of Their Use by the 8th Air Force, Sep 45. SigC 413.44 RCM Gen 3 ET 2757.

[63] Dir SCL, Suppl Rpt to CSigO, 1935, Proj 88-G.

imaginations of the scientists conducting it than Signal Corps efforts were allowed to do. Experimentation at Fort Monmouth had to be directed toward an immediate application, toward developing a specific and practical piece of equipment. For large research, the continuing policy was always to turn to commercial concerns and to get it done by contract. Much of the early work on Army radar constituted an exception to this normal procedure.[64] During 1936, Lt. Col. Roger B. Colton, Maj. John H. Gardner, Jr., of Colton's office, and Lt. Col. Louis B. Bender, Colton's successor as officer in charge of the Research and Development Division, were to visit the principal companies to see what they had and whether they could take over the Signal Corps work. The companies were pessimistic about the possibilities of the work, and the decision was accordingly to continue it in the Signal Corps Laboratories.[65] This was a forthcoming arrangement, and was concerned only with getting the work done. First, the direction it would take had to be decided. Early 1936 determined this matter.

Just at that time a deterrent befell thermal research and development which was not to be overlooked. Both the Signal Corps and the Corps of Engineers models of thermal equipment were declared inadequate for detecting aircraft.[66] The method was acceptable for detecting ships. The Coast Artillery Corps, which was the using arm for the thermolocator that the Signal Corps had developed, wished to be sure of warning of the approach of vessels to the nation's harbors and coast defenses, and for that reason the Signal Corps equipment and projects remained in force. But warning of enemy bombardment planes? That was a different matter. The Corps of Engineers, withdrawing from

thermal detection, sought to turn to radiowave projects, and the Ordnance Department once again came forward to put in a claim of its own. In this area, though, the line of demarcation was sharp. Radio, as Maj. Gen. James B. Allison, the Chief Signal Officer just then, reminded everyone, has but a single medium for transmission. "For this reason it is a cardinal principle that every endeavor must be made to centralize control of radio matters in a single agency wherever practicable."[67] Moreover, Signal Corps radio-wave work was just about to come into its own. Allison won his point. Not only was his responsibility for thermal detectors sanctioned, but he was charged with responsibility for radiolocation development as well.

The victory was clouded, for he was given no funds, although he asked for less than a single SCR-268 cost after Pearl Harbor. Taking up the Colton-Hershberger memorandum which urged the pulse method, Blair had forwarded it to Allison's office. In the general field of radio methods of detection, Blair had noted the Navy was "far in advance of . . . any other known agency."[68] He indicated regret that radio-detection work was only a subproject of thermal-detection

[64] Davis hist cited n. 44, rev. Ch. V, p. 21.

[65] Ltrs, CSigO to TAG, 23 Oct and 6 Nov 36, sub: Airplane detection devices. SigC 311.6.

[66] Coast Artillery Bd Proceedings, Ft. Monroe, Va., Proj 1060, Thermal Direction Locators (Heat Detectors), 17 Mar 36.

[67] 14th Ind, CSigO to TAG, 12 Dec 35, on Memo, Chief of CAC for CSigO, 4 Jun 34, sub: Development of heat detection device. SigC 311.6 (6-4-34).

[68] Ltr, Dir SCL to CSigO, 12 Feb 36, sub: Radio-optical position finding of aircraft, with Memo, Hershberger for Dir SCL, 27 Jan 36, sub: Detection of aircraft by radio-optical methods. SigC 413.44. The Navy was working on a set which would give protection for fifteen miles through fog and other disturbances.

work at the Signal Corps Laboratories, and asked for the money to give it full standing. Allison accordingly sought the funds. The Chief of Coast Artillery, vigorously supporting him, held that "the Army has before it today no more important development project than that of finding positive means for the detection of aircraft"; but Army feeling was rather general that whatever funds could be obtained should be applied to known commitments, not to uncertainties. The War Department conceded the importance of the project, but could only rule that the money "must be provided by the curtailment [within the Signal Corps] of other less pressing developments." [69] This meant taking it out of moneys already allotted to something else.

The other developments under way at that time in the Laboratories included many items which were to become important in the tactical signal communications of World War II, among them the first Field Artillery and Infantry walkie-talkies, the vehicular radio sets SCR-193 and SCR-245, a shielding system for suppressing radio interference in tanks, the sound-powered telephone, the throat microphone, and improved field phones, field wire, assault wire, and loading coils. [70] The top priority given to radiolocation would affect them all, and although the opening of the new Squier Laboratory building had improved conditions at Fort Monmouth, there was still only a small staff.

But devoted to their work, as they had need to be, the Fort Monmouth engineers had been accomplishing much with little. On 15 May 1936, with the moneyless permission of the War Department, pulse-echo detection became a high-priority job. Using a design which Hershberger had entered in his notebook in February, the

Laboratories commenced construction of the first Signal Corps pulse equipment. The microwave equipment had not been able to surmount the difficulty of inadequate strength in the transmitter and receiver, and had been abandoned in favor of very high frequencies. [71] By the end of June, the engineers had built a "breadboard model" of a portable, 75-watt, pulse transmitter. [72] Colton joined them as executive officer in August, and Capt. Rex V. D. Corput, Jr., was assigned as officer in charge of the Radio Section. In Washington the Chief Signal Officer was asking for a reconsideration of his plea for special funds. Hershberger left in October and a few months later joined Dr. Wolff at the RCA Laboratories in working with 9- and 10-centimeter waves generated by a magnetron and echoing from objects a mile and a half away. Wolff demonstrated the equipment in Camden to both Army and Navy officers. [73]

The request for outside funds was once more denied. The work would have to be supported at the expense of other projects. Allison took the necessary step and diverted $75,741 of fiscal year 1937 money. [74] The sum became available in November.

[69] Ltr, Chief of CAC to ACofS G-4, 24 Sep 36, sub: Airplane detection device, and 1st Ind, TAG to CSigO. SigC 413.44.

[70] Davis hist cited n. 44, p. 34.

[71] Roger Colton, "Radar in the United States Army: History and Early Development at Signal Corps Laboratories, Fort Monmouth, N. J.," *Proceedings of the Institute of Radio Engineers*, No. 331 (November, 1945), p. 742.

[72] SigC R&D hist cited n. 37, Vol. IV, Pt. 2, Proj 12-6.2, p. 7.

[73] Henry E. Guerlac, Hist Div OSRD, Radar, Sec. A, Ch. VIII, pp. 31–34 (in consecutively paged copy, pp. 344–47). Photostat of 1945 MS in SigC Hist Sec File.

[74] Historical Report of the Signal Corps Engineering Laboratories, Folder 5, Ch. X, p. 232. SigC Hist Sec File.

Many more engineers were now occupied with the task. Whereas it had been full-time work for one man, it became at least half-time for more than fifteen. Colonel Blair moved everything, including the beat-detection work, into the Radio Section, and Paul Watson, its civilian chief, became director of the project. The day for the first test approached rapidly. A receiver was added, and the transmitter's frequency changed from 133 megacycles to 110. On 14 December 1936 the men loaded the transmitter into one truck, the receiver into another, and set out for a site near Princeton, where the traffic to and from the Newark airport provided many targets. There they saw the device record the echoes of the pulses which they were directing into the flight path. Crude and experimental as it was, it was radar. The transmitter and receiver were a mile apart, and the equipment tracked the airplane for only seven miles, but it was radar at last.

The Naval Research Laboratory was now quite reticent, although soon to disclose its experiments to the Bell and RCA Laboratories. For the past year its confidential progress reports had become secret and therefore inaccessible. The reason for such security was of course that the Navy's pulse experimentation, parallel to the Army's, but in advance of it and assured of financial support, had suddenly shown the dramatic promise which characterized it wherever scientists were investigating it. The Naval Research Laboratory had been able to demonstrate the method to Admiral Arthur J. Hepburn, Commander in Chief of the U.S. Fleet, that fall. In February, Charles Edison, Assistant Secretary of the Navy, in company with Admiral William D. Leahy, saw another demonstration. The Signal Corps considered renewed

consultation, but the December tests decided against that step. Through the following period, nonetheless, naval aviation lent its co-operation, in concert with that of the GHQ Air Force, to the testing of the Signal Corps equipment. The two air services provided blimps and airplanes to be detected, over and over, while the Laboratories crews tinkered with it.

Everything came to a head in the following spring. May 1937 is a turning point in Army technical history. What later became the SCR-268, first U.S. Army radar, was shown then to a number of important persons with such effect that it became one of the top military secrets of the nation. It was a short-range radiolocator for controlling searchlights. The immediate purpose in constructing it had been to locate airplanes at night, in range, elevation, and azimuth (distance, height, and direction), accurately enough so that a Coast Artillery battery's searchlight would instantly pinpoint the plane when the apparatus turned the light on. Given this purpose, the Signal Corps apparatus came into being with a quality which no other system possessed. It was mobile. By contrast, the British equipment, meeting a different function, had taken shape as an immobile series of high towers.

During their first trials of the device, the Radio Section men had built two models, one of 110 megacycles and the other of 240, the latter in an effort to reduce the cumbersome amount of antenna that was necessary.[75] These were very high frequencies, but not, of course, microwave frequencies. Only when the more powerful transmitter tubes came into being would radiolocation become microwave radar and the marvelous advantage of compactness be achieved. At

[75] Davis hist cited n. 44, p. 48.

these lower frequencies, the equipment made its test appearance. The 110-megacycle apparatus employed a heat detector, because the specifications still required it. The Laboratories men had improved the thermotheodolite during the year just past by mounting six thermopiles in a 60-inch searchlight reflector; so they used it as an intermediary, to focus and specify for the searchlight the information which the radiolocator had picked up. A much more significant feature was the directional antenna array, which consisted of a number of rods arranged so that the radio waves would be canceled in the directions which were not being searched, strengthened in those which were. In order to swing and tilt them in a broad scanning of the sky, the engineers mounted them on the chassis of sound locators from which they had stripped away the listening horns. Sound detection of aircraft became archaic in the American Army at that moment.

On 18 and 19 May 1937 General Allison, Maj. Gen. Archibald H. Sunderland, who was the Chief of Coast Artillery, and Brig. Gen. Henry H. Arnold, at that time the Assistant Chief of the Air Corps, watched the future SCR-268 show what it could do. A week later the demonstration was repeated for Secretary of War Harry A. Woodring, several senators and representatives from the Congressional Committees on Military Affairs, and Maj. Gen. Oscar Westover, Chief of the Air Corps. On the first occasion the weather was so bad that the heat locator was of no value at all; the radiolocator found the airplane in four out of seven passes. At the May 26 demonstration the weather was better and the score was excellent.

Even the most extraordinary technical advance looks crude from the point of view of its later stages of improvement,

and the performance of May 1937 at Fort Monmouth would have been completely inadequate for the war which was on its way, but this was four and a half years ahead of the Pearl Harbor crisis. If luck, engineering skill, and appropriations held, the device might be ready by the time the yet undesignated enemy attacked. At its debut, its potential importance was plain to be seen. Secretary Woodring declared that "all the members of the [inspecting] party were a unit in praising the remarkably satisfactory result attained." [76]

The Laboratories men themselves were more critical. They saw that the equipment would have to give a continuous tracking rather than a point-by-point report, that it could not be brought to bear against low-flying airplanes, and—a nearly insuperable problem—that it could be jammed. Moreover, this was a Coast Artillery set, a set designed to point searchlights and then antiaircraft guns at an approaching airplane; but an enemy bomber would be only five minutes away by the time the locator detected it. This was not enough time to get interceptors up into the air to meet the hostile craft. What the Air Corps wanted, and immediately requested, was a detector with longer range. The military characteristics formulated for an Air Corps set, upon Signal Corps recommendation, required it to be capable of an early warning range of 120 miles.[77] In this undertaking was the inception of the SCR-270 and the SCR-271. One mobile, the other fixed, they were the early-warning companions to the gun-laying SCR-268. The Army entered the

---

[76] Ltr, SW to CSigO, 2 Jun 37. SigC 413.44 Detector 12-F, Folder 3.

[77] SigC Technical Committee Case 151, 12 Jul 37. SigC Hist Sec File.

war with these three radars and continued them in use throughout the conflict.

Administrative Signaling

The development of radar in the Signal Corps came about as part of the Signal Corps' responsibility to tactical communications. The SCR-268 was in the broadest sense a piece of communications equipment, informing a coastal gun position of the nearness of an airplane. It was a part of the tactical signaling which engaged Signal Corps efforts in all of the arms of the service—in the Infantry, Cavalry, Field Artillery, and Air Corps, as well as in the Coast Artillery for which it had been devised. Administrative signaling was quite another thing. The Army as an army wanted tactical communications equipment: mobile, individual, secure. The Army as an agency of government, a complex apparatus of thousands of persons many of whom had no tactical duties at all, wanted administrative communications: fixed, interrelated, continent-spanning, day-in-day-out channels of business. In peacetime years and, as the global scale of the oncoming conflict determined, in war as well, this was the most important single function of the Corps. It was the one field of military communications where the Signal Corps authority was supreme, both in tradition and prospect.

The Signal Corps itself did not wholly realize the fact that in a considerable way it **was** becoming a communications industry right within the Military Establishment. Elsewhere in the Army, many other persons had been slow to catch up to the change which the 1921 reorganization had overtaken and confirmed. Some held the view that a peacetime Signal Corps was a luxury. Had not its wartime mission been

allotted to each of the other arms? And surely there was "nothing about telegraph, telephone or radio that requires special training in time of peace. . . ."[78] Maj. Gen. Johnson Hagood, whose opinion in the 1920's this was, acknowledged that in past performance the Signal Corps had been "wonderful," but felt that the time had come to dissolve it. Others, citing the nonmilitary Washington-Alaska Military Cable and Telegraph System, agreed that the function of Army communications was wholly tactical, and that since that function had been dispersed the Signal Corps was left with nothing to do. Even in the War Department, some were unaware of the Corps' record of practical service. Secretary of War John W. Weeks, for example, did not know (nor had any particular reason to know) that his message center was paralleled by one in the Office of the Chief Signal Officer in another part of the Munitions Building; the duplication was revealed when General Squier sent up for permission to hire a messenger boy.[79]

Encouraged to do so by Congress and American business, the Army was in the habit of thinking of fixed communications systems as private enterprise. The Army could rent or lease them in time of war, but otherwise they belonged outside the government. In the Civil War, Western Union had declared this point of view. In the 1870's and '80's, the wire strung through hostile Indian country had never been considered the Signal Corps' merely because Signal Corpsmen had put it up. The Washington-Alaska Military Cable and Telegraph System had monopolized

[78] Maj. Gen. Johnson Hagood, *The Services of Supply* (Boston and New York: Houghton Mifflin Company, 1927), p. 379.
[79] Ltr, CSigO to SW, 28 Oct 20, and 1st Ind, 1 Nov 20. SigC 311.2 WD Msg Ctr 1, 1920–29.

Alaska communications on terms mutually convenient to the government and to commercial fishing, lumber, mining, and shipping interests. To resist a British state-subsidized combine which gave evidence of controlling long-range communications, President Wilson had encouraged General Electric, American Telephone and Telegraph, Western Electric, Westinghouse, and United Fruit to form the Radio Corporation of America, a private combine.[80] All of these instances demonstrated the established custom. In reducing the Military Establishment and other governmental agencies after World War I, Congress required them to go to private commerce, industry, and banking—the Signal Corps, for example, being kept dependent upon the communications industry.

Yet whether in private or public form, communications services were as necessary to Army administration as to that of any civilian department of the government. It was inevitable that they would be essential to the daily routine, and a matter for consolidated, specific assignment. The advent of radio, heralding big, swift communications, and its addition to the cable, telegraph, and telephone already in existence made technical message sending too complex to assign to any but a technical service. In fact, the first move toward it came concurrently with the 1921 reorganization of the Army. In Plan White, one of the "color" series of war plans, the General Staff proposed a network of Army radio stations, operated exclusively by military men and connecting the staff with all corps area headquarters except the First, and with certain key cities. The intention was to provide the Army with both alternate and auxiliary means of communication in case internal strife or national disaster broke or interrupted the commer-

cial facilities upon which it depended.[81]

The War Department Radio Net thus came into being. A control station in Washington was designated WVA and manned by the 17th Service Company.[82] The original equipment was a 1½-kilowatt transmitter mounted on a 1½-ton truck at the Army War College two miles away; the station crew operated it by remote control.[83] With the subsequent use of additional transmitters at the Arlington naval radio installation, the net expanded until a five-station linking was carrying about fifty messages a day. Measured in terms of original sent traffic, it totaled 3,868,362 words the first fiscal year.[84]

This was the first element of an Army radio system which was to grow steadily, span the world, and comprise both tactical and administrative networks. The tactical networks would include the Air Alert Net, both fixed and mobile, for air defense; the Coast Artillery, for harbor defense fire

---

[80] Maj. Gen. George S. Gibbs, "The Influence of the Control of International Communications on the Conduct of War," Signal Corps Bulletin, No. 55 (July–August 1930), p. 7. This article appeared again in 1933 (Signal Corps Bulletin, No. 70, January–February, 1933, pp. 2–18) under Maj. Gen. Irving J. Carr's name.

A detailed story of the beginnings of the Radio Corporation of America is to be found in Chapters 9–12 of Gleason L. Archer's History of Radio to 1926 (New York: The American Historical Company, Inc., 1938). A second volume Big Business and Radio (New York: The American Historical Company, Inc., 1939), brings the account of the radio industry up to World War II.

[81] Ltr, TAG to CSigO, 12 Mar 21, sub: App. 10 coms War Plans White. AG 381 Misc Div.

[82] Redesignated the 17th Signal Service Company per War Department General Order 5, 23 March 1925.

[83] Interv, SigC Hist Sec with Charles Murray, ACS Div, OCSigO, 7 Sep 45.

[84] Ten years later, in 1933, it was 26,500,058, and yet another ten years after that, 216,145,629 words, enough to send the complete text of War and Peace every day in the year and twice on Sundays.

control; and others as need arose—in maneuvers, for instance. The administrative
would include, first of all, the War Department Radio Net of fixed stations located
in Washington and at the headquarters
of each corps area and department; next,
and in logical extension from this control
net, individual ones for each corps area
and department to connect its headquarters with garrisons and posts in its territory; third, the Army transport net, linking the vessels with each other and with
shore stations; and ultimately, the network of the Army Amateur Radio System.
Thus the military radio system would
become an integral part of the command
communications system, extending from
general headquarters through the chain
of command to the smallest unit in the
field, and an integral part also of the
administrative system. Its name in World
War II, when it reached maturity, fused
these functions, and it became known as
the Army Command and Administrative
Network.

While a radio net was thus being
formed, the War Department's telegraph
business was originating in two places: in
the Office of the Secretary of War and in
that of the Chief Signal Officer. The discovery of this obvious duplication, together with the example of yet another
duplication in the fact that the Navy had
a communications center of its own, led
Secretary Weeks to propose a merger.[85]
Both General Squier and the Navy demurred, but the Army wire and radio
centers did combine to produce a War
Department Message Center. This was the
second principal step in systematizing
Army administrative communications.
WVA and the two telegraph offices merged
in order to handle all of the military communications traffic—collecting, receiving,

sending, and distributing—in Washington. Whether accomplished by radio,
cable, or telegraph, the traffic came
through the Message Center and was
assigned to the supervision of the Signal
Corps. The War Department Message
Center opened on 1 March 1923. Set up
as a field agency despite the fact that it
was not "in the field" but in the Munitions
Building, it became by tacit working
agreement in the Signal Corps a section of
the Plant and Traffic Division next door.[86]

A third government message center was
to have been run by the Post Office Department, but the Army and Navy joined
forces to quash it while still not uniting
their own.[87] Nevertheless, the War Department Message Center had immediately invited other agencies of the government to use the War Department Radio
Net,[88] and commencing with the Veterans
Bureau, the Departments of Justice and
Agriculture, and the Bureau of Internal
Revenue, they did so, to such an extent
that by the end of the 1920's War Department radio was handling dispatches,
which would once have gone by commercial telegraph, for more than fifty agencies
of the government.[89]

The War Department Message Center
rapidly became the vital organ of the Signal Corps. It represented to Washington
a palpable reason for the Corps' being.
Despite the recurring problem of getting
enough men and equipment, successive
chief signal officers guarded control over

---

[85] Oakes study cited n. 4(2), p. 9.
[86] Memo, Capt Carter W. Clarke, O/C WD Msg
Ctr, for Exec Officer OCSigO, 29 Sep 38. SigC 320.22
17th Sig Co.
[87] Oakes study cited n. 4(2), pp. 9–10.
[88] Ltr, Actg Chief Coordinator WD to SW, 6 Apr
23. SigC 676.3 Gen 2, 1922–23.
[89] *Historical Sketch of the Signal Corps (1860–1941)*, p.
107.

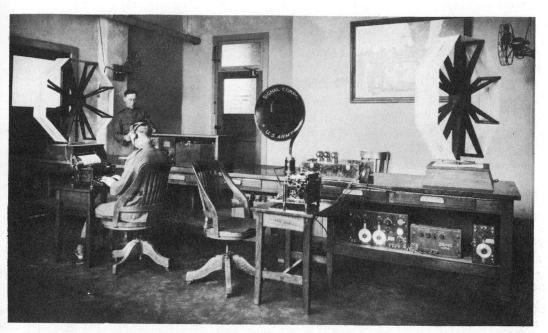

THE WAR DEPARTMENT MESSAGE CENTER. *Early radio facilities at the Munitions Building above, and the Message Center in May 1941 below.*

it against any attempt to modify or dilute it.[90] In 1925 General Saltzman lost authority over the 17th Signal Service Company, but regained it at the end of the year. In 1926 amendments to the National Defense Act, which had cut the Signal Corps strength to 2,165, curtailed the hours of operation at Station WVA. The War Department Radio Net had been slowly increasing in importance, but now had to forego any thought of matching the Navy Department's twenty-four-hour schedule. The loss of operating hours was regrettable because one reason for establishing the net had been to give experience to soldiers who were taking communications training. To select the appropriate means for transmitting a message demanded a thorough knowledge of the channels of communication available at the Message Center; a good man had to know what burden he could put upon any of the several means without congesting them and the degree of security which each afforded. Moreover, communications apparatus changed rapidly.

Medium-frequency, high-power transmitters like the SCR-140 replaced the original continuous-wave sets and then gave way to high-frequency, low-power equipment. The use of these followed a trend established by amateur operators and the Navy. The first equipment of the sort in the War Department Radio Net consisted of eleven crystal-controlled sets built in the Signal Corps Laboratories from Navy specifications and installed in 1926. They were temperamental, and Capt. Guy Hill was the only man then stationed in Washington who could master their whims, but they outdated the old high-power, long-wave transmitters.

By the time when, on 30 November 1928, WVA changed its call letters to the neatly appropriate WAR, the control station was using transmitters not only at Arlington but also at Bolling Field, Washington Barracks, and Annapolis. Nine Coast Guard transmitters—1 kilowatt, high-frequency—improved the network's sending, and in the following year the establishment of 10-kilowatt amplifiers in San Francisco eliminated the last relay points between the east and west coasts. Washington, San Antonio, San Francisco, Panama, Hawaii, and Manila now all had 10-kilowatt transmitters. WAR was taking care of one sixth of the Signal Corps' radio business, and the radio service was becoming the equal of the telegraph. Without counting the stations of the Alaska system, there were 154 in the Army system.[91]

Like anything else, the repeated urge for modernization in the Message Center and Radio Net was offset by handicaps. Everything had to be wrung from meager appropriations but that was the usual story. More to the point in the late 1920's was the fact that the Navy's insistence limited the Army to an antenna power of 10 kilowatts; and this turned out to be a disguised blessing.[92] Being barred from greater antenna power, the Signal Corps turned to greater antenna refinement,

[90] (1) Memo, CSigO for ACofS G-1, 17 Oct 23, sub: AR 105–25 SigC tg, cable, and radio msg sv. SigC 311.2 WD Msg Ctr 1. (2) Ltr, Exec Officer OCSigO to All Corps Area and Dept Sig Officers, 6 Jan 36, sub: Msg ctr, and Ind, Col Walter E. Prosser, Sig Officer Eighth Corps Area, to Col Dawson Olmstead, 30 Jan 36. SigC WD Msg Ctr 2.

[91] CSigO, *Annual Report, 1929*. There were 16 in the War Department net, 46 in the corps area and department individual nets, 28 in the Air Corps net, 21 for harbor defense, 15 for Army transports and other Quartermaster vessels, and 28 for mine planters and other Coast Artillery vessels.

[92] Joint Army-Navy Committee on Army-Navy Coms, Communication Procedure, Ch. II, 22 Aug 21, superseded by Ch. VI, Sec. B, 16 Aug 28. SigC 311.23 Joint Bd Serials.

with the result that it succeeded in beaming the signal, for the first time in government radio. Beaming, or directing the signal precisely to the point of reception,
made maximum use of the allowable
power, whereas broadcasting had wasted
it. WVA thus got continuous, high-frequency channels of a range long enough
to reach across the continent and overseas.[93] Other improvements took place.
The first transmitting station to be built
by the Army was set up at Fort Myer and
went on the air on 20 March 1930. After
January 1931 a site at Battery Cove, near
Alexandria, Virginia, became a remote receiving station.[94] Up to that time, noise inside and outside the Munitions Building
had often made radio reception so trying
that message traffic would pile up all
through the day, to be taken care of only
when the relative peace of night had arrived. The Message Center was simultaneously allowed to make itself over. The
Navy communications center had already
done so, and some improved equipment
from Navy yard shops aided the conversion. Wire teletype had begun to come in,
as a matter of universal preference and in
imitation of commercial practice. This
equipment and all of the cable and telegraph facilities were rehabilitated. In
radio the administrative net attained to
twelve high-frequency positions and two
medium-frequency positions which could
all be monitored from a single control
point, and WAR had achieved a twenty-
four-hour schedule with other stations in
the net, although not yet with full schedules in the incoming direction.

Special unemployed legislation made it
possible to use fiscal year 1932 funds
before the expiration of the 1931 year in
order to begin replacing some telephone
equipment which was older than World

War I. The legislative gesture was much
too feeble, and the replacements had to be
made over a period of fifteen months and
from place to place throughout the Army
telephone system; yet, complete at something less than would be an impressive
total in World War II, they were welcome
as being one more little toward an ultimate much.[95]

It was more difficult to keep trained
men in the Message Center, when civilian
communications offered less regimenta-
tion and better wages, than in any other
part of the Signal Corps. In 1928–29, for
example, just before the business index
plunged, 40 percent of the operators on
hand at the beginning of the twelve-
month period were lost to the Signal
Corps when it ended, and had been replaced by tyros. One of the more disturbing aspects of such a situation was that
there was no way of meeting emergencies
and an Army which is not equipped with
an infallible manual of witchcraft in order
to meet a situation which nobody expects
is no Army at all.

With a sidelong look at the Navy,
which was walking along the same route,
the Signal Corps moved toward closer
relations with civilian radio hams. The
amateurs were making radio the province
of every enthusiast in the nation. "Their
highest ambition is to reach halfway

---

[93] 1st Lt. Wesley T. Guest, "Rehabilitation of the
Army Radio Net," Signal Corps Bulletin, No. 66
(May–June 1932), pp. 32–35.

[94] (1) Memo, Capt Frank E. Stoner for Gen Gibbs,
29 Dec 30; (2) 3d Ind, TAG to CSigO, 26 Jan 31, on
Ltr, OCSigO to TAG through QMG, 8 Jan 31, sub:
Temporary location of remote radio receiving station.
SigC 676.3 Battery Cove 1, 1930–39.

[95] Twenty-two new switchboards (51 positions), 2
automatic systems (2,000 lines), 26 underground con-
duits, 33 underground cables (buried wire), 13 aerial
cables (wire pole lines), 7 lines for target ranges, 6 for
fire-control positions, and 8 miscellaneous projects.
CSigO, Annual Report, 1932, p. 19.

TRANSMITTERS AT STATION WAR *are being inspected by David Sarnoff of RCA (left) and Capt. Frank E. Stoner.*

round the world . . . with a 10-watt set," Maj. Gen. George S. Gibbs commented in an early broadcast, and went on to praise them for many advances.[96] Short of controlling a large organization all under military regulation, a circumstance the Signal Corps could not possibly hope for, a ready-made civilian auxiliary was the best bulwark possible. With the hams, the Signal Corps developed the co-operative program known as the Army Amateur Radio System.

Springing from the recollection of the work of civilian radio operators in World War I, the relationship had begun in 1925 with a visit which Lt. Col. Frank J. Griffin and Capt. Tom C. Rives had paid to the headquarters of the American Radio Re-

lay League in Hartford, Connecticut.[97] What they discovered had impressed them and had confirmed Rives's belief that Signal Corps training should tap this source. The lack of men for military communications was not to be put down to a lack of interest in radio, for league membership had increased rapidly. Most of the members had Department of Commerce transmitting licenses, and their stations stood comparison with commercial and governmental outlets.

[96] Gen Gibbs, address on Station WBZ, Boston, 15 Mar 28.

[97] K. B. Warner, Secy ARRL, Proposed Plan of Co-operation Between the Signal Corps, USA, and the American Radio Relay League, as Determined at Conference at Hartford, Conn., 24 Mar 25. SigC 311.23 A/N Radio Procedure 1, 1924–32.

In fact, the radio amateurs were amateurs only in the sense that they worked for pleasure rather than for pay. They had long since graduated from Ford spark coils to tube transmission on continuous wave, and they spoke casually about making two-way contact across the Atlantic despite their limited power and against heavy atmospheric and artificial interference. Their pioneering on the short waves had opened new channels which had proved reliable for daytime long-distance use, and they had explored and utilized the high frequencies which commercial interests had rejected. Accordingly, the Signal Corps began seeking out small groups in several of the corps areas, and, with their co-operation, indoctrinating them in military radio procedures and holding weekly radio drills. The groups merged, and the Army Amateur Radio System came into being. At first it was unsuccessful. An unlucky burden of administrative detail fell upon each of the hams serving as local representatives. Then a noteworthy job in the 1928 Florida hurricane, when WAR and an amateur at West Palm Beach had worked together to keep a circuit open, gave AARS new impetus. By slanting it away from the Army and toward the Red Cross, its sponsors were able to keep it alive. Operating on Monday nights except during the summers,[98] and with its control station moved to Washington, the AARS expanded from 300 to 500 members, then to 1,100 in 1935, to 1,700 in 1939, and ultimately to 2,400, when the Pearl Harbor attack suspended all amateur radio activity in the United States.

But WAR's connection with the radio amateurs was only periodic—a matter of immediate local or remote national emergency. It still did not put men at the operating positions for routine daily and nightly work. The problem remained. When war began in September 1939, there were sixty-three civilians and forty-three enlisted men in the Message Center. Even this number existed, however, only because appropriations had touched bottom and had had to go up again. Funds had been drastically cut five years before, at the very time when the advent of the Civilian Conservation Corps and the order requiring the Air Corps to carry the mail had crowded the channels with flight messages and triple-C traffic. The Signal Corps had been obliged to warn other government agencies that free message service must come to an end with the fiscal year 1935.

Because half of the total business came from outside the War Department and because none of the agencies, understandably enough, had provided in their estimates for money to pay for it, the Bureau of the Budget had had to come forward with a special temporary allowance. Thereafter, a rate of nine mills a word went into effect, and the civilian agencies took most of their business elsewhere. The military administrative traffic increased, however, and the effort to handle it was no easier than before. Commercial enterprise went on, also, picking off the men trained at government expense, and leaving the Signal Corps to try to perform technical jobs without the technicians for them.

General Allison protested in 1936:

While the Army has been struggling with unsatisfactory communications in spite of the best efforts of zealous and intelligent personnel, the American Telephone and Telegraph, Western Union, Postal, RCA and Mackay

---

[98] Radio had not yet reached the stage where it was dependable. Heavy interference often obscured it and summers nearly closed it out.

Companies have been earning an international reputation . . . because . . . men . . . thoroughly trained for their jobs are able to secure long life from the expensive equipment which is required in modern communications. . . . The Army has . . . [an] organization of part-time signalers. . . . It is extravagant to entrust expensive signal equipment to men who do not fully understand it, and it is idle to expect partially trained operators to give the rapid service which is demanded by a modern army.[99]

With the aid of the Civil Service Commission, the Office of the Chief Signal Officer inaugurated civilian recruiting measures which improved classifications and allowed for training on the job. The effect was almost immediate: men withdrew from the 17th Signal Service Company, became civilians, and continued at their jobs in the Message Center at better pay. At the approach of World War II, the 17th had the status, moreover, of a separate company, except that it was under the Chief Signal Officer for duty assignments.[100] The situation continued to be tense in all of the other stations of the Radio Net; in a fifteen-month period in 1937 and 1938, they lost 456 trained specialists.

Largely as a result of improved equipment, operators who did stay were able to multiply speed by two, then by three. In September 1933 the Public Works Administration allocated $176,170 to the War Department for the Signal Corps to spend on physical improvements.[101] This made it possible to continue renewing the threadbare telephone and radio systems of posts and garrisons. The Plant and Traffic Division blocked out the money in twenty-five projects, half of them being for the Air Corps. "This work is of great benefit to the Army," one officer stated. "It has enabled the Signal Corps to place worn-out, obso-

lete (and in many cases pre-war) telephone systems in first class condition. It has expanded facilities to the point where all activities requiring telephone communication can be furnished such service." [102]

PWA expanded rapidly, and within its first year (fiscal year 1934) had distributed $343,614,628 to the War Department.[103] For seventy-seven projects which were supported either by direct allotment or by suballotment from the Quartermaster, Air, and Engineer Corps, the Signal Corps employed $1,801,766 of the whole War Department allocation. Many of the projects were for fire-control communications in the antiaircraft gun batteries and harbor defenses of Pearl Harbor and the Panama Canal. Another grant of $207,-366, apart from the sums for construction

---

[99] CSigO, *Annual Report, 1936,* pp. 19–20.

[100] M. E. Boswell, The 17th Signal Service Company: A Component of the War Department Signal Center from World War I Through World War II, Oct 45, p. 26. SigC Hist Sec File. Of the forty men who made up the company as it generally was in the late 1930's, one third were assigned to the Photographic Laboratory, the other two thirds served as the Message Center, at the AARS station and the transmitting station at Fort Myer, and at the remote receiving station at Battery Cove. SigC 320.22 17th Sig Sv Co, *passim.*

[101] Ltr, Maj Kenneth P. Lord, Finance Dept, to CSigO, 16 Oct 33, sub: Apportionment of National Industrial Recovery funds. SigC 475.7 (PWP) Funds 1, 1933–34.

[102] (1) Schedule of obligations attached to Ltr, OCSigO to WD Budget Officers, 15 Nov 33, sub: Preparation of schedules of obligations (Green Sheets) for funds received from Federal Emergency Admin of Public Works. SigC 475.7 (PWP) Funds 1, 1933–34. (2) OCSigO R&W Sheet, Plant and Traffic Div, initialed "RBC" [for Maj Colton], to Exec Officer, 7 May 34. Same file.

[103] This was part of a larger sum of $1,371,388,345 set aside for federal projects, and that sum in turn was part of a total of $3,300,000,000. Ltr, Harold L. Ickes, Federal Emergency Administrator of Public Works, to SW, 16 Jan 34, with OCSigO status rpt, 22 Jan 34. SigC 475.7 (PWP) Rpts, Jan–Feb '34.

of fixed communications, provided aircraft tactical radio.[104]

The windfall of Public Works Administration and Works Projects Administration funds rescued the communications from falling behind. In the nerve center at Washington and in the outlying stations, the effect was gratefully felt. High-speed equipment appeared in places other than the original two, Washington and San Francisco. Although it was still manual and not automatic, it was an improvement, and Hawaii, San Antonio, Atlanta, and Chicago profited from it.[105] Diamond-shaped, or rhombic, directive antennas arose at the Fort Myer transmitting station and receiving rhombics at Battery Cove, each an asset by virtue of providing the most possible with the least amount of power; gradually the net was enhanced with others.[106] Noise and fault locators and vacuum tube keyers made a commendable difference. WAR had kept a channel open for radioteletype, so in 1937 the equipment was installed as a venture in the Second Corps Area station in New York. Washington hoped to provide either leased teleprinter or teletypewriter exchange (TWX) service to other sections of the country, quite apart from any such facilities within the regional communications systems. The net began to think also of adding to its own group of networks those of the National Guard, the districts of the Civilian Conservation Corps, and the police.

Necessity forced more and more expansion upon fixed Army communications despite the opinion, long held in the Signal Corps itself and enforced in the 10-kilowatt limitation, that in case of war the Navy's radio system would become global whereas the Army's would be confined to the corps areas and departments. Yet to meet a world-wide war, the War Department Radio Net and Message Center were antiquated.[107] All equipment, either Boehme (high-speed) or straight key, was still operated by hand. Radioteletype had not yet come into general use, and for most of the stations was only in prospect. The system needed emergency power equipment, independent of the commercial supply, as well as additional channels similarly independent of leased lines.[108] And for all that it was a number of years since General Gibbs had announced, "Facsimile transmission has come, television is a demonstrated fact, and high-speed radio transmission and reception we have in our hands to use whenever the volume of traffic justifies its installation,"[109] his forecast had still not come wholly true.

In the Signal Corps' unique field agency, WAMCATS, the Washington-Alaska Military Cable and Telegraph System, a

---

[104] The Air Corps sought radios for each of 24 fighter airplanes, 30 light bombers, and 46 medium and heavy bombers. The principal requirement was for the airborne sets SCR-183 and SCR-187 and for the ground radio SCR-188. Ltr, Brig Gen Oscar Westover, Actg Chief of AC, to TAG, 8 Dec 33, sub: AC requirements program from Public Works funds. SigC 475.7 (PWP) Supplies.

[105] Signal Corps Information Letter, No. 2 (July 16, 1934), p. 13.

[106] Ltr, Maj Van Deusen, Exec Officer OCSigO, to TAG, 22 Mar 34, sub: Installation of antennas at WAR, and 9th Ind, 4 Jun 34. SigC 676.3 Fort Myer, 1932–39. The National Capital Park and Planning Commission asked for the Battery Cove site in order to make a park for Alexandria, but was denied. Ltr, Harry H. Woodring, Actg SW, to Frederic A. Delano, Chm National Capital Park and Planning Commission, 25 Jul 36. WDGS G-4 26616–16.

[107] Maj Gen Harry C. Ingles, Speech at Centennial of American Telegraph Association, 24 May 44. SigC AC 352.13 Speech Material, 1943–44.

[108] Memo, Capt Clarke, O/C WD Msg Ctr, for CSigO, 23 Feb 37. SigC 676.3 WAR (WDRS), 1936–39.

[109] Gibbs (and Carr) article cited n. 80.

similar set of changes took place. Wireless, first supplementing wire, came actually to supplant it. A network of cable, telegraph, and radio at the end of World War I, the system became one of cable and radio ten years later (the telegraph being discontinued in 1928) and of radio alone by 1934. In 1930 the cable began to go out of use, despite the fact that in 1924, at a cost of $1,500,000, the earlier one had been replaced with a new one. An appropriation of $200,000 bought radio equipment to serve in its stead. The Seattle–Ketchikan portion of the cable was abandoned on 31 December 1931, and the Ketchikan–Seward portion in 1934.[110] Time thus wholly transmuted the original system of the year 1904, a system of 2,100 miles of cable, 1,500 of land line, and only 100 of wireless space spanning. By 1936 there was no longer any way to keep even the name. It was changed to Alaska Communication System. Veteran employees went into mock mourning[111] for the days before radio had assumed command, and WAMCATS fell back into the past to join the vanished Aviation Section and Myer's *Manual of Signals.*

Radiotelephone made a limited Alaskan debut in 1931, when transmitters were put in at Marshall and St. Michael, two outposts of the Norton Sound region where wireless had been essential from the beginning of the century. Boehme high-speed automatic equipment appeared upon the Anchorage–Seattle circuit in June 1933. Simultaneously, the imponderables of the budget affecting Alaskan communications as everything else, the War Department ordered thirteen stations closed; but because they were necessary, the Signal Corps sold the equipment to the communities concerned and provided

the operators for it almost as before.[112] The system as a whole had been saved from sale to private interests only because the enabling legislation had been tabled.[113] In 1936 increasing traffic brought a regrouping of twenty-five stations into six nets, all stations of a net working on the same frequency and Anchorage serving as the control. After July 1937 radiotelephone facilities had become universal; connected to the long lines of the American Telephone and Telegraph Company, they made it possible to reach any point in the world from Juneau or Ketchikan.

Peacetime Procurement Planning [114]

In providing administrative communications the Signal Corps performed a basic peacetime service. War would raise tactical communications to the same importance, then redouble the doubling,

---

[110] (1) *Historical Sketch of the Signal Corps (1860–1941)*, p. 103. (2) Pamphlet, Alaska Communication System, 1900–1950, p. 26; (3) First Draft, Alaska Communication System History, p. 130. SigC Hist Sec File.

[111] Hist cited n. 110(3), p. 99.

[112] CSigO, *Annual Report, 1934,* p. 6.

[113] (1) Ltr, Patrick J. Hurley, SW, to Joseph W. Byrns, Chm HR Committee on Appropriations, 25 Mar 32. WDGS G-4 29284. (2) CSigO, *Annual Report, 1931,* p. 1.

[114] In the series UNITED STATES ARMY IN WORLD WAR II the full-length study of military procurement, procurement planning, industrial mobilization, manpower uses, logistics, and other aspects of the whole subject of supply is contained in the following: (1) John D. Millett, *The Organization and Role of the Army Service Forces* (Washington, 1954). (2) Richard M. Leighton and Robert W. Coakley, *Global Logistics and Strategy: 1940–1943* (Washington, 1955). (3) R. Elberton Smith, Army Procurement and Economic Mobilization, and (4) Byron Fairchild and Jonathan Grossman, Industrial Relations and Labor Problems. The last two volumes are now in preparation.

again and again, toward infinity. Of this fact, even in limbo, the Army's communications branch was sure. The War Department Message Center, the War Department Radio Net, the Army Amateur Radio System, leased wire lines, garrison and field systems, and the Alaska service, contained both a continued response to the calls of peacetime and a rudiment for a wartime communications system which would meet a wartime mission. The future was tacitly imposed on the present. At times between the two world wars, the day was sufficient without a tomorrow, especially a threatening one; but awareness of the next day, the next fiscal year, the next war never disappeared. No military agency could afford to forget that however well it had met its charge in the recent war, however adequately it did its duty currently, it would fail unless it could find some way to calculate and be ready for the future. Although the Army might recede from the public mind, the public would nevertheless expect it to be equipped on demand for an emergency.

The future was peculiarly difficult for the Signal Corps. In order to accomplish its mission, the Corps had to be a supply arm as well as a technical arm, a supply service as well as a technical service, and the obligation to be so was to the future even more than to the present. In being responsible for every dry battery the Army needed, precisely as the Quartermaster Corps was responsible for shoelaces and the Medical Department for aspirin, the Signal Corps was its own best customer.[115] The demands of the rest of the Army, however, particularly of that shadowy Army of the successive Protective Mobilization Plans, had evermore to be taken into account as the foremost obligation.

Tangible signal material had to be on hand for the daily demands; imagined supplies had to be on paper for a distant exigency. Tangible or imagined, they were a problem.

The apparatus of the Signal Corps is technical to the highest degree. This observation was made with great earnestness in 1919, at a time when radio was just coming into its own.[116] Succeeding years confirmed the view, with emphasis. Communications instruments are precision instruments, individual, complex, so subject to constant modification as to be new one year, out of date the next. They demand exact engineering, exact manufacture, exact testing to bring them to the delicate efficiency expected of them, and exactly trained men to use them to best advantage. For these reasons, Signal Corps anticipation of its future mission was equivalent to knowing the futures of the Army, the electrical industry, and electrical science.

The supply function was thus always both actual and theoretical, the actual straitened, the theoretical unbounded. For *supply* was as big a word as *communication*. It could be split three ways, resplit a dozen. In its broad reaches it touched budgeting and contracts, raw materials, allocations, critical items, and priorities, machine tools, spare parts, patents, industrial mobilization, and manpower. Its enormous range and detail offered a career in itself, within the larger career of the Army. Men like Elder, Hildreth, Cuny, Bush, and Pigg could be thought of as career colonels in supply within the Signal Corps as Olmstead could be con-

---

[115] The policy was set in 1920. WD GO 61, 22 Nov 20, Sec. II, and WD Supply Div Memo 1049, 22 Nov 20.

[116] WD, *Annual Reports, 1919*, Vol. I, Pt. 1, p. 1282.

sidered an administrative careerist or Milliken a specialist in training.[117]

At the top level of definition, supply comprised planning, procurement, and distribution. Planning was the duty assigned to planning sections both in Washington and the field, procurement was done (at least after 1925) from the offices of procurement districts, and distribution was made from depots and depot sections. Planning formed the future of supply; procurement and distribution were ordinarily linked because they represented the immediate moment.

For many years, equal boxes on the organization charts of the Office of the Chief Signal Officer showed "procurement," "storage and issue," and "procurement planning,"[118] the first two representing the actual or current work going on in supply, the third the hoped-for. The three boxes were not really equal, for the nebulous long-range work possessed much more significance than the palpable, day-in-day-out purchase and issue did. Given the stripped and shivering body military of those years, what fatness there was, was all in dreams. Two thirds of the orders which the Signal Corps placed in 1920 were for less than a hundred dollars, and one fourth for less than ten. Both procurement and distribution were often merest routine.[119] Corps area signal officers kept their units provided with what the peacetime budgets and their own initiative made possible. Signal depots and signal sections of depots catalogued, repaired, and issued signal equipment as they were directed to, and tried to keep life in what was stored. Stockpiles were so meager that ten years after the Armistice the largest depot section, New York, held only 4,000 items for issue and the smallest, New Cumberland, 41.[120]

Procurement, a function which in World War II created one billion-dollar Signal Corps after another, was then work-

---

[117] Eugene V. Elder studied at the Army Industrial College and the Harvard Graduate School of Business Administration, commanded the Philadelphia Procurement District between 1943 and 1945, and before and after that assignment spent more than fifteen years in the supply organization of the Office of the Chief Signal Officer. From 1929 on, Raymond C. Hildreth's duties were those of a supply officer. They culminated with command, successively, of the Sacramento and Lexington Signal Depots. Clifford D. Cuny, who was one of the first to take the Harvard course under the arrangement begun in 1923, was a Signal Corps supply specialist from the end of World War I through World War II. George P. Bush made his career in this field principally for twenty years. His capacities spanned planning and expediting, storage and issue. Albert M. Pigg's career lay most consistently of all in supply, from 1 January 1920, with an assignment to the Signal Corps General Supply Depot in Washington, D. C., to 15 May 1946, when he completed a two-and-one-half year tour at the Holabird Signal Depot, Baltimore.

For many years before Dawson Olmstead became Chief Signal Officer, his assignments gave him administrative experience. He was a student at the Command and General Staff College and the Army War College, officer in charge of the Washington-Alaska Military Cable and Telegraph System, executive officer to General Allison and General Mauborgne, president of the Signal Corps Board, and commandant of the Signal Corps School. Charles M. Milliken was for two years a student and for five years an instructor at the Command and General Staff College, for another four years was assistant commandant of the Signal Corps School, and, after an interval of a year as chief of the Operations Branch and its successor, the Field Service, in the Office of the Chief Signal Officer, was for the next six years, as a brigadier general, the officer commanding the Signal Corps training activities at Camp Crowder, Missouri, and Fort Dix, New Jersey.

[118] E.g., the charts for 30 September 1922, 1 November 1928, 26 December 1929, and 9 November 1939. The box titles varied, but their meaning remained the same.

[119] Capt. Wilton B. Persons described the peacetime procurement process in "Signal Corps Supply," a Signal Corps Bulletin article, May–June, 1933.

[120] Memo, Maj Dawson Olmstead, Chief Supply Div OCSigO, for CSigO, 8 Jan 29, sub: Outstanding accomplishments in SigC Supply Sv, 9 Jan 28–9 Jan 29. SigC 400 Gen 5.

ing in terms a thousandth part as large.[121] The years between the wars limited distribution to a bedrock meaning, a matter of bin-stock items and control space, shipping tickets and memorandum receipts. The handing out of items as they were asked for, a giant's duty when procurement became gigantic, was correspondingly dwarfed in time of peace.

Planning was a thing the other way around. The press of war might allow little time for it, but the stretch of postwar (or prewar) years offered a long opportunity to plan to the last crystal. There was no night-and-day shipping schedule to keep abreast of; maintenance was free of the special problems, like protection against fungus, which war in strange theaters imposed; the signal supply catalogue contained only 2,500 items and seldom needed to be revised.[122] Not only the entire country but overseas stations as well were served from three procurement districts. Contracting was minor, and educational orders, the special contracts devised to educate manufacturers in the Army's needs, remained in the cocoon. Allocation, scheduling, expediting, which were all vital parts of a wartime supply machine, in peace had small importance. Supplying the day's needs built up good experience, but anticipating tomorrow's created knowledge in advance of experience. Planning surveyed a whole region from requirements and standards to estimates of plant capacity and sources of manpower. It dealt in major potentials.

Certainly World War I had demonstrated the need for planning in the whole field of supply, including industrial mobilization, an area which before that time neither foreign armies nor the U.S. Army had seriously considered.[123] All through the final offensive of 1918, there had been dangerous shortages of many kinds; the munitions program had been inadequate; confusion had existed among the various supply agencies at home and abroad; some factories had fallen behind because of too many orders, others had not been equal to the orders they got. A man in the street might have thought that the Allies had won because they were so good that the enemy had to give up, but the persons responsible for supply had breathed a sigh of relief. The war had ended just soon enough to forestall a breakdown. If, for instance, all of the American combat forces had actually been engaged for a full month together, the Signal Corps would have needed 63,000 miles of wire to maintain their communications. But the best production figure for any month was only 8,000 miles.[124]

Peacetime procurement planning started off immediately at the close of World War I, from a series of conferences with businessmen in which Brig. Gen. William Mitchell of the Air Service and Col. Charles McK. Saltzman, the Assistant Chief Signal Officer, took part.[125] Legislation was the next stage. Saltzman helped to draft an enabling paragraph which would oblige the armed services to under-

---

[121] The amounts of Signal Corps purchases from 1920 through 1935 remained in sums which fluctuated between one and two million dollars. E.g., 1926: $1,031,484; 1930: $2,299,181; 1935: $1,688,633.

[122] James V. Clarke, Contract Adjustment in the Signal Corps, 1 July 1939–15 August 1945, MS, 1946, p. 9. SigC Hist Sec File. See also Col H. B. Ferguson, CE, Lecture G-4 Course 47, Army War College, 26 May 22. Army War College Record Sec.

[123] [Dwight F. Davis] ASW, Mass Procurement, lecture delivered before the Army War College, 20 Jan 23. SigC Proc Plng Sec File.

[124] 1st Lt. Frank W. Bullock, "Wire Industry Vital to War Planning," Signal Corps Bulletin, No. 66 (May–June 1932), p. 6.

[125] Hall hist cited n. 4(5), pp. 88–89.

take procurement planning, Secretary of War Newton D. Baker endorsed it before Congressional hearings, and it was made one of the 1920 amendments to the 1916 National Defense Act. The same legislation authorized an assistant secretary of war, responsible for all military procurement and for mobilization of industry and materials.[126]

Planning, explicitly authorized, was of course implicit in both of these functions; but whereas military procurement was part of the civilian economy, and long accepted, industrial mobilization was new and ominous. Wherefore, the two parts of this assignment diverged. Business, the accepted guide of government at that period, put the emphasis upon procurement and bridled at the shackling possibilities of mobilization planning. Whether in its military or its civilian aspects, mobilization planning called up such possibilities. In spite of the fact that military planning is planning for some place not here and at some time not now with men who are not yet in uniform and with materials which are not yet in production, it implies present conscription; and conscription is hard to achieve even when the threat to the national security is at hand, let alone in the afterglow of a war to end all future wars. The military phase of procurement planning, reflecting that of actual procurement, involved estimating requirements, allocations, contract schedules, and so on; but the larger economic phases took planning into such fields as stockpiling strategic and critical materials, converting plants for wartime manufacture, financing new factories, and awarding contracts according to local supply of power, to ease of access, to availability of labor.

The need for superagencies, controlling the civilian elements of military power, could be prophesied. Assistant Secretary of War Dwight F. Davis, for example, was aware of a necessity for a war industries board, a price control committee, apparatuses to administer labor, food, fuel, transportation and communication, a war finance corporation, and a war trade board.[127] There was no getting away from these parts of the plan if there was to be a plan at all. The initial group of fifty officers working in the Assistant Secretary's office at first devoted their attention to the military requirements of a procurement program and let the economic phases go; but it became apparent that computing the needs of a military force was not to be achieved while the equation was filled with x's. Wide-scale procurement planning took firm root. The War Council, the Joint Army and Navy Munitions Board, and the Army Industrial College became its agents. Maj. Laurence Watts was the first Signal Corps officer to be assigned to the Industrial College for training. Its lecturers during its first years included not only Watts, 1st Lt. Byron A. Falk, Maj. Roy H. Coles, Capt. Alfred M. Shearer and other Signal Corps officers engaged in the problems of supply mobilization, but also civilian communications chiefs like David Sarnoff of Radio Corporation of America and J. J. Carty of American Telephone and Telegraph.

Acting under the Assistant Secretary's office, the lower echelons organized procurement planning programs of their own. The supply list which the Assistant Secretary assigned to the Chief Signal Officer's responsibility reiterated signal, meteorological, and photographic items as custom

[126] 41 Statute 764, sec 5, 4 Jun 20.
[127] ASW lecture cited n. 123.

already established.[128] To plan for their procurement, the Office of the Chief Signal Officer opened a section headed by Maj. Francis G. Delano, with Capt. Edward F. French and Lieutenant Falk as his assistants.[129] For most of the 1920's there were three officers and two clerks in the section. In accordance with boundaries which the Office of the Assistant Secretary of War had fixed for fourteen industrial districts, the Signal Corps also established three procurement districts and assigned an officer in each of them to carry out procurement planning which was distinct from that of the Office of the Chief Signal Officer. The officers were Capts. Ralph R. Guthrie, Alfred M. Shearer, and George P. Bush, and they served respectively at New York, Chicago, and San Francisco. These three sites were chosen because, as Assistant Secretary Davis explained, "the Signal Corps districts are necessarily built up around those existing facilities such as General Electric Company, the Westinghouse Electric Company and the Western Electric Company, dealing in electrical equipment."

In Washington and afield, then, the Signal Corps undertook the planning of primary and secondary requirements, the surveying of industry, and the imaginary apportioning of war contracts. Furthermore, it sought Reserve officers as procurement experts; this was a part of the work in which, as elsewhere, the official policy was to look to industry. The rule of thumb in Signal Corps planning was to expect 50 percent of the required manufacture to come from the area of the New York Procurement District, 40 percent from Chicago, and 10 from San Francisco.[130] Telephone equipment came principally from the Chicago region, radio from New York.

All planning led to the secret strategic plans of the General Staff's War Plans Division, and was based upon the probable requirements of a mobilized army and the survey of industrial power. Personnel mobilization plans were to take care of the former and supply planning the latter. The War Department Mobilization Plans commenced in 1919; and 1920, 1924, 1928, and 1933 plans followed before Protective Mobilization Plans took their place. The supply plans were at first known by the names of colors—Green Plan, Tan Plan, and so on—and ultimately as Industrial Mobilization Plans.

At first, supply planners attempted to survey industry by means of questionnaires. They were markedly unsuccessful. They were rebuffed as meddling, presumptuous, or simply "dumb."[131] The Army War College began the use of questionnaires with an endeavor in 1921 to get replies to what it called an industrial inventory. When the effort failed, the General Staff ordered the supply agencies to gather their own information. Repeating the attempt with its own industrial mobilization questionnaires, the Signal Corps had no better luck. U.S. Steel, Westinghouse, and General Electric were

---

[128] The Signal Corps' responsibility for radar lay in an early regulation's specifying "all methods of determining the direction or range of artillery, radio stations, aircraft, or marine craft." AR 105–5, 14 Jan 22, Duties of the Chief Signal Officer, par. IV b.

[129] Lt Col George P. Bush and Martha E. Manning, History of Procurement Planning, 1920–1940, MS, 1942, p. 21. SigC Proc Plng Sec File.

[130] The New York District represented the Office of the Assistant Secretary of War's areas 1, 2, 3, 4, 5, 6, 7, 10; Chicago, areas 8, 9, 11, 12, 13; and San Francisco, area 14. OCSigO Office Memo 74, 20 Dec 22. WD Industrial Mob Plan, Dec 23, Annex 5, Chart 2. In March 1933 the War Department substituted four procurement zones for its original fourteen.

[131] Capt Albert M. Pigg, Monograph on Reports of Survey, 1935, p. 3. Proc Plan Sec File, Industrial Mob Br, P&D Div, OCSigO.

among the large companies to show un-
willingness to answer them. The War
Department registered an ineffectual re-
taliation against brusque treatment by
promising to shut out un-co-operative
businessmen in case of war. This was
comforting, but did not fill the void where
the answers should be. Moreover, there
was dispute over such basic riddles as the
reserve of materials: whether to plan for
the maximum emergency or for whatever
modest contingency Congress was likely
to agree to.[132]

The procurement problem stemmed
straight from the mobilization problem.
The War Department Mobilization Plan
work, which had commenced in terms of
an Army of six and a half million men
while production was still geared to war
effort,[133] had dwindled to a million men
on M Day, a million and a half six months
later. On this basis, the planners working
in the Assistant Secretary's office toward
the 1924 revision of the plan were computing requirements, but could hardly
know the conditions under which they
would be needed. In a dinner address,
General Squier offered lump sums to give
an idea. Each month, it seemed to him,
the Signal Corps would probably need
7,000 radio sets and 12,000 telephones;
19,000 miles of galvanized iron wire and
76,000 miles of insulated wire; 20,000 storage batteries and 200,000 dry batteries.
He even mentioned 60,000 pounds of
pigeon feed.[134] So, would the war be short
or long? local or global? soon or never at
all? The Signal Corps' part in planning
had to be related to the answers to these
questions, to the reserve of raw and manufactured materials, to manpower, transportation, and industrial potential. In
order to answer them the planners needed

to get replies to their questionnaires. Industry pointed out that the Army could
not expect answers without knowing what
to ask—and the circle was complete.

Conferences with industry, a second
attempt, were hamstrung by the reluctance of business representatives to speak
frankly in front of their competitors. This
reaction was not surprising. One of the
important tools of supply planning was the
report of survey, and the report of survey was
panoramic enough to daunt a man whose
factory it analyzed.[135] Yet until the good
faith and serious purpose of military
planners were accepted by business, there
could be no real information on which to
base a plan. After a period of several years,
the Signal Corps officers on planning duty
built up the confidence of industrialists,
and business representatives did consent
to disclose production rates, plant capacity, and other figures. They stipulated,
however, that they speak in private and to
a Regular Army officer, not to a civilian
who might be hired away by a competitor

---

[132] Bush and Manning hist cited n. 129, pp. 77–78.

[133] WD Pub Relations Br, Statement by Brig Gen
Harry L. Twaddle Before the Truman Committee,
24 Apr 41. AG 381 (11–29–40) Sec 1.

[134] Maj Gen George O. Squier, Wartime Procurement and Procurement Planning in the Signal Corps,
address at dinner for ASW, N.Y., Feb 23. SigC PP
Basic Plan for Proc.

[135] Reports of survey were supposed to show
"parent or subsidiary firms, executives, ownership,
capitalization, normal products, production machinery, normal suppliers and subcontractors, sources
of supply for raw materials, number of employees,
power and transportation facilities available, a complete listing of the Signal Corps items which, in the
judgment of the Planning Officer, the plant would be
capable of producing, the *preferred* items for production, that is, the items for which the plant was considered to be best suited to produce economically and
in the quantities needed, and finally, a recommendation by the Planning Officer as to 'allocation' of the
facility." Bush and Manning hist cited n. 129, p. 85.

for the sake of the information he had obtained.[136] Under no circumstance was industry asked for information without clear approval from the Office of the Assistant Secretary.

Consultation with industry was further hampered by the fact that officers had no expense account to depend on so that they could travel to a plant in order to survey it firsthand. Ordinarily, they prepared reports from the information on file near them, and the result was sometimes remote from fact. The farther away history moved from World War I, the less significant was any report based on the industrial potential which had existed at its close. Most industries had converted their factories wholly to the uses of peacetime and could no longer be considered available for war production without extensive reconversion. As this situation developed, the *factory plan* came into being. Wherever a survey became obsolete, planning officers sought to replace it with a construction plan, for building a new factory, or an expansion plan, for altering an existing one. These plans held the kernel for the arrangements whereby the federal government later subsidized the expansion of industry during and somewhat before the 1941–1945 war. A factory plan was made if the industrial capacity for an item was determined to be less than twice the amount which the requirements of the Mobilization Plan made necessary. (In the Office of the Assistant Secretary of War, the standard planning policy was that half of the industrial capacity would be the maximum allowed to military use, the other half being reserved to the civilian economy.) Planners estimated production in twenty-four-hour units because full-time operation would be the rule of war, but computed it at two and one-half rather than three times the production figure of a peacetime eight-hour shift because they felt sure that efficiency in the second and third eight-hour periods of the twenty-four would not be up to the standard of the first.

In the preparation of factory plans, the Signal Corps asked for the industrial surveys which the Bureau of the Census had compiled with an expertness and detail that no small service could approach. Statutory secrecy imposed upon them made them inaccessible, however, and the planning sections were accordingly obliged to cover the same ground for themselves. Moreover, factory plans were of less use to the Signal Corps than to services like Ordnance which required special military manufacture almost totally unrelated to civilian use.

The most valuable device for Signal Corps planning was the *item-procurement plan*. It came up in the same set of circumstances which produced the report of survey but accomplished a different purpose. It shifted the point of view from plant to item and from report to plan. The reports of survey were in no sense plans. They were supposed to reflect the existing situation, plant by plant, of the communications industry. The item-procurement plan (or, simply, procurement plan, as it came to be called) separated the problem into the actual materials themselves, by considering the requirements of the military system singly, whether as raw resources or as manufactured products, and synthesized future procurement in that way.

One of the commodity committees of

---

[136] Pigg monograph cited n. 131, p. 5.

the War Department of which the Signal Corps held the chairmanship was that for mica.[137] As an insulator—as a component of radio condensers, as an essential to commutator segments in motors and generators—mica was vital; and since only a small proportion of the total amount mined was useful and since several branches of the Army counted upon it, there had to be careful planning for an adequate supply in case of war.[138] It accordingly received special study. So did quartz crystals for radio transmission, crude diamonds for wiredrawing, and other raw materials.[139] For manufactured items, similar studies had to be made. Storage batteries, a common enough product, were of continuous importance to the Signal Corps. A 1926 item-procurement plan for them began by scrutinizing and trying to define the strategic mission of storage batteries, then moved into detail, first describing the basic lead-sulphuric acid and nickel-iron-potassium types, next listing the models which the Signal Corps would need. Continuing, other sections of the plan discussed critical components, critical raw materials, production tools, labor requirements, and contract policy. The plan closed with a graph which charted the manufacture of batteries from the beginning of the process to the end.[140]

These plans had limitations. Not only were lists of critical materials likely to change abruptly, but new methods of manufacture or advances in the field of electricity could fast make them out of date. For instance, the advent of better magnetic steel altered the whole area of procurement of field telephones. An even more important change occurred when the use of metal for vacuum tubes made the shielding process unnecessary. The rapid obsolescence which was the Jonah of communications equipment made it hard to merge the individual item plans into a comprehensive view.

Military uses often set a standard much higher than commercial manufacturers maintained in their product; hence a plan ordinarily had to be written with custom-built apparatus in mind. Maj. George P. Bush and others held that war would require mass production, even of radio, yet attempts in that direction were frustrated by the very attributes which render radio a valuable and delicate instrument.[141] Another barrier to mass production could arise from the fact that companies would probably not use interchangeable components to an extent which would make it possible for several factories to join in quantity production. The New York Procurement District anticipated difficulty in subcontracting the manufacture of high-frequency equipment for this reason—that the prime contractors would use proprietary parts and features.[142]

Machine tools posed another dilemma. Should the Signal Corps try to keep up its supply of them, an effort which would involve almost yearly replacement, or should an equivalent amount of money and time be spent on developing better methods and models, in the hope that there would

---

[137] The Signal Corps was also represented on the commodity committees for ferroalloys, nonferrous metals, optical glass, rubber and rubber goods, steel and iron, and wire and cable. CSigO, *Annual Report, 1930*, p. 56.

[138] Capt Alfred M. Shearer, Tentative Plan for the Production of Mica, 1929. SigC FM-137.

[139] CSigO, *Annual Report, 1928*, p. 18.

[140] "A Typical Signal Corps Plan for the Procurement of Supplies," Signal Corps Bulletin, No. 37 (January, 1927), pp. 31–40.

[141] H. D. Hausmann, Procurement Planning and Industrial Mobilization, 1920–1940, Pt. II, pp. 258ff. OCSigO Industrial Mob Br File.

[142] Rpt of N. Y. SigC Proc District, 35, 8 Jul 35. SigC Annual Rpts.

be enough advance warning for the nation to retool its factories? After World War I, the Signal Corps took over a large quantity of tools, jigs, and dies which were so soon outmoded that the second choice was inescapable; and machine tools had to be added thereafter to the planned production of an item.

In 1929, when the new administration of Herbert Hoover came into power, a reorganization in the Office of the Assistant Secretary of War took industrial mobilization planning out of the experimental cycle which it had been in thus far. Under this influence and in the ascendancy of item planning, the Signal Corps' procurement mobilization principles were gradually crystallizing. Planners tried to reduce the problem to two considerations: where to find each item and at what rate to expect it. For a third factor, where it would be used, the point of reference was always the mobilization plan.[143] All requirements were classified according to the probable difficulty of meeting them in time of war. Class I item-procurement plans, the highest of three orders, demanded approval in the Office of the Assistant Secretary lest there be a conflict with other services or with civilian needs. The accumulation of hundreds of Class I, II, and III plans[144] had developed a conception of an ideal production plan as a progression in which an item would be standardized, the demand for it settled, its specifications drawn up, plants allocated to its manufacture, factory layouts determined, all special machine tools and contributory items provided, an educational order let to determine the rate of production and encourage the training of the labor force, the costs computed, and the whole thing stored up until M Day invoked it.[145]

Nobody knew it, but an M Day was moving nearer. In retrospect, events before 1929 seem a long backing away from World War I, those after it a long approach to World War II. The mid-point between wars arrived with the great economic depression which began in October 1929, eleven years after the close of World War I, ten years before World War II opened. The depression dealt a blow to supply planning and purchase. The Signal Corps placed only 2,400 orders in the fiscal year 1930.[146] There were not even funds with which to send officers to the Harvard Graduate School of Business Administration, as had been the case since 1923.[147] The Supply Planning Section was cut. Reports of survey became so unstable as to be almost wholly useless, and visits to plants in an effort to bring the statistics up to date turned into mournful walks through empty shops and past halted belt lines. But although industry offered little to survey, planning went on in much the same fashion as before. In 1930 the Signal Corps settled upon a policy of industrial surveys every year, every three years, or every five, depending on the rapidity with which the factory's product changed.

At the same time, two years of effort

---

[143] Until 1930, specifically Annex 5 to the plan.

[144] By 1939 the files of the Procurement Planning Section, Office of the Chief Signal Officer, contained plans for 1,160 items. Officers charged with current procurement seem to have neglected this treasure of information, however, and to have procured signal material without regard to the long view contained in it. Bush and Manning hist cited n. 129, p. 89.

[145] Capt L. J. Harris, Problem 11, Army Industrial College 1935–36 course, Suppl Rpt 4, pp. 7–8. Army Industrial College File.

[146] By contrast with 74,000 at the wartime peak in 1943. Brig. Gen. Calvert H. Arnold, "Industrial Mobilization and the Signal Corps," *Signals,* I, No. 3 (January–February, 1947), 10.

[147] Provided for in paragraph 127a of the National Defense Act, 1923.

culminated in statistics on the weight, volume, and cost of the tactical signal equipment a wartime military machine would use in units from a platoon all the way up through a field army. This task completed, planners turned to presenting the computations in the form of charts, for the greater convenience of corps area signal officers in their own planning and purchase of equipment. For a period, these *war planning equipment charts* unofficially took the place of tables of basic allowances. They could not serve forever, though, and in the fall of 1934 Capt. Albert M. Pigg and his associates—Pigg by then the Procurement Planning Section's only officer—began to prepare tentative tables of basic allowances upon the basis of discussion with all arms using signal material. The discussion was careful enough to result in nearly definitive work, so that Signal planning reaped two benefits. In the first place, it enjoyed the advantage of up-to-date information until the official tables of basic allowances appeared; and in the second, when that time came, most of the Signal Corps' contribution was ready. The old supply plans named for colors were falling into the discard meanwhile, although unluckily not until a good deal of time and energy had gone into attempts to revise them. Further work on these plans stopped in 1934, and they were replaced altogether in 1937 by the first of the Protective Mobilization Plans.

In anticipation of the new Protective Mobilization Plan and to try the usefulness of existing plans, Signal Corps supply agents were everywhere asked how ready they thought they were. Long lists of questions went out in 1936 to each echelon— the Office of the Chief Signal Officer, the New York and Chicago Procurement Districts, the signal sections of the New York, Chicago, and San Francisco General Depots, the corps area signal offices, and the signal sections of corps area supply points. For Wire W-110, for example, the questions included these:

Which items procured by other supply arms and services must be considered in procuring Wire W-110?

What will be the procedure, if any, to insure the required flow to manufacturers of manganese, rubber and tin required for Wire W-110?

What procedure will be followed in placing contracts for Wire W-110 and . . . in making payments therefor?

Have all the facilities capable of fabricating Wire W-110 or its component processes been surveyed . . . ?

Have plans been made so that production can be shifted from one geographical area within a district to another . . . ? To another procurement district?

How much wire is the depot planning to stock in wartime? Where?

Will this wire be stocked as loose coils, on reels DR-4, on reels DR-5? What proportion?

How will overseas shipments be made? [148]

Procurement planning had gone far in the years it had been in existence. These were searching questions, making plain the extent to which Signal Corps requirements were interbound with those of the rest of the Military Establishment, American industry, and civilian life. They called up the whole supply apparatus of the Signal Corps: the depots, the procuring agencies, the overseas suppliers. Planning, indeed, revealed that procurement itself was half planning. The most difficult thing of all was to calculate the rate. The last (1933) War Department Mobilization Plan did not allow enough time for equipping the troop units which it projected. It was unrealistic in its apprehension of

---

[148] Bush and Manning hist cited n. 129, pp. 62–64.

engineering difficulties, oversanguine in its estimate of the amount of war production to be drawn from an industry far removed from war.

The only certainty about procurement was that it was a long process—many thought too wrapped with red tape to be able to move at all [149]—and the greatest contribution which planning could make would be to hasten it. Almost no one then realized what later experience eventually proved—that the time lag from drawing board to end of production for military electronics equipment is normally from four to eight years.[150] A schedule for the SCR-194 showed that four and one-half years had advanced it only to the edge of manufacture. Proposed 23 June 1932, the SCR-194 had traversed various routes of approval and amendment, service test and modification, standardization and specification, to final authorization from the Office of the Assistant Secretary on 18 January 1937.[151] Bidding, award of contract, manufacture, inspection, acceptance, delivery, and that ultimate test, the approval of actual use, were yet to come.

More than for any other reason, the Protective Mobilization Plan was developed because it promised to speed things up. The first one was prepared in the anxiety engendered by the newest Japanese attack upon China, which followed German and Italian demonstration of strength in Spain, which followed Italian force against Ethiopia, which followed Japan's Manchurian conquest at the outset of the decade. Assuredly, there was no want of urging for planning. Whether a new approach would produce good results remained to be seen. In any case, the years devoted to predecessor plans were far from wasted. If the work on the new basis was as valuable, it would produce priceless knowledge of methods and techniques, priceless experience in computing requirements, gauging sources of supply, revealing possible shortages in materials or components, and estimating facilities which would be depended upon for manufacture. The ultimate value of two decades of procurement planning would lie not in perfected blueprints, ready instantly to fill the breach when the emergencies were proclaimed, but in the men it had trained.

---

[149] Brig Gen Alfred W. Marriner, USAF Ret., ruefully made this point in an interview with the author, New York, 12 February 1950.

[150] A conservative estimate allowing two to four years for development, one to two years from development until production begins, and one to two years for completion of production. MS Comment by Maj Gen Roger B. Colton, Ret., 14 Sep 53. SigC Hist Sec File.

[151] Hausmann study cited n. 141, Pt. III, p. 79.

CHAPTER III

The Scope of the Signal Corps

The Chief in Office

For a Chief Signal Officer between wars to suppose what his Corps might be at full reach and range took an act of the imagination. From 1924 to 1937 General Saltzman, General Gibbs, General Carr, and General Allison spanned a period when neither World War I nor World War II was close, yet all of them were expected to know their service not only as it existed but also as it ought to exist for a major conflict. The circle of their fiscal yearly duties was concentric to a larger circle which they could only guess at. Everything they did might shorten or extend the radius. Each Chief followed in a kind of episcopal succession derived from the past but deferring to the future; each in turn took his place at the head of an agency which had antedated him far enough so that he could not mold its dogma but which would also postdate him in assigning his acts to the body of permanent tradition. The primary charge laid upon each of them was to act in terms of what might lie ahead, because if war materialized, the nebulous outer limits would become real.

It is not surprising that the constricted limits they worked in appeared sometimes to be the whole reality. The Chief himself could often give his time in office an importance it did not actually have, to the extent of his awareness that he had been set in place to hold the organization together and to advance it if circumstances called upon him to do so. Maj. Gen. George S. Gibbs was of this sort, a man of capacity whose career matured at a point when there was least for him to do. Both the recollection and the prospect of a wartime Signal Corps being uppermost in a good Chief Signal Officer's administration, the guiding principle was conservation, retention, preservation. Empire building might well have been easier by comparison. Maj. Gen. Charles McK. Saltzman even found himself obliged to deny the assertion that the Military Establishment was "standing by in idleness and wastefulness." [1] He met this threat, and turned to the next, where "One and Two Per Cent Clubs," economy devices of the Coolidge and Hoover administrations, were demanding that he pare the skin from a budget which he felt had already lost its flesh. Both he and his successor, Gibbs, made the cuts, but they both put the equivalent amounts back into their budget requests for the ensuing years. [2] Gibbs also balked at a proposed sale of the Washington-Alaska Military Cable and Telegraph System; and he reorganized the whole administrative structure of his command so that he could leave it, he hoped, well decentralized the better

---

[1] CSigO, *Annual Report, 1926*, p. 1.
[2] CSigO, *Annual Report, 1926,* App., pp. 68–70, and *Annual Report, 1927,* App., p. 23.

to resist the onslaught of either Congress or war.

To take care of the responsibilities charged to the Chief, his office was usually arranged in four divisions: Personnel, Research and Development, Supply, and Special Service, the latter including such miscellaneous activities as the photographic, pigeon, and meteorological services. Little change in this basic organization took place in the 1920's; the principal one was that General Saltzman organized a Training Division apart from Personnel.[3]

During the fiscal year 1930, however, something of a real reorganization was undertaken by General Gibbs. Declaring in his annual report for that year that he had wanted to make the Office of the Chief Signal Officer a genuine "head office," he explained that he had "centralized supervision and decentralized operation" by closing the Washington, D. C., signal depot and moving four laboratories to Fort Monmouth.[4] Current purchasing had already been shifted to the procurement districts; and Monmouth was well established as the center for training. Gibbs's small Washington headquarters of twenty-one officers and fifty-three civilians stepped out of the general organizational pattern of the 1920's and into one which lasted a comparable time in the 1930's. It comprised the Personnel, Research and Development, Supply, and Training Divisions, added Plant and Traffic, for the administrative communications duty, and made photography and meteorology into separate divisions by dissolving the old catchall, Special Service. With these seven divisions the Office of the Chief Signal Officer continued up to the end of the decade and the threshold of the new war. Then, under expansion, the peacetime pattern served like a basic blue-

print. The double scope of the Signal Corps between wars, the daily challenge to a Chief Signal Officer of those days to see his organization as acorn and oak at the same time, could scarcely have materialized with more force than actually did develop. A dozen small and quiet field agencies grew to over four dozen which, although dependencies, were often as large as their progenitors of the 1920's and 1930's; and the Office of the Chief Signal Officer alone reached a size greater than the Washington and field activities together had once been. (Chart 2)

The December 1929 reorganization anticipated the larger view by its redesignation of the Training Division as the War Plans and Training Division. Actually, its principal work continued to be training. It was responsible for the program of Signal Corps interrelation with ham radio enthusiasts.[5] It scheduled the special one-year assignments of officers who studied at the Massachusetts Institute of Technology, the Harvard Graduate School of Business Administration, the Yale Sheffield School of Electrical Science, at other universities, in Los Angeles with the moving picture industry, at the Command and General Staff School and Army Industrial College, and with the division itself in the Signal Intelligence Section—all as part of the very real trend to specialize the officers of the Signal Corps. For want of anyone else to do so, it supervised the instruction of pigeons as well as of human beings. In the

---

[3] Courtney R. Hall, The Development of the Office of the Chief Signal Officer, Pt. I: 1917–43, p. 50. SigC Hist Sec File.

[4] CSigO, *Annual Report, 1930*, p. 2, and accompanying orgn chart.

[5] (1) Maj. David M. Crawford, "The Army Amateur Radio System," Signal Corps Bulletin, No. 47 (March, 1929), pp. 39–45. (2) AARS Revised Gen Plan, pars. 2 and 5, and AARS Regulations, Secs. I, VI, VII, VIII.

School and Literature Section, the division concerned itself with the revision of past training doctrine and the formulation of new doctrine; extension courses were one of its innovations which the Army generally adopted. There were never as many as a dozen civilians, including those working at codes and cryptograms, in the War Plans and Training Division, and the whole complement of officers was three, then four, then five, and ultimately seven by 1937. Maj. David M. Crawford was the first officer in charge; Maj. Spencer B. Akin succeeded him in 1932 and Maj. William S. Rumbough followed Akin in 1935.[6]

The reorganization plan also moved fiscal duties up to the Executive Office. There the Fiscal Section devoted itself primarily to the budget, a process managed over a range of at least three years. If, for example, the Research and Development Division and the Laboratories were readying a program, the preparations were not for the current fiscal year nor even for the next but for the one after that. In the last six months of 1934, Major Blair, Maj. Hugh Mitchell, and others projected the fiscal year 1937 development program. By 1 January 1935 they were ready with two sets of estimates, maximum and minimum figures, which they had discussed with Maj. Stewart W. Stanley, chief of the Fiscal Section and which, through him, they were prepared to defend before the G-4 Division of the General Staff. G-4 then reached a compromise figure which General Carr, the Chief, forwarded to the War Department, his own officers being obliged to defend it again, item by item. This stage resulted in another calculation, which went into the War Department budget and, in August, was presented before the Bureau of the

Budget. Having been approved there, with further modifications, it came before the Appropriations Subcommittee of the House of Representatives and finally, in early 1936, to the floor of Congress. Debate in each house and Senate-House conference preceded its passage and its signature by the President. Then it became official and, on 1 July 1936, took effect as a part of the fiscal year budget for 1937.

As a matter of fact, the Signal Corps' 1937 appropriation marked the end of the era of impoverishment, for before that fiscal year ended the total reached $5,587,357.[7] A large part of it, however, went toward the intensive program to put radio in every military airplane. Only a fifth went to the communications mission, a seventh to the pay of civilian employees, and in every case except the special expenditure for the Air Corps the Chief Signal Officer and his staff could use the funds only on a monthly basis.[8] If a telephone construction project were to cost more than one twelfth of the total amount appropriated for telephone construction projects, it would have to wait until enough money for it accrued. This sort of arrangement set limits to administration which no Chief Signal Officer of the period could escape. It heightened the importance of routine, of detail, of slowness to take action. The Army between wars was not a big business, but an enterprise conserved for bigness, its agents trustees for a critical and universal public.

---

[6] Capt Frederick Reinstein, The Development of Military Training Branch, OCSigO, 1929–1945, pp. 2–7. SigC Hist Sec File.

[7] CSigO, *Annual Report, 1937*, p. 7. Part of the new accretion of funds reflected the appointment, two years before, of Gen. Malin Craig as Chief of Staff. General Craig had lent personal support to the increase because he especially valued communications.

[8] Ltr, CSigO to Sig Officers All Corps Areas and Depts, 2 May 36. SigC 676.1, Jan 25–Dec 39.

All procedure had to be standardized, and co-ordinated with the standardized procedures of other agencies.

Suppose that the Chief of Cavalry wanted the Chief Signal Officer to provide him with a radio which troopers could mount upon guidon staffs.[9] He first offered a tentative description of its military characteristics agreed upon by his service board. The Signal Corps Technical Committee reviewed these and passed them on to G-3 and G-4. The concurrence of these staff sections permitted the item to appear in the budget requests for the ensuing fiscal year, to pass through the channels just described.

With the appropriation in hand, the Chief Signal Officer assigned the project to one of the Laboratories or to a commercial organization. Thereupon the developing laboratory started a test model, sending in monthly reports the while. With the model in hand, the Signal Corps and the Cavalry, together with the Infantry or any other component also interested, conducted a service test, the reports of which, after a month or a year, found their way back to the laboratory or the business firm, so that the design might incorporate all modifications called for. The project engineers tested the redesigned model and, if the alterations were satisfactory, the Signal Corps Technical Committee recommended that the guidon radio be standardized for production. With the Office of the Assistant Secretary of War supervising the scheduling, a basis of issue would be determined from the needs of the Cavalry and the plans of the General Staff. The stage of final specifications then would arrive, although not without thorough discussion, including suggestions from industry; and at last the Signal Corps could invite bids, let the contract, follow the item through its manufacture, pay for it, and issue or store it according to the requisitions made.

Next to getting money, the great problem for these Chief Signal Officers was getting personnel. The effect of horizontal or across-the-board cuts, as often as not at a time when the duties were doubled, was to close out all hope of promotion for years; as a result, some civilians and many enlisted men whom the government had spent thousands of dollars to train took the first opportunity to leave.

In 1927, the 2,165 enlisted men in the Signal Corps, representing 1.8 percent of the enlisted strength of the Army, were distributed not only in the United States but also in Alaska, the Canal Zone, the Hawaiian Islands, and the Philippines. The greatest number, 864, was assigned to the 11 signal service companies in the United States and the next largest, 530, to the remaining tactical organizations within the continental limits: that is, to the 51st Signal Battalion, the 1st and 2d Signal Companies, and the 1st Signal Troop. The Hawaiian garrison took 320 men, Panama 215, Alaska (for the cable and telegraph system) 187, and the Philippines 63. Sixty percent of the assignments were to the Signal Corps' administrative, or at any rate nontactical, functions.

Ten years later, in 1937, the distribution of enlisted strength was unchanged: 60 percent administrative, by this time assigned in 14 signal service companies, and 40 percent tactical, now not only in the 51st Signal Battalion and the 1st Sig-

---

[9] The reality that grew out of this supposition was the SCR-511, although by the time it emerged for general use there was no longer any thought of carrying it on horseback. Hist Sec E&T Divs OCSigO, History of Signal Corps Research and Development in World War II, 1945–46. Vol. VIII, Pt. 2, Proj 814–B. SigC Hist Sec File.

nal Troop but also in 6 (rather than 2) signal companies and the new provisional Radio Intelligence Company. A 1,200-man increase which had come about during ten years was confined almost entirely to the continental assignments, leaving the garrisoning overseas little altered. For Hawaii there were 340; for Panama, 250; for the Alaska Communication System (and this did include the men stationed at the Seattle headquarters), 185 where there had been 187 a decade before, and for the Philippine Islands, 60.[10]

Officers were a more stable force. Rank carried attributes of social acceptance and authority which made all the difference in choosing whether or not to stay with a military career. In the long economic depression this intangible influence melted before the more telling desire just to hold a job. Then there were fewer resignations. A study completed in 1936 advanced the possibility that the Signal Corps would have a hard time filling up its officer allotment in the decade from 1939 to 1949.[11] What was expected was that many officers would reach retirement during those years and that the Signal Corps would be confronted with the fact that the years of economizing had robbed it of successors for them. For there were few opportunities for young men to enter the corps of Regular Army officers during the years when the World War I officers were still thoroughly active and filled all the places allowed except a few at the bottom for each year's West Point graduates. The Signal Corps was a popular choice at the academy, and because of its technical exactions was likely to secure cadets from the upper scholastic levels, but it was not enough that this was the case.

Until the Thomason Act [12] was passed in 1935, no new officers came in except by transfer from other branches or from the Military Academy, and even under the new legislation only one or two men a year could be beckoned from civilian life. At no time between the wars did Signal Corps officer strength reach the authorized 300.[13] In July 1937 General Allison was asked to submit "some feasible plan that would permit a decrease in the number of Signal Corps officers on duty in the District of Columbia without impairing the efficiency of the Office of the Chief Signal Officer." [14] In view of the fact that there were then only 21 officers on the Washington staff, and only 265 in the entire Corps, Allison's opposition to the proposal can be imagined. He had only just got through recommending that his supply of officers be increased by 54.[15]

The Regular list always looking too short to them, the Chief Signal Officers maintained a commissioned Reserve by means of Affiliated Plan arrangements and Reserve Officers' Training Corps units. For most of this period the roster totaled between 2,000 and 2,500 names.[16] Some training of Reserve officers was undertaken at Fort Monmouth during the summer encampments of the Citizens' Military Training Corps, 412 appearing for this duty in 1928. Signal Corps ROTC units were located at the Massachusetts, Carnegie, and Georgia Institutes of Technology, Cornell University, and the state

---

[10] CSigO, *Annual Report, 1927*, App., pp. 19–20, and *Annual Report, 1937*, p. 2.

[11] CSigO, *Annual Report, 1936*, p. 1.

[12] PL 408, 30 Aug 35, 74th Cong. See also WD Bulletin 9, par. II, 22 Oct 35.

[13] Capt Wilson G. Burden, Mil Pers Br OCSigO, Signal Corps Strength, Nov 45, p. 8. OCSigO Career Management File.

[14] Ltr, ASW to CSigO, 8 Jul 37. SigC 322.08 Gen.

[15] Ltr, Gen Allison to CofS, 17 Mar 37, sub: SigC troops. In same file.

[16] Burden study cited n. 13, p. 10.

ROTC STUDENTS *are shown above arriving at the railroad station at Fort Monmouth and below in a field training class.*

universities of Ohio, Michigan, Illinois, Wisconsin, and Minnesota. These were the principal source of Reserve officers, producing 156 second lieutenants in a typical year, 1928.[17]

By a well-established arrangement a large share of the officers in the Reserve came from the communications industry, especially from the operating rather than from the manufacturing companies. It was perfectly natural that a communications agency should find its officers among communications men. Certainly one would expect Reserve chaplains to be clergymen, and in a profaner sphere the Signal Corps was quite as specialized. In the same way that the medical departments of the armed services answered to the American Medical Association, so, although to a less marked degree, the American Telephone and Telegraph Company and the Radio Corporation of America had a prominent position in the Signal Corps.

Col. Ira D. Hough and Lt. Col. Carroll O. Bickelhaupt, on temporary active duty in 1934, prepared a prospectus which recommended that enlisted communications specialists be recruited in time of war by a group of Reserve officers "selected from the personnel of the four large communications companies." The other two were the Western Union and Postal Telegraph-Cable corporations; but neither of these matched the importance of AT&T in wire or of RCA in radio. Colonel Hough and Colonel Bickelhaupt proposed that thirty-six of thirty-eight recruiting officers be Reservists from the telephone and telegraph system, and allowed radio one in New York and one on the Pacific coast. Recruiting from the 6,000 or more "so called independent telephone companies," they said, "could and probably would be handled through the Bell Telephone Com-

panies with which they are connected."[18]

If businessmen thus proposed partial control of the supply and assignment of Army personnel, Army men were comparably willing to have it so. Private industry could place its officials in the Reserve and the Army could encourage its Regular officers to be businessmen. A Reservist could be a businessman in olive drab and a Regular a soldier in a grey flannel. At about this same time Major Rumbough, for example, although not a businessman-officer,[19] recommended that the radio course be divided into three periods so that student-officers might spend the middle stage working for RCA or Mackay, in association with the RCA or Mackay Reservists.[20]

Both sides were at pains to make certain that the public did not become aware of any agreement between them in the matter of mobilization, but the interrelationship between the Signal Corps and the giants of the commercial communications networks was fundamental to any Chief's administration.[21] The Signal Corps Laboratories, as has been pointed out, were in frequent connection with the Bell Laboratories. Both military and civilian personnel attended schools of the Bell System.[22] Manpower and industrial mobilization planning was necessarily based upon commercial capacities. Military expansion

[17] CSigO, *Annual Report, 1928*, p. 17.

[18] Col Ira D. Hough and Lt Col Carroll O. Bickelhaupt, Signal Corps Enlisted Communications Specialists Requirements for a Major Emergency, 20 Apr 34. Personal file of Bickelhaupt.

[19] In retirement after World War II, he became principal of the Falls Church, Virginia, high school.

[20] Ltr, Maj Rumbough to CSigO, 12 Oct 36, sub: Practical radio course for officers. SigC 352.11 Gen 2.

[21] Ruth Sadler, Mil Pers Br OCSigO, History of the Signal Corps Affiliated Plan, Aug 44, p. 17. SigC Hist Sec File.

[22] CSigO, *Annual Report, 1928,* p. 18.

yielded to commercial priority in setting up the terms and conditions under which War Department facilities were provided with such special services as long lines and teleprinter networks, the Signal Corps ordinarily fulfilling that half of its mission which pertained to domestic communications by leaving them in the hands of the private companies.[23] And commercial communications men crossed back and forth into the military preserve, military men into the commercial—General Gibbs, for example, having become the executive head of Postal Telegraph—in a way which blurred the demarcation line between them.

To umpire communications after the model of the Interstate Commerce Commission's authority over transportation facilities, Congress created the Federal Communications Commission in 1934. Hitherto jurisdiction over domestic communications had been shared by the ICC, the Post Office Department, and the FCC's predecessor, the Federal Radio Commission, which dated from 1927, and to which still another chief signal officer, General Saltzman, had been appointed. All forms of domestic communications now were brought under the supervision of the new agency. In many aspects of his work a Chief Signal Officer came into contact with the FCC, usually at second hand but nonetheless with registered effect. The frequencies which he reallocated throughout the using components of the Army he received from the commission. Equipment developed in the Laboratories conformed to airport control allotments or to standards approved by the commission. The amateur radio operators upon whom he depended for an initial source of skilled manpower were licensed by the FCC. The Alaska Communication System made direct recommendations to the commissions on all applications for service in the northern territory.[24] New developments like frequency modulation, so vital to military communications, were repeatedly examined and arbitrated before the commission.

As a rule, the Chief Signal Officer acted or was instructed in such matters through representation on a variety of boards and committees designed to deal with them. It was through the Interdepartment Radio Advisory Committee that General Allison participated in the 1937 hearings before the Federal Communications Commission which ultimately reserved 43 percent of the 30–300 megacycle band for government television use.[25] Consultative agencies existed on international, national, interdepartmental, joint Army-Navy, and interservice levels as well as within the Signal Corps command itself, where the Chief had the Signal Corps Board and the Signal Corps Technical Committee for expert counsel. For the Signal Corps Technical Committee, the chairman and vice-chairman were the chief and assistant chief of the Research and Development Division. In a similar fashion, the commandant and assistant commandant of the Signal Corps School were the two first officers on the Signal Corps Board, which made up its membership with three, four, or five other Signal Corps officers. The board had its headquarters at Fort Monmouth and was probably the most important of all the committees and boards at

---

[23] E.g., 1937, Agreement Between the War Department and the American Telephone and Telegraph Company. SigC 676.1 WD Agreement.

[24] *Fifth Annual Report of the Federal Communications Commission—Fiscal Year 1939,* pp. 3, 6, 68, 81, 83.

[25] A decision which drastically affected the FM development discussed in pages following, especially Chapter VI.

the disposal of the Chief Signal Officer; whenever he directed it to do so, it undertook cases which concerned equipment, method, organization, or any other subject which required its deliberations.

To improve his knowledge of the problems and demands of his fellow services, General Allison added a Communication Liaison Division to his office in 1936, a move prompted by aviation, the new force in warfare. The principal problem of the Communication Liaison Division was to get frequencies for this growing arm of the service, whether for the GHQ Air Force, the various wings, or the Aircraft Warning Service. The Communication Liaison Division made a fresh start in fields which were also formed in the Interdepartment Radio Advisory Committee, the Communication Appliances Committee of the Army and Navy Munitions Board, the Joint Army and Navy Board, and the various technical committees of other branches of the service. On most of the technical committees—Quartermaster, Engineer, Medical, Chemical Warfare, Ordnance, and, most important of all, Air Corps—the Signal Corps had membership. All were intended to reconcile the interests of the various arms which were concerned with the developing of equipment. At top echelons, the Army and Navy Munitions Board and the supreme war planning agency, the Joint Board, called upon the Chief Signal Officer and his staff and agencies for both the seeds and the fruits of his administrative direction.

Outside the Military Establishment the Chief's connections thinned but nevertheless led to other departments of government, to the Congress, to the scientific, engineering and industrial worlds, and to international relations. In the period when accords on many subjects were growing

out of the Hague Conference and the League of Nations, the Chief Signal Officers sent one or another member of their staffs, most frequently Major Crawford, or went themselves, to meetings in foreign capitals. From the preliminaries in Washington, in 1920, of the International Conference on Electrical Communications and from its Provisional Technical Committee discussions in Paris the next year, there followed a series of congresses in Rome, Brussels, The Hague, Copenhagen, Madrid, Lisbon, Bucharest, and other cities. Inter-American relations produced similar meetings in the capitals of the Western Hemisphere. To most of these the Signal Corps sent a delegate.

Pictorial Communication

Thus from the details of their immediate suite of offices to the world panorama of communications, General Saltzman, General Gibbs, General Carr, and General Allison pursued the interests and assignments of their position. Their main business was always communications, the large segments being research and development, training, planning, supply. The smaller segments were such interests as photography, cryptography, meteorology, pigeons. Any of these was a side line, a fact which underscores the change in the Signal Corps which World War II was to produce, for no one of them could have been called a side line after that war was over. Pigeons practically disappeared from military use; meteorology, transmuted into "sferics," became a major concern of science; and the other two activities were so raised up to and merged with the main function that they were no longer adjuncts to communication but veritable forms of it. Cryptography looked odd in the prewar world but perfectly natural in the general secrecy of the mid-century, when communication was as often cryptic as clear. Photography promised to become the most immediate form of all, short of speaking to a man face to face. Development of facsimile and television to a point where transmission of a scene was possible at the moment of its occurrence might all but undermine writing, and return the human race to the use of pictures.

Although facsimile and television were much farther along than the general public realized, so long as the communications industry held back their development, in effect they had no practical existence for the Signal Corps. Photography was limited to the indirect forms of communication, and for military purposes these were associated with minor functions or with major functions in a minor way. Publicity and record were the minor, intelligence and training the major. Chief Signal Officers were curators of a large collection of still pictures assembled from photographs made by the Corps of Engineers, the Medical Corps, the Air Corps, the commercial news services, civilian government organizations, and the Signal Corps itself. These interservice pictures provided detail upon hundreds of items of equipment, especially for illustrations of technical manuals, supply catalogues, and film strips, and stored up a mass of source material for G-2 analysis.

The Signal Corps' own pictures, the bulk of the collection,[26] had followed the tradition of Mathew Brady through the 1917–1918 war without loss of artistry or significance. As time replaced the immediate shock of these photographs with the poignancy of remoteness, it became evident that they were a national record of great value. World War I was the first conflict to be photographed widely with the motion picture camera as well, and not only did the results aid combat intelligence and stimulate pictorial instruction but they also brought cinema audiences close to the sight of battle for years after the Armistice. Nevertheless, although the Signal Corps' files of historical still and motion pictures had permanence, change often reduced their importance, especially for G-2 use. Technical photographs were outmoded by technical advances. Photographs taken in the name of publicity and morale were the most ephemeral of all; when their occasion was past, they became either waste paper or dead items in the record file.

With the end of World War I and the return from France, the war-trained photographers and laboratory technicians vanished into civilian life, leaving only a small staff in Washington, a cameraman or two for each corps area, and a unit on duty at the Signal Corps School. A mere remnant retired to Washington Barracks; and nothing could illustrate the pinch of postwar retrenchment more than the fact that the Signal Corps Photographic Laboratory building there, designed for three stories, leveled off at two in 1919. The new training program dwindled to a single course in still photography, which was periodically crowded from the curriculum.[27] In 1927, reinstating the course after a lapse, the Signal School made the attempt to teach the elements of both still and motion picture photography in four months, but obliged its instructors to ignore the existence of the new sound

---

[26] Including the transparencies for color prints, which Maj. Edgar Russel had made in 1910.

[27] Signal Corps Bulletin, No. 35 (August, 1926), p. 50.

techniques until the next year, when the school was able to double the time of study and add a lecture series in the theory of sound pictures. Graduates spent a few more months at the laboratory in the Army War College and then were assigned to corps areas or departments.

Demands for photographic service mounted slightly as the facilities for it declined. In 1925 the Signal Corps was ordcrcd to be the Army's outlet for all pictorial publicity.[28] The Photographic Division of the Office of the Chief Signal Officer opened an agency in New York City to deal with the press but was never in a position to be effective. Requests also came in for new training films, the distance from World War I having made the old ones absurd. In 1928 the War Department designated the Signal Corps as the producer of these films and set forth the procedures for them but stopped short of allocating funds.

The motion picture industry's investment in silent pictures had been jeopardized by the sudden appearance of talkies. Before they converted production to all-talkies, however, the large companies were dubbing in sound effects and dialogue and issuing the patchworks which resulted. Taking a leaf out of their book, Capt. Alonzo P. Fox of the Signal Corps Photographic Laboratory contrived to purchase two sound projectors and bring a few of the old silent films up to date. Naturally, the result was a makeshift, particularly awkward because the projectors had to be cranked at a steady rate of twenty-four frames a second to correspond with the normal speed of talking, whereas the projection rate for the silent film was sixteen frames.

The next step was to make new films,

devised from the outset for sound. In 1929 there was money to hire a commercial agency. Fox Movietone News owned a truck that seemed suitable and, as an experiment, was engaged to produce a trial motion picture of Infantry maneuvers at Fort Benning, Georgia. The Fox equipment was not so mobile as it had been expected to be, however, and took all shots and managed all effects from the observation post alone. Inevitably, the maneuvers maneuvered out of sight and the commercial cameras ground away at scenery. The Signal Corps cameramen pursued the infantrymen on foot, and later the technicians interwove the successful parts of the two versions; but temporarily the Photographic Division abandoned the idea of producing training films by commercial contract.[29]

Yet it was obvious that Signal Corps photography would have to be dependent upon the film industry. Even if the Laboratory had been able to acquire fine equipment, there were no photographers prepared to cope with its complexities, and the Signal Corps School was incapable of instruction in them. G-3 could promise no more than one or two hundred dollars for tuition at any trade school to which the Signal Corps might send its officers.[30] Subsidization would have to be sought elsewhere. In the Research Council of the Academy of Motion Picture Arts and Sciences the industry had an agency which could sponsor just such arrangements. The Army had been lending itself

[28] WD GO 26, 30 Dec 25.
[29] Interv with Willard W. Jones, Special Proj Br E&T Div OCSigO, 2 Mar 48.
[30] Memo, Maj Crawford for Pers Div OCSigO, 15 Jul 30, sub: Photographic courses. SigC 352.11 Photographic Courses.

MOTION PICTURE CAMERA CREW *photographs a sequence for a training film at Fort Benning, Georgia.*

o a succession of boy-gets-girl films with a military setting, and had reason to hope or reciprocal relations.[31] Confronted by Lt. Col. Walter E. Prosser with a request o sponsor Signal Corps officers for annual photographic training in Hollywood, the Research Council agreed to do so. It paid or the training from funds contributed by he Association of Motion Picture Producers of America, and in the fall of 1930 Capt. Frederick W. Hoorn went to the west coast, the first of seven officers thus scheduled.[32]

With its first sound camera, an RCA product, the Signal Corps, in April 1933, undertook its first feature-length production in sound. That the film should justify he $3,300 expense of the new equipment

was important. For this reason, the Pictorial Service decided to capitalize upon the experience just past, and to photograph the infantry at Fort Benning again. The picture became TF-13, Signal Communications Within the Infantry Regiment, and except for the problem of maintaining uniform density and for a new difficulty that manifested itself in the processing (the racks and tanks which had

[31] In D. W. Griffith's *America,* not of this type but one of the most ambitious historical films of the period, Maj. Jonathan M. Wainwright appeared briefly, many years before taking the central role in the Corregidor drama.

[32] Summary Report on Photographic Activities of the Signal Corps Since August 4, 1941, in the Fields of Motion Pictures and Visual Aid, 26 Feb 43, pp. 374–76. SigC APS Div File.

served well enough for 16-millimeter film required that the new 35-millimeter strips be cut, developed in sections, and spliced), all went well.[33]

Subsequently, Maj. Melvin E. Gillette, returning from the Hollywood course to resume the directorship of the Photographic Laboratory, was able to get funds for machines which performed the developing and printing under automatic controls of time and temperature. He also secured a special-effects printer by means of which the laboratory could produce dissolves, fades, and trick shots.[34]

Because many of the training films of these years were taken not in a studio, but out of doors, control of sound was laboriously learned. "Progress in this activity is necessarily slow," said a contemporary statement.[35] "The whole field of educational talking films is a new one, with little material available as a guide in methods of presentation." The technicians had to discover how to shut out the whistling of the wind or the chirping of birds and where to catch the noise of cannon fire.[36] Gradually they became sufficiently familiar with the mechanical processes to spare more time and thought to the substance of the narrative.

In response to continuing demand for training films, the War Department set a yearly production rate of twenty. Although this number was so modest that it allowed for barely one to an arm or service, the Signal Corps had not produced so many in ten years, let alone in one. Rather than ask the laboratory to take on such a program of field work, Major Gillette, by this time the officer in charge of the Photographic Division, went to Fort Monmouth to organize and head a Training Film Field Unit, the first of the sort, in June 1937.[37] To discharge a central duty

of photographic communication, he had a staff of three enlisted men and one civilian.[38]

Communications Contradictions

The concealed nature of major areas of Signal Corps work, notably in research and development, prevented them from being fully weighed and estimated, and rendered the whole scope somewhat indistinct. A diffused impression also arose from the addition of apparently unrelated assignments which blurred the outline of the main mission. There was indeed a lack of cohesiveness in a mixture which tumbled photographs and pigeons, secret inks and weather balloons in with communications, and advocates of neat spheres of administration could object that a Chief Signal Officer's responsibilities were too diverse. The administrators themselves, however, found that the most burdensome anomaly of all still derived from this paradox: that while the past war posed the problems the next held the answers. The

---

[33] The cast included 1st Lt. Claude B. Ferenbaugh among other assignments, he held that of postwar commanding general of the Military District of Washington.

[34] Major Hoorn devised an improvement upon which the Signal Corps sought a patent until intervention by the Eastman Company led to its abandonment. His method endeavored to substitute continuous for intermittent motion of film, as it passed through the aperture of the projector. If it had been successful it would have resulted in a much wider range of images and in great optical accuracy, an advantage of importance to scientific work like that performed in the Signal Corps Laboratories. SigC File 072 [Patents] Hoorn, Maj Frederick W., 29441.

[35] CSigO, *Annual Report, 1932*, p. 31.

[36] At the point of reverberation, not at the muzzle of the gun, although the finished production would make the roar simultaneous with the belch of smoke.

[37] Notes. SigC Hist Sec File.

[38] Fort Monmouth: An Outline of the Principal Activities of the Only Signal Corps Post, p. 17. SigC Hist Sec File.

fact that their fellow chiefs of other arms and services labored under the same uncertainty made it no easier to solidify. World War I lived on, World War II was yet inscrutable.

Thus at the same time that the Signal Corps was supposed to be modernizing itself to serve the new mechanized Army, it was also supposed to maintain an Army Pigeon Service. To think simultaneously in terms of vehicular radio and a formula for mash required more flexibility than the average administrator was willing to attempt. Yet both were a part of a Chief Signal Officer's domain; and who was to say either that vehicular radio would be possible or that birds would be outmoded in the communications of a war to come? Homing pigeons belonged to an earlier tradition as much as the Army mule and, in a small way, were as persistently laughed at, yet made a very good agent of communication, as reliable as many and more discreet than most. The Army mule was not to be wholly displaced by mechanization; nor was the pigeon.

The basic contradiction was to be observed in other areas. In radio intelligence, for instance, a table-of-organization unit was at last authorized in 1937, but was unprovided with modern equipment and therefore limited to much that was obsolete. Again, although an Aircraft Warning System represented a firm look into a risky future, and radar, which would give it substance, was already at hand, so long as aircraft warning was conceived in terms of fixed continental positions it was also characterized, so far as the Signal Corps was concerned, by conventional fixed wire. This persisting paradox deserves closer illustration.

After the Armistice in 1918, 35 of 110 Signal Corps pigeon lofts remained in op-

eration. General Squier authorized the expenditure of five thousand dollars to replenish and improve the stock, and the Pigeon Breeding and Training Center at Fort Monmouth bought, through the chief of the British pigeon service, 150 pairs of the best European strains and bred them with 200 good specimens retained from the war. Five thousand dollars was a considerable sum to spend all at once upon any form of communication, and if pigeons were to go out of date the expenditure would be hard to justify. If they were not to be any more out of date than the bayonet or the steel helmet, a communications chief would be rash not to keep them in force. In any case, pigeon communication remained a part of the Signal Corps' charge, and in the next two decades the quality of the birds improved steadily. Such money to spend on them, though, was not available again. The number of lofts dwindled to sixteen in 1928 and to eight in 1938.[39] The entire Army Pigeon Service consisted of a dozen enlisted men, who were stationed at Forts Monmouth, Benning, and Sam Houston, and in the Canal Zone, Hawaii, and the Philippines. Fanciers and racing enthusiasts made a very large civilian public, but for military communication "pigeoneering" lapsed into obscurity. The airplane as well as the radio made pigeons look ill-suited to the era.

When early Kelly Field pilots had taken them into the cockpit on training flights from San Antonio to Austin, the birds could deliver messages calling for relief, the relief could arrive and the air-

---

[39] (1) CSigO, Annual Report, 1942, p. 309. (2) Army Pigeon Sv Agency, The Homing Pigeon, draft of revision of TM 11-410, 1943; (3) SigC Hist Sec, Military Use of Pigeons Between Wars, p. 19. SigC Hist Sec File.

planes be repaired and on their way by the time that word could get through by telephone or telegraph. In the later years, when cockpits had closed against the winds of high speeds, when concrete had replaced grass airfields and beacons and directional radio guided a pilot, the pigeon seemed to have no service to perform for him. Nor for many others.

A dozen years after the war, the pigeons at Fort Sam Houston, Texas, having rendered their wartime quarters unhabitable, the building was razed, and in this case the birds were moved to empty barracks which were no newer, but were cleaner. This transfer was an exception. Ordinarily, as the lofts fell into disrepair they were not replaced, until necessity developed a mobile loft—a Chevrolet station wagon somewhat remodeled, screened, and accommodating fifty pigeons in baskets— which the 11th Signal Company at Schofield Barracks, Hawaii, tried out and approved in joint Army-Navy maneuvers in February 1932.[40] At that time the cost to the Army of a Chevrolet station wagon was $569.92, and the materials to convert it at the Signal Section of the New York General Depot amounted to $130 more. After several months of planning and some transferring of funds, the Office of the Chief cleared the way for the expenditure and procured two more vehicular lofts, one for Fort Sam and the other for Quarry Heights in the Canal Zone. With this development, the Army Pigeon Service reached a peacetime limit. Except for an unpublicized experiment at Monmouth in breeding birds to fly at night.[41] the status of pigeon communication could not advance much further.

With radio the opposite held true. Little used in the 1917–18 war, radio might be the principal means for communication in another. Informed Signal Corps opinion did not really think so, but the change of doctrine which brought about the mobile army created the demand to find out. Certainly communications would have to keep up with the troops, no matter how or how fast they moved. The initial test came in Texas, in the fall of 1937, when the entire Military Establishment focused its regard upon experimental maneuvers there of the new infantry division. Called triangular because it assembled a division out of three regiments, without brigades, rather than out of four, paired off in brigades, this organization of a combat division had been in the mill for many years. General Pershing had recommended it. The talk of mobility and the need to streamline the fighting machine had at last brought it forward. Staff officers were hoping to reduce to 13,500 a combat organization which in 1918 had numbered more than 28,000.[42] The signal complement would be halved from 40 to 20 officers and from 1,000 to 500 men. A great challenge would lie in assembling replacements months in advance of any emergency call for them, because the reduction was what looked then like an absolute minimum.[43]

With some anxiety, in view of the importance of the tests, the Signal Corps began to ready its only full-strength bat-

---

[40] (1) Memo, Brig Gen Halstead Dorey, CG 2d Div, for CG Eighth Corps Area, 17 Nov 31, sub: Proj for pigeon-loft building, with 1st Ind, Eighth Corps Area to TAG, 5 Dec 31. SigC 454.8 Pigeon Lofts 1, 1917–Jul 42. (2) Memo, Capt Evan D. Cameron, 11th Sig Co Hawaiian Div, for CSigO, 10 Mar 32, sub: Rpt on Chevrolet mobile pigeon loft of 11th Sig Co. SigC 454.8.

[41] SigC Cir 10-4, Wash., D. C., 1 Sep 36, pp. 1 and 4.

[42] *Annual Report of the Secretary of War, 1937,* p. 6.

[43] Signal Corps Information Letter, No. 16 (January 12, 1938), p. 18.

MOBILE PIGEON LOFT

talion. Typical of the battalion's circumstances was the fact that not a model of any new radio development, especially in the short-range, high-frequency, lightweight versions, was available. The best that could be done was to convert SCR-194's into SCR-195's and to assemble some SCR-209's from components in stock, a process which yielded seven sets. In a convoy of fifty-five vehicles, the 51st Signal Battalion left Fort Monmouth on 21 July 1937, and reached San Antonio on 2 August.[44] Maj. Stephen H. Sherrill commanded the 51st, and Maj. Harry E. Storms, Maj. Garland C. Black, Capt. Elton F. Hammond, Capt. Gilbert Hayden, and Capt. Robert W. Raynsford were among other Signal Corps officers on hand.

The tests were scheduled in three stages. The first emphasis, through August and September, fell upon the separate units, specifically the signal platoons; but most of the two months passed in close order drill, parades, inspections, and athletic contests.[45] Training was scarcely more specific in the second stage, which continued for two weeks and was devoted to combat teams, the men being urged to find "points of cooperation" with each other. Only in the third period, which occupied a month's time, did the new triangular division emerge for trial. Accordingly, the Signal Corps got few answers

[44] A History of Fort Monmouth, New Jersey, 1917–1946, pp. 59–60. SigC Hist Sec File.
[45] Signal Corps Information Letter, No. 16 (January 12, 1938), p. 19.

to the question of the proportionate importance of tactical wire and tactical wireless.

The Texas tests would have been significant, however, if they had done nothing else than to hint the possibility that the conduct of communications in another war might bog down in dormancy and complaisance. Signal Corps feelings had been roughened by an Associated Press statement to the effect that motorization of the Army had made the existing military communications equipment obsolete.[46] The official release from which the story had been written had already stated much the same thing. Many of the lessons which Signal Corps officers said they had learned in Texas were so trivial as hardly to be lessons at all. Some officers saw nevertheless that wire, the queen of World War I combat communications, was going to have to take a consort for World War II. Both in front-line and in mobile communications, where wire would be left behind and where its security systems were slow and cumbrous, there was a new field for radio. Even beyond combat communications and into the need for long-range, secure, and generally fixed administrative communications, radio would have a large place. But how large?

Generally speaking, wire was too well established for radio to have much opportunity to compete. Ready at hand as a prime element in the national defense was the great commercial wire system, long-range, apparently secure, and fixed. The defense of the United States was the principal mission charged to the Army, on a directed assumption that the nation would be defended on its own soil rather than across oceans and continents. Aerial assault, for example, would be intercepted at home, with home-based airplanes, civilian home guards, troops on home ground. Accordingly a vast communications system already in existence was an integral part of defense and basic to the Signal Corps' calculations. In these estimates, warning against the approach of an enemy would require no special communications equipment which could not be improvised or provided locally.[47]

Plans called for a series of observation posts and information centers along the national frontiers. Each frontier had been marked off into sectors, and each of these was to have its own Aircraft Warning Service. A sector AWS, in turn, was divided into zones containing an information center and ten or twenty observation posts. Except that the alarm would be broadcast over commercial radio, the commercial wire system would serve as the whole communications net, with regular telephone service to and from the observation posts and with leased telephone and teletypewriter circuits, including teletypewriter exchange service, everywhere else.[48] The networks of the state police, the Forestry Service, and the Coast Guard, as well as facilities of railroads, oil companies, and public utilities might be auxiliary; for the most part, however, the American Telephone and Telegraph Company would provide communications for the entire national system.

The earliest organized Aircraft Warning Service exercises occurred under these proposals at Muroc Lake, California.

[46] Signal Corps Information Letter, No. 15 (October 7, 1937), p. 10.

[47] AG Ltr to CG First Army et al., 21 May 35, sub: AA defense of continental U. S. AG 660.2 AA (5-15-35) (Misc.) E-M.

[48] Col Carroll O. Bickelhaupt, Use of Commercial Communications Systems in the Aircraft Warning Service, 18 Nov 37. SigC Hist Sec File.

AN AIRCRAFT WARNING SERVICE FILTER CENTER *during a practice alert at Charleston, South Carolina.*

Civilian observers spaced about eight miles apart reported plane sightings to the information center, which sent out orders to military commanders and air raid warnings to civilian defense agencies.[49] Although successful in demonstrating the participation of civilians as observers, an aspect of aircraft warning which lost importance in later astonishing developments, the Muroc Lake tests faltered as arguments for the use of existing commercial lines. The average time required for transmitting a report that a plane had been sighted was five minutes, far too slow to be of any tactical value in sending up interceptors.

In antiaircraft defense outside the country, radio developments had a somewhat better opportunity. Panama had chief importance, and the Signal Corps was asked to engineer a system there of 20 searchlight command posts, 24 antiaircraft batteries, 36 automatic weapons positions, 8 automatic weapons command posts, and 7 group command posts. Hard upon new developments, however, a War Department board studying the Canal Zone defenses proposed a five-year program for a unified signal communication system "whenever the proper equipment was perfected."[50] The equipment was of

---

[49] Summary of the Cooperation of the Southern California Edison Co. in Providing for an AWS for GHQ AF Maneuvers in 1937, Incl 7 with AG Ltr to CG First Army *et al.*, 23 May 40, sub: AWS continental U. S. AG 660.2 AA (5-22-40) M-WPD.

[50] (1) AAF Hist Study 42, Air Defense of the Panama Canal, 1 Jan 39–7 Dec 41, pp. 49–50. AF Archives. (2) Sig Office, PCD, Unit Hist, Signals, Panama Canal Department, Vol III, No. 24, pp. 8–9.

course the new pulsed detector which the Signal Corps Laboratories were just then designing, primarily for antiaircraft searchlight control. Despite this promise, the conception of the use of radio, even in radio communications only, was still limited. With a scheme of fixed defenses in mind, radio's mobility appeared to be an attribute of no consequence, and objections to it arose from a supposedly fundamental lack of security, the necessity for electrical plants at every station, and the requirement for specially trained operators. At various stages in the ensuing war, swift ground or air action disposed of the first objection by rendering it unimportant. Vehicular radios and handie- and walkie-talkies eliminated much of the second by making the generators as movable as the sets. The degree to which voice replaced continuous wave went far to solve the third.

Communications Spheres of Interest

Provision for radar was probably the most important part of the Panama aircraft warning plan. In terms of the era, however, there was significance in the Signal Corps Board's recommendation that the Corps install and maintain the equipment but that the Air Corps operate it. For the discrepancy in the scope of the Signal Corps was measured more uncomfortably in relations with the Air Corps than at any other point. Love and friction made a prevailing climate for Signal Corps-Air Corps liaisons almost all through the period of the two world wars. It is a major theme. The ties were close but strained. Army aviation had been the Signal Corps' offspring, and now bid fair to be its arbiter, having grown to a height which dwarfed that of all other components of the service but the Infantry.

The initial estrangement of divorce was receding far into the past when another contention arose to replace it, derived from the sense of the future which simultaneously separated and united the Signal Corps and the Air Corps. Each had in its possession one of the new wonders of the age: the Air Corps the means of flight and the Signal Corps the means of communication through space. From the inevitable time when the airplane and radio came together, skirmishes set in anew. To the Air Corps, the Signal Corps was slow and unimaginative in adapting radio to aviation, particularly to air navigation. To the Signal Corps, the Air Corps' restiveness on the subject appeared grounded upon a desire to take over a province of great prestige. General Gibbs was leaving office at just about the time when the aircraft radio controversy commenced, in 1931; Maj. Gen. Irving J. Carr departed in 1934 with it still going on; Maj. Gen. James B. Allison forced it to a top-echelon decision before he left in 1937; and Maj. Gen. Joseph O. Mauborgne, who had been on the scene as the commanding colonel of the Aircraft Radio Laboratory, became Chief in a succeeding false calm.

As might be supposed, the scene of the controversy was a Signal Corps installation on an Air Corps base. Up to 1931, the small Aircraft Radio Laboratory staff at Wright Field was devoting its effort largely to aircraft communication, as distinct from navigational radio. The laboratory was a potential site for advances in both fields, and important work on radio beacons had already come from it; but navigationally it was behindhand. At Wright Field then was Lieutenant Hegenberger, one of the pair of Army pilots who had made the pioneer flight from California to Hawaii four years earlier. Navigational radio aids specially rigged for that flight had been so helpful that Hegenberger was a determined spokesman for equipping all Army airplanes with radio, at least to the degree of enabling them to tune in on the beacons and ranges then multiplying along the nation's airways. "In the first and last analysis," it seemed to Hegenberger, the matter "concerns the effectiveness of the Air Corps to carry out its mission as an arm of the National Defense. Avigation is a paramount problem in carrying out all phases of this mission." [51] Upon this conviction, in the summer of 1931 the Air Corps organized a Navigational Instrument Section in its Equipment Branch at Wright Field, located it in the same building with the Aircraft Radio Laboratory, and placed Lieutenant Hegenberger in charge.

The Signal Corps assumed that the section was only intended to supervise the service testing of navigational instruments after the Aircraft Radio Laboratory had developed them. Under this impression, Captain Rives, the head of the laboratory, lent the Air Corps section a civilian Signal Corps employee who had begun to work on a radio compass. But the co-operative relationship altered and darkened. It began to appear that the new section was undertaking the actual development of the compass. The employee lent to the Air Corps was not coming back. The Aircraft Radio Laboratory went ahead with one form of radio compass, the Navigational Instrument Section with another. Very soon "a deadly serious fight was going on." [52] Lieutenant Hegenberger locked up his part of the building, his engineers charging that Signal Corps technicians were appropriating their circuits; the ARL officers and civilians, in turn, felt that the compass being developed under

Lieutenant Hegenberger was actually their own, and that Army regulations clearly gave the Signal Corps sole responsibility for such development. They pointed to AR 850-25. "While the Air Corps officers appear to be conversant with the provisions of AR 850-25," Rives remarked, "they seem either hesitant as to how to proceed under them or else they do not desire to comply. . . ." [53]

The Equipment Branch sought first to challenge this regulation with another ("Under AR 150-5, the Air Corps as the using arm is authorized to carry on any purely experimental development which it sees fit to do. . . ."),[54] then to change or even to ignore it, holding that the thing to do was to get aircraft radio and not allow regulations to stand in the way. Matters grew so strained that at one time Rives went to the commander of Wright Field, Brig. Gen. H. Conger Pratt, and requested a court of inquiry into the charges being made against him and the ARL.

In the midst of all this, a recommendation that all Signal Corps development work of whatever nature be consolidated at Fort Monmouth arrived like a thunderbolt. Col. Arthur S. Cowan, then commandant at Monmouth, and Major Blair,

[51] Memo, Capt Albert F. Hegenberger, AC, for Maj Edward L. Hoffman, AC, President of Subcommittee to AC Tech Committee, 21 Dec 34, sub: Disputed functions of research, development, procurement, etc., between AC and SigC. AF 413.44 ARL Orgn, Change, Research, Developments, 1931–38, USAF Mat Comd Central Files.

[52] Ltr, Brig Gen Tom C. Rives, USAF Ret., to G. R. Thompson, SigC Sec OCMH, 8 Jan 50. SigC Hist Sec File.

[53] Ltr Memo, Capt Tom C. Rives for Maj Colton, 11 Aug 34. SigC 413.684 RDF's 7, Jan–Aug 34.

[54] Memo, Maj Hoffman, AC, Chief Equip Br Mat Div, for Chief Mat Div, 14 May 34, sub: Radio and navigation development. AF 413.44 ARL Orgn, Change, Research, Developments, 1931–38, USAF Mat Comd Central Files.

the Laboratories chief, urged that the ARL be returned to the status of a liaison unit and that the whole research and development activity for the Air Corps be centered upon Monmouth, where the Signal Corps did research and development for all of the other arms. The merging of the scattered laboratories of the Signal Corps had been General Gibbs's policy, and if unopposed would fill in one more major chink in the structure. From the standpoint of sound administration and with plenty of good precedent, General Carr was inclined to favor the consolidation; but before ordering it he sent Blair with 1st Lt. Gilbert Hayden (still another Signal Corps officer who was to be identified with the Aircraft Radio Laboratory) to Wright Field, "for a thorough investigation . . . from all angles. . . ." [55]

A major shift in the Signal Corps Laboratories' research and development activity underlay the proposed transfer. Hitherto, the Signal Corps had given out contracts for the design of separate pieces: an antenna, a power generator, a telephone. Now the tendency was toward assemblies rather than single items: a whole field telephone system, a complete radio set. Blair and Cowan felt that the Laboratories could best pursue such a policy of system design and standardization, keeping in close touch with university and commercial laboratories, and purchasing commercial samples for study, but avoiding contracting for the central research work. The Signal Corps should design more of the Army's electric equipment itself and depend less upon industry. Cowan in fact maintained that the Signal Corps Laboratories alone, and no other organization, commercial or military, had any adequate conception of the Army's entire communications system. [56]

At Wright Field Blair confirmed his opinion that the Air Corps relied too much upon commercial development. He thought this "the easier but less effective procedure"; although it was possibly "entirely justified by the fact that it is rendering essential assistance to the relatively new airplane industry," it could not eliminate the necessity for just such a plant for laboratory research, testing, and installation as the ARL represented. He felt sure that ARL could best function in close association with the other Signal Corps research organizations, especially because at present it was "neither adequate nor properly constituted to do development and design work. It is primarily organized for the work of consultation, installation and test." [57] At Fort Monmouth, it seemed to him, development for all arms could be co-ordinated, items simplified and standardized, and economy and general satisfaction be realized.

The men most immediately concerned, the staff of the Aircraft Radio Laboratory, did not at all agree with Major Blair's minimization of their contribution. That they were primarily organized for development and design work was exactly what they wished to maintain. Rives was convinced that the move would be wrong. Despite his current vexations, which might well have prompted him to clutch at a way to break free of them, he argued that development for the Air Corps had its first cause in service to the Air Corps,

---

[55] Historical Report of the Signal Corps Engineering Laboratories, July 1930–December 1943, pp. 19–20. SigC Hist Sec File.

[56] Ltr, Col Cowan to CSigO, 3 Jun 32, sub: Reduction in number of R&D projs. AF 322.081 SigC Activities, 1932–45, USAF Mat Comd Central Files.

[57] Ltr, Maj Blair to CSigO, 27 Jun 32, sub: Visit to Wright Field. AF 322.081 SigC Activities, 1932–45, USAF Mat Comd Central Files.

and that such service could be rendered only in proximity to the Air Corps. This was another proof that those who dealt with the Air Corps felt, almost as much as did the Air Corps itself, that its problems were unique, that a fundamental difference existed between it and the other arms. The equipment used by ground arms had an elemental first cousinship. Equipment to be used in the air invoked another element as well, and must not be contemplated apart from the terms and conditions of the air. An antenna array which might be a comparatively simple development for ground use could become an extremely difficult one when it had to be attached to the outside of an airplane.

Col. William L. Bayer, who, like Rives, Murphy, 1st Lt. Francis L. Ankenbrandt, and so many others, was a Signal Corps officer made familiar with the problem by close assignment to the Air Corps, later explained:

Airplanes are rather precisely engineered and anything which affects the outside contours or weight distribution is frowned upon. [Consider] the enormous vibration to which parts or accessories are subjected; and . . . the difficulty of high voltage apparatus at the low pressure of altitude. These are in addition to the normal space and weight limitations. . . . There is at least three to four times as much engineering involved in the developing of electronic equipment for air use as for . . . the ground.[58]

Not only did Rives think that the Signal Corps and Air Corps should and could be able to work out their disagreements and produce aircraft radio equipment at Wright Field, but he anticipated that withdrawal of the Signal Corps would leave the arena wholly in possession of the Air Corps, which would very soon thereafter gain the entire responsibility for

aviation radio. He and his colleague, 1st Lt. Herbert G. Messer, who was the only other Signal Corps officer on duty in the depressed and skeletonized Aircraft Radio Laboratory of January 1932, accordingly concluded that the disadvantages of a consolidation at Fort Monmouth would far outweigh any advantages.[59] They got telling support from the Air Corps. Upon inquiry from Washington, General Pratt's engineers came up with the same argument: that separating the research from the aircraft themselves would present an impossible situation, because no airborne device could be properly designed without constant flight experience and testing; and in Washington itself, Maj. Gen. Benjamin D. Foulois and Brig. Gen. Oscar Westover, Chief and Assistant Chief of the Air Corps, expressed the strongest opposition.[60] This was the view which won out. The move to Fort Monmouth had no support at Wright Field, from either service's representatives there, and could not take place without it.

The Navigational Instrument Section continued with its development of the radio compass, and bulwarked it with an entire blind-landing program which included, by a strange irony, a project for using microwave gear to prevent airplanes from colliding with each other or crashing into unseen obstacles. The irony dwelt in

---

[58] Comment written by Col Bayer, JCS, to SigC Hist Sec, Aug 49. SigC Hist Sec File.

[59] Ltr, Capt Rives to CSigO, 7 Jan 32, sub: Consolidation of SigC ARL and SCL at Ft. Monmouth. AF 322.081 SigC Activities, 1932–45, USAF Mat Comd Central Files.

[60] (1) Ltr, Gen Westover to Gen Pratt, Chief Mat Div, 10 Jun 32; (2) Maj Fred H. Coleman, AC, and Capt Albert B. Pitts, AC, Mat Div Engr Sec Memo Rpt 54-4-67, 28 Jun 32, sub: Proposal to move SigC lab from Wright Field to Ft. Monmouth. AF 322.081 SigC Activities, 1932–45, USAF Mat Comd Central Files.

the fact that the project[61] might have become airborne radar, years before anything of the sort was developed, if the air and ground radio work actually had been in the close contact which Blair had urged. The Monmouth laboratories went so far as to hint that they had microwave work in progress which might "eventually be adapted as an aid for the prevention of collisions,"[62] but the preradar experiments there remained isolated by secrecy, and the collision-prevention project withered under low priority for several years until the Air Corps Technical Committee discontinued it altogether.

The quarrel over navigational equipment had blazed right through this, and had become a conflagration. Lieutenant Hegenberger's superior, Maj. Edward L. Hoffman, had entered it, although Hegenberger was by no means superseded. *Signal Corps* and *Air Corps* were now being used generically, each supposed to represent only one point of view. The Signal Corps (to speak in this mode) maintained that all devices employing vacuum tubes and radio circuits fell within its domain. The Air Corps insisted that the only concern which the Signal Corps could have with Air Corps equipment was with communications devices in the most direct and limited sense.

"In the beginning, the Signal Corps, as its name implies, was charged with communication," Hoffman said. "They first had the wig wag, heliograph; later the telegraph, telephone, and now, radio, [where] they should confine their efforts to communicational radio. . . ." He in no way considered that the Air Corps should be obliged to follow the procurement procedures of the other arms, seeking out the pertinent service, describing what was wanted, and asking to have it developed.

"To go through military channels" would render the Air Corps "powerless." He emphasized this point, and broadened it to include the Air Corps' connection not only with the Signal Corps but with all other "auxiliary branches."[63]

The Signal Corps did not think itself auxiliary, but rather as much a part of the Military Establishment as any other arm or service. Nor did Major Hoffman's point of view, although it was destined to mature into official Air Corps doctrine, have the solid home support which he counted upon. At the next level above him, Lt. Col. Robert E. M. Goolrick posted a dissent, coming to the root of the matter by observing that navigational radio involves sending and receiving radio waves, just as any other kind of radio does. Goolrick said he believed it wrong in principle to charge two Army agencies with the same thing, and saw no reason why, since the experience and competent personnel for the work were to be found almost entirely with the Signal Corps, the Air Corps

---

[61] "*Collision Prevention:* provide a means of showing on a single indicator the location of other aircraft within a range of 15 miles giving the bearing in azimuth throughout 360° with an accuracy of 15° and elevation within a range of plus/minus 30° from the horizontal with an accuracy of 5°. It is suggested that acorn tubes and micro rays be used for this purpose and that individual antennas be limited to 7" in length and that the total drag of the antennas and reflectors (if used) not exceed six pounds at 250 MPH." Ltr, Capt Hegenberger to Chief Engr Sec Mat Div, 24 May 35, sub: Avigational radio development program for ARL, Item 6. AF 413.44 ARL Orgn, Change, Research, Developments, 1931–38, USAF Mat Comd Central Files.

[62] Ltr, Gen Westover to CSigO, 27 Sep 33, sub: Co-ordination of AC research work with SigC, and 1st Ind, Maj George L. Van Deusen, Exec Officer OCSigO, to Chief AC, 21 Oct 33. In same file.

[63] (1) Ltr, Maj Hoffman to Chief Engr Sec Mat Div, 8 Jun 33, sub: Handling of radio apparatus by SigC and AC; (2) Memo, Hoffman for Chief Mat Div, 14 May 34, sub: Radio and navigation development. In same file.

should not permit its radio equipment to be developed as all the other branches of the service did. "It only requires a little cooperation on the part of the Air Corps to make such a system work," Goolrick observed.[64] Which was much the opinion of the War Department, when the controversy flared up that high. Called upon to cite regulations, The Adjutant General pointed to AR 850-25, and specifically to paragraph 10 *d* on established procedures,[65] complaining as he did so that "the interests of the Government would be served better if the Air Corps and Signal Corps would cooperate with each other. . . ."

Allotment of Public Works Administration funds to the Air Corps to finance the radio compass program increased the stake, and the travail when the President called upon the Army to fly the air mail increased the bitterness, for Air Corps spokesmen were inclined to charge the Signal Corps with a part in the fiasco.[66] Conciliatory statements in the report of the special War Department board of investigation headed by the World War I Secretary, Newton D. Baker, made careful note of the fact that "the most effective and efficient communication equipment should be provided for the Army Air Corps," and balanced the account by observing that "the radio equipment that has been provided by the Signal Corps has proved effective"; but these remarks had small opportunity to temper the disagreement.[67]

With continued angry interchange, the two sides charged bad faith. "As a result of the Signal Corps handling radio, we couldn't fly the Air Mail as well as commercial lines and we still can't," Major Hoffman exclaimed. "When I hear Indianapolis talk to Dallas right now, I wonder if the Air Corps will ever be able to do as well, with the Signal Corps handling the radio."[68] Hegenberger added other arguments and Rives and Messer jointly answered them, protesting: "Other arms have accorded the Signal Corps their wholehearted support in development work rather than setting up development establishments of their own in the effort to be independent of all contact with other arms. The Signal Corps and the Air Corps can also get the desired results if their respective personnel have the will to work toward this end in full cooperation."[69]

Matters had reached their worst by the turn of 1934 into 1935, as General Allison succeeded General Carr. Allison took direct action by proposing a conference to General Foulois. The Chief of the Air Corps agreed, and at the conference surrendered the program, acknowledging that all radio development at Wright Field should be centered in the Aircraft Radio Laboratory under Signal Corps direction.

---

[64] Memo, Col Goolrick, Actg Exec Officer Mat Div, for Chief Mat Div, 22 May 34. In same file.

[65] AR 850-25, 15 Jul 31. Paragraph 10 *d* states that the military characteristics for any item to be developed will be formulated by the using arm and coordinated through the appropriate technical committee. Ltr, TAG to CSigO, 18 Jul 34, sub: Radio direction compass. AG 413.68 (7-14-34) Misc. (D). Also in SigC 413.44 Compasses 1, 1919–34.

[66] Ltr, Gen Pratt to Chief AC, 5 Feb 34, sub: Purchase of radio compasses or RDF's. SigC 413.684 RDF's 7, Jan–Aug 34.

[67] U.S. Special Committee on AC, *Final Report of War Department Special Committee on Army Air Corps*, 18 Jul 34, p. 50.

[68] Maj Hoffman, comments on Memo of Capt Rives for Maj Hoffman, 8 Dec 34, sub: Disputed functions of research, development, procurement, etc., between AC and SigC. AF 413.44 ARL Orgn, Change, Research, Developments, 1931–38, USAF Mat Comd Central Files.

[69] Memo, Capt Rives and Capt Messer for President of Subcommittee to AC Technical Committee, 19 Dec 34, sub: Reply to Hoffman's Memo 12-6-34 and Hegenberger's Memo 12-8-34. In same file.

The Air Corps completed the contracts let with the Public Works Administration money, but made no other arrangement to enter into either the development or the procurement of radio equipment.

An insubstantial victory never looked more substantial. The Air Corps expansion undertaken in the ominous shadow of 1938 made inroads upon it which all but reversed it. At the time, though, regulations had been vindicated. Behind that fact fell into place all other parts of the dispute: whether the Signal Corps had been so laggard in its duty as not to begin development of airborne radio to any adequate degree until stirred up to do so; whether the Air Corps had raided Signal Corps prerogatives and picked Signal Corps brains; these and others receded behind the essential law and prophet.

General Allison subsequently went out of office in the satisfying persuasion that the problem had been resolved. He complimented his successor, Mauborgne, and told him: "I feel that we have accom-

plished a result that will reflect with great credit upon the Signal Corps and the Army as a whole, and I hope very much to the benefit of the Air Corps, whom we serve." General Mauborgne took office in the equally hopeful prospect of a return of good feeling. He was a new Chief Signal Officer, Maj Gen. Oscar Westover a new Chief of the Air Corps, and Westover had praised his "spirit of cooperation" as director of the Aircraft Radio Laboratory.[70] The clash of interest was still there, however, muffled though it was by well-wishing and good intentions. The essential disharmony remained to grow clamorous again and to renew a question of Signal Corps boundaries.

---

[70] (1) 5th Ind, Gen Allison to Chief AC, 26 Feb 35, and 6th Ind, Gen Foulois to TAG through CSigO, 11 Mar 35, on Ltr, TAG to CSigO, cited n. 65. (2) Statistical Sec SigC Aircraft Sig Sv, Signal Corps Aircraft Signal Service History and Activities Compiled as of 1 July 1943, p. 2. SigC Hist Sec File. (3) Ltr, Gen Westover to TAG through CSigO, 9 Jun 37, sub: Rpt of functioning of ARL. AF 413.44 ARL Orgn, Change, Research, Developments, 1931–38, USAF Mat Comd Central Files.

CHAPTER IV

The Army in Abeyance

There was an almost imperceptible change in the Army as the Signal Corps shifted leadership for the last time before the emergency.[1] The state of the world made the Military Establishment uneasy. The League of Nations had sickened upon Mussolini's success in Ethiopia to the point where Germany's reincorporation of the Rhineland had aroused no counteraction. President Roosevelt had suggested a quarantine of dictatorships. Spain's civil war was producing studies of German and Italian methods and weapons in the Army service journals. Deeply concerned Navy and Army intelligence watched a curtain of secrecy fall around the Japanese-mandated islands between Hawaii and the Philippines, while at the same time Japan renewed a war of conquest in China. The extension to Tokyo of the previous year's Rome-Berlin Axis left other capitals paralyzed; no move to build up a military organization reached a popular hearing even in the nations nearest to thě danger. However, the danger was strong enough to begin beckoning the Army away from the void over which it hung suspended and into the crystallizing national policy. Individual services like the Signal Corps were not yet affected, but there was evidence that they would be, and that was sufficient to change the atmosphere.

As a functioning agency, the Signal Corps performed its task adequately. Existing administrative communications were sound; a large part of the expansion to occur in them could take place in terms of what had been tried and found good. It was as a planning agency that the Signal Corps had its work to do. The impetus to all Army planning, the demand above all others, was the challenge to have the right equipment with men trained to use it.

Signal Corps preparations walked on these same two legs: equipment and men. Its own problem of equipment loomed from the radiation spectrum itself, which held an infinite number of combinations. There were times when every one of them promised to materialize, relegating items to obsolescence with as much indifference as crude pulse radar was showing to the finest sound detectors. Boehme radio was another case in point. If it was to be replaced, a good deal of specialized skill would go out the window and, as with radar, a shift in equipment would shift the plans in personnel and training. The chief perplexity in setting the gauge for expansion, in either equipment or strength, was that no one could move it much without coming into the range of another's expanding interest. Sometimes the obstacle was industry, sometimes the Congress, sometimes a riddle of research, sometimes statistics of manpower, sometimes one of the co-ordinate arms or services.

The population growth of the District of Columbia area in the 1930's had made land scarce. At Fort Myer, the activities

---

[1] General Mauborgne succeeded General Allison on 1 October 1937.

of the Cavalry were more and more restricted to the equitation field itself. Col.
George S. Patton, Jr., the commanding
officer at Myer, objected on learning that
the increase in the Army communications
net, which had already crowded the transmitting station there part of the way out
onto the equitation field, would require
the station to encroach still further or
burst. General Mauborgne expressed the
urgent hope to put up a rhombic antenna,
in order to accomplish point-to-point
transmission to Seattle. Patton opposed
not only the rhombic but the whole Signal
Corps installation and sought to have it
propelled from the post which bore the
first Chief Signal Officer's name. Mauborgne prescribed a temporary rearrangement of facilities and meanwhile sounded
out the Navy upon the possibility of getting antenna space on the land of the
naval Arlington radio station just adjoining. He learned that the Navy would in
fact discontinue its station there and let
him have it; and in anticipation of the
transfer he obtained the Navy's permission to put up the Seattle rhombic and
another one to Puerto Rico as well. Colonel Patton objected to this arrangement as
much as to the first proposal, declaring
that the Navy site had been a part of Fort
Myer twenty-five years earlier, and ought
to be again. All of the radio towers and
telegraph poles with which WAR had encumbered the post should be swept from
view. In any case, he needed the Navy
buildings. The Adjutant General offered
to split the site, so that the buildings went
to Patton and enough land for the rhombics to Mauborgne. Now the Navy's willingness was fast ebbing, and no longer
took the form of outright transfer but only
of an offer on a revocable basis. This
was unsatisfactory, but further pressure

brought all negotiation to an end. Since
the Chief Signal Officer's original request,
enough time had elapsed to bring the
nation up to within a year of war, and in
the shadow of that emergency the Navy
withdrew its offer altogether.[2] Here was a
sample of how strong the administrative
tug and pull was to get anything at all.
This was but a local expansion, however
importunate, and the Signal Corps' energy
in urging it yielded to others' energy in
resisting it. Other circumstances might
reverse the roles.

One or two instances of expansion from
outside sources met similar resistance, this
time on the part of the Signal Corps. In
the spring of 1938 aircraft warning exercises, similar to the earlier ones at Muroc
Lake, were staged within the domain of
Southern California Edison Company,
the large public utility concern there. In
the Signal Corps' opinion, the claims
made for the exercise were unrealistic.
Eighty observation posts, principally
manned by the Edison Company's employees, had theoretically intercepted all
approaching aircraft and had kept March
Field inviolate. Actually, the practice airplanes had flown a straight course along
the line of observer stations. The Signal
Corps also felt that the communications
provided under the arrangement with the
company were inadequate. In that California sector they might do, but in most
places it would be necessary to use the full

<hr/>

[2] (1) Ltr, OCSigO to TAG, 23 Feb 39, sub: Transmitting antenna, WD Msg Ctr, transmitting station,
Ft. Myer, and 3d Ind, Col Patton to CG Third Corps
Area, 9 Mar 39, and 6th Ind, CSigO to TAG, 11 May
39; (2) Ltr, CSigO to Dir Naval Com, 11 May 39,
sub: Transfer of Arlington radio station from Navy
to Army. SigC 602.3 Arlington. (3) Same file, *passim.*
(4) Pauline M. Oakes, The Army Command and
Administrative Communications System, Part I: War
Department Radio Net, 1920–1940, Oct 45, pp.
103–07. SigC Hist Sec File.

range of facilities offered only by the telephone and telegraph system. The big disadvantage in using the communications of the electric power utilities was that whereas neighboring telephone lines intercommunicated, neighboring power lines ordinarily did not.

If the Signal Corps was unimpressed with Southern California Edison's contributions to the exercises, the company was equally vehement about their value. Its view was that the tests had been such a success that the Federal Communications Commission ought to allow expansion of the company's radio network. Submitting an aircraft warning program which encompassed this plan, A. A. Hopkins, an officer of the company, raised two sore points, implying that in this specific field, at least, radio could do the work of wire and Edison could do the work of the Signal Corps. "From what I have seen of this branch it is not abreast of the public utilities, either in equipment or personnel," he commented. The company envisioned sixteen fixed and forty mobile radio stations under its control, which it would be willing to associate with a system where the Signal Corps would not "enter the picture in any form." To this proposal Hopkins got the indorsement of the GHQ Air Force, which recommended that the War Department make every effort to persuade the FCC to grant the extra radio frequencies for the expansion of the company's network. Noting "one or two dirty digs at the Signal Corps," Brig. Gen. George V. Strong, at that time the head of the War Plans Division of the General Staff, sent the proposal on to General Mauborgne.

The Signal Corps had communications responsibility throughout the series of aircraft warning services, as the Air Corps had for interception, both being subordinate from place to place to the frontier or department commander concerned. This was established fact. In addition, General Mauborgne knew that the heavily secret pulse-radio detection equipment had stunning promise and that the Laboratories were nearly ready with the long-range model which the Air Corps had requested after the dramatic demonstration of the SCR-268. In any event, he was dubious about the ability of radio to serve as the core of an administrative communications system, and certainly not ready to see a commercial organization improve its position by climbing upon the Army's shoulders.

I am of the opinion [he replied] that while the War Department recognizes the practicability and desirability of utilizing the wire and radio facilities of power companies to save telephone company lines for other uses, no assistance should be given such companies towards securing radio frequencies from the Federal Communications Commission for their use. I think this is an underlying motive back of this proposal on the part of the power companies of southern California.[3]

Nevertheless, he did balance his objection. To a special committee appointed by the President to survey the power facilities of the nation, Mauborgne expressed the hope that it would direct some attention to the use of the utility companies' networks in the defense communication of large cities.[4] He could not risk committing the Signal Corps wholly to one course of action or association, and his emphasis upon the importance to the Army of a

---

[3] (1) Ltr, A. A. Hopkins to [Gen Strong], 19 Jan 39; (2) Memo, Strong for Mauborgne, 21 Jan 39; (3) Memo, Mauborgne for Strong, 27 Jan 39. SigC 676.3 (AWS) Gen 1. (4) AG Ltr to CSigO, 10 Mar 39, sub: AWS. AG 660.2 AA (3-8-39) (Misc.)-E.

[4] Memo, CSigO for ACofS G-3, 6 Jan 39. SigC 676.3 (AWS) Gen 1.

nationwide network of commercial telephone and telegraph might be construed as marrying the Signal Corps to the AT&T till death them did part. He took a stand against any connection, whether illicit or blessed by law, which would deprive the Signal Corps of all freedom of action in dealing with the great commercial wire system.

Hearings were beginning just then on a Senate resolution to investigate the state of the telegraph industry. The Postal Telegraph and Cable Company was seeking reorganization under the Bankruptcy Act, with engulfment by Western Union in prospect. However anemic it had hitherto been, the existence of Postal had preserved the appearance of competition in the industry. Absorption of the company would render the telegraph system a monopoly, Continental having already dropped from view. Short of governmental subsidy to Postal, however, the merger was inevitable, and a subsidy was unacceptable because it would put the government into competition with a private business. Thus the prospect of a single telegraph system, which actually materialized in 1943, had to be accepted.

To the next stage, the extension of this merger to consolidation with the telegraph and teletype systems of the telephone companies, opposition could be vigorously entered.[5] "In time of war we contemplate a great use of the latest fast means of communication: for instance, the teletype," Mauborgne explained, testifying also to the importance of double-tracking the telegraph network so that it and the telephone system could both bear a vast wartime traffic.[6] Commercial communications would be called into heavy use in emergency, especially in the corps areas, which would feel the first burden of mobilization.

The Army expected to rent and lease a "tremendous amount" of commercial wire,[7] not only in the East but also in thinly populated sections of the United States where the profits were so low that only the possibility of competition kept circuits in being.

A final point in the War Department's opposition to any commercial expansion which would put the whole wire system under single control was the belief that only competition could encourage the introduction of new models of equipment. This was a matter corresponding in interest to the vital need for assurance that there would be plenty of circuit lines, because much of the equipment for the Army fixed communication system was adapted directly from commercial stock.[8]

Everyone's ox was gored, everyone's shoe pinched when it came to creating a military establishment in abeyance. Interruptions to plans could come politically as well as in any other fashion. The Congress appropriated $220,000 in 1939 for a new laboratory building at Fort Monmouth. This was a satisfaction, but a difficulty arose from the fact that the construction had been authorized for two years. Now

[5] Ltr, SW to Chm FCC, 18 Dec 39. SigC 483.1 Gen Telegraphy 3.

[6] *Hearings Before the Subcommittee of Senate Committee on Interstate Commerce,* Senate, 76th Cong, 1st Sess, To Authorize a Complete Study of the Telegraph Industry, 22–23 May 39, pp. 27–29.

[7] Ordinarily, telegraph and teletype circuits were leased, telephone circuits rented. TWX service was engaged as needed, whether on twenty-four circuits between continually busy administrative centers or on circuits between infrequently called points where traffic was diverted from the civilian pattern only when need arose.

[8] (1) Maj Gen Joseph O. Mauborgne, Signal Communications as a Requisite of Command, lecture delivered at Army War College, 4 Apr 38, pp. 5–6. SigC AC 352.13 Speech Mat, 1943–44. (2) Senate Rpt 529, 76th Cong, 1st Sess, *Study of Telegraph Industry.* (3) AG 676.2 (5-20-39) (1), *passim.*

that the money was in hand for it, the situation had changed so much that Brig. Gen. George H. Brett, commanding the Air Corps Materiel Division, declared that there was reason to "feel very bitter" that a new laboratory building was to go to the Monmouth installation rather than to Wright Field, "where it is so sorely needed." The Signal Corps acceded, changed its plan, and obtained rulings from the Judge Advocate General and the Comptroller General that the appropriation could be spent in Ohio rather than in New Jersey. G-4 withdrew the advertisement for bids on the intended construction at Fort Monmouth and substituted advertisements for the work to take place at Wright Field. This action drew objections from New Jersey. Representative William H. Sutphin took exception to the Judge Advocate General's opinion, and was immediately joined by Senator W. Warren Barbour. The New Jersey State Building and Construction Trades Council passed a unanimous resolution protesting the transfer of the construction from its state to another. Under these combined pressures the Acting Chief of Staff, Brig. Gen. Lorenzo D. Gasser, yielded and directed G-4 to return the proposed construction to Fort Monmouth.[9]

The expansion overriding all others was that of the Air Corps. Not a service of the Army or Navy escaped jostling in that process. Statutory recognition of it began in 1939 with an appropriation to the Military Establishment of a third of a billion dollars to carry it out. The Signal Corps allotted 90 percent of its available money to procurement under the legislated program. Almost every item in the Signal Corps budgets for the next fiscal year reflected the Air Corps' needs, supplemental estimates to the regular budget calling for

more than five million dollars' worth of airborne communications, and for nearly another million to buy Air Corps equipment used on the ground.[10] Fixed equipment, both for navigation and control, had to be planned for the new Army Airways Communications System. In such a modest item as the budgeted amounts of signal equipment needed at the various service schools, the Air Corps required $120,000 worth, the other arms not half so much.[11] For the first time, the Signal Corps also sought funds to cover a 10 percent reserve supply of extra sets and spare parts, so that pilots would not be obliged to fly without radio whenever the equipment needed repair.

What the Signal Corps would have liked to do was to equip the Air Corps completely, stock a good reserve in each signal section of each air depot, and then begin to operate a supply system without any of the makeshifts and inadequacies which halfway measures produced. It had an orderly scheme for achieving an organization which would procure, issue, store,

[9] (1) Memo, Col Clyde L. Eastman, Exec Officer OCSigO, for CSigO, 27 Jul 39. AAG 322.081 SigC-Liaison-Mat Div (Establishment of SigC Proc District at Wright Field, lab and warehouse), AAF Mat Comd Central Files. (2) Ltr, CSigO to TAG through Chief of AC, 16 Sep 39, sub: Substitution of ARL building Wright Field for extension to SCL Ft. Monmouth, and (a) 1st Ind, Chief of AC to TAG, 22 Sep 39, and (b) 2d Ind, TAG to CSigO, 18 Oct 39; (3) Msgs, William H. Sutphin and W. Warren Barbour to Judge Advocate Gen, 11 and 13 Sep 39; (4) Memo, ACofS G-4 to CofS, 2 Oct 39, sub: SCL Ft. Monmouth, and associated memos, 12, 13, and 18 Oct 39. AG 580 (3-31-26) (1) Sec 3E, Aviation Expansion. (5) Publication 394, 75th Cong, and Publication 164, 76th Cong.

[10] Hearings Before the Subcommittee of Committee on Appropriations, HR, 76th Cong, 1st Sess, On the Supplemental Military Appropriation Bill for 1940, statement of Gen Mauborgne, 22 May 39, pp. 158–72.

[11] Ltr, CSigO to Chief of Inf et al., 31 Mar 39, sub: SigC equip required for sv schools, and 1st Ind, Chief of Inf to CSigO, 12 Apr 39.

and maintain all the signal equipment that the Air Corps used. This scheme might have been realized if the war had not exploded it and many similar plans. The first step had been accomplished under Air Corps prodding when the signal air depot sections had been raised from the single functions of repair to full-statured supply units.[12] This was paper preparation for the time when they would be called upon to store, repair, and issue equipment on a greater scale than was in prospect.

When Air Corps expansion sharpened the prospect, the Signal Corps took a second step and commenced to fill out the outlines of the sections by decentralizing to them some of the authority of the big supply centers. The main depots at Brooklyn and Chicago held pre-expansion supplies, principally of ground arms signal equipment, and were inconvenient to many of the Air Corps bases, both old and new, wherefore it seemed a necessity to build up the air depot sections. To make considerable Signal Corps investments in the midst of Air Corps holdings was a risk. It exposed the sections to the inevitable day when they would be taken over by the Air Corps—padlock, bin-stock, and barrel. The fact that they existed solely to serve the Air Corps would become the logical reason for transferring them to the Air Corps, a change which the approach of the war delayed but which came about later when the end of the war was in sight.[13] It was therefore broad necessity rather than narrow self-interest which developed such signal sections as those at Fairfield, Ohio, and San Antonio, Texas, which were inherent parts of the Wright and Patterson Field, Randolph and Kelly Field air centers.

A third step followed when General

Mauborgne suggested that in order to eliminate any contractual delay arising from mere distance he would set up a new section at Wright Field and move the procuring of air signal equipment there from the New York Signal Corps Procurement District. At a conference with their opposite numbers in the Air Corps, Signal Corps officers went still further and agreed to a major commitment of Signal Corps supply in the Dayton area, Fairfield becoming the focal depot section of all the air signal depot sections and the proposed procurement section becoming a procurement district, equal partner with those in existence since the early 1920's. General Mauborgne, however, denied approval of the procurement district, because he felt that, along with the Fairfield build-up, a section was enough.

The whole project then progressed, as things always did, to the matter of funds. To have found the money for the ideal furnishing job, propeller hub to tail assembly, which the Signal Corps would have liked to do for the Air Corps would not have been much further out of reach than to underwrite a small office and 25,000 square feet of warehouse space. But the need for the office and warehouse was so fundamental that General Brett urged that it be considered a part of the equipment expansion. The Signal Corps accordingly reopened its supplemental estimates for the next fiscal year and inserted a request for the funds. Coupled with the request for the new laboratory

---

[12] Ltr, Actg CofS GHQ AC to TAG, 17 Dec 36, sub: SigC supply secs in AC depots, and 2d Ind, CSigO to TAG, 29 Dec 36. AAG 322.081 SigC Activities, 1932–45.

[13] WD Cir 429, 3 Nov 44. See OCSigO, Report of Transfer of Signal Corps Communications Equipment Peculiar to the Army Air Forces, 31 Mar 45. SigC Hist Sec File.

building at Wright Field, and piled on top of the original hope to have a new laboratory building at Fort Monmouth, it forced a choice which General Mauborgne met by deferring the Monmouth construction, bestowing upon Wright Field the $220,-000 which was to have been spent upon it, and asking for yet more to build a warehouse at Patterson.[14] Then the objection raised by the New Jersey legislators forced still another revision of the budget and introduced another request to take care of the Signal Corps Laboratories construction also.

Of all branches of the service, the Air Corps was also most in need of training films. It had only three. Between March and May 1939, the Signal Corps schedule for training films to be produced by mid-1941 was extended from forty to sixty reels, the increase representing what the Air Corps sought.[15] The Signal Corps' capacity for making training films stood further in abeyance than most of its other activities. The photographic course at the school had yielded only three graduates the year before and had been eliminated in favor of direct experience on the job at the Photographic Laboratory.[16] The Training Film Field Unit at Fort Monmouth was newly organized and understaffed. Senior instructors at West Point had studied the existing training films and recommended that eighteen more be made—none for the Air Corps.[17] Eighteen made as large a program as could be considered for a long time ahead, frivolities like films of the military contingent at the New York World's Fair being officially discouraged.[18]

In attempting to satisfy the requirements of the ground arms first, the unit came under criticism from the Air Corps, which asked for a change in Army regulations to permit the organization of its own motion picture agency.[19] The request took off from the argument that Signal Corps photographers were not authorized to make the aerial shots which no Air Corps training film could do without. Since experience had shown that the Signal Corps could neither keep one set of photographic equipment for the Air Corps and another for all the ground arms nor maintain photographic units at every air base in the Military Establishment, the Signal Corps compromised. The Air Corps might make the sequences involving aerial photography but the Signal Corps would go on being responsible for the whole.[20] To implement the agreement, the Signal Corps then established Training Film Field Unit Number 2 at Wright Field and placed Maj. Frederick W.

_____

[14] (1) Ltr, Chief of AC to CSigO, 4 Apr 39; (2) Ltr, Chief of AC to CSigO, 17 May 39, sub: Handling radio equip-expansion program, and Inds, 1–9. AAG 322.081 SigC-Liaison-Mat Div.

[15] (1) Memo, Actg CSigO for All Divs OCSigO, 27 Mar 39, sub: Tentative dir WD program FY 41. SigC 111 FY 41 Tentative Dir 1. (2) Memo, Exec Officer OCSigO for Pers and Tng Div *et al.*, 2 May 39, sub: Preliminary estimates FY 41. SigC 111 FY 41 QMC 1. (3) Mauborgne statement cited n. 10, pp. 170–71.

[16] Robert L. Eichberg and Jacqueline Quadow, Combat Photography, 1945, p. 5. SigC Hist Sec File.

[17] Ltr, Brig Gen Jay L. Benedict to TAG, 24 Apr 39, sub: WD tng films, 004.52-TF West Point, and 2d Ind, CSigO to TAG, 27 Apr 39. SigC 004.52-TF USMA (4-24-39).

[18] Ltr, CO Hq Camp George Washington to CG Second Corps Area, 7 Aug 39, sub: Films of mil activity N. Y. World's Fair, and 5th Ind, CSigO to TAG, 1 Sep 39. SigC 004.52 Mil Activity N. Y. World's Fair (8-7-39).

[19] Summary Report on Photographic Activities of the Signal Corps . . . in the Fields of Motion Pictures and Visual Aid, 26 Feb 43, p. 443. SigC APS Div File.

[20] Ltr, Chief of AC to TAG through CSigO, 4 Apr 39, sub: Proc of ground photo supplies for AC use, and 1st Ind, CSigO to TAG, 12 Apr 39. **SigC** 004.52 Authority.

A TRAINING FILM FIELD UNIT *at work on a film for the Air Corps.*

Hoorn, just back from a Panama assignment, in charge. He had only one other man, one camera, and a basement room, and unhappily met passive resistance at the field.[21]

Training-film photography was thus a fledgling. Tactically, photography was nonexistent. Maj. A. E. Holland, a Reserve officer on temporary active duty, prepared a study which emphasized public information, propaganda, troop information, and historical record as the wartime functions of military photography. He did look ahead, nevertheless, to problems of tactical equipment and organization. In the former case he urged the development of a lightweight sound camera, and in the latter proposed that photographic units be identically organized, then assigned in varying strength to field

headquarters, base laboratory, zone of interior, and theaters of operation.

The report was well received, but laid away because the Photographic Division was in no position to put it into effect.[22] It was not possible to make sure that any report would be read and applied to the future. Another, in this instance a reaction to the Southern California Edison aircraft warning plan, never got beyond the immediate range of the Office division where it was prepared, despite the fact that the

---

[21] Ltr, Maj Hoorn to Capt R. T. Schlosberg, O/C Photo Div OCSigO, 4 Nov 38. SigC 004.52 TFFU Wright Field Personal Correspondence.

[22] (1) Maj A. E. Holland, Report: War Plan for Signal Corps Photographic Division, Incl to Memo, Capt Schlosberg for Holland, 18 Jul 38, sub: Active duty tng. SigC 000.7 Publicity Photo Div, Nov 29–Mar 39. (2) Interv with Holland, 15 Mar 48, Washington, D. C.

Signal Corps Board wanted to use it in connection with an important study brought on by the imminence of the new SCR-270 radar. The report was denied to the Board "pending staff action," which was to say, "Because there is only one copy and no typist to make another." The Board of course went ahead and wrote up its study as scheduled, but without any light which might have been shed upon it by the other material.[23]

Yet whatever the brake, large or trivial, foreign or home-grown, the Army was perceptibly getting into motion. Each succeeding report of the Chief of Staff or of the Secretary made the fact plainer. More than in the panoramic generalities, the acceleration could be surely measured in the details, the minutiae of the process—such as rhombic antennas encroaching upon equitation fields.

One of the preparatory devices was the educational order, and the Signal Corps, although slow to take it up, ultimately placed two dozen of them.[24] Western Electric, General Electric, Stewart-Warner, Stromberg-Carlson, Farnsworth, U.S. Rubber, Roebling, Anaconda, and others on Signal Corps survey lists got the orders, although few of those companies were subject to education in the sense meant. In announcing the plan, Louis Johnson, the Assistant Secretary of War, explained that the intention was to instruct a manufacturer in the demands which war might make and to instruct the military agencies in the amounts and rates of production which they could look forward to.

This pair of conditions had little interest for the Signal Corps and its manufacturers. The connection established with industry was so close and the industry itself so closely grouped that there was not much doubt where production orders would go. The Ordnance Department, which seems to get the credit for conceiving educational orders, had observed this circumstance in both the Signal Corps, which had a commercial communications industry to count upon, and the Air Corps, which had a commercial aircraft industry. Ordnance was interested in finding out how much munitions expansion the nation's industry could absorb. There was no civilian market to spur ordnance development and manufacture, and time of war would require production of weapons by manufacturers who had never made anything like them.

This was not the problem for the Signal Corps, or at any rate was not thought to be. Undiscerned in its most chilling possibilities but at least detected on the horizon was the contest for raw materials which educational orders could not resolve. Mica, quartz, rubber, and silk were all going on the strategic list.[25] In the competition for them the most orderly plan would falter. Yet it was still too early for critical shortages to be apprehended very clearly. The Signal Corps Laboratories had turned down acetate in favor of pure silk for telephone insulation and the outer wrapping of the telephone cord, although a number of concerns had indicated their willingness to use the substi-

---

[23] Ltr, SigC Bd to CSigO, 24 Jun 39, sub: Study on AWS, and 1st Ind Reply, 28 Jun 39. SigC 676.3 (AWS) Gen 1.

[24] (1) Ltr, Louis Johnson, ASW, to CSigO et al., 20 Jun 38, sub: Program under educational order legislation; (2) Ltr, Col Harry K. Rutherford, OD, Exec Officer Plng Br OASW, to CSigO et al., 21 Jun 38, sub: Educational orders; (3) [Capt Byron S. Falk, SigC], Educational Orders, 1936–37, MS. OCSigO Proc Plng Sec File.

[25] Office of the Assistant Secretary of War Under the Protective Mobilization Plan and the Industrial Mobilization Plan, 15 Jul 39, pp. 16–18. AG 381 Mob Plan.

tute; and the Infantry was insisting upon latex insulation of field wire, although it had the double disadvantage of being produceable by only a few companies and of demanding a highly strategic material.[26]

Beginning with the 1939 fiscal year, Congress made an annual sum of $2,000,-000 available for educational orders and before the fiscal year was out amended the legislation to permit $34,500,000 to be spent on them within three years.[27] The Signal Corps' action was to settle upon orders for items which required little retooling of the plant production line. Because its equipment, like that of the Air Corps, was likely to change overnight and require a whole new manufacturing process along with the change, there was no question of placing an order to educate a manufacturer in a course of production which might never be used again. Accordingly, Signal Corps procurement planners decided to emphasize the two items which were least likely to change, the two which were also the backbone of signal equipment: wire and telephones. The basic design for field wire 110-B and for the EE-8 field telephone had not changed for ten years (and continued unchanged in the war which followed).

Once begun, the educational orders were a success. They streamlined specifications and indicated that the production rate could rise by forty or fifty times. The cost of the field wire program was $63,000, a comparatively small expenditure for such large returns. As a direct result of this program, the Signal Corps placed other orders for items like switchboard, cord, and radio equipment for which requirements were known to exceed the surveyed capacity.[28] The program was a success only by prewar standards, however. The ultimate goal was underestimated by so

much that the effort toward it fell very far short. The 1924 mobilization plan had guessed at a need for 4,000,000 dry batteries monthly six months after an M Day; the 1927 plan had knocked the guess down to 1,500,000; the 1939 estimate put it back and moved it beyond, to 5,000,000; but the production during the ensuing war twice reached 21,700,000. Although it had perceptibly increased, procurement was still under tight rein. The value of Signal Corps obligations in 1939 was $6,000,000 but in 1943 it was $3,000,000,-000. The amount obligated to procurement for Signal Corps research and development in 1939 was a thousandth of what it became in 1943.[29]

The Army could not read the future any more closely in terms of manpower. Mobilization estimates were a thoroughgoing piece of guesswork—thoroughgoing, but guesswork. Any plan, even the most carefully engineered, had its feet in a bog, its head in a fog. Yet the ability to respond when events put the nation on guard, then at defense positions, then on a full war footing would have been unattainable without the plans. Calculations of the rate at which personnel could be obtained

[26] (1) SigC 400.1141 Gen 17, *passim.* (2) L. H. Drake and F. W. Thomas, Production Div Phila SigC Proc District, Industrial Summary: Signal Corps Procurement of Wire and Cable With Recommended Operating Procedures, 16 Jan 46, p. 13. SigC Hist Sec File.

[27] Publication 639, 75th Cong, 1st Sess, 16 Jun 38; amended in Sec. 13 of Publication 18, 76th Cong, 1st Sess, 3 Apr 39.

[28] Brig Gen Calvert H. Arnold, Chief P&D Div OCSigO, Procurement in the Signal Corps, lecture given in Army Industrial College, Washington, D. C., 26 Feb 46, pp. 2–3. SigC Hist Sec File.

[29] (1) Henry C. C. Shute, Production Div Phila SigC Proc District, Industrial Summary: Signal Corps Procurement of Dry Batteries With Recommended Procedures, 15 Jan 46, pp. 7, 50. SigC Hist Sec File. (2) Arnold lecture cited n. 28. (3) OCSigO P&D Sv, Dry Batteries Supply and Demand, Mar and Apr 45.

started off, like equipment-rate calculations, from whatever facts could be gathered. The numbers, being few, were quickly arrived at.

Three and a half square divisions scattered over 130 Army posts pretty much typified the land power of the United States. There were sixty-two air squadrons, all half a dozen years behind the fierce Luftwaffe. There was no independent battle fleet in the Atlantic, and Japanese naval strength surged in the Pacific. The 188,000 Regular Army men in the three and a half divisions, in the sixty-two air squadrons, and in a multitude of administrative, service, and technical assignments constituted the nucleus of an initial protective force. This force was to be ready to defend the United States, Panama, and Hawaii within thirty days of the mobilization call. At the second stage, the Protective Mobilization Plan would assemble 700,000 more men, in consonance with the Industrial Mobilization Plan necessary to equip them. Third, augmentations would create a total force of 4,000,000 within about thirteen months from the start of the process. The god of war being willing, planned mobilization could replace an overwhelming influx with an even and balanced growth.[30]

The Signal Corps had approximately 1.5 percent of the officers and 2 percent of the enlisted men of the Regular Army. In the initial protective strength, this was the Signal fiber. Strength was not a matter of simple measurement, however. Personnel figures appeared in several guises; one could cite authorized strength, appropriated strength, allotted strength, active duty strength, and still none would represent the actual strength. Authorized strength was the figure set forth in the National Defense Act and its amendments. It was wide of the mark, for the appropriations each year stopped well short of maintaining it. The original figure authorized to the Army in the Thomason Act, for one example, was 1,000, but the 1940 budget pared it to 500.[31] An authorization was a promissory note; an appropriation was a savings account. Appropriations went to the War Department as a whole, and the shares of the individual services were allotted, usually in portions a bit less than their appropriated strength. From the allotted figure one subtracted those who were in school, in transit, or in hospital—men and officers who were spoken of as being "in the pipeline" between active duty assignments. Subtract them, and one reached the active duty figure, still not the actual strength, for the absence of a substantial number on special details lowered the sum further. Actual strength could have been calculated only by totting up morning reports, a process which was not practicable. When determined, it would have been a long distance from the most sanguine authorization and not very near to the most liverish.

By the end of June 1939, when the 1940 fiscal year commenced, the Signal Corps' strength was still not above 4,000. (The peak of war strength would put ninety men in the place of every one.) The totals in the end-of-the-year reports were 3,687 enlisted men and 248 officers (248 was exactly the commissioned strength listed

[30] (1) *Logistics in World War II, Final Report of the Army Service Forces, 1 July 1947* (Washington, 1948), p. 116. (2) WD Public Relations Br, Statement by Brig Gen Harry L. Twaddle Before the Truman Committee, 24 Apr 41. AG 381 (11-29-40) Sec 1.

[31] *Hearings Before a Subcommittee of the Committee on Appropriations,* HR, 76th Cong, 1st Sess, On the Military Establishment Appropriation Bill for 1940, statement of Lt Col W. P. Wattles, 7 Feb 39, p. 659.

a dozen years before, and in the intervening time the total had been lower). What
this represented was in effect actual
strength, as an analysis of the second figure shows: 288 officers held commissions
in the Signal Corps; 56 of the 288 were
detailed elsewhere, principally to the Air
Corps; 232 Signal Corps officers were
therefore on active duty with the Signal
Corps; but in addition 16 had been detailed to the Signal Corps from other
arms; thus, 248. In the authorized figures,
one officer out of every half dozen was a
ghost. The allotted officer strength, the
Signal Corps' portion of the 12,760 Regular Army officers provided for in the fiscal
year 1939 appropriations, was 262; and
this paper figure was 38 officers short of
the 300 theoretically permitted under the
National Defense Act amendment of the
year before. The difference between the
authorized number of officers and the
number actually present to do the Signal
Corps' business was thus 52—the 16⅔
percent discount on the promissory note.[32]

To the military strength of the Signal
Corps one could add the civilian employees. In 1939 there were 863, working
in the laboratories, the depot sections, the
Chief's office, through the continental
United States, and beyond in its territories. Statutory paradoxes caused civilian
strength to wilt a bit, too. The Classification Act provided for systematic increases
in salaries, but the appropriation acts year
by year contained a clause which in effect
nullified the increase except for those with
the lowest seniority and sometimes with
the least competence. At the opening of
the fiscal year 1940, the outlook for civilians somewhat improved, with Congressional appropriation for small rises in pay
and a modest hope that ultimately employees could dream of sixty-dollar pro-

motions every four years.[33] Counting its
civilians lifted the Signal Corps closer to
five thousand than to four, but this could
hardly be called a prefiguration of a major
military service of a major power. A company of Galahads equipped with Cadmean
dragons' teeth would have been more
like it.

Mauborgne pressed the contention that
Signal Corps increase under a defense
mobilization would have to be large. In
the first place, he argued, the Signal Corps
was a three-in-one in the Army; a combat
branch, a supply branch, and a headquarters branch, in the headquarters function
alone taking responsibility for signal intelligence operations, training-film production, and the War Department Message
Center. Second, the Signal Corps also
served joint Army-Navy policies, as the
recent need to create a Communication
Liaison Division demonstrated. Third,
wartime indicated an important role in
civilian radio, and, as for wire, would
oblige the Signal Corps to become a leading stockholder in long-distance telephone
lines, teletypewriter exchanges, and facsimile circuits.[34] At that, the conception
was drawn in terms of a solely protective
force. Tests of the new triangular division
were conducted at peace strength and
under the assumption that the United
States could be involved only in protective
warfare. Secretary Woodring currently
took pride in the reduction of mobilization plans "to sensible working propor-

---

(1) SW, *Annual Reports, 1939, 1940, 1941*: Table A
in each case. (2) Capt Wilson G. Burden, Signal Corps
Strength, Nov 45, p. 8. OCSigO Career Management
File.

[33] Pers Control Book of the CSigO, FY 39. OCSigO
Central Files.

[34] Ltr, Gen Mauborgne to TAG, 24 Sep 38, sub:
Mob Plans WD Offices in Washington, D. C. SigC
381 Gen 10, 1938.

tions." Eighty percent of the important nonradio items required for inactive units were for the Coast Artillery, a defensive arm.[35]

Even under this assumption the Signal Corps would need many persons. In radio the demand would be for specialists who had never been missed when all that was required was the twiddling of a screwdriver to free a circuit. Even the men who started off untrained would have to show some knowledge of radio engineering. In view of the fact, however, that the nation was richly supplied with wire and all of its advantages, radio was not dominant in Signal Corps mobilization plans. Wire was, especially in administrative communications which were much the larger part of Signal Corps responsibility.

The fact that the administrative system had now pretty generally changed over from telegraph to teletype was a matter of great pride. There were dissenters who felt that the Signal Corps and the communications industry were making a mistake in discarding Morse. Two promoters represented this point of view obliquely—"technical etiologists" who proposed to lift the Postal Telegraph Company from its fatal illness, restore it to health, and within two years transform it into a flourishing source of at least 50,000 trained Morse operators for the Army to draw upon.[36] They believed that the Signal Corps was wrong to imitate the big commercial wire trust in giving up telegraph for teletype, because teletype would be unadaptable to tactical situations.

Despite the forlornness of the etiologists' proposal to rouse a dead horse, gallop forward, and tilt at lances with the giant Bell, there was a point to be made in favor of retaining Morse. Wire might have outgrown telegraphy, but radio had

not. Voice radio was not yet common; most message sending over wireless went by *dit*'s and *dah*'s from the clicking key. The days were coming when because of this fact hundreds of thousands of young men—at Fort Monmouth, Camp Crowder, and the aviation cadet centers, for example—would be learning "code." Air operations would employ it heavily; and on the ground advanced tactical communications would frequently need it and so would much of the administrative system. Fifty thousand telegraphers could then have been welcomed. In a setting of defense, they did not figure, first because the Army's need for skilled "fists" could presumably be met from its own ranks and those of the organized amateurs, and second because the theater of action, the home scene, would enjoy the full resources of a universal wire system of telephone and teletype.

The big commercial wire system was a central part of the Signal Corps' plans. Of the 20,000,000 telephones in the nation, the Bell System operated 80 percent; 6,000 independent companies operated the others. In December 1938 General Mauborgne invited officials of AT&T to a conference. As a result of the discussion and a joint study by Carroll O. Bickelhaupt of the company and the war plans unit in General Mauborgne's office, a new

---

[35] (1) Signal Corps Information Letter, No. 21 (April 10, 1939), pp. 10–14. (2) Congressional hearings cited n. 31, statement of Harry W. Woodring, 24 Jan 39, p. 2. (3) Chart: Important Non-Radio Items Required for Inactive Units, 28 Nov 38, Incl with Memo, Exec Officer OCSigO for ACofS G-4, 30 Nov 38; (4) Memo, Exec Officer OCSigO for ACofS G-3, 28 Sep 38. SigC 381 Gen 10, 1938.

[36] 2d Ind, Exec Officer OCSigO to TAG, 9 Apr 38, on Ltr, Frank Payne and D. Sherrill Talmage to CofS, 4 Apr 38, sub: Dangers to national defense with recommendations for averting leading causes thereof. SigC 381 Gen 10, 1938.

Affiliated Plan crystallized, evolving in relation to the Protective Mobilization Plan. The PMP mapped out the organization of seven signal battalions in addition to the Regular establishment's two, a signal construction battalion, two independent signal companies, and three signal depot companies. It looked ahead also to expansion of the Office of the Chief Signal Officer, organization of a GHQ signal service and of a GHQ Air Force signal battalion, and provision of commissioned and enlisted personnel to four field armies and the headquarters of the Atlantic, Pacific, and Gulf frontiers. Augmentations of the PMP contemplated thirty more signal battalions and seventeen more signal companies. All of these would require telephone men.

The joint commercial-Army planning assumed that the Signal Corps would grow to 18,500 in the initial phase of mobilization and to 62,500 when the augmentations were complete. Bell had 78,800 male employees under forty-five. According to expectation, Affiliated mobilization would probably take 5,659; the rest would stay with the system, whose position in the defense plan discouraged the withdrawal of more. Of the 5,659 Affiliated men from Bell, 143 would serve in the Chief's office, the procurement districts, laboratories, schools, training centers, and corps area headquarters. Everyone else would be assigned to units. To nondivisional units. That is to say, to outfits primarily concerned with the administrative wire system, supply, and pole-line construction.[37]

Divisional signal units, whose men would be performing tactical signal functions, had an allotment from the Protective Mobilization Plan of 469 officers and 11,390 enlisted men, organized in fifty-four signal companies for Infantry divisions and twelve signal troops for Cavalry divisions and a thirteenth for the Cavalry Corps. When mobilization brought these units to life, they would need cadres around which to grow. The intention was to put trained specialists in as the nucleus, because the remaining members of the organization would be new to their tasks. At any stage before mobilization, most of the potential cadremen were detailed to duties in which they could be replaced. Upon mobilization, according to plan, they would transfer to the field, taking their skills and their good physical condition to the new units, while limited-service personnel or civilians moved in behind them.

There were many possibilities for the Signal Corps in such a plan. Many Army assignments did not require a technician. Noncombatants, whether men or women, could undertake them. One of the greatest advantages in changing over to teletype in the administrative wire system lay in the fact that the machine absorbed much of the technical burden and required of the operator only that he could type. The Signal Corps had employed women with great success as telephone operators in World War I; women would also serve expertly as typists, code clerks, laboratory assistants, and in a multitude of other zone of interior occupations. The "basic" civilian, like the "basic" soldier, would be most in demand; but accountants, lawyers, industrial specialists, statisticians would join echelons of technicians, engi-

---

[37] (1) Ruth Sadler, History of the Signal Corps Affiliated Plan, Aug 44, pp. 20–21. SigC Hist Sec File. (2) [Carroll O. Bickelhaupt *et al.*], Report: Procurement of Signal Corps Personnel From the Bell Telephone System in an Emergency; (3) Ltr, Actg CSigO to TAG, 8 Aug 39, same sub. SigC 381 Affiliated Units 6.

neers, and scientists. If war were to make the Signal Corps' military strength grow at a rate of ninety to one, it would increase the civilian strength in a nearly comparable proportion. But the time had not yet come for that. The present outlook was modest. In Signal Corps estimates, it was 1,376. This was the number of positions held by its enlisted men which the Signal Corps presumed civilians could fill. General Mauborgne doubted that a civilian could replace an officer. The positions set up to effect the civilian replacement of enlisted men would assign them as everything from janitors at $1,080 to radio, sound, and telephone engineers at $3,200. If all 1,376 positions were filled by civilians, the Congress would have to appropriate $2,253,920 every year to pay their salaries.[38] But no one could move just yet, whether Congressman, general, or common citizen. These were plans, not action, the abeyance, not the world war; and there were few persons who were eager to hurry them into effect.

---

[38] (1) Memo, Exec Officer OCSigO for ACofS G-3, cited n. 35(4). (2) 1st Memo Ind Reply, 30 Aug 39, on Memo, Actg ACofS G-1 for CSigO, 25 Aug 39. SigC OT 322 Gen, 1941.

CHAPTER V

Equipment Search and Research

If manpower must remain in abeyance, such was not wholly the case with matériel.[1] Plans could be made for the amassing of signal equipment without some of the anxious implications of war which attended plans for manpower. In the first place, a large bulk of the Signal Corps' equipment was almost indistinguishable from that which bore the nation's daily interchange of commerce, news, entertainment, and correspondence. In the second, the equipment which was developed solely for the uses of war tapped electrophysical knowledge of the widest consequence and had a way of giving off peaceful by-products. The challenge of communications equipment was a challenge in technology. In this sense it stood apart from the search for communications men, although not farther away than the use which communications men had for it. Occasionally developments like radar broke ranks, and appeared ahead of a specific demand for them. Otherwise the technological patterns of use determined, or at the least molded, the equipment.

The determinants in producing signal equipment were accordingly the requirements of the Signal Corps itself and of the tactical users. The attributes of the Signal Corps mission were largely administrative and the equipment required to carry it out was therefore likely to be of commercial or near-commercial models. The problems they created, certainly large enough, were principally problems of procurement—of planning the equipment, searching it out, and making sure that enough would be on hand. The technical challenge resided in the other area of equipment especially, the equipment for tactical use in the field—by the Infantry platoon sergeant, the Coast Artillery searchlight station, the nine-man crew of a heavy bomber, the regimental message center. In this part of its responsibility the Signal Corps took orders from the Infantry, the Coast and Field Artillery, the Cavalry and Armored Force, the Air Corps. One or another of the using arms such as these asked for equipment of a particular sort to meet a particular anticipated need; or the Signal Corps suggested to them that it would be a good thing for them to have if it could be developed.

Wire

To those who used the communications equipment, whether it was of wire or wireless design mattered less than whether it got the message through. Generally speaking, wireless only hovered at the edge; wire had the central place. The superla-

---
[1] See Appendix, "Signal Corps Equipment, World War II."

tive research which enabled a radio signal to be relayed from a front-line handie-talkie all the way back to the Chief of Staff was at least a dozen years in the future.[2] Even then, such a feat would not be accomplished without wire at several points. In 1939 there was no question that wire was the primary means of communication, likely to be dominant in both tactical and administrative uses. That it lent itself to secrecy (radio having to broadcast everything it knew) was only one mark in its favor. It also enjoyed the advantage of long establishment and the related advantages of well-known and abundant instruments. The lapse of years since World War I had allowed time to solve many of the problems of military wire and to make wire equipment and wire organization familiar throughout the service, while to all those coming into the Army it was the familiar means of communication known everywhere in the nation.

The list of Signal Corps wire items in this year between the Munich blitz and the panzer blitz began with the wire or cable itself and opened out three ways, into telegraphy, telephony, and the new teletyping. Telegraphy was characterized by the fact that it sent its messages in Morse code. The telephone instrument carried the human voice. Teletypewriters transmitted messages in printing, or in inked or perforated symbols which were a specialized substitute for printing. Each of the three forms had its equivalent radio version. Radioteletype was too new to take into account. Radiotelephony was the area upon which the most concerted effort centered. Radiotelegraphy was temporarily the farthest along of the three, as was to be expected in the normal course of development, which achieves code transmission before voice. Wire telegraphy still held the field in many uses; the six-pound manual telegraph set TG-5 was a familiar item of equipment in World War II. At the main points of a communications system, however, wire teletype now replaced wire telegraph; and radiotelegraph forced a total abdication of wire wherever it could not go—into the air, or in a wireless region like so much of Alaska. Wire telephony was uppermost in all employment of voice communication. Wire teletype was so well liked that it had even regained ground from radio, by widely supplanting the Boehme high-speed system.

The standard field wire which the Signal Corps offered was W-110, the standard assault wire, W-130. These were lightweight twisted pairs with limited capacity and range, but they could be laid rapidly from reels carried by the construction crewmen or payed out from the rear of a truck.[3] A mile of twisted-pair field wire weighed 130 pounds, the same amount of assault wire, 30 pounds. The reels upon which wire was wound varied in size. Two men could carry a small one, turning it as they went in order to dispense the wire. The RL-27A, for example, an axle, weighed but 5 pounds, although when loaded with a half mile of wire, at the outset of a wire-laying stint, it was heavy indeed. The RL-31 weighed 30 pounds and was also hand-cranked. The large, gasoline-powered RL-26, which replaced horse-drawn wire carts, had to be carried in a vehicle, because, when it was loaded with two miles of W-110, it weighed nearly 600 pounds.

[2] Brig. Gen. Wesley T. Guest (Chief of Sig Plans and Opns Div OCSigO), "Planning Integrated Signal Communications," and Col. Edwin R. Petzing (Chief Engr and Tech Div OCSigO), "Engineering the Integrated Communications System," *Radio and Television News*, December, 1950.
[3] TM 11-487, Electrical Communication Systems Equipment, 2 Oct 44, p. 118, par. 614.

LAYING FIELD WIRE *from the horse-drawn cart (above) and from the truck-mounted RL–26 (below).*

The battery-powered telephones used in the field were like standard commercial ones. Development was complete on the universal stand-by of the ensuing war, the EE-8A. The sound-powered telephone, that interesting return to the first principles of Alexander Graham Bell, had met with some success in the testing of the Navy and commercial models, and now became the TP (for telephone)-3. It was later modified so that the bell which gave its position away to an enemy was replaced by a small light. Any field telephone was carried about in a stout case, made of leather until the oncoming rationing forced the use of cord and fabric instead.

Although the wire, reels, and telephone instruments of tactical communication had changed considerably since World War I, no comparable redesign had occurred in switchboards. The Laboratories could have set up projects for new ones except that there was already more pressing business. There were three basic types all taken from French models of World War I. The BD (for board)-71 had six "drops," [4] the BD-72, twelve; both were regimental boards. For division headquarters there was a 40-line unit, the BD-14. All of these field switchboards were heavier than they needed to be, partly because of the storage battery which was necessary if the board were to be part of a common battery system. Although it was helpful if a field telephone could operate in such a system, so that it could be put on a desk or hung on a wall, ordinarily its prime use was in circumstances where there were no desks or walls and where a local battery, just to serve the switchboard, was enough. These switchboards worked on local batteries only: that is, they depended upon the dry cells contained in each field telephone set

A BATTERY-POWERED TELE-PHONE, *the EE-8A. (Photograph taken in 1943.)*

and in the board itself. The originator of the call had to crank the handle which rang up the switchboard operator, who in turn cranked up enough energy to ring the telephone of the person being called.

The switchboards for the next higher echelons were in course of development. The Signal Corps Laboratories had recently begun work on the BD-89, for use between the division and corps headquarters. A replacement for the BD-14, it was a compact 60-line unit which could be used in part or in whole, either as a few sections or as the entire set all at once. For

---

[4] That is to say, six lines. The drop is specifically the small shutter above the plug opening, or jack. When someone rings the switchboard, the ringing energizes an electromagnet to release the shutter, which drops and thereby signals the operator to plug in for the call.

A TWELVE-DROP SWITCHBOARD, *the BD-72, in a communications dugout.*
(Photograph taken in 1943.)

the field army there was to be a full telephone central set, the TC-1. Its switchboard, the BD-80, had been in process
since 1933, three models having been received for testing in January 1938. It, too,
was planned for partial use as required,
with multiples up to six installed side by
side; its capacity was 100 lines. The field
telephone central sets like the TC-1 were
usually transportable by truck, and when
in place provided a complete telephone
exchange for headquarters requiring the
capacity of three-position BD-80's. The
fixed telephone equipment of the rear
areas was of course like any of the great
central office sets to be seen in the city ter-

minals of the Bell System, as the administrative wire telegraph and teletypewriter
equipment was similarly to be seen in the
offices of Western Union.

The Signal Corps Laboratories had
looked into the possibilities of using teletype in the field as well, starting in the
early 1930's when it was called telegraph
printer and when the industry first
changed over to using the sort of teletype
which spun out the message on paper
tape. Other armies, the German, for instance, were exploring the same possibility. When page teletype replaced tape
commercially, the Laboratories tested
several page models. Of these, the Tele-

type Corporation equipment seemed best and, slighty altered, became standardized as the TG-7. With auxiliary parts such as power supply and rectifier, the TG-7 formed both the mobile field teletypewriter, EE-97, and the fixed equipment, EE-98. The military teletypewriter employed the neutral system, which required fewer parts than the polarential system generally used in commercial teletypewriters. Neutral operation alternated pulses of current with breaks when no current flowed. Each letter which the transmitting operator struck on his keyboard was translated, according to the five-unit code, into a combination of current flow (mark) and of current break (space). This coded combination actuated the corresponding combination at the receiving teletypewriter, which automatically typed the letter almost at the same instant as the transmitting operator was typing it many miles away.

The biggest problem in the early development of a military field teletypewriter was a reliable power supply which would put out the stable flow of current necessary for mark-and-space operation. The cycle rate could be twenty-five a second or sixty a second but in any case had to be unvarying. Even so little as a 3 percent shift of frequency would affect the printing, for the electrical impulses had to keep both the sending and receiving printers in perfect synchronization. Of six commercial power units that the Signal Corps Laboratories had tested, none proved satisfactory. The resultant efforts to develop a reliable field generator led to the PE-77, a 70-pound d-c generator. Frequently the 300-pound PE-75 which provided commercial alternating current was also used to power the mobile teletypewriter set EE-97. The fixed EE-98 was identical

with the EE-97, except that it lacked this power unit. Being intended for fixed use, it could be plugged into commercial power lines.[5]

This was the outline of U.S. Army wire equipment just before World War II. Of the imminent foes, neither Japan nor Italy was comparably developed; and what was known of German equipment made this pattern look entirely adequate. The Germans employed light and heavy wires similar to the Signal Corps' 130 and 110. Whereas W-130 was a double conductor, much of the equivalent German light wire consisted of a single strand, and the return was by way of the ground, a method which the American Army did not employ.[6] The two-conductor light wire, which the Germans did have, used the metallic return that was universal in American practice. As for field cable, the Germans had produced one item of marked importance. Manufactured in lengths which could be

[5] (1) Signal Corps Information Letter, No. 1 (April, 1934), pp. 7 ff., No. 10 (July, 1936), pp. 13–17, No. 13 (April, 1937), pp. 8–9, No. 15 (October, 1937), p. 7, No. 18 (July, 1938), p. 12, No. 22 (July, 1939), p. 12, No. 24 (January, 1940), p. 9. (2) Signal Corps Technical Letter, No. 38 (January, 1945), p. 24. (3) SCL, Annual Reports, 1936, pp. 21–22, 1937, p. 31, 1938, pp. 33 ff., 1939, pp. 42 ff., 1941, pp. 30–31. (4) Historical Report of the Signal Corps Engineering Laboratories, pp. 149–56, 161–62; (5) Hist Sec E&T Divs OCSigO, History of Signal Corps Research and Development in World War II, 1945–46, Vol. V, Pt. 1, Proj (510)2-4, Pt. 3, Proj 532 (4.32.1), Pt. 4, Projs 574-A, 574-B. SigC Hist Sec File. (6) Rpt, C&E Coordination Bd OCSigO to Chief Com Coordination Br, 26 May 42, sub: Case 17 types of W-110 concentric vs. parallel lay. SigC C&E Case 17 Com Coordination Br Types of W-110. (7) TM 11-487, Electrical Communication Systems Equipment, pp. 55 ff. (8) Maj. Gen. Roger B. Colton, "Army Ground Communication Equipment," Electrical Engineering, LXIV, No. 5 (May, 1945), 173–74. (9) Interv, SigC Hist Sec with Col James D. O'Connell, CO SCEL, Belmar, N. J., 14 Apr 47.

[6] Partly because it makes the line easy to tap, by electrical induction. FM 11-35, Signal Corps Intelligence, 2 Sep 42, pp. 17–18.

readily handled in the field, their cable could be laid quickly and joined by means of pluglike connectors two inches in diameter. Loading coils which much increased conductivity, range, and general efficiency could be inserted into the connector. This was the subsequently famous four-conductor or "quadded" cable captured and copied by the British and still later adapted by the Signal Corps as *spiral four*.

Standard German field telephone sets were a No. 26 and a No. 33. No. 26, powered by two battery cells, utilized a hand-cranked magneto generator and a buzzer for calling; it weighed about fourteen and one-half pounds. No. 33 used only one battery cell and weighed twelve and one-half pounds. The Signal Corps' superior EE-8 weighed but about ten pounds. For small-scale switching in the field, the German army had a two-line board which measured only six by six by two inches and had been developed to the stage of replacing the bell or buzzer with a light. The Signal Corps had nothing so convenient until well along in the war, when the small plastic SB-5 was produced. The Germans used two types of lightweight ten-line switchboards, one with shutter indication, the other with audible calling, which compared to the Signal Corps' regimental BD-71 and BD-72. The heavy field switchboard, for thirty lines, fell in the same category as the American division boards, BD-14 and BD-89. In communications for their higher units, both nations were replacing hand-keyed Morse code with teletypewriters, the Germans having adopted the Siemens and Halske telegraph printers as standard.[7]

Radio

Wire was the primary means of communication because so much of the entire activity was administrative and rear-area traffic. For combat, however, an area was now forming between the divisional wire and the light assault wire where conventional means were being supplanted. The twin doctrines of mechanization and mobility promised to send troops out of reach of the rear wire very soon after a campaign began; and so long as they might be moving, there would have to be a link between the men at the back where the fixed equipment was and the men at the front with the sound-powered telephones and the lightest wire. Ultimately, this link was accomplished either by spiral-four cable or by radio relay. To the astonishing degree that voice radio came into use, however, displacing telegraphy and wire telephone everywhere in the forward echelons, radio became the dominant tactical communications equipment.

Until that stage was reached, the radio equipment which the Signal Corps provided was a subordinate or an appendage to the wire system. Radios were designed for the specific uses of artillery batteries or infantry divisions or interceptor squadrons; they were modeled according to a conception of warfare which did not require that they be able to bear the main load or to intercommunicate extensively. For the most part, the radios worked on tone or continuous wave signals and in the middle and high frequencies. Develop-

---

[7] They also used radioteletype in the war. See Mobile Field Interrogation Unit 2, Prisoner of War Intelligence Bulletin No. 2/18, 9 Dec 44, p. 18. OCMH Foreign Studies Br File.

TM-E 30-451, Handbook on German Military Forces, 1 Sep 43, pp. 159–83. This handbook describes equipment in use several years earlier than 1943. The tables outlining German radio sets, opposite page 168, are identical with tables drawn up by the British, entitled German Wireless Transmitters and Receivers, and extracted from Periodical Notes on the German Army, No. 22, Jun 40. SigC ET 413.44 German Sets (Wireless Transmitters and Receivers), Copy 5 of 7. T 1324.

ment had reached the stages beyond, but the equipment in the hands of the troops necessarily represented a point several years behind research. The hand-cranked generator was usual, the small loop antenna common, and manual tuning nowhere replaced by pushbutton control. The equipment was generally bulky and heavy, even pack sets being "two-man portables" often enough, and *vehicular* sets being more precisely *transportable* by horse or truck, from which they were removed to the ground before setting up in business. In none of these aspects was the equipment obsolete; almost all of it was soundly designed and much of it was in wide use in the forthcoming war. It was obsolete only in the laboratory, where engineers perceived a multitude of refinements which could be made in it, and, overshadowed by the threat of war, felt pressed to put them into effect.

The chief users of the tactical wireless equipment were the infantry division with its supporting ground and air artillery; the cavalry division and later the armored; the coastal defense site; and the air group or squadron. The three oldest sets—no older than much of the wire equipment, although they could not, like the wire, go through an approaching war unchanged— were the SCR's 131, 161, and 171. The remarkable SCR-131 did see some wartime service in training camps, but with its companion sets had already been overtaken by later development. These three were continuous wave, short-range, loop antenna, portable or semiportable, regimental sets, the 131 being intended for the Infantry and Cavalry, the 161 for the Field Artillery, and the heavy 171 for ground-to-air control and even division headquarters use.

A second group of ground radios could be distinguished by their intended use for point-to-point and ground-to-air communications, as well as by the fact that they employed the superheterodyne receiver. These were the series 177–78–79 and the 188. They, too, were designed for stationary ground use, but at longer range. All were heavy enough to need to be carried about in a vehicle, or, in the instance of the 179, which was an already obsolete version made for the Cavalry, by a horse. The SCR-177 was primarily a Coast Artillery Corps set, the 178 was for the Field Artillery, and the SCR-188 was thought of as an Air Corps set. The transmitters had power up to 75 watts, which was sufficient to send Morse code by continuous wave or tone signals for distances approaching one hundred miles, especially in the air, where the signal could be received much farther than ground receivers could discern it. The voice transmission of these sets was limited to twenty miles or so. Utilizing the upper reaches of the middle frequencies and the lower reaches of the high frequencies, they operated chiefly in the region just above the broadcast band, except for the 188. This Air Corps ground set, originally calibrated for the range between 6,200 and 7,700 kilocycles, subsequently extended its frequency coverage down to 1,500 kilocycles and up to 12.5 megacycles. Any of these sets, each weighing hundreds of pounds, had to be operated from the ground, drawing its power from a gasoline-driven generator and a dynamotor and radiating its signals from an antenna supported by a thirty-foot mast.

The same disadvantages attached to comparable radios in other armies—the German 80 W.S.2, for example—but the knowledge that such was the case in no way diminished the compelling need to overcome them. Thus, although the SCR-177 and the SCR-188 were in frequent use for several years to come, the function

THE SCR–131 *in operation at Fort Monmouth in 1941.*

which they were principally intended to serve was changing as dramatically as all other aspects of the use of air power, and as a result they seemed far out of date when highly portable sets, mobile sets, crystal-controlled sets, and frequency-modulated sets appeared. Under the pressure not only of the Air Corps but of the Armored and Infantry arms, the drive for equipment to meet the sudden new tactical concepts replaced most of the Signal Corps radios in the 100 series, filled the 200 series, left the 300's and 400's almost entirely open in case daring changes should be reconsidered and drastic decisions recalled, and went on to the 500's and 600's for a whole scale of brilliant development.[8]

The rapid change was very greatly more marked in airborne radio, which was still an almost wholly new field. If the SCR-

[8] (1) Signal Corps Information Letter, Nos. 1–16 (April, 1934–January, 1938), *passim* under Development of Equipment. (2) SCL, Annual Report, 1941, p. 71. (3) R&D hist cited n. 5(5), Vol. VIII, Pt. 3, Projs (823) 10-11, 833-A. (4) C&E Cases No. 3, Purchase of 1500 Additional SCR-288 Radio Sets, 15 Nov 41; No. 6, Substitution of Radio Set SCR-284 for Radio Set SCR-290 for the Coast Artillery Corps, 14 Nov 41; No. 55, Tab D, Signal Equipment Suitable for Standardization Within and Between Corresponding U.S. Army and British Commonwealth Army Units, 18 Nov 42. SigC Files. (5) TM 11-227, Radio Communication Equipment, 10 Apr 44, *passim*. (6) Interv, SigC Hist Sec with Capt W. W. Van Winkle (formerly assigned with com systems in Panama), Signal Corps Sidelights, Vol. I, Pt. 1, pp. 222–26. SigC Hist Sec File. (7) CSigO, Annual Report, 1945, p. 398. (8) History of the Philadelphia Signal Corps Procurement District, III, 627 ff. SigC Hist Sec File.

131 continued in use, its contemporaries in air equipment did not. Aviation in 1939 was too different from that of the 1920's for items to be carried over from the earlier period. The old 134, the liaison set for bombers, had been replaced by the 187 and a 287 modification. The SCR-187 had been initiated at the first inauguration of Franklin D. Roosevelt, when it was used in a nationwide broadcast of an air view of the ceremony; and in the next year, 1934, SCR-187's had been aboard the pioneer flight of Air Corps bombers to Alaska. This long-range airborne communications equipment was very sound. Its transmitter was so dependable that it was employed for ground use as well, as a component of that work horse of early vehicular radios, the SCR-193. Its receiver was notable as the first airborne receiver to incorporate the superheterodyne circuit successfully. The 187 did not begin to be replaced until late in the ensuing war, and even then the receiver component continued in use on long-range aircraft. One of the reasons for its long life was its adaptability to frequency changes. For instance, to obviate the development of a new set whenever the Air Corps shifted to a different frequency band, the Aircraft Radio Laboratory used plug-in tuning coils, so that all that was needed in order to change frequency was to remove one coil assembly and plug in another.

The opposite number of the long-range liaison set was the short-range command set, in this period the SCR-183. Like the SCR-187, the 183 had been designed to operate on the 12-volt storage battery then standard in aircraft. By this time, a 24-volt battery had become standard, and accordingly an SCR-283 was being readied to supplant the 183, just as was true of the 287 and the 187. The SCR-183 weighed somewhat less than fifty pounds. This was

one point which outmoded it, for aviators had a dread of anything that increased the weight of their craft. "The attitude of most of the flying people," a Signal Corps officer remarked with rueful bias, "was that when war came, the radio equipment would be left out of the plane and the corresponding weight would be used to carry more machine gun ammunition or more bombs." [9] Another mark against it was that its maximum range—a continuous-wave range—was forty-five or fifty miles. The newer pursuit planes could pass beyond that in a few minutes of flight. True, the pursuits were still on the drafting board, and hard reality kept the SCR-183/283 in standard service until 1943.

Nevertheless, aircraft radio design had to keep up to aircraft design, and accordingly the Air Corps Technical Committee proposed a command set of a radically different sort, which the Signal Corps began to develop as the SCR-240. This was a noteworthy departure. Nothing like it had yet been introduced in ground equipment; for both the transmitter and the receiver were to have crystal control, in the new sense of a presetting of the crystals for automatic finding of the frequencies. To extend the range of a command set outward toward one hundred miles, as would be true of the SCR-240, was a great advantage, but it was an even greater one to make possible a quick and easy selection of channels. Relieved of the tedious and delicate business of dial tuning, the operator would have only to flick a switch or press a button. Inasmuch as the operator in a pursuit craft was the pilot himself, this was an improvement which the Air Corps awaited with understandable impatience. The 240, however, was not destined to fill the bill. Its development, standard-

[9] Interv, SigC Hist Sec with Lt Col W. G. Eaton, SigC, ARL, 25 Oct 44.

ization, and procurement lost time all along the way, and two years elapsed before the Signal Corps let contracts for it.[10] Only a few SCR-240's were produced before they, with their 24-volt partner, the SCR-261, gave way to the crystal-controlled command set of the World War II period: SCR-522.

Meanwhile, the search for a satisfactory command set took two other turns. First, the Signal Corps standardized one of its own Aircraft Radio Laboratory high-frequency models which the Navy was already having manufactured. Designated SCR-274-N, for *Navy*, despite its origin in Signal Corps design, it became one of the most widely used command sets of the war. Although it was manually tuned and weighed seventy-five pounds, it had the advantage of a range which reached out to 150 miles. The Aircraft Radio Corporation, Colonial Radio Corporation, and Western Electric built thousands of them, the last alone turning out 100,000 by the end of 1944. Plans for another command set, which was to have been the very high frequency SCR-264, faded; but they did result in a model which illustrated the Laboratories' first attempt to move above the conventional, crowded, high frequencies into the then almost untapped very high frequencies.[11]

To the command, or short-range, sets and the liaison, or long-range, sets which provided airborne communications, radio compasses added a navigational complement. Navigational radio was an outgrowth of World War I direction finding, which had taken two divergent paths, one for signal intelligence to follow in the locating of enemy radio stations, the other to develop the means by which both ships and airplanes might take bearings upon radio communication stations. It was the second form which included both the radio compass in the airplane and the navigational aids on the ground. On an instrument panel, the airborne compass looked like the familiar magnetic compass, although it pointed not to magnetic north but to the ground transmitter to which it was tuned. The radio compass, SCR-186, which had threatened to split the Aircraft Radio Laboratory apart had now become a dead issue, and the SCR-242 was the model in general use. A radio compass was necessarily light—the one used with the SCR-274-N weighed only six pounds—but the ground navigational aids were proportionately heavy because they had to receive a comparatively weak signal from an aerial distance. The ground set which the Signal Corps then had in use was a Navy item. A cumbersome apparatus mounted on a tower, and employing a large H-shaped Adcock antenna which had to be rotated by hand, it was nevertheless excellent equipment, and, after there had been deliberation over it until the war was already begun, it did get into wide service.

_____

[10] Exhibit A to Memo Rpt, Lt Col Alfred W. Marriner, Asst Tech Exec Air Mat Div, for Tech Exec, 6 Aug 41, sub: SigC deficiencies. AF 322.081 SigC Activities 1932–45.

[11] More than anything else, the crystal problem seemes to have blocked early German development of very high frequency airborne transmitters. The Germans used only the lowest frequencies of the VHF band, those between 38.2 and 42.6 megacycles. In the course of the war, they did use frequencies running above VHF into the UHF span. They did so, for example, in radio link equipment comparable to the so-called antrac (AN/TRC) sets of the Signal Corps. (1) Interv, SigC Hist Sec with 1st Lt Lloyd A. Severson, Signal Corps Sidelights, Vol. I, Pt. II, p. 309. SigC Hist Sec File. (2) MID WDGS, Mil Attaché Rpt 59499, London, 4 Aug 43, sub: German UHF beamed coms radio type, with incls. (Inclosure 2 dates the examination of the captured equipment at 7–14 December 1942.) SigC 413.44 German Sets (ET) T 1324.

The development of radio compasses, radio beacons, radio ranges, and other types of navigational equipment had led also to apparatus for instrument landing systems, by which "blind" pilots could be precisely lined up with the airstrip, directed down the glide path, and safely landed. The equipment had to be accurate to the nth degree and the ground components highly mobile so that they could be shifted from one runway to another as the wind changed. The Aircraft Radio Laboratory had begun to work on the earlier forms of this equipment, particularly devices to indicate angle of descent, and to show, on the compass itself, deviations to left or right. Microwave indicators held the most promise, and, awaiting only the delayed approval of the National Academy of Sciences, the Signal Corps and Air Corps had already chosen Sperry Gyroscope equipment developed in collaboration with Stanford University and the Massachusetts Institute of Technology.

All of this radio gear, whether for air or ground, was essentially for heavy tactical use rather than for the light, mobile, and lower-echelon demands in sight since the Texas maneuvers had tested a new ground conception and the Spanish conflict had demonstrated a new and deadlier capacity of air power. There were in addition to these dozen sets or so another half dozen which were becoming as important singly as many of these together. They were the sets of the immediate future: the vehicular radios SCR-193 and SCR-245, the first walkie-talkies SCR-194 and SCR-195, and the last long-range ground set before the achievement of coupling range to motion, the SCR-197. Even more significant of the prospect were the beginnings of frequency modulation, the Link FM equipment SCR-293 and SCR-294. The impact of emergency gave all of these sudden impetus.[12]

Radar

But the most futuristic of all radio sets was unquestionably radar. Few knew about it, but those who did were certain of its importance. The two years of development which had followed the dramatic tests of May 1937 had consolidated the SCR-268 and brought forth two other models of ground detector equipment, the mobile SCR-270 and the fixed SCR-271. These were the first generation of descent from the parent equipment; and, like them, all of the future airborne radar, MEW radar, and radar countermeasure devices of the Army, each creating families of its own, traced their heritage in a direct line from the SCR-268.

The early demonstration had been successful enough to provide justification for the first serious expansion which the Laboratories had been able to undertake in anticipation of the war. Promptly a Radio Position Finding Section had been formed, to work solely on improving the SCR-268. The day after the demonstration, the project engineers had begun to dismantle the

---

[12] (1) Signal Corps Information Letter, No. 1 (April, 1934), p. 9, No. 2 (July, 1934), p. 9, No. 9 (April, 1936), pp. 10 ff., No. 7 (October, 1935), p. 9, No. 13 (April, 1937), p. 8, No. 16 (January, 1938), pp. 12 ff., No. 17 (April, 1938), p. 11, No. 18 (July, 1938), p. 16, No. 20 (January, 1939), p. 23, No. 21 (April, 1939), p. 8. (2) ARL, Annual Reports, 1931, pp. 23, 32, 34, 1932, Projs 6, 9, 10, 1933, pp. 16, 21, 23, 1934, pp. 13, 19–20, 1937, p. 11, 1938, pp. 7, 18, 1939, pp. 9 ff., 19, 1940, p. 22. (3) R&D hist cited n. 5(5), Vol. III, Pt. 2, Proj 304-A, Vol. I, Pt. 3, Proj 105-A, p. 7, Proj 101-A Proj 304-B, p. 7. (4) John A. Miller, *Men and Volts at War; the Story of General Electric in World War II* (New York: McGraw-Hill Book Company, Inc., 1947), p. 158. (5) Ltr, Asst Chief of AC to CSigO, 10 Oct 39, sub: Proc of instrument landing system, with 19 inds. SigC 160 Gen Contract 26.

equipment preparatory to moving it, because the Chief of Staff, Gen. Malin Craig, although impressed by it, had also been impressed by what he felt was an inadequate amount of secrecy for it. After a brief period of negotiations, the equipment had been established at Fort Hancock on Sandy Hook, where, along the holly-grown dunes of the lonely spit reaching toward one of the most densely populated areas of the world, Captain Corput, the project officer, and Paul E. Watson, the civilian chief of the new section, set the scene of the work.

In many ways Sandy Hook was a natural choice. Fort Hancock was a reservation of the Coast Artillery, for whom the work was being done. The spot was, moreover, not far from Fort Monmouth, and, because it lay athwart heavily traveled military and commercial air routes, would have the same advantage for detecting airplanes by radio pulses as it had had several years previously for detecting ships by heat transmissions. Finally, the location had the advantage of being a peninsula from which the curious could be easily warded off, inasmuch as there was but one land approach. Disadvantages, however, were almost as great. Sandy Hook barely clears the ocean; so that the effort to get the antennas up high enough led to expedients like the use of four 100-foot spruce poles, and, a little later, to a request for room in the Coast Guard lighthouse station at Navesink, where the Atlantic Highlands reach a peak of 225 feet. Sandy Hook also was wholly exposed to the weather—a baking summer heat, an icy winter, and seasonal gales which reached their peak in the devastating hurricane of September 1938. The most distinct drawback of all was the mere fact of the transfer; it caused a loss of several months

which, to the impatience of the principal customers, the Air and Coast Artillery Corps, had to be added on at the other end of the research span.

The initial stage after the move had settled down involved a thorough redesign. Continuing to test the equipment in the laboratories, after the important visitors had departed, the project engineers proved to themselves again what they already knew: that there was much to be done before the device could be called an accurate antiaircraft aid. The thermal element almost immediately proved disappointing, and the step-by-step motor which powered the vertical antenna broke down. "You will see," Lt. Col. William R. Blair explained to General Allison, "that the equipment is still mechanically crude and not very reliable, but it is remarkable that most of our troubles have been mechanical rather than radio. . . ." [13] The pulse-and-echo theory was as sound as the theory of the compression engine. It needed only the mechanical contriving to make it work. Both Blair and Allison moved off the scene just then, Allison leaving office and Blair being overtaken by an illness which caused his retirement a year afterward.

Along the mechanical labyrinths indicated, the growing staff continued the work. One engineer remade the transmitter, another experimented with a cathode-ray oscilloscope receiver, another built antennas. Among those who made significant contributions, although not necessarily this early, were Harold A. Zahl, who pioneered in the development of an ultrahigh-frequency vacuum tube; James Moore, who principally worked out the valuable double-tracking or lobe-switching system;

---

[13] Memo, Dir SCL for CSigO, 26 May 37, sub: Tests of AA detection apparatus. SigC FM (SCL) 413.684 Proj 113.

John J. Slattery, who constructed transmitter antennas; John Marchetti, who contributed to the final design of the keyer; Melvin D. Baller, who developed the final form of the SCR-268's transmitter; John Hessel, the engineer of some of the earlier models of the receiver; and Arthur Vieweger, Robert Heller, and Paul Watson, the chief, who made equivalent contributions to what became the SCR-270.[14]

A detachment of men of the 62d Coast Artillery Regiment, Antiaircraft, stationed at Fort Hancock, augmented the manpower, not merely by guarding the secret site but also by helping to build the equipment and try it out. They were representative of the skilled enlisted man who would be expected to cope with the new detector, and it was invaluable to see how they met its problems. Their commander, 1st Lt. Albert F. Cassevant, also threw in his lot and built an experimental transmitter which worked well enough to be put to use in the course of the ensuing service tests.[15]

The project continued at first in both the 110- and 240-megacycle versions, and with the heat-detector unit as well. All three disappeared before the third and final type of the set had been achieved. For the oncoming service test, which had been set for the end of the fiscal year, June 1938, the availability of tubes determined choice of the 110-megacycle model over the 240-megacycle, which could go no farther, it appeared, without a specially designed transmitter tube. To generate the enormous amount of power needed to send a pulse hard enough so that there would still be something left of it when it rebounded was a matter of the greatest concern. A series of tests on all available high-frequency tubes was resolved temporarily in favor of the RCA model used at the

May demonstration, despite the fact that it took such excessive voltage that its average life was less than twenty hours. A transmitter using six tubes instead of the original two was decided upon, and a model built after the RCA transmitter design. Meanwhile, the Laboratories let a contract to Westinghouse for a more powerful tube.

Interested visitors watched the progress of the work. In January 1938 the Chief Signal Officer came and departed well satisfied; in February the General Staff sent another representative; and in March the Chief of Coast Artillery paid a call. By this time, a number of odd, desolate buildings, half hangar, half barn, had been planned for the gale-swept reservation. They had to be high, because they were antenna shelters; and except for nails, they could contain no metal much above ground level because of the misleading echoes which metal would produce in the equipment. Both Western Electric and Westinghouse were to take up firsthand positions at the site, the government to put up eight of the antenna shelters for the former company and a large trapezoidal structure for the latter.

Experiments and dry runs increasingly pointed toward final elimination of the thermal element. Its claim had been accuracy. Project engineers now believed that they could achieve a comparable accuracy without so much trouble. A method known as lobe switching, suggested by the principle of the radio range station, brought

---

[14] Heller subsequently drowned while on duty in Panama for the installation of some of the first SCR-271's. Watson died in 1943.

[15] Cassevant's long experience with radar later caused him to transfer from the Coast Artillery Corps to the Signal Corps, where, among other assignments, he subsequently became commanding officer of the Evans Signal Laboratory.

about this change. Whereas two towers of a range station transmitted an *A* signal and the other two an *N,* thus creating two dot-dash and two dash-dot lobes of coverage which merged at their outer margins and told the pilot that he was "on the beam," the same principle, applied to the detector equipment, suggested building the receiving antenna in double array, each to cover the lobe of the angle at which it was erected. An antenna system which could be switched from one lobe to another received not one echo but two, which could thus be co-ordinated on the oscilloscope with considerable precision. Again, the theory was sound, and again, the challenge lay in solving the mechanical difficulty.

In June 1938, Colonel Colton became director of the Laboratories.[16] At the same time, the opening of a new fiscal year made an opportunity to redefine the program, to give substance to developments which had been apparent all through the past year. The work split four ways, although with the emphasis still almost wholly upon the original project, the one now officially designated SCR-268 in a secrecy as impenetrable as the Fort Hancock site. What emphasis was left was directed to the first offshoot, which was to become the SCR-270/271. The Radio Position Finding Section was not yet in a position to do much about the third and fourth segments of the radar program. These two projects merely left room to expand in later on. The main work had not reached them. The third was intended to explore the avenue left open by the experiments, earlier in the decade, to detect enemy surface vessels as they approached a friendly coast; it eventually led to equipment called the SCR-296.[17] Experience with radar having already been sufficiently dazzling to sug-

gest that anything might be possible, the fourth was a miscellaneous category, from which emerged in time, and among other items of equipment, the range-finder SCR-547.

Although the work had begun with the single goal of producing a searchlight-laying device for antiaircraft batteries, there had been many evidences that the equipment ought to go beyond that stage and lay the guns directly, without the intermediary of searchlights. If specifications could be changed in order to permit it, and if the forthcoming service test could be hurdled, there was hope that the primary project would mature as a short-range, mobile gun layer. Since the Naval Research Laboratory was much more advanced than the Signal Corps in short-range radar, as much consultation occurred as mutual secrecy tolerated.[18]

The entry of the Air Corps as an interested customer determined the need for a model of longer range, to provide early warning to interceptor squadrons. A change was taking place in this area also. Mobility, important to a detector in use by an antiaircraft crew, did not seem essential to one intended to scan at long range from a permanent defense site. Range rather than mobility was the prime requirement there. In theory, an airplane 93 miles away could be detected at a thousandth of a second,[19] but an airplane 930 miles away would take ten times as long to be detected: a full hundredth of a second. These were the postulates; but the

---

[16] Lt. Col. George L. Van Deusen and Capt. David E. Washburn had served as interim directors.

[17] SCEL hist cited n. 5(4), pp. 316–18.

[18] Interv, SigC Hist Sec with Gen Mauborgne, Ret., Washington, D.C., 1 Dec 48.

[19] I.e., the radio impulse traveling at the speed of light, 186,000 miles per second, and going out from the detector and coming back to it.

increasing speed and range of aircraft, and hence the need to find them earlier and farther, was a sharp reality. Watson was accordingly designing the great fixed towers which became characteristic of the SCR-271, in the hope of extending the range as far as line-of-sight coverage permitted. Mobility was nevertheless quite urgent enough to be retained in the specifications, and as a result the Air Corps equipment, soon after it became a separate project, subdivided into what became known as the SCR-270 and the SCR-271, the mobile and fixed early warning detectors.

The need for mobility had forced SCR-268 development into higher megacycle bands: from 110 as far as 240, although it settled at 205. Because the early warning equipment did not have to be primarily mobile, it could work with the large antenna which the use of longer waves made inescapable. The SCR-270/271 work started out with the RCA long-wave transmitter first built before the gun-laying and early warning functions had become distinct. In August 1938 a preliminary model found a bomber at seventy-five miles, but more was looked for as of the time when the Westinghouse tube would be ready. This item now belonged to the 270/271 effort; the contract had been let with the specific anticipation that, although the work in progress at the time might not need such tubes, the long-range detector certainly would. In October, the company delivered the first samples,[20] and there was hope that the range specification could be more than doubled. It was set at 50 miles, and the engineers wanted to extend it to 120. Many of the engineering problems on the equipment were made simpler by virtue of the SCR-268 work which had already occurred.

The circuits were in 110 megacycles, for example; and for another, there was no need for double-tracking accuracy, or hence, for lobe switching. Even height finding was not called for in the Air Corps' original specifications.

Experiments to use a single antenna system for both transmitting and receiving began in that same autumn, and by spring were consolidated in a noteworthy contribution made by Dr. Zahl, who, by applying the spark-gap principle to the joint switching mechanism, for the first time made it possible to switch the power from the transmitter to the receiver and back again. The design of the SCR-270/271 was good enough altogether for the transmitter to serve all through to Okinawa and the end of the war. Okinawa was not thought of then. At the outset of the project, Panama was the first-priority destination as soon as the equipment could be made.

The Fort Monroe weather was overcast and uncertain in November and December 1938, just as in 1919, when it had frustrated Hoffman's early thermal tests at nearby Langley Field. As a result, the heat-detector unit did not prove itself. More than 4,000 readings brought the conclusion that the SCR-268-T1 fell short of the mark in accuracy. The specifications called for a maximum deviation of one degree in both azimuth and elevation, but the average error was nearly four degrees (70.9 mils) in azimuth and more than two in elevation. Actually, the error was not so great as that, for the figures averaged readings taken at all angles. It was then imperfectly understood that radar's sharp eyesight became blindness at low

---

[20] The Signal Corps nomenclature given to the tube was VT-122. It remained standard in all World War II SCR-270's and 271's.

RADAR. *The SCR-268 is shown above in action in the Nettuno area of Italy, and the SCR-270, below, is shown installed in the Ryukyu Islands.*

angles. From this point of view, a short-range set was especially likely to fail. Yet although the azimuthal error was indeed bad, the elevation error was not: it was close enough to the deviation allowance to be encouraging. The heat-detector element nevertheless could not survive this demonstration, and again and finally went out of the specifications for both of the Coast Artillery Corps detector projects, this and the SCR-296. The engineers willingly dispensed with it, for lobe switching gave them a much better substitute.

If the SCR-268 had faltered in this aspect, however, in others it had won through. For the first time, the flight of artillery shells was reflected upon an oscilloscope; and, after a bad moment when a relay jarred open, the equipment appeared to be rugged enough to withstand the shock of nearby gunfire. Its range, furthermore, was distinctly superior to what was required, another fact which led to the stepping-up of work on the longer-range SCR's 270 and 271. An experimental pressure-cabined bombardment airplane, precursor of the B-29, had flown in to Langley from Wright Field; and this short-range set tracked it to thirty miles. The most unexpected triumph of all came during trials with a B-10-B which was being used in one of the regular night tests. The pilot was supposed to keep within a 180-degree arc over land; but without realizing that he was being blown off course·by a high gale he got sixty miles out to sea before he surrendered to the urgent warnings of the SCR-268 engineers who had him exactly plotted on the oscilloscope. This misadventure helped to persuade Air Corps opinion that the equipment could be considerably more than an intermediate accessory to air patrol.

Radar gave promise of patrolling at as long a range as an airplane could, at the same time giving the skies a much finer combing. Most noteworthy, however, was the fact that in this return of the hapless B-10 to the safety of land, radar heralded its use as an aid to air navigation.

In little more than a month after the service test was over, the Coast Artillery Board wrote up its decision. Electronic detectors would replace their sound locators so soon as they could be standardized and produced in quantity. The time lapse between a service test and general field use put this prospect some distance into the future, and sound locators did not forthwith collapse on the junk heap, to be replaced by the newest thing in radar. Even farther in the future was the hope to eliminate searchlights. Searchlight-control radar remained standard throughout the oncoming war.[21] Further, since the device could give an ack-ack crew the data for firing, the board could hope to put aside the searchlight specification, in order to plan in terms of the magic invisibility which was its true spirit.

With lobe switching reducing the antenna size, a 205-megacycle SCR-268-T2 model was ready by May 1939. It was never service tested, because the beginning of war in September left no question of the priority of the early warning set. Instead, Type 3—the SCR-268-T3, a genuinely mobile set even if short of what had been hoped for—was quickly standardized and put into production on the unimpeachable ground that something would be better than nothing. The SCR-268 "assumed an odd role" in the war.

Nobody liked it very much but everybody wanted it very badly. . . . Its performance

---

[21] AN/TPL-1.

was satisfactory for pointing searchlights, although it was considered too bulky. It was not quite accurate enough for precision gun-laying, but it was the only available American set that permitted an effective antiaircraft barrage through overcast. Its power gave it greater range than necessary for either of these . . . purposes, but not quite enough . . . for . . . early warning. . . .[22]

By June 1939 the early warning radar was undergoing daily tests from the two-towered Navesink lighthouse station, the "Twin Lights" of the coastal region. It tracked Mitchel Field aircraft out to ranges approaching 150 miles, but no more than 80 could be relied on. The first of the Westinghouse tubes had now been built into the transmitter. It was a very large water-cooled triode, oscillating at the 110 megacycles determined for the equipment; at its peak, it gave the extraordinary output of 100 kilowatts. However, 110 megacycles indicated a wavelength of nearly nine feet and proportionately large antenna size. If electronic detection were to achieve variety and flexibility, large rotating antennas and huge towers were out of the question. The British were using even very much longer waves; their emerging Chain Home system, a chain of 240-foot and 350-foot towers fencing in the homeland, housed radar constructed in the 23-megacycle band.[23] But with thirty times as much area to protect, the continental United States could not consider anything so fixed. Microwaves looked like the answer. The original research had begun in microwaves. If a tube could be evolved which empowered microwave transmissions, the whole course of radar development could change.

The two versions of the early warning equipment were now confirmed. It was the SCR-270 particularly which was being tested from the Twin Lights station; the set was to be trailer-mounted and at least as mobile as trucks and highways could make it. The other series, the SCR-271, was intended for fixed locations, usually in permanent buildings. The course of the war which made fixed radar vital to the United Kingdom passed it by so far as the United States was concerned. The SCR-268 and 270, not the SCR-271, were sets which saw the wider use, for the very fact that they were movable, and the SCR-270 remained standard throughout the war. In that final peacetime summer it was approaching its service test, at a rate considerably accelerated over the schedule of the SCR-268. Whereas more than a year and a half had elapsed between the day when the original 268 was shown to the high command and the day when the Fort Monroe readings began, the SCR-270 service test and its preliminary unveiling were almost simultaneous.

This event took place late in the year. The war had begun in Europe; Poland lay conquered. Again Secretary of War Woodring, Gen. George C. Marshall and Maj. Gen. Henry H. Arnold, and other official visitors were present for a demonstration. This time two models of equipment were used and two sites chosen, one being Twin Lights, the other, West Peak in Meriden, Connecticut, a thousand-foot rock formation not far from the center of the state. From the eastern tip of Long Island to the New Jersey coast beyond Atlantic Highlands, the two sets tracked target aircraft, one following the northeastward course, the other the southwestward, and consolidating their information by

---

[22] Harry M. Davis, The Signal Corps Development of U.S. Army Radar Equipment, Pt. II, 1945, pp. 96–97. SigC Hist Sec File.

[23] Rowe, *One Story of Radar*, p. 32.

telephone for it to be plotted. At one point, the Twin Lights station suddenly went off the air, but a sigh of relief followed when Secretary Woodring was discovered to have brushed the stop button on the rectifier unknowingly. Continuing tests through December proved the set, and in May 1940 the Army adopted it.

Thus the Army arrived at the onset of war in possession of radar. Barely in possession, but in the race with competitors. British radiolocation research jumped ahead under the stimulus of war, just as did American work two years later, when the United States felt the impact. Lord Beaverbrook picturesquely compared the Chain Home system to the golden cockerel which crowed at the enemy's approach. In the close alliance formed by war, Britain opened some of its secrets to France. Neither the Soviet Union, Italy, nor Japan had radar, but in 1940 the Japanese began to employ pulsed radiations and by 1942 produced early warning sets comparable to the SCR-271 and 270, these being the Taichi-6 and 7 respectively.[24] Germany had not only the Wuerz-

burg and Freya, but also other types in process at various stages from blueprinting to initial manufacture. When the combatants began to use airplanes in World War I, the Wrights' invention was eleven years old and had been in the public domain during that time. When World War II began, radar was less than four years old and a heavy secret. To those confronted with the problem of getting American radar into full-scale action in the conflict, the comparison had some point.[25]

---

[24] *Taichi* means *land-based*. R. I. Wilkinson, "A Short Survey of Japanese Radar," *Electrical Engineering*, LXV (August–September, 1946), 370–77 and 455–63.

[25] A number of sources other than those already cited for this section are pertinent to it, the work of the late Harry M. Davis, in fact, being continuously valuable. Among the sources are: (1) Davis, The Signal Corps Development of U.S. Army Radar Equipment, 1945, Pts. II (already cited) and III; (2) A Brief History of the Development of Aircraft Detection Equipment by the Radio Position Finding Section of the Signal Corps Laboratories, Ft. Monmouth, N. J., 1945; this appears also as Chapter X of the Historical Report of the Signal Corps Engineering Laboratories; (3) A Brief History of Early Radar Development in

the U.S. Army, 1945; in a slightly abridged form, this is to be found also under the title Early Radar Development Work by the Signal Corps. All in SigC Hist Sec File. (4) Ltr, President SigC Bd to CSigO, 22 Nov 39, sub: Demonstration of SCR-270-T1 scheduled for 29 Nov 39, Incls 1 and 2, draft speeches. SigC CE 334 Case 312, Folder 1. (5) Interv, SigC Hist Sec with Arthur L. Vieweger, Tech Staff Evans Sig Lab, Belmar, N. J., 15 Apr 47. (6) Notes on German Radar and on Ultra and Infra-Red Equipment, 29 May 45, 6824 DIC (MIS)/M. 1168. OCMH Foreign Studies Br File.

The following are printed sources: (7) Harold A. Zahl, "From an Early Radar Diary," *Coast Artillery Journal*, XCI, No. 2 (March–April, 1948), 8–15. (8) Roger B. Colton, "Radar in the United States Army: History and Early Development at the Signal Corps Laboratories, Fort Monmouth, N. J.," *Proceedings of the IRE* [Institute of Radio Engineers], III, No. 11 (November, 1945), 740–53. (9) "Radar: the Technique," pp. 142, 144–45, 196, and (10) "Radar: a Primer," p. 140, both in *Fortune*, XXXII, No. 4 (October, 1945). (11) I. E. Mouromtseff, "A Quarter-Century of Electronics," *Electrical Engineering*, LXVI, No. 2 (February, 1947), 171–77. (12) M. J. Kelly, "Radar and Bell Laboratories," pp. 221–55, (13) "Radar: a Story in Pictures," pp. 256–82, and (14) F. R. Lack, "Radar and Western Electric," pp. 283–94, all in *Bell Telephone Magazine*, XXIV (1945–46). (15) "The SCR-268 Radar," *Electronics*, XVIII (1945), 100–108. (16) David O. Woodbury, *Battlefronts of Industry, Westinghouse in World War II* (New York and London: J. Wiley, 1948), pp. 104 ff., 268 ff. (17) A. H. Sullivan, Jr., "German Electronics in World War II," *Electrical Engineering*, LXVIII, No. 5 (May, 1939), pp. 403–09.

PART TWO

THE LIMITED AND UNLIMITED EMERGENCIES

CHAPTER VI

The Pace of Emergency

The whole military arithmetic multiplies "Men, Material, and Me," the useful catch phrase of West Point lectures. Infinite variety resides in them. Apart from Me—a matter of personal concern, vital but up to the individual—the other two represent the aims of military preparedness at any stage. Men and equipment, equipment and men, are the two ends of the same quarterstaff, the striking power of the Army.

To the 1939 Signal Corps the problem of men was not so much acquiring them as training them. Numbers were less significant than capability. The organization was certainly smaller than it wanted to be; but so long as war stood off at a distance there was no prospect of extreme increase, and the important thing was to make sure that the men on hand could execute the signal mission. This mission was performed with equipment which in the case of the Signal Corps was always specialized and often intricate enough to throw the whole schedule of training well back of the point at which an emergency would create a demand for finished products. The readying of equipment could be measured at the successive stages of laboratory test, service tests, field tests. The relative preparedness of the human side of the equation could be tried out in field problems, maneuvers, and ultimately in "games" whose imitation of war approached the actuality.

Since its reduction after World War I, the Signal Corps tactical mission had stood virtually unchanged. Tactical theory had not. New developments pressed in, particularly ground mobility and air power. The provisional Infantry division typified one, the accelerated importance of aircraft warning, the other. In the persisting point of view of the Signal Corps, both gave more exigency to the old question never settled to its satisfaction, the argument for a unified field signal system. Communications were by nature single, and responsibility for them ought not to be divided: in essence, this was the Signal Corps position.

Still spelled out in the words of 1921, the Corps' ground tactical mission carried down only through the divisional level. During two decades when no higher echelon than a division existed, and when even divisions existed only in fractions, this arrangement seemed effectually to wipe out all Signal Corps tactical responsibility and to alter its position as a combat arm. Responsibility for construction, operation, issue and basic maintenance stopped short of the brigade; and from there on, the Infantry, Artillery, and Cavalry, not the Signal Corps, carried communications forward "to the barbed wire" (the Signal Corps could never forget that General Pershing had given his signal officer, Brig. Gen. Edgar Russel, responsibility "for all communications from St. Nazaire to the barbed wire").[1] Controlling their own communications, the combat arms moreover devised their own signal organization and conducted their own signal training.

Apparently, then, the tactical duty of the Signal Corps was chiefly a matter of developing and supplying equipment which it was not to use, and of training men whom it was not to supervise. Signal Corps officers frequently found themselves wishing that the whole determination rested with them. They felt that they could be trusted to know what was best, because they were the Army's communications experts.

The Signal Corps was charged with the training of specialists and of special units. Such technical supervision, carried throughout the field forces,[2] was a duty of long standing, and existed in other technical services, but it often put the Signal Corps in a quandary. When developments advanced signal equipment into the realm of electronics and signal tables of organization to the stage where specialists and special units were listed well front in the order of battle, as seemed to be foreshadowed in radar, aircraft warning companies, and radio intelligence companies, there was one problem. When, on the other hand, improvements made signal equipment simpler, then the Signal Corps' argument for specialists was weakened and, in its effort to control tactical communications, it had less reason to plead operational complexities and the need for detailed training. If, for example, page teletype were to supplant Boehme, or pushbutton voice sets take the place of continuous wave, then the Signal Corps mission could be almost limited to development, installation, and maintenance. These were service functions, not tactical.

Yet the Signal Corps had always been an arm as well as a service. Was it to abandon its dual role? Should not the Signal Corps once again furnish all communications in the Infantry, and communications in the Field Artillery at least through the regimental level? "It is not my intention to present any new argument," General Mauborgne wrote to General Craig.[3] "The War Department is thoroughly familiar with the entire subject and what has been done." He merely wanted to say that he had learned that an informal survey taken during the Texas tests of the proposed triangular division had shown the Infantry predominantly in favor of the Signal Corps view, the Field Artillery against it, and corps area commanders "about equally divided pro and con." Why not effect a compromise, "turning over Infantry communications to the Signal Corps and leaving Field Artillery communications unchanged? "[4]

He had no more success in extending Signal Corps tactical boundaries than any of his predecessors had had. The General Staff did declare his proposed signal company satisfactory for the new division, allowed a division signal officer a small reserve of signal troops to move about from one duty to another, and gave radio intelligence companies a place in the table of organization for field armies. But the General Staff did not change its view that field communication is an instrument of field command, and that communications

[1] Memo, Maj Gen George S. Gibbs, Ret., for Gen Marshall, 27 Jun 40, sub: Sig coms requirements in preparation for war. SigC 381 Gen 16, Mar–Aug 40.

[2] FM 100-5, Tentative Field Service Regulations: Operations, 1 Oct 39, par. 86.

[3] AG Ltr to CSigO, 24 May 37, sub: SigC troops for test of proposed inf div. AG 320.2 (5-5-37) (Misc.)-C.

[4] Memo, CSigO for CofS, 13 Jun 38, sub: Coms for Inf and FA. SigC 676 Gen, 1918–38.

troops should belong to the field arms in which they serve.[5]

Uniform training and co-operative staff action were therefore all the more worth stressing. Actual use of the walkie-talkie or the sound-powered telephone, as well as the simple training required for them, would be in the hands of the forward troops. Use of SCR-268's, 270's, and 271's would require special training, of units which the Air Corps or Coast Artillery Corps would probably take over. Middle- and long-range transmitting and receiving equipment and all the network of wire where tactical communications approach the strategic would, like radar, require the closest possible technical supervision. For tactical signal officers who might feel frustrated by an apparent obligation to make up systems composed of differently trained men, the answer would lie in their ability to serve two masters: their branch of the service and their field assignment. The obligation of officers assigned within the Signal Corps itself was to think in terms flexible and various enough to satisfy the needs of all arms and integrated enough to respond to the entire Signal Corps mission.

Somewhat the same situation existed with aircraft warning. It should have been expected to fit squarely within the framework of national military planning. Unlike the triangular division, which was a weapon being forged to strike an offensive blow, an aircraft warning system was a defensive measure. Defense of the homeland in the most unassailably moral sense it was, and therefore public support was not lacking for it. Nevertheless, the Aircraft Warning Service was something of a maverick within the armed forces. Nobody was quite sure who owned it. Responsibility for air defense, including the

Aircraft Warning Service rested with the commanding generals of the four continental armies and of the overseas departments.

Studies made in 1931 for erecting a warning service upon the existing Anti-Aircraft Artillery Intelligence Service had produced the conclusion that it would be a mistake to assign anything so extensive to a single arm or service, because it would embrace both military and civilian agencies and would merge telephone, telegraph, and radio facilities.[6] Aircraft warning was a command function, like tactical communications. In relation to it the Chief Signal Officer found himself in much the same position as with Infantry or Cavalry responsibility. There had to be aircraft warning equipment to suit both the Coast Artillery Corps and the Air Corps. The Signal Corps was preparing ultimately to offer SCR-268's, 270's, and 271's, but no frontier or sector commands existed, as must be the case if these radars were to be assigned, their sites chosen, and their crews trained. The general assumption was that individual aircraft warning services would cover the nation's coastal frontiers and oversea possessions, in terms of large, fixed defense installations. Already composed of sound locators, searchlights, harbor artillery, mines, and

<hr>

[5] (1) AG Ltr to CSigO, 3 Aug 38, sub: Requirements for SigC pers. AG 320.2 (3-2-38) (Misc.)-C. (2) WDGS WP&T Div, Texas Infantry Division Reorganization Training Tests, Sec 3, Signal Communication, pp. 95–109.

[6] Eventually the Air Corps came to be the party most concerned, although especially after the invention of radar the Signal Corps was scarcely less involved. (1) Memo, ACofS WPD for ACofS G-3, 30 Nov 31, sub: G-3 study 6 Nov 31 on rpt of joint AC-AA exercises Langley Field Mar 30. WPD 3640. (2) Arthur P. Watts, History of the Air Defense Command, pp. 92–98, and Apps. 1, 4, 5, 6. AF Archives COMD-AD-AAF-HI, 26 Feb 48 (1804-1).

interceptor airfields, these aircraft warning sites would be further enhanced by the new electronic detectors.

The aircraft warning program was up for study simultaneously with the communications problem of the new ground army. The Signal Corps was told to plan aircraft warning companies for both the fixed defenses and the mobile forces, "making the maximum use of existing facilities, including commercial, military and naval installations." [7] Extensive preparation for detector sites, information centers, and the aircraft warning units began in the summer of 1939. At the same time, the last of the series of peacetime maneuvers got under way.

Testing Tactical Communications

War was now close enough so that maneuvers seemed less strange to the localities where they occurred, although often still unwelcome. Citizens who denied the approach of war were likely to object to the presence of any army at all; and those who felt it near found no comfort in the thought of being defended by this one. To the altogether uninitiated, the maneuvering was no more than a few summer Guardsmen picnicking in the open and staying off the highway when told not to jam up the Saturday traffic to the beach.

Faced with shortages in equipment and personnel, signal officers usually drew on the local market for both. Thus, as often as not, exercises which had been designed to train the Army under modern conditions of war used a civilian wire communication system, with rented civilian equipment and with pole lines constructed by civilian crews, and dependent largely upon civilian switchboard girls, teletypewriter operators, telephone installation and

maintenance men, linemen, and clerical help.[8]

When communications troops arrived for maneuvers, their officers ordinarily had only about three weeks to train and organize them into headquarters signal sections, first in groups according to their duties and later as signal sections under supervision of the signal officer. Location of command posts was a lame compromise. Commanders realized that sites in the field would give valuable training, afford a basis for testing equipment and for ferreting out weaknesses in organization, put factors of time and space in proper perspective, and give desk officers a feel of the ground. But the proper thing was not easy to do. Communications troops were required not only to conduct the theoretical problem but also, as an immediately practical mission, to put in a communication system for the umpires and keep it going; construction by commercial contract was unrealistic; temporary lancepole lines were undependable in bad weather; and a want of enough leased trunk lines between army and corps would in part defeat the object of the exercise. Consequently, command posts often were placed, not in actual field position, but instead in the nearby town or on the military reservation, in order to be served by the existing cables.

Troops were still practicing with old equipment and often setting themselves

---

[7] (1) AG Ltr to CSigO, 10 Mar 39, sub: AWS. AG 660.2 AA (3-8-39) (Misc.)-E. (2) WPD file 3640, *passim*. The Chief Signal Officer submitted an initial study on 26 June 1939 and estimates on 28 August and 3 November 1939.

[8] See, for example, (1) Wisc. Telephone Co., Communications Report, Second Army Maneuvers, August 1-31, 1940; (2) Traffic Dept, Southwest Bell Telephone Co., Report on Commercial Telephone Communications for Anti-Aircraft Warning Service, U.S. Army, etc., 7-11 May 40. SigC 354.2 Second Army.

problems which had mellowed out of World War I. To make an exercise look like even a moderate success, commanders assumed existence of conditions which some of them knew would not exist when the troops were committed to war. The few airplanes sounded like eggbeaters, and in any case the maneuverers fought a ground war. Except in the airplanes and for the horse cavalry, radio was wholly contingent upon wire. There was no frequency problem with wire, whereas the radio art as it then stood, with every band allocation crowded, did not permit operation of an entire army net without interference. One maneuver report after another emphasized the importance of wire—wire in constantly increasing amounts, because good voice communication was to be vital to any army whose improved vehicles allowed it to stretch over a wide area. Yet if troops were to traverse a wide area, a wireless system would seem to be indicated, and gradually the reports began to present this view also. "There is a real need for securing new data on the use of radio in a war of movement," a Third Army signal officer had anticipated long before, and he was not alone.[9]

The summer of 1939 was no climate for war plans and war maneuvers. Talk of foreign quarrels emphasized the fact that they were foreign. Defense measures such as a program for 5,500 airplanes blew gustily about in Congress; the military held up a wet finger, not sure what the weather was to be and remembering the last tempest uncertainly. Newsreels of a mighty parade down the Champs Elysées suggested that France had an invincible army; and the fact that there had been no world war after any of the crises of the past decade softened the alarm felt as the Germans produced a sinister six-month

schedule of them. March 1938, September 1938, March 1939 had threatened and passed over. There was no reason to know that September 1939 would bring the final crisis.

Remarks made by Maj. Gen. Hugh A. Drum in anticipation of his first Army maneuvers showed the state of things military clearly enough. "The First Army as it has taken the field this month," he said, "is not in fact an army." It was a collection of individual units, partially equipped, "woefully short" in almost everything which experience suggested was essential. There were no corps or army headquarters. Division headquarters were skeletons. If he filled in the gaps with antiaircraft and coastal defense troops, and from the National Guard, the ROTC, and the Reserve, he did so by sacrificing their normal duties and training them in functions other than those they needed practice in.[10]

Yet the exercises must be held, whatever their shortcomings. In them, in an effort to imagine a situation which did not exist, which nobody wanted to exist, but in which the Army found its reason for existence, the mission of each branch of the service stood out clearly. It was hard to know whether the mission were being executed. How know, for instance, whether you were successfully killing any of the men opposite you when you had distinguished none of them as enemies? Devoid of the fears and suspicions which alone give war a meaning, war games had fundamentally none. Much of the routine aspect of Army peacetime maneuvers

[9] Ltr, Col James H. Van Horn, Sig Officer IV Corps, to CSigO, 23 Oct 36, sub: Rpt on Third Army command post exercise. SigC 354.2 Third Army, 1936.
[10] *Congressional Record*, 76th Cong, 2d Sess, LXXXV, App., p. 237.

came directly from this lack of source. They were a double negative.

Negatively they could test many things. If, for example, assault wire worked in Wisconsin, it might or might not work in Burma; but if it did not work in Wisconsin, it could certainly not be counted upon for the ruggeder use of war. Even the prospect of maneuvers could show up wants. The two especially urgent signal equipment needs wcrc radio communication for vehicles in motion, and wire systems which could carry heavy message traffic at longer ranges than customary. Wire systems always took precedence in the maneuver planning. Consideration of teletypewriter equipment was much in the foreground because of the obvious need to speed up telegraphy. The TG-5 was right enough for the telegrapher himself, but field commanders were loath to use it because of the inconvenience of having to write the message out by hand and get an operator to pound it out. The Signal Corps Laboratories had been tentatively working on their lightweight field printer for several years.[11]

Now the First Army maneuvers, at Plattsburg in upper New York State, toward the end of August 1939, put commercial teletype equipment to field tests. Colonel Colton, who was there as an observer, thought it impracticable in rapidly moving situations and urged continued development of the Laboratories' field printer, the TG-7-T3, which he preferred to any of the commercial printers then in use.[12] To the extent that the maneuvers had been heavily dependent upon leased teletypewriter service, he was right, for no army could afford to assume that the Bell System would be on hand wherever needed. Colton also felt that the chief signal deficiency during the Plattsburg

maneuvers was the lack of standardized telephone switchboard facilities at division, corps, and army level. Everyone praised the EE-8 field telephone, and Colton spoke well of W-110 field wire. Army and corps message centers at Plattsburg handled no radio traffic. Their radio was set up only on an emergency basis, so supplementary to wire that it was not called into use at all during the maneuvers.

But despite the pre-eminence of wire, vehicular radio was a much more pressing question. Artillerymen and infantrymen alike used the obsolescent loop-antenna ground radio sets SCR-131 and 161, as well as the longer-range 171. The operators themselves rather liked these old radios because they could take hard knocks with very little need for repair. But they were continuous-wave sets only, and like the field telegraph made it necessary for all messages to be written out upon a blank form and then sent in International Morse code. Voice communication was to be desired, and to a degree it was available. The SCR-193 and SCR-245 were vehicular equipment with which it was possible not only to communicate at sixty miles by the conventional continuous wave, but also to get fifteen-mile communication, by voice and while in motion, over the headset and microphone. These were standard equipment, but the sounds received were often forced to swim through a sea of static.

For its maneuvers, the First Army had been provided with too few SCR-245's and, at that, with no homogeneous sets. In at least one case, an organization went all

---

[11] Signal Corps Information Letter, No. 9 (April, 1936), p. 12, and No. 14 (July, 1937), p. 9.

[12] Ltr, Col Colton, Dir SCL, to CSigO, 20 Oct 39, sub: Observers' rpts on First Army maneuvers at Plattsburg 20–26 Aug 39. SigC 354.2 First Army 3, 1938–Oct 39.

the way through the maneuvers without benefit of vehicular radio. This was the 1st Tank Company. About a week before departure for Plattsburg, the company had received ten SCR-245's, but the sets lacked cords and could not be installed.[13] The Signal Corps had been able to issue components only piecemeal as they were developed and procured, now a transmitter, now a receiver, now an antenna, now a battery. Public economy still required the Army to exhaust old equipment or parts before obtaining and issuing anything new. Consequently, field units had to request individual components over a period of several months before they could assemble any kind of set, and the result was generally heterogeneous. Ordinarily, moreover, the field troops had not sufficiently trained their men to install the radios. The only unit which met this problem at all well was the 7th Cavalry Brigade (Mechanized), probably because of the presence of Capt. Grant A. Williams, an officer who claimed a pioneer's part in the development of tank radio.

In this field, the SCR-193 and 245 were not ideal. Williams said that "the old SCR-193 . . . bears almost the same relations to communications as the Springfield Rifle does to the Infantry." [14] It added 200 pounds to the vehicle which carried it and had to be manually tuned, with the ever-present likelihood of cutting in upon somebody else's frequency. Signal Corps engineers got much experience in suppressing vehicular radio noise from their troubles with the 193, which they could never get to work satisfactorily in a moving vehicle until they discovered ways of eliminating the crackling static created both by the tank's electrical system and by the friction of the treads.[15]

Along with the SCR-177 and 188, the stationary ground sets, the SCR-193 and 245 were among the early Signal Corps equipment to employ the superheterodyne receiver. Hitherto, Army receivers had used only the tuned radio-frequency circuit, which was simple and sturdy but not very sensitive. When the initial patent rights to superheterodyne radio expired and better tubes began to be made, the Signal Corps Laboratories had developed two new receivers, and it was the second of these, the BC-312, which both the 193 and the 245 employed. The SCR-245 was even heavier than the SCR-193, and its operator had to manipulate no fewer than seven tuning regulators. But at the wish of the Infantry, Cavalry, and Field Artillery, the Signal Corps had equipped it with both crystal and master oscillator circuits. As the Laboratories' initial step toward the use of crystals to control the frequencies in combat radio, the SCR-245 had specific significance; and in any case, despite their cumbersomeness or interference or the annoyance of having to assemble them in driblets, both of these vehicular radios were points of advance.

A really promising pair of items of Signal Corps equipment in 1939 maneuvers was the SCR-194 and 195. They were the first walkie-talkies. They were the Laboratories' earliest experiment in short-range radiotelephone transceivers, the

---

[13] Memo, Capt James D. O'Connell, O/C Radio Com Projs SCL, for Dir SCL, 16 Oct 39, sub: Comments on First Army maneuvers Plattsburg. In same file.

[14] Ltr, Col Grant A. Williams, Ret., to Dr. G. R. Thompson, OCMH, 31 Dec 49, p. 9. SigC Hist Sec File.

[15] Yet even after the advent of its successor SCR-506, the 193 remained in very wide use for infantry divisions. Of the nine vehicular sets assigned to the radio section of the signal company of an infantry division as late as 1944, eight were SCR-193's. TM 11-227, Radio Communication Equipment, 10 Apr 44.

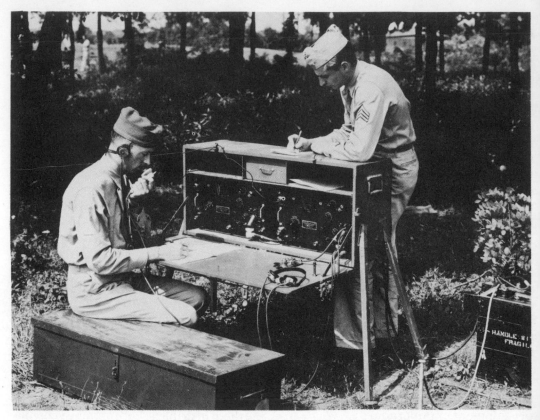

THE SCR–177. *Receiving position showing the BC 314–C and BC 312–C receivers.*

fused word *transceiver* indicating alternate transmitting and receiving on the same two tubes. Crystal calibration was built into them. The 194 operated in a Field Artillery frequency range of 27–52 megacycles. The 195 was set at 52–65 megacycles for the Infantry. Both were thus experiments in very high frequency. Designed for use on the ground, in a vehicle, or on a soldier's back, model sets weighing about twenty-five pounds had been tested as early as 1934. At that time the Laboratories had decided to take out tone transmission, for Morse code, and make them voice sets only. In this way they became field radiotelephones, and shadows of

things to come. Equipped with dry batteries and whip antennas, revised models had passed Infantry and Field Artillery service tests in 1935 and 1936, and were supposed to have gone into production and first issue in 1937. Short of being produced under a wartime program, however, and issued to a wartime army, they remained all but nonexistent. The interesting difference between them and some of the other items developed during the mid-1930's was precisely in their promise. They were distinct efforts at mobility, notably divergent from conceptions of immobilized warfare.

The SCR-194 and 195 represented,

moreover, determined attempts to break through the frequencies barricade. The frequency bands allotted to military use seemed chock-full. To serve the conventional ground arms with them had appeared to be as much as could be hoped for. Then when the expansion of the Air Corps began, when Infantry communications were pinpointed almost to the individual soldier, and when an armored force took shape, the demand for frequency allocation threatened a nightmare. When the 1st Armored Division, for example, wanted one hundred radio channels, the Radiofrequency Control Section could assign only forty-five. At that, "the congestion which will occur within the Armored Force will be extreme," the section chief, Maj. Wesley T. Guest, commented. "[It will] tax to the fullest extent the capabilities of the SCR-245 and SCR-193 sets." [16]

The efforts to escape overcrowding had been prodding radio to notable advances. One was the increasing attractiveness of crystal control, because a process which disciplined a radio, as crystals could, into remaining strictly upon its own frequencies saved other sets from cross drift and somewhat eased the congestion simply by helping to get the most use out of each frequency. Along with this, the effort to open more channels had driven radio development into ever higher frequency bands. Supposing a channel to be 10 kilocycles wide (10,000 cycles), there would be 100 channels in the span of 1 megacycle (1,000,000 cycles). Thus if equipment could be successfully set at megacycle calibrations, there would be room in the very high frequency and ultrahigh-frequency bands for all sorts of special purposes. To the Signal Corps, parceling out the Army's allotted bands, so much to one service, so

much to another, this meant that while the long-range corps and division sets had to remain where they already were, a whole segment of short-range sets all the way to platoon radios could be transferred. The lower section of the frequency band would be relieved; the upper section would not be filled up for some time.

This line of reasoning presumed an orderly development. It did not take into account an upheaval in communications which would throw upon American military radio a burden as big as the globe. The Laboratories engineers had turned their attention to stretching the rigid allotment by developing equipment in the very high (or ultrahigh) ranges, when peace exploded. The Germans roared into war, the United States entered a limited emergency.

FM

One cast of opinion, within both the Signal Corps and its using arms, held that war abroad and maneuvers at home argued for basic changes, possibly for a whole new body of equipment to meet the new tactical organization and doctrine now winning acceptance. Colton, being in a position to do so as director of the Laboratories, and urged by Watson, Capt. James D. O'Connell, Hessel, William S. Marks, and others, frankly set about to create a demand for more effective radio communications, especially for better stabilized tuning and for radio sets which could be precisely held to frequency by the use of crystal control. Assembling into a display almost everything which the Laboratories had ready, he started it off to

[16] Memo, Maj Guest for CSigO, 19 Aug 40, sub: Armored Force radio com. SigC 413.44 Armored Force (Sets) 1, 1940.

the combat arms.[17] "Compared to the equipment that was to come, his 'bag of tricks' was small indeed. He did have an SCR-245 with an actual bona fide crystal, an SCR-197, an enormous thing in a truck tractor and a big house trailer, some primitive forms of microwave beam equipment and a pilot model of a . . . Police set built under Armstrong." [18] The destination was Fort Knox, Kentucky, headquarters of the Mechanized Cavalry Board. For three weeks in October and November, 1939, the Signal Corps showed its equipment. Ultrahigh-frequency models in 400, 600, and 1,200 megacycles were the particular object of pride.

But what was most to ease the problem of frequency congestion, although its early limitations and untried potentialities as yet denied it more than a scattering of Signal Corps support, was also on display at Fort Knox. It was frequency modulation. Army radio equipment was amplitude-modulated. If all that could be done to escape overcrowding was to move development from high frequencies to very high and from very high to ultrahigh, the ultimate prospect was not encouraging. A solution to the problem of producing a radio free from interference and static involved not merely moving to very high frequencies but finding better ways of using them as well. Stormy weather, lightning, and summer humidity all affected radio reception, and the roaring, sputtering, and snapping set up by the unshielded spark-plug system of gasoline engines made vehicular radio almost impossible. Skilled operators in attendance upon the fixed equipment at a remote receiving station could often capture a message through static and interference but were resigned to being blacked out from time to time. Vehicular radio was constantly beset. Even

when the truck or command car which carried it was not in motion and its engine not running, any other vehicle passing by caused trouble and a march column made the radio all but unusable.

Edwin H. Armstrong appeared to have found a solution. He had by this time been making contributions to radio science for thirty years, his name being spoken with Marconi's. His more recent experiments had come to a visible climax in a great steel tower transmitter set on the Palisades at Alpine, New Jersey, and overlooking the Hudson opposite Yonkers. This was the first frequency-modulation transmitter. The electronic industry had soon begun following up Dr. Armstrong's invention, and the General Electric Company had made FM receivers and erected two FM transmitters, one on the roof of its plant in Schenectady, the other on the thirty-one-story State Office Building in Albany, fifteen miles away.

In the autumn of 1938 Comdr. Joseph R. Redman, USN, had seen the General Electric equipment tested in Schenectady. "He believes thoroughly," Colonel Crawford told General Mauborgne, "in the future of frequency modulation as applied to the requirements of the military serv-

---

[17] (1) SCL, Annual Report, 1940, pp. 24–25. (2) Interv, SigC Hist Sec with Maj Gen Roger B. Colton, Ret., New York, N. Y., 14 Feb 50.

[18] Ltr, Williams to Thompson, cited n. 14, p. 4. "Colonel Williams' description of the last named set was an error. It was originally intended for aircraft work." MS comment by Dr. Edwin H. Armstrong, 17 Nov 51. SigC Hist Sec File.

Maj. Gen. James D. O'Connell subsequently pointed out that the "bag of tricks" was a sizable one at the time, representing major accomplishments in FM. The microwave beam equipment was primitive only in the sense that it represented the earliest form of practical microwave radio. Actually, in production at the Signal Corps Laboratories, it was running ahead of the radio art of those days. MS comment by Gen O'Connell, Deputy CSigO, 1953. In same file.

DR. EDWIN H. ARMSTRONG *receiving the Legion of Merit from Maj. Gen. Harry C. Ingles, Chief Signal Officer, in 1946.*

ices, particularly aircraft," and added his own recommendation "that the Signal Corps investigate frequency modulation with a view to possible adaptation for Army needs." [19] The Signal Corps did so at once. Redman's suggestion of airborne applications prompted the dispatching of Lt. Col. Hugh Mitchell, director of the Aircraft Radio Laboratory, to look at the Schenectady equipment. At the same time, Oliver Lewis, a radio engineer in the Research and Development Division, expressed his opinion that the disadvantages of FM "far outweigh any advantages claimed for increased power and freedom from noise interference." In part, he cited

the wide frequency band which satisfactory operation would require, and Maj. Tom C. Rives agreed with him. [20] The continuous incubus of Signal Corps engineers was frequency congestion; they could not be expected to shake it off readily.

For some fifty miles in the vicinity of the transmitters at Schenectady and Albany, Mitchell rode in an automobile

---

[19] Memo, Col Crawford for CSigO, 8 Oct 38, sub: FM. General Mauborgne added a note on the same date, directing the memo "to R&D: for consideration." SigC 413.44 FM 1, 1938–39.

[20] Memo, CSigO for Dir ARL, 12 Oct 38, sub: FM, with Buckslips, Oliver Lewis to Maj Rives, and Rives to Lt Col Louis B. Bender, 12 Oct 38. In same file.

containing a receiver capable of picking up AM signals as well as the FM. The contrast was impressive, especially in the suppression of noise and interference. The signals from the two FM transmitters did not overlap, although they were being radiated simultaneously on the same 41-megacycle frequency. One transmitter operated with an output of 50 watts, the other with three times as much, yet the receiver would pick up now one, now the other, the stronger always eliminating the weaker despite the slight difference between them, whereas an AM signal needed to be a good twenty times stronger than any other competitor on the same frequency. Mitchell passed his enthusiasm on to Mauborgne in a long and detailed report. Not only was the prospect of noise suppression in view, but with FM the same frequencies could be used over and over again in areas not very far apart. Mitchell had no doubts about the immediate desirability of setting up a frequency modulation project at once in the Aircraft Radio Laboratory.[21] Presently a diversion of funds would enable the Signal Corps Laboratories to add FM to their active projects. And from the Research and Development Division, Rives recommended that the Signal Corps test it for use as ultrahigh-frequency command equipment, mechanized vehicle equipment, and as a replacement for the SCR-194 and SCR-195.[22]

On 27 and 28 April 1939 the Aircraft Radio Laboratory tested airborne FM receivers upon transmissions from the Schenectady and Albany transmitters and also from the original FM tower in Alpine. The Signal Corps representatives were again impressed.[23] Mitchell expanded the Aircraft Radio Laboratory project for the very high frequency command model SCR-264 so that the new set would be both amplitude- and frequency-modulated, and at the same time gave General Electric an order for FM sets. But frequency modulation did not find airborne applications. Even two years later, by mid-1941, General Electric had not delivered the equipment. Throughout World War II airborne radio remained amplitude-modulated.[24]

Thus it was that frequency modulation would make its great military contribution in the field of vehicular radio. Deprecation from Western Electric-Bell Laboratories was overborne by endorsements from his own staff, and Colton directed the Signal Corps Laboratories to buy an FM receiver from General Electric and to make a mobile 50-watt transmitter. When the Fort Knox show came up, the receiver was not very sensitive, and the transmitter was not very reliable because it was reactance-modulated. Armstrong's aid and pocketbook willingly entered the scene, and a set was hastily put together and flown to Kentucky.[25] It was not by any means the center or cynosure of the collection because at this early period in FM development, the equipment failed to demonstrate marked superiority for military use. A few months later much better performance was obtained. The Signal Corps therefore put more of its time and

---

[21] Ltr, Col Mitchell to CSigO, 1 Nov 38, sub: Demonstration of FM vs. AM sigs. In same file.

[22] Memo, Maj Rives for Col Bender, R&D Div, 20 Apr 39, sub: Rpt on demonstration of AM-FM at Schenectady 13 Apr 39. In same file.

[23] Memo, Capt Gilbert Hayden, Chief of Com Unit, for Dir ARL, 3 May 39, sub: FM tests at Schenectady. In same file.

[24] ARL, Annual Report, 1941, Proj 47, Item 3, p. 15.

[25] Intervs, SigC Hist Sec with Col James D. O'Connell, Dir SCEL, Shark River Hills, N.J., 14 Apr 47, and Dr. Edwin H. Armstrong, New York, N.Y., 13 Feb 50.

persuasive efforts into demonstrating the other items up for view. Somewhat to his surprise Colton encountered almost more demand for better radio than he had expected. Captain Williams had been exploring crystal control and similar possibilities with other radio enthusiasts, a course which had led him to Fred M. Link, a young promoter and small manufacturer of special emergency mobile radios. Link's company had built the amplitude-modulated radios for the Connecticut State Police, and was due to get the contract for their frequency-modulated sets in the year following.

Few demonstrations can have brought together the inventor, potential civilian and military users, and manufacturers as the Fort Knox occasion did. The audience as a whole was paying scant attention to FM because it was not yet ready to prove its case. A heater to provide an ample supply of boiling water for field kitchens excited much more interest, thanks to "an enterprising Quartermaster Officer who crashed the Signal Corps demonstration and temporarily stole the show." [26]

On the afternoon of 16 November 1939, frequency modulation received its first demonstration before an all-military audience. A Link police transmitter and receiver provided the AM contrast. The results seemed not altogether conclusive. "Frequency modulation," read a subsequent report, "gives some promise of providing a somewhat greater discrimination against ignition interference than the peak noise limiter used in amplitude modulation. It does not appear in its present state to be a complete cure-all which will permit noise-free reception of weak signals in the immediate presence of [an] unshielded ignition system." [27]

For some months after these Fort Knox

demonstrations, the Signal Corps Laboratories were unable to push FM. "Enthusiasm was high, but the means available did not permit all-out pushing." [28] Radar research at the time outweighed radio and the Radar (RPF) Section at the Laboratories got the lion's share of available funds. Radar funds could no longer be diverted to communications, and therefore radio development was much slowed down from November 1939 to August 1940. [29]

Meanwhile, Signal Corps radio engineers, having to content themselves with a "wait and see" attitude, watched the commercial progress of Armstrong's new development. Colonel Mitchell, Director of the Aircraft Radio Laboratory, said early in 1940, "Frequency modulation equipment which we have on order with General Electric has not been delivered to date so our information on the subject is limited for the present to work performed by others." [30]

As the Fort Knox disappointment had shown, the earliest versions of FM were

[26] MS comment by Gen O'Connell cited n. 18. The amusing intrusion of the water heater was attributed by Col. Grant A. Williams to Capt. C. Elford Smith, Quartermaster of the 7th Cavalry Brigade. To quote Williams: "He [Captain Smith] had purchased a type [of inversion gasoline heater] developed in the upper Middle West for use in freezing weather to keep water in the tanks used for watering cattle from freezing. He had set three of these up in G.I. cans and the water boiled furiously . . . attracting far more attention from the spectators than the radio, much to the disgust of Col. Colton. Ample hot water was something all could appreciate, radio was still a mystery to all except a few experts and higher commanders." Ltr, Williams to Thompson, cited n. 14, p. 4.

[27] SCL Engr Rpt 701, Summary of Demonstrations and Tests of Radio Communication Equipment, 25 Nov 39, p. 9. SCEL, Ft. Monmouth.

[28] MS comment by Gen O'Connell cited n. 18.

[29] MS comment by Maj Gen Roger E. Colton, Ret., 19 Nov 51, p. 7. SigC Hist Sec File.

[30] (1) Ltr, Col Mitchell to Maj Armstrong, 26 Apr 40. SigC 413.44 FM 1, Jan–Sep 40. (2) SCL, Annual Report, 1940, Proj 10-a, p. 25.

less efficient than they later became. The first sets used reactance modulation, which was not very stable and which could not operate in motion. Vehicular FM became really practicable for the Army with Armstrong's perfection of phase shift. At first, too, the power output compared unfavorably with that of AM sets. At the time of the Fort Knox demonstrations, it took 50 watts of FM to equal 10 watts of AM.[31] A year later the relation reversed in favor of FM. There was a very serious drawback in the fact that a single FM channel required a band many times wider than an AM set needed. Since it was not yet widely comprehended that a good many FM transmitters could all "work" the same frequency—this being the attribute which would have erased the objection—and since frequency channels were at a premium, the Office of the Chief Signal Officer was prompted to plug its ears against frequency modulation and listen through static. These considerations, which made some Signal Corps officers reluctant to adopt FM too hastily during early 1940, may have been further conditioned by the fact that the large radio chains and much of the communications industry opposed it, and were successful, indeed, in delaying its general acceptance even after World War II. Frequency modulation threatened them because it gave promise of reopening commercial broadcasting to competition.[32] Amplitude modulation protected the commercial chains against encroachment because the Federal Communications Commission could not permit a rival station to begin broadcasting on a frequency which would interfere with the established station. In stocks of home radio sets, all amplitude-modulated, there was also a very large investment.

The Chief Signal Officer could not of course commit his organization to FM until he had proof that it was unquestionably superior in military short-range radios and until he knew that industry was able to manufacture intricate FM equipment in vast quantities. He had to know that frequency modulation was going to be good enough to warrant total discard of the SCR-131, 178, 194—standard and well-tried sets. He had to be sure that each of the arms wanted it enough to be willing to come together on a few models, for the War Department's annual appropriations made him believe that multiplicity was out of the question. Finally, crystal control would be vital for very high frequency

[31] It should be noted that the 10 watts of AM was the unmodulated power. When the transmitter was modulated, the peaks would go up to 40 watts power. MS comment by Armstrong cited n. 18.

[32] RCA and its subsidiary, National Broadcasting Company, particularly resisted FM. See: (1) Deposition of Paul A. de Mars, 2 Jan 42, Interference No. 79, 216, Armstrong vs. Hansell, U.S. Patent Office, Washington, D.C., p. 186. (2) *Hearings Before Committee on Interstate and Foreign Commerce*, Senate: 78th Cong, 1st Sess, On S. 814, A Bill to Amend the Communications Act of 1934, and for Other Purposes, 3 Nov–16 Dec 43; 80th Cong, 2d Sess, On S. 2231, A Bill to Limit AM Radio Broadcast Stations to 50,000 Watts and to Provide for Duplication of Clear Channels, 5–23 Apr 48; 80th Cong, 2d Sess, On Certain Charges Involving Development of FM Radio and RCA Patent Policies, 30 Mar, 23 Apr, 12–13 and 21 May 48. (3) *Hearings Before Subcommittee of the Committee on Interstate and Foreign Commerce*, Senate: 80th Cong, 1st Sess, On S. 1333, A Bill to Amend the Communications Act of 1934, and for Other Purposes, 17–27 Jun 47; 81st Cong, 1st Sess, On S. 1973, A Bill to Amend the Communications Act of 1934, as Amended, 16–17 Jun 49. (4) *Hearings Before Committee on Interstate and Foreign Commerce*, HR, 80th Cong, 2d Sess, On H. J. Res. 78, A Joint Resolution Relating to Assignment of a Section of the 50-Megacycle Band of Radio Frequencies for Frequency Modulation (FM), 3–4 Feb 48.

(5) [Milton B. Sleeper, ed.], *FM Radio Handbook* (Great Barrington, Mass.: FM Company, 1946), Ch. I (Testimony of Major Armstrong before Senate Interstate Commerce Committee, 6 Dec 43), pp. 2, 6. See also (6) "Revolution in Radio," *Fortune*, XX (October, 1939), 86 ff.

radio. The frequency would have to be found precisely, because no manual tuning could do in a jolting tank or jeep. Conversion of Army radio equipment to FM in any degree at all would call for quantities of crystals, machine-cut to the thousandths of an inch in thickness. But quartz crystal was an item of major strategic importance; almost the whole supply came from Brazil, and there was yet no proved method for producing crystals synthetically. Another year went by before demand forced the decision.

Moves During the Winter

As the abrupt spectacle of the September conquest of Poland dimmed, the sense of urgency which it had brought to military preparations in the United States faded. Western Europe was supposed to have settled into a contemptibly ineffective war behind the Siegfried and Maginot Lines. U. S. plans were adequate if they met hemispheric defense. That in itself was a long martial step away from defense solely of the continental United States and outlying possessions, but, to mention signal units alone, there were not enough for the tactical communications of even one army in one land area. To contemplate manning the western Atlantic from Greenland to Brazil and the eastern Pacific from the Aleutian to the Galápagos Islands was out of the question although only a year away.

The Protective Mobilization Plan envisioned relatively local limits to any theater of operation, and thought of field forces in terms of the four regional armies and the GHQ reserve. It assumed, among other things, that special organizations or equipment would not be necessary, and that air superiority would be maintained.[33] It did not recognize the extent to which air

superiority might depend upon special radio and radar services almost as important as the airplanes and pilots. Signal Corps officer requirements under the Protective Mobilization Plan totaled only 319: 106 to serve with troops in the United States, 22 with National Guard divisions, 48 for overseas service, 67 in the Office of the Chief Signal Officer, 30 for corps area commands, 10 for detail to the Air Corps, 31 for detail or assignment to other offices of the War Department, and 5 for liaison with the schools of other services.[34] Overseas garrisons were not included in the initial protective force, nor did any provision exist for mobilization assignments of enlisted men.[35]

Despite what was generally called "expansion," [36] the situation spoke of unreadiness, inadequate supply, obsolete equipment. Substituting vicarious for first-hand experience, the Army did its planning and training by guesswork, hoping that the guess was good. There was cautious development of the triangular division, the mechanized Cavalry, and the Aircraft Warning System. In the Signal Corps there was cautious assessment of FM and crystal control.

Along with other arms and services the Signal Corps campaigned for recruits, not very successfully. The campaign sought to

---

[33] Memo, Col Harry L. Twaddle, Actg ACofS G-3, for CSigO *et al.*, 10 Feb 41, sub: GHQ reserve troops. G-3/44984, and also SigC 326.21 Gen 1, Jan–Jul 41.

[34] Memo, CSigO for ACofS G-1, 14 Feb 40, sub: Budget of SigC officers WD PMP 1939, with 1 incl. SigC 381 Gen Mob 15, Jan–Feb 40.

[35] 1st Ind, CSigO to CG Fourth Army, 10 Aug 40, on Ltr, CG Fourth Army to CSigO, 2 Aug 40, sub: Mob assignments Fourth Army hq. SigC 381 Mob Assignment Gen 2.

[36] E. g., "The Signal Corps Expands," an official release at a time when expansion could be measured in inches. Signal Corps Bulletin, No. 107 (January–March, 1940), pp. 51 ff.

lure the unskilled young man with the offer of technical training, a dignified approach which often foundered on the young man's lack of an elementary education. There was no way to remove this obstacle. To send and receive messages, he had to be able to read and write. The promise of Reserve strength was comparably uncertain. The Signal Enlisted Reserve Corps, a perfunctory organization still on the books from World War I, had dwindled in a statutory half-light from a peak never better than 118, and now contained nine men. It disappeared in the general 1940 suspension of reserve enlistments. The Regular Army Reserve had been reestablished the year before as a preparedness measure, and offered real encouragement.[37] Yet it held only 473 signalmen. The Officers' Reserve Corps contained 2,200 Signal Corps names; it was a certainty that not all of them would be available in an emergency. Although some 1,700 radio operators were members of the Army Amateur Radio System and a few thousand more had received AARS training, they could not be counted in precise strength figures because there was no way of knowing how many would be eligible for Army service, nor any provision for channeling into the Signal Corps those who were.[38]

Tables of organization in general were of little help. The allotment of men depended upon appropriations. Seldom did the allotments fit the tables, and Col. Dawson Olmstead said flatly that tables were so detailed and so rigid that scarcely a unit in the Army followed its table of organization. He recommended that the tables be abandoned entirely in favor of organization charts, personnel allotments being cited on the charts as a guide. These charts would specify organizations, but

the commander could determine the assignment of his available strength. Noting a weakness in this plan as it pertained to the assignment of specialists, Mauborgne nevertheless sent it to the War Department with his concurrence, but tables of organization continued in use and it became not a whit less difficult to effect changes in them.[39]

The 51st Signal Battalion turned out to be the nucleus for what expansion was taking place or about to take place. Its contribution toward the future of the Army became clear after the United States was involved in the war, when 82 percent of its 1939–40 complement had become officers and 16 percent sergeants of the three highest grades.[40] In the last three months of 1939 the battalion gave up eight officers and fifty-three enlisted men to form cadres for new units, including, for the first time in many years, another signal battalion, the 62d, activated at Fort Sam Houston. The prewar expansion persistently borrowed from the left hand to fill the right. The 1st Radio Intelligence Company, less than a year after its own activation, supplied a cadre of eight men for the 3d when that company was organized in October. Students from the Signal Corps School often filled up the ranks of the 51st when it was needed at working strength. Improvising a unit in this fashion, to meet the demands of an exercise and

[37] "Today the number enrolled exceeds 20,000 men." SW, *Annual Report, 1939,* p. 28.

[38] Pauline M. Oakes, Army Command and Administrative Communications System, Pt. II, 1945, p. 61. SigC Hist Sec File.

[39] Ltr, Col Olmstead, President SigC Bd, to TAG through CSigO, 1 May 40, sub: Simplification of T/O's, and 1st Ind, CSigO to TAG, 9 May 40. SigC 320.3 Gen 9, 1940.

[40] Interv, SigC Hist Sec with Lt Col Frank E. Herrelko, Phila., Pa., 12 Mar 47.

then to be dissolved, was a misleading practice because it made things look better than they were. Certainly it served no useful training purpose, because an improvised organization lived for its day only and then died.[41]

Following the Plattsburg maneuvers, the 1st Signal Company left Fort Monmouth to winter in Georgia. Unexpected snow and ice added discomfort and, presumably, greater value to the field training, but so low was the strength of the company that forty-nine recruits had had to be assigned. They were given four weeks of concentrated training before being put on signal duty.

The new signal aircraft warning company emerged with the first of the year. Having just seen the SCR-270 tests at Navesink, Secretary Woodring announced that a command would soon be set up in the northeastern part of the United States to prepare warning and defense against air attack. The new command would coordinate Air Corps pursuit planes, Coast Artillery Corps antiaircraft guns and searchlights, and Signal Corps detection and communication equipment. This was the first move to give specific character to the Aircraft Warning Service. For the initial tactical defense frontier within the Aircraft Warning Service the War Department designated the nation's most valuable and concentrated target area, the area approximately that of the First Army. The Signal Corps now knew a little better where it stood with the aircraft warning function. Instead of serving an amorphous coast-to-coast paper organization, it would serve an Air Defense Command whose headquarters were at Mitchel Field, Long Island, and whose chief, Brig. Gen. James E. Chaney of the Air Corps, would be an immediate subordinate to General Drum.

Not only would it provide radar and other equipment but supply and train the aircraft warning units as well.[42]

The very first such unit was not for the northeast Air Defense Command, after all. That headquarters came into being on 26 February 1940,[43] whereas on 1 January the War Department had established a Signal Company, Aircraft Warning, Panama and had ordered it to get ready for transfer to the spot which defense strategy most wanted to guard. Created with an authorized table of organization of ninety-three men, this company went into training. At the secret preserve, the men practiced the strange and uncertain business of electronic detection, using the fixed version, the SCR-271, and without any promise that there would be radar for them by the time they got to the Canal Zone.

For General Chaney's new command, General Mauborgne planned two aircraft warning companies.[44] One unit would be designated a Signal Company Aircraft Warning, the other a Signal Company Operation. The former would have six officers, the latter five, and each 125 enlisted men. Three of the officers would be Regular Army men, the remainder Reservists called to duty for this assignment. The 250

---

[41] Col Owen S. Albright, "Army Signal Communication, Army-Navy Landing Exercise, Fourth Army, January 15–22, 1940," Signal Corps Bulletin, No. 108 (April–June, 1940), pp. 44–66.

[42] AG Ltr to CG First Army, 23 May 40, sub: AWS continental U. S. SigC 220.3 ADC.

[43] For an account in full, see (1) Watts hist cited n. 6(2). (2) Wesley F. Craven and James L. Cate, eds., The Army Air Forces in World War II, Vol. I, Plans and Early Operations: January 1939 to August 1942. (3) Stetson Conn and Byron Fairchild, The Defense of the Western Hemisphere, a two-volume subseries in preparation for the series UNITED STATES ARMY IN WORLD WAR II.

[44] Memo, CSigO for Air Defense Bd, 25 Jan 40, sub: Orgn of SigC troops for ADC. SigC 220.3 ADC.

enlisted men would derive, the Chief Signal Officer hoped, from an increase of that amount in the Signal Corps. The Signal Company Aircraft Warning would operate both the detector equipment and the information center, and organize and supervise the ground observer system. The Signal Company Operation would install, maintain, and operate the usual signal facilities other than its twin company's special equipment. To an extent, it still was true that, as Signal Service troops of an Air Defense Command, these companies were neither Signal Corps fish nor Air Corps fowl. Their commander was to be Maj. Paul S. Edwards, signal officer on General Chaney's staff.

Mauborgne assured General Strong of the War Plans Division that, if the War Department could recruit the 250 men and authorize them to the Signal Service of the Air Defense Command by the end of February, they could be trained and ready for the July maneuvers.[45] This was a real promise, because there was only one SCR-270 to train them on. It was for lack of another that the men destined for Panama were using a 271. The General Staff had authorized the construction of a second 270 set, but no one would see it before May.

General Mauborgne called attention to the fact that each of the men must be trained in Signal Corps specialties before he could begin team training for his role in the Air Defense Command. In order to get them through the curriculum of the Signal Corps School without delay, he offered to give priority to the men of this group over all others who were waiting for the course. He estimated a schedule of forty-five days for school training, thirty for combined training, and then assignment to field or maneuver training. The

Laboratories thought the minimum time to train them even sketchily to install and maintain an SCR-270 was ninety days.[46] Few military men and few civilians were acquainted with the intricacies of the new development, because it had no commercial counterpart.

Conforming to these plans in most details, the 1st Aircraft Warning Company, Signal Corps, and the 1st Operation Company, Signal Corps, came into existence on 1 March 1940. The Signal Corps had got a 1,600-man increase under the Protective Mobilization Plan in February, so that there was no question of its carrying the further request for the 250 men. The 1,600 were hypothetical, the 250 had to be real; but there was still no question. Signalmen from other units manned the two new companies.

The center of Signal Corps attention to the aircraft warning program now shifted to Fort Monmouth, where Olmstead, as commandant of the school, undertook the work in co-ordination with the Air Defense Command.[47] Suppressing his dislike for tables of organization and tables of basic allowances, he began to have them prepared for aircraft warning companies all over the defense zone. To serve in Puerto Rico: 4 radar stations linked by

[45] Memo, CSigO for Gen Strong, 27 Jan 40, sub: SigC units for ADC. SigC 381 Gen-Mob 15, Jan–Feb 40.

[46] OCSigO R&W Action 2, R&D Div to P&T and Supply Divs, 31 Jul 41, sub: AWS technicians Panama. SigC 353 Gen MT-38, Feb 39–Dec 41.

[47] (1) AG Ltr to CO Ft. Monmouth, 27 Feb 40, sub: Activation of SigC cos. AG 320.2 (2-12-40) M (Ret) M-C. (2) Memo, CSigO for Lt Col Harry L. Twaddle, ACofS G-3, 2 Feb 40, sub: Allocation of increase of 1,600 enlisted men in PMP for SigC. SigC 381 Gen Mob, Jan–Feb 40. (3) 2d Ind, CSigO to Chief of AC, 27 May 40, on Ltr, Capt John L. Hitchings, CAC (Cav), to TAG, 20 May 40. SigC 676.3 (AWS) Gen 1. (4) Ltr, CSigO to CG ADC, 10 Jun 40, sub: ADC. SigC School Hq 220.3 ADC.

radio and (with one exception) by wire also to the information center. To serve in Alaska: 4 stations all communicating with the information center by radio. To serve in Hawaii: 8 stations, 3 communicating to the center by wire, 5 by radio. For the United States itself: 10 frontier companies, of which 5 would have 2 stations each, 3 would have 3 stations each, and 2 would have 4 stations each. Such was the Signal Corps schedule for aircraft warning. The number of men needed for the frontier companies alone was 3,786.[48]

Fortunately, strength was now accumulating. Enlisted rolls had increased to six thousand and the ratio of officers to enlisted men was one to twenty. Four times as many Reserve officers were taking fifteen-day tours of duty as had the year before. Revitalization of the Reserve had begun, officers being weeded out because they were over the maximum age for the rank which they held. One hundred and forty-seven names fell under the red pencil. Nevertheless, the Reserve officer rolls contained the names of 173 who had been commissioned within the year, and 13 cadets in the Military Academy were due to be appointed in the Signal Corps at the end of the term, so that there was both Reserve and Regular new blood.[49]

In May, the men of Signal Company, Aircraft Warning, Panama left for the Canal Zone. The SCR-271 with which they had trained followed them.[50] For Alaska and Hawaii, two more aircraft warning companies, similarly named, entered the activation stage of planning. Although there was no radar for them, and would be none until well on into 1941, these units were at least to prepare the sites and set up communications nets.

At a time when the British were about to use radar in order to detect the prein-

vasion Luftwaffe, American aircraft warning was part of an unreal cotton-batting world. To say so is not to diminish the stature of the defense effort, which had scarcely begun to grow at all, but merely to place it in time. Antiaircraft exercises alerted several Southern States in the second week in May. They occurred in a state of mind which urged that "the utmost care [be] employed . . . not to leave any feeling of alarm or uneasiness over the purposes behind these maneuvers." Even when the circumstances were predetermined, civilian observers already posted, and the bombers flying only two miles a minute, it took forty-five seconds to report them from fairly close by.

Subsequent history gives mournful overtones to the words of that period, when peace was the declared aim and it was still possible to say, "Experience in matters of this nature [seems to have] considerable merit, especially in view of the current situation in Europe."[51] It was a period when the chairman of the House Subcommittee on Military Appropriations thought the nation might "hope" to have a "defense" force "in the next two or three years."[52] General Mauborgne felt that he could assure an inquiring Senator

[48] (1) Ltr, CSigO to Comdt SigC School, 23 May 40, sub: T/O and T/BA for aircraft warning orgns; (2) 10th Ind, CSigO to TAG, 20 Sep 40, on Ltr, CO Harbor Defenses of Puget Sound and 14th Coast Artillery to CG 9th Coast Artillery District, 27 Jul 40, sub: Aircraft warning cos; (3) Memo, OCSigO for G-3 Sec WDGS, 24 Oct 40. SigC 676.3 (AWS) Gen 1.

[49] SW, *Annual Report, 1940,* App. B.

[50] In June. It went into operation at Fort Sherman, guarding the Caribbean approach to the Canal, early in October, thus becoming the first radar in the American defense system. Davis, History of the Signal Corps Development of U.S. Army Radar Equipment, Pt. III, pp. 33–37. SigC Hist Sec File.

[51] Southwest Bell Telephone rpt cited n. 8(2), p. 14.

[52] Statement by Hon. J. Buell Snyder in *Congressional Record,* 76th Cong, 3d Sess, 3 Jan 40–3 Jan 41, LXXXVI, 316.

that "the Signal Corps development program is progressing as rapidly as funds appropriated for the purpose will permit," but had to say once again, as so many times in the past, that "many development projects are inactive due to lack of funds which, if activated, would insure more rapid progress in the equipment of Signal Corps units with modern communication apparatus." [53] And General Marshall, the new Chief of Staff, spoke very bluntly to a House of Representatives subcommittee. "We have not been allowed to learn how to fight, except theoretically," he charged. "It is important that we do learn." [54] His words contained the paradox in which the whole nation struggled. With perfect military propriety, he pressed for the most unmoral pursuit the human race is addicted to.

The Weight of Field Demands

In the narrower sense, he was not referring to war at all but to the first of the great Louisiana maneuvers, which was about to engage 60,000 troops along the Sabine River boundary with Texas. Preceded by IV Corps maneuvers at Fort Benning, this May exercise tested tactical communications more thoroughly than anything else had since World War I. As a result, it re-emphasized their inadequacy. The absence of numbers of men all properly trained and equipped raised the specter of failures which could occur in war.

The 51st Signal Battalion again doubled and redoubled in brass. General Allison had remarked one time to an audience at the Army War College that they probably knew every man of the 51st by name, because the battalion had had to furnish communications at every maneuver in the country. [55] In large-scale

maneuvers the battalion men were sure to be spread thin, for they not only had to set up the administrative and tactical systems for the army but also provide aircraft warning communications and man the signal supply depot. What strength was left over went to corps communications. Again, they had only a few men left for corps use. This was a deficiency in strength, and in the echelons beyond Signal Corps responsibility there was a degree of deficiency of training. Most important of all, there was a default in equipment.

Mobility and air power, indeed, had outrun signal tactical equipment. Speed, wide separation, and frequent change characterized all the units of the striking force which the Army was trying to imitate from the object lesson overseas; and these characteristics had to exist under the constant threat of air attack. Equipment which had seemed possible in the summer of 1939 was antediluvian in the spring of 1940.

Just as the Sabine River maneuvers were commencing, Germany tore the cotton-batting world apart again. The maneuvers took place almost in loneliness, because the eyes of spectators were turned toward the grim and rapid disaster sweeping through northwestern Europe. For that sort of fighting, the conventional tactical communications system being shown at maneuvers was unsuitable. It was, for example, still heavily dependent upon

---

[53] Memo, CSigO for ACofS WPD, 3 Feb 40, replying to Ltr, Senator Elmer Thomas (Okla.), Chm Senate Appropriations Subcommittee in charge of WD, to SW, 15 Jan 40. SigC 676.3 (AWS) Gen 1.

[54] *Hearings Before the Committee on Appropriations*, HR, 76th Cong, 3d Sess, On Military Establishment Appropriation Bill for 1941, 23 Feb 40, p. 44.

[55] "Organization Day of the 51st Signal Battalion," Signal Corps Bulletin, No. 105 (July–September, 1939), p. 108.

LOCATOR EQUIPMENT AT THE LOUISIANA MANEUVERS

commercial systems. Given a situation where no commercial facilities were available, what would happen? A Signal Corps colonel took note of the fact that division-to-corps wire communications were hampered during these Southern maneuvers, despite the fact that the area was one which already had commercial communications. Although more than most battle areas would be likely to provide, they were less than signal officers were used to. Yet, granted "warfare of this nature," the colonel conceded, "the limited amount of wire communication that was available was probably what might be expected. . . ." Extending one probability into another, he went on: "It is doubtful whether much reliance can be placed in time of war on the extensive use of commercial communications systems, especially"—adding one more possibility—" in areas where the civilian population is unfriendly." [56]

The maneuvers brought out varying views of wire equipment. Colton had spoken well of the field wire W-110 in the 1939 New York maneuvers. But in 1940 Maj. William O. Reeder, who was then signal officer of the IX Corps, reported

[56] Lt Col Edgar L. Clewell, "Signal Communications in Fourth Corps During Spring Maneuvers, 1940," Signal Corps Bulletin, No. 109 (July–December, 1940), pp. 31–32.

The amount spent in renting commercial communications facilities for the maneuvers conducted by the four armies that year (over $100,000 by the Third Army, $98,000 by the First, and lesser amounts by the Second and Fourth) would have met the enlisted payrolls of two signal battalions for a year. SigC Bd Case 327, 25 Jul 40, sub: SigC units required for the Army and T/O's and T/BA's for these units. SigC Files.

that W-110 showed up poorly in Louisiana. Wet weather cut its talking range in half. Its insulation suffered damage from motor traffic, and from cows, which found the insulating compound much to their taste.[57] The insulation had been vulcanized either too much, so that it grew brittle and cracked easily, or not enough, so that it tended to melt and become sticky. Reeder felt that the Laboratories had developed the wire with too much of an eye to the theories of electrical properties and too little to the realities of field use, and recommended, among other things, that "quibbling over the dielectric capacity of field wire insulation should be dropped in favor of finding an insulation that will resist the mass effect of modern truck transportation passing over the wire."[58]

The 1940 maneuvers reversed Colton's 1939 stand on field teletypewriters. Commercial printers worked well. They handled, for instance, nearly half of the IV Corps message center traffic in Louisiana. Reeder urged that the "development of a field printer should be discontinued at once in view of the proven excellence of the teletypwriter now standard in the Bell System." The Signal Corps Laboratories did not drop their own design of a light field printer but did adopt the TG-7, the the model built by the Teletype Corporation, and began development of a switchboard for field teletype, BD-100, and a complete teletypewriter center set, TC-3. Of telephone switchboards, the divisional BD-14 appeared entirely inadequate. The number of incoming calls often averaged 150 an hour for hours on end, and overtaxed the operator beyond endurance.

Both Colton in 1939 and Reeder in 1940 put wire far ahead of radio. Colton had summed up the observations of Signal Corpsmen at the 1939 New York maneu-

vers to the effect that the greatest need was standardized switchboard equipment for headquarters. Reeder in 1940 stressed the need for better field wire, together with repeaters to increase its range and H carrier systems to increase its traffic capacity. That they followed the established view, relying on wire for message centers and regarding radio as a stand-by, was to be expected, since Signal Corps responsibility was to communications in higher headquarters, which were relatively fixed. In the Louisiana maneuvers the IV Corps message centers handled but 296 radio messages out of 8,977 messages in all.

Even more to the point in Signal Corps thinking was the fact that wire offered far less chance for interception than radio did. When radio was used, too often messages went out in the clear. The temptation to use plain English over radiotelephones was nearly irresistible. To go on the air at all, even in code, gave away the location of the radio transmitter to any listening post equipped with good direction-finding equipment. And to encode or encipher a message was time consuming, especially when the Army was using a field code widely condemned as archaic. Troops simply would not use it. Without a mechanical cipher device which would be fairly secure from the prying of enemy cryptanalysts and which might encipher

---

[57] Pigs, by contrast, preferred spiral-four cable. They liked what advertising would call its chewy goodness. A Signal Corps lieutenant who recalled Reeder's remark suggested that it would be a good idea to lay W-110 in pig country and spiral four in cow country. Memo, 1st Lt G. W. Good for Maj Arthur A. McCrary, 21 Oct 42, sub: Rpt of sig activities during Second Army maneuvers 12 Oct. SigC 451.7 (RL-31) No. 2, 1940–43.

[58] Annex Rpt 10, Maj Reeder to IX Corps, Rpt of Third Army Maneuvers, 1940. AG 353 (10-20-38) Sec 1-E Rpts on 1940 Army Maneuvers.

and decipher at the rate of five words a minute, Reeder declared, "the radio is more dangerous than it is useful." [59]

Security considerations could not, however, keep radio merely an emergency adjunct to wire in tactical uses. Co-ordination of fighting machines in rapid motion, whether on the ground or in the air, required radio contacts. Obviously wire was impossible. What was needed was redesign, for tactical radio communications were failing too often. Contact between vehicular units was poor. Contact with airplanes was worse: an army headquarters could not communicate directly with them; battalions and regiments, using the SCR-161, could receive continuous-wave signals from an airplane but could not readily answer except by spreading colored panels upon the ground. There was an immediate need to lengthen the range of corps and division equipment and to get it to work on wheels. A radio which had to stop, hoist its antenna, generate power, and get everything all set before it could serve the corps and division headquarters was outdated if meanwhile the headquarters were rolling on ahead of it, moving farther out of range with every minute. "A hundred miles in motion" was the catchword.

Another demand existed for close-range sets: pack sets for the Infantry, tank sets for the embryo Armored Force, air-to-ground and air-to-air sets for the Air Corps. "Walkie-talkie" and then "handie-talkie" became the catchwords there. Changes were in order if the methods, organization, and equipment of tactical communications were to meet the exigencies of the new war of movement.

Signal Corps policy had supposedly been fixed for the past two years against appeals for a wider use of crystals; but the claims made for them kept breaking through with fresh importunities. The apparently unyielding circumstance which had set the policy was that the world's deposits of good quartz were almost entirely in Brazil. Joint study undertaken by the Supply and Research and Development Divisions had produced the reluctant belief that neither would the quartz already imported and on hand meet the initial demand if crystal control were to be extensively introduced nor would a continuing demand be assured of an uninterrupted supply in case of war. Nevertheless, mobile radio seemed to call for nothing else, and the pressure for crystals increased.

More and more, the staff at the Laboratories felt that a way must be found for a greater use of crystals than the visible supply seemed to countenance. Finely cut quartz, able to prevent a frequency from drifting, had such value that even partial crystal control promised to free Army radio from the domination of frequency meters and to make radio as easy for nonsignalmen to use as a telephone. With a prospect of thousands of unskilled users not very far in the future, this was a strong talking point. Thus the Laboratories recommended crystals for the SCR-197. The Office of the Chief Signal Officer said no, because the SCR-245's were about to take a large amount. Colton pursued the matter, and cited Dr. H. C. Dake, editor of *The Mineralogist,* to the effect that "there seems to be no reason why domestic quartz crystal could not be used." This was a mistake, for the Research and Development Division asked both the National Bureau of Standards and the Naval Research Laboratory for comment on Dake's

---

[59] *Ibid.*

opinion. They agreed in repudiating it. Only Brazilian quartz was of sufficiently high quality to produce the piezoelectric effect. Yet whatever the obstacles to getting them, crystals seemed to be the only door opening upon good vehicular radio, and essential to very high frequency development and frequency modulation.[60]

The Signal Corps had made little progress in testing frequency modulation. The technical staff in the Office of the Chief tended to think conservatively, absorbed by problems of frequency allocation and of assigning military frequencies in such a way that no two transmitters in a given area could interfere with each other.

Col. Louis Bender, the head of the Research and Development Division, went with General Mauborgne and Major Rives to look at a demonstration staged in the Washington Hotel through the efforts of Armstrong and engineers of the Stromberg-Carlson Company, and remained passive. This was on 12 January 1940, and on the next day he went to another in the auditorium of the Smithsonian Institution, where Armstrong showed that his FM equipment not only would transmit with high fidelity but could simultaneously accommodate a teletypewriter channel. Bender commented: "This was an interesting demonstration, but I see little practical value in it." RCA was promising television in order to obtain new frequency allotments from the Federal Communications Commission, and Bender suspected that the purpose of Armstrong's demonstrations was to win Army backing in FM's struggle for the same frequencies. He acknowledged frankly that nothing of the sort had been hinted, but did think that "the frequency modulation people" probably would offer to strike a bargain in the 44–56 megacycle band. But, he concluded, "We are not nearly so ready to make use of it [FM] as the broadcast people appear to be." [61]

The Infantry and Field Artillery had got quite the opposite impression from the conferences which had followed the Fort Knox demonstration. The Field Artillery Board was sufficiently convinced to be thinking of FM as "the most promising line of future development." The Infantry joined with equal enthusiasm, and, since the mechanized Cavalry was already on record, three powerful arms of the service were now urging the Signal Corps to exploit the possibilities of FM without delay for use "across the forward fire-swept areas." The Research and Development Division rebuffed them with the contention that "the radio system referred to, while attractive in some respects, has certain known deficiencies that make its use . . . questionable." Anyway, whose job was it to bring out the Army's communications equipment? Was it not the Signal Corps? Of course, replied the other arms, but surely it was proper that they not be required to wait for whatever the Signal Corps produced for them but instead be able to exchange queries and suggestions in mutual interest? Shrewdly enough, and capitalizing upon the difference of opinion within the Signal Corps itself over frequency modulation, the Field Artillery cited the Signal Corps Bulletin's own wholehearted appreciation of it. Colonel Bender privately observed that he did not at all consider the Bulletin authoritative, and maintained that the

---

[60] SigC file 413.44 Crystals 5, 1940, *passim*.

[61] (1) OCSigO R&W Action 1, "WTG" [Wesley T. Guest], Com Liaison Div, to R&D Div, 29 Aug 40, sub: Assignment of radio frequencies. SigC 413.44 Development 9, 1940–41. (2) Memo, Col Bender for CSigO, 15 Jan 40. SigC 413.44 FM 1, Jan–Sep 40.

THE SCR–195, WALKIE-TALKIE

Radio Corporation of America had "developed some pertinent facts that the enthusiasts for this system had conveniently forgotten to publicize [and which] took much of the wind out of the broad claims made." [62]

Colonel Bender did concede that frequency modulation might yet be found helpful, especially in vehicular and air uses. Since vehicular uses—forward, mobile uses where a quiet radio could be a godsend—were exactly what the ground arms had in mind, they were left the winners of the debate: the Signal Corps Technical Committee would have something ready for them by May. But there was a wide gap between this modest first victory and any general capitulation. In the long run, FM got no further than primarily tactical ground uses; it did not establish itself in naval, air, or (except for certain radio link equipment) ground administrative applications. In the immediate run, Bender warned the Chiefs of Infantry and Field Artillery that they could expect no funds to be available until more than a year had passed.

With this or other considerations in mind, the Laboratories matched the hesitant attitude of the Research and Development Division. When in advance of the maneuvers the Laboratories outlined the requirements of the using arms, they proposed the SCR-245 for tanks, its frequency range moved up to 3,700 kilocycles; the 131, with a voice channel added, for rifle platoons; the 161 and 171 on 2,000–6,000 kilocycle range for Field Artillery tactical uses, and so on.[63] Colton's report that year, as director of the Laboratories, made a point of the fact that lack of funds had prevented any development of FM. He had passed up an opportunity to

send an observer to New York in April for a special test of the Armstrong equipment, despite the fact that General Mauborgne had thought it a good idea.[64] Thus, neither in the Washington headquarters nor at Fort Monmouth was the Signal Corps extraordinarily alert to the possibilities in frequency modulation.

Meanwhile, under Armstrong patents, the Radio Engineering Laboratories of Long Island City, New York, had built twenty-eight FM radio sets incorporating the phase shift improvement. Put to use in the First Army's summer maneuvers of 1940, they at once intensified the demands from the field. Simultaneously, the Connecticut State Police tried out the FM radios which Link had recently begun building, also under Armstrong patents. The immediate success of these new police sets added to the pressure. In rapid order, the Chiefs of Field Artillery, Infantry, and Coast Artillery asked the Chief Signal Officer for service test sets. Further pressure was in store from the successor to the mechanized Cavalry, the Armored Force. The Link police sets were about to become

---

[62] (1) Ltr, Office of Chief of FA to TAG through Chief of Inf, 2 Jan 40, sub: Improvement of Inf-FA liaison radio com, with 6 inds among TAG, OCSigO, Chief of Inf, and Chief of FA, 12 Jan–27 Apr 40, and associated OCSigO R&W's. SigC 413.44 Development 9, 1940–41. (2) Capt. K. M. Soukaras, "Frequency Modulation," Signal Corps Bulletin, No. 107 (January–March, 1940), pp. 24–30.

[63] (1) Ltr, Col Colton to CSigO, 1 May 40, sub: R&D recommendations by FA, Inf, and CAC; (2) OCSigO R&W Action 4, J. M. [Mauborgne] to Exec Officer 13 Mar 40, sub: FM hearings. SigC 413.44 FM 1, Jan–Sep 40. (3) SCL, Annual Report, 1940, pp. 24 ff.

[64] (1) Ltr, CSigO to Dir SCL, 14 Mar 40, sub: Demonstration of FM equip; (2) Msg, Mauborgne to Lab Ft. Monmouth, 9 Apr 40; (3) Msg 76 WVPAC 9 WD, Colton to Signals, Washington, D.C., 9 Apr 40. SigC 413.44 FM 1, Jan–Sep 40.

the prototypes of the SCR-293 and 294, the small, short-range vehicular sets which were to go into the tanks of the 1st and 2d Armored Divisions. They were the Army's first FM.[65]

There remained the other of the two most urgent equipment needs, a truly mobile, long-range, 100-mile radio set. The development had proceeded only so far as the laboratory model of the truck-and-trailer SCR-197 contained in the Fort Knox exhibit of the preceding fall. The origin of the SCR-197 went back several years to a request from the Air Corps for a big and powerful radio which might be transported in a truck or airplane. The set had originally been planned to operate on the ground over a universal frequency range, and to possess sufficient power whether on continuous wave, tone, or voice to attain a distance "approximately equal to the transmitting range of the radio set installed in aircraft to which it must communicate." This meant a power output of hundreds of watts if the set were to equal from the ground the range of the airborne liaison radio SCR-187. An output of 300 watts had first been offered but had failed to satisfy needs.

In requesting a still more powerful set, the Air Corps had made the important recommendation that it be installed for operation, not temporarily on the ground, but permanently in its truck and trailer transport. The Signal Corps Laboratories had accordingly followed this proposal. The engineers blueprinted the set so that a 400-watt transmitter, antenna equipment, rectifier, and emergency gasoline generator would all go into a single truck, and so that the trailer would hold two receivers, two telegraph printers, and a forty-line telephone switchboard. Remote

control equipment, field wire, and telephones were included in order to permit the trailer message center to be located as much as seven miles away from the transmitter truck.

By 1939 the project, "Radio Equipment for Moving Stations," was in order. The Signal Corps arranged with the Quartermaster Corps for truck and trailer, installed the equipment for the Plattsburg maneuvers, reported that it worked "very satisfactorily," and contracted with the Federal Telegraph Company to begin manufacturing it. Unluckily, the SCR-197 was soon proved somewhat less than satisfactory. Field forces found that the mobility of the carriers was poor; the truck was underpowered for its load and the trailer was overcrowded. There were bugs in the transmitter; the power supply did not work well. Above all, the transmitter

---

[65] (1) Ltr, Col Crawford to CSigO, 19 Sep 40, sub: Frequency assignments for 25-watt mobile radiotelephone equip. SigC 413.44 FM 1, Jan–Sep 40. (2) Col. John C. Moore, Signal Officer Headquarters, Second Corps Area, Governors Island, New York, reported on these sets without particular enthusiasm on 17 October. Ltr, Col Moore to Col Colton, 17 Oct 40. SigC 413.44 Radio Sets, Armored Force Bd File, Folder 2. (3) Ltr, 1st Lt J. J. Davis, 80th FA Regtl Com Office, to CG 6th Div, Ft. Snelling, Minn., 27 Aug 40, sub: Radio recommendations, and 1st Ind, Lt Col Clift Andrus, CO 80th FA, 18th FA Hq, Ft. Des Moines, Iowa, to CG 6th Div, 30 Aug 40; (4) Ltr, Chief of FA to CSigO, 19 Aug 40, sub: FM equip, and 2d Wrapper Ind, Col Colton to CSigO, 6 Sep 40; (5) Ltr, Chief of Inf to CSigO, 19 Sep 40, sub: Test of FM radio; (6) 1st Ind, Chief of CAC to CSigO, 4 Oct 40, on Ltr, Col William S. Bowen, President CAC Bd, to Chief of CAC, 12 Sep 40, sub: Commercial FM radio equip; (7) OCSigO R&W Action 1, W. T. G. [Guest], Com Liaison Div, to R&D Div, 19 Aug 40, sub: FM system rpt of test by FCC, and Incl Memo, E. L. White to Chief Engr of FCC, 16 Aug 40, sub: FM system of Conn. State Police. SigC 413.44 FM 1, Jan–Sep 40. (8) SCL, Annual Report, 1941, Proj 11-9.3, p. 83. (9) Ltr, CSigO to Dir SCL, 11 Sep 40, sub: Radio sets for armored forces. SigC 413.44 Armored Force (Sets) 1, 1940.

could not operate while the truck was in motion.[66]

Yet the Signal Corps had taken a step which interested not just the Air Corps but all of the rest of the Army, and especially the mechanized Cavalry. One of four basic types of vehicular sets which Williams and others of that service were proposing was a voice-and-continuous-wave, long-range radio of this sort. The concept of a large transmitter which could operate in a moving truck seemed to lie in the realm of fantasy, although most communications men were familiar enough by now with medium vehicular transmitters such as the 193 and 245. The May 1940 Third Army maneuvers, and the German blitz across western Europe, led military observers to realize that the Army must have a radio—self-contained, power and all, in a truck and trailer—which would be able to transmit and receive over ranges of at least 100 miles even while the truck and trailer bounced along highways or byways. Either the SCR-197 must be made truly mobile, or a new and better set must be developed.

The Third Army maneuvers brought signal matters to a head. "There were numerous and painful failures of signal communication . . . which subjected the Signal Corps to continuous criticism." [67] What had the criticisms been? "Generally inadequate"; "complete reorganization necessary"; "inadequate and insufficient"; "complete modernization necessary"; "certain modifications necessary"; "present facilities inadequate"; "generally inadequate." Courtney H. Hodges and Adna R. Chaffee had been among the critical generals; Olmstead, Ingles, Clewell, Reeder, and Matejka among the critical Signal Corps observers. Signal communications were inadequate not

merely for the oncoming war but even for a play war, which, although the largest yet staged by the peacetime Army, was still not comparable to the sort of force which was just then overpowering northern and western Europe. The Signal Corps position was that little more could have been expected. Manpower shortage had accounted not only for the wide and expensive use of commercial facilities, but also for the absence of trained signalmen. It hardly needed to be said, either, that when the telephone company's men were hired, the telephone company's men got the training.

The principal concern, though, was not yet a matter of training, but of personnel and equipment. There lay the prime insufficiencies. From the Chief's office an urgent appeal went out to the Signal Corps Board. Undoubtedly, the appeal explained, the War Department would be calling for a thorough report, so the board must be ready with the answers. If Congress authorized the Army to expand to 375,000, including men for two armored divisions, the Aircraft Warning Service, GHQ aviation, and universal mobility, the Signal Corps must know exactly what units to ask for. Board membership was high-powered just then. Olmstead was president and Colton, Ingles, Milliken, and Back were members. All soon became

---

[66] (1) SCL, Annual Reports, 1937, p. 13, 1938, pp. 24–25, 1939, p. 30, 1940, pp. 23–24. (2) C&E Case 12, Mobile Communication Centrals, 9 Jan 42, p. 9. SigC Files. (3) Memo, Lt Col David E. Washburn for O/C R&D Div, 15 May 41, sub: Radio set SCR-197 in C&E Case 27 reduction in types of equip. SigC C&E Case 27. (4) Hist Sec E&T Divs OCSigO, History of Signal Corps Research and Development in World War II, Vol. VIII, Pt. 4, Proj 832-A, p. 5. SigC Hist Sec File.

[67] SigC Bd Case 327, 25 Jul 40, cited n. 56.

For a brief description of these maneuvers see Lt Francis G. Smith, History of the Third Army, Hist Sec AGF Study 17, 1946, pp. 6–7.

generals and Olmstead, Ingles, and Back became Chief Signal Officers. They received the case on 11 June and reported it out on 25 July.

In personnel, they made two kinds of recommendations. One was to increase the number of signal units, the other to increase the number of men in each unit: a signal battalion, for example, being strengthened by ninety-eight more enlisted men and three more officers. "The many difficulties experienced in our peacetime maneuvers are not due to deficiencies in the proper allotment of tactical signal communications to Army units but due to the fact that the signal organizations required are generally not in existence and those that are active are too small to perform their functions." A simple citing of percentages proved this assertion. Whereas during World War I signal units had represented 4.5 percent of the total, and in foreign armies the proportion was comparable,[68] the National Defense Act permitted them to constitute only 1.8 percent of the Army. In May 1940 there were four authorized signal battalions. Double that number, the Board said, and the annual expense of hiring temporary maneuver communications will be cut three fourths. What was more important, communications soldiers would be serving and training with each of the field armies, ready for "the sudden dispatch of an expeditionary force" as in 1917.

As before, the Signal Corps intended to rely to a degree upon National Guard units. The National Guard then had eighteen signal companies, one signal troop, and one signal battalion (the 101st in New York); and two Guard infantry battalions were to be converted into signal battalions.[69] For a citizenly duty such as

aircraft warning, the Guard units would be especially suitable. They could study the SCR-270 in their armories, and in the field could practice against observation planes, which had metal fuselages like bombers and were much less scarce. Reaffirming the plan for aircraft warning companies, in the GHQ reserve and elsewhere, which would be large enough to man seven stations apiece, the Board urged that two-station, three-station, and four-station companies be organized in the Guard for every state where the Aircraft Warning Service was setting up an SCR-270 or 271. Thus a Guardsman would join in the air defense of his own section of the country, quite simply defending his own home in the tradition descended from Lexington and Concord.

Not only were strength recommendations to be made. The Board had also a matter of equipment before it. Anyone aware of the swinging door which the Germans had opened upon France at Sedan and had closed at Dunkerque could see that changes in all types of American military equipment would be necessary in order to meet the standards which the Germans were imposing. Equipment changes, the Signal Corps Board said, must be brought about immediately. *"Time is the essence,"* they underlined it. June 1940, like June 1942, was a period when everyone expected the worst at any minute.

Colonel Olmstead had returned from Louisiana with the controversial 100-

---

[68] E. g., the proportion of the Royal Signals to the British Army as a whole was 4.1 percent in 1939, 5.1 percent in 1945. Col T. B. Gravely, The Second World War, 1939–1945, Army: Signal Communications, British War Office, 1950, p. 13. Copy in OCMH.

[69] Signal Corps Bulletin, No. 109 (July–December, 1940), p. 3.

miles-in-motion set in mind: a super-vehicular radio, a large van load of radio-telephone and radiotelegraph apparatus. This project he laid before General Mauborgne, who turned it down. Although commandant at Fort Monmouth and number two man in the Signal Corps, Olmstead accepted the decision and prepared to go back to Red Bank. Maj. Frank C. Meade, who was well down the line in rank but strategically located on the staff of the War Plans and Training Division of General Mauborgne's office, proposed instead that Colonel Olmstead write a justification for his idea which, rather than striking head on and falling back, would come in through a side door, clear the Signal Corps Board, and hope for success with a chorus of approval behind it.[70] Meade was not merely artful in making a suggestion of this sort. Olmstead was president of the Signal Corps Board, and as its head was of course able to exert considerable weight in its proceedings; but in this matter he had the strong support of the other members. They concurred in the need for 100-miles-in-motion ground radio.

In doing so, they did not abandon the emphasis upon tactical wire communications to which they subscribed along with most other Signal Corps officers, of both older and younger groups. Their recommendations included not only the big radio but also portable power for field teleprinters; switchboards for field teletype; repeaters for field telephone systems; wire-throwing devices for dispensing W-110 in a hurry; and, with only two dissents, trailers in which field message centers could be established and taken wherever the troops went.[71]

The Board report did not forsake wire for radio, or the complementary relationship of one with the other. But the recommendations in wire equipment were all tributes to mobility; and in urging tactical mobility for long-range radio, the members went so far as to declare that for much of the time the new triangular divisions and their combat teams would have to depend wholly upon wireless. The Signal Corps was proud of the SCR-197 as a long-range radio; but the 197 would not do, either for the Infantry or for the Armored Force. "The Board believes that Radio Set SCR-197 is *not* suitable radio equipment for an armored division and urgently recommends that the use of this set be regarded as a temporary expedient until a vehicular set capable of operation in motion and with sufficient range to meet requirements can be developed."[72]

So they declared for "Olmstead's baby" (a term applied with emotions varying from impatience to tempered admiration), which was to be a stopgap put together from military and commercial materials on hand. In a panel truck, a light one-and-a-half such as laundries or florists use, Laboratories engineers would bring together a Hallicrafter HT-4 transmitter, of 450 watts, the antenna rig, and the original Signal Corps superheterodyne receiver, BC-312, plus the BC-342. A two-wheeled trailer cart would hold the power equipment.[73]

---

[70] Interv, SigC Hist Sec with Brig Gen Frank C. Meade, Ret., Chicago, Ill., 12 Sep 49.

[71] This trailer development resulted in the K-35; the field teletype switchboard became the BD-100; the repeaters, EE-89 and 99.

[72] 1st Ind, Col Olmstead to CSigO, 19 Jul 40, on Ltr, OCSigO to SigC Bd, 13 Jul 40, sub: T/O for sig com, armored div SigC Bd Case 328. SigC 320.3 Armored Force and Armored Div, 1940–43.

[73] One of the most interesting of all the equipment recommendations was based on the Board's belief that a single standard trailer could be used "for all Signal Corps purposes where it is necessary to make equipment entirely mobile."

In the meantime, conferences under the aegis of the General Staff were considering the needs of both the Air Corps and the Armored Force. The program for raising the Air Corps to a strength of fifty-four combat groups by 1 April 1942 [74] was increasing the pressure upon the Signal Corps. At first, discussion gave some thought to creating a large number of skeleton signal aviation units, scattering them widely throughout the Air Corps, and bringing them gradually up to strength as the Signal Corps turned out trained technicians. No doubt such thinking was influenced by the universally necessary practice of carrying organizations on paper until an emergency should force their activation as live units, but now an emergency was here. A new plan concentrated all of the trained signalmen available for Air Corps assignment into a few signal aviation companies of full strength, rather than into many skeletal ones. The Signal Corps would make an effort to include a variety of specialists in each, and the Air Corps, assigning one company apiece to each wing or higher command, would detail detachments to signal maintenance, to service as air base platoons, and so on. This plan seemed to offer the double advantage of administrative simplicity and of maximum use of personnel. [75]

The forces of change soon obscured it. General Arnold of the Air Corps headed it into a new direction by outlining "a scheme for . . . a complete ground system of Signal Corps communications all the way from GHQ to the foremost air unit, and practically paralleling Army and other systems." Mauborgne was not convinced that such duplication of facilities was necessary, and suspected that Arnold's purpose was to use the results of the committee's study to capture a force of Signal Corps units. Moreover, he knew that a Signal Corpsman operating a ground radio for the Air Corps might often be getting fifteen dollars a month less than he would if he "wore an Air Corps hat cord" while doing the same kind of work. Yet the suggestion was too near to the Signal Corps' dearest hope to be opposed. Mauborgne directed Lt. Col. Richard B. Moran to play ball to the extent of studying the matter. [76]

Looking toward the advent of the Armored Force, which was due to be created in July, he began also to confer in Maj. Gen. Frank M. Andrews' office with Brig. Gen. Adna R. Chaffee. General Andrews was then G-3 and Chaffee the architect of the new armored command. Mauborgne asked for a statement of Armored Force requirements which he might study. He had in mind the fact that the new signal troop, mechanized, which had just reached the table-of-organization stage, was in process of being superseded by the signal company, armored division. The Signal Corps Board had revised the strength of an armored signal company from 4 officers, 141 enlisted men, to 4 officers, 196 enlisted men, and then had revised the revision in order to ask for 6 officers, 206 enlisted men. Before Mauborgne got the statement he asked for, the War Department moved the figures up to 6 officers, 218 enlisted men. [77]

[74] AG Ltr to Chief of AC, 29 Jun 40, sub: Army's first aviation objective. AG 580 (6-28-40) MF.
[75] Memo, Col Clyde L. Eastman, Exec Officer OCSigO, for ACofS G-3, 16 Jul 40. SigC 320.3 GHQ AF C&E Equip Gen.
[76] Ltr, Lt Col Cedric W. Lewis, Sig Officer GHQ AF, to CSigO, 13 Aug 40, and Reply, 16 Aug 40. SigC 676 Gen 1, 1940–42.
[77] Memo for File by Maj Washburn, 20 Jun 40, sub: Conference on formation of armored (panzer) div (continuation of conference started 10 Jun 40). SigC 320.3 Armored Force and Armored Div.

Two omissions were already apparent, nonetheless. The radio section of the company would need more men; and it looked as if there would not be enough drivers for the vehicles assigned. "This is the same outstanding weakness that occurs quite generally in Signal Corps tables of organization," warned Maj. George I. Back, then secretary of the Board. "In all other arms and services chauffeurs are provided for all self-propelled vehicles." [78]

Chaffee mentioned the 100-miles-in-motion equipment. Such a development, Mauborgne felt, would demand a redesigning of antenna and transmitter—in short, a fresh start. How could a makeshift be expected to serve? Mauborgne thought of signal equipment in terms of the complete, complex, and beautiful product it often was. He displayed the affectionate perfectionism of the engineer and technical scientist. He did not quite see that the Signal Corps could neither go into the war with some of the equipment it had nor take the usual length of time to develop replacements. At his urging, Chaffee agreed to accept SCR-197's even though they would need to come to a halt in order to permit communication, but he strongly hoped that the Signal Corps would be able to come forth with a substitute which would continue to work while moving. [79]

Chaffee's requests epitomized the new Army. Everything he spoke of turned upon the principle of tactical swiftness. When Mauborgne raised the question of the amount of wire communication a mechanized division would need, "General Chaffee stated that the only time that wire would be used would possibly be at night or in rest areas." [80] In agreeing to try the SCR-197 until something better was ready, he computed his need at five to a

division, rather than the three which the Signal Corps estimates called for; the Signal Corps representatives yielded, pointing out that this meant two more vehicles and ten more men in the armored division table of organization and equipment. Because his forces would be subject only to radio control, Chaffee asked for as many frequencies as could possibly be allotted to him. And, reaching the climax, he sought an FM command set for every two scout cars he had.

For the Research and Development Division, Colonel Mitchell deplored such a request. "The number of radio sets estimated for an armored division appears to be quite high," he cautioned. "Channel congestion and interference may be expected, particularly where more than one armored division is . . . in the same general area." [81] Succeeding weeks consolidated the decision nevertheless, and a final conference on the whole matter, shifted to General Chaffee's headquarters at Fort Knox, produced characteristics for an entire vehicular series with the initials of the Armored Force and combining the past year's requests from the two components—Mechanized Cavalry and Infantry

---

[78] 1st Ind, Maj Back to CSigO, 22 Jun 40, on Ltr, CSigO to President SigC Bd, 20 Jun 40, sub: T/O for sig co armored div. SigC 320.3 Sig Co Armored Div.

[79] Memo for File by T. C. R. [Maj Tom C. Rives], R&D Div OCSigO, 13 Jun 40, sub: Conferences on formation of armored (panzer) divs. SigC 320.3 Armored Force and Armored Div, 1940–43.

[80] Memo for File by Washburn cited n. 77. The Armored Force planners were underestimating their need for wire. "Later in action in Northern Europe the Armored Divisions of First Army used almost as much wire as an Infantry Division (something we could not visualize at that time)." Ltr, Williams to Thompson, cited n. 14, p. 13.

[81] OCSigO R&W Action 1, Col Mitchell, Dir R&D Div, to CSigO, 26 Jun 40. SigC 320.3 Armored Force and Armored Div, 1940–43.

Tanks—which had merged to make the new command.

For AF-I, the projected 100-mile set, the Laboratories tried to convert the SCR-197 to permit communication on the march, but the effort met with only partial success. The Signal Corps Board recommendation was rushed into development, and matured in eighteen months into the SCR-299, one of the most usable journeyman sets of the war.[82] In the war, ironically enough, the SCR-197's were stopgap equipment, whereas the stopgap equipment which had been proposed to do what the 197 could not do served throughout the conflict.

To serve as AF-II, a reliable, 40-mile, medium-range set, the Signal Corps offered the SCR-193 and the SCR-245; they were yet new and others liked them,[83] but they did not suit the user, either. Tanks were too cramped to have space for them and tank crews too busy to adjust the delicate controls. Smaller size and simpler operation looked mutually incompatible, because crystal control, which could introduce easy tuning, would probably require more space. Two-way police radios temporarily provided a solution, especially after being acclaimed during the Second Army's Wisconsin maneuvers in August. In advance of those maneuvers the Signal Corps leased a 50-watt fixed set and twenty-five vehicular sets of $7\frac{1}{2}$ watts, all amplitude-modulated, from the Galvin Manufacturing Corporation, assigned the fixed equipment and a dozen of the vehicular sets to the umpires, and turned over the remaining ones to the cars of the reconnaissance squadron. Everyone was delighted, although the sets were instruments of essentially shorter range and were AM. The usual communication distance with

them, depending upon the terrain, was from ten to thirty miles. It was the elimination of all intricacies of tuning which was a boon. Anyone could use them, without previous experience or training.[84]

The advantage of crystal control for the mobile forward uses was now so apparent that the time had arrived for a major decision. The other sets in the Armored Force series called for crystals, too. In the case of the AF-III, the Signal Corps was asked to produce a short-range radio for use at from five to seven miles. The AF-IV was to be even smaller and to have an even shorter range. Both emerged as FM radios in the remarkable SCR-508-9-and-10 series.

The era in which sullen peace had flared into urgent war preparations had begun in a professional sense, it was now possible to see, with a reorientation of tactical theory. The mobile Infantry, the alerting Air, the mechanized Armor were now discernibly emerging, and these "500" radios epitomized their demands, for they were compact and crystal-controlled; they were frequency-modulated; they carried the human voice; and they brought airborne command maneuverability to vehicles on the ground. The only flaw in them was that they were still nearly two years off—and time was short.

---

[82] (1) SCL, Annual Report, 1941, pp. 89–90. (2) Ltr, Defense Aid Sec OCSigO to British Air Comd, Washington, D. C., 16 Jan 42, sub: Mobile W/T equips. SigC 475.7 No. 5. (3) S. I. Nieman, "Vehicular Radio," Signals, I, No. 7 (September–October, 1947), pp. 28–34. (4) Oliver Read, "The Army's SCR-299," Radio News, XXX, No. 2 (August, 1943), 17 ff.

[83] Far on into the war. E.g., Maj S. T. Martin rpts, Jan–Dec 44. SigC 413.44 RDF 2.

[84] Lt Col Leland H. Stanford, Sig Officer Second Army, Final Rpt, Tab 12, Vol. II of Report of the Second Army Maneuvers August 1940. AG 353 (10-20-38) Sec 1-E Rpts on 1940 Army Maneuvers.

CHAPTER VII

The Propulsion From Limbo

Accumulating Production

Shortness of time in 1940 was not a fact the armed services could conjure with but a guess they must submit to. Enough time had followed the first declaration of emergency for them to begin to brace themselves. The collapse of continental Europe shook not only their attitudes but intellectual positions throughout the country. The amount of room left in which to pursue national policy had markedly shrunk. At its center was the nation itself, with the territories and dependencies. At the next layer was the hemisphere; and farthest out, Great Britain and such shreds of the Continent as Vichy France. Policy, including military policy, took the shape of these three outlines.

At the core, preparedness was based upon defense of the United States, in a wider conception upon hemispheric defense, and, in the least defined area, upon the possibility of preserving those potential allies which had not yet gone under. The second conception was generally replacing the first, and was conclusively confirmed in September by the announcement of the exchange of destroyers for bases in British western Atlantic possessions. The third conception, confirmed in the Lend-Lease Act of March 1941 only after many weeks of earnest debate, was still quite out of reach. The immediate goal was to assemble men and material

within the national region and in the aims of the Protective Mobilization Plan and its associate, the Industrial Mobilization Plan.

Material in the mass being less malleable than men, time pressed, if at all, harder upon the production program than upon the schedule for raising and training the new Army. Industrial mobilization plans contemplated that American war production would need about two years to reach a satisfactory output—an optimistic estimate.[1] The burden of bringing it about was the three-way concern of the Army, industry, and the public at large. It was particularly incumbent upon the Army and industry; for public sentiment, increasingly unsettled by events abroad, was being reflected in Congress by substantial grants of funds to the military organization and in both the legislative and executive branches by unreserved encouragements to capital. Endeavoring to give the Army what was needed, individual Congressmen called repeatedly for estimates upon which they could base supplemental appropriations, often faster than the military agency itself was prepared to move. In the

---

[1] (1) Troyer S. Anderson, "Munitions for the Army, 1940–1945," *Infantry Journal*, LIX, No. 4 (October, 1946), p. 14. (2) R. Elberton Smith, Army Procurement and Economic Mobilization, a volume in preparation for the series UNITED STATES ARMY IN WORLD WAR II.

Supply Division of the Office of the Chief Signal Officer, members of the staff found themselves working long hours to provide these estimates. Capt. Eugene V. Elder in one week prepared thirty-nine budgets for signal units.[2]

None of these was in existence, yet almost all were to be combat organizations. War had not materialized, but the necessity was present in the reinforcement of the Panama Canal Zone and similar defense actions being taken. The decision to establish Borinquen airfield, Puerto Rico, invoked the need for a signal depot, installation of the post and administrative wire and wireless systems, stations and networks for airport control and the Army Airways Communications System, and accordingly for all the signal units required for the work. In a dozen other cases of the sort, units being created had to be equipped—equipping being a considerably longer process than creating and an expensive one to the taxpayer: hence the estimates. All deficiency appropriations for the fiscal year 1940—$10,000,000 worth—were going for equipment, and $5,128,185 of the basic appropriation of $7,828,804; so that all together the Signal Corps was spending approximately $15,000,000 on defense material.[3]

When General Mauborgne appeared at hearings for the 1941 appropriations, however, the lull in the war had not yet been broken by the German invasion of Denmark and Norway, let alone by the catastrophe to France. He asked for $11,000,000 less than the amount obligated throughout the preceding year. There would not be so much need for equipment, he reasoned, when the demands for aviation expansion, augmentation of the Canal garrison, and Protective Mobilization Plan requirements had been

met.[4] It seemed to him that whereas 1940 was proving a costly fiscal year, 1941 would be a normal one like 1938 or 1939. It seemed so to the House Appropriations Committee, too, which reduced an Air Corps request for 166 airplanes to 57 and then nearly eliminated the Signal Corps' budget item calling for radio equipment for the 57. Before the fiscal year 1941 ended, the Signal Corps was going to have $256,652,964 available; and in 1942, it was to have more than $3,500,000,000.

Signal Corps requirements, therefore, were not yet great enough to tax the productive capacity of industry, and far from enough to sound out its limits. The industrial and military economies were both almost at the starting line. In May the Office of the Chief Signal Officer provided the Assistant Secretary of War with a list of obstacles to mass production which the planning staff foresaw in the event of a greatly enlarged procurement program. First on the list was a personnel shortage, a shortage of both officers and civilians. Two-week active duty periods of limited numbers of Reserve officers were not to be thought of as training enough officers to meet an emergency. As for civilians, the Signal Corps would need accountants, industrial engineers, statisticians, lawyers, and inspectors to deal with a large-scale procurement program. It would need them in a hurry, already trained, in larger numbers than the Civil Service lists could provide, and freed of the constricting provisions of legislation which held down Washington employment. The function

[2] Interv, SigC Hist Sec with Col Eugene V. Elder, Washington, D. C., 28 Sep 49.

[3] *Hearings Before the Subcommittee of the Committee on Appropriations*, HR, 76th Cong, 3d Sess, On the Military Establishment Appropriations Bill for 1941, HR 9209, p. 643.

[4] *Ibid.*, p. 641.

was one which could not very well be transferred away from the Chief's Office.[5]

The next obstacle was the system of making contracts, especially the requirement for competitive bids, which the Signal Corps procurement officers considered inefficient in both time and money. Their opinion was that they lost weeks in waiting for bids to come in and thereafter compounded the loss of time, first because the obligation to make the award to the lowest bidder sometimes prevented making it to a bidder who, they felt, was already "tooled up" and trained to produce the order, and second because they could not farm out the contract to several bidders at one time. The Signal Corps was also feeling the pressure for other changes in the contractual relationship between government and business. Mauborgne reported that his contracts officers were finding manufacturers reluctant to bid on military orders before they were guaranteed protection against rising costs and wages. He endorsed the proposed introduction of an escalator clause, a formula to protect the contractor's margin by allowing for changes in material and manpower costs during the life of the contract.

A third reservation was still at the stage of possibility. The repeal of the arms-embargo provisions of the 1937 Neutrality Act and the substitution of a cash-and-carry policy presumably opened the way for other armies than our own to buy on the American market. The Chief Signal Officer foresaw a time when foreign orders might occupy American manufacturers to such an extent that the Army's augmented procurement program would come off badly. He felt misgivings that manufacturers upon whom he counted would prefer foreign orders because of larger profit, and that if they accepted Signal Corps

contracts at all, they would do so only on schedules of delayed delivery and at greatly increased prices. He recommended special legislation which would require contractors with the government to deliver War Department orders before foreign orders whenever the interests of the defense program demanded it.

In the ultimate analysis, all of the problems came to a head in materials and manpower, just as they did in the Army in equipment and men. It seemed probable that government control over raw materials would be necessary. The War Department's list of strategic materials now included those which had been merely "critical" a few months before. Nine of the fourteen items on the list were widely used in Signal Corps equipment. The combination of large foreign orders with increased military procurement at home would result in serious shortages. The shortage of skilled toolmakers and artisans created by the depression years in which there had been little demand for them was beginning to show up in delays. In this view from the Signal Corps, accordingly, the Congress must permit the Secretary of War to suspend labor legislation limiting the workday and the work week.[6]

Toward legislative curbs upon business and industry, Signal Corps spokesmen were generally disapproving, not liking the Vinson-Trammel Act's imposition of a

---

[5] Memo, CSigO for ASW, 10 May 40, sub: Pers for proc in an emergency. SigC 381 Gen.

[6] (1) Memo, CSigO for ASW, 15 May 40, sub: Measures to expedite proc. SigC 400.12 Gen. (2) Mob Plan OASW under PMP and IMP, 15 Jul 39, pp. 16–18. AG 381. (3) Byron Fairchild and Jonathan Grossman, Industrial Relations and Labor Problems, a volume in preparation for the series UNITED STATES ARMY IN WORLD WAR II. (4) Hearings Before the Subcommittee of the Committee on Appropriations, HR, 76th Cong, 3d Sess, On the Military Establishment Appropriation Bill for 1941, 23 Feb 40, p. 99.

12-percent profit ceiling upon contracts for military air material, liking even less any proposal to tax excess profits, and conversely supporting the escalator clause, cost-plus-a-fixed-fee contracts, provision for easy amortization, 30-percent advances at the outset of contracts, relaxation of terms for Reconstruction Finance Corporation loans, and government underwriting of private plant expansion. Their point of view was fixed by lifelong association with business and industry in both military and commercial circles, and sharpened by such legislative proposals as one which would have required the Secretary of War to oversee and approve every purchase made for more than one hundred dollars. (Lt. Col. Clifford D. Cuny described this bill as "particularly obnoxious.")

On the other hand, Congress was obliged to make sure that so vast a governmental spending agency was held within the public interest. At a time, for example, when small business was the subject of efforts to improve its place in the expanding military procurement program, Representative John W. McCormack of Massachusetts elicited the information that the Signal Corps had obligated $8,000,000 in contracts with five large companies, especially General Electric, during the calendar year 1939.[7] The Signal Corps had its closest relations particularly with the "Big Five": General Electric, Western Electric, Westinghouse, RCA, and Bendix.[8] The Eastman Kodak Company was the prime producer of photographic equipment.

"Our big push in procurement did not begin until September 1940," Robert P. Patterson later recalled before the Truman Committee.[9] Along with a number of other actions urging maximum production after the Allied disaster of May, President Roosevelt set up an Advisory Commission to the Council of National Defense to help guide the production program about to be set in motion. The Industrial Mobilization Plan had envisioned something more like an administrator than an adviser,[10] and ultimately the administrators—William S. Knudsen, Donald M. Nelson, James F. Byrnes, Jesse Jones, Henry A. Wallace, William L. Batt, Harold L. Ickes, Harry Hopkins, William N. Jeffers, and others— did appear. But for the time being, the

---

[7] (1) SigC File .032 Legislation 7, 1939–40, *passim,* especially: Ltr, SW to Chm HR Judiciary Committee, 4 Apr 39; Memo, CSigO to ASW, 21 Apr 39; OCSigO R&W Action 1 by CDC [Lt Col Clifford D. Cuny], 2 Feb 40; Ltr, CSigO to TAG, 4 Mar 40. This file comments upon HR's 4236, 7545, 8152, 1082, 8509, 4236, 74th Cong, 1st Sess, and S. 59, 3515. (2) Memo, CSigO for ASW, 10 Aug 40. SigC 160 Contracts Gen 30. (3) Memo, Current Proc Br OASW to CSigO *et al.,* 18 Sep 39, sub: Closing agreement formula developed by Treasury to facilitate work under contracts affected by the Vinson-Trammel Act; (4) 1st Memo Ind, OCSigO for ASW, 27 Sep 39, on Memo, OASW for CSigO *et al.,* 23 Sep 39, sub: Direct current proc. SigC 160 Contracts Gen 26. (5) Brig Gen Calvert H. Arnold, Procurement in the Signal Corps, lecture given in Army Industrial College, 26 Feb 46, p. 3. SigC Hist Sec File. (6) Ltr, Hon. John W. McCormack to SW, 31 May 40; (7) Memo, CSigO for ASW, 7 Jun 40, with Incl, draft of Ltr to McCormack and ASW, 14 Jun 40. SigC 400.13 Gen.

[8] The "Big Five" was a catch phrase in Signal Corps procurement to refer to the giants with whom it made most of its contracts. Like the "Big Ten" of university football which for a time became the "Big Nine," the "Big Five" in many uses became the "Big Four," Bendix being omitted as not of equivalent gigantic stature, although the Signal Corps had considerable business with the Bendix Corporation, especially when acting as the Air Corps' procurement agent. Another variation in the use of the term was that Western Electric, Graybar Electric, and their controlling company, American Telephone and Telegaph, appeared interchangeably.

[9] *Hearings Before Special Committee Pursuant to Senate Resolution 71,* 77th Cong, 1st Sess, Investigation of the National Defense Program, 15 Apr 41, Pt. I, p. 21.

[10] Senate Doc 134, 76th Cong, 2d Sess, *Revised I.M.P.,* 24 Oct 39.

direct responsibility, as well as much of the power, for the defense production program was in the hands of the Assistant Secretary of War. With the 1940 presidential campaign, Henry L. Stimson succeeded Harry Woodring as Secretary of War, and Patterson joined Stimson as Assistant Secretary. Patterson, then, was the official with whom the Signal Corps and other supply agencies worked.

It was just as well to have in Patterson a new broom, for the explosion abroad had made debris of most previous planning. Everything had to be reconsidered. The supply planning groups of the Signal Corps had begun the period of limited emergency with the strength of former months unchanged. Maj. James H. B. Bogman and five women clerks comprised the Procurement Planning Section in the Office of the Chief Signal Officer, and there was one planning officer in each of the three active Signal Corps Procurement Districts. This staff had spent much of 1939 endeavoring to meet the terms of the revised Protective Mobilization Plan going into effect on 10 April 1940. In the interests of acceleration, Bogman had acquired his first officer assistant, Capt. Robert E. Burns, that spring, but still needed a production engineer who could help guide the planning through the maze of electronic developments.

Their planning now identified two signposts not hitherto marked. One was the fact that the Protective Mobilization Plan revision provided reasonably accurate tables of basic allowances for the first time; the other, that a Strategic Materials Act had authorized the stockpiling of strategic and critical materials.[11] Now the relaxing of peacetime contractual regulations in the procurement of experimental, test, and secret equipment constituted another ad-

vantage to them, for planners had consistently anticipated that in time of emergency they would be allowed to drop open bidding and replace it by the direct or negotiated awards which they felt sure would be a short cut.

Except for radio compasses and wire and cable, foreign orders were proving negligible. The cash-and-carry policy denied U.S. material in any abundance to almost every nation, because those which might have afforded the cash did not have or could not spare the navies to carry the material. The few foreign orders were proving of positive benefit, however, contrary to expectations, particularly because they helped to alert both the Signal Corps and its manufacturers. The latter usually notified the Chief Signal Officer even before requesting a Munitions Board permit to sell, and the Chief Signal Officer either urged manufacturers to follow military design where possible or himself released the design to the interested nation, as in the case of granting the British access to the aircraft radio compass. Release of a design to one country permitted the manufacturer to sell it to any other nation, and so to increase his productive potential even while he committed current operating capacity. Thus production of military signal equipment in greater quantities than the Signal Corps would absorb was slowly placing industry in a better position to meet war.

The Signal Corps had been slow with educational orders, partly because of the assumption that the half-dozen companies dominating communications manufacture were well in command of the situation. Inquiry now showed such disturbing facts

[11] (1) Pub. 117, 76th Cong, 1st Sess. (2) Report of Second General Procurement Planning Conference, 9–14 Oct 39. SigC FM 186 Plng Gen ASW.

as a serious shortage of machine tools and of men trained in the skill to use them. Again, for field wire, that subject of more than twenty years of supply planning, there appeared to be only two companies in the United States capable of making it; and neither had done so. Under suggestion from the Office of the Assistant Secretary, the Signal Corps now reversed its position on educational orders and entered upon the first of a series: a contract with John A. Roeblings' Sons for 500 miles of W-110-B wire a month. Eventually eleven firms learned through educational orders to make this wire, at a combined rate of 8,500 miles a month.[12] This was still far from enough. How far, could be measured by the fact that the planning which followed World War I had called for twice as much.

To be awarded an educational order, a company had to complete a detailed production study which showed a scheme for conversion of the plant to emergency military production and listed in full the machine tools, dies, jigs, fixtures, and gauges needed, with indications of where they could be obtained; components and accessories to be purchased from designated contributory sources; and the number of workers, with the time required for training them. Under the terms of the order, the manufacturer also estimated what the cost of manufacture in quantity would be if the "educational" method were employed on a mass production line. In short, the award of an educational order could give the Procurement Planning Section the information that production surveys had not drawn out.

The stand-by equal in importance to wire, the EE-8 telephone which the entire Army used, constituted another invitation to educational orders. American indus-

try's capacity to produce it was fifty a day. Its manufacture involved hand cutting and sewing of leather cases; special processing of kangaroo skin used in the cover section of the case; individual production of plastic parts, like the handles, which could be mass-made; and altogether a watchmaker's skill on the part of the artisans. The cord was figuratively strangling production of the telephone, because only one manufacturer knew how to make it. Educational orders which set three facilities to work on the EE-8-A developed new sources of supply for the cord and streamlined the manufacture by introducing machine sewing and finishing of the cases, substituting cowhide or even processed canvas for the kangaroo, and devising rapid assembly lines. Maximum daily production rose from 50 to more than 2,000.[13]

Military radio equipment, often having little in common with civilian items, presented a serious procurement problem even when ordered in small lots, let alone in quantities. Radio is never wholly amenable to mass-production techniques. Its manufacture is essentially not an industry, but a craft; and radiomen echo this feeling when they speak of their work as the radio

---

[12] (1) Report on Problem No. 3, Analysis of Basic Industry, Committee E, The Machine Tool Industry, 1938–39 course, Army Industrial College, Dec 39. (2) H. D. Hausman, Procurement Planning and Industrial Mobilization, 1920–1940, Pt. II, p. 162 and *passim.* OCSigO Industrial Mob Br File. (3) "The Crowell Board [Brig Gen Benedict Crowell, Chm] Report on Educational Orders for Peacetime Munitions Production," *Army Ordnance,* XX, No. 117 (November–December, 1939), 167–70. (4) Maj J. H. B. Bogman, Chief of OCSigO Proc Plan Sec, A Procurement Study of the Influence of Educational Orders on Wire W-110-B, 21 May 40; (5) 4th Ind, CSigO to ASW, 4 Jun 40. SigC 160 Contracts Gen 29.

[13] (1) Lt. Col James H. B. Bogman, Current Problems in Signal Corps Procurement, Army Industrial College Short Course 3, Jul–Sep 41, pp. 14–15. (2) Hausman study cited n. 12(2), Pt. II, pp. 240 ff.

art. Radio manufacture had become an industry, undeniably, but industrial mass production had brought such a cheapening of the product that workers in the big plants would have to be trained to do better work. They were so used to a standard which cut corners, eliminated certain parts, adulterated others, accomplished the wiring or soldering hastily, and assembled components without the necessary repeated testing of both the individual parts and the whole radio that, confronted with a call for carefully made equipment, they had no experience with which to start. It was desirable to apply mass-production techniques in order to meet a wartime demand for military radio, but there was a serious risk that they would turn out botched equipment. To satisfy the extraordinarily technical requirements of the armed forces, companies which had been making thousands of radios would have to learn to make thousands of good radios. Toward this end, their employees would have to be metamorphosed from assembly-line automatons to painstaking craftsmen: an irony quite the reverse of the need in EE-8-A telephone manufacture.

For this reason as much as because the field was considered to have been finally partitioned by a few companies, it had been against Signal Corps policy to place educational orders for radio. Bogman's office now had a production engineer who had reinforced this policy by reporting that it was impractical to compute radio requirements under the Protective Mobilization Plan because design changed too fast. Accordingly, the Signal Corps withheld educational orders until designs could be frozen long enough to make the production test worth while. But May 1940 changed that. General Mauborgne sought $2,665,000 for educational orders to cover

nine of the most important items of radio equipment which the Signal Corps procured for troops.[14]

The Chief Signal Officer had already asked the Senate, on May 10, to restore funds permitting the fifty-seven aircraft to be equipped with radio. Six days later President Roosevelt threw all previous estimates to the winds by asking for 50,000 airplanes within the coming fiscal year. At the same time funds became available to let a secret contract for $1,000,000 worth of SCR-268 searchlight-control radars. The sum was unheard of for investment in a single item, and industry was unprepared to deal with it. A few of the great companies had worked with radar on an experimental basis in their laboratories (RCA notably, as General Electric had with FM), but they were reluctant to contract for large-scale production of sets. Eventually Western Electric took up the contract.

There was more in this incident than the frequent refusal of industry to participate in the defense program unless all risks were removed and top profits guaranteed. Manufacturers did sometimes accept contracts which later proved to have disadvantageous specifications. This was almost the situation—a situation rescued for a happy ending—with reference to a contract which the Allen D. Cardwell Manufacturing Company made to produce frequency meters. A frequency meter is an essential in electric communications; and the one which the Cardwell firm produced turned out to be "super-delicate" and "of the most accurate precision." In

---

[14] (1) Milton B. Sleeper, "War Revises Radio Industry," *FM* [later *FM and Television*], II, No. 6 (January–April, 1942), pp. 5–6. (2) Proc Plan Sec Supply Div OCSigO, Data for Bi-Weekly Conference, 23 May 40. SigC PP 381 Plans Acceleration, May 40.

making it so, the manufacturer had accepted requests from the Laboratories not actually incorporated into the specifications; this had thrown him far behind schedule; and he became liable to heavy damages despite the undenied fact that he had produced a much better item than the government had contracted for. After due negotiation, he obtained a remission of damages, but the call was close.[15]

In taking up the million-dollar SCR-268 contract, Western Electric was in no such danger. It had a cushion of capital resources, its own laboratories, a firm understanding with the Signal Corps, and an almost impregnable position in the national business economy.

With this order for radar and the prospect of equipping 50,000 airplanes, the Signal Corps passed a milestone on the way to the tremendous procurement program of World War II. In the ensuing month, the New York Signal Corps Procurement District alone let more than $2,000,000 worth of contracts.[16]

It became evident that in order to meet the quotas of the new fiscal year's up-stepping procurement, one-shift plants would have to go onto two-shift schedules, two-shift plants go to three. It became further evident that plant space as well as plant manpower must grow, and on June 25 Public Law 664 authorized government financing of such expansion through the Reconstruction Finance Corporation. The Signal Corps' first arrangement of the sort was for the Bendix Radio Corporation, in the production of radio compasses, frequency meters, direction finders, and other items of the Air program.

On June 27 the President established the National Defense Research Committee "to correlate and support scientific research on the mechanisms of warfare" and

to contract with individuals, educational or scientific institutions, and industrial organizations for studies, experimental investigations, and reports. NDRC was the forerunner of OSRD, the Office of Scientific Research and Development, and the chief civilian governmental agency to which the Signal Corps looked during the war.

On June 28 Public Law 671 effected more of the measures which military procurement had looked for: in this case, priority of Army and Navy contracts over civilian and export contracts, and suspension of the provisions of the Walsh-Healy Act[17] at need, particularly the limitation to an eight-hour day.

And on July 2 Public Law 703, another in the urgently mounting list "to expedite the strengthening of national defense," greatly enlarged the area where negotiated contracts would be permitted. The charge was now definitely upon big industry and the Military Establishment to equip the nation for war, for major curbs hitherto applied in the public interest had been removed.

At first, the War Department handled this grant of authority with extreme caution, the Office of the Assistant Secretary drawing up and distributing rules to govern it. Negotiated contracts involving $500,000 or more, as well as cost-plus-a-fixed-fee contracts, could be made only with the approval of the Assistant Secretary and subject to the further approval powers, if he exerted them, of Donald M. Nelson, the chairman of the Advisory Commission to the Council of National

---

[15] SigC File Contract W-227-SC-1723, *passim*.

[16] Ltr, Actg O/C N.Y. SigC Proc District to CSigO, 18 Jul 40, sub: Monthly status rpt. SigC 400.13 Gen 18.

[17] See Fairchild and Grossman hist cited n. 6(3).

Defense. A set of standards stated by the commission would guide the War Department's procurement, Patterson announced. Speed was the foremost of them, but not to the extent that the devil could take the hindmost. The military economy was cautioned to maintain itself wholly within the civilian economy, statutory guarantees to labor being preserved, commitments toward social welfare being safeguarded, and industry and venture capital being protected by government subsidization at every possible point.

In August, letters of intent were developed, to expedite production still further by anticipating even negotiation of a contract; a letter of intent gave a manufacturer assurance that the government would bear any costs resulting from getting production under way. The manufacturer would not be out of pocket if the subsequent negotiation failed to produce a contract. In actual fact, a letter of intent was as good as a contract, for a procurement agent who had committed the government to the initial expense was not likely to see it go for naught. Contract restrictions were still tight enough so that the procuring agency was reluctant even to acknowledge an occasional bad bargain and terminate it, with the result that once in a while good time and money were thrown after bad. And always beyond the awarding and completion of a contract stood the General Accounting Office, requiring to be satisfied on any changes, any extensions, any remissions, any exceeding of sums.[18]

The Mirrors of Defense Effort

Half glare, half shadow, the emergency provided an imperfect light by which to look at preparedness measures, but there was no doubt of the elements to prepare. There were simply the elementary one-and-one: men and equipment. The men would come from the nation as a whole. Equipment must come from those who manufactured it. Procurement of men was a universal issue, far beyond the reach of the Signal Corps or any other single agency, although all eyes turned for its solution to the forthcoming conscription. The burden of equipment, however, lay directly upon those charged with assuming it. As in 1941 the provision of men was uppermost of the two essentials, so in 1940 was the provision of equipment. The probability that *defense* would prove to be an urgent euphemism for *war footing* subordinated everything else to the necessity to amass material.

Thus the specific procurement demands of the customers, especially of the Air and Armored branches, forcibly turned the course of signal development into some

---

[18] (1) *Hearings Before the Subcommittee of the Committee on Appropriations,* HR, 76th Cong, 3d Sess, On the Military Establishment Appropriation Bill for 1941, HR 9209, p. 655. (2) *Hearings Before Special Committee Pursuant to Senate Resolution 71,* 77th Cong, 1st Sess, Investigation of the National Defense Program, 15 Apr 41, Pt. I, pp. 27–29. (3) Memo, CSigO for ASW, cited n. 6(1). (4) Arnold lecture cited n. 7(5), p. 3. (5) Bogman course cited n. 13(1), p. 10. (6) Col George P. Bush and Martha E. Manning, History of Procurement Planning, 1920–1940, MS, 1942, p. 19. OCSigO Industrial Mob Br File. (7) Memo, Dir Current Proc Office OASW for CSigO, 10 Jun 40, sub: Approval of important purchases by Council of National Defense; (8) Ltr, ASW to CSigO, 12 Jun 40, sub: 1941 proc program; (9) Memo, Dir Current Proc Office OASW for CSigO, 13 Jun 40, sub: Approval of important purchases. SigC 400.13 Gen. (10) Memo, ASW for Chiefs of WD Supply Svs, 27 Sep 40. SigC 160 Contracts Gen 31. (11) Ltr, Dir SCL to CSigO, 24 Sep 40, sub: Contract W-1077-SC-320 Sound Products, Inc. SigC 160 Contracts Gen 30. (12) 1st Ind, Lt Col Clifford D. Cuny, OCSigO, to Chief of Audit Div GAO, 29 Oct 40, on Ltr, Chief of Contract Exam Sec GAO to CSigO, 7 Oct 40. SigC 160 Contracts Gen 31.

channels it had not yet taken. The example of foreign, civilian, and naval new material was increasingly bearing upon the laboratories of both Monmouth and Wright. The probable use of hundreds of standard commercial models of communications equipment almost without change drastically modified the freedom of choice also. Often these influences conflicted. In procurement there was no sole cast of countenance. Many lines cut across the main furrows.

Emergency was a galvanic word, but it had not brought a unified effort into existence—the sort of well-muscled national right arm which the posters showed to be brandished against danger. With the loss of continental Europe, many more persons in the United States had doubts about the remoteness of the war, yet much was unready. A part of the public, part of the Congress, part of the business world, part of the military world was apathetic; other parts were divided against themselves. A nation accustomed to peace was resisting war. In Congress, the first peacetime conscription in the nation's history was being hauled back and forth between the goals of necessity and liberty. In commerce and industry, many executives were waiting for their own terms to be met. In the Army, mobilization and procurement had picked up but little momentum, and that at an uncertain rhythm. The place to measure it was in the experience of the last war and in the tryouts of the next.

Asking a former Chief Signal Officer, General Gibbs, for his opinion on preparedness measures which the communications service could take, General Marshall heard, among other things, that the country's communications specialists, particularly the 48,000 members of the American Radio Relay League, should be

theoretically allotted without delay, so that the Signal Corps could know what strength it had to count upon in competition with Navy, air, and ground force communication.[19] "This personnel must be highly trained to perform useful service," Gibbs emphasized. "Poor service is worse than a disappointment. It may bring disaster."

General Mauborgne, his successor, estimated that he could substantially equip and maintain the signalmen for an army of 1,200,000 by 15 November 1941, of 2,000,000 by 1 June 1942. He hedged his bet by pointing out the probable absence of enough men trained to carry out the program, by citing manufacturers' resistance to the Vinson-Trammel Act and the cost-accounting system required by the Treasury Department, by expressing his hope to see strikes repressed by legislation, and by voicing concern over a quick shortage in raw materials if foreign demands were allowed to grow.[20]

For the time being, until the issue of Selective Service should be settled, he had no way of knowing whether he was right or wrong in manpower estimates. In equipment, field exercises revealed some of the answers. Before maneuvers were complete, there was an occasion under the Protective Mobilization Plan to look at tactical signal equipment again. Which were the absolute essentials? Their procurement must be expedited, if there were any question that a state of war would put them in short supply.

Looked at on a basis of total cost, radio was the essential, without quibble: the

[19] Memo, Maj Gen George S. Gibbs, Ret., for Gen Marshall, CofS, 27 Jun 40, sub: Sig coms requirements in preparation for war. SigC 381 Gen 16, Mar–Aug 40.

[20] Memo, CSigO for ASW, cited n. 7(2).

dozen major points of expenditure were all for radio sets. Looked at so far as quantities of items were concerned, radio was nothing of the sort: the vital needs were in wire and, remarkably, in visual equipment. Radar and vehicular radio were dominant; so were flashlights, panels, and telephone instruments. It is of sufficient interest to cull from the whole listing of Signal Corps essential items the top dozen in several categories, for the illustration it offers of divergent interests, conflicting demands, good and bad guesses. Listed according to their total procurement cost in each case, the twelve leading items in the Signal Corps' estimates were:[21]

SCR-245 (vehicular radio)	$7,080,000
SCR-274 (aircraft command set)	6,450,000
SCR-268 ("radar"—searchlight controller)	5,180,000
SCR-259 (soon abandoned aircraft liaison set)	4,180,000
SCR-193 (ground forces)	2,822,400
SCR-177 (ground-to-air)	2,400,000
SCR-283 (aircraft command set)	2,400,000
SCR-270 and SCR-271 (aircraft interception "radar")	2,275,000
SCR-287 (aircraft liaison set)	1,980,000
SCR-210 (receiver only)	1,668,800
SCR-269 (radio compass)	1,400,000
SCR-183 (predecessor and partner to SCR-283)	1,320,000

Listed according to individual cost, these items led:

SCR-270 and SCR-271	$65,000
SCR-268	35,000
SCR-197 (truck-and-trailer long-range radio)	20,000
Sound-ranging equipment, GR-3	11,000
Telephone central TC-2	8,000
Spotting set PH-32	7,000
Truck and earth borer	6,200
SCR-177	4,800
SCR-188	4,800
SCR-259	4,400
SCR-287	4,400
SCR-193	4,200

Listed according to unit quantity:

Flashlight TL-122	176,526
Lamp LM-35	72,000
Clip TL-123	50,000
Headset HS-23	30,000
Panel AL-120	25,000
Wire W-110 (mile lengths)	22,000
Chest BC-5	16,000
Head and Chest Set HS-19	14,000
Cord CD-190	14,000
Telephone EE-8	8,000
Panel AL-119	8,000
Filter Equipment RC-32	6,000

After the last of the series of maneuvers, General Marshall put another question. Having asked what the Signal Corps thought it ought to do (Gibbs had doggedly replied with the traditional plea for unified responsibility), he now asked what it could do. The Germans were apparently using radio a great deal, all the way down to companies. Was the Signal Corps going to pursue that? Commercial equipment was probably better than that of the Signal Corps. Was the Signal Corps prepared to contract for it on a large scale? Would it not be well to imitate the Air Corps practice of competitive design? And how was the Navy handling its communications procurement? Marshall was disturbed that the maneuvers of the summer—first each of the armies, starting with the Third in Louisiana during May, then all four in August—had shown tactical signal communications to be inadequate.[22] The onus of inadequacy was not solely the Signal Corps'—combat communications was a field in which the Signal Corps largely took, rather than gave,

---

[21] Incl with AG Ltr to CSigO, 12 Jun 40, sub: Expediting program for critical items (PMP) and essential items (existing units)—SigC. AG 112.05 (6540) M-D, and also in SigC CH 11-106 Proc Program, 1941.

[22] Memo, CofS for CSigO, 7 Sep 40. OCS 16281-6.

orders—but, Marshall asked, within the limits which were the Signal Corps' responsibility, were things as good as they should be?

Signal Corps observers, still as much worried as in the preceding year's maneuvers, said "No." Bluntly: "The reputation of the Signal Corps is at stake." [23] This was the conclusion after the Camp McCoy, Second Army exercises at Wisconsin, although the man who made it, Lt. Col. Richard B. Moran, qualified it by advancing the familiar demand for more men. It was "pitifully inadequate," he felt, to assign only part of a battalion to do everything, as the 51st Battalion detachment had been expected to do at Camp McCoy. But there was even less strength in equipment than in troops: fewer than half a dozen vehicular sets; no Aircraft Warning Service, let alone aircraft warning equipment; and a tendency on the part of the tactical air cover, after waiting for good weather, to ignore its radio and drop messages over the side.

Maj. Jerry V. Matejka was another Signal Corps officer who was obliged to take note of improvisations and inadequacies. At both the First and Second Army operations he had observed "a general lack of modern . . . radio . . . particularly of vehicular sets such as the SCR-245, which . . . assume great importance in rapid movement of troops." [24] Although he was told that telegraph printers, the improvement which had been strongly recommended in the 1939 maneuvers, were sending messages from the divisions back to the corps, he found out that they were not in use at all. The whole wire system was still based upon easy access to local facilities; men of the 51st had spent half of July, ahead of the Camp McCoy maneuvers, in building a

pole line tributary to the one already settled into the Wisconsin countryside, running circuits to the airports, and connecting with the telephone buildings in Sparta and other nearby towns. [25]

Truth to tell, however remote this action was from Attu or Tunisia, it was not a world away by any means. Typical of American military operations is the fact that wherever they do not find the scene they are used to, they create it. In the sense that a barn "improves" an acre of land, they "improve" the Aleutians or the desert or the jungle with buildings, roads, vehicles, and an abundance of mechanical equipment which sooner or later brings into being the kind of situation where the teletype in the general's field office works as matter of factly as if there were not a thousand miles of undeveloped land outside. Thus many of the signal communications men of the forthcoming war would be set down in conditions at least as established as those of the various maneuvers. As for the men who would be the first on a scene not yet provided with all the conveniences, there was ample reason to presume that they could meet the test, summoning both the stamina for hardship and the ingenuity for mechanical improvisation.

At these same much-criticized Second Army maneuvers, for example, an infantry officer noticed that men of the 11th Infantry, wanting a vehicular set, had mounted an old SCR-171 in a half-ton truck, rigged an antenna, and contrived a

[23] Lt Col Richard B. Moran, SigC, Rpt on Exec No. 5, 2d Army Maneuvers, Camp McCoy, Wisc., 24–27 Aug 40. SigC 354.2 (2d Army) No. 2, 1938–3 Mar 41.

[24] Memo, Lt Col Jerry V. Matejka for Brig Gen Lesley J. McNair, 30 Aug 40. AGF 324.2 Maneuvers 1, 1940–41.

[25] Rpt, Participation of the 51st Signal Battalion in 2nd Army Maneuvers, 1940. SigC 354.2 (2d Army) No. 2, 1938–3 Mar 41.

power supply out of dry batteries they had salvaged from SCR-195's. Thus transformed, the 171 not only got around in its own vehicle but even functioned a bit when the truck was in motion.[26] In little instances of this sort lay much encouragement.

They could not be permitted, however, to lighten the burden of the Signal Corps, which was the duty of seeing that equipment did not have to be improvised or men worked at double duty. Enough equipment, enough men. . . . The peacetime conscription bill was closer than ever now; that should open the supply of men. For equipment, mass procurement was similarly near. The valuable upshot of the maneuver season was that leading categories of new equipment distinctly emerged. The catalog of "essentials" became a thing of the past wherever it emphasized anything outside these categories. Teletype. Vehicular radio. Air radio. Radar.

Unknown to the men on maneuvers, air radio and radar developments of the most extraordinary kind were under discussion on an interservice, international scale. The Armored Force was suing for and getting Signal Corps commitments to vehicular radio with all the drive of a new organization. The Air Corps was suing for and getting its radio equipment with all the force of the Air Corps. The ground arms saw clearly the desirability of communications which could move: walkie-talkies, radio in motion, light wire, compact teletype. The final report on the First Army maneuvers epitomized this awareness, counting off its elements: 100-miles-in-motion, abundant wire above the regiment, abundant radio below, mobile teletype for divisions and corps, and especially—FM.

FM Confirmed

Word of mouth was bruiting the merits of FM. Some of the support came from the field, some from the Signal Corps, some from manufacturers. Among the last were those whom Armstrong had licensed to use his patents, plus the inventor himself, who took every opportunity to lend the Army his equipment. He had provided the First Army's maneuvers with the twenty-eight sets from the Radio Engineering Laboratories, which was his own outlet. In part, a demand had been sown within the Signal Corps. The demand which settled the matter, however, came from the field arms, for no amount of drive either from manufacturers or from individual proponents in the service could establish FM tactically if the tactical users did not want it.[27]

They did. Against such remarks as the Laboratories', that there was "no need at the present time for the development of any special frequency modulation equipment,"[28] chiefs of one component after another were persisting in their inquiries, and the Signal Corps' own chief, General Mauborgne, occasionally added his. The

[26] Ltr, Maj I. M. Oseth to Chief of Inf, 16 Sep 40, sub: Rpt by inf observer at Second Army maneuvers 24–27 Aug 40. AG 353 (10-20-38) Sec 1-E Rpts on 1940 Army Maneuvers.

[27] On all of these points, see intervs, SigC Hist Sec with: (1) Col Edward A. Allen, SigC Bd, Ft. Monmouth, N. J., 10 Feb 50; (2) Dr. Edwin H. Armstrong, New York, N.Y., 13 Feb 50; (3) O. M. Brymer, Government Sales Representative Western Electric Corp., New York, N.Y., 15 Feb 50; (4) Maj Gen Roger B. Colton, Ret., New York, N.Y., 14 Feb 50; (5) C. M. Jansky, Jr., Radio Engr Consultant, Washington, D.C., 16 Nov 50; (6) Fred R. Lack, Vice-President Western Electric Corp., New York, N.Y., 15 Feb 50; (7) Fred M. Link, Link Radio Corp., New York, N.Y., 15 Feb 50.

[28] 1st Ind, Maj Rex V. D. Corput, Jr., to CSigO, 12 Sep 40, on Ltr, CSigO to Dir SCL, 19 Aug 40, sub: FM equip. SigC 413.44 FM 1, Jan–Sep 40.

general pleasure in the twenty-eight sets tried out at maneuvers was such that the signal officer of the Second Corps Area (which served the First Army) pressed for permission to keep them.

No one in the Signal Corps who was concerned with the FM decision wanted to approve these sets just yet. Colonel Colton cited the need for "further tests looking to authorized tactical use." Major Guest in the Communications Liaison Division raised the question of frequencies again, saying that the available ones were already "barely adequate" for the authorized equipment, the SCR-194. The prospect of a radiotelephone at hand in every Army car unsettled him, too; the convenience of it suggested that the demand would be enormous. Colonel Moran, in the War Plans and Training Division, recommended that the sets be used only under the specific authorization of the Chief Signal Officer; and Colonel Mitchell, for the Research and Development Division, agreed that "continued use for tactical purposes cannot be countenanced." Temporarily, they went back to the builder.[29]

With noteworthy unanimity of time and circumstance, however, the demands consolidated immediately after the close of the maneuvers season. In much the same way that a captain in a mechanized cavalry brigade had raised one call from the grass roots, a lieutenant in a field artillery regiment raised another. "[Although] the present type of transmission used in the Army is called amplitude modulation," 1st Lt. John J. Davis, communications officer of the 80th Field Artillery Regiment at Fort Des Moines, argued, ". . . an entirely new type of transmission called frequency modulation . . . has many distinct military ad-

vantages." The sets could be smaller and lighter, he said; they operated over such a wide band that the network possibilities were manifold; they did not compete for the crowded bands, but transmitted in the ultrahigh-frequency area; they did not require exclusive frequency assignment, for if transmitters of equal power were operating on the same frequency, only the nearest would be heard; they were difficult to jam; and—a "self-evident" advantage—they were free from vehicular interference and atmospheric shutdowns. The Chief of Field Artillery agreed to the extent of saying that Davis expressed "almost the unanimous opinion of artillery commanders that field artillery communications are archaic and woefully inadequate." [30]

At that date, the SCR-194 was the standard radio for light and medium gun batteries and the fifteen-year-old SCR-161 for regiments. For vehicular use, the Field Artillery employed the SCR-245, when it could get one. Both the old and the new were amplitude-modulated; and the Radio Corporation of America, the solid opponent of frequency modulation, was manufacturing another AM set intended to replace the 161.[31]

---

[29] SigC File 413.44 FM 1, Jan–Sep 40, *passim.*

[30] (1) Ltr, Col William S. Bowen, CAC Bd, to Chief of CAC, 12 Sep 40, sub: Commercial FM radio equip, with 1st Ind, Chief of CAC to CSigO, 4 Oct 40; (2) Ltr, Chief of Inf to CSigO, 19 Sep 40, sub: Test of FM radio; (3) Ltr, Lt Davis to CG 6th Div, 27 Aug 40 sub: Radio recommendations, with 3d Ind, Chief of FA to CSigO, 3 Oct 40; (4) Ltr, Chief of FA to CSigO, 19 Aug 40, sub: FM equip, with 2d Wrapper Ind, Col Colton to CSigO, 6 Sep 40. SigC 413.44 FM 1, Jan–Sep 40.

[31] The SCR-285, then under development, but so similar to the SCR-284 that it was subsequently dropped. Hist Sec E&T Divs OCSigO, History of Signal Corps Research and Development in World War II, 1945–46, Vol. VIII, Pt. 3, Proj. (823) 10–11. SigC Hist Sec File.

Signal Corps equipment policy had seldom had such a decision to make. Disruption theatened the vital relation between research and procurement. If research went ahead with a development not supported by the Signal Corps' major outlets for manufacture, how could the item be procured in the quantities which a war would impose? If procurement made sure of mass production by remaining within the fold of the mass producers, would not the Army be denied one of the most promising communications advances in years? There were many cross currents to the decision. For example, even the inventor himself questioned whether FM would lend itself to small portable sets—which, because they were small and portable, had transmitters of possibly too low power. The SCR-509 and SCR-510 later banished doubts on this score, when the Signal Corps Laboratories revived reactance modulation and combined it with crystal control.[32]

Another deterrent to quick decision appeared in the fact that a decision had to be made on crystals first. The pressure for them was becoming all but irresistible. At ever more frequent intervals it unsettled established policy and reopened closed verdicts. To the near consternation of a considerable body of opinion both in the Signal Corps and in industry, the Armored Force asked for 100 channels for its tank sets, the AF-III, any 10 to be available in advance of an operation. Mechanization indicated the need for that much choice, because moving vehicles would cross into many assigned frequency areas. Experience had shown that it was extraordinarily difficult to change frequencies on a master-oscillator vehicular set when the vehicle was in motion. The simplest possible means of operation was essential, and

the Armored Force therefore felt that crystal control was the obvious answer: immediate, pushbutton finding of the frequency at the center of the channel.

So did the Signal Corps. But theory came up against practice. A 10-crystal radio posed as delicate an engineering challenge as a 24-jewel watch. That challenge could be met, but what of the still brittle fact that quartz was one of the most strategic of strategic materials? If crystal control were to be introduced everywhere at the rate the Armored Force was proposing, not all the quartz in Brazil might be enough. Surveys in the Laboratories and the Procurement Planning Section of the Office of the Chief Signal Officer counted up all the known sources, even to the amount in American museums.

The Signal Corps made up maneuver test models with everything the Armored Force officers wanted, almost expecting that such an array of quartz would discourage them. The more crystals, went the argument, the more space required in the set; therefore the larger set; therefore the more space which an already crowded vehicle would have to sacrifice to it. Could every tank make room for a cubic foot of crystals? That was the approximate amount which 100 channels would necessitate. Lt. Col. Edward A. Allen, the signal officer of the Armored Force, himself felt that there was no need for so many channels; 6, rather than the 10 being sought, would give a comfortable scope in which to plan an armored operation. The problem was not comparable to that of a

[32] (1) Memo, Maj John Hessel, SigC, for Col Eugene V. Elder, 1 Nov 42, sub: Pertinent info concerning development of SCR-300. SigC 413.44 (SCR-300) No. 1, 1942. (2) MS comment by SCL [Mar 42]. SigC Hist Sec File. (3) John J. Kelleher, "VHF and Microwave Military Communication Systems," *Signals*, I, No. 4 (March–April 1947), 44–48.

mobile police radio system, as some of the enthusiasts seemed to think. All cars of a police system worked on the same channel, and each set needed to receive only that one. Armstrong, Colton, Allen, Fred R. Lack of Western Electric, and others would all have recommended fewer channels, and eventually the Armored Force did drop its requirement from 100 to 80. But General Chaffee and his staff held firm to the center of their demand, which was for crystals. Whether 100 or 80, tank-set channels must be crystal-controlled.

Laboratories proponents of crystals sought a firmer bulwark. Their belief in American quartz had not been supported by the careful judgment of the National Bureau of Standards, the Naval Research Laboratory, and the Signal Corps' own Research and Development and Supply divisions. This time, the Laboratories obtained an estimate from some of the companies in the market. Although not leading crystal suppliers, three companies (Western Electric, Radio Corporation of America, and American Gem and Pearl) calculated that they could get a million and a half radio crystals out of the contemporary U.S. stockpile of Brazilian quartz, and that Brazil could provide 600,000 more a year. Once again, the Office of the Chief Signal Officer divisions refigured the supply. They could arrive at nothing like such large figures. Their arithmetic showed 480,000 rather than 1,500,000 and 300,000 rather than 600,000. If this were true, the Signal Corps could not commit itself to an extensive crystal program. It viewed with alarm any such prospect, and urgently reminded the Laboratories that this was the case. Colton assured the Washington offices that he had not been flying in the face of their policy. "As a matter of fact," he declared,

"we did not suggest the use of crystals originally to the Mechanized Cavalry." Even so, Laboratories opinion was markedly favorable to crystals, and the using arms were all but clamoring for them. Maj. James D. O'Connell succinctly said, "Without crystals, you have radio; with them, communications." Along with the Armored Force went other users of vehicular radio. Even the Air Corps was building up to the SCR-274 and other very high frequency equipment which would tax the crystal supply.

Almost suddenly, a way out appeared. O'Connell, Colton, and Lack, consulting on the matter, proposed that the Signal Corps underwrite a new method for making four crystals out of every one. Fine cutting and a reorientation to the use of crystals smaller than hitherto thought feasible would quadruple the supply. In addition, there was a possibility that "seeding," or growing artificial crystals around a core in a laboratory solution, would provide a synthetic abundance in case the natural supply should be cut off. The matter was given to the National Defense Advisory Committee. Every interested agency of the Signal Corps recalculated the visible supply and the invisible demand, figuring the latter in association with the Laboratories' insistence that if crystals were to be used at all they must not be used partially or meagerly. On a basis of four for one, it might be possible to go ahead.

The long discussion culminated on September 18 and 19, at conferences held at the Signal Corps Laboratories over Armored Force equipment.

. . . It was concluded that . . . the United States' stock pile of quartz plus one year's supply from Brazil, was sufficient quartz for 1,000,000 normal size crystals. If an extra stage of amplification is used, crystals can be cut to ¼ normal size and if half the amount above were cut to the ¼ size, we would have 2,500,000 crystals available. It was estimated that the Armored Force could be equipped . . . using only about 9% of the immediately available supply. . . . A total of 405,000 crystals for Types III and IV and IV-a sets for the Armored Force . . . is only 10.1% of the 4,000,000 crystals (¼ size) available in the United States plus one year's supply from Brazil.

On September 25, the Office of the Chief Signal Officer approved a 100-channel type III and a 50-channel type IV. The decision had been made, and Army vehicular radio was committed to crystals. It was satisfying to contemplate, and risky. O'Connell, later assigned the wartime mission of fulfilling the program decided upon in 1940, had a success which removed all doubts; but on at least one occasion he looked at the predictions which he and his colleagues had made and ruefully observed: "For a good laugh, read this." [33]

In this fashion one major problem, crystal control, had been settled or at least alleviated. The decision closely related to it, where and how much to use frequency modulation, remained formally unresolved, but was actually so close to an answer that in the minds of many it, too, was a settled issue. First, the Radio Engineering Laboratories sets of the late summer maneuvers moved to the forefront again. The Signal Corps Laboratories agreed to ask for only three of them, and Lt. Gen. Hugh A. Drum successfully dislodged the other twenty-five for "urgent" use in infantry command and staff cars and in infantry-artillery liaison. "It is assumed," he assumed, "that crystals could be furnished and the sets adjusted so that they could be operated on a fre-

quency that could be authorized." [34] At this, the entire Signal Corps gave a sigh. Shortage, however, had not put off the Armored Force; neither could it the Infantry; and along with agreeing to provide the crystals, the Signal Corps assigned the 37–39 megacycle band to the twenty-five sets.

Thus was the field demand making itself felt and covering in a stride or two the conventional, slower route toward acceptance which Army regulations obliged the Signal Corps to follow. The Armored Force, like the Infantry, also demanded similar sets. The Signal Corps was reluctant to permit Captain Williams to borrow six Link police sets, as he had asked. There was no reason to do so, the Laboratories maintained, when Armored Force specifications were still for amplitude modulation (accordingly, the Signal Corps' first order upon Western Electric for three service-test samples of the AF-III radio, the SCR-508, called for amplitude modulation). In addition, there was some feeling that the sets would certainly be less satisfactory than could be developed in the normal course of research on the "500's." Moran suggested that it would be a good idea to let the Armored Force find out for itself; and Mitchell commented, "We are

[33] (1) SigC File 413.44 Crystals 5, 1940, *passim*. (2) Brig Gen James D. O'Connell, Deputy CSigO, personal file on crystals (untitled), *passim*. (3) MS comment by Maj Gen Roger B. Colton, Ret., 19 and 24 Nov 51; (4) Ltr, Col Williams to Dr. Thompson, 31 Dec 49; (5) Ltr, John Hessel, Chief of Br SCEL, to Colton, 30 Nov 51. SigC Hist Sec File. (6) Intervs cited n. 27. (7) M. L. Melia, The Quartz Crystal Program of the Signal Corps, 1941–1945, 1945, *passim*, especially pp. 1–20. SigC Hist Sec File. (8) Vance Hilliard, "Radio Telephones Guide the 'Blitz Buggies,' " *Bell Telephone Magazine*, XXIII (1944), 52 ff.

[34] 4th Ind, Col Crawford to Sig Officer First Army, 3 Dec 40, 5th Ind, Gen Drum to TAG, 5 Dec 40, and 7th Ind, CSigO to TAG, 4 Feb 41, on missing basic Ltr. SigC 413.44 FM 1, Jan–Sep 40.

getting a bear by the tail but it can't be helped." Federal Communications Commission engineers contributed to the resolution of the problem by producing a favorable report of the FM sets installed in the cars of Connecticut State troopers. They had tested the sets in the presence of Link, the manufacturer, and Dr. Daniel E. Noble, the designer. The report won the support of Guest,[35] in the Office of the Chief Signal Officer, and he forwarded the papers to Colton for "earnest consideration." Colton, O'Connell, and several of the civilian radio engineers went off to Connecticut to have a look for themselves. The look strongly favored FM. Next, the Signal Corps Laboratories ran off tests of their own, late in 1940. FM was confirmed as more efficient and more effective in short-range mobile radio. At once the Signal Corps asked Western Electric to build FM versions of the SCR-508. Superior FM radios for the Armored Force became assured.[36]

This plunge into frequency-modulated radio together with the commitment to crystal control constituted two daring ventures by the Signal Corps and its Laboratories. The more basic decision, upon which all higher-frequency radio awaited, involved crystals of quartz. The decision was made in the face of great odds; the great need for simple dependable tuning was pitted against a critical scarcity of quartz and wholly inadequate facilities for producing the crystals. There were many misgivings and doubters. "One day in 1943," Colton subsequently reminisced, "when it looked as if we would have to shut down many of our radio manufacturing lines [for lack of crystals], I could not but remember their warnings."[37] But the warnings fortunately went unfulfilled.

Pending the manufacture of Western Electric's SCR-500 series of FM radios, the Link Connecticut police sets were standardized in 1941 as the SCR-293, transmitter and receiver, and the SCR-294, receiver only. They did not, of course, meet the military requirements for which they had not been designed. They were experimental, four- and five-channel sets, never intended for field use, but for training. Such, however, was the exigency of the production, the long route between deciding upon an item of equipment and getting it abundantly into the hands of troops, that the SCR-293 and 294 not only got first to North Africa but were also the first frequency-modulated radios any-

---

[35] Guest, like Bender, harassed with frequency allocation problems (too few frequencies available for the multitudes of army radio needs), had hitherto viewed FM skeptically because of the very wide frequency band width each FM radio channel requires.

[36] (1) OCSigO R&W Action 1, W. T. G. [Guest], Com Liaison Div, to R&D Div, 19 Aug 40, sub: FM system rpt of test by FCC, and Incl Memo, E. L. White to Chief Engr of FCC, 16 Aug 40, sub: FM system of Conn. State Police. SigC FM 1, Jan–Sep 40. (2) Ltr, F. H. Schnell, Radio Engr Radio Sec Conn. Police, to Bureau of Criminal Info and Statistics, 21 Oct 40, sub: Request of Col Colton, Dir Ft. Monmouth. Copy in SigC Hist Sec File from file of Edwin H. Armstrong. (3) SCL File, Proj 11-9.3-12, Rpt, 16 Dec 40. (4) R&D hist cited n. 31, Vol. VIII, Pt. 1, Proj 802-A, and Pt. 2, Proj (812) 11-9.3, pp. 6–7. (5) Ltr, Col Colton to Maj Edwin H. Armstrong, 16 Nov 40. SigC 314.7 Armstrong-Colton FM Folder, SigC Hist Sec File.

[37] MS comment by Gen Colton, 19 Nov 51, p. 3. SigC Hist Sec File. Armstrong wrote in 1944:

"I think it is no overstatement that the decision to rely on FM in the mobile and portable fields of use was probably the most difficult decision in the history of radio which anyone was ever called upon to make. History will show . . . that the decision which you made was the correct one." Ltr, Armstrong to Colton, 29 Jun 44. SigC 314.7 Armstrong-Colton FM Folder, SigC Hist Sec File.

Speaking of . . . the problem of obtaining crystals by the millions, Williams wrote, "Col. Colton . . . in my opinion is responsible, more than anyone else, that we eventually had an adequate supply." Ltr, Williams to Thompson, cited n. 33(4).

where in combat use. A National Guard separate tank battalion hastily equipped with them in the state of Washington reached the Philippines only to be captured a month or two later.[38]

The stopgapping SCR-293 and 294 symbolized the Signal Corps' and the Army's FM commitment as a whole. Like many such decisions, this one was expediently compromised. That the demand could be fragmented and dispersed, satisfied in part and without alienation of essential sources of manufacture, helped the Signal Corps to meet it. First, the "500" series for the Armored Force began to stem from the Type III plan, the Armstrong-Noble-Link police sets for the Connecticut troopers, knowledge of Navy experimentation,[39] the direct assistance of Armstrong, and the work of the Signal Corps Laboratories. Setting up the "600" series for the Field Artillery appeased a second demand. For the three other principal combat branches, there were other answers. The Coast Artillery was sponsoring radar. The Infantry was getting a dramatic addition at each end of the scale: handie- and walkie-talkies for short-range use, and truck-and-trailer SCR-299's for 100-miles-in-motion.

But the Air Corps, the largest and most exacting customer of all, wanting dozens of radio wonders for missions unimagined in ground warfare, wanted no FM. This was a wry but not unexpected reaction. In ground-to-air communications, frequency modulation was no more than 10 percent better than amplitude modulation, a difference which the Air Corps did not believe warranted a vast and fundamental change. Another talking point which FM lost with the Air Corps was its freedom from static interference, for Army airplane engines had long been shielded. Its sup-

porters responded to the first of these criticisms that 10 percent could be as much as an inch on the end of a nose, and to the second, that shielding was expensive, hampering to aircraft design, and less than impressive in operation. They also offered a suggestion which grew out of the discovery that an AM receiver tuned slightly to one side of an FM frequency can hear the FM. Colonel Allen, among others, hoped that the Air Corps would introduce this change, especially for tactical air support communications, so that the air cover could hear the mechanized ground.

Nothing came of the proposal, however. Air radio remained amplitude-modulated. So did Navy and British equipment. British radio engineers steadfastly maintained that hills or buildings obstructed FM signals,[40] although a vehicular transmitter or receiver is expected to move and therefore is only briefly interrupted. The U.S. Navy's fundamental objection to FM was no more nor less than a heavy commitment to the established design, but there also existed a mistrust of the "capture effect." That is to say, the belief that the nearer transmitter would capture the air for itself caused naval apprehensiveness that an admiral might find himself blocked out by a junior lieutenant. The question of capture effect was never raised during the ensuing war, when even the Navy ordered thousands of frequency-modulated ship-to-shore sets; and of

[38] (1) SCL, Annual Report, 1944, p. 83. (2) Ltr, Col Colton to Maj Armstrong, 2 Nov 40. SigC Hist Sec File. (3) Interv, SigC Hist Sec with Link, 15 Feb 50.

[39] Ltr, T. McL. Davis, Radio Engr NRL, Anacostia Station, to Chief of Bureau of Engineering, via Dir NRL, 3 Jun 40, sub: Rpt on demonstration of FM vs. AM model CXAB transmitter and CXAC receiver. SCL File S-13.

[40] The British later adopted FM as standard in forward Army units.

course it was one of the features of FM which the ground forces considered a boon.

First Answers in Air Radar

The Navy's requirements were formed not by ground but by water, and the air was yet another element. Like the Navy, the Air Corps could plead a uniqueness in dissenting from what suited the ground arms—and did so, whenever airplanes were spoken of as flying artillery or cavalry. Aviators had now won usual acceptance of the fact that air responsibilities, training patterns, and equipment were divergent. Yet years of making themselves heard had put a shrillness in the Air Corps voice which somewhat overemphasized uniqueness. In the field of signal communications the shrillness at times became stridency, for there the doctrine entered the central area of Signal Corps-Air Corps relations. The Signal Corps had no operational responsibility in the air like that which it possessed among the ground forces. The Signal Corps' air duty was to install, maintain, and operate administrative radio only, at GHQ, wing, and base headquarters, but no more.[41] Otherwise, the Air Corps held control over communications operations, tactically everywhere and administratively in the newly organized Army Airways Communications System. The chief point at which the Signal Corps met (or split from) the Air Corps was therefore the development and procurement of equipment.

In their separate views of this mission, some of the Signal Corps officers remained earth-bound, some of the Air Corps officers never touched the ground at all. Some, on both sides, were slow to realize the significance of airborne electronics, and fliers as

a class were impatient with most of it. Leaders of the air service, however, were restlessly alert to every hint of technical advance from commercial or foreign sources, to anything which the services supplying them might not have proposed, to developments with which other armies or other branches of the Military Establishment of the United States might put them at a disadvantage. They felt their mission keenly, and by the time that the emergency was reaching mid-course, the keenness was becoming razor sharp so far as the Signal Corps was its object. It first pricked the thin skin grown over the wounds of the dispute about navigational equipment. As a result of the decision made then, the impetus for development was expected to come from the Signal Corps, especially from project officers and engineers of the Aircraft Radio Laboratory.[42]

The task of equipping 50,000 airplanes a year posed a dramatic reversal to this convention, which further actions broke into too many pieces ever to put together again. For the Signal Corps, such an expansion of the Air Corps involved, in the first place, a staggering number of command and liaison sets. At the same time, air navigation items began to divide and multiply like amoebae before the demands of the defense program. They became the hub of airborne development for a time, and within their own category the radio compass, the issue of the former day, was replaced as the focus of attention by the radio altimeter.

Paradoxically, air navigation radio might have become the field in which the

---

[41] AR 105-15, Signal Communication, General, 17 Apr 40, par. 3. h. (3) (a) (b) (c).
[42] Comment by Col William L. Bayer, SigC, on MS of SigC Hist Sec, Aug 49. SigC Hist Sec File.

Air Corps adopted frequency modulation, for until mid-1940 most of the altimeter experiments made at the Aircraft Radio Laboratory employed the beat method of radio reflection, a method in which the modulation of frequency is inherent. Of the many navigational devices under development at ARL, including several originally undertaken in the rival Navigational Instrument Section before the clearing of titles, one to prevent collisions had given way to a twin brother called obstacle detection. In the collision-prevention project, ARL had touched pulse radar, and in its successor it approached beat radar. Both then took second place to a radio altimeter which also used the beat method and proved to be the forerunner of airborne radar in the United States. No one in ARL or anywhere else had any knowledge that this was the case. *Radar* was a term not yet devised. The ARL projects were radio projects, and that in itself was sufficiently venturesome. It was still true that, in relation to its position five years later, little was known about how radio behaved in the air.

Aviators were using the barometric or aneroid type of altimeter. It was not only imprecise but of no help to blind flying, because it measured altitude from sea level rather than from the ground underneath the airplane at a given moment. What was wanted was a device which would give a continuous account of the terrain below— a terrain indicator, an absolute altimeter. In a period when most of them still preferred to fly by the seat of their pants, airmen did not welcome another dial on the instrument panel, and certainly did not want anything which increased the weight of the airplane so much as to alter its performance.[43] Nevertheless, the Air Corps

took great interest in the projected radio altimeter, which promised to follow the actual terrain closely by reflecting radio waves against it and measuring the time required for them to get back to the airplane. If this could be accomplished, the radio altimeter would then be the foremost navigational aid, so important as to be called "the greatest single invention in aviation radio,"[44] and with its importance enhanced by the further, exclusively military possibility that it could be the pivotal aid to air bombardment. High-altitude bombing was the Air Corps' single most controversial mission; to accomplish it, bombsights would be of little use at great heights, however, unless the altitude were exactly known. A barometric altimeter gave a bombardier only a rough approximation of height and even then required that his maps tell him what the elevation of the land target below might be. To measure height exactly, far above the target, called therefore for radio reflection.

As if condemning itself, the Aircraft Radio Laboratory's first radio altimeter was a low-altitude set. It was good below 3,000 feet, but the Air Corps Technical committee had specified one which would function up to 15,000. The Western Electric Company came forward with another beat altimeter, good up to 12,000 feet. Tests of this set confirmed the realization that airborne radio reflection equipment held other possibilities than measuring the distance to the ground, for when its output was shown in an oscilloscope, the contours of the terrain stood revealed. Still, 12,000 feet was too low.

---

[43] (1) ARL, Annual Report, 1938, Proj. 31, Radio Absolute Altimeter RC-24, p. 35. (2) Interv, SigC Hist Sec with Maj. E. A. Massa, ARL, 9 Oct 44.
[44] Roberts, *Aviation Radio*, p. 292.

But the Navy, likewise interested in developing an altimeter for an exact fix on a target, had turned from beat to pulse. This was a true irony, because the Navy was not interested in high-level bombardment, where pulse was at its best, and the ARL, trying for high-altitude equipment, was using low-level devices. Secrecy was so fast that Navy altimeter engineers knew no more about their own service's principal radio reflection work than did the ARL men about the SCR-268, 270, and 271. At the Signal Corps Laboratories, pulse radar remained ground radar; at the Aircraft Radio Laboratory, air radar remained beat radar. Having now learned of the Navy altimeter work, furthermore, ARL voluntarily continued with beat, in order not to duplicate what the Navy was doing.

The ARL director, however, Colonel Mitchell, strongly recommended that the laboratory should investigate the Navy work, specifically the model under contract to the Radio Corporation of America. For a while, lack of money delayed the Signal Corps' joining the Navy-RCA project; and the delay came just at the time when the British, as the Aircraft Radio Laboratory was soon to learn, were commencing to make long strides in airborne radar. Up to this time, although unknown to each other, American and British radar had progressed equally in both ground and airborne applications. The U.S. work, compartmentalized, now fell behind, for without interrelation or even consultation, ground pulse radar was shut up in secrecy at Fort Hancock, airborne beat radar at Wright Field, and airborne pulse radar at the RCA Laboratories in Camden.[45] RCA, competing with Bell-Western Electric, was just as secretive about its work as

was either of the Signal Corps laboratory centers.

The company demonstrated the Navy pulse altimeter twice at Wright Field, and each time the Signal Corps officers there longed to have the money to buy it. It looked the best of all that they had seen thus far, even to offering a possibility of reviving the moribund double project for obstacle detection and collision prevention, because it could indicate objects in front of an airplane as well as below. The Air Corps was equally anxious to have it. But "the approximate price for one equipment has been placed at $20,000," Mitchell's successor, Maj. John H. Gardner, Jr., reported. The Signal Corps disconsolately cast about for funds, even turning to the Air Corps for assistance, only to be reminded of chapter and verse in the 1937 concordat. By pooling all available funds from four projects, Gardner got $7,000 together; the joint arrangement with the Navy was made; and finally the Air Corps did enter, after all. The Radio Corporation of America put the price down to $14,800, and with a total sum of $32,000 there was enough to purchase two sets.

Thus the pulse altimeter crept in through the back door. Although the purchase contract was let in April 1940, the models were not received until that autumn, nor the first service tests made possible until January 1941. The device was good, for all that, which was what counted. It weighed only 90 pounds and was accurate to .005 percent up to 20,000

---

[45] Promptly after the first successful demonstrations of the SCR-268, the Research and Development Division of the Office of the Chief Signal Officer had imposed secrecy upon the ARL radio reflection projects, but without fully explaining why.

feet. The Signal Corps quickly standardized it as the SCR-518 and, working with
RCA, ultimately got it down to 30 pounds
and up to 40,000 feet.[46]

The pattern of pulse and beat work in
the Aircraft Radio Laboratory's altimeter
projects amply illustrated the fluctuations
of research. ARL's early work with pulse
had had a low priority because of absence
of Air Corps support. Since the laboratory
was a servant to the Air Corps, and the
Air Corps felt certain that it did not want
anything heavy, which seemed to be all
that pulse could offer, this decision was
perfectly within bounds. Yet the Air Corps
would now soon adopt airborne pulse in
various British and commercial forms developed during the time when the Signal
Corps work had been suspended.

Another contradiction lay in the fact
that beat altimeters, too, could have
served an air arm well. But in this case,
the obstacle was a major concept of the
Air Corps. The planners of the Air Corps
associated low-level air attack with air
support of ground operations, and associated this, in turn, with subservience.
They took up instead the concept of high-
altitude bombing, where their independence was unchallenged and where their
contribution would be undeniably valuable under prevailing strategic plans of
continental defense.

High-altitude bombing naturally associated to itself pinpoint accuracy: hence
the emphasis upon precise instruments for
computing altitude, for determining a target through the intervening overcast lying
between the airplane and the earth, and
for minutely integrating the data affecting the release, trajectory, and detonation
of the bomb. The last of these three types
of equipment, the precision bombsight,
the Air Corps put wholly in the hands of

the Sperry, Norden, Bendix, and other
commercial concerns. The first two, radio
or radar altimeters and BTO, or bombing-through-overcast, were sought not
only in commercial development but also
in the work of the Aircraft Radio Laboratory, the Telecommunications Research
Establishment of the United Kingdom,
and the Radiation Laboratory of the wartime Office of Scientific Research and
Development.

The possibilities of following land contours which the radio altimeter had indicated led without delay to the initiation
of a BTO project at the Aircraft Radio
Laboratory. Afterward, when the work at
the Fort Monmouth laboratories had been
made fully known to them, the ARL engineers expressed the opinion that perfection
of airborne detection and tracking, upon
the basis of ground detection and tracking, should certainly have come first. To
try to begin bombing before finding the
target was to put Z before A. Nevertheless, the development of BTO equipment
began as altitude work and with a series
of commercial items all on the beat prin-

[46] (1) Interv, SigC Hist Sec with John Keto, Chief
of Electronics Subdiv ARL, USAF Mat . Comd,
Wright-Patterson Air Base, Dayton, Ohio, 20 Jul 49.
(2) Interv, SigC Hist Sec with Col Bayer, Washington,
D.C., 26 Apr 50. (3) ARL, Annual Reports, 1936, p.
14, 1937, p. 30, 1938, p. 35, 1939, pp. 34–41, 1940,
pp. 45–53. (4) Henry E. Guerlac, Hist Div OSRD,
Radar, Sec. A, Ch. VIII, pp. 31–34 (in consecutively
paged copy, pp. 344–47). Photostat of 1945 MS in
SigC Hist Sec File. (5) Signal Corps Information
Letter, No. 25 (April, 1940), p. 11. (6) Ltrs, Col
Mitchell, Dir ARL, to CSigO, 8 Nov 38, sub: Western
Electric radio absolute altimeter, and 26 Jul 39, sub:
Radio absolute altimeter, with 1st Ind, CSigO to Dir
ARL, 29 Jul 39, bearing a note initialed L. B. B.
[Louis B. Bender]; (7) Ltr, CSigO to Dir ARL, 10
Aug 39, sub: Radio altimeters; (8) OCSigO R&W
Action 1, R&D Div to Exec Officer, 6 Sep 39; (9) Ltr,
Chief of AC to CSigO, 20 Oct 39, sub: UHF radio
ranges, with 4 inds; (10) Ltr, Dir ARL to CSigO, 24
Nov 39, sub: Radio type absolute altimeter. SigC
413.44 (RB-1514) SCR-518.

ciple. In view of the emphasis upon high-altitude bombing, this was fated to be a wrong approach. A beat altimeter would be useful for low-level attack, because it could be exact right down to the ground, as the pulse type could not be. It could not follow upward with the pulse altimeter, though, which could be extended into the high altitudes where the Air Corps wanted its bombers to fly.

The bombing-through-overcast project started as a stab in the electronic dark and not until the war was already exploding in Europe. Because of the defensive concept which dominated American strategy, the range specification was not great, the maximum target distance being set at 500 miles. Also in defensive terms, the prime urgency for the device lay in the ability to attack submarines, raiders, and other vessels. Recollections of the first U-boat war were sharp; the second war had commenced with a demonstration, in the German pocket battleships, *Deutschland* and *Graf Spee,* of the danger of raiders; and American involvement, of any kind, would expose U.S. shores, military convoys, and sea commerce.

Sizing up the problem for which they were to try to find an answer, the Aircraft Radio Laboratory engineers noted that the project fell into three stages: first, to find means to navigate the bomber to the vicinity of the target; second, to locate the target precisely; and third, to bomb it. In the case of area bombing, the second stage mattered little; but area bombing of a surfaced submarine was idle. The egg had to be laid in its periscope. Hence, the precise fix of the target was the center of the problem. With a radio (or radar) altimeter, a bombardment crew could take the airplane near the target. With a bombsight, they could strike the target. The

middle stage, finding it exactly, was the challenge.

The earliest proposals to meet it were of three kinds. The RCA Laboratories suggested automatic triangulation of radio beams, thereby bringing up to date for the new war the ground radio goniometry of the old one. The International Telephone Development Corporation proposed position finding by the intersection of very narrow, ultrahigh-frequency beams.

It was partly in this connection that General Arnold, the Air Corps chief, insisted upon inquiry into the possibilities of a portable radio range. "We wasted a lot of effort on it," Col. William L. Bayer recalled.[47] But for a time, the hopes of both the Signal and Air Corps were centered in the notion of the portable range, of ultrahigh-frequency design. "This appears to offer great possibilities as an aid in area bombing, particularly when the objective cannot be seen," Mauborgne thought. The Air Corps even, with an untypical clumsiness, sought details from the embassy of the German Reich. When further examination, however, brought out the fact that it required special marker beacons, and because there seemed little prospect of getting an enemy to co-operate in his own destruction by putting the beacons up, the idea died a-borning. In any event, the development would have cost $100,000, and the Signal Corps, with Air Corps approval, preferred to try, for one fifth of that sum, for a test model of the RCA pulse altimeter.

A third approach hazarded was the use of a pathfinder plane to fly below the overcast and direct the bombers flying above it. This notion was quickly disposed of, the second more slowly; hesitatingly,

---

[47] Bayer comment cited n. 42.

the project directors settled upon the first. There was a wavering toward a scheme for letting a television camera down through the cloud stratum in order to relay the target information photographically to the bombardier, but Mauborgne ruled against it and urged research into radio reflection.

Following up this direction, the Aircraft Radio Laboratory looked into the available commercial equipment first. Time was short, and the International Telephone crossbeam equipment would have to serve unless something better proved itself soon. In March 1940, ARL tried out a beat device prepared by the Sperry Company and, in August, one developed by Western Electric. The project engineers tried both of these in the air, and in the latter instance hooked up an oscilloscope as well. The equipment indicated a real possibility for sharp beam transmission, but the reflections on the screen were imprecise and the range simply too short. Yet radio reflection using the pulse method invariably produced equipment which was too heavy. Aircraft design could not allow it. ARL thus continued to look for ways to give beat equipment the range needed, because no one could yet visualize the other solution of making pulse equipment light of weight.[48]

The range and altitude increases in airplanes which made BTO not only possible but desirable had been accompanied by increased speed. Pilots, artillerymen, and others were taught to recognize aircraft by looking at them, carefully distinguishing the shape and position of the nacelles, the set and sweep of the wings, the single, double, or triple style of the empennage; but high speed, great altitudes, and night flying threatened to make much of the instruction meaningless. Particularly in view

of the fact that antiaircraft artillery crews now had in radar the means for learning of the presence of airplanes but did not have the means to tell which were friendly, it was vital that a way be found for swift mechanical recognition. Airplanes were already falling victim to the fact that their own side could not distinguish them as friends. Over the Thames estuary, that very spring of 1940, Spitfires had shot down a Coastal Command reconnaissance Hudson, and a Hurricane had brought the crewmen of a French Potez to their deaths.

Solution of the problem became the object of a third principal navigation project in the Aircraft Radio Laboratory. Intelligence reports had revealed something of two devices which the British had in use. One of these, called pip-squeak, signaled for fifteen seconds of each minute over one of the channels of the command set which the British airplanes used. The other, a device which gave its name to all development work in this line in the future, responded to the great Chain Home radars. It was the Mark I version of an IFF, *identification, friend* or *foe*. Hearing of these, the Air Corps asked the Signal Corps to set up Project 63C.[49]

The project engineers gave some

---

[48] (1) Ltr, Chief of AC to CSigO, 20 Oct 39, sub: UHF radio ranges, and 1st Ind, CSigO to Chief of AC, 16 Dec 39. AAG 676.3A Wireless Radio Systems. (2) Ltrs, Dir ARL (Mitchell) to CSigO, 21 Mar 40, sub: BTO, and to Col Bender, OCSigO, 11 Apr 40; (3) Ltrs, Dir ARL (Gardner) to CSigO, 14 Jun 40, sub: Detection through overcast, and 29 Aug 40, sub: Tentative specification proj 61C, with Incl, Tentative Specification, A Device for Detecting and Tracking Objects Through an Overcast, 9 Aug 40. SigC RB-1910.

[49] Ltr, CG GHQ AF to Chief of AC, 27 Apr 40, sub: Airplane identification, with Incl, Extracts from G-2 rpts regarding identification of aircraft, and 1st Ind, Actg Chief of AC to CSigO, 11 May 40. SigC 413.44 Identification 1, May 40–May 41.

thought to equipping airplanes with resonant antenna rods, in the hope that these would reflect ground radar pulses sharply enough to make a positive identification on the radar scope. This solution required that a ground search set be obtained for experiments, but at that time the only SCR-270's in existence were the actual laboratory models. Manufacture had not yet begun. In any case, the 1st Aircraft Warning Company was relying heavily on the equipment for training. An attempt was made to move a detachment of the company to Ohio to help the identification project, but the air defense program as a whole was a matter of greater urgency than any of its parts. In order that the testing of the resonant rods would not have to mark time, the engineers mounted the antennas on a B-18 and flew to Fort Hancock. They made a number of test flights over Sandy Hook, and tried out antennas which were resonant to the SCR-268 as well as to the SCR-270.[50]

The results were encouraging, but meanwhile a General Electric-Navy design had shown itself to be better. It was a system providing for interrogator-responsors on the ground and "transponders" in the aircraft, and had the great advantage of using its own frequencies instead of those of the radar set. This arrangement made it usable with any radar, whereas the resonant-rod system could be used only with the type to which it was geared.[51] American development called this device RR, for *radio recognition*; but the time was at hand when it would become Mark IV IFF. For British airborne developments, and British names with them, were at that very time about to unite and mingle with American research and equipment in an extraordinary and dramatic alliance.

The Tizard Mission

No other part of the Army was to figure in this union more closely than the Air Corps, and the Air Corps drew the Signal Corps along in its slipstream. The Battle of Britain was about to open, the expected mass attacks being prefaced by coastal bombings. Each passing week which was apparently building up to another dread climax was also indicating that British air defense possessed a vital secret. In addition to the Spitfires, searchlights, barrage balloons, flak curtains, there was something else. In the United States, popular conjecture worked at large, but electronic scientists and the inner circle of government could pin the answer down. On the British side, there was a similar shrewd understanding of the areas of research which other countries might be exploring. But the intelligence channels which inform one government of another's secret activity run in only one direction. Both countries had every motive for opening up a two-way passage, defense being the common denominator in their policy.

Upon instructions from his government, the British Ambassador to the United States, the Marquess of Lothian, broached the matter. The British "would greatly appreciate" it, Lord Lothian said, if the Americans, being given the "full details of any [British] equipment or devices, . . . would reciprocate by discussing certain secret information of a technical nature which [the British] are anxious to have urgently." A startling rearrangement of Atlantic power was even then being com-

---

[50] Ltr, Lt Col John H. Gardner, Jr., Dir ARL, to Comdr R. P. Briscoe, Asst Div NRL, 25 Sep 40, sub: Special flight tests at Ft. Hancock. In same file.

[51] R&D hist cited n. 31, Vol. II, Pt. 1, proj. 203-A, pp. 8–11.

posed, under the color of the exchange of destroyers for island bases. What was asked was that the two nations break tradition in another field, in order to exchange carefully guarded technical information.

Lothian hoped to avoid the show of a bargain; and, indeed, there was no need for any, because unlike the plan for the United States to take over the strategic defense of the western Atlantic, this agreement would not be—could not be—submitted to public discussion. In fact, he proposed to the President, "Should you approve the exchange of information, it has been suggested by my Government that, in order to avoid any risk of the information reaching our enemy, a small secret British mission consisting of two or three service officers and civilian scientists should be despatched immediately to this country to enter into discussions with Army and Navy experts." Thus only a few would be party to the vital secret, and of those few, all would be "perfectly open" in telling what they knew, without jockeying for leverage.

Some on the American side were suspicious of this; some, even, subsequently felt that they had been required to surrender national advantage. The Army and Navy held back their hearty concurrence. "[The proposal is] aimed at getting full information in regard to our airplane detector, which apparently is very much more efficient than anything the British have," was the Army's point of view, which nevertheless also recognized that the British had their own detector and gun layer, as well as the pip-squeak system for identifying aircraft.

Some on the British side were inclined to assume that they had little to learn from the Americans. The relation would be an exchange of British headwork for American handwork. Lothian made it plain that what Great Britain was particularly anxious for was permission "to employ the full resources of the [U.S.] radio industry . . . with a view to obtaining the greatest power possible for the emission of ultra short waves." [52]

This statement directed American concern to patent rights and to the demands which might be made upon industry. Its deepest significance, which was contained in the reference to "the greatest power possible for the emission of ultra short waves," was temporarily passed over, not to be understood until the actual discussions brought it out. Both sides had more to learn about the other than they realized. The truth was that probably neither would have brought electronics to the maturity it quickly reached had they not got together. And had electronics lagged in the crucial two years before the free powers joined military forces in Africa, the effect upon the war would have been grave.

However much basis existed for misgivings, the circumstances of the moment overrode them. The air was electric with peril. The President therefore lost no time in approving the plan, and, so soon as they could be chosen and prepared, the members of the secret technical mission set out. The mission was given the name of its chief, who was Sir Henry Tizard, rector of the Imperial College of Science and Technology and adviser to the Ministry of Aircraft Production, and the other civilian members were equally close to

[52] (1) *Aide-mémoire*, the Marquess of Lothian to the President, 8 Jul 40; (2) Memo, Gen Strong, ACofS WPD, for CofS, 19 Jul 40, sub: Gen interchange of secret tech info between US and British Government. WPD 4340, Exchange of Info with British Government.

their country's research effort and to the unnamed equipment which was fending off the Germans.[53]

Along with three officers of the Royal Air Force and Navy, this group arrived in the United States late in August 1940. They were scheduled to confer first with the Army (which was to say primarily the Signal Corps) and the Navy, then with the civilian National Defense Research Committee. On September 2 Tizard and Professor R. H. Fowler met the armed forces representatives, in General Mauborgne's office. The principal guest was Maj. Gen. Joseph A. Green, the Chief of Coast Artillery, the branch for which American military radar had been instituted. Maj. Wallace G. Smith, specially detailed there by General Arnold, represented the Air Corps. The Navy had sent three junior officers. The seasoned radar men were in the Signal Corps contingent. It was an extraordinary moment. National security, the most powerful of official taboos, was about to be lifted.

Neither the Army nor the Navy had caught up with the unusual circumstances of the Tizard Mission enough to authorize full disclosure, with the result that talk was fenced at the outset. Another result, ultimately of astonishing effect upon the position of the Signal Corps, was that, with the British scientists speaking more fully and being unhampered by the necessity to disclose how much of what they were describing existed, a seed of suspicion imperceptibly took firm root. Quite without any Machiavellian intent on anybody's part, the impression arose, never thereafter to be dislodged, that Signal Corps equipment was inadequate, insufficient, belated, lamely derivative, and unworthy of any place in the same league with British equipment.

Hindsight makes it possible to say what position each was actually in at the time. Both had pulse radar equipment for the ground (although far from enough of it to be emancipated from sound locators)[54] and both possessed the basic types, the searchlight-control, gun-laying, and early warning sets. American searchlight control was probably better than that of the British; neither gun-laying set was good; the aircraft detectors had reached equal, if differing, stages of development. That of the British gave a better definition on the oscilloscope and also indicated the height of the target to some degree. U.S. technicians were still in the process of working out height-finding characteristics, but they had devised lobe switching and antenna tilting, and their equipment was mobile.

In airborne radar, both nations, again, had been working in basic types, except that only the Americans had created an altimeter. Apart from the altimeter, these types represented efforts at air-to-surface-vessel detection, air-to-air detection or

[53] They included Professor J. D. Cockcroft, nuclear physicist at Cambridge University, adviser to the War Office and chief of the team which had installed the Chain Home radars; Dr. E. J. Bowen, the chief expert in airborne radar at the Bawdsey Research Station; Messrs. Wallace, Pearce, and Nutt; Mr. C. R. Fairey, aircraft manufacturer; and Professor R. H. Fowler, the representative in Canada for the British opposite number to National Defense Research Committee, the office of the Director of Industrial and Scientific Research. Ltr, Air Commodore G. C. Pirie, Air Attaché British Embassy, Washington, D. C., to Col John A. Crane, Foreign Liaison Officer, WDGS, 12 Aug 40. SigC 350-05 Brit Tech Mission 1 (RB-1156).

For more about the Tizard Mission, see Baxter, *Scientists Against Time,* Ch. VIII, *passim.* See also Rowe, *One Story of Radar.*

[54] See, for example, Gen. Sir Frederick A. Pile, *Ack-Ack: Britain's Defence Against Air Attack During the Second World War* (London: Harrap, 1949), pp. 151, 313 ff.

interception, and identification of friend from foe: respectively jargonized as ASV, AI, and IFF. In the airborne types, however, the Americans had used beat reflection in their experiments. The British had airborne pulse equipment, to which the Americans were just turning after their disappointments in the beat method, at that early stage of imperfect understanding of its possibilities. Moreover, Great Britain had airborne pulse equipment beyond the development stage and actually in operation. The sets were plaguedly heavy and cumbersome, like the U.S. experimental models, but they were in service in the war. All in all, therefore, Great Britain and the United States had followed separate routes to approximately equivalent spots, eleven months of touch-and-go warfare having put the British a milestone or so farther along. None of this was precisely assessed at the time, and the tally of British items made an enormous impression.

At the first meeting, both sides began somewhat guardedly, referred to their facsimile, teletype, and speech-scrambling devices, and arrived rapidly at the fact that radio reflection was a mutual secret. It was, as a matter of fact, not a secret at all. The Japanese had just begun to shift from the Doppler method to pulse;[55] the *Graf Spee,* scuttled so soon after the outbreak of war, had had radar; and the British themselves had shared much of their own work with Frenchmen now subject to German pressures. A very long distance intervened, nevertheless, between the fundamental principle, which was known in so many scientific circles, and the applications of it, wherein secrecy was vital, and wherein lay a victory in a deadly race.

When the Signal Corps representatives

heard that the British had apparently solved the baffling problem of satisfactory airborne radar, they were immediately impressed. It was air-to-surface-vessel equipment, Tizard disclosed; it worked on the pulse principle, as the Aircraft Radio Laboratory experimenters had believed would have to be true; and, although details would have to be forthcoming from another expert more familiar with them, it used a 200-megacycle wavelength. Two hundred megacycles indicated a wavelength of a meter and a half, with correspondingly long antenna, one of the very things that the Signal Corps had been trying to get away from; nonetheless, the British had about fifty sets already installed and operating, and the equipment had shown that it could find surfaced submarines within a radius of five miles and a considerably larger target like a battleship as much as forty miles away. Such a development had tangibly brought British radar down from the eleven meters of the enormous, fixed Chain Home towers to one and one-half.

American radar, which was mobile, had got down as far; but, Mitchell explained, the Aircraft Radio Laboratory "had never tried pulse transmission in the air." [56] Colton interposed that possibly the Signal Corps Laboratories had slighted microwave pulse, but to go up into the superhigh frequencies introduced "extreme difficulties"—one of which, Mitchell came in again to say, was a reliable vacuum tube. The problem which they had in mind was that microwaves, which may

<hr/>

[55] R. I. Wilkinson, "Short Survey of Japanese Radar," *Electrical Engineering,* LXV (August–September, 1946), 370–77.

[56] Lt Col Hugh Mitchell, Notes on the Meeting with the British Mission, September 2, 1940. SigC 350.05 Brit Tech Mission 1 (RB-1156).

be expressed also in very short wavelengths—roundly, 10 centimeters—would use proportionately short antennas. To receive an echo from a pulse sent out over a very large antenna mounted on a height or a tower was one thing, but to achieve a good echo from small antenna equipment would be quite another. In the first instance, the transmitting area was big enough to accommodate an outsized tube which could produce outsized power, and send the pulse out hard enough for some of it to be left to be caught on the rebound. In the second instance, everything would require a smaller scale yet the power would have to be as great as ever. Mitchell thought that a small tube developing big power ought to be feasible, but acknowledged that it had not yet been "completely developed."

All of this no doubt fascinated Tizard and Fowler. They had brought over a model of just such a tube. British electronic research, goaded by exigency which American research had not yet felt, had turned to and solved the problem with a tube which time later showed to be the greatest single contribution to radar.[57] It was the resonant-cavity magnetron, an electronic vacuum tube, a tube specially created for a new science.

In 1928 the Japanese scientists Yagi and Okabe had discovered that a split-plate magnetron could oscillate at extremely high frequencies, yielding wavelengths as short as 2½ centimeters; but the power output was very low. The same had been true in 1931 and 1932 of the Westinghouse 10-centimeter magnetron. But from the split-plate magnetron a research team at the University of Birmingham had now evolved a multicavity magnetron, which not only produced microwaves but produced them with force. This resonant-cavity magnetron thus was at hand, internationally, ready to give life to a multitude of microwave radar devices. It was the heart of the transmitter; the klystron tube, which amplified the echoes of the pulse, was the equivalent vital organ in the receiver.[58]

On the cavity magnetron, accordingly, the two great powers came electronically together. At their second meeting, this time in Ohio, at the Aircraft Radio Laboratory, both sides showed much less reticence. The Signal Corps had got G-2 clearance to reveal practically all classified technical developments, including homing and instrument-landing methods, means of aircraft recognition, bombing-through-overcast, filter control networks, absolute altimeters, underwater and ground sound ranging, artillery spotting, and everything else in the whole range from wire throwers to "death rays."[59] The British delegates explained that their electronic establishment had made considerable progress with 600-megacycle (½-meter) equipment, but this frequency was still not far enough up in the spectrum. Later in the war it turned out that in many uses, the longer radar waves were preferable to the shorter. The 11-meter Chain Home stations, for example, could detect the German rockets of 1944 and

[57] Although far from being "the most valuable cargo ever brought to our shores," as one historian permitted himself to say in an unguarded moment. Baxter, *Scientists Against Time*, p. 142.

[58] (1) "Unseen Victories of Radio; Secret Manufacture of Radar Equipment," *Record of British War Production, 1939-1945* (London: London *Times*, 1945), p. 18. (2) I. E. Mouromtseff, "Progress in Electron Tubes," *Electronics Digest*, No. 6, pp. 41–42. (3) Harry M. Davis, The Signal Corps Development of U.S. Army Radar Equipment, Pt. III, 1945, pp. 9–13. SigC Hist Sec File.

[59] Ltr, CSigO to Brig Gen Sherman Miles, ACofS G-2, 3 Sep 40, sub: Exchange of SigC info with British Mission, and Memo Reply, 4 Sep 40. SigC 400.3295.

1945 better than microwave equipment could.[60]

But both nations had long-wave radar. What they wanted was the microwave applications. The 200-megacycle British air-to-surface-vessel detector was limited simply to finding the vessel; a visual bombsight took over from there. Pinpoint bombing would require radar of no more than one tenth that wavelength. The same thing was true of any other form of precision bombardment. Wellingtons, making attacks upon Germany which motion pictures like *Target for Tonight* suggested were ruinous, actually were dropping two thirds of their bombs at least five miles wide of any worth-while target.[61] Great Britain felt an urgent incentive to work out also an airborne set capable of detecting other aircraft: an AI. Here, the large antennas which they had managed to make the best of in ASV were quite out of the question, for the airplanes to carry AI would not be big patrol bombers. They would be fighters, and small. Anything larger than microwave antennas would also project too broad a beam for this purpose, because the earth would intercept the pulses which one wished to be repulsed only by objects in the air.[62]

Radio could never reach variety and flexibility until it could get rid of great weight and length and size, without losing any of the power which went with those qualities. This was a matter of developing a giant's strength in a dwarf's arm. The resonant-cavity magnetron ultimately wrought the feat and revolutionized what was already a revolution.

But the magnetron was so new that the blueprints were still wet. Deep anxiety showed in the haste with which the Tizard Mission had been dispatched to obtain mass production of the magnetron in the

United States' industrial outlay and multiform application of it in the United States' fertile research organizations. The newest of these, the National Defense Research Committee, was about to set up a Radiation Laboratory at the Massachusetts Institute of Technology; to this agent would be handed the challenge of microwave radar. The Aircraft Radio Laboratory would limit its own microwave efforts to engineering the equipment; and the Signal Corps Laboratories would keep their research below about 600 megacycles, the area of relatively long-wave radar in which the SCR-268, 270, and 271 had demonstrated the Monmouth laboratories' authority. The immediate future of radar, which lay in pulsed microwaves, above all in their airborne applications, became the specialty of Division 14 of the Radiation Laboratory, as well as of its only real rival in the United States, the Bell Laboratories, where the first American version of the British resonant-cavity magnetron took shape in the closing months of 1940.

This commercial development was of course a Signal Corps choice; there was no question of the Signal Corps' having abdicated its prominence in radar. The ensuing connection between the Aircraft Radio Laboratory and the Radiation Laboratory became extremely and necessarily close; and the Signal Corps Laboratories afterward entered the microwave field in connection with Division 14's gun-

---

[60] Because layers of air at different temperatures can refract microwaves as a prism refracts light; thus an aerial object passing from one layer into another may disappear from the scope altogether. Interv, SigC Hist Sec with Col Rex V. D. Corput, Jr., Dir Sig Plans and Opns Div OCSigO, Washington, D.C., 16 Feb 49.

[61] Churchill, *The Hinge of Fate*, p. 279.

[62] "The Evolution of Radar," *Engineering*, CLX (August 31, 1945), 176–77.

laying set, SCR-584, the hairbreadth hero of the Anzio beachhead.[63]

In this summer after Dunkerque, however, with the Luftwaffe and the Royal Air Force building up to the Battle of Britain, urgent attention was settled more upon air devices than ground. While the Tizard Mission remained in the United States, there was much discussion about IFF. Air combat over the British Isles daily demonstrated the need for it. The presence of increasing numbers of airplanes in the sky compounded the risk that friendly ones might be shot down, foes allowed to penetrate. How important it might be to know one from the other, Pearl Harbor would show. IFF could have drastically diminished that disaster.

Still an unknown number of months short of a war of their own, the Americans had an identification development in initial stages only; this was the RR, the Navy's interrogator-responsor system of radio recognition. The British had gone from their Mark I model of an IFF to a Mark II version—also in initial stages— but relied principally and riskily upon a system of direction finders which intercepted a plane's coded radio transmissions, took bearings upon them, and, from a general knowledge of both code and position, identified the craft. Both the Mark I and the Mark II of the British IFF involved merely a receiver-transmitter aboard the airplane. Normally in a receiving position, the set commenced to transmit when a radar signal alerted it, returning another signal along with the normal echo. The effect was to intensify the reflection which the airplane itself was making on the oscilloscope of a ground detector.[64]

The first order of business after the opening talks with the Tizard Mission was to follow the British example and put pulse equipment, however cumbersome, in the air. The visiting scientists had acknowledged that their own airborne pulse radar had to be "nursed along in order to keep in operation."[65]

The Signal Corps had the means to do as much as that. Arrangements promptly got under way for elements of an SCR-268 to be tried out in an airplane. There was no question of including its antennas. "No one ever believed airborne antennas (Yagis) would be feasible at 2 or 3 meters [the SCR-268's antenna length]. Even when the British sets were first received at ARL there was much doubt as to whether anyone would take up a U.S. plane with them."[66] The engineers on the project temporarily rigged up a single horizontal dipole and mounted it on the nose of a B-18. Then, since an airplane could go to the radar set more easily than the radar set could go to the airplane, the engineers had the B-18 flown to Red Bank airport, where they attached the receiving antennas along the sides of the fuselage. There followed a hurriedly designed transmitter, the SCR-268 receiver, a commercial oscilloscope, a modulator to pro-

---

[63] (1) R&D hist cited n. 31, Vol. IV, Pt. 3, Proj. 424 12-15.1, pp. 4–6. (2) Historical Report of the Signal Corps Engineering Laboratories. SigC Hist Sec File. (3) Guerlac hist cited n. 46(4), in consecutively paged copy, pp. 699–719. (4) Baxter, *Scientists Against Time*, pp. 114–15.

[64] (1) Ltr, Col Gardner, Dir ARL, to CSigO, 9 Sep 40, sub: Exchange of SigC info with British Mission. SigC 350.05 Brit Tech Mission 1 (RB-1156). (2) Notes on Meeting With Members of Sub-Committee No. 3 (NDRC) and British Mission, 3 Oct 40. SigC 334.8 Notes on Meetings With British Mission (RB-2214). (3) Louis N. Ridenour, "The Future of Radar in Artillery," *Coast Artillery Journal*, LXXXIX (September–October 1946), 23–32.

[65] Mitchell notes cited n. 56.

[66] Bayer comment cited n. 42.

vide 4,000 pulses a second, and a gasoline-powered generator.

On October 2, a date coincident with the departure of the mission, preparations at Red Bank were complete. Bad weather prevented test flights there, the B-18 went back to Wright Field for no better luck, and it was the beginning of November before airborne trials could commence. In advance of them, the crew kept the bomber on the ground and shot pulses at a basic training plane five or six miles distant in the air. The results were distinct, for the basic trainer reflected pips upon the oscilloscope. Had the B-18 been flying, this application would have approximated AI. On November 4 it did fly, from Wright Field over Lake Erie. Now the equipment was being tested as an ASV. Up in the air, it surpassed the 6 miles of the ground test and attained 17 against an ore boat, 23 against shore lines and islands. This was only half the distance the British claimed for their ASV, but for a first try it was encouraging. That the patchwork of components worked well at all was proof of the soundness of the SCR-268 and of the engineering skill which had adapted it.

The Aircraft Radio Laboratory experimenters were under no illusions about what they had.

For practical aircraft use the transmitter, keyer, receiver, indicator and power supply would all need to be completely redesigned mechanically. . . . Until a pulse less than a micro-second is obtained with the [Signal Corps Laboratories] equipment or until equipment modeled after the 500 megacycle [Naval Research Laboratory] pulse altimeter . . . is completed, flight tests on aircraft detection will be suspended.[67]

This was the view of the ARL director. The Air Corps view at Wright Field was more sanguine, with the chief of the Experimental Section declaring that "the results obtained from this equipment were very encouraging and show that a means of detection of surface vessels from airplanes is available. To be made practicable, this equipment needs only to be reduced in size and weight."[68]

British ASV arrived at the field within a fortnight of the Lake Erie tests, though; and, inasmuch as it was supposedly ready to be Chinese-copied, it was given right of way over any attempt to modify the SCR-268 for the same purpose. Thus the airborne SCR-268 experiment did not bear fruit as it might have, if it had been tried several months sooner. The Aircraft Radio Laboratory did continue the work, with a number of sets under the nomenclature SCR-519; one of these utilized the lobe-switching technique of the SCR-268, but none of them materialized. The first ASV and AI radars to see service in the Air Corps were copies of British designs.

Great Britain had first experimented with putting radar aboard aircraft in 1937.[69] The Signal Corps had had radar by then. What were the obstructions which had so long blocked the Americans? Lack of free communication must bear part of the responsibility. No doubt can remain that with a readier flow and exchange of knowledge, American Army radar would have had a much shorter infancy. "The 268 projects were kept so *secret* that few at ARL knew of them. I did not," was the remark of Col. William L.

[67] Ltr, Col Gardner to CSigO, 6 Nov 40, sub: Detection of water-borne target Proj 61C-1. SigC 400.112 Location of Waterborne Target.

[68] Memo, Lt Col Franklin O. Carroll, AC, Chief of Experimental Sec Mat Div, for Chief of Mat Div, 20 Nov 40, sub: Location and tracking of water-borne target (part of BTO proj). AF 413.44 BTO, 1939–40, USAF Mat Comd Central Files.

[69] "Radio-Location Convention," *Engineering*, CLXI (March 29, 1946), 307.

Bayer, one of the half dozen who first tested the SCR-268 components over Lake Erie. Lack of funds, absence of basic research, unflagging Air Corps attempts to absorb the Aircraft Radio Laboratory also contributed barriers. But the main reason why nobody up to this point had got pulse radar up into the air was doubtless that nobody had thought of it—a reason which directs admiration toward the British scientists. "It is easy to say now that the weight and size limitation might have been overcome but it would not have been easy to visualize the 268 as flyable. How the British [imagined] it still baffles me.." Bayer's tribute came from a man who knew the problems.

Assessing the relative progress of British and American radar is a matter of balancing one extreme against the other. In the first place, radar research in the two countries differed significantly in origin, and this difference may be assumed to have advanced airborne radar rather more in the United Kingdom than in the United States. British radar was developed from the first for Royal Air Force uses.[70] In the Signal Corps development the interests of the air had been secondary, if not in demand at least in point of time. No radar undertaking specifically for the Air Corps had begun until after the Coast Artillery set, the SCR-268, had shown itself to be good. Then, although expressing itself vigorously in favor of the work, Air Corps policy had made little more room for electronics than for radio. This observation is no sooner stated than it is overmatched by another, which must also be taken within the context of the era. Research and development for the Air Corps which was carried on in other branches was no more hampered than in the Air Corps itself; the list of airplanes with which the Air Corps

entered the war suffered even more by comparison with foreign design than did many other categories of equipment. And this exception must in turn be excepted to. No part either of the Army or of the public thought to fight the sort of war which called for the impossible, at once—a war fought close to the shores and thousands of miles away; an air, ground, and sea war; a high-, middle-, and low-altitude war; a tropical war and an arctic war; a long war and a succession of short wars. It could not justly be expected that everybody would be ready for everything, everywhere.

The Germans were not, even after half a dozen years' head start. Neither were the British. If British scientists suggested that Britain was advanced in all forms of electronics, they were drawing a long bow. If the members of the Tizard Mission talked about what they were going to have as if they already had it,[71] they did so possibly because, being scientists, they thought of the blueprint as the end product. In the field, in action in the Battle of Britain, "radio-location was in its infancy," "the teething troubles with radar were enormous," "it was bitterly disappointing," "the S.L.C. radar sets, designed for searchlight work, were not due to come forward until the end of February [1941]," and so on.[72]

Hard on the heels of the Tizard Mission's arrival in the United States, American observers left for Great Britain. They reported with conviction on what they saw. In the extreme of Signal Corps Labo-

[70] (1) "Radar," *Flight*, XLVIII (August 23, 1945), 208–11. (2) "Radar," *Mechanical World*, CXVIII (August 24, 1945), 216–20.

[71] Interv, SigC Hist Sec with Col Corput, Washington, D.C., 16 Aug 49.

[72] Pile, *Ack-Ack: Britain's Defence Against Air Attack During the Second World War*, pp. 151, 173, 183, and *passim*.

ratories opinion, gullibility and superficial knowledge misled some of the observers, especially in the Air Corps, into seeing more in British radar than actually existed or would be suitable to the very different needs of the United States. The Laboratories radar men came to this conclusion after they learned that the Chain Home's range was less than they had at first understood, that its height-finding qualities were rough, and that the whole gear sacrificed mobility.[73]

Against any line of argument which might have belittled British accomplishment simply in order to exalt the U.S. achievement stood not only the fact that the British had radar much farther in use but also the fact that they had it more efficiently in use. The Telecommunications Research Establishment represented a pool of scientific knowledge from which Army, Navy, and Air alike might draw.

British methods of research and development were sometimes more flexible and appropriate than American methods. Their scientists did not carry the laboratory work on a project too far or continue it too long. When a Mark I had emerged, they cut short further development, and the interested arm or service tried out the equipment, incomplete though it was. Meanwhile, the laboratory would start working on a Mark II, incorporating changes in it as the tests of Mark I showed the need for them. Mark III would presently succeed Mark II. In this way, a series of improved versions might come out rapidly, logically, and with a minimum of misunderstanding between technicians who might otherwise grow too remote from immediacy and users who might be oblivious both of the problems and the difficulties of solution.

The actual military organization for

aircraft detection in Britain was highly effective also; it showed few of the shortcomings which often left the impression, especially in 1941 and 1942, that the American equipment, rather than its operation, was inadequate. Moreover, although the Germans attacked the Chain Home from the beginning, the stations were hard to damage. General Chaney, a special observer of the Battle of Britain, visited one of the CH sites a day or two after an attack which had knocked out two legs of a tower, burned some of the buildings, and killed several girl operators. The station still functioned, guy wire holding up the tower, and there were wooden dummy towers adjacent, both to confuse the enemy and to serve in the event of further emergency.[74]

Chaney was an Air Corps officer, one of several who became devotees of British radar.[75] Major Edwards, a Signal Corps representative, also liked British design and recommended immediate purchase of the IFF and ASV equipment, as well as of the very high frequency command radios which the Royal Air Force used.[76] By far the most important sizing up was a quick trip undertaken jointly by Maj. Gen. Delos

---

[73] Intervs SigC Hist Sec with: Col Corput, Washington, D.C., 16 Aug 49, Col Gilbert Hayden, Dir Electronics Subdiv, AF Mat Comd, Wright-Patterson Air Base, Dayton, Ohio, 21 Jul 49; W. G. Eaton, Tech Asst Electronics Subdiv AF Mat Comd Wright-Patterson Air Base, Dayton, Ohio, 22 Jul 49; Maj F. L. Holloway, SigC, Electronics Div ARL, Dayton, Ohio, 4 Oct 44; Lt Col Albert F. Cassevant, Dir, and John J. Slattery, Evans Lab, Belmar, N.J., 10 Feb 50.

[74] Interv, SigC Hist Sec with Maj Gen James E. Chaney, USAF Ret., Washington, D.C., 14 Jul 49.

[75] On Air Corps interest in British equipment, see Martin P. Claussen, AAF Hist Div, Development of Radio and Radar Equipment for Air Operations, 1939–1944, and AAF Hist Study 50, Materiel Research and Development in the Army Air Arm, 1914–1945. Air Hist Archives, Air University.

[76] Msg, Brig Gen Raymond E. Lee, US Mil Attaché, London, to MID WDGS, 22 Oct 40, sub: Radio equip. Air Intelligence Library US 9510.

C. Emmons of the Air Corps and General Strong, the chief of the War Plans Division of the General Staff.

Emmons and Strong found an England which everyone presumed would be invaded and which some feared would succumb. They were therefore all the more impressed by the evidences of order, system, and progressive refinement which they saw in the British defenses and scientific establishment. The design, construction, and organization of the command posts which formed the corpuscles of British defense struck them particularly.

The secret of the success of the operations [there, they noted] is rapid, reliable and accurate channels of communications. The British have installed a very elaborate system of communications, consisting of the telephone, the teletypewriter and the radio. This . . . must have been extremely expensive and required years, but it is the framework upon which the defenses of Britain are built. If England successfully resists an invasion it will be because of this. . . . The fact that an airplane can be picked up by a radio watchman and its position, direction of flight, and so forth reported to a fighter station in a matter of seconds is illustrative of the care with which this system has been designed and of its value.[77]

Emmons and Strong also learned of the AI and ASV, respectively the air-to-air detector and the air-to-surface-vessel detector. They did not see an AI, and the British confessed that it was "in limited use at the present time." Actually, the first one had just been ordered.[78] They saw the pip-squeak method of identification, with its use of a visual signal, a plume of smoke shot from the tail of the fuselage when the airplane was coming over a friendly anti-aircraft battery or wanted to signal that it was about to attack. And above all, they saw the three principal sets, roughly corresponding to the three which the Signal

Corps had developed. They liked all three, and urged that the Signal Corps delay not an instant in dispatching a man to learn from the British book.

Thus one of the most significant Signal Corps involvements of World War II began. In less than two months' time from the arrival of the Tizard Mission, Signal Corps research had forsworn the sandspit isolation where it had wielded its own radar and had been irrevocably committed to full participation in a world conflict. Departing from the United States to return to England, Tizard said:

From our point of view our visit has been a great success, and I hope it has also been of value to [the Americans]. The British Government are only too anxious to have as full as possible cooperation in all scientific and technical developments and I hope the interchange of important technical information will not cease or diminish on our departure.

It did not. Under the example of the leaders of the two nations, President Roosevelt and Prime Minister Churchill, co-operation was the order of the day in all enterprises, an order unchanged year after year. The Tizard Mission and the simultaneous Minerva-birth of the National Defense Research Committee (Dr. Vannevar Bush was Jupiter) had pointed up one form of co-operation aside from the international. This was the desirability for collaboration between soldiers and civilians. Englishmen associated from the beginning with the Telecommunications Research Establishment have not hesitated to say that its great work could never have brought so many victories had the Air and

---

[77] Memo, Gen Emmons, CG GHQ AF, and Gen Strong, ACofS WPD, for CofS, 25 Sep 40, sub: Observations in England. G-4 No. 4368.

[78] "The Evolution of Radar," *Engineering*, CLX (August 31, 1945), 244–45.

War Ministries not recognized their dependence upon civilian intellectuals who were following what often seemed undisciplined courses of thought. Science had advanced by the co-operation of scientists, and military science could advance only by encouragement of the same freedom of investigation and intercourse. At the least, the double collaboration between science and army, Great Britain and the United States, rescued millions of persons from agonized prolongation of the war.[79]

---

[79] (1) Ltr, H. T. Tizard to Brig Gen Sherman Miles, Actg ACofS G-2, 30 Sep 40. SigC CE British Equip. (2) Rowe, *One Story of Radar*, Foreword by Air Marshal Lord Tedder and *passim*.

CHAPTER VIII

Selective Service

All through that summer of 1940 the Burke-Wadsworth bill was under intense debate. In the year since the Army had totaled 174,000, Congress had moved the ceiling up to 210,000, then to 227,000 with an additional National Guard strength of 235,000. The authorized Army thus stood short of the half million which represented the initial protective force of the current plan for mobilization. At the rate at which German power was threatening, support in depth would need to be built behind the authorized defense establishment. Legislation under discussion in the midst of the excitement of May and June, when every overseas safeguard appeared to be crashing, contemplated a lift in the allowed ceiling to 255,000, then to 375,000. The figure was still not enough. The Military Establishment felt that the American public and their representatives would not fail to see that at the very least the defense of their own hemisphere rested upon the United States and that the Selective Service program set forth in the Burke-Wadsworth measure ought to be passed. Speed was the watchword, from that point of view.

To the nation as a whole, the decision struck too deep at the roots to be taken hastily. Every principle of the country's history said "No" to peacetime conscription, and only a reluctant "Yes" to any conscription at all. The last forced association of the civilian public with the military had also left a residue of wariness which was still perceptible. Yet it was vital that bygones be bygones. Danger was real, and universal. Except legalistically, the era was not peacetime: it was an uneasy grace for preparation, which might be put to an end at any moment. The existing Army and Navy were not the force which would be defending the country: they were a sketch whose outline and bulk must be filled in by the citizenry.

At last the step was agreed to, a first step but a long one, which authorized an armed service of 1,400,000 men. Of these, 630,000 were to come into service through the process tactfully referred to as "selection," 270,000 more through the National Guard, the civilian army thus coming to 900,000. For the rest, Congress raised the Regular Army ceiling to 500,000.[1] With whatever regrets at putting tradition aside, and with whatever jokes, both raucous and rueful, about it, the public at large supported Selective Service, and on 16 September 1940 the act became law. On October 16, males between twenty-one and thirty-six registered. By Thanks-

---

[1] "Biennial Report of the Chief of Staff of the United States, July 1, 1939, to June 30, 1941," SW, *Annual Report, 1941*, pp. 48–53.

giving, the first "selectees" were drawing equipment.

Signal Strength

If equipment involved first creating the items, then getting them, manpower was a problem solved the other way around. The thing was to get the men first—a matter the public was now complying with— and then to create them. They had to be created, to begin with, as a standardized machine, a "You're in the Army now" mass; next, as units in the mass, a stage which to the Signal Corps suggested construction battalions, aircraft warning companies, wire platoons; and last and most importantly, as the trained soldier, the specialist, the man who could be counted on to work a bad radio signal, the man who could take a clear photograph, the man who could catalogue depot stock, the man who could keep cryptographic information secret. Manpower was a matter first of numerical strength and then of training.

At the end of the fiscal year just closed, 30 June 1940, Signal Corps strength had stood at 6,543.[2] To come up to strength in the Selective Service expansion, the Signal Corps had 30,000 to go. Every man must figuratively move far enough apart from every other man to give five new men space between. At the end of the next fiscal year, the 6,000 strength should be 36,000. If the same proportions were applied to the Signal Corps as to the Army as a whole, approximately 7,200 (20 percent) of the 36,000 would be National Guardsmen; 12,600 (35 percent), Regular Army personnel; and 16,200 (45 percent), civilians drafted under the Selective Service law.

If the Signal Corps could have had its way, all of them would have been specialists. That was quite out of the question; since it took even the Army from five to fifteen months to specialize a man, the result represented invested wealth. Still, there was no bar against trying to get as many as possible. For this sort of strength, the ranks of the existing Regular Army did not offer much of a reservoir, because both in total size and in apportionment of quotas among its competing branches the Army was strictly regulated. Recruitment also met with little success, particularly when the Marine Corps, the Air Corps, and the Navy were passing the king's shilling at the very doors of the draft boards. And Selective Service men were in service for only a year, most of which would have to be spent in training them. Otis tests were likely to disqualify the less intelligent of the new soldiers; and of the

---

[2] No personnel calculation is sure at any number greater than 1. The conflict among official sources makes it necessary to strike a mean among them on occasion. At other times, it is advisable to select one source and adhere to it. On this basis, the figures contained in Signal Corps Strength, a monograph (Nov 45, OCSigO Career Management File) by Capt Wilson G. Burden, have proved very generally useful.

To make a quick comparison possible, the following figures are brought together:

				SigC percentage of Army
		30 June 1939		
Army officers...	13,814	SigC officers...	248	1.7
Army EM.....	174,079	SigC EM.....	3,687	2.1
Army strength..	187,893	SigC strength..	3,935	2.0
		30 June 1940		
Army officers...	14,677	SigC officers...	282	1.9
Army EM.....	249,441	SigC EM.....	6,261	2.5
	264,118		6,543	2.4
		30 June 1941		
Army officers.	94,103	SigC officers..	1,945	2.0
Army EM....	1,361,462	SigC EM....	34,451	2.5
	1,455,565		36,396	2.5

brighter ones, few showed any interest in an Army career. Further to handicap it in the race for specialists, the Signal Corps had no high ratings to offer for inducement as the Navy had for its communications men, yet the requirements for signal training were about comparable to those for officer candidacy.[3]

Nevertheless, and despite a slow start, Selective Service, once set in motion, like the sorcerer's broom brought thousands of men in, and thousands upon the thousands, imparting to the parched Army first a sense of incredulity, then one of delight, then, with the flood unstanched and running over, something like dismay. The influx did take just this form. The National Guard was mobilized promptly, in swift orders from September on; then for several months few came into the service except voluntary enlisters. The nation had to set up a mammoth apparatus of draft boards, the registered men had to fill out questionnaires and take physical examinations, and the Military Establishment had to get as much construction done in a hurry as it could achieve. This was negligible, and men arrived at old and new posts alike which had no housing for them. With a relative smoothness creditable to the whole country, however, the machinery of conscription went into gear and by 1941 every community was sending off its tribute. If they were not specialists, they were manpower, and it was this fact that drove in with such engulfing force. In January the strength of the Signal Corps grew to 16,000; by April it rose to 32,000.

Nor was there any difficulty in filling up the officer ranks. As the demand widened, so did the possibilities for meeting it. Mobilization of the National Guard brought scores of new officers into the Signal Corps. At the outset of 1941, there were fourteen vacancies in the Thomason Act allotments, which provided another possibility. Still another opened in the opportunity to commission a few officers in the Reserve, tacitly for the statutory five-year period only, but practically making them very accessible in case of a need which would override all normal considerations.

For any active duty short of war, the span of service of non-Regular officers, as of non-Regular enlisted men, was a year. No Reserve officer could be recalled without his consent unless a state of war existed. Sometimes this was a vexing provision. The Bell System, thought of by the Signal Corps as the best potential source of Reserve officers, used the ground that war had not been declared in resisting requests for them.

From the one-year limitation also arose the odd fact that the demand for officers was greater than the need, simply because it was important to have a successor on hand before a Reserve officer went back to civilian life; overlaps of several months could come about in this way. With whatever cross-purposes and delays, however, the Reserve list constituted the immediate source of officers beyond the National Guard addition, and stopped the breach until officer-candidate training began. By March there were 69 Reserve officers on duty with the Signal Corps, of whom eight

[3] (1) Ltr, CG Hq SCRTC, Ft. Monmouth, to CSigO, 22 Jul 41, sub: Recruiting for Regular Army. SigC Hq SCRTC 341 and also in WD 341 Gen Recruiting 2, Apr–Dec 41. (2) 1st Ind, CSigO to TAG, 12 Feb 40, on Ltr, TAG to CSigO et al., 8 Feb 40, sub: Loss replacements. SigC 381 Gen Mob, Jan–Feb 40. (3) Frederick Lewis Allen, "Drafting This Army," Harpers, CLXXXIV, No. 1106 (July, 1942), 113 ff.

were in the field grade and 61 in the company grade.[4]

Because the Signal Corps looked for experience, officers in the field grades were hard to get. The company ranks were easier to fill. A hundred or 150 automatic additions came into the Reserve at each graduation season from the Reserve Officers' Training Corps. To meet the main objective of Signal ROTC units, which was to produce a young man qualified to command an infantry or cavalry communications platoon, there were 350 advanced and 1,400 basic signal ROTC students in eleven universities. Many of these, because their classroom instruction had not yet rubbed off, were thought to be superior technically to the National Guard officers. Whether they were or not, the ROTC was an essential reservoir: when, for example, G-1 proposed that Fort Monmouth train 50 ROTC students in the summer of 1941, the Chief Signal Officer recommended that Monmouth take eight times as many. Again, Signal Corps planners were agreed that the 10-percent increase in the Reserve allotment was too low, and urged that the figure be raised to 25 percent. A few officers materialized from the Army Amateur Radio System; and a few more entered the Signal Corps upon graduation from the Military Academy. Of the 425 cadets graduated in the class of 1941, 17 went to Signal Corps units.

This tally of auxiliary sources brought the list back again to Selective Service and the creation of officers from among its numbers. So long as the existing Reserve was being called up, Selective Service was still not thought of as offering a quick prospect of officers. But the time was not far away. Even had all 1,809 officers on the Reserve list been available, consenting to return for a year, experience had shown that probably fewer than half could meet the charge of active duty. Some were overage in grade and not susceptible to being lifted a grade, some had dependents whom they could not leave, some would fail the physical examination. In June the War Department ruled that men classified 1-A by draft boards would not be eligible for commissions under the Affiliated Plan. Few Affiliates were in 1-A status, anyway, so that the Affiliated potential was not much narrowed, but the order did serve to direct further attention toward the untapped springs of the selective conscription.[5]

---

[4] (1) Carroll O. Bickelhaupt, Vice-President AT&T, Brig Gen, SigC, Ret., excerpts from office diary, *passim*, e.g., 26 Feb, 4 and 17 Sep, 1 and 7 Oct 40, 9 Jan, 12 Mar, and 28 May 41. SigC Hist Sec File. (2) Ltrs, TAG to All Corps Area Comdrs, 28 Oct 40 and 19 Nov 41, sub: Allocation of Selective Sv men to arms and svs by reception ctrs. AG 324.71 (10-28-40) EA and (11-19-41) EC. (3) 1st Ind Reply, 31 Dec 40, on Ltr, CSigO to Comdt SigC School, 16 Dec 40, sub: Tng of candidates for commissions in SigC Reserve; (4) Memo, Maj Frank C. Meade for CSigO, 16 Jan 41, sub: Proc of officers for SigC units and installations. SigC 353 Gen, MT-38 Feb 39–Dec 41. (5) Robert R. Palmer, Bell I. Wiley, and William R. Keast, UNITED STATES ARMY IN WORLD WAR II, *The Procurement and Training of Ground Combat Troops* (Washington, 1948), p. 327.

[5] (1) Ltr, CSigO to TAG, 13 Jan 41, sub: Recommendation for transfer of SigC Reserve officers to Thomason Act status. SigC 326.21 Transfers. (2) Memo, Brig Gen William E. Shedd, ACofS G-1, for CofS, 30 Oct 40, sub: Officer candidate schools. AG 352 (9-19-40) (1) Sec 1. (3) Ltr, TAG to CSigO, 5 Jun 41, sub: Appointment of Reserve officers in Affiliated units and installations. AG 381 (5-29-41) RE-A. (4) Ltr, CSigO to Comdt SigC School, 13 Nov 40, sub: Tng of civilian components ROTC students and CMTC candidates at exempted stations 1940, with 1st Ind Reply, 16 Nov 40, and Ltr, CSigO to TAG, 18 Nov 40, same sub. SigC 381 Gen 17. (5) Ltr, CSigO to TAG, 23 Jun 41, sub: Assignment of graduates 1941 class U. S. Mil Academy. AG 210.31 (4-22-41) Sec II. (6) SigC Bd Case 446, Controlled Items, 13 Oct 41. SigC 400.12 Controlled Items 14. (7) Ltr, CSigO to TAG, 25 Mar 41, sub: Active duty tng for SigC Reserve officers having Affiliated status, with 1st Ind Reply, 8 Apr 41. SigC 326.21 and also in AG 353 ORC (3-25-41) M. (8) Ltr, CSigO to TAG, 7 Jul 41, sub: Officers' peacetime proc objective for mob SigC. SigC 381 Gen 18.

When the mass influx of men into the Army commenced in the spring, the total active duty officer strength of the Signal Corps was 320. Approved plans called for 2,715 officers, 1,700 of whom, in the grades of 1st and 2d lieutenant, were made necessary by aircraft warning plans alone: most of these were destined for the Electronics Training Group, a unique project already well formulated and about to take shape. Into the enlisted ranks Selective Service was pouring thousands of inductees, not only doubling the strength between January and April but climbing uninterruptedly beyond that point to the mark of the Initial Protective Force allocation. This was the projection of Signal manpower in mass.

The next stage, while the first continued beyond the goal of the initial force and beyond that and still beyond, was the creation of units from the mass. This process called into use the cadre system of withdrawing from old units enough trained men to make the framework for a new one, then filling in the spaces. Though the established unit might feel anguish at seeing its working pattern disrupted, its sense of identity violated, there was small doubt that the best way to absorb thousands of new men was not to isolate them but to work them in among those already initiated into Army mysteries.

The Signal Corps had five types of units. By far the most important to its mission were the organizations for providing all of the standard forms of signal communication; much less numerous were supply and repair units; and then, making up only a sliver, came signal intelligence, photographic, and pigeon organizations. Every unit of whatever type was open to the full and upheaving force of emergency preparations.

The triangular division, the motorization of the Cavalry, and the expansion of air activities all called for new units, new types of units, and differences in established units. A new signal repair company was growing out of the wide variety of developments in equipment. A signal company, signal depot was on the way in order to meet different methods of supply operation. The signal troop, mechanized, which had just reached table-of-organization stage, was in process of being superseded by the signal company, armored division. More aircraft warning companies—still an experiment—were being created; and there were units to be designed for air divisions, air wings, and air bases.

Even before the draft legislation had passed, the Signal Corps had forecast the activation of twenty-eight signal aviation companies and five signal aviation maintenance companies. Under the pressure of the times, unit after unit was brought into being, cadre upon cadre withdrawn upon which to shape them. In addition to the 51st Signal Battalion, for many years the only unit of its kind, a dozen more arose. Beside the original 1st Radio Intelligence Company, half a dozen other radio intelligence companies came into existence. A dozen signal companies served with infantry divisions, and more than a dozen signal aviation companies with air wings. Under the cadre system, units propagated by a sort of vertical fission. In three months' time, the long-established 15th Signal Service Company gave up 66 men. The structure of the 1st Aircraft Warning Company was created by combining a cadre of 30 from Fort Monmouth, 10 culled from other stations, and 43 recruits. Eight organizations were drawn upon to provide a 14-man detachment of the 12th Signal Service Company for Jamaica.

Almost no unit, new or old, was up to table-of-organization strength; and all of the new depended heavily upon the seasoned cadremen and such experienced men as might come in from industry.

The Protective Mobilization Plan took it for granted that for several months after a war began, the Army would have to make the best of units at peacetime strength. In the case of the division signal company, the difference was 150 enlisted men rather than 202, and 6 officers instead of 8. In bloc after bloc, the second manpower stage appeared, as the Signal Corps activated units to meet its obligations to the Protective Mobilization Plan. Inescapably, paper obstacles and red tape hindered the process. To get new patterns authorized was difficult; to develop tables of organization for them, in view of the fact that they were untried, was also difficult. G-1's table of occupational specialists became obsolete rather quickly. In some categories it omitted essential specialists, in others it allowed for too few. And all cases necessarily awaited a full revision of the Protective Mobilization Plan, because each change set up so many others that to admit one threatened to disrupt the plan.[6]

Along with the activation of units according to plan, others came into existence in response to an emergency which cut across the most orderly provisions. Simultaneously with Selective Service, the continental commitment of the United States openly became hemispheric. The defense range moved outward to Newfoundland, Labrador, Greenland, and Iceland, and from Florida passed over the Caribbean arc; on the Pacific side, it swept most of the coast of North and South America. The Hawaiian and Philippine Islands and the unfortified scattering which included Guam, Wake, and Howland extended the commitment far beyond the hemisphere.

Mobilization—for that is what was occurring—demanded task force and theater units for all of these areas. In February Secretary Stimson approved the organization of three task forces, numbers 1 and 2 to occupy bases in the Caribbean and number 3 to join Canadian forces in the defense of Newfoundland. A few months later the War Department created a pool of units for these task forces, and gave it priority in equipment, training, and organization.

The signal component of this pool included four battalions, a construction battalion and two construction companies, an operations company, a photographic company, a pigeon company, two depot companies, a repair company, four radio intelligence companies, three aircraft warning companies, three air companies, and eight air platoons. In the same way that these and other units sprang into being from many sources, so they divided among the steadily growing number of

⁶ (1) Ltr, TAG to CSigO *et al.*, 8 Feb 40, sub: Loss replacements, and 1st Ind Reply, 12 Feb 40. SigC 381 Gen Mob, Jan–Feb 40. (2) Ltr, Budget Office WD to Chief of Estimating Agencies WD, 2 Jun 40, sub: Suppl estimates for increase in strength of Regular Army from 280,000 to 375,000. SigC 111 Suppl FY 41, No. 1. (3) "Editor's Observation Post," Signal Corps Bulletin, No. 109 (July–December, 1940), p. 107. (4) Ltr, Chief of AC to TAG, 30 Aug 40, sub: Provision of sig maintenance cos aviation for air divs operating in support of an army or expeditionary force. AG 320.2 SigC (8-30-40). (5) Pers Div OCSigO, Charts 1–9, 1 Mar 41, sub: SigC units First Army, SigC units Second Army, etc. SigC 063.1 Charts. (6) Capt Frederick Reinstein, Study of Signal Corps Officer Schooling, 1939–1944, 1945, App. A, Growth—Army and Signal Corps. SigC Hist Sec File. (7) Signal Corps Information Letter, No. 21 (April 10, 1939), pp. 10–12, and No. 25 (April 10, 1940), p. 24. (8) Memo, CSigO for Lt Col James R. Townsend, WPD, 2 Jun 41. SigC 381 Gen 18. (9) Ltr, President SigC Bd to CSigO, 25 Jul 40, sub: Occupational specialists required for WD PMP 1940. SigC FM 381 SigC Bd.

regions being brought under the protection of the United States. Whether in areas long inside the defense perimeter or newly included, they served in another kind of limbo, neither peace nor war. Alaska, for example, a huge subcontinent, had only one aircraft warning company (which had arrived at Fort Richardson, the raw new base at Anchorage, on 14 March 1941) and that company had no radar. Neither did the Signal Company, Aircraft Warning, Hawaii.[7]

Signal Training

Throughout the peacetime years Signal Corps technicians, along with occasional communications men from the rest of the armed forces or from foreign armies, had got their training at the Signal Corps School at Fort Monmouth. Fitted into a galaxy of northern New Jersey communities, a region of ocean resorts, manufacturing, estates of the retired, and homes of commuters, Monmouth was the particular center and epitome of the Signal Corps.

The laboratories which had developed Army radar represented one chief aspect of the post, the school the other. Enlisted men assigned there to study took a ten months' course; the officers' work lasted nine months. Enlisted men followed the radio or wire curriculum much as in a trade school, without emphasis upon textual learning but with a great deal upon direct tradesmen's applications. Although the curriculum had shown little variation from year to year, the 1935 move to adjust the student's advancement to his ability and the concomitant 1936 establishment of a continuous schedule had primed the school for what was coming.

The training given to officers—foreign, Regular Army, National Guard, and Reserve—was correspondingly matter-of-fact and directed toward producing communications officers rather more than signal officers. It anticipated, that is to say, that they would be concerned with tactical more than with administrative signal work. This seemed a sensible orientation because relatively few Regular officers of the Signal Corps ever got to the school but perforce learned their administrative duties on the job. Developments were to prove, however, that there were flaws in the assumption that tactical communication, which was not the essential responsibility of the Signal Corps, could be allowed to fill the course of study at the expense of administrative communication, which was. To some degree, the tactical subjects were too much based on the war of the past; to a greater one, administrative signaling was not properly appraised in terms of the war ahead; one result was that the World War II need for great communications systems with an abundance of heavy equipment and a complex organization of personnel, took the Signal Corps by surprise.

Tactical instruction consisted of lectures, conferences, and field exercises; technical instruction proceeded by means of conferences and workbench exercises on equipment. Chalk and a blackboard necessarily served in place of the ample training aids of the forthcoming wartime instruction; simple true-false, multiple-choice, and

---

[7] (1) Ltrs, CSigO to TAG, 29 and 31 Mar 41, sub: Orgn of emergency expeditionary forces; (2) Incl, Signal Corps Equipment for Emergency Expeditionary Forces, 10 May 41, with Ltr, CSigO to TAG, 21 May 41, sub: Orgn of emergency expeditionary forces. SigC OT 381 Gen Emergency Expeditionary Forces. (3) AG Ltrs, 27 Feb and 28 Aug 41. In same file and also in AG 381 (2-27-41) M-D-M and (7-28-41) MC-E-M.

completion questions made up the examinations, as would continue to be the case. Noncommissioned officers gave the courses in the Enlisted Department; after a perfunctory briefing in training methods, Signal Corps officers conducted the officer courses. The commandant paid weekly visits to the classrooms, and liaison officers detailed from the Infantry, Cavalry, Field Artillery, and Marine Corps watched the instruction.[8]

Then came the limited emergency of September 1939. Word went out that the standard course for officers must not be rescheduled after the current one came to an end; the War Department held that the Army had too few officers to allow them time for special schooling during a growing crisis. The order set a deadline of 1 February 1940. To come within it, and to end coincidentally with the conclusion of the nine months' course, the Signal Corps School scheduled an extra one only a third as long.

When February arrived the situation had changed enough to permit a second three months' course, which thirty-three National Guard and Reserve officers were completing when alarm at the desperation of France and the Low Countries darkened the emergency in May. More and more of these officers were entering the service, and for them—and theoretically for any new West Point graduates who could be spared for it—the school now made the three months' training period a continuing part of its program.

For Regular Army officers, the deepened emergency cut allowable training still further, to one month, whereupon, making a virtue of a necessity, the Officers Department arranged for one-month bird's-eye views of wire, radio, radio intelligence, aircraft warning, photography

and pigeons. Cursory as this training was, it was nevertheless to make of the rare individual who elected it a one-eyed man in the kingdom of the blind. The 65-percent increase in the school's officer enrollment which 1940 showed over 1939 was accounted for almost entirely, however, by National Guard and Reserve students.[9]

During the same 1939–40 period, a similar set of adjustments occurred in enlisted training. G-1 directed that except for a few courses intended to train radio and telephone electricians and teletypewriter repairmen, the ten months' course for enlisted men must be curtailed after 10 July 1940; most students thenceforth entering the Enlisted Department would have to come under a different regimen. The first response to the change was to organize a replacement pool at Monmouth, giving a five months' basic course, and the second was to institute a four months' schedule in the Enlisted Department. This, too, so shrank at the crisis abroad that as of the deadline, 10 July 1940, and in concert with an Army-wide action, the Signal Corps set up a schedule designed to train enlisted signalmen in three months.

This drastic decision provided "the most important announcement at the Signal Corps School since the middle

<hr />

[8] (1) Interv, SigC Hist Sec with Maj Gen Francis H. Lanahan, Jr., CG Ft. Monmouth, 10 Feb 50. (2) Capt Frederick Reinstein, Study of Signal Corps Enlisted Schooling, 1939–1944, 1945, pp. 2–3, (3) Study of Signal Corps Officer Schooling, 1939–1944, 1945, p. 6, and (4) Summary Chapter on Signal Corps Training, 1939–1944, 1945, p. 2. SigC Hist Sec File. (5) OCSigO Instruction Cir 2, 1 Sep 39.

[9] (1) Brig. Gen. W. O. Reeder, "Training at Fort Monmouth, World War II," *Signals,* I, No. 5 (May–June, 1947), p. 6. (2) SigC School, Commandant's file of graduates. SigC 352.17 Ft. Monmouth. (3) Ltr, TAG to CSigO, 7 Oct 39, sub: Proposed closing special sv schools and C&GSS. AG 352 (10-3-39) M-C. (4) SigC File 353 Ft. Monmouth, *passim.*

1930's." [10] The "ninety-day wonders" whom it produced were to be rivaled only by the ninety-day-officer wonder, as objects of easy ridicule in every branch of the service where the experiment was tried. Maj. Gen. Spencer B. Akin, a postwar Chief Signal Officer, whose experience with them dated from the opening days of the war in the Philippines, recoiled from the recollection.[11]

Yet after a long shaking down—a period when unfortunately many products of highly uncertain training had to be shipped out, and gave such men as Akin basis for exasperation—the process more than proved itself. The best argument for it was that there was no other way to do. Beyond that elementary fact, however, lay unexpected advantages in obtaining thousands of signalmen on a production-line basis and in capsuling instruction to a point often emulated by the teaching profession itself. The inescapable trait of so short a course was specialization. Singleness is a better word, for there was no question of a new man's becoming a signal specialist in the old sense of the term. He was singled out first for wire or radio, and then for an individual capacity in either field. The Enlisted Department divided its wire course into new subcourses for cable splicers, frame men, inside men, local and common battery installation and repair men, line foremen, power men, manual switchboard installers, local and common battery wire chiefs, and teletypewriter maintenance men. The objective of the new radio courses was to qualify a man to become a repairman, a teletypewriter operator, or the operator of a field or fixed station.[12]

Categorizing the broad radio and wire training into lesser specialties was an attempt not only to train men faster but also to train more of them at the same time, to meet the passage of Selective Service in the fall. The consequent pressure on the buildings of the school and replacement pool threatened to burst out the roofs. For Fort Monmouth had thought of itself as crowded ever since it had been Camp Alfred Vail in World War I. It had been obliged to use nearby private property and the sides of the public highways for field exercises, and equipment was still being accommodated in the temporary hangars erected in 1917. Housing was scarce enough so that a portion of the garrison had to live off the post and in quarters which cost as much as 30 percent more than their rental allowance or commutation. Something had to be done, for the national registration for the draft was coming up in October. First conservative estimates told the school to prepare to train 299 officers and 3,755 enlisted men, specified as *fillers* (224 officers and 2,455 enlisted men) and *replacements* (75 officers, 1,300 enlisted men).[13]

In the use of these terms lay a needless and harmful confusion. It caused many misunderstandings in Army personnel administration throughout the war. Practi-

[10] Maj Gen Frank E. Stoner, SigC Speech to American Signal Corps Association, N. Y., 27 Feb 46. OCSigO Info Br File.

[11] Interv, SigC Hist Sec with Gen Akin, Washington, D.C., 18 Oct 49.

[12] (1) 2d Lt. George M. Simmons, (Inf) SigC, "The Enlisted Men's Department Signal Corps School," Signal Corps Bulletin, No. 108 (April–June, 1940), pp. 108 ff. (2) History of the Eastern Signal Corps Training Center (Ft. Monmouth, 1945), p. 16. SigC Hist Sec File.

[13] (1) Memo, CSigO for ACofS G-4, 8 Dec 41. SigC 601.1 Ft. Monmouth. (2) Signal Corps Information Letter, No. 1 [new ser.], (December 1, 1941), p. 43. (3) Ltr, Inspector Gen Second Corps Area to CG Second Corps Area, 26 Feb 40, sub: Annual inspection Ft. Monmouth. IGO 333.1 Ft. Monmouth, FY 40 (2-26-40). (4) A History of Fort Monmouth, New Jersey, 1917–1945, p. 86. SigC Hist Sec File.

cally, the two groups need not have been separately labeled, for the officers would get officer training and the enlisted men would get enlisted training, whatever their assignment afterward was to be. While they were in training, they would be students; after they had been assigned to units, they would be signal or communications specialists or nonspecialists.

Whether they were fillers or replacements was a matter which hinged upon no more than whether the unit to which they were assigned was just being formed or was already in existence. Fillers went to an incomplete unit to fill up the spaces around the cadre. They were sorted out and told off to their jobs when they reached the unit; before that stage, they were men in the mass, a bulk allotment. Replacements were singled out as individuals. Commanding officers requisitioning replacements were asking for specific men to take over specific duties left vacant by their predecessors. Inasmuch as the Army at the beginning of the emergency was so small that it possessed few units, there was little need for replacements. Instead, the need which the Selective Service system was designed to meet was for fillers, in the hundreds of units to be created. Mobilization planning referred to these men as replacements—men new to the service, who would be assigned to units new to the service, where nobody had preceded them in the assignment, and where, indeed and in many cases, even the assignment itself was so new that it had never existed before.

For all the new soldiers, whether they were to be fillers or replacements, the first stop was a reception center; the second, unless they were sent directly to a unit to learn their job while they worked at it, was likely to be the replacement training cen-

ter. So far as reception centers affected its problem, the Signal Corps was concerned only in getting its quota of the incoming men. To set up a replacement training center, however, in dimensions far exceeding the simple replacement pool which Fort Monmouth had already established, constituted a sharp and inescapable obligation now that the Protective Mobilization Plan was gradually being put into effect.

The Signal Corps' first proposal to meet the requirement, a proposal made in May 1940, was for a 15 September activation and a complement of 750. Part of the staff would come from the resident 51st Signal Battalion; the total proposed overhead included a lieutenant colonel, 8 captains, 7 1st lieutenants, 5 Reserve 2d lieutenants, 154 enlisted men, 8 civilians, and Quartermaster and Medical detachments. The May plan had the ill luck to be offered just as the German triumph over western Europe made it certain to be rejected as inadequate. The War Department began thinking of twenty-one such replacement training centers, all to be established in the rest of 1940 and 1941.

The next Signal Corps plan, submitted in August, proposed a capacity of 5,000. In the Signal Corps School, there would inevitably be expansion beyond the startling, and just announced, figure of 831 enlisted students, because some of the men to be at the new replacement center would be transferred to the school after their basic training. Fort Monmouth would have to swell like the frog in Aesop, although every effort would be made to expand it without bursting. By comparison with the sprawling communities attained by 1943, the layout was cautious. The familiar training center was implicit in it: the classroom and workshop build-

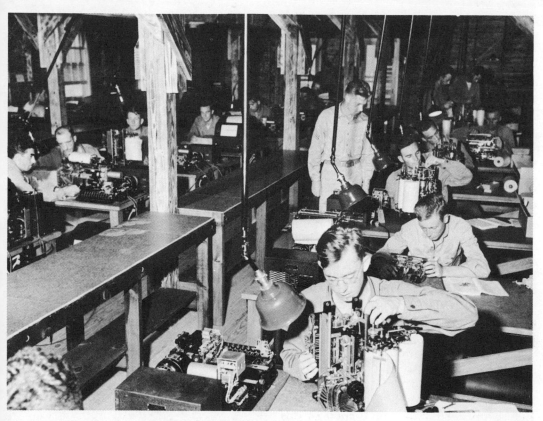

TRAINING IN TELETYPEWRITER MAINTENANCE. *(Photograph taken in 1942.)*

ings, each 20 by 100 feet, surrounding an instructors' building; the barracks, bath houses, and latrines; the recreation halls, kitchens, and mess halls; the headquarters buildings; the post exchanges; the hospital area; the fire department, the guard house, and military police station; the utilities preserves; and so on, to a full-scale training post like any of those known to millions of men within the following years.

The new training facility would represent almost from its opening more persons than were present at all the rest of Fort Monmouth. Garrison strength stood at 2,300 when the draft registration took place. According to plan, it would rise to 3,500 by January 1941 and to 11,000 by March, when the Replacement Training Center would be open. Rapidly the calendar was drawn. March 15 was to be the activation date. By April 1, buildings were to be completed, on an area near Fort Monmouth to be leased or bought. On April 15, the first group of a thousand "selectees" would arrive for training; on May 1, a thousand more; on May 15, a thousand more; on June 1, a thousand more; and on June 15, the last thousand, bringing the center up to capacity. Nobody was scheduled beyond June, because the Selective Service and Training Act was due to expire by the time the June entrants completed their courses. Out of each thousand, 142 men were to have specialist training. All of the rest would be nonspecialists: that is, simple technicians as distinct from expert technicians.[14] To train these men—5,000 instead of 750— the staff would include 146 officers, 1,340 enlisted men, and 12 civilian clerks. Hence the garrison increase by January.[15]

December 1940 plans advanced the proposed activation date by two months, drawing it up from March 15 to January 15. This change also slashed the length of the proposed training period from one year to one quarter and raised the capacity to 7,000. Replacement Training Center men would be ninety-day products, too, and there would be many more than from the school.

The post commandant, Colonel Olmstead, leased 131 acres adjoining the reservation and began to put into effect an authorization for a 500-man barrack. Before any earth had been turned for this building, blueprints for others had nearly used up the allowance, and the Signal Corps negotiated for two more parcels of land along Oceanport Creek. For a moment the expansion wavered, the War Department needing further sanction from the Bureau of the Budget; General Marshall had even announced that it would be necessary to delay the opening of several of the Army's new replacement centers. Then the department decided to cut a corner everyone had hoped to avoid, and to open them with the bare minimum of "essential housing"—a term which did not include classrooms.[16] Late in January, Fort Monmouth reported that essential housing for 800 men was ready; so were the bunks and bedding for thousands

more—stored in the barracks because there were not yet any warehouses. The Replacement Center was officially open, with Col. George L. Van Deusen as com-

---

[14] The breakdown was as follows:

Specialists

TOTAL	710
radio electricians	200
installer-repairmen	200
radio operator specialists	100
teletypewriter maintenance men	50
cable splicers	50
telephone operator specialists	40
telephone and telegraph power men	30
frame men	20
inside men	20

Nonspecialists

TOTAL	4,290
linemen	1,600
radio operators	1,000
message center clerks and messengers	580
teletype operators	320
telephone operators	200
automobile mechanics	170
cooks	150
supply and general clerks	100
pigeoneers	100
photographers	70

Source: Ft. Monmouth hist cited n. 13(4).

[15] (1) Memo, CSigO for ACofS G-3, 24 May 40, sub: Requirements for SigC Enlisted RTC, Ft. Monmouth. SigC 381 Gen 16. (2) *Congressional Record,* LXXXVI, 536 (4 Aug 40). (3) Ltr, CG Ft. Monmouth to TAG, 16 Oct 40, sub: Disbursing Office Finance Dept at Ft. Monmouth. SigC 381 Gen 17. (4) Ltr, CSigO to Comdt SigC School, 12 Aug 40. Ft. Monmouth File. (5) Capt Frederick Reinstein, Signal Corps Training in World War II: Background and First Six Months of War, 1917–1942, 1944, *passim.* SigC Hist Sec File. (6) Ltr, OCSigO to Comdt SigC School, 1 Feb 41, sub: Tentative layout for a SigC tng ctr theater of opns, with accompanying inds, and Incl to 3d Ind. SigC 381 Gen 18, Jan–Dec 41. (7) Ltr, Asst Chief of Fortification Sec Office of Chief of Engrs to CSigO, 30 Jan 41, sub: Engr construction. Office Chief of Engrs, Com and Records Br File 600.13 War Construction, Pt. 1, Serials 1–65.

[16] (1) 4th Ind, TAG to ASW, 13 Dec 40, sub: Acquisition of land, Ft. Monmouth, without basic Ltr. AG 680.1 (11-2-40) MD. (2) Memo for File [Fiscal Officer OCSigO], 11 Dec 40. SigC 601.1 Ft. Monmouth. (3) Ltr, TAG to ASW, 11 Oct 40, same sub, with 1st Ind by Budget Officer WD, 11 Oct 40. AG 680.1 (9-18-40). (4) AG Ltr, 16 Dec 40, sub: Deficiency in funds for emergency construction. AG 600.12 (12-7-40) M-D (Sec 1-E).

manding officer, and on 27 February the men began to arrive.[17]

After nineteen years at Fort Monmouth, the 1st Signal Company left to make way for them and join the 1st Division. In succeeding months, the 51st Signal Battalion, the 1st Radio Intelligence Company, the 1st Operations Company (Aircraft Warning) and the cadre of the 1st Aircraft Warning Company also moved out. Drafted or newly enlisted, the men who physically replaced them came from the reception centers, where their days had been a succession of queues for filling out forms, queues for assembling a uniform, queues for getting a haircut, queues for inoculation, and queues for more forms, which they now replaced with formations. Within three days at the end of February and the beginning of March, 1,300 new soldiers appeared.

Gradually, the Replacement Training Center emerged from mud and confusion. In the midst of both and in defiance of them, the training program commenced, with lectures in sex hygiene, military courtesy, and the articles of war, with close-order drill and ritual calisthenics. Things were too feverish for orderly plans to be going into effect—the Chief Signal Officer hastily asked for another replacement training center, which he would locate at Neosho, Missouri—but the ultimate intention was that men would arrive weekly, according to quotas set by The Adjutant General, that they would stay for thirteen weeks, and that the training schedule would be staggered according to the entrance schedule: at the time when one group of men had reached their thirteenth week of training, a second would be in their twelfth, a third in the eleventh, and so on.

After the new soldier had spent the first

three weeks learning how to march and how to wear his uniform, how to salute and how to do push-ups, how to pitch a shelter tent and how to meet inspections, how to put on his gas mask and how to fire a pistol, he began from four to eight weeks' training as a basic signalman.

A lineman, for example, learned the maintenance of small switchboards, field telephones, and repeating coils, along with such essential abilities as how to count the number of pairs in a cable terminal, how to lay field wire, and how to set and climb a pole for an open-wire line. (Climbing poles was not as easy as it looked; many a novice "burned" one before he mastered the technique.) A lineman also discovered how to attach crossarms, brackets, pins, and insulators; to string and to tie wire, to place guy lines and to lay cables; and to identify various types of wire.

A message center clerk learned to encode and decode messages; to release pigeons; to read maps marked with common military symbols; and to know the organization of the unit in which he would serve. Pigeon men—or pigeoneers, as the Signal Corps called them—could not be completely trained within the twelve or thirteen weeks' period, but they could become competent in feeding and handling the birds. Field radio operators were supposed to emerge with the ability to send and receive messages at a rate of at least twelve words per minute—a word being commonly measured as a five-letter group—as well as to know the elementary installation and maintenance of Signal Corps radio sets and, if possible, touch typewriting. The switchboard operator had to understand traffic diagrams and of course to be able to operate either a local

[17] Hq Ft Monmouth GO 11, 14 Jan 41.

ENLISTED MEN LEARNING OPEN WIRE CONSTRUCTION. *(Photograph taken in 1942.)*

or a common battery switchboard. Expert typists were selected for training with the teleprinter and teletypewriter. Motion picture cameramen studied lighting and angles of focusing, in addition to the use and repair of their cameras. Draftsmen were required to have a general knowledge of layout plans and wire plans employed in the construction, the installation, the repair, and the daily use of wire communications systems.[18]

With Selective Service only a one-year experiment until the act was extended, General Marshall had warned that the success of the entire program might depend upon the efficient operation of replacement training centers. Political re-

percussions would be sure if the students thought ill of the methods or contents of the courses. Marshall had further cautioned that time allowed for only the most essential subjects; no matter how interesting any other material was, the instructors had to forego it.

Since Fort Monmouth had already packed the school curriculum tight in the

---

[18] AG Ltr to CSigO *et al.*, 23 May 41, sub: Revision of mob tng programs, with inds and following incls: Training Program, Signal Corps Replacement Training Center, Basic Subjects—Common to All Training Battalions, and MTP 11-2, Signal Corps Mobilization Training Program for Signal Corps Enlisted Replacements at Signal Corps Replacement Training Centers, 1941. AG 381 (5-20-41) MT-C, and also in SigC 381 Gen 18.

ENLISTED MEN LEARNING POLE CLIMBING. *(Photograph taken in 1948.)*

process of reducing most of it to three months or less, this problem affected the Signal Corps primarily in the matter of finding instructors. Army teaching was an assignment which offered little hope for promotion and none for genuine recognition—reasons enough why Regulars, with their careers to think of, shied away from it if they could. The school pressed some of its recent graduates into service, along with Reserve officers. The result was sometimes not successful, for the new instructors began their work without much opportunity to become familiar with its subject matter, let alone to sense the art of teaching.

School officials also drew up a list of minimum requirements in technical per-formance and knowledge, added a week's work in training methods to the Enlisted Department course, and revised a few manuals which dealt with new equipment, such as TM 11-450 on early warning radar. The texts had to be clear because as often as not there was no equipment available for explanations and demonstrations. Priorities set just before the draft had put service schools twelfth on the controlled-materials list and had made no provision to supply replacement centers. Even when the War Department relaxed the ban a little, training facilities could get equipment only after all of the needs of tactical units had been met. Fundamentally, though, every shortage was merely academic so long as the teachers were unacademic, every corrective gesture was a stopgap awaiting the time when the instructors had the skill as well as the name.[19]

As for officers in training, the supply to the Signal Corps would now have begun to run short had General Staff policy not imposed the innovation of officer candidate schools. Soon after the beginning of 1941 it became evident that the available sources would not be adequate in the almost certain event of a prolongation of the emergency. The foreseeable need alone, the need for 2,715, was an enormous number for an agency used in peacetime to one tenth that all together. The Regular Army, Reserve, and retired lists carried the names of 2,136, but the sum of those who were actually eligible for duty or already serving was not much more than 940. Hence the deficit was something like 1,775. The solution could lie only in something more extensive than a 70-officer limit at the school and more permanent than an officers' training camp. An Officer Candidate Department for the school was necessary.[20]

In April, therefore, the new enterprise was set up, and Capt. Charles L. Olin, 1st Lt. William B. Latta, and several students in the Officers Department prepared course outlines for the 500 candidates due to arrive on the first of July. They put the development of officerly qualities foremost in the curriculum, and sandwiched technical training in wherever there was any time for it. There was no time at all for sleep. The ninety-day program was specifically designed to bring out a candidate's qualities of leadership under discomfort, stress, and actual harassment.

As at other officer candidate schools, those privileged to undergo this torment achieved it by being personally selected,

not by applying. The officials' principal objection to admitting applications for officer candidacy was that a man ought not to make his way in except by winning the approbation of his commanding officer; but it was also true that General Marshall feared that opening the lists to application might upset the Army's policy of racial segregation. The Signal Corps Replacement Training Center, for example, was white. In June 1941 the new Officer Candidate Department officially came into being, with Maj. George L. Richon as director and Olin and Latta as assistants.[21]

While the Officer Candidate Department was coming to a head, the school was setting up still another department, the fifth, this one being for training in aircraft warning. A board of officers appointed to consider it recommended at the end of March that it give maintenance training only, to a maximum of 100 students, at least until such time as two roadblocks could be cleared away. One of these was that there was no room for any

---

[19] (1) Memo, ACofS G-3 to CSigO, 29 May 41, sub: Methods of instruction and tng; (2) Ltr, CSigO to Comdt SigC School, 6 Jun 41, same sub, with 1st Ind, Comdt SigC School to CSigO, 13 Jun 41. SigC 352.11 Ft. Monmouth (HQ 353). (3) OCSigO WP&T Div Diary, 5 Dec 40. SigC 353 Gen MT-38, Feb 39–Dec 41. (4) Ltr, CSigO to TAG, Nov 40, sub: Distribution of controlled items of equip; (5) Ltr, TAG to Chiefs of Arms and Svs *et al.*, 22 Jan 41, sub: Distribution of controlled items of equip to RTC's, with incl. SigC 381 Controlled Items of Equip 2, Jan–Feb 41.

[20] (1) Memo, Chief of WP&T Div OCSigO for CSigO, 16 Jan 41, sub: Proc of officers for Sig units and installations. SigC OT 322 Gen; (2) 1st Ind, Comdt SigC School to CSigO, 31 Dec 40, on Ltr, CSigO to Comdt SigC School, 16 Dec 40, sub: Tng of candidates for commissions in SigC Reserve. SigC 353 Gen MT-38, Feb 39–Dec 41.

[21] (1) Memo, Gen Shedd, ACofS G-1, for CofS, 12 Oct 40, sub: Officer candidate schools; (2) Memo, CofS for Maj Gen William Bryden, 28 Oct 40, same sub. AG 352 (9-19-40) (1) Sec 1. (3) SigC Tng Ctr hist cited n. 12(2), p. 22.

more than 50, the number which had been first tentatively spoken of; the other was that nobody knew very much about aircraft warning equipment yet, nor had any opportunity to find out while it was so scarce. The school put 5 enlisted men through a short course in radar maintenance immediately, and then sent them to the Radio Division of the Enlisted Department to learn what they could about radar operation. This was enough for a start. The pressing situation permitted no more.

On June 2, the Aircraft Warning Department opened, with Maj. James W. Green, Jr., as director. No one knew quite how much could be promised, but so far as anyone could tell, the work would commence 1 July, with a class of 10 officers and 40 enlisted men, and a possibility of borrowing an SCR-270 so that these radar students could see a radar. Ultimately, the enlisted students would be given both operational and maintenance training, the officers maintenance training only, and the staff might expect to have two SCR-268's and three SCR-270's as demonstration equipment. No later than the arrival of the fourth four-month class, however, the capacity of the Aircraft Warning Department would have to be 400.[22]

Needless to say, the commandant had to look for more land. He had originally intended to locate Aircraft Warning on high ground at the west end of the post. Then the board's advice to allow for 100 students instead of 50 had made that area too small; in any case, the cost simply of installing the utilities there would have been as much as the combined cost of utilities and thirty acres at the south of the post, in an even more private spot for the secret training.

Now not only was the size of the Aircraft Warning Department growing to 400, but in the wind was the prospect of a total of 900, the extra 500 to be added to the Enlisted Department. This increase was to be made at the expense of the Replacement Training Center, which the commandant was authorized to reduce from 6,007 to 5,007; and he could shorten the Replacement Training Center courses a little, crowd the men a bit more, and house some of them in winterized tents; but the situation still and plainly called for more land and more housing.

The 500-man barrack allotted to the Replacement Training Center while it was on paper had never been built. Now, partly to provide space for it, the commandant asked to buy 10 acres in addition to the 131 already under lease. He got approval at last, and by December permission to buy the leased land—the whole parcel for $50,000—but then a wartime Fort Monmouth was ranging far beyond this stage.[23]

As of the late spring of 1941, the post had changed markedly from its appear-

---

[22] (1) SigC School Staff Memo 3, 2 Jun 41. Ft. Monmouth File. (2) Proceedings of Board of Officers Convened at Fort Monmouth Pursuant to Special Orders No. 75, Headquarters Fort Monmouth, 31 March 1941. SigC 601.1 Ft. Monmouth.

[23] (1) Ltr, CG Ft. Monmouth to CSigO, 31 Mar 41, sub: Acquisition of additional real estate for reservation at Ft. Monmouth; (2) Ltr, Comdt SigC School to CSigO, 5 Apr 41, sub: Location of building for Aircraft Warning Dept, with 1st Ind, CSigO to TAG, 8 Apr 41, and 2d Ind, TAG to USW, 21 Apr 41, to rpt of proceedings cited n. 22(2); (3) OCSigO R&W Action 1, WP&T Div to Exec Officer, 15 Apr 41, sub: Status of proposal to purchase 30 acres (Maida) 4 acres (Eckhardt) for site of Aircraft Warning Sec SigC School; (4) Ltr, CG Ft. Monmouth to CSigO, 1 Apr 41, sub: Transfer of tactical units now stationed at Ft. Monmouth; (5) Ltr, CG Ft. Monmouth to QMG, 29 Jul 41, sub: Additional land Ft. Monmouth, with 11 inds. (6) Memo, OCSigO to Comdt SigC School, 23 Aug 41. SigC 601.1 Ft. Monmouth.

ance of a year before. The heavily increased school population filled gaps left only momentarily by departing tactical organizations which had been there for years. Fort Monmouth encompassed the Signal Corps Board; the Training Film Production Laboratory with the 20th Signal Service Company; the Signal Corps Band; the Pigeon Breeding and Training Center; the Signal Corps Laboratories; the Signal Corps School, consisting of the faculty, the 15th Signal Service Battalion, and a group of student officers; and the headquarters, band, and five battalions of the Signal Corps Replacement Training Center. Brig. Gen. Dawson Olmstead was commandant, Lt. Col. William O. Reeder

was assistant commandant, and Brig. Gen. George L. Van Deusen was the Replacement Training Center commander. The total post population was more than 6,000; 5,775 were in training at the end of May. The ending fiscal year had witnessed the training of 293 officers, 2,144 enlisted men in the Signal Corps School, and of 1,806 new Selective Service soldiers in the Replacement Training Center. It was a year which had distinctly reflected the national emergency.[24]

----

[24] (1) Pers Div OCSigO, Chart 9, Signal Corps Units, War Department Overhead, Fort Monmouth, N. J., 5 Apr 41. SigC 063.1 Charts. (2) SigC Tng Ctr hist cited n. 12(2), p. 23. (3) Reinstein monographs cited n. 6(6), n. 8(2), n. 8(4), and n. 15(5).

CHAPTER IX

Working for the Ground Forces

Just before the fiscal year ended, the limited emergency broke all bounds and was declared unlimited. The difference was scarcely noted, for emergency was reflected throughout the armed forces. Not at all a world to itself, at every point the Signal Corps felt the stirring and pressure. Soldiers left their training center for destinations as far outside the immediate range as the defense establishment had spread. In the Laboratories, research accepted the governing of every part of the Army. Signal supply channeled a multitude of ground and air demands, for wire and radio uses, to interior and foreign areas. The slow complexity of the great defense program made all the more remarkable whatever order emerged from it. The grand design was not yet clear; the goal looked fateful, but still general. To keep its segments distinct, to keep the lines of interrelationship serviceable at all of the stages beyond the simplest, made a surprising problem, increasing daily with the strength of the ground and air arms. Communications were as diverse as the number of communicators. Both the ground and the air defined new uses continually.

The Pigeon Service

Many of the ground demands, whether in supply or training, were rather more familiar. Nonelectrical means were rapidly disappearing in air communications, and air force requirements involved special problems in organization with which no one felt at ease; but ground needs were somewhat more diverse and still held room for nonelectric methods.

Thus pigeon communication, an uncomplicated activity, had a secure if minor place in the company of its intricate counterparts. In exercises and maneuvers, the ground arms habitually employed pigeons as a means of communication from small units theoretically located at inaccessible spots. The Camp McCoy maneuvers of 1940, for example, had developed "an immense respect" for them. In Hawaii, the departmental commander had asked for them; and in Alaska also, the chief of the new defense command, Brig. Gen. Simon Bolivar Buckner, Jr., had interested himself in their value in remote regions, especially in the chilling and rugged wildernesses where pilots might be forced to land. Vilhjalmur Stefansson, the noted authority on the Arctic, Frederick C. Lincoln, expert of the United States Fish and Wildlife Service, and others advised the Signal Corps on a plan for the use of pigeons there. The effort failed through no more hazard than ordinary delay: birds which had been started on their way to Buckner's new Fort Richardson while

PIGEON LOFTS AT FORT MONMOUTH, *the scene of pigeon training experiments.*

they were still young enough to be trained were grandfatherly when they arrived.[1]

Innovations at the Monmouth Pigeon Center—where the appropriation was $2,490 more in 1941 than it had been in the year before—were similarly undetermined of their final success, and similarly plagued with an aspect of absurdity. A joke revived from World War I hinted that the Signal Corps was crossbreeding pigeons with parrots so that the birds could say their messages, with angels so that they could sing them, and with Western Union boys so that they could sing and salute, too. The actual experiments were rather more likely to succeed. The pigeon experts were making a serious effort to train the birds to work at night, and to fly out from

their home lofts as well as back to them. In effect, one experiment crossbred the pigeon with a nighthawk and the second with a boomerang.

In no way inconsequential, the work was supported by an increasing and general agreement to organize separate pigeon

[1] (1) Rpt of Pigeon Officer Second Army Maneuvers, 31 Aug 40, and associated papers. SigC 354.2 2nd Army Maneuvers, 11–31 Aug 40. (2) Memo, Maj Gen William H. Wilson, CG Hawaiian Div, for TAG, 3 Jan 40, sub: Schofield Barracks Pigeon Loft, with 1st Ind, TAG to CSigO, 17 Jan 40, 2d Ind, OCSigO to TAG, and OCSigO R&W Action 1, CSigO to Exec Officer. SigC 311.91 Gen, 1940–41. (3) Ltr, Gen Buckner to CSigO, 23 Dec 40, sub: Pigeons; (4) Ltrs, Stefansson to Gen Mauborgne, CSigO, 2 Oct 40, and Reply, 19 Oct 40; (5) Ltr, Lincoln to Stefansson, 23 Oct 40; (5) Correspondence, 6 Mar 41–12 Jan 42, *passim.* SigC 311.91 Alaska, 1940–42.

companies to serve field commanders. Plans went forward to create the first—although it was temporarily called the 2d Pigeon Company—of these units at Camp Claiborne, Louisiana, in June, and to draw at least two of the officers from that considerable group of persons who especially admired these birds. Pigeon fanciers all over the country had sought to lend fine stock to be bred with the pedigreed strains in the Signal Corps lofts at Fort Monmouth, Fort Benning, and Fort Sam Houston. Many enthusiasts in the breeding and racing of pigeons had seen service in 1917 and 1918, and some were now coming back into the Signal Corps for duty in the emergency, among these being the officers for the new company and those performing the experiments at the Pigeon Breeding and Training Center.[2]

With the first addition to its cadre, the new unit, redesignated the 280th Pigeon Company, made a reconnaissance trip to Vicksburg, reconnoitered along the Mississippi River, and after a little while took part in the summer maneuvers. Pigeons from the Fort Sam loft were winning long races by flying distances as great as 600 miles within 17 or 18 hours. Both there and at Fort Benning the signal officers received instructions to breed young stock for the 280th, first for the maneuvers, then to replace a 75-percent loss of birds during them. The 280th for a time had 800 or 1,000 pigeons on hand at the beginning of a month and only 250 or 275 survivors at its close. In the Hawaiian Department, the loft was transferred from Schofield Barracks to Fort Shafter in an effort to reduce losses: the birds had been flying into wires, disappearing into a eucalyptus grove near the loft, and even colliding with the aircraft of the adjacent base.

Yet there was no suggestion that the Signal Corps ought to drop pigeons from its list of communications means. By mid-summer, the Pigeon Breeding and Training Center was able to report progress. The experiments as yet had no tactical value since their range had not got beyond a dozen miles, but the trainers had accustomed an increasing number of birds to fly at any hour and to cover a two-way course at six in the afternoon, a good meal providing the spur. At the close of the breeding season all of the pigeons lent by civilian owners were returned, and thenceforward the Signal Corps bought birds at two dollars apiece. In nine months during 1941, the center bred and shipped out 2,150 to tactical units everywhere.[3]

The Photographic Service

The force of the times which gave even the Pigeon Center a modest importance at

[2] (1) History of the Eastern Signal Corps Training Center, 30 Oct 43. SigC Hist Sec File. (2) Memo, OCSigO for TAG, 24 Sep 40, sub: Additional Reserve officers for Pigeon Sv of SigC, with 1st Ind Reply, 10 Oct 40. Sig C 311.91 Gen, 1940–41. (3) 1st Lt C. A. Poutre, SigC, Pigeon Fanciers and the National Emergency, paper prepared for convention of International Federation of American Homing Pigeon Fanciers, Asbury Park, N.J., 1941, pp. 13, 73. (4) Memo, Maj John K. Shawvan, SigC, for Public Relations Br WD, 4 Feb 41, with incl; (5) Memo, Lt Col Bertram J. Sherry, Sig Sec, N.Y. Gen Depot, for Lt Col George P. Bush, Supply Officer Sig Sec N.Y. Gen Depot, 25 Feb 41, and Reply by Lt Col Kirke B. Lawton, WP&T Div OCSigO, 1 Mar 41. SigC 311.91, 1941.

[3] (1) History of the 280th Signal Pigeon Company, Ch. I. SigC Hist Sec File. (2) WD Bureau of Public Relations Press Release, 27 Jun 41, Army Signal Corps Pigeon Establishes a Flight Record. SigC 311.91, 1941. (3) SigC 311.91 Ft. Benning, 1941–42, *passim.* (4) Memo, Lt Col A. W. Smith, Office of Sig Officer Hawaiian Dept, for Lt Col Carroll A. Powell, Sig Officer, 16 Aug 41, sub: Informal rpt on inspection of pigeon lofts at Schofield Barracks, T. H., with 1st and 2d Inds, and Reply by Maj Francis H. Lanahan, Jr., OCSigO, 8 Nov 41, sub: Pigeon Sv for Hawaiian Dept; (5) Memo, Maj Shawvan, O/C Pigeon Breeding and Tng Ctr, for Maj Francis E. Kidwell, OCSigO, 25 Jul 41. SigC 311.91, 1941.

the great Signal Corps training installation markedly changed and increased photography. Every part of the service was a seller's market for photography. Wherever civilians were being transformed into soldiers, the Army wanted training films in quantity. To meet the demand required the Signal Corps to expand both the training program and the production program. In 1936 the War Department had hesitated to schedule production of twenty training films a year. Now in 1941 there was a program of 192 subjects alone, any of which might require as many as five training films. The resources of the Signal Corps were small. Few officers had had the year's sponsored training with the Research Council of the Academy of Motion Picture Arts and Sciences. Production space was small at Fort Monmouth and minuscule at Wright Field.

Lt. Col. Melvin E. Gillette, the Signal Corps' top officer in photography, proposed consolidating the Photographic Laboratory with the Training Film Field Unit Number 1 and the photographic instruction given at the Signal Corps School, focusing them all at Fort Monmouth as a Training Film Production Laboratory. Pending this change, Gillette arranged with the Henry R. Luce interests to take over some of the training. In February 1941 *The March of Time* began a new seven-month course in motion picture filming and editing; it dealt with the expository and hortatory sort of film which was the closest commercial parallel to what the Army would need. For still photographers, *Life* commenced a nine-week course in June.

Meanwhile, Gillette began to hire civilian instructors, because uniformed ranks yielded too few who were competent to do the work.[4] He had assumed that motion picture men would be coming into the service through the draft, reach the Replacement Training Center, and qualify for these or similar courses. Some time elapsed, however, before he learned that the instructions for diverting such men toward the Signal Corps had been garbled, and that clerks at the reception centers had missed the point altogether. This misunderstanding corrected, another block appeared in the personnel procedural maze: classification assignment lists had recognized only a few of the aspects of photographic work; cutters, for instance, had been given a number, but scenario writers had not. They were being assigned to information offices rather than to training-film production. The corrective action for this was highly informal but effective. The Photographic Division sought out scenarists and men of other essential but unnumbered specialties and coached them to say that they were cutters when they filled out the occupational questionnaires. At the Wright Field Training Film Field Unit Number 2, Lt. Col. Frederick W. Hoorn and his man of all work had been joined from the Reserve by Maj. A. E. Holland; together they patrolled the reception area to make off with any new arrival who could take photographic training. Since the Wright Field command had not been able to provide them with a building, they got an evacuated Civilian Conservation Corps barracks on a memorandum receipt. By late summer they were at work on twenty-three projects which involved fifty-two films.[5]

---

[4] Summary Report on Photographic Activities of the Signal Corps Since August 4, 1941, in the Fields of Motion Pictures and Visual Aid, 26 Feb 43, pp. 16–95. SigC APS Div File.

[5] Interv, SigC Hist Sec with Maj Holland, SigC, Ret., 15 Mar 48, Washington, D. C.

The Monmouth installation was weighted down with a far greater load of work, but had a far larger staff. A force of 20 officers, 178 enlisted men, and 31 civilians was formed into seven crews to make training films and three teams to do film bulletins. This Training Film Production Laboratory was also quartered in an unsuitable building, a frame warehouse neither fireproof nor sound-repellent which had no indoor stage. Just at the same period, Paramount Pictures put on the market its large studio in Long Island City, the Astoria studio where hundreds of films had been made in the era of silent pictures. Gillette lost no time in urging its purchase.[6] He had approval in hand for construction of a production center at Fort Monmouth, but this opportunity offered something better and half a million dollars cheaper. The Office of the Chief Signal Officer entered negotiations forthwith.

While the crowding at Fort Monmouth and Wright Field, coupled with obstacles created by early draft procedures, held both training and production below their desired point, the Office of the Chief began to put plans into effect to relieve the situation by using the resources of the great west coast industry. The restrictions governing the appointment of Reserve officers had somewhat affected this relationship. In a kaleidoscopic business, persons moved about enough so that it was not possible for them to meet the requirement that they hold at all times a civilian position exactly comparable to the one which their Reserve commission would indicate. Because change and intervals of detachment from any studio were so common, the Signal Photographic Laboratory, GHQ, a unit intended to call for twenty-six officers under the Affiliated Plan, had never been strong.

The two Reserve officers with whom the Signal Corps dealt especially were Nathan Levinson, Warner Brothers' pioneer sound engineer, and Darryl F. Zanuck, vice-president of Twentieth Century-Fox. Both men were officers of the Research Council of the Academy of Motion Picture Arts and Sciences. Zanuck, the council chairman, sponsored the Affiliated unit and also organized himself, Levinson, and John O. Aalburg, sound director for Radio-Keith-Orpheum, into a component of the Chief Signal Officer's Advisory Council, that group of industrialists which was intended to take a leading part in the forming of Signal Corps policy. Levinson, the Academy Research Council vice-chairman, took over the selection of officers for the Affiliated unit as well as the obtaining of the enlisted cadre. He did so quickly.[7]

The Signal Corps was not yet ready to call it into service but did want to link the training of the unit with Hollywood's share of the training film production program. Affiliation, however, had agreed to an expedient advocated by Col. Carroll O. Bickelhaupt of the Bell System and Col. William C. Henry of the independent telephone companies which would keep men selected for the enlisted cadres unaware of their selection until their unit was activated. The Signal Corps could not bring together the men of the Signal Photographic Laboratory, GHQ, to work on a film without letting them know of their mobilization assignments. The Sec-

---

[6] Memo, Gillette for O/C Photo Div OCSigO, 2 Oct 41, sub: Consolidation of motion picture production. SigC APS File.

[7] (1) Ruth F. Sadler, History of the Signal Corps Affiliated Plan, Aug 44, pp. 81–94. SigC Hist Sec File. (2) Interv, SigC Hist Sec with Samuel J. Briskin, Vice-President Paramount Studios, 3 Aug 49, Los Angeles, Calif.

TRAINING FILM UNDER PRODUCTION *at the Astoria studios of the Signal Corps.*

retary of War agreed to an exception, and the men were notified; but no sooner was the information out than rumors followed of a government scheme to take over the amusement industry and to name Cecil B. DeMille, then a major in the Signal Corps Reserve, as some sort of potentate of pictures and rajah of radio. *Variety* straightened the matter out, but not before the gale had blown away any illusions that the public shared the Signal Corps' and industry's regard for the Affiliated Plan.[8]

The planning for Hollywood production of training films got under way in the Research Council late in the fall of 1940. The large studios notified Secretary Stim-

son that they would produce the films at cost. Capt. Charles S. Stodter, one of the seven Signal Corps officers who had had a Research Council fellowship, set up a liai-

[8] (1) T/O 11-94. (2) Ltr, OCSigO to TAG, 6 Jul 40, sub: Affiliated positions in SigC orgns; (3) Ltr, Col Otis K. Sadtler, OCSigO, to Col Bickelhaupt, 11 Dec 41; (5) Ltr, Gen Mauborgne to Zanuck, 14 May 40, with incls. SigC 381 Affiliated Units. (6) Ltr, CSigO to TAG, 26 Oct 40, sub: Use of pers of Affiliated SigC units in producing tng films; (7) Memo, ACofS G-1 for TAG, 5 Nov 40, same sub. AG 381 (1-1-40) Sec 1 PMP, 1940. (8) Incl to Ltr, Col Levinson to Maj Frank C. Meade, OCSigO, 4 Dec 40. SigC 381 Mob Gen 15. (9) Tab 1 of Tab D to Memo, Col Henry L. P. King for Deputy CSigO, 23 Oct 42, sub: Pers requirements. SigC 320.22 Enlisted Strength, MT-25. (10) Hollywood *Daily Variety*, November 22, 1940.

son office to advise the council in the further selection of candidates for commissions under the Affiliated Plan, to provide the studios with military consultants whom they might need during the course of the filming, and to negotiate the purchase of the films as they were completed.

The work commenced immediately, without waiting for the financial arrangements to be made. In fact, to avoid delay, Zanuck had authorized his own studio to go ahead with the first two scenarios as soon as the War Department had them ready. After a few months, mutual adjustments appeared. Scenarios became the function of writers rather than of officers; the branch of the Army for which a film was being made provided the scenarist with an outline only. To allay criticism that the work was not being evenly distributed, the Research Council rotated the assignments among the participating studios in a rough alphabetical order somewhat disrupted by exceptions. The original plan to contract for the films died under some of these exceptions, contract terms not being compatible with a large commercial production schedule of which the Army's part was small and subjoined. Stodter consequently used purchase orders. Under this system, the Research Council offered the finished product—which a contributing studio had fitted into its schedule when a stage and a production company became available—to the government at a fixed price. If the Chief Signal Officer accepted it, his liaison officer issued the purchase order against allotted funds, which the finance officer of the Fourth Army paid out. The Signal Corps was also free to reject a film outright or to turn it back for revisions.[9]

The initial admixture of altruism thus disappeared from the arrangement, which solidified instead into more familiar forms. The studios based their price on four items: first, studio overhead; second, direct costs such as the expense of script writing, titling, cartoon animation, shipping, and travel; third, such indirect costs as appeared in the maintenance of the Signal Corps Liaison Office and additional staff and rent required for the Research Council in connection with the work; and fourth, an amount to meet current expenses on training film projects in progress.

Final accounting later established the industry's contention that the Research Council paid out more than it charged the program under the fourth item; and for the later investigation conducted by the Truman Committee of the United States Senate, the Research Council was able to argue other actual savings in the salaries of producers, directors, and actors, in sound-recording royalties, in the use of existing sets and so on. On the film Safeguarding Military Information alone, the government was said to have saved nearly $20,000.[10]

In any case, speed was more important than economy. It was essential that masses of men coming into the Army, to be trained in mass, take major parts of their instruction from mass media like the films. Four basic pictures, Sex Hygiene, Personal Hygiene, The Articles of War, and Military Courtesy and Customs of the Service, were in demand for all reception centers. It was a fruit of the arrangement with the Research Council that the Signal

---

[9] Summary rpt, cited n. 4 pp. 377–81.

[10] Hearings Before Special Committee Pursuant to Senate Resolution 71, 77th Cong, 1st Sess, Investigation of the National Defense Program, Pt. 17, Army Commissions and Military Activities of Motion Picture Personnel, Jan–Apr 43, pp. 7100–110.

Corps was able to distribute these within the first six months of the draft, the first two being ready by March.[11]

In July Zanuck went to Washington to apprise General Marshall directly of Hollywood's part in the defense effort. The Chief of Staff, who was interested in the training power of films, agreed to send him upon a tour of training camps and service schools to report how extensively and how effectively they were using pictures. The Operations and Training Division of the General Staff, in the person of its director, Brig. Gen. Harry L. Twaddle, opposed the survey, and to a degree so did the Office of the Chief Signal Officer. Twaddle doubted that the trip could "accomplish any useful purpose" and in any event asked that he and the Signal Corps send their own observers along. Marshall preferred to leave the itinerary to Zanuck, as well as to let him choose his associates. The Hollywood producer, with two other Reserve officers and prominent members of the motion picture community, went to installations in California, Washington, Wyoming, Kansas, Oklahoma, and Texas, and returned a report at the end of the summer which was summarized and sent, at the Chief of Staff's order, to all replacement centers.[12]

Zanuck reported a "complete absence of coordination between the production, distribution and use of training films." He supplied such familiar details as the facts that equipment was short and that training officers were less than resourceful in limiting the use of films to rainy days and then showing one after another in dreary succession. Had this been all, his report would scarcely have created any interest. The whole military scene was a scene of inadequacy; few commanders needed to be told that. Zanuck recommended that

all silent and otherwise obsolete films be withdrawn, that no more than one picture be shown at a session and that none be more than half an hour long, that lifelike details and humor be introduced into the scripts, that professional actors tide the picture over the dull parts—likely to be the explanations—by giving them the benefit of variety in manner and inflection. Although these were certainly helpful and practical suggestions, they, too, were not his main point. This was that the Army should either drop its training film program altogether or standardize and run it according to the methods of the motion picture industry. He proposed that the War Department designate an individual with Army-wide powers to set up a complete distribution system like the one used by commercial producers. In this apparatus the director-in-chief would have a representative at each post, responsible only to him and charged with supervising the films and projection equipment, and a staff of traveling supervisors, one for each branch of the service.

Thus the Zanuck survey once again advanced a question which was basic in Signal Corps, and, indeed, in Army policy. Should civilian industry administer and possibly even determine the equipment of the military service? In this case, should Hollywood do all of the films the Army needed? Or should the Signal Corps go on making a sizable share of them? The sur-

---

[11] CSigO, *Annual Report, 1932*, p. 315.

[12] (1) Msg, Zanuck to CofS, 22 Jul 41, Reply, 26 Jul 41, and Msg, Zanuck to CofS, 27 Jul 41. AG 413.56 (7-23-41) Tour of Inspection of Army Camps in re Study of Effect and Value of Army Tng Films. (2) Memo, Gen Twaddle for CofS, 24 Jul 41, sub: Proposed inspection tour of US Army camps by Zanuck. OCS 19966-38. (3) Ltr, CofS to CG's RTC's, 22 Sep 41, with Incl, Summary survey of Zanuck's rpt to CofS, 22 Aug 41. OCS 19966-46.

vey urged that the training film distribution program be centralized to the extent of making one officer on each post solely responsible, and solely responsible in turn to the national administrator of the whole. Since this individual would probably be an executive of the industry commissioned into service, the direction of the recommendations was clear.

As on any basic question, there was a difference of opinion. In the opinion of some, training film production was not a proper function for the military; training films were manufactured items as much as radios or cameras. It had never been Army policy to compete with civilian industry, nor should the policy be changed. Commercial producers, eastern as well as western, could make any kind of Army film wanted, according to specification, just as they made films to train salesmen or factory workers.

In the Signal Corps this view was taken, for example, by Lt. Col. Kirke B. Lawton, who believed that the Army should confine itself to training photographers in both still-picture and motion-picture field techniques, and to maintaining laboratories to process their work, meanwhile leaving the production of films to industry.[13] Colonel Gillette, who had made the recommendation that the Signal Corps buy the Astoria plant for a place in which to expand, felt quite otherwise. What he proposed was a liberation of the Signal Corps training film program from the benevolent despotism of the Motion Picture Academy's Research Council. He urged that the Signal Corps break away by renting its own liaison office in Hollywood rather than accepting one from the industry; by hiring its own employees from among persons free from obligation to the industry; by having scripts pre-

pared, not in the studio, but in the branch or service school which was going to use the film. In sum, he questioned the unwritten agreement of ten years' standing which gave the Research Council the exclusive supervision of all training film production for the Army which the Army did not do itself. This arrangement restricted competition to the extent that the Research Council did not represent all of the companies capable of bidding for training film production contracts. In his estimation, the whole arrangement could invite Congressional investigation.[14]

The Signal Corps was responsible for completing 370 reels in the next year, a production load approximating that of a large commercial company equipped with twenty or thirty stages and a staff of three or four thousand. Even without Astoria, although with a staff increased to 500, the Monmouth installation was turning out two thirds as many films as a large studio of this sort would, and at very much lower cost.

Understandably, there was strong support, including that of General Twaddle, for keeping the activity within the Signal Corps. On the other hand, the Chief of Staff and some of the field generals favored settling all film production upon the motion picture industry. One of their points of approach which the Gillette argument, they felt, left unsatisfied was that not the quantity but the quality of training films set their value. Quality was not to be measured in reels any more than a book is

---

[13] Interv, SigC Hist Sec with Col Kirke B. Lawton, Chief of Fiscal Div OCSigO, 5, 8–9 Mar 48.

[14] (1) Memo, Col Gillette for Col Sadtler, Chief of Opns Br OCSigO, 21 Nov 41, sub: SigC Hollywood Office; (2) Attachment 4 to Memo, Maj Thomas D. Hodge, Control Div OCSigO, for Deputy Chief of APS, 20 May 43, sub: Analysis of rpt of Inspector Gen tng film production. SigC EC 062.2 Tng Films.

measured in the number of pages. To these supporters of the Zanuck survey there was a strong appeal in his contention that soldiers' films could be made interesting, that training could proceed without tears, or worse, yawns. Gillette contended that the Signal Corps could do as much if provided with indoor studios and stages, improved shop and recording equipment, and a great increase in qualified writers and editors. But this brought the discussion back to the question of whether the Army should seek to put itself upon a comparable production level with civilian facilities. The decisions which finally emerged included the purchases of 500 projectors, an increase in the number of film libraries from 90 to 140, and the commencement of a full photographic record, including foreign pictures, of contemporary developments and experiments.[15]

Tactical and Administrative Service

That this program was to cost more than $430,000 was one sign that starvation rations were a thing of the past. As had not been true for many years, money was coming in plentifully. During the fiscal year 1941 the Signal Corps Laboratories, for example, were able to grow five times as big as they had been in 1940. In April the Signal Corps submitted its contribution to the general augmentation of the Mobilization Plan, in which the basic assumptions now were that the mythical M Day would occur somewhere during the last three months of 1941 and that everyone in the Army as of that date would stay in. The Signal Corps School and Replacement Training Center, steadily preparing the communications technicians for the growing forces, esti-

mated that they would be coming out of the thirteen-week and sixteen-week hoppers at a rate well over 500 every Monday. Two summer months alone were expected to turn out nearly 6,000.[16]

Expansion was of course too recent to make its effect felt immediately. There was a lag in the developmental field, and an even longer one in procurement, which nothing could reduce. Planners in the Office of the Chief Signal Officer asked for a month's warning on the mobilization of division signal companies, knowing it to be very likely that ostensible "refresher" time would have to be devoted to giving many of the men their first acquaintance with communications work. And until the Laboratories could perfect replacements and the factories produce them, the equipment and the trickle of procurement of the years just past had to suffice. Such items as were on hand were parceled out among all of the branches calling for them; many became controlled items and were distributed only under a system of priorities, although they might go back in date almost to World War I. All of the new items were on the way, some so far from development that their ultimate manufacture was barely discernible, others slipping so easily from one stage to the next that there was even a chance that they

---

[15] (1) Memo, ACofS G-3 for CofS, 14 Nov 41, sub: WD tng film program. OCS 19966-57. (2) Memos, Maj Gen Barton K. Yount, CG West Coast AC Tng Ctr, for CofS, 6 and 21 Oct 41, sub: Tng films and strips. OCS 19966-46 and AG 413.56. (3) Summary rpt cited n. 4, passim.

[16] (1) Ltr, OCSigO to Actg ACofS G-3, 14 Apr 41, sub: Mob schedule for SigC units in AMP, 1941, with Incl, Troop Basis for Computing Supply Requirements, Augmentation Mobilization Plan, 1941. SigC 381 Gen 18. (2) 2d Ind, Hq SCRTC through Comdt SigC School to CSigO, 12 Apr 41, on Ltr, TAG to CSigO, 4 Apr 41, sub: Completion of tng of March load at RTC's. AG 324.71 (4-4-41) M-C.

might be ready by the time that World War II drew America in. Despite the sudden flush of relative wealth, the Signal Corps could not at once heap its partners-at-arms with abundance; but their needs were uppermost, development having advanced or started in a hundred directions, and procurement in a dozen.

In October and November of the preceding fall, the Cavalry and the Signal Corps had agreed upon a short-range radio to be constructed, with its antenna, around a guidon staff; the trooper would hold it upright with the lower end of the staff resting in a saddle boot. This guidon radio, the SCR-511, was to become one of the best of the walkie-talkie types—although not much used by men on horseback. Rather, it proved out as a set for cavalrymen and infantrymen alike and engineers as well, all of whom used it in vehicles if they could, as a pack set otherwise.[17] But at the same time that cavalrymen approached the Signal Corps for this portable guidon set, infantrymen had asked for an even more portable and compact, equivalently short-range radio for paratroopers to use. On this, the development was phenomenally rapid. By mid-February the Galvin Corporation demonstrated equipment which filled the bill. Weighing only five pounds, and promptly accepted in substantially its original form, it became the SCR-536 and probably the best-known item of all Signal Corps equipment in the war: the handie-talkie. The initial order to Galvin, later that year, was for 3,500 of them.[18]

The Laboratories were also progressing with the Armored Force "500" sets. The first models of the SCR-509 and 510[19] had arrived at Fort Knox, and the Armored Force gave them a thorough drubbing to make sure that they were sturdy. A motor-

cyclist with a 510 on his machine ended a two-hour ride in a severe spill which injured the man, damaged the motorcycle, and left the radio unaffected. This was proof not so much of the set as of the mounting by which it was held to the luggage carrier, for a second SCR-510 attached without the special mounting was all but shattered. Yet a third, similarly without shockproofing, survived being thrown to the ground from a scout car by a very heavy jolt and, reinstalled in the car, worked perfectly.[20]

So two more 500's were on their way. Others were already part of the Armored Force organization. As it was planned, each tank had both a radio and an interphone system. With headsets at their ears and microphones at their throats, crewmen could intercommunicate and intracommunicate. In a regiment of 108 tanks, all would have interphone equipment, just as in a bombardment airplane, and the company commanders would have SCR-508's (a transmitter and two receivers), battalion and platoon commanders SCR-528's (a transmitter and one receiver), and all the rest SCR-538's (receivers only). A model of the tank under procurement for this purpose, the new medium

---

[17] (1) Hist Sec E&T Divs OCSigO, History of Signal Corps Research and Development in World War II, 1945–46, Vol. VIII, Pt. 2, Proj. 814-B. (2) First Partial Report of Cavalry Board on Test of Radio Set SCR-511, Ft. Riley, Kansas, 25 Nov 41. SigC 413.44 (SCR-511) No. 1, 1940–41.

[18] (1) Ltr, Chief of Inf to CSigO, 28 Oct 40, sub: Lightweight pack radio equip for opn from parachutes. SigC 413.44 (SCR-536) No. 1, 1940–41. (2) SCL, Annual Report, 1941, pp. 72–73.

[19] Alike except for power supply, the 509 operating from dry batteries so that it could serve as a portable set, whereas the 510 was wholly vehicular.

[20] Rpt of Armored Force Bd, Proj. No. 104, Service Test of SCR-510-T1, AF Type IV-A, and SCR-509 ( ), AF Type IV, 5 May 41. SigC 413.44 (SCR-509) No. 1, 1940–42.

PORTABLE RADIOS DEVELOPED BY THE SIGNAL CORPS *included the*
SCR-536 (left) and the SCR-511 (right).

M3, went on display at the Aberdeen Proving Ground in April for the scrutiny and comments of representatives of the Air Corps, the Signal Corps, and the Ordnance Department.[21]

W-130, the light assault wire, posed a problem if it were to be manufactured in mass quantities. It required a special latex insulation for which a single manufacturer controlled the patent. The answer was to spread the patent. This the owner agreed to do; under educational orders, two other companies joined his in the W-130 manufacture; the Defense Plant Corporation built the factories for all three; and the result was a ready potential of 6,300 miles of the wire a month.[22]

Introduction of the teletypewriter at field maneuvers had accented a different side of the wire question. The Army needed a cable which would combine the long range of open wire, strung on poles, with the ease of field wire, which did not possess the range but was speedily laid. The need was filled in time to meet the approaching demands of field teletype for just such characteristics. In this case, the solution came from the Germans, unwillingly. British Commandos had just captured some new cable and under the agreement reached in the course of the Tizard Mission sent samples of it to the Signal Corps Laboratories. This became

[21] Notes on Meeting at Aberdeen Proving Ground, Maryland, April 10, 1941, attached to OCSigO R&D Div Buckslip, S. E. P[etrillo, Associate Radio Engr R&D Div] to Col Mitchell and Maj Washburn, 16 Apr 41. SigC 413.44 V. 1 Special 1, 1940–41.

[22] Lt Col James H. B. Bogman, Current Problems in Signal Corps Procurement, Army Industrial College Short Course 3, Jul–Sep 41, 29 Jul 41, p. 6.

the renowned *spiral four,* a superlative cable consisting of four insulated conductors wound spirally about a central core.[23]

As for the instruments which the wire served—the telephones, switchboards, and teletypewriters which the past year's maneuvers had thrown into a sharp, clear light—they were the center of the stream of supply to the ground forces, becoming so usual, so abundant, so effortless that they would be more and more taken for granted the more they approached their goal, imitation of the human voice and eye. By this time the Signal Corps Laboratories had largely completed work on the sort of switchboards which Colton and Reeder had pointed out as the most urgent of tactical communications needs in 1939 and 1940 maneuvers: 100-line BD-80's which could handle heavy traffic and yet operate simply, from the modest power sources likely to be available in the field. These now began to reach the Infantry. The new corps and division switchboards did not; and in the area where Infantry communications *were* Infantry communications, the Laboratories altogether forewent the development of new switchboards.

Many things had to yield to the radio and radar developments, and the small switchboards were among them. Although the two decades in which BD-71's and 72's had been in use had not wholly outmoded them by any means, the Infantry Board was undeniably right in saying that they could both be materially improved. The chief disadvantage was their weight— fifty-six pounds for one, seventy-nine for the other. There was too much else to do, however, and supplies of the BD-71 and 72 ran into the thousands, and manufacturers long used to making them could turn out thousands more upon demand.

Moreover, having reached maturity long before, wire held its ground against change to an extent which was out of the question for radio. Major O'Connell demurred at "burdening the fighting troops with at least twice the switchboard weight" necessary, and protested that "repeatedly since 1920 the development of a better switchboard unit has been put off"; but since the Field Artillery was relatively satisfied and the several arms which used the boards were not entirely agreed upon the characteristics of a replacement, the work continued to be put off in favor of more vital research.[24]

In any event, by the onset of the maneuver season, it was evident that field teletypewriters were on their way to becoming standard tools of military communication; and though they did not take the place of a good telephone switchboard system, they were superlatively welcome in their own right. An observer at the VII Corps maneuvers declared that "the telegraph printer is beginning to get the distinction it deserves. Seventh Army Corps kept the six . . . machines in constant operation." The old telegraph suddenly was revitalized. The new equipment made it possible once again to write over wires at a speed equal to the demand of military

[23] (1) R&D hist cited n. 17(1), Vol. V, Pt. 1, Proj. (510) 2-4. (2) C&E Case No. 21, Long Range Tactical Cable for Field Armies. SigC Files.

[24] (1) R&D hist cited n. 17(1), Vol. V, Pt. 3, Proj. (532) 4-32.1. (2) Historical Report of the Signal Corps Engineering Laboratories, pp. 156–57. SigC Hist Sec File. (3) TM 11-487, Electrical Communication Systems Equipment, pp. 60, 64. (4) Ltr, Lt Col Harris M. Melasky, Chief of Test Sec Inf Bd, to President Inf Bd, 7 Mar 41, sub: Replacement for BD-71 and 72; (5) 3d Ind, Col Colton, Dir SCL, to CSigO, 17 Jul 41, on Ltr, President Inf Test Bd to Chief of Inf, 13 Mar 41, same sub; (6) Memo, Capt L. B. McConaghy for O/C R&D Div OCSigO, 22 Dec 41. SigC 413.42 (BD-71 and 72) No. 2, 1940–41.

operations, and without much more inconvenience or loss of time than would be true of talking over a telephone.[25]

As usual, maneuvers were providing a good school for tactical training and a good testing ground for tactical supply, research, and development. The longer the nation stood aside from actual war, the better the opportunity for a Signal Corps to judge itself. The first 1941 exercise occurred off Puerto Rico between January 25 and February 14. The Navy and Army joined in a problem to test an assault upon an island; Culebra, which lies just east of Puerto Rico, was chosen. Maj. Francis H. Lanahan, Jr., the Signal Corps observer at the exercise, noted that "it was immediately apparent that the Army contingent had not brought sufficient radio personnel" or the right kind of equipment, and laid the blame upon Admiral Ernest J. King for having imposed his own plan without consulting or informing the Army in the least.

This was irksome but not conclusive, for it was still possible to distinguish the terms in which the Signal Corps ought to be thinking. The signal teams, with which the Army element, the 1st Division Task Force, was provided, might better be replaced by a regimental headquarters company, Lanahan felt. These teams had signal flags, panels, tactical wire, and radio. The semaphore flags would have helped to dispel the initial confusion on the landing beach had the men been practiced in them; their usefulness in the ensuing war developed in just that way. Panels did not prove out, although the slow airplanes of the day made them look feasible at this time, as did the accustomed use of aviation as a sort of sky cavalry. Wire equipment, including the new W-130 assault wire, was satisfactory. Radio—

SCR-131's and the preliminary walkie-talkies, the SCR-195's—was less so, but without any basic fault attributable to radio itself. The 131's were out of date by many years, and porcelain antenna insulators in the 194's and 195's were easily broken. Modernization amended one and phenolic insulators the other.[26] The uninterrupted trend toward radio left no doubt that it was welcome everywhere; in all of the maneuvers of 1941, it came into far more use than in 1940.

The war in Europe and the 1940 maneuvers, particularly the one which had involved the First Army and the IV Corps in November, prompted Lt. Gen. Walter Krueger to wish plenty of radio on hand for the maneuvers of his Third Army in Texas, where he took command in the spring. He wanted to blanket every part of his force with radio communications— the advanced reconnoitering elements, the reconnaissance airplanes, the command posts, and all—so that he might move freely without losing touch with any unit of his command. In order to bring this about, his signal officer, Col. Spencer B. Akin, went so far as to write out of channels for three SCR-193's, which neither the Third Army nor the 52d Signal Battalion had been authorized to have. The SCR-193 was a controlled item, short in supply; so that the best General Mauborgne could give him was advice to make

---

[25] Ltr, Lt Col William S. Rumbough to President SigC Bd, 8 Aug 41, sub: Use of tg printers and associated equip. SigC 413.41 (BD-100) Tg Printers Associated Equip.

[26] (1) Maj F. H. Lanahan, Jr., Report on Joint Minor Exercise, Culebra, P.R., 25 Jan–14 Feb 41, in Final Report, 1st Division Task Force, Army & Navy Joint Exercise No. 7, 1941, Vol. II, Annex B. AG 354.2. (2) Memo, Actg ACofS G-4 for ACofS G-3, 21 Jul 41, sub: Rpt on Army-Navy Minor Joint Exercise No. 7, 1941. SigC 354.21 (12-7-39) Sec 1 (a).

sure that the next table-of-basic-allowance requests included them.[27]

Working for the ground forces was a two-way business. The employer had to make his needs clear. "Without exception," according to two Field Artillery officers at the Second Army maneuvers the next month, there was an undeniable shortage of radio sets. (Without exception, it would continue, until production caught up with demand halfway through the war, and despite strenuous efforts to overcome the deficiency sooner.) There was also a want of spare parts, but piecemeal issue contrarily encumbered some units—although in the case of a regiment which had thirty-two SCR-194's, all incomplete, excess was no boon.[28]

Lt. Col. Fred G. Miller, commander of the 50th Signal Battalion, brought thirty years of experience to bear when he declared that the tables of allowance and organization were both meager, both "too superficial to perform the . . . mission of the signal battalion with the modern army." There were not enough enlisted men or officers for a peacetime organization, let alone for war, Miller thought. Grades were too few and too low for a technical service; and not a day passed that a technician was not taken off to do kitchen police duty. Miller believed that the tables provided for too many general cargo vehicles and too few of specialized value. To give a battalion only 2 radio and 12 wire vehicles while allowing 55 for cargo purposes was "all out of proportion as to numbers and types, and based on no sound fundamental plan." Furthermore, to put all of them, plus the drivers and the mechanics, in the headquarters and headquarters company of the battalion was comparable to putting all the guns of an artillery battalion in the headquarters and

none in the gun batteries. The tables omitted teletype, repeaters, and power units essential for a higher headquarters and certainly for the self-contained unit he thought a signal battalion should be: so organized and equipped that it could load everything into its own vehicles and be prepared to set up army or corps headquarters communications without delay.

The Second Army commander threw his weight behind Colonel Miller. Office of the Chief Signal Officer responses to him were reasonable; they represented simply a difference in point of view. Miller spoke as the man in the field charged with a tactical mission. Lawton, who answered him, did so from the point of view of the headquarters man, not having to meet a tactical situation firsthand as a division signal officer did, but required to cope with a general situation broadly, as an officer in the field was not. He called attention to new tables which authorized a battalion twenty-four wire and four radio vehicles. Several other new types were on the way, all specialized to haul poles, to accommodate cable reels and poles together, to serve cable repair, and so on. Everything else Miller had mentioned was assuredly either under procurement or under study. If it had not appeared in the field, the reason was that the Signal Corps' policy, learned by its own long experience, was not to put any item into the tables of organization and allowances until a unit which requisitioned it could be sure of

[27] Ltr, Col Akin to Gen Mauborgne, 19 May 41, and Reply by Col Clyde L. Eastman, Exec Officer OCSigO, 23 May 41, sub: Radio equip Third Army. SigC 413.44 (SCR-193) No. 3, 1940–43.

[28] Ltr, Lt Col Rex·W. Beasley and David S. Rumbough, FA, through Chief of FA to TAG, 16 Jul 41, sub: Second Army maneuvers in Tenn. AG 353 (5-15-41) 3-C 2d Army Maneuvers 1941.

getting it. This left the opposition unconvinced but the point had some validity all the same.[29]

The Office of the Chief Signal Officer did agree that far too little equipment had been issued to battalions for training, but inasmuch as henceforth all of the men for such units were to be learning their signaling in the Signal Corps School and Replacement Training Center, that difficulty was disposed of. Training in the communications units beyond the point where direct Signal Corps responsibility in the ground arms stopped was another matter. Certainly the Infantry, the Cavalry, the Armored Force, and the Field Artillery would have to see to it that the draftees being poured in to fill up their ranks learned on the job, with equipment on hand, the communications tasks they were assigned to perform. From the Signal Corps point of view, observer after observer at the succeeding maneuvers noted a lag. Training had not caught up with manpower. Their reports unconsciously confirmed the impression of critics that the maneuvers were a dream play in which lackadaisical recruits, drafted for a year, performed by rote motions which had never been suitably justified to them or even explained; where "dead" men sought the shade of a pine tree, to chew the needles while they awaited the umpire; where crudely lettered fluttering cloths labeled a truck a tank, or a World War I Springfield a .30-caliber machine gun.

In that summer, the Germans had just delivered another heavy blow and the Japanese were getting set for one of their own. The signal units at Tennessee maneuvers could get no nails, screws, or plywood for their field message centers, and chipped in to buy them. Cord was a universal shortage. Headquarters provided

itself with 20 representative messages, which the communications men had practiced often enough to memorize. Some of the Morse operators could send as many as 10 words a minute. But not all. The 33d Division had held a five and one-half weeks' course which 178 men had completed, but in which only 36 had attained a code speed of 15 words. An operator who could manage to take in only 15 words a minute at a code classroom table could not do much better than 10 under field conditions. Panel crews knew the technique of panel communication, but had never had any practice with an authentic airplane. The 33d Signal Company and the 58th Signal Battalion both failed in the reading of maps and aerial photographs. Yet by specific statement, "the morale, enthusiasm, soldierly attitude, willingness to learn, on the part of the enlisted men [were] highly commendable."[30] Training had simply not got started.

One device to stimulate it which occurred to signal officers was for each corps and division to seek out commercial communications men who might be serving in other duties. Col. John C. Moore, First Army signal officer, reiterated the concern of Miller, the Second; Akin, the Third; and Col. Joseph J. Grace, the Fourth Army signal officer. The Washington *Post* correspondent at the First Army's Carolina maneuvers charged that "radio fell

---

[29] Ltr, CO 50th Sig Bn to CSigO, 22 Oct 40, sub: Inadequate T/O's and T/BA's Sig Bn, with inds 1–14. AG 400.34 (7-21-39) (1) Sec 1 T/BA's—Equip for Posts, Camps and Stations.

[30] (1) Ltr, Sig Officer VII Corps Tng Ctr, Camp Forrest, Tenn., to CG VII Army Corps, 25 Jul 41, sub: Sig com tests of 33d Div and corps troops; (2) Memo, Col Moran for CofS GHQ, 29 Jul 41, sub: Mob tng test, Camp Forrest, 22–25 Jul 41, sig com. SigC 381 Gen 18. (3) *Hearings Before the Subcommittee of the Committee on Appropriations*, Senate, 77th Cong, 1st Sess, On HR 4050, 20 Mar 41, p. 24.

down repeatedly, delaying messages which would have changed the course of battle." This immediately alerted the Chief Signal Officer. Was it true? It was, said Moore. "Our one great fault"—he was speaking of the First Army—"is lack of training." He described breaches of radio discipline and inspection, and remarked, "I seldom see an officer standing by listening to radio transmission to correct procedure." He extended his remarks to take in wire: "I am appalled at the great percentage of wire failures due to lack of training in its laying and maintenance. . . . Some of our officers are seized by panic when they are confronted with the need of wire from army to corps and corps to division, thinking that the job is too big for us." From the state of Washington, and anent maneuvers there in August, Grace disclosed that the 202d Signal Depot Company at Fort Lewis had handled nothing but paper signal supplies, a training assignment which did not train. He suggested transferring the unit to special duty at the corps area depot in San Francisco, where the men could work with real equipment. Lt. Col. Raymond C. Hildreth, in the Supply Division of the Office of the Chief Signal Officer, disagreed. "To load up one or two corps areas with a field army or more . . . is not reasonable. . . . The armies should establish their own depots and necessary repair shops." [31]

The Signal Corps had both sides to consider. Making sure of field communications was half of a mission whose other half was administrative. The corps areas often carried out the administrative duty, especially at a stage when the nation's military effort was almost entirely confined to home soil. Over much of the face of the country, and possibly in the South more than anywhere else, the region of the

Fourth and Eighth Corps Areas, the defense program was making quick, deep changes. In the industrial East and Middle West a general expansion of plants was beginning, in order to take care of the production demands of war. Civilian though they were, their purpose was military and naturally tapped military services at many points. Huge reception or training areas like Fort Dix, New Jersey, or Camp Grant, Illinois, were filling, expanding, filling to new limits, and expanding again, at a rate which left them perpetually unfinished. Raw settlements for thousands were appearing everywhere, panoramas of newly sawn lumber and bulldozed land; and in some localities the nearby towns, long saddened by economic adversity, were at a loss to cope with them. Depots, arsenals, harbor gun sites, and military hospitals made other parts of a scene of unlimited emergency; and all bulwarked hundreds of existing posts and stations which, if small, were growing large, and if large, enormous. Where the region was undeveloped, the Engineer, Quartermaster, and Signal Corps were challenged to produce complete systems of roads, sewage disposal, electricity, and telephones. There was equivalent work of a different kind in commercial and manufacturing areas; meagerness of facilities was not the problem, but defense was expanding so many offices and factories that even the most extensive systems were taxed.

Funds for the new emergency construction went as a rule to the Quartermaster

---

[31] (1) Ltr, Col Sadtler to Sig Officer First Army, 1 Nov 41, with Incl, clipping from Washington *Post*, 28 Oct 41, and Reply, 7 Nov 41, sub: Pers and radio equip First Army maneuvers. SigC 354.2 1st Army Maneuvers, 1941. (2) OCSigO R&W Action 2 (Supply Div to WP&T Div), 26 Sep 41, sub: Rpt concerning sig com pers within Fourth Army. SigC 354.2 Fourth Army, Jan 41.

General or Chief of Engineers, who in turn made suballotments to the Chief Signal Officer, to cover the cost of the telephone part of the construction plan. This the Wire Section of the Plant and Traffic Division prepared, and ordinarily delegated its execution to the signal officer of the corps area concerned. Telephonically, the term *plant* refers to the mechanical apparatus, taken as an entity, which the process requires. At times, signal officers rented the plant for a defense project intact from the local telephone company; at other times, Signal Corpsmen entirely installed and maintained it. The decision which to do was taken upon the basis of long-standing practice. Just as in Adolphus Greely's days in the frontier West, the Signal Corps did not go where commercial systems were already established and install competing systems, but rather went where they were not: a direction which implied commercially unrewarding or pioneer and rugged circumstances, and a purpose for which the Plant Engineering Agency was created later on, in the war.

The expansion going on as of midspring of 1941 called for $5,594,150 worth of telephone plant, especially in the Fourth and Ninth Corps Areas. Seventy-seven of 213 projects all told were for Air Corps installations. The rest were all for the Ground Forces, in the various guises which defense expansion took. Mushrooming troop housing called for 59, almost evenly divided among new posts, old posts, and replacement training centers. A program of 26 projects was scheduled to supply telephone service to Ordnance and Chemical Warfare facilities. For the Medical Department there was a list of 10; these were to serve large hospitals, of a thousand beds or more, which it was agreed ought to have plants separate from

the general post switchboard. Storage depots, reception centers, special facilities of all kinds needed consideration. The cable plant for harbor defense, for example, amounted to three or four times what was normal for the same number of telephones in a different activity. The conduct of fire, particularly of the great fixed guns, necessitated constant communication between the gun crews and the observers or spotters. These were not the conditions which radar would bring about, but radar was not yet established in most Coast Artillery stations.[32]

When there was an occasion to join Army with non-Army areas, other agencies of the government were involved and other considerations entered than those of the Signal Corps, G-4, a corps area, and the Bell System. When $868,250 for switchboard and telephone construction in defense-housing areas, included in the Signal Corps' 1941 supplemental estimates, was cut to $75,000 by the Budget Advisory Committee and restricted to guard and fire-alarm telephones, straightening the matter out called in the Federal Works Agency and the Public Buildings Administration. This situation was usual, not unique; and the increased intertwining of the national interest with the military was to make it universal. In the face of the demands of defense housing, a working agreement and mutual understanding were highly important. Many of

---

[32] (1) Incl, Major Building Construction Projects Involving Telephone Systems, 23 Apr 41, with Ltr, OCSigO to Sig Officer First Corps Area, 25 Apr 41, sub: Tp construction; (2) Ltr, CSigO to The Surgeon Gen, 3 May 41, sub: Opn of separate switchboards in larger hospitals, and 1st Ind Reply, 3 Jun 41. SigC 676.1 Gen 11. (3) Maj John C. Grable, O/C Fire Sec P&T Div OCSigO, Address Before N. Y. Chapter of American Institute of Electrical Engrs, Newark, N. J., 6 Feb 41. SigC 676.1 Gen 10.

the commissioned and noncommissioned officers of a rapidly growing post had to live in a defense-housing development, whereupon the question arose of connecting them by telephone with the post itself. A commander could think of many situations when it would be inefficient, and of some when it would be serious, not to be able to get in touch with the post complement during off-duty hours. In all instances where the defense housing stood on a military reservation the Signal Corps simply gave the Bell System blanket permission to install home telephones and connect them, over Signal Corps poles if necessary, with the nearest commercial exchange—not, of course, with the post system, although in many cases the use made of the two was much the same.[33]

At a camp or post it was also important to have adequate public telephone service. Off-duty use of the public telephone was especially high at reception centers and training stations. Men wanted to call their wives and mothers, and, since most of them were on duty during the day, they needed to have phones available to them between evening mess and tattoo. They preferred booths, too, rather than the publicity of a telephone on an open wall. Nevertheless, it was often impossible to make sure that morale was served as it ought to be by plenty of booths and phones. The Bell System estimated from its reports of usage that three or four per thousand men would take care of the demand, but long queues were a regular occurrence at the evening peak, and whenever movement orders were out, the rush to the telephone became an elemental force. At most posts—at 129, up to that time—the men also had access to the public telegraph, Western Union or Postal or both, so that the strain was partly shared by the older commercial facility.[34]

Part of the task in analyzing any request for a telephone project lay in discovering whether existing equipment was actually being used to the maximum, as the circumstances unquestionably required. A post signal officer might unwittingly be allowing inefficiences because he was new to his job and unfamiliar with Army procedure. From time to time, he perhaps might send in requisitions in round numbers, almost a sure indication that some of the order would be left over. At some posts, the drive to expansion created temporary or deceptive demands which soon evaporated but still withheld telephones from active use. With the adoption of new standards, there was always a tendency to get rid of everything except the newest equipment, despite the fact that much which was of substitute or recently obsolete quality was good enough.

---

[33] (1) Ltr, CSigO to QMG, 30 Sep 40, sub: Tp construction at new cantonments. SigC 676.1 Gen 9. (2) Ltr, CSigO to Sig Officer Hawaiian Dept, 5 Feb 41, sub: Tp construction in connection with Public Building Administration projs. SigC 676.1 Gen 10. (3) Ltr, Sig Officer Fifth Corps Area to CSigO, 22 May 41, same sub, with following inds: 1st Ind, OCSigO to TAG, 27 May 41, 3d Ind, QMG to TAG, 7 Jul 41, 4th Ind, TAG to CSigO and CG Fifth Corps Area, 17 Jul 41; (4) Memo, CSigO for ACofS G-4, 19 Jun 41, sub: Tp sv defense-housing proj; (5) Memo, Lt Col Paul C. Gripper for Tp Sec and File OCSigO, 19 Jun 41; (6) Incl, Defense Housing Fire Alarm Systems, with Memo, Maj W. W. Carlton, QMC, for Col Gripper, OCSigO, 20 Jun 41. SigC 676.1 Gen 11. (7) Ltr, Asst Dir Defense Housing to Maj James P. Hill, G-4, 24 Jun 41; (8) Ltr, TAG to CSigO, 17 Jul 41, sub: Installation of tp sv in defense-housing projs on mil reservations; (9) Ltr, CSigO to Sig Officers All Corps Areas and Depts, 23 Jul 41, same sub; (10) Memo, Actg CSigO for Brig Gen Albert E. Brown, Office of Deputy CofS, 2 Sep 41, same sub. SigC 676.1 Gen 12.

[34] (1) Ltr, Commercial Engr AT&T Co. to All Gen Commercial Managers, 16 Apr 41, with Incl, Public Telephone Service in Military Camps. In same file. (2) Memo, P&T Div for Com Liaison Div OCSigO, 21 May 41. SigC 483.1 Gen.

Signal officers turned in serviceable EE-5's and BD-9's and 11's even when depots were unable to provide the models intended to replace them. To all officers in this duty, the Chief Signal Officer sent out word that they ought to check to see what excess equipment there might be, to recondition it, put it on inventory, and send it to other posts where there was a shortage.[35]

Most post telephone systems contained three parts, the main one being the central administrative switchboard and the other two being comprised of a target-range system and an emergency system for reporting fires and explosions. The fire department, the motor pool, the commanding officer, the officer of the day, and the post physician could all be alerted from the alarm system, which was essentially a conference circuit that the operator kept open as long as was necessary. A specific type, which became necessary with the building of cantonments housing 50,000 men or more, reported all fires to the central fire station and made it possible for remote guard posts to report in to the main guardhouse. Target-range systems varied from a modest support for rifle practice to 100-line separate switchboards with telephones scattered throughout the target area and connected by tie lines to the main system of the post. This central administrative post telephone system was itself either small or large according to the size of the camp. If it went above 500 lines, every effort was made to install automatic, dial equipment. Usually the outside plant was lodged underground, although at any impermanent post the wire was simply strung on poles shared with the electric lighting. In the spring of 1941 there were 189 administrative post telephone systems with 60,000 telephone connections, and by the time that all of the temporary addi-

tions then in view were completed, there would be 274 systems and 125,000 telephones.[36]

Supply Service

No one knew by then whether M Day had slipped past unnoticed in the increasing activity. The Protective Mobilization Plan was thrown awry, its calendars unsettled. There had been no declaration of war, and yet the readying of the nation's manpower and productive economy was farther advanced than an uncompromised peace would have produced. Contrariwise, the record of the nation's potential enemies gave warning that there would be no correct transition from peace into war, but rather that one day would arrive with abrupt notice that a state of war had existed for several years. In that case, the national war effort was far behind.

The absence of a yardstick made it a problem to know how much to order, and for whom. "It has not been possible, in many cases, to obtain any basis whatever for the computing of requirements," the Signal procurement planning officer complained.[37] Realistic estimates had to allow for the requirements of friendly nations, but in that black year their needs changed with their fate almost from hour to hour. Estimates also had to predict the supply of new items to new units, a guess with a large margin for error even when both the items and the units were well understood. Current requirements were already surpassing the greatest volume anticipated

[35] (1) Msgs, CSigO to Sig Officers All Corps Areas, 13 May 41. SigC 381 Controlled Items of Equip 4, May 41. (2) Ltr, CSigO to Sig Officers All Corps Areas and Depts, 2 May 41, sub: Construction and maintenance of tp systems. SigC 676.1 Gen 11.
[36] Grable address cited n. 32(3).
[37] Bogman course cited n. 22, p. 4.

when the Protective Mobilization Plan was new. The sum allotted to the Signal Corps for radio equipment alone had reached $148,638,747 by February 1941: that is to say, with the fiscal year little more than half gone, the outlay for radio had already been more than twelve times the total for the whole fiscal year 1940. As Akin and many another had learned, the supply of almost everything was short. BD-14's, the old SCR-131's, 161's, and 171's, and other familiar equipment stood in the critical list along with the radars. Not until January 1941 was the Supply Division able to report that the fiscal year 1940 procurement of SCR-177's, 193's, and 245's was complete, and this procurement was for mere fractions of the quantities desired for 1941.[38]

A closely revised forecast for the Munitions Program at the outset of the fiscal year in progress had ranged the field to list more than a dozen standard radios; telegraph, telephone, and telephone central office sets; all of the switchboards; field wire; reels; flash-ranging and sound-ranging apparatus; theodolites; cryptographic machines; and yet other items beyond these. The spread in cost of individual items was as remarkable as their variety. It extended from 45,000 telephone sets at $40 apiece and 80,000 miles of field wire at $50 a mile toward SCR-177's and 188's which cost $4,800 an item, to sound-ranging GR-3's at $11,000 apiece, and out to the radars SCR-268 at $35,000 and SCR-270 at $65,000.[39] All of the estimates of the period were directed toward the 2,000,-000-man Army contemplated with Selective Service. As that Army did not materialize at once, neither did the equipment. The explanation was interwoven with the contemporary scene. Raw materials had a great deal to do with it; priorities entered

in; sources of labor were vital; design and patent, essential; allocation and expansion of facilities, basic.

Even plant security was a factor. With its record in formulating aircraft plant protection in World War I, and as a supply arm markedly responsible for the procurement of secret and expensive equipment, the Signal Corps was particularly aware of the need for a system to guard defense production against both accidental and intentional interruptions. Promotion of security was a national concern and the Signal Corps' part in it comparably minor, but comparably necessary, too. The War Department periodically sent to the Federal Bureau of Investigation a list of plants working on important military contracts, and with each list forwarded specific requests for surveys from one or another of the supply services.[40]

If, for example, a contract officer in the New York Signal Corps Procurement District wanted to make sure of a plant in New Jersey which was working on aircraft radio, his request for a survey joined those from other supply arms on a list in the Office of the Assistant Secretary of War. G-2, the official liaison with the Federal Bureau of Investigation sent the list to the Plant Protection Survey Division of that agency. The reports of the FBI agents were

---

[38] (1) Ltr, Henry L. Stimson to Senator Henry Cabot Lodge, Jr., 20 Feb 41. X-ref sheet in SigC 413.44 Gen 15, Jan–Aug 41. (2) OCSigO R&W Action 1, Supply Div to R&D Div, 12 Jun 40, sub: Expenditure program covering critical and essential items FY 41. SigC RP-111 (ET-111) Program FY 41, pp. 1–29. (3) Rpt, Lt M. M. Kilgo to Col Mitchell, O/C R&D Div, 29 Jan 41. SigC 413.44 Gen (Set) 13, Jan–Jun 41.

[39] Critical Items on Munitions Program of June 30, 1940. SigC MB-111 (ET-111) FY 42 (Expenditures Program FY 42).

[40] *Annual Report of the Attorney General, 1940,* pp. 152–53.

detailed, sometimes hundreds of pages long. When the bureau had described the hazards in a given plant and made its recommendations for eliminating them, its duty and authority ended. Beyond that, except that a plant expansion could always reopen an FBI survey, security lay in the hands of the manufacturer and the agency of government with which he had a contract.

For some time in the emergency, the Signal Corps' formal organization for plant protection consisted only of a liaison officer, Major Bogman, who was primarily assigned as the officer in charge of procurement planning. Informally, the inspectors in the procurement districts took over the responsibility; they went in and out of plants which were working on Signal Corps contracts, and thus could most readily follow up the FBI surveys. When orders began to mount past the point where inspectors could continue to handle the extra duty, the Signal Corps established a plant protection section in the New York district, the largest of the three Signal Corps procurement districts. This action anticipated by some weeks instructions from the new Office of the Under Secretary to do just that. The Under Secretary authorized the Signal Corps to assign seventy-five civilians and fourteen Reserve officers to plant protection.

On the part of the manufacturers, there was a certain amount of passive resistance. Some, like the Du Pont Company, were accustomed to using the same frame of thought as the Federal Bureau of Investigation; but in general, even manufacturers who attempted to carry out the recommendations of a survey interpreted them rather freely. One plant engaged in work upon classified equipment bought safes to hold the drawings and blueprints, then pasted the combinations on the outside. Another manufacturer surrounded his plant by a fence with locked gates, but provided keys to children accustomed to taking a short cut to school through the grounds. A third management, warned of a fire hazard, placed barrels of water and buckets at frequent intervals, then, to discourage mosquitoes from breeding in the water, poured oil upon it. The manager of still another defense plant, which had hired a substantial force of guards, agreed that it was a good idea to require written reports from them describing the delinquencies they had observed but pointed out that it was not practicable because few of them could read or write English. After a conference of procurement officers with major industrialists and the director of the Plant Protection Survey Division of the FBI, the security in plants of prime contractors gradually tightened. Eventually a clause requiring both prime and subcontractors to conform to specified standards of plant protection and make their factories accessible to Signal Corps inspectors became a part of every instrument of procurement.[41]

Security, of course, was much broader even than in its effect on defense production. The telephone company employees

[41] (1) Plant Protection Conference, 22–24 May 1941, Washington, D.C. SigC FM 004.02 Plant Protection Conference 43, May 41. (2) Memo, Actg ACofS G-2 for CSigO, 3 Apr 40, sub: Designation of liaison officer, and 1st Ind Reply, 5 Apr 40. SigC FM 004.02 Protecting Guarding Gen 32, Jan 40–Dec 41. (3) Industrial Mob Div Phila. SigC Proc District, History of the Plant Protection Section. SigC 004.003 Hist of Plant Protection Sec. (4) Memo, CSigO for USW, 28 Feb 42, sub: Plant protection; (5) OCSigO R&W Action 1, Maj Gen Dawson Olmstead to Brig Gen Roger B. Colton, Chief of Supply Sv, 27 May 42, sub: Contract clause for plant protection, and Action 4, Facilities and Materials Div to Proc Div, 28 May 42; (6) Memo, OCSigO for SigC Contracting Officers, 27 May 42, sub: Contractual provisions. SigC FM 004.02 Protecting Guarding 45, 1941–43.

engaged in putting in a phone system at a defense plant or on an Army reservation had to be cleared and identified before they were admitted. And many offices of government tightened their organization, warned their employees against talking about their work, scrutinized them for evidences of subversive behavior, issued new badges, put new force into secrecy regulations. As was to be expected of a people of easy, casual, and unsuspicious approach to one another, the new policy was more honored in the breach than the observance. Even generals could not always remember that a "secret" telephone was not secret. But good will and intelligence accomplished what regulations never did, with the result that the nation went through the war with few such instances of negligence or sabotage.

Lt. Gen. John L. De Witt, in command of the Ninth Corps Area, had proposed that the War Department exclude aliens from Army employment, arguing that inasmuch as the Congress had expressly barred them from the Panama Canal, from aircraft plants, and so on, common caution demanded that they be denied jobs at any Army post. The Presidio of San Francisco was his headquarters; many west coast citizens mistrusted Orientals; and newspapers at the time were detailing the activities of the German consul, Fritz Weidemann, whose office windows overlooked the Golden Gate. What General De Witt suggested, however, was extralegislative action. Moreover, the Signal Corps, being asked for an opinion—and agreeing in general—pointed out that "if such exclusion were applied indiscriminately to skilled and unskilled labor at overseas depots and Army posts, serious delay in the completion of construction projects and installation of Signal Corps

equipment thereat might result." And so it might. A project like the new $660,000 warehouse at Schofield Barracks had employed noncitizen laborers, and the Caribbean and Latin American defenses depended upon local hiring. In short, the challenge to a supply arm was to protect itself against spying and sabotage without crippling itself by ruling out the contribution of thousands of trustworthy persons.[42]

In any event, the Signal Corps was more concerned with the general possibility of a labor shortage than with any of the details. Although this was a matter almost wholly outside its scope, it was of firsthand interest. When the Office of the Under Secretary established a Labor Section where policy could be formed for the whole War Department and integrated with the action of other parts of the government, the Signal Corps welcomed it, for complex matters quite beyond a small branch of the Army had been building up and then halting in the jam of the channels ahead of them. One of the fiercest pertained to the Fair Employment Practices bill, which the Signal Corps opposed with a somewhat narrow statement of self-interest subsequently submerged by the bill's passage. Civilian and military agencies alike, the Departments of Interior and Labor, the

---

[42] (1) Ltr, CSigO to Sig Officer Second Corps Area, 15 Apr 41, sub: Identification of Bell System employees at arsenals and posts. SigC 676.1 Gen 11. (2) Memo, Actg Dir Naval Coms for Col Sadtler, 30 Oct 41. SigC 380.01 SMI CED 1941–43. (3) OCSigO Memo No. 2, 3 Jun 40. SigC 230 CP. (4) AG Ltr to Chiefs of Arms and Svs and CG's Corps Areas and Depts, 31 Jan 41, sub: Credentials and identification badges. AG 344 (1-28-41) M-B-M. (5) AG Ltr to same, 24 Jun 41, sub: Procedure in discharge of subversive Civil Service pers. AG 230 (6-18-41) C-B-M. (6) Ltr, CG Ninth Corps Area to TAG, 18 Jul 40, sub: Exclusion of aliens from employment on Army posts; (7) Memo, OASW for Chiefs of Supply Arms and Svs, 1 Aug 40, same sub, and 1st Ind, OCSigO to OASW, 13 Aug 40. SigC CP 014.31 Alien Employment.

Civilian Conservation Corps and the National Youth Administration, the Civil Aeronautics Administration, and procurement planning groups within the armed forces, had been examining the labor prospect and coming up with the expected conclusion that there might be a deficiency. Skill was what the Signal Corps was especially interested in; and as Affiliated Plan discussions with the American Telephone and Telegraph Company had noted, the depression had reduced it by 25 percent. So far as the recurring surveys could make sure, the first reopening of industry under the demands of emergency had trained enough skilled workers to restore 15 percent of the loss. The nation had to make the rest up, and create more, if the rapidly accelerating requirements of the current period were to be met, not to speak of what would be needed in case of war.[43]

But for the time being, shortages in raw materials looked more immediate than shortages in the labor supply. Gradually, as 1941 lengthened, one after another developed, in quartz crystal, steatite, tungsten, tantalum, mica, aluminum, carbonyl, rubber. The materials supply could not keep pace with the production demands of wire, cable, insulating machines, insulating materials, resistors, commutators, dynamotors and tubes, of glass envelopes, carbon anodes, tungsten filaments, magnets, metal stampings, diamond dies, and disks of copper oxide and selenium.

Beginning of work on the multicrystal FM and VHF sets produced an instant sharp increase in the quartz requirement; the Procurement Planning Section estimated a need for 300,000 pounds for the forthcoming fiscal year. The section was deeply worried about getting it, because the nation's authorized stockpile was only

106,000 pounds and less than half of that had been collected. Production of the essential wafers remained at laboratory level, carried on in twenty-nine small plants by craftsmen who did most of the cutting by hand. Yet without quartz-plate oscillators, there could be no effective control of radio frequencies, no pushbutton tuning; without quartz-plate resonators, long distance lines and ocean cables could not transmit hundreds of messages at once. The supply of raw quartz had to be dramatically increased, or the processing of crystals had to be simplified for mass production, or the Army would have to economize on their use.

At a meeting which the Office of Production Management held with representatives of the Treasury, the Bureau of Mines, the Bureau of Standards, the Army-Navy Munitions Board, and the Signal Corps, the discussion was concerned primarily with the basic shortage of raw quartz. The Office of Production Management set broad quotas of 300,000 pounds for civilian needs, 600,000 for military, the latter amount to include the Signal Corps' requirement. Through its Metals Reserve Company, the Reconstruction Finance Corporation, which was also charged with stockpiling rubber, was responsible for building up the supply of raw quartz. Those present at the conference of the Office of Production Management agreed that the Brazilian supply, which was

[43] (1) Lt Col James I. Heinz, Labor Officer OCSigO, Report of Labor Office, OCSigO (1945). SigC Hist Sec File. (2) H. D. Hausmann, Procurement Planning and Industrial Mobilization, 1920–1940, Pt. III, pp. 172–82. OCSigO Industrial Mob Br File. (3) Memo, ASW for Chiefs of Supply Arms and Svs, 25 Feb 41, sub: Labor Section OUSW. SigC FM 004.02 Labor 19, Jun 40–Dec 41. (4) Ltr, OCSigO to TAG, 23 May 41, sub: Bill S-1400, 77th Cong, 1st Sess. SigC 032.

almost all there was, ought to be solidly underwritten, with no chance for it to get into other hands, by a credit to the Bank of Brazil which would cover half of the anticipated purchases. Japan had taken far the greatest part of the Brazilian export for a long time, until Britain suddenly moved ahead in 1940; but in that year, Japan's purchase was still five or six times greater than that of the United States. The American Gem and Pearl Company, which had a South American cartel arrangement, had now once again begun to sell more quartz to the Japanese than ever, and in June informed the Army— the company president telling Bogman— that they had just tripled their order.[44]

Meanwhile, the Signal Corps and the Bureau of Standards looked toward two further goals: the most efficient use of the quartz already on hand, and the possible development of artificial quartz. There was no perceptible expansion in the United States of manufacturing facilities, although the limited capacity was coming under scrutiny. All of the raw quartz in the world was of little use unless it could be precisely cut into crystal slivers. The truth was that neither supply officers nor manufacturers nor the Reconstruction Finance Corporation were universally educated to the magnitude of the conflict about to encompass them. At the beginning of that year, Signal Corps opinion believed that the production facilities were sufficient. Zenith and Emerson, among manufacturers, said so, as did General Cable—in this last case despite a general knowledge that a British demand would tax the market as never before.[45] As late as July Lt. Col. James H. B. Bogman was reporting that "the available manufacturing capacity of the communications industry" had not yet been overtaxed and that

"expansion of facilities . . . has been necessary in only one or two instances."[46] Actually, various points of the communications industry were already clogging.

For the Congress had admitted foreign orders almost without limit to the production plant. This act was the cause of the greatest of all of the debates over the degree to which the United States should commit itself in the war. Not even the struggle over Selective Service had aroused and prolonged so much controversy as the proposal to put the country's industrial capacity at the service of all opponents of the Axis powers. On one side, narrow interest dilated at the prospect of commercial profit, and broad interest responded to the opportunity to aid and comfort allies without making an alliance. On the other side, narrow interest shrank from sharing the nation's own vital reservoir with others who might drain it, and broad interest dreaded the risk of a step which might pitch the United States forthwith into war. The controversy culminated in March when the Lend-Lease Act was passed.

----

[44] (1) Conference Rpt, 22 May 41. SigC 314.7 Data on Bi-Weekly Conferences OCSigO Proc Plng Sec, May 41. (2) M. L. Melia, The Quartz Crystal Program of the Signal Corps, 1941–1945, 1945, *passim;* (3) Quartz Crystal Coordination Sec Gen Development Br OCSigO, Handbook for the Manufacture of Quartz Oscillator-Plates, 20 Aug 42. SigC Hist Sec File. (4) Proc Plng Sec Supply Div OCSigO, Daily Historical Record, 11 Jun 41. SigC 314.7 Proc Plng Sec Daily Hist Record, 1 Jan–13 Jun 41.

[45] (1) Memo, Capt Eugene V. Elder for Lt Col James T. Watson, Jr., Fiscal Div OCSigO, 7 Jan 41. SigC CH 11-101 Defense of Proc Activities under Various 1941 Appropriations. (2) Andre E. Gerard, The Story of Supply in the Signal Corps in World War II: Pt. III, Production, 1945, p. 24, and (3) Activity and Participation of the Signal Corps in Foreign Procurement and Lend-Lease, p. 85. SigC Hist Sec File.

[46] Bogman course cited n. 22, p. 8.

Beforehand, there had been a long stage when any foreign orders which entered the ken of the Signal Corps came from the foreign purchasing missions. In effect, this meant Great Britain, many other powers being either submerged or isolated and Soviet Russia remaining beyond the pale until an uneasily common cause lowered the bars. During that period, the Signal Corps did not know how much foreign purchases cut into its market. In the first place, there was no single report of them. Not only did the Royal Corps of Signals, the Admiralty, and the Royal Air Force all buy signal equipment, but they might do so through the British Supply Board in Canada, the British Purchasing Commission in the United States, or one of their own officers sent out on a special assignment. In the second place, only if the equipment were classified against espionage was it necessary for the Army-Navy Munitions Board and the Signal Corps to designate the manufacturer.[47] Otherwise, the purchasing mission could place the contract anywhere, and, unless it happened to go to a Signal Corps prime contractor, the Signal Corps would have no knowledge of the transaction. Until 1941 nine tenths of Signal Corps equipment was commercial. Foreign purchasing commissions could of course buy any of it. Nine tenths of it, also, comprised processed raw materials and unassembled components.

Signal Corps procurement dealt almost exclusively with the large companies, confident that they would always consult the Chief Signal Officer before accepting a contract for end items and would in no way permit foreign orders to interfere with the delivery of U.S. Army equipment.[48] But most of the signal equipment, being not only commercial but also fractional,

was manufactured by secondary or subcontractors of whom the Signal Corps had no knowledge at all. When the foreign orders came in, they were usually for these items—wire, batteries, tubes, microphones, ceramic insulators, crystal oscillators, tantalum sheets. Because many were made of critical materials, their uncontrolled manufacture intensified shortages.

Thus the whole foundation of communications equipment could have been undermined before a threat was suspected. Practically, nothing of the sort happened. Before lend-lease, the cash-and-carry principle drastically limited foreign purchase, and, afterward, procurement vision was refocused. Nevertheless, the inability of the Signal Corps to know the extent of foreign orders of vital components served to throw procurement planning further askew. If, along with ordnance, aircraft, and certain strategic supplies, communications equipment had been included in the Munitions Control Act of May 1, 1937, the opportunities for sounding out and "educating" lesser firms by means of foreign orders would have been much greater. As it was, the Tizard technical mission had somewhat stimulated purchase beyond the ordering of quantities of routine components, but the chief effect, as a result of the Air Corps' discovery of British equipment, had been reproduction of the foreign designs, again with little educative advantage to Signal Corps procurement.

---

[47] (1) Ltr, CSigO [to All SigC Field Agencies], 7 Dec 39, sub: Clause in contracts regarding secret, confidential, or restricted projs. SigC 160 Contracts Gen 27. (2) Ltr, ASW to RCA, 24 Jul 40. SigC 072 Patents 9.

[48] Memo, Actg CSigO for ASW, 18 Mar 40. SigC 032 Legislation 7, 1939–40.

With lend-lease, everything commenced to look different—except shortages: the consecutive shortages of labor, materials, and plant facilities, and the ultimate shortage of end products. Communications equipment became "defense articles" along with almost everything else.[49] All of the orders for Army signal equipment once placed by foreign nations now went to the Signal Corps to place. To handle lend-lease in the War Department—so far as policy was concerned, the actual operation devolving upon the various technical services—the Office of the Assistant Secretary of War set up a Defense Aid Division [50] within a month of the enactment of the legislation. Before Pearl Harbor, and until the Services of Supply materialized three months after Pearl Harbor, this division was one of the mentors of Signal Corps supply activity. Another was the Statistics Branch, to which the supply services reported their procurement progress or backsliding every week.

The Signal Corps' portion of the first $7,000,000,000 appropriation for lend-lease was nearly $225,000,000.[51] Even the cumulative total of the past three fiscal year appropriations fell short of that. The first authorized request for signal equipment under the new legislation came in just the day before the huge sum was approved. It was a British request for 35,000 more miles of telephone wire. The Signal Corps had covered more than half the distance toward the Mobilization Plan's goal of 101,853 miles of field wire W-110. This came in addition. The General Cable Corporation had a contract to manufacture 57,917 miles, Anaconda Wire and Cable, 20,729. They were the chief recipients of the British order for wire, as well as for 200,000 feet each of cable. In the wireless category, a large order had gone to the Bendix Radio Corporation for thousands of aircraft radio compasses, SCR-269A's, under two contracts which totaled $2,075,363.[52] Lend-lease production, then war production, soon overshadowed these contracts. For the time being, they provided a chance to build up and test the capacity of these companies, even though the chance was of less than first importance because there was little doubt that large companies would work at peak capacity in any event.

Considering all of the influences upon Signal Corps procurement, what was its status? Or, better, its progress? General Mauborgne felt that he was doing well. He believed that his agency's supply procedure and supply organization were "efficient and adequate to meet the present emergency and . . . sufficiently flexible for such future eventualities as can now be foreseen." [53] That was at the halfway point of the fiscal year and a year before Pearl Harbor sharply cast up accounts.

One way of looking at the procurement record was that whereas at the end of the fiscal year 1940 there had been little radio equipment on hand and only a million and a half dollars' worth of wire equip-

---

[49] Sec 2a of PL 11, 11 Mar 41, 77th Cong.

[50] At a later date, it became the International Aid Division of the Services of Supply and still later, the International Division of the Army Service Forces.

[51] PL 23, 27 Mar 41, 77th Cong.

[52] Incl, Foreign Orders for Communication Equipment, to Ltr, Chief of R&D Div OCSigO to Dir SCL, 4 Apr 41. SigC 334.8 Army-Navy Munitions Bd. See also R. Elberton Smith, Army Procurement and Economic Mobilization, a volume in preparation for the series UNITED STATES ARMY IN WORLD WAR II.

[53] 1st ind, CSigO to ASW, 11 Dec 40, on Memo, ASW for Chiefs of Supply Arms and Svs, 6 Nov 40, sub: Review of orgn, procedures, and methods pertaining to proc. SigC 400.13 Gen 20.

ment, by the end of the 1941 year the Signal Corps' manufacturers would have delivered more than $28,000,000 worth. Another way was that by virtue of the inevitable lag between signing a contract for equipment and getting delivery of the finished product, this $28,000,000 actuality would look meager by contrast with the expectation. During the fiscal year 1941 the Signal Corps would be letting contracts for equipment up to the amount of $223,000,000, or, bluntly, $195,000,000 more than it would be getting from its contractors.[54]

Between these two views lay a discrepancy; and a persisting misinterpretation, coupled with the frequent protests of the Air Corps, established an impression that the Signal Corps was in default as a supply service. The Signal Corps contributed to this impression by placing its contracts within too narrow a range of manufacturers and by a less energetic approach than the situation warranted. Yet some of the discrepancy would have been expected as an inevitable part of the procurement lag.

At the time when General Mauborgne wrote his opinion, the Signal Corps procurement districts had obligated about three fourths of the 1941 funds. They assumed in most cases that deliveries of equipment would keep up smoothly with the Protective Mobilization Plan. The PMP requirements for the EE-8 field telephone, for example, totaled 63,593. Six manufacturers were delivering 56,678 of them, and in addition 39,708 were already on hand in the depots or in actual use. Nevertheless, even these simple statistics, which looked like the innocent flower, held a serpent under them. Beneath any such figures of ostensible progress lay the exasperating complexity of procurement.

The 56,678 new EE-8's had not all been delivered, but were in the process of being delivered. The 39,708 on hand were not all brand-new; they included World War I EE-4's and 5's.

The situation was much the same for field wire. The Signal Corps had indeed provided fifty thousand of the hundred thousand miles of W-110 which the Protective Mobilization Plan required. Fiscal year 1941 contracts specified that 70,498 additional miles would be delivered by the end of June: more than enough to meet the PMP. But there was yet all of the lend-lease demand. Again, the PMP required 764 portable field generators, used for charging storage batteries. The contract called for delivery of 680 of them to begin in January. Actually, delivery began in mid-April. Another important item was the standard telephone central office equipment. The Signal Corps had arranged for 36 of these sets; but at the moment there were none on hand, and deliveries were not to commence until February.[55] In short, figures showing estimates or even quantities actually let to manufacturers on contract could never be taken as the equivalent of deliveries.

Change kept altering the procurement outlook as much as delay. Orders for 3,855 of the SCR-131's, 161's, and 171's which had been "critical" in June simply because nothing else was ready were canceled late in the year in favor of SCR-288's. This was the set which the Swedish Government had ordered; the manufacturer was tooled up for it; and until production could begin on the new American

---

[54] CSigO, Annual Report, 1942, p. 77.

[55] Statistical Br OASW, Weekly Statistical Report Summary, No. 22, 30 Nov 40, pp. 23–25: text summary, Procurement of Signal Corps Items—Nov 16, 1940. OASW Files.

sets which were due to replace the old series, it made an acceptable stopgap. Accordingly, the supply program classified it under "limited procurement" and the 131, 161, and 171 under "limited standard." [56] Changing circumstances also showed in a sequence on the SCR-245. A requirement for 1,237 had dropped to 589 on the Munitions Program list; by the end of the fiscal year the set was no longer "critical"; and by October 1941, 919 were stricken from the First Supplemental Program for fiscal year 1942. Production of the SCR-245's was necessarily quite a different thing. Between the middle of August and the first of October, just before Pearl Harbor, the Signal Corps issued 1,035; and by the end of the year nearly half [57] of all the 245's ever built had been delivered. Thus the manufacture continued for more than two years after planning had foreshadowed its end. The equipment itself continued in use throughout the war.

As rapidly as possible, new items were moved forward to take the place of the old, sometimes as stopgaps, most often as full replacements. Equipment unknown when the fiscal year was beginning, barely developed and standardized when it was half gone, filled the planning lists as the new supplemental programs were prepared. The Fifth Supplemental for 1941 asked for 2,849 handie-talkies, for instance; the $15,000-apiece, 100-miles-in-motion SCR-299's neared production; and the Field Artillery's "600" series pressed for manufacture. [58]

But after a slow start, Selective Service was increasing the procurement demands by 75,000 men a month. Delays in delivery were proportionately serious. It became important to know just what and how much was actually coming off the assembly lines. The lump figure for "radio sets, ground," gave way to statistics for specific items, the most closely watched being the new sets toward which Infantry, Cavalry, Armor, and Artillery were making their plans and training the incoming men. The last week in the calendar year, a month after the Chief Signal Officer had expressed confidence, sounded warnings. There was no delivery of the radars SCR-268, 270, and 271; none of the short-range SCR-288, the temporary replacement for the SCR-131, 161, and 171; none of the long-range SCR-197, the temporary stand-by until the SCR-299 could be made ready. Apart from radio, there was no delivery of the portable switchboards BD-71 and 72; of the GR-3 and 4; of the M-134; of the TC-2. [59] In the case of the SCR-197, a change in the truck which transported it was causing the delay. A shortage of tuning units had held up delivery of the Air Corps command set, the SCR-183. Contractors for the radio direction-finder SCR-206 and for a battery charger, SCR-169, had not yet furnished satisfactory samples. The manufacturers of the SCR-177 and the theodolite ML-47 explained that difficulty in obtaining com-

---

[56] Ltr, TAG to CSigO, 13 Nov 40, sub: Radio sets for FA and Inf. AG 413.44 (11-8-40) M-D, and also in SigC 413.44 Gen Sets 12, 1940.

[57] 4,927 out of a total production of 11,513.

[58] (1) OASW, Weekly Statistical Report Summary, No. 23, 7 Dec 40, p. 21. OASW Files. (2) OCSigO R&W Action 1, Scheduling Div to Proc Div, 29 Oct 41 and 24 Dec 41, sub: Third Suppl Program FY 42; (3) Memo, Col Cuny, Proc Div OCSigO, for OUSW, 7 Jul 41, sub: Addition of item. SigC MB-111 (ET-111) FY 42 (Expenditures Program FY 42). (4) Memo, Maj E. Blair Garland, Exec Mat Br OCSigO, for Actg CSigO, 4 Oct 41, sub: Rpt of major items of program during week ending 5 P.M., 3 Oct 41. SigC 319.1 Weekly Progress Rpts (Evaluation Br), 1941.

[59] OASW, Weekly Statistical Report Summary, No. 28, 11 Jan 41, containing SigC rpt through 28 Dec 40. OASW Files.

ponent parts and materials made it impossible for them to meet their delivery schedules. And these shortages were indeed showing up: in aluminum; brass; iron dust; mycalex, an insulating material; and carbonyl E, essential in the making of radio tuning coils.

Things promised better as spring approached. The first factory-built SCR-268 arrived in the week ending February 28. (Almost four years had elapsed since this radar's great day of revelation.) In March delivery of the SCR-206 and SCR-288 commenced, with 5 sets each. Delivery of the SCR-193 resumed with 15 sets, and 34 of the SCR-245's appeared. Production of the EE-8 was flowing in the thousands; field wire W-110 reached 5,980 miles in one week. Two hundred fifty Air Corps command sets, both the 12-volt SCR-183 and its 24-volt twin, the SCR-283, came from the assembly lines the first week in March, and in the second week the first five liaison sets arrived. The Supply Division took an optimistic tone and informed the Assistant Secretary that "the Signal Corps procurement program is showing very satisfactory progress." [60] Even so, an aluminum shortage had "made it necessary to revise some delivery schedules," several contractors had been "slow getting into production," and delinquencies were impressive. They involved nearly 10,000 sets of 25 items.

Thus the supply program hung in balance, looking well, looking ill. In the midst of an emergency it represented the Signal Corps' chief service to the fellow arms— more immediate than research, more insistent than training. It had to be done well, but it was "exceedingly difficult," the Signal Corps pleaded. By the end of May, shortages in minor parts and accessories were holding up nearly 3,000 of the commonest ground radios, all standardized and familiar so long that nothing except a shortage could have detained them in the factories. Similarly, hundreds of the FM police sets hastily legitimized in the expectation of quick manufacture, were being retarded not by reason of their newness but for lack, in one model, solely of microphones, in the other, solely of whip antennas. For other new equipment, never before manufactured, let alone manufactured in quantity, mere shortages were compounded with technological difficulties. In self-extenuation, the Signal Corps supply spokesmen went over familiar ground now become stonier than ever: "Before contracts can be awarded, it is necessary to develop and built test models; after testing and standardization, the contractor must tool for quantity production; months necessarily elapse between the time a new item is engineered and its production in quantity is achieved." [61]

[60] *Ibid.*, No. 41, 12 Apr 41, Sec. 4.
[61] *Ibid.*, No. 49, 7 Jun 41, Sec. 4.

CHAPTER X

Working for the Air Forces

Air communications procurement was exploring two streams. One headed in toward the Signal Corps' own developments, like the standard ground-to-air radio, the SCR-188, like the SCR-270 radar, or even like the SCR-268 radar which had not been designed for air use but was now being importantly diverted to it. The other stream was the transoceanic current from Britain, which the Air Corps watched for signs of CH, CHL, ASV, IFF, AI, GCI, PPI, and a swell of very high frequency command and direction-finding radio.

With the Munitions Program, the Air Corps had gone up into the hundreds, and then the thousands, of airplanes; the associated requirements in communications equipment had risen into the thousands and then the tens of thousands. The Air Corps wanted more than 8,000 SCR-274's: a thousand more of a single item than the sum of all of the equivalent radios which the ground forces desired. Air requirements listed 1,910 frequency meters, 2,656 radio compasses, 7,398 interphones, and 15,218 command and liaison sets. By the time of the departure of the Tizard Mission some of these were going under contract; by the turn of the year 21,354, apart from radio compasses, were underwritten with 1941 funds. If the manufacturers met their schedules, all would be well except for the fact that there was much more to Air Corps supply than

the requirements of the Protective Mobilization Plan.

For the Air Corps, the dream of British equipment had arisen overnight into an unsubstantial palace, iridescent with Arabian Nights promise. Had the Signal Corps had a genie to build it, nothing could have been more welcome. But stubborn fact ruled the fancy. On top of the principal obstacle, the inherent intricacy of signal equipment, reality reared another: the double intricacy of foreign signal equipment. Even so, at the strong urging of the Air Corps, which like Aladdin believed in genies, the Signal Corps undertook to surmount the second obstacle. Promptly upon receipt of Major Edwards' message from London urging the purchase of samples of the very high frequency radios and of three principal Royal Air Force radars, the Signal Corps entered the procurement channels to obtain $100,000. This was to procure the three radars, respectively of the airborne-interception, air-to-surface-vessel, and identification-friend-or-foe types; one ultrahigh-frequency direction finder; one searchlight director; one gun layer; one pipsqueak; one command radio TR-1133; and the "micropup" tubes and other components to go with them.[1] In an effort to put the cavity magnetron to use to de-

[1] Memos, CSigO for ACofS G-2, 24 Oct, 29 Oct, and 8 Nov 40, sub: Purchase of British equip. SigC 413.44 Purchase of British Equip (RB-2331).

velop a practical 10-centimeter set, the first of these, airborne interception, was already under study at the new Radiation Laboratory, which the National Defense Research Committee had established at the Massachusetts Institute of Technology.

At the same time, the Signal Corps also gave high priority at the Aircraft Radio Laboratory to its own airborne-interception project, partly because of a feeling that it would lead to the bombing-through-overcast equipment upon which the Air Corps centered its immediate interest.[2] Airborne-interception, bombing-through-overcast, and air-to-surface-vessel efforts had all been present in the hurried experiments which the Signal Corps had made to put pulse radar into the air after talking with the Tizard group. In the SCR-268 the U.S. Army had its own searchlight director and a potential gun layer. As for airborne radio, very high frequency possibilities were well understood.

The Chief of the Air Corps was embarked upon a major campaign, far outstripping these initial moves on the part of the Signal Corps. Saying to the Deputy Chief of Staff that "beyond a doubt the British detectors, both ground and air, are much farther advanced than those we are developing in the United States," he recommended not only that they be reproduced but that production cease on the American equipment.[3] Maj. Gen. George H. Brett, General Arnold's second, concluded also that despite "many wonderful pieces of equipment," the United States was behind in radio and radar. "Every effort should be made to force the Signal Corps," he said, "to a practical and logical development which will give us equipment usable under war conditions."

Aroused, the Signal Corps persuaded General Arnold to modify his criticism of the ground detectors.[4] General Mauborgne called a special meeting of the Signal Corps Technical Committee to consider "the relative merits of the British aircraft equipment (AI, IFF and ASV) and the like equipment proposed for use of the U.S. Army." In the hope of "frank discussion as to the proper course of action," he invited representatives from Chemical Warfare, Quartermaster, Engineers, Field and Coast Artillery, and the Office of the Assistant Secretary; from the Navy; from the National Defense Research Committee; and of course from the Air Corps. Brett directed the air spokesman, Lt. Col. Alfred W. Marriner, who for years had found himself assigned to spearhead the opposition to the Signal Corps, "to lay the cards on the table" at the conference. And Arnold, having directed Brett, replied that "if no action toward remedying our troubles results from that conference, I want to know about it so that I can take some other action."

Under the impression that the latest form of that dazzlingly new radar, AI, was already in production in Great Britain, and under the further impression that the Radiation Laboratory's 10-centimeter AI-10 would be available "in quantity" by the late summer or early fall, Marriner pressed the Signal Corps for equal speed. Signal Corps representatives either did not know or had no opportunity to say that the British equipment was still in its

[2] Memo, CSigO for Deputy CofS, 2 Dec 40. SigC 350.05 British Tech Mission 1 (RB-1156).

[3] Memo, Gen Arnold, Chief of AC, for Maj Gen Richard C. Moore, Deputy CofS, 28 Nov 40, sub: British detectors, with penciled note upon a copy of this memo. SigC 413.44 British Equip Gen 1 (RB-1151).

[4] Papers, *vide passim,* attached to Office Chief of AC Routing and Record Sheet Action 1, Gen Arnold to Gen Brett, 6 Feb 41, sub: Air defense com plan. AAG 676.3A Wireless Radio Systems.

early forms and that the AI-10 could not possibly be in use in six or eight months' time. In fact, one reason that it could not be was that the Air Corps was refusing the Radiation Laboratory the test airplanes and pilots.[5]

Marriner urged that the British ASV and IFF be obtained without a moment's delay: the ASV so that the Air Defense Command could begin training with it, and the IFF for the vulnerable areas of the Panama Canal and elsewhere. Maj. Gilbert Hayden of the Aircraft Radio Laboratory interposed a description of American IFF and said that General Electric and the Radio Corporation of America were at work upon it, but Marriner held the opinion that the British model could be copied and issued long before the other. As for ASV, the Signal Corps could not get it past a rigmarole of British security, did not in fact receive it for three months after this time, and could not get an airplane to test it with until another four months after that.[6] The newness of all of this equipment, the crucial life-and-death newness, imposed heavy secrecy upon it. With its component parts, it had to be handled, shipped, guarded with all of the time-consuming and frustrating precautions which a high classification imposes. And beyond all that, Great Britain was particularly concerned that no single factory see any more than a few segments of any set, so that its function would not become apparent until final assembly at a government armory or laboratory.

No one, even in Britain, knew just what equipment was best, just how to operate it most effectively, or what portions of it were being rendered obsolete by the rapid succession of late models. A case in point was the ground control of interception, the GCI, a development which had just commenced to shoot like a comet out of the panoramic oscilloscope; and the panoramic oscilloscope, or the plan position indicator, the PPI, was so new itself that it was barely understood. Actually the only radars which Great Britain had in production were the huge search sets CH and CHL, the gun director GL-1 and the IFF Mark I. The others were principally hand-built models or blueprints.

The terms in which the Air Corps spoke, however, were those of the leading generals whose responsibility for air defense of the nation led them to wish to overleap oceans and to telescope time. For his Air Defense Command Maj. Gen. James E. Chaney wanted the AI and other night interception equipment, the very high frequency control system, antijamming measures, and altitude indication on the existing U.S. ground radars; and he used phrases like "immediate action," "at the earliest possible date," "at once," "expedited by all available means," and "immediate solution."[7]

Late in December the British assembled what they could of the equipment which Edwards had ordered. They included their airborne interceptor in a Mark IV version and their command radio, the TR-1143; but they were at first unable to provide the ASV, the IFF, any of the three

[5] Msg EXP-T-252, Admin Exec Wright Field, signed [Brig Gen Oliver P.] Echols, attn: Col William F. Volandt, 27 Nov 40. AAF Proj MX-68 Installation of AI Equip in B-18A Airplane, 1940–41, USAF Mat Comd Central Files.

[6] Interoffice Memo, Col Gardner, Dir ARL, for Tech Exec Mat Div, 30 Jun 41, sub: Airplanes for test installation of British ASV equip. AAF 413.44 ASV British Radio Equip, 1941–43, USAF Mat Comd Central Files.

[7] Incl Ltr, Gen Chaney to ACofS G-2, 15 Dec 40, sub: Observations on trip to England, p. 31, with Ltr, Actg ACofS G-2 to CSigO, 12 Feb 41, sub: Final rpt of CG ADC. SigC (RD-438) ET 676.3 AWS Defense Comd Observation on Trip to England, 1941.

other detectors asked for, or the ground elements which went with the TR-1143. At that, some of the equipment was being made specially for the shipment.[8] This was a starter, though, and none of the Signal Corps and Navy equivalents was ready for production. Possibly several months could be gained. The Signal Corps followed up by putting in a supplemental estimate for $2,646,000 to procure more of the British equipment for test. In the Air Corps view, the equipment was already successful and required no tests. Brett felt that the amount ought to be used instead to begin quantity procurement. Marriner repeated the need for a much quicker system of service testing and standardizing than the Signal Corps had. He proposed that the two services emulate the British in bringing research and test close together, specifically by setting up a streamlined test unit at Patterson Field, adjacent to the development going on at Wright Field. "We can get nowhere," he reiterated, "unless . . . action is taken *now*." [9]

There was a nervous interim. The Air Corps assigned a bombardment airplane to the testing of the AI-10, which the Radiation Laboratory and a number of manufacturers were progressively assembling. Wright Field engineers put a plexiglass nose on the bomber, a B-18, in order to make it serve, although the AI-10's were of course headed for use in pursuit and attack. The first fifteen after the service-test model were to go either into A-20's or the experimental Black Widow heavy pursuit, the P-61.[10] The general tension put the AI-10's designers in Boston and the P-61's engineers in Dayton somewhat at odds, and the airmen momentarily became the minority when the Signal Corps rejected their assertion that the Radiation Laboratory's work had overborne the Air-

craft Radio Laboratory's own AI project.[11] Flight test for the AI-10 was set for February 15. It was expected also to determine much of the bombing-through-overcast equipment. No BTO contract had been let, but there were two parallel ones for ASV, producing models to be tested on March 15. This was acceptably tight scheduling.

But what could be done about the British equipment? It had been shipped, but had got only as far as Canada. The shipment now included an ASV, the Mark II IFF, the command set with pipsqueak, and "an old type airplane detector." The latter was the Mark IV AI, not old at all except for a mistaken impression that a Mark VI had replaced it. Eager to get the devices, Gardner and Hayden from the Aircraft Radio Laboratory and Lt. Col. Tom C. Rives from the Research and Development Division in the Office of the Chief Signal Officer went to Ottawa, saw them, made arrangements for their inviolate passage through the customs, and returned to Wright Field and Washington to await them again. Two things looked disturb-

[8] (1) Rpt 42067, Mil Attaché, London, to ACofS G-2, 3 Jan 41, sub: Shipment of British sig equip; (2) Memo, CSigO for MID G-2, 25 Nov 40; (3) Paraphrase of Msg 620, Mil Attaché, London [to WDGS G-2], 30 Dec 40. SigC 413.44 Purchase of British Equip (RB-2331).

[9] AAG File 676.3A Wireless Radio Systems.

[10] Office Chief of AC Routing and Record Sheet Action 1, Gen Brett to Gen Arnold, 24 Jan 41, sub: Aircraft-detector equip. AAG 413.4-B Com Equip, 1941.

[11] (1) Memo Rpt by Lt Col Franklin O. Carroll, Experimental Engr Sec, and Capt Marshall S. Roth, Aircraft Projs, 20 Jan 41, sub: Conference on present status and development of AI equip; (2) Ltr, Maj Howard Z. Bogert, Chief of Tech Staff AC Mat Div, to Tech Exec (attn: Col Marriner), 17 Jan 41, sub: Recommendation for AI Proj Officer, with 1st Memo Ind, Col Gardner to Chief of Tech Staff Mat Div Wright Field, 22 Jan 41, sub: ARL Proj 61C-4. In same file.

ingly sure as a result of the firm British insistence upon dispersed manufacture. First, there were no complete blueprints for ARL to study. Second, American reproduction of the sets would be retarded— possibly for nine months.[12] Adding the three months which had already passed since Major Edwards, in England, had first ordered the sets, this would make a year's delay which air defense plans had not counted on.

On Long Island, General Chaney, and in England, Maj. Gordon P. Saville, who had just visited the experimental GCI site at Durrington, arrived at a crystallized pattern of what the Air Defense Command wanted.[13] It took shape as a complex of the equipment they had seen demonstrated in both England and America, all of it interrelated, every item affecting the contribution of other items, and all being components in a single, regional operation: the British AI and IFF responding to the American SCR-270 or 271, the American AI-10 integrated with the British very high frequency command system, the outmoded Chain Home imported along with the barely born GCI, the Fleet Air Arm's ASV put into use as well as the U.S. Navy's altimeter. The outline of the pattern was firm. Nowhere in the top command, however, had it yet been realized that the organization of a continental fighter command system called for co-ordinated planning far beyond anything realized thus far. Brett proposed a committee to study the problem in which General Arnold, General Chaney, and Lt. Gen. Delos C. Emmons of the GHQ Air Force would overbalance General Mauborgne and an undesignated man from G-2. Not only would the concern be broader than that, but it would cut across all arms and services of the Army, across the gulf between the Army and Navy, and across the sovereignties of nations.

For the time being, General Arnold felt that air defense was getting "nowheres fast."[14] He complained that Antiaircraft rather than the Air Corps seemed to be getting the priority for all of the SCR-268's. The Signal Corps had developed them entirely for the Coast Artillery Corps and a long-range but equally mobile SCR-270 for the Air Corps; there had been no previous intimation that the air arm would want any of the 268's. But now it appeared that they could be valuable as a stopgap until the Air Corps' own model, the 270, could be equipped with what the 268 had and the 270 did not: the capacity to indicate the height of a target airplane. Arnold requested twenty sets, but General Mauborgne, doubtless having in mind that SCR-268's were still almost as rare as men who knew how to operate them, objected that the detector's short range would require too many sets to cover a given area and thus drain off too many troops. At this, "he was informed by General Brett that he was a procurement man and not a tactician and that Signal Corps should procure what the tactical people required." Sir Hugh Dowding, who was present along with Dr. Vannevar Bush, Dr. Karl Comp-

---

[12] (1) Memo, Col Rives, R&D OCSigO, for O/C (Lt Col Hugh Mitchell), 10 Feb 41, sub: Inspection of British sig equip in Ottawa. SigC 413.44 Purchase of British Equip (RB-2331). (2) Memo, Mitchell for CSigO, 18 Feb 41; (3) Ltr, Mitchell to Dir ARL, 19 Feb 41, sub: Shipment of British equip from Ottawa. SigC 413.44 British Tech Mission 2 (RB-1157).

[13] (1) Henry E. Guerlac, Hist Div OSRD, Radar, Ch. A-VI, n. 67 (in consecutively paged copy, p. 293). Photostat of 1945 MS in SigC Hist Sec File. (2) Incl 1, Memo, Maj Saville for ACofS G-4, 28 Jan 41, in Tab A to Immediate Action Sheet, TAG to Chief of AC, 3 Jun 41, sub: Air defense equip (AG 452 (5-24-41) MC). AAG 413.4-B Com Equip.

[14] Office Chief of AC Routing and Record Sheet Action 1 cited n. 4.

ton, Dr. Alfred Loomis, and the Signal Corps-Air Corps principals at the conference where this took place, agreed that the Air Defense Command needed the 268's even if they had to be taken from the antiaircraft artillery, and the twenty were assigned to Chaney.[15]

The Signal Corps Laboratories undertook to increase the range of the SCR-268[16] and to give height finding to the SCR-270 without destroying its mobility. In neither instance were they endeavoring to make the sets into GCI's. One was a searchlight director, the other an early warning set; neither was designed for ground control of interception. But the Air Corps observers had seen what they thought were comparable radars doing GCI work in Britain, and wanted GCI. The set must provide all-around coverage of the sky within a range of 70 miles, must show the position of targets continuously, and must spot them at 40 miles with an accuracy within 3 miles as to direction and within 1,000 feet as to elevation.[17] GCI had just emerged from the Chain Home Low and was still under development; only the peril to their island had required the British to put it into operation while by all normal standards it would still have been in the laboratory. Mauborgne asked for details on it at once,[18] but there was none of the equipment to spare.

For this reason the engineers at Fort Monmouth undertook the modification. They achieved a preliminary GCI span of 70 miles with the short-range SCR-268, and Mauborgne told Robert Lovett, the special assistant to the Secretary, soon to become the Assistant Secretary for Air, that he believed the 268 would most quickly provide a substitute, pending the actual GCI.[19] There was no doubt of the

need for a height finder attachment for the 270, although development had gone all the way past the specification and laboratory stages without it. Chaney had spotted its absence during a visit to Fort Monmouth with General Emmons and Maj. Gen. Frank M. Andrews. His recommendation ground through channels for months—so long that the Laboratories had only just set up the necessary project. To modify the 270 further according to what they could learn of the British GCI, the project engineers prepared to try two antennas on different frequencies and then, applying the method used on the Chain Home Low detectors, to try them at different elevations; but whatever the Laboratories did they could never make their 268 and 270 into something which was quite different.[20]

[15] Memo, Maj Kenneth N. Walker, AC Plans Div, for Brig Gen Carl Spaatz, 27 Jan 41, sub: ADC. AAG 676.9-A AWS Sites.

Present at the January 25 meeting were Arnold, Brett, Chaney, Mauberg [Mauborgne], Edwards, Meade, Smith, Marriner, Saville, Drs. Bush, Loomis, and Compton, Sir Hugh Dowdey [Dowding], and Squadron Leader Hignett.

[16] Memo, Col Mitchell for CSigO, cited n. 12(2).

[17] Ltr, TAG to CSigO, 25 Feb 41, sub: Equip for air defense. SigC (RD-428) ET 676.3 AWS Defense Comd Observation on Trip to England 1941.

[18] Memo, CSigO for ACofS G-2, 7 Feb 41. SigC 413.44 British GCI (RB-2330).

[19] Memo, CSigO for Special Asst to SW, Lovett, 14 Mar 41, sub: Special radio signaling and detector apparatus. SigC 413.44 Purchase of British Sets (RB-2331).

[20] (1) Ltr, Col Colton to CSigO, 4 May 40, sub: Determination of altitude of approaching aircraft (FM (SCL) 413.4 P. 12-i), with inds, especially No. 6, Gen Chaney, ADC, to CG First Army, 28 Jun 40, and No. 9, Gen Arnold to CSigO, 18 Jul 40. SigC 413.44 Gen Research 1 (to Apr 41) RB-1172. (2) SCL, Annual Report, 1941, Proj. 12-10, p. 23. (3) Harry M. Davis, History of the Signal Corps Development of U.S. Army Radar Equipment, Pt. III: Long Range Radar—SCR-270 and SCR-271, 1945, pp. 67–70; (4) Hist Sec E&T Divs OCSigO, History of Signal Corps Research and Development in World War II, 1945-46, Vol. IV, Pt. 3, Proj 423-B. SigC Hist Sec File.

For GCI was an innovation among innovations. The British engineers had not only replaced the several fixed antennas of the Chain Home with a single rotating antenna, used both for sending and receiving, but at the same time had hit upon a new type of oscilloscope, the PPI. This Plan Position Indicator, the very heart of GCI, was a type of cathode-ray tube whose time base, or light beam, rotated like a watch hand from the center of the round tube face in synchronization with the turning of the antenna. Echoes appeared as points or smears of light along the beam as it rotated several times a minute. The coating of the scope provided a phosphorescent afterglow, so that a target reflection remained visible until the next rotation renewed its intensity, and incidentally revealed any change in the position of the target. Thus, this PPI scope actually painted a round maplike picture of the sky around the radar. Elevation was determined by auxiliary equipment including an additional antenna and scope. Obviously, for controlling fighter planes sent aloft by day or night to intercept enemy craft, the GCI with its PPI would be far better than the very high frequency system, including the Aircraft Warning System and long-range detectors, with its cumbersome and time-consuming direction finding and plotting-board representation of aircraft, all of which occupied so many persons and so much interlinking telephone and switchboard equipment. The GCI operator would need merely to study the PPI, watch his own airplane echoes (identified by IFF) and the enemy plane echoes (not identified) in order to radiotelephone proper instructions as to the direction, height, and speed of the enemy. Night and clouds would be no hindrance. The operator could coach a

fighter equipped with AI to within a mile or two of an enemy plane, to close in for the kill, even in inky darkness.

Anticipation of GCI and PPI dazzled Air Corps observers in England at the turn of 1940–1941 hardly less than their first glimpses of CH, IFF, AI, and VHF had amazed them a few months earlier. By February Chaney was listing GCI among the priorities he wanted for his Air Defense Command. Saville, who had inspected the original, was especially insistent. And, as with other British equipment, the airmen wanted it copied by the Signal Corps "at once and as is," although the British had but a few experimental models all together—in combat, it is true, but still under development. Again, the Signal Corps would request plans and a model, and again it would be months before the British could send over an actual set.

The Air Corps had got its case on record and had stated it before the civilian and military planners immediately concerned with it. The sum of General Arnold's position was "that the Air Corps was badly in need of detector equipment for tactical use and required equipment right now for training purposes even though it was not the ultimate type which would be produced." [21] It was as blunt as that. The Signal Corps was a supplier to the Air Corps. This was what the Air Corps urgently needed. Let the Signal Corps find the means of getting it, fast. In the stale air of routine procurement, the Air Corps' glamorous folklore to the effect that the difficult could be done at once and the impossible very soon afterward was like ozone. Even those who knew it was heady breathed it eagerly. Summoning G-4 to

[21] Memo, Gen Arnold for Lovett, 25 Jun 41 (recapitulating remarks of 25 and 28 Jan 41). ASWA 413.44 Radio Equip.

set up an amenable board, General Arnold imposed a rigid schedule upon the Signal Corps. The twenty SCR-268's were first; they were to be delivered in little more than six weeks. Second came the long-range detectors, a matter to Arnold either of 270's with height finders or of copies of the CH and CHL. Third was the VHF fighter complex: the direction finder, the pipsqueak, and the ground and airborne communications equipment. Fourth was IFF. For this and the three other principal forms of airborne radar, AI, ASV, and BTO, his estimate, based upon a force of 12,000 airplanes, amounted to $137,000,-000 worth of equipment: 500 AI-10's, 501 ASV's, 1,501 BTO's, and 9,240 IFF's.[22]

Chaney, who was planning air defense maneuvers for May, listed his needs in different order—AI's first of all (and he meant the British Mark IV version, not the American 10-centimeter set which the Radiation Laboratory was readying), then the pipsqueak contactor, then IFF and ASV, and last of all the short- and long-range ground detectors. He spoke of this to General Mauborgne in Secretary Stimson's office, with Lovett present. He wanted an assortment of 100 contactors, IFF's, and ASV's, and by May; so that the net effect, regardless of priority, was the same. General Mauborgne protested that the Signal Corps had all of these developments under study, in versions which he maintained would be improvements upon the British models. He acknowledged that the pipsqueak might be easy to copy but saw no way to procure the other items in anything less than six months. Lovett therefore turned a direct plea to the British Air Commission for a 100-set assortment; Secretary Stimson verbally instructed the Chief Signal Officer to buy 5 AI-IV's, 50 ASV's, and 100 IFF's; the

Air Commission promised to cable to England to the Ministry of Aircraft Production to ask whether anything could be released; and the Navy and Air Corps informally agreed to split whatever ASV's there might be on a 40-60 basis.[23]

Out at the Aircraft Radio Laboratory, the first British samples arrived, the IFF Mark II, ASV Mark II, and AI Mark IV reaching Wright Field under guard from Ottawa on February 22. Chaney enlarged his wants beyond the May maneuvers, in order to meet his Air Defense Command's part in the 12,000-plane program, and General Mauborgne put through a request for a diversion of funds to pay the bill. It came to 240 pipsqueak contactors ($100 apiece), 100 IFF's ($2,500 each), 80 AI-IV's ($10,000 each), 51 DF's (at $3,500 a set), and 50 ASV's ($6,000 each). Chaney reiterated, "I cannot recommend too strongly the extreme urgency for the earliest possible action," and added his belief that all of the British equipment was "ready for immediate procurement."[24]

The reply from the British Ministry of Aircraft Production came in. It appeared that 5 AI-IV's could be made available, 50 ASV's and 100 IFF's. Almost simultaneously, Lovett heard that the Navy had

[22] Ibid.

[23] (1) Memo, Lovett for SW, 15 Feb 41, sub: Urgent radio items in aircraft defense program; (2) Ltr, Lovett to Sir Henry Self, Dir Gen British Air Commission, Washington, D.C., 17 Feb 41; (3) Undated Buckslip from Office Secy of Navy; (4) Ltr, Air Vice Marshal G. B. A. Baker, British Air Commission, to Lovett, 24 Feb 41. ASWA 413.44 Radio Equip.

[24] (1) Memo, CSigO for CofS, 20 Feb 41, sub: Proc of British types of equip for test and tng purposes. SigC 413.44 Purchase of British Sets 1 (RB-2331). (2) Ltr, Gen Chaney to TAG, 24 Feb 41, sub: Air defense equip, in Tab A to Immediate Action Sheet, TAG to Chief of AC, cited n. 13(2). (3) Ltr, Col Gardner to CSigO, 18 Mar 41, sub: Shipment of British com equip. SigC 413.44 Purchase of British Equip (RB-2331). (4) Ltr, TAG to CSigO, cited n. 17.

set aside 16 direction finders for the Signal Corps and the Federal Communications Commission. These two items of news were greeted with rejoicing, and with an understandable feeling of triumph on the part of Lovett, who told Chaney: "With any luck at all, and unless the westbound shipments are interrupted by sinkings, we hope to get some of these sets for you in spite of the statement which you heard that it could not be done. I am going to keep a constant follow-up on this, as I think a little competition may stimulate the Signal Corps to a more realistic approach to the Air Corps needs." [25]

Yet serious limitations existed in each category. They showed how far these items were from being ones which the American defense establishment could count on within a few weeks, and how much farther from being items which American industry could promptly begin to produce in mass. Regarding the airborne interception equipment, over and above the fact that Britain had been able to spare only 5 of the 100 asked for stood the fact that "detailed drawings are not available," and the further fact that "component manufacture is required"—that is, that unknown equipment must be broken up for manufacture, with no scheme to assemble it by afterward. The British spokesman heavily emphasized this necessity, and Sir Henry Self, the Air Commission's chief, also rehearsed patent agreements and commercial rights.[26] In the instance of the gear for identification, friend or foe, adjustments in wavelength had to be made if the sets were to work with American detectors. With the air-to-surface-vessel sets, there was the possible obstacle of having to arrange manufacture in Canada. From all of the equipment, the aerials would be missing, because of course, as was under-

stood at the Aircraft Radio Laboratory, each aerial would have to be made especially for the American airplane on which it was to be used. And finally, there had been "no mention" of spare parts. Lovett asked General Mauborgne to "make arrangements to obtain from the British a small quantity for maintenance." [27]

Thus if the haze lifted even a little, it disclosed that at least some of the obstacles the Signal Corps was talking about were real. After a month when both engineering and procurement of the items which had arrived from England had been baffled by the inflexibility of British security, Mauborgne sought General Staff aid toward a compromise. What he proposed was to disperse the manufacture within the several plants of a giant company. The Air Corps' Materiel Division itself supported him, reporting a "most discouraging" experience. The British "never give us specific authority to use their equipment and their indefinite commitments are always nullified by restrictions as to method of manufacture to insure secrecy and protect patent rights." Duplication was not to be readily accomplished under any circumstances. As is necessarily characteristic of any effective research organization, British research did not stay fixed. It developed. In some cases, the British engineers had not yet devised one of the

[25] (1) Ltr, Air Vice Marshal Baker to Lovett, 28 Feb 41, sub: Special radio signaling and detector apparatus; (2) File Memo for Lovett, 20 Feb 41; (3) Ltr, Lovett to Chaney, 5 Mar 41. ASWA 413.44 Radio Equip.

[26] (1) Ltr, Self to Gen Arnold, 15 Mar 41, sub: Special radio signaling and detector apparatus (AI Mark IV); (2) Ltr, R. H. Fowler, British Purchasing Commission, to Col Mitchell, 17 Mar 41. SigC 413.44 Purchase of British Equip (RB-2331).

[27] Memo, Lovett for CSigO, 8 Mar 41, sub: Special radio signaling and detector apparatus. AAG 413.4-B Com Equip, 1941.

components; in others, they made con-
tinual changes—in frequency ranges, for
example.

When yet another Air Corps observer
in England, this time Maj. Gen. Barton K.
Yount, recommended that "British equipment be adapted and manufactured 'as
is'" Colonel Mitchell came down hard.[28]
Strictly speaking, any exact reproduction
was impossible, he argued; the basic measuring systems of the two countries were
different, and all the dies and gauges and
components would incontrovertibly have
to be changed from one to the other. Be it
said that this was a far more literal reading of "as is" than any Air Corps officer
probably had in mind; the fact remained
that mere copy work was much more intricate than might at first be imagined.
Differences in technological and industrial measurements were going to require
extremely close co-operation during the
war; and afterward, when the United
States' alliances grew even stronger, the
standardization of measurements was to
become one of the most essential points for
agreement.

General Staff intervention won success.
The Ministry of Aircraft Production relaxed its stipulations sufficiently to grant
permission for the IFF to be adapted to
the frequency of American radars and for
the airborne interception set to be manufactured by components in the separate
factories of such a firm as Bell or Westinghouse. At the same time, the ministry released for American manufacture two of
the elements in the very high frequency
system, these being the ground direction
finder and the airborne command set, as
well as the wonderful Plan Position Indicator, the essential center of GCI. With
considerable caution, the Signal Corps
allowed itself to say that the way looked

clear now, if it could be sure of getting the
samples to alter and to copy. A detailed
letter went to G-4 and another to the Special Assistant; the net effect of so many
new, strange, and marvelous items was impressive. Having consulted Colonel Marriner first, General Arnold told Lovett,
"This looks OK to me."[29]

The dream of easy equipment had now
reached its zenith. Behind was the stage
of great expectations, unheard explanations. Here was the point of attack, and
just ahead lay fulfillment. The Air Corps
thought it understood fairly well what its
communications requirements were. The
Signal Corps was not so sure. "No determination . . . can be made until the
Signal Corps receives notification as to
quantities and types of aircraft."[30]

Air procurement began to occupy a col-

---

[28] (1) Memo, CSigO for ACofS G-2, 17 Mar 41,
sub: Proc of British type sig equip to US. SigC 413.44
Purchase of British Equip (RB-2331). (2) AC R&W
Action 4-E, Mat Div to Com Engr Div, 25 Mar 41,
sub: Standardization of radio equip between Army,
Navy, and British; (3) Memo, Col Rives, SigC, and
Lt Col Wallace G. Smith, AC, for Chm SigC Tech
Committee, 7 Apr 41, sub: Subcommittee SigC Tech
Committee (OCSigO 413.44 ADC). AAG 413.4-B
Com Equip, 1941. (4) Memo by Col Rives for File, 7
Apr 41, sub: Conference. SigC 413.44 British Equip
Gen 1 (RB-1151). (5) Memo, Brig Gen Sherman
Miles, ACofS G-2, for ACofS G-4, 27 Mar 41, sub:
Rpt of Maj Gen B. K. Yount; (6) Memo, Col Mitchell
for CSigO, 3 Apr 41. SigC 413.44 Purchase of British
Sets (RB-2331).
[29] (1) Ltr, Air Vice Marshal Baker to G-2 WDGS
(Lt Col Thomas D. Finley), 29 Mar 41, sub: Special
radio signaling and detector apparatus; (2) Ltr, Baker
to CSigO, 1 Apr 41. SigC 413.44 Purchase of British
Equip (RB-2331). (3) Memo, CSigO for ACofS G-4,
17 Mar 41, sub: Air defense equip. AAG 413.4-B
Com Equip, 1941. (4) Memo, CSigO for Special Asst
to SW, Lovett, 17 Mar 41, sub: Special radio signaling
and detector apparatus. SigC 350.05. (5) Penciled
note initialed "HHA" [Maj Gen Henry H. Arnold],
26 Mar 41, on copy of Memo, Lovett to Mauborgne,
18 Mar 41. ASWA 413.44 Radio Equip.
[30] OASW, Weekly Statistical Report Summary,
No. 41, 12 Apr 41. OASW Files.

umn of its own in the Signal Corps reports, equal in extent and detail of presentation, though still not in number of items, to the portion dealing with procurement for the ground forces. The equipment was to be brought together from three sources— Signal Corps, British, and miscellaneous— and, at this stage in between the Washington planning offices and the production assembly lines, appeared to divide itself among the Signal Corps Laboratories, the Aircraft Radio Laboratory, and the Radiation Laboratory. The Signal Corps items included all of the main communications, navigation, meteorological, and air photographic equipment, and the ground elements of radar. The British specialties were airborne radar and very high frequency radio. The remainder was made up miscellaneously, the most prominent item being the AI-10.

To demonstrate their AI-10 at the stage it had attained by mid-April, the Radiation Laboratory set up a trial run and invited the interested parties, among them the Air Corps officers Marriner, Wallace Smith, and Hobart Yeager, the Signal Corps officers Mitchell, Gardner, and Bayer, and an observer from the British Central Scientific Office. There was some difficulty in arranging for a pilot, but once that was out of the way the trial flights took place and the laboratory set worked well.[31] Well enough, in fact, for the Air Corps to schedule it for procurement forthwith. This action left the civilian scientists and the Signal Corps officers gasping. There were a dozen hurdles to leap before any procurement. Standardization, for one; before that, a service test; and, had both of those processes been accomplished, there still was the basic circumstance that airborne interception equipment was meant to serve night

fighters, and the Air Corps had no night fighters. P-61's were so far from rolling down the assembly lines that it would be 1944 before any of them saw action. The airplane which Wright Field had provided for the demonstration was a B-18, a slow bomber, not a fast fighter. The Air Corps had no existing airplane which would not have to be considerably modified if it were to use the AI-10. The answer would have to be for the Air Corps to devise one more form for its remarkable, protean A-20 light bomber, giving it enough of the necessary characteristics to serve as a night fighter.

To the Signal Corps, then, the demonstration was only preliminary to the conventional procedures which would lead, after some time, to a service test, and after more time, to standardization for manufacture. Here the Radiation Laboratory commenced an exercise in rapid fabrication which seemed to reflect upon the Signal Corps' methods. On what engineers described as a "crash" basis, the Model Shop of the laboratory began the custom building of thirty sets.[32] Only assembly-line building would serve in the long run, but for the immediate demand the Model Shop could turn out enough to go around. While the Signal Corps, following unspectacularly after the edge had been taken

[31] (1) Draft Memo, initialed "H.M." [Lt Col Hugh Mitchell], sub: Status of AI-10 development, attached to OCSigO R&D Div Buckslip, also initialed "H.M.," 16 Apr 41, bearing notes relative to SigC's policy of reducing NDRC projs to practice, after Radiation Lab had completed basic research. SigC 413.44 SCR-520 No. 1 AI-10 (RB-1378). (2) Msg E-656, Exec (EM) to Tech Exec Wright Field, 7 Apr 41. USAF Mat Comd Central Files, Proj MX-68. (3) Ltr. R. O. Jones, British Air Commission, to CSigO, 7 Jul 41, sub: Provisions for secrecy of British equip reproduced in US. SigC 413.44 Purchase of British Sets (RB-2331).
[32] Memo, Col Rives for Col David M. Crawford, 18 Jun 41. SigC 413.44 SCR-520 No. 1 AI-10 (RB-1378).

off, was placing a $1,016,700 contract with Western Electric to build thirty models for service test, Wright Field took the laboratory demonstration model and tested it in a B-18. Although testing laboratory sets was an admired British practice, both the Radiation Laboratory and the Aircraft Radio Laboratory objected vehemently. Dr. Karl Compton declared that the Air Corps test board's report revealed "a pretty complete lack of understanding." Mitchell expressed surprise "that the Air Corps intended to *service test* this particular equipment as it was obvious that [it] would not pass. . . ." Regarding the test board's criticism that only a highly skilled man could work the set, he remarked that "the user better get busy now and do some training." [33]

The situation was embarrassing, because the Air Corps had overpowered the Signal Corps order for 30 sets by an order for 500, made out in advance of the hasty test and under the assumption that its success was a foregone conclusion. In Loomis, Compton, and other members of the National Defense Research Committee the Air Corps momentarily found doughtier, and more tellingly placed, adversaries than the Signal Corps, with the result that the test board was effectually overruled. A compromise disavowed the board by approving the AI-10 and supported it by reducing the order to 165—"for installation in 165 P-61 planes." [34] But this was not enough of a concession to NDRC, and the order for 500 was continued in addition to the order for 165.

Further to complicate the matter, the Signal Corps had also contracted, upon General Chaney's order, for the manufacture of 80 of the British airborne interception sets, the AI-IV, and then, before these went into production at Western Electric,

for 500 more, at a further request from the Air Corps. The sets, designated SCR-540, proved inferior to the British prototype and, when the Air Corps accepted them only with reservations, no more were made. The AI-10, standardized after considerable conversion as the SCR-520, replaced them. In expectation of the wide use of this 10-centimeter equipment, both Americans and British suspended further work upon long-wave airborne radar; and the SCR-540, the only long-wave airborne interceptor to be produced in any quantity, was relegated principally to training planes. [35]

The course of the AI-10 in manufacture effectively demonstrated that quantity production of such a mechanism can be as complicated and prolonged as the labora-

---

[33] (1) Service Test Report of Board of Officers Appointed Per Paragraph 9 Personnel Orders No. 152 WD Office Chief of AC, 2 Jul 41, signed by Lt Col Reuben C. Moffatt and Majs Hobart R. Yeager, William L. Bayer, and Gordon P. Saville. AAG 413.4-C Com Equip. (2) Memo, Col Mitchell for H. H. Bundy, Special Asst to SW, 23 Jun 41, sub: Radio set SCR-520-AI-10; (3) Ltr, Col Gardner to CSigO, 25 Jun 41, sub: Sv test of AI-10 equip. SigC 413.44 SCR-520 No. 1 AI-10 (RB-1378).

[34] (1) Memo, Chief of AC for Chief of AAF, 9 Jul 41, sub: Sv test of AI-10; (2) Incl Memo, Bundy for SW, 11 Jul 41, with Office Chief of AC Routing and Record Action 1, Chief of AC to Chief of Mat Div, 25 Jul 41, sub: In re AI-10—airborne detector; (3) Memo, Bundy to Lovett, 21 Jul 41, with attached correspondence; (4) E. M. McMillan, B-18-A Report—February 13 to July 22, 1941, 5 Aug 41. AAG 413.4-C Com Equip. (5) Memo, Col Rives for Chief of Mat Br AC, Wright Field, 24 Nov 41, sub: Differences between NDRC AI-10 and radio set SCR-520. SigC 413.44 SCR-520 No. 1 AI-10 (RB-1378).

[35] R&D hist cited n. 20(4), Vol. II, Pt. 3, Proj (205), 71-1.
"Long" radar waves are not to be confused with long radio waves. The latter are several thousand meters long, whereas radar waves begin at about 10 meters (a point at which radio waves are very short) and become progressively shorter until they are at the border of heat. The right-hand margin of the radiation spectrum indicates the difference.

tory research upon it. The British establishment, which had been making progress with a microwave AI set of its own, ordered the American version instead, to mount in its Beaufighters, whereupon its engineers ran into the familiar difficulties of adapting foreign equipment. The Radiation Laboratory undertook to alter a few sets especially for British use, because some time would intervene before Western Electric could finish the American order and start the British order. The two nations had agreed from the beginning of the Tizard Mission that British calls upon American production would yield priority to American needs.[36]

The Radiation Laboratory also turned to adapting the AI-10 to ASV uses: that is, to make the night airborne interception equipment into equipment for air search of the sea. This work, especially supported by the Navy, succeeded so well that the Air Corps pressed for copies of it and the Signal Corps responsively standardized and ordered it as another in the immediate series, the SCR-517. Subsequently this air-to-surface-vessel radar led to bombing-through-overcast radar, in just the progression the Signal Corps experts had hoped might result.

Quite distinct from the long-wave ASV and BTO efforts at the Aircraft Radio Laboratory, the SCR-517 was of course microwave equipment adapted from a 10-centimeter set. Almost all of the microwave development fell to the Radiation Laboratory according to the understanding reached at the time of Tizard's visit and of NDRC's formation of the Microwave Committee. At the same time, the Aircraft Radio Laboratory was converting the British ASV-II, a long-wave set, to an American version, SCR-521. When the set was tested in B-17's and B-25's without any great success, it was obvious that here again was an instance of the vicissitudes of attempting to apply equipment to circumstances for which it was not designed.

Colonel Gardner, the director of the Aircraft Radio Laboratory, forecast that the microwave SCR-517 might come off production lines about as quickly as the SCR-521, and urged everyone to consider carefully whether it would be worth while to go ahead with the adaptation of the British set. The antenna layout, the disposition of components, the circuit wiring, the power supply all had to be modified for American use, and the switches, plugs, sockets, tubes, and other parts peculiar to British manufacture would be almost certain to cause production bottlenecks. Although these were characteristic Signal Corps objections, any careful research and supply agency would have been remiss not to make them. On the other hand, the Air Corps, charged with the almost impossible task of becoming a major striking force in no time at all, could not risk being left without an essential tool. Accordingly, the Air Corps backed both ASV sets, and the SCR-521 was manufactured along with the SCR-517. By the end of the year, the Signal Corps had placed orders for thousands of the SCR-521's, with Philco and the Canadian facility, War Supplies, Limited. They came into considerable use in the antisubmarine warfare of 1942, and

---

[36] (1) Ltr, Col Hugh Mitchell to Dr. Alfred Loomis, Radiation Lab, 18 Aug 41; (2) Ltr, Air Marshal Roderic M. Hill, British Air Commission, to Dr. Carroll Wilson, Liaison Officer NDRC, 3 Sep 41; (3) Extract from Maj Bayer's Rpt, 11 Sep 41; (4) Ltr, Air Marshal Hill to OCSigO, 13 Dec 41, sub: AI in British Beaufighter aircraft; (5) Memo, Col Rives for Chief of Mat Br AC, Wright Field, 14 Dec 41, sub: Expediting critical contracts. SigC 413.44 SCR-520 No. 1 AI-10 (RB-1378).

some of the American aircraft in the Southwest Pacific theater had them as late as 1944.[37]

Identification, friend or foe—IFF—raised a new kind of controversy. After choosing the Navy-General Electric form of radio recognition in preference to its own, the Aircraft Radio Laboratory had turned it into three more units in the "500" series of radars. The SCR-515 was to be the airborne component, and the SCR-532 and 533, respectively, for short and long ranges, were to be the ground elements. This IFF gear was not, like that of the British, dependent upon certain radars, but could be used by itself as a sort of beacon system in any situation: between ships, between ships and aircraft, between ships and the shore, between ground and aircraft, and between aircraft themselves. The circuit was all but instantaneous, so that the question "Who are you?" was asked and answered with the speed of light and, visibly on the ground oscilloscope, with the form of light. The Aircraft Radio Laboratory tried out service-test models of the 515 (two thousand dollars), the 532 (twenty thousand dollars), and the 533 (fifty thousand dollars) and found them satisfactory enough to contract for 150 of the first, 10 of the second, and 11 of the third. If the equipment were good at all, these amounts were wholly inadequate, and in two months' time they had indeed risen: respectively, to a hundred times as many of the first and third and to two hundred and fifty times as many of the second.

Meanwhile, the Signal Corps' laboratory engineers modified the British IFF for use specifically with the SCR-268 and 270, as in Britain it was used specifically with the CH, CHL, or GL radars. It was the Mark II version, an airborne trans-

pondor only. In its American form, it received the designation of SCR-535. Because of the fact that it had to take the time to sweep a range of frequencies instead of having a precise allocation all to itself, it was not instantaneous. Nor, in either version, could it be used apart from the detectors to which it was attuned. Thus the American IFF, which came to be known as Mark IV, had the double advantage of independence and instant response. It was also probably superior to the succeeding British model, Mark III, which improved upon and supplanted Mark II.[38]

Nevertheless, the Mark IV sat the war out. When the likelihood began to appear in 1941 that American airplanes might soon enter battle areas, the British wanted them to carry Mark III, which they intended to introduce when it was ready. A struggle thereupon developed between the two allies, opening with a conference in the British Central Scientific Office in Washington on July 1. The British representatives pointed out the possibility of disastrous confusion in the event of combined allied campaigns by sea or air. Even though they recognized the advantages of

---

[37] (1) Interv, SigC Hist Sec with Col G. E. Metcalf, ARL, Wright Field, Ohio, 2 Oct 44. (2) R&D hist cited n. 20(4), Vol. II, Pt. 3, Proj 205-B, pp. 5–6, and Vol. II, Pt. 5, Proj 209-B, pp. 13, 16–17. (3) ARL, Annual Report, 1941, Proj 61C-1.4, p. 5. (4) Ltr, Col Gardner to CSigO, 25 Jul 41, sub: SCR-517 and SCR-521; (5) Memo, Col Rives for Chief of Mat Br AC, Wright Field, 13 Dec 41, sub: Expediting critical contracts. SigC 413.44 SCR-521 No. 1 (RB-1379).

[38] (1) R&D hist cited n. 20(4), Vol. II, Pt. 2, Projs 203-A and 203-C, Vol. IV, Pt. 5, Proj 462-A. (2) C&E Case No. 4, Identification and Recognition Equipment. (3) ARL, Annual Report, 1941, Proj 63C, Airplane Identification, pp. 7–8. (4) Memo, Col Mitchell for CSigO, 21 Aug 41, sub: Development and proc of radio recognition equip (Navy type ABA equip). SigC 413.44 Identification 2, Jun 41–Jun 42 (RB-1165).

CAMOUFLAGED IFF EQUIPMENT *of an American antiaircraft artillery group installed near Folkestone, England.*

the American system in principle, the British spokesmen felt it had not yet been proved in combat. The American point of view was that the equipment the British were speaking of had not been, either. Mark II had been in combat, but not Mark III. So long as the British had not yet made the change-over, why not skip Mark III and settle upon Mark IV if it were a better set? The thousands of Mark IV's on order represented an investment of millions of dollars.[39] Favoring their Mark III, which they said they could supply to America almost immediately, the British amassed technical arguments to which the name of Watson-Watt lent

weight.[40] On the American side, a Joint Radio Committee studied the problem, the Navy at first stating "quite positively . . . that the British system was objectionable," then relaxing its stand. The Army

[39] Incl, Notes on Conference on Coordination of American and British I.F.F. Held at B.C.S.O., July 1, 1941, at 4 p.m., with Ltr, C. G. Darwin, Dir British Central Scientific Office, to CSigO, 3 Jul 41. SigC 413.44 SCR-515 No. 1 (RB-1374).

[40] (1) Robert Watson-Watt, Scientific Adviser on Telecommunications British Air Ministry, Memo, Identification and Recognition in RDF, 9 Sep 41, with Ministry of Aircraft Production Buckslip, I. Horsfold to Maj Hayden, 24 Sep 41; (2) Unsigned Memo on American IFF Proposal, 19 Aug 41, with same Buckslip. SigC 413.44 Identification 2, Jun 41-Jun 42 (RB-1165).

followed the Navy's lead at both stages, since the Navy's stake in the outcome was greater.[41]

The argument was drawing to an unsatisfactory compromise on the very eve of Pearl Harbor. It appeared that in the Atlantic American ships and airplanes alike would have to carry both the Mark III and the Mark IV, an unwieldy arrangement at best and impossible for pursuit planes. In the Pacific, the Navy was planning to use only the Mark IV, on the assumption that tests to begin aboard the *Hornet* on December 8 would prove successful.[42] The compromise went into the ash can on December 7. The Pearl Harbor disaster found the United States virtually without IFF. If American airplanes and American search radars had been provided with it, the two Signal Corpsmen at the Opana SCR-270 would have been able to alert the Oahu garrisons. As it turned out, Col. Hugh Mitchell, in the Research and Development Division of the Office of the Chief Signal Officer, noted frantically that no IFF's—even the SCR-515, which by the time of Pearl Harbor had been on order for half the year— would be available for months. The Signal Corps quickly modified the Mark II's which were on hand and rushed them to the Philco Corporation, where a select group of the company's engineers and production men, working in a locked garage under guard, hand-built twenty-six sets in three weeks. In fact, Mark II and its American counterpart became the universal Allied IFF until Mark III replaced it in 1943. Mark IV was held in reserve in case Mark III should be compromised. That occasion never came, and the American sets were never used.[43]

War engulfed this multimillion-dollar waste. There were other losses, still in the emergency period well before the war. The Air Corps canceled an aircraft liaison radio, the SCR-259, after the Signal Corps had already begun to procure it. In that instance, the loss was a modest $4,000,000 or less. General Electric was again the company concerned, as with the IFF. The Air Corps, which was spared the rebuke that had been prepared for it, had sought the cancellation on the ground that the radio was not a part of the intercommunications complex which the Air Corps desired to make common with the British.[44] The VHF complex, on the other hand, went through the conventional process, even to a separation and assignment of the components according to the established division of Signal Corps laboratories. The air parts remained at ARL, the ground went to the Monmouth laboratories. Fortunately, they proved relatively easy to convert to American use. The airborne component, the TR-1143, became the SCR-522; the ground components, including the transmitters, re-

[41] Unsigned Document, C&E Div OCSigO, 21 Nov 41, sub: Proc of identification and recognition equip SCR-515, 532, and 533. SigC C&E Case 4 Proc of Identification and Recognition Equip SCR-515, 532, and 533.

[42] Memo Rpt of Radar Subcommittee of the Inter-Service Coms Bd, 6 Dec 41. In same file. See also documents in SigC RB-20, 106 IFF Equip.

[43] Memo, Mitchell for CSigO, 10 Dec 41. SigC C&E Case 19 Emergency Interceptor Equip for AC. (2) "Radar: The Industry," *Fortune*, XXXII, No. 4 (October 1945), 146. See also Baxter, *Scientists Against Time*, p. 150. (3) R&D hist cited n. 20(4), Vol. II, Pt. 2, Proj 203-A, pp. 11 ff. The United States Navy further insisted upon the production of Mark IV because it would become indispensable in case the enemy overwhelmed the British Navy. MS Comment by Gen Colton, 14 Sep 53. SigC Hist Sec File.

[44] (1) ARL, Annual Report, 1941, Proj 49, p. 16. (2) AAG File 413.4-C Coms Equip, *passim*. (3) Memo, Brig Gen Eugene Reybold, Actg ACofS G-4, for CofS, 19 Jul 41, sub: Standardization of aircraft radio equip. G-4 No. 27963-184.

ceivers, and direction finders, became part of the Air Defense Command's sector control system: the SCS-2 or 3 being an assemblage of the direction finders and the information centers associated with them, on the one part, and of the transmitters and receivers and the communications centrals they served, on the other part. The SCS-2 was semifixed, the SCS-3 entirely mobile.[45]

Long before this, everyone who had anything at all to do with airborne radar equipment must have made up his mind that it was an intricate business which became more intricate with every month. And yet each new model was but an extension of the original strikingly simple conception. All of these items had their beginning and their continuation in the basic ground detectors. It was for this reason that General Arnold had put the ground detectors at the top of his list of urgent electronics requirements. This meant the American mobile short-range SCR-268, the mobile long-range SCR-270, and the fixed long-range SCR-271; or it meant the British fixed long-range system, Chain Home, the fixed short-range system, Chain Home Low, and their most recent descendants, ground-controlled interception and gun-laying sets.

In pursuit of its policy of distributing its eggs in order to be sure that at least one basket got to market, the Air Corps was asking for all of these. One of the moves the Chief Signal Officer made was to seek out a Canadian detector called the Night Watchman. Apparently interpreting his inquiry as a letter of intent, Canadian production started upon the order, whereupon the Signal Corps confirmed it with a formal contract. A Canadian combination of the British CHL and GCI also entered the Signal Corps radar lists as the SCR-

588.[46] These were side excursions. With much more direct aim, the Signal Corps still hoped also to get the GCI itself—the Air Corps had put in an order for 210 of them—and if possible the even less known and certainly less satisfactory GL. The foremost effort of all centered upon the attempts to convert the SCR-268 into an Air Corps set and to provide the SCR-270, which was already an Air Corps set, with height finding.

The conversion of the SCR-268 led to the SCR-516. The work took place in the Fort Monmouth-Fort Hancock area rather than at Wright Field, for this equipment was of course born and bred at the Signal Corps Laboratories. First the engineers lowered the pulse rate and increased the power, with the result that they attained the desired seventy-mile range. Then, to improve the set's ability to measure altitude as low as to within five degrees of the horizon, they mounted longer antennas upon a low wooden tower. They were pleased with the results, and felt sufficiently confident of the merits of the equipment so that an ambiguous performance at the Carolina maneuvers did not shake their view. Much later, they were able to add a plan position indicator also

---

[45] (1) Memo, Col Rives and Lt Col W. G. Smith, AC, for Chm SigC Tech Committee, 7 Apr 41, sub: Subcommittee SigC Tech Committee. SigC 413.44 ADC. (2) Ltr, OCSigO to Dir ARL, 29 May 41, sub: Air defense equip. SigC 413.44 British Equip Gen 1 (RB-1151).

[46] (1) Ltr, CSigO to Dir Gen British Air Commission, Washington, D.C., 5 May 41, sub: Purchase or loan of British secret equip. SigC 413.44 British GCI (RB-2330). (2) Ltr, Col Clyde L. Eastman, Actg CSigO, to Canadian National Research Council, 15 May 41, sub: Purchase of RDF equip from Canadian Government. SigC 413.44 British Equip Gen 1 (RB-1151). (3) SCL Files 12-11, Intermediate Range Low-Angle Detector (British Type GCI), 12-11.1, American Equivalent of GCI Equip SCR-527-T1, 1941–42, and S-32.3, Proc of Radio Set SCR 527-A, 1941–42.

and thus bring the SCR-268 as close as it ever got to being a GCI.[47]

Pending the arrival of a bona fide British GCI, specifications were prepared as well as could be done in the absence of drawings, and General Electric started in upon them. The company had completed a test model when definite word came through that the British equipment was on its way. A conference agreed that it must be adopted and produced at once, deviating "only to the extent necessary to utilize American materials to expedite production" and to be accommodated to American power sources. Otherwise, it was to be an exact copy. Notwithstanding, Signal Corps officers preferred the SCR-268 or its stepchild, the SCR-516. Inspecting the GCI in England, Major Hayden acknowledged its "convenient and usable" way of supplying target data, but declared that the SCR-268 was more accurate. Tests at Lakehurst and Sandy Hook bore him out in his opinion, Colton and Lt. Col. Frank C. Meade, who were there, recommending against the GCI. Brig. Gen. Clinton W. Russell, chief of staff of the Air Force Combat Command, who warned against indiscriminate adoption of British equipment, and officers of the Air Defense Section, GHQ Air Force, concurred in the recommendation. A ponderable body of opposing opinion prevailed, however, and asked the Signal Corps to procure it at once without any further loss of time in service testing. Thus an SCR-527 was launched, the American copy of the GCI, and ultimately 200 were produced.[48]

SCR listings were becoming astronomically hard to keep up with. The array was becoming a constellation and the constellation a galaxy. At the center, though, at least for the Signal Corps, were still the

SCR-268 and the SCR-270/271. The Air Corps' strong doubts of them got forcible utterance at the Louisiana maneuvers in the person of Lovett. The Assistant Secretary for Air turned in an adverse report of the SCR-270 because none of the four sets he inspected could detect airplanes approaching at levels below 3,000 feet. Colton and Maj. Rex V. D. Corput, Jr., were given an opportunity to defend the radar they had shepherded almost from infancy. They maintained that the sets instead had shown good normal performance, detect-

[47] (1) Davis hist cited n. 20(3), Pt. II, pp. 106–09. (2) SCL, Annual Report, 1941, Proj 12-10, p. 23. (3) R&D hist cited n. 20(4), Vol. IV, Pt. 3, Projs (424) 12-10.1 and 12-10.2. (4) SigC File RB-24, SCR-516. (5) Personal Papers of John J. Slattery, SCL. Evans Sig Lab File.
[48] (1) Ltr, Col Colton to CSigO, 19 May 41, sub: Proc of special radio set SCR-527-( ); (2) Ltr, Air Marshal Hill, British Air Commission, to Col Mitchell, 8 Sep 41, sub: GCI equip; (3) Maj P. E. Watson, O/C Field Lab 3, Record of Demonstration and Minutes of Meeting—British GCI Equipment, 12 Nov 41; (4) Ltr, Maj Joseph A. Bulger, Actg Exec 1st Interceptor Comd, to CG AFCC, 28 Nov 41, sub: Rpt on comparison of British GCI and SCR-516-A, with 1st Ind, Gen Russell to CSigO, 13 Dec 41; (5) Rpt of Meeting with GE Representatives at SCL in Connection with GCI Equipment, signed by 1st Lt Earl J. Atkinson. SigC 413.44 SCR-527-627-12K (RB-1381) No. 1. (6) Memo, Col Colton for CSigO, 12 Aug 41, sub: Conferences on urgent program (OCSigO 400.-112). SigC (ET) 676.3 AWS, 1942. (7) Memo for File, signed by Cols Crawford, Mitchell, and Rives, and Maj Corput, SigC, and by Lt Col W. G. Smith and Maj Saville, AC, 14 Aug 41, sub: Rpt of Conference—GCI equip. SigC 413.44 British GCI (RB-2330). The Signal Corps Technical Committee approved the military characteristics on 15 August, Meeting No. 198-A. (8) Ltr, Maj Hayden to OCSigO, 13 Sep 41, sub: Summary of equip and equip plans. SigC 413.44 Gen Memo—London—Maj G. Hayden (RB-2164). (9) Col Meade, Memo for Record, 18 Nov 41, sub: Result of visit to Ft. Monmouth and Lakehurst 13–15 Nov. SigC RB-19 (105) GCI Equip. (10) OCSigO R&W Action 1, Air Coms Div to Opns Br and Mat Br C&E Div, 1 Dec 41, sub: Proc of SCR-527 or similar set, and (11) Action 4, R&D to Opns Br through Mat Br, 13 Dec 41. SigC RB-23 (110) Radio Set SCR-527. (12) R&D hist cited n. 20(4), Vol. IV, Pt. 3, Proj (424) 12-11.

ing airplanes at distances up to 100 miles. Actually, such a record surpassed the performance of the British detectors and did so without having to be immobilized atop huge towers.[49]

These words fell upon deaf ears. General Arnold learned from Air Marshal Sir Arthur T. Harris that a model of the Chain Home radar could be spared for the United States to copy, and made haste to accept. As Chief of the new Army Air Forces, created in June 1941, and as a Deputy Chief of Staff as well, he was now established so far above the Chief Signal Officer that he moved directly to get the set without waiting for the Signal Corps. The British Air Commission did wait, however, and then after a month of delay said what the Chief Signal Officer doubtless would have liked to say: Chain Home was so enormous and bulky that it would take months just to erect the antenna towers. The Air Commission members suggested that since a mobile model was being installed on the eastern coast of Canada the Signal Corps might better make comparative tests with it. Thus brought together under equal conditions, the British and American sets proved wholly comparable. The Chief of the Army Air Forces therefore concluded that "the installation of the CH equipment is extremely complicated and does not appear necessary due to the information now available." But this was a curbstone opinion. It was not intended to be final. The interceptor commands into which the Air Defense Command had been transformed continued to ask that the SCR-270 be replaced.[50]

The Signal Corps, at the very vortex of all the criticisms and demands pertaining to Army electronics, felt none too sure sometimes of its own basic sets, but did not

lose at all its conviction that there were objections to some of the proposals which the Air Corps advanced. It was the Signal Corps' business to know technical matters, to make technical recommendations, and to seek technical improvements; and to this extent there was nothing surprising in the objections. Yet the Air Corps, at a vortex of its own, had reason to insist upon some sort of equipment, however technically defective, rather than none at all. The struggle between the two services really came down to this one question, therefore: was it possible to get equipment faster than the Signal Corps was getting it? The record of delay, misapplication, and duplication as the huge Air Corps program got under way between January and June suggested that it would have been better to confine all efforts to speeding up the routine of development, service testing, and procurement which the Signal Corps followed, rather than to interrupt, divert, and attempt to remake it. In the roar and din of war preparations this opinion could not be heard, especially when the Signal Corps' voice became weaker with every access of power to the Air Corps, and hoarser with every suggestion that its opinion was scarcely a disinterested one.

Late in June, with the fiscal year ending, Assistant Secretary Lovett made himself the vessel of a concentrate of Air Corps exasperation and called attention to the

---

[49] (1) Memo, Lt Col Eugene V. Elder for Col Colton (containing Maj Corput's remarks), 19 Sep 41; (2) Memo, Colton for Gen Olmstead, 19 Sep 41. SigC SPSTP 10 CSigO.

[50] (1) Memo, Chief of AAF for TAG, 25 Sep 41, sub: Proc of British CH unit. OCS 20648-35. (2) Ltr, TAG to CSigO, 29 Sep 41, same sub. AG 413.68 (9-25-41) NC-G. (3) Ltr, Air Marshal Hill to ACofS G-2, 11 Nov 41, with 4th Ind, Chief of AAF to TAG [22 Dec 21]. SigC 413.44 British Equip Gen 1 (RB-1151).

fact that the Air Corps' February training requirements for British equipment had not been met. The British had had them "in current production" and had agreed to supply them. As the law and Army regulations necessitated, their procurement had been "turned over to the Signal Corps." Yet "to date these items have not been received." There the indictment paused. The Air Corps spokesmen either did not know or did not believe that there were many more reasons why the items had not been received than intolerable procrastination on the part of the Signal Corps. It was an error to have thought that the items were "in current production in England"; some were not in production at all, others were being crash-built, none were to be had just by feeding an extra order to the assembly line. It was an error to suppose that, in the absence of samples and drawings and without technical conversion and adjustment, the items could be immediately applied to American use, especially since many of the airplanes to employ them were still on paper. The February requirements, here left unspecified, had included 50 ASV's, 80 AI-IV's, 100 IFF's, and 240 contactors. The "rough estimates" which the Assistant Secretary of War for Air passed on listed 400 ASV's, 500 AI-IV's, 500 IFF's, and 2,000 contactors. Lovett strengthened his remarks with the implication that the matter must be taken out of Signal Corps hands.[51]

Secretary Stimson's special assistant, Harvey H. Bundy, queried the Signal Corps, asking for a résumé of all the air and ground radar which the Signal Corps was either developing or procuring. Colonel Mitchell replied with no waste of time, capsuling the work on the SCR-268, the SCR-270 and 271, the SCR-516, the AI-10, and BTO, and enumerating the orders for GCI, GL, AI-IV, and ASV. The unintended gist of his report was just what the Air Corps protested: that everything was on order and nothing on hand. Yet the Air Corps asked for its communications and detection equipment for "all airplanes on hand or on order." [52]

This was impracticable from a Signal Corps point of view. The Signal Corps could not contract for sets until it knew what commitments had been made for the airplanes in which the sets were to be installed or for which they were to be used on the ground. General Mauborgne agreed with his critics regarding the need for efficiency in the radar program, and broadened his own remarks—nearly his final official ones in the dispute—by calling attention to the mutual interest of Army air, Navy air, and the Royal Air Force. "Many of the airborne equipments will be standard for all three services," he pointed out, and urged "adequate administration and coordination of this whole series of projects." The time had passed for this sort of co-ordination. (Historically, it had not arrived.) General Mauborgne felt sure of his ground, because Under Secretary Patterson had just congratulated him on his "success . . . in effecting the placement under contract with industry of the largest peace-time program of National Defense procurement in the history of this country." [53]

---

[51] Memo, "R.A.L." [Robert A. Lovett] for Harvey H. Bundy, Special Asst to SW, 24 Jun 41, sub: Special microwave devices. ASWA 413.44 Radio Equip.

[52] (1) Memo, Col Mitchell for Bundy, 26 Jun 41. SigC 413.44 British Equip Gen 2, Jun–Jul 41 (RB-1152). (2) Ltr, Chief of AC to CSigO, 26 Jun 41, sub: Proc of detector and air defense equip. SigC RP-400.12 Proc Program Gen.

[53] (1) Ltr, Gen Mauborgne to Bundy, 10 Jul 41, sub: Needs for expediting proc of special detection equip. SigC 676.3 AWS ET 1, 1942. (2) Ltr, Patterson to Mauborgne, 2 Jul 41. SigC Hist Sec File.

But the Air Corps, despairing of Signal Corps capabilities, was turning more and more toward finding its own solution. Things came to an outburst in August, erupted, and left wreckage all about. With the concurrence of Brig. Gen. George C. Kenney, assistant chief of the Air Corps Materiel Division, and of Brig. Gen. Henry J. F. Miller, chief of the Maintenance Command, and with the explanation that it was "in line with the directive from . . . General [Oliver P.] Echols," chief of the Materiel Division, Colonel Marriner prepared an arraignment for General Brett.

He began by striking out at the "lost motion," the "red tape," the "rigmarole" of the "whole development program" carried on by the Signal Corps for the Air Corps. Citing in particular the SCR-268 and SCR-270, he charged that the Signal Corps had given "comparatively little thought" to the Air Corps' use of them, leaving the former with a short range and the latter without any means for indicating elevation "even though we asked for this indication . . . early in 1937." (The SCR-268 was not an Air Corps radar; its short range was intentional, to give it the accuracy required of a searchlight director or gun layer. The SCR-270 specifications had omitted height finding until 1940, when Chaney alerted a request for it.)

Colonel Marriner came directly to grips by reviving the old quarrel over the control of air navigational equipment, repeating the contention that because it was equipment developed just for the Air Corps, the Air Corps should develop it. On Signal Corps supply, his comments were very severe: "It is antiquated, slow and cumbersome, extremely inefficient and entirely inadequate for these times of speed." He described the slow crawl of a requisition for standard command and liaison radio, a description which could have been illustrated as pertinently by what was happening just then to a number of Navy scout bombers, which the Air Corps was taking into its own list as A-24's. Intended for the Philippines, they were delayed so long for installation of radio that they never got there.[54]

"For some years we have endeavored to correct . . . deficiencies" in signal supply, Marriner went on, always being frustrated by arguments of the Chief Signal Officer which "we never could understand. . . . After considerable long discussion, General Brett finally succeeded in getting a Signal Corps liaison officer [assigned to Wright Field] on supply distribution, but the Chief Signal Officer never gave him enough authority to act in any way which might be of assistance to us. . . . The main point . . . is that in no case have they taken the initiative. In all our joint discussions we seem to get the Signal Corps out of their lethargy, but just when we think something will be done they go back to sleep." From development and supply he went on to procurement, and found the same "lethargy" and "lack of boldness and imagination" there. "Something must be done *now*" to bring order to this "most chaotic mess of all the messes. . . ." The solution he had in mind was to give the Air Corps responsibility for every aspect of Air Corps communications: its development, standardization, procurement, inspection, storage, issue, operation, maintenance, repair and replacement; for communication, meteorology, navigation, photography, detect-

---

[54] AAF ATSC Hist Office, Radio and Radar Supply, Maintenance and Training by the Air Service Command (Dayton, 1944), pp. 8–12. USAF Archives 201-41 (2802-3A).

MAJ. GEN. JOSEPH O. MAU-
BORGNE. *(Photograph taken in 1937.)*

ing, bombing, search, identification, and
instrument landing; for radio, radar, and
wire; for ground and air.[55]

The heat grew intense. Speculation and
rumor flew about. General Mauborgne
was due to retire at the end of September
after four years as Chief Signal Officer.
Suddenly the Deputy Chief of Staff, Maj.
Gen. Richard C. Moore, got in touch with
General Olmstead at Fort Monmouth.
Olmstead came to Washington, General
Marshall examined him searchingly, and
General Mauborgne was relieved of his
statutory responsibility six weeks early.[56]
He was directed to spend his remaining
time as Chief Signal Officer making visits
to Signal Corps activities throughout the
United States, and left Washington almost
immediately. General Olmstead took up
his duties as Acting Chief Signal Officer.
He immediately initiated extraordinary

efforts to satisfy the demands of Secretary
Stimson, Assistant Secretary Lovett, General Marshall, and General Arnold. On 15
August, only a week after the Air Corps
had presented its bill of particulars, a
single meeting of the Signal Corps Technical Committee standardized fifteen of
the new radio and radar devices.[57] The
sweeping action confirmed the British air-
to-surface-vessel, airborne interception,
ground-controlled interception, identification—friend or foe, and very high frequency command equipment. It also approved the American airborne interception, identification—friend or foe, and
ultrahigh-frequency command equipment. There were three more for the Coast
Artillery, but all of these others—twelve
sets out of the fifteen—were for the Air
Corps.

Having the advantage, the Air Corps

---

[55] Memo, Asst Tech Exec AAF Mat Div for Tech
Exec, 6 Aug 41, sub: SigC deficiencies. AAG 322.081
SigC Activities 1932–45, USAF Mat Comd Central
Files.

[56] Four years later, General Marshall had forgotten
any pressing reason for the action. In the hearings
before the Joint Congressional Committee investigating the Pearl Harbor attack, Senator Ferguson of
Michigan, questioning him on a meeting of the "little
war cabinet" held with the President on November
24, 1941, asked whether the appointment of General
Olmstead had any particular significance. Quoting
from Secretary of War Stimson's diary, Senator
Ferguson read: "On November 24, 1941 I had a talk
with General Olmstead, whom I recently promoted
to be chief signal officer." Said Ferguson, "Were you
having trouble with the signal officer that you were
going to get a new one?" General Marshall replied
that he did not think the appointment of a new Chief
Signal Officer had anything to do with the White
House meeting. General Mauborgne's term was
about to expire—"I think it expired, and we were
bringing in General Olmstead as his successor." *Pearl
Harbor Attack: Hearings Before the Joint Committee on
the Investigation of the Pearl Harbor Attack*, Pt. 3, p.
1279.

[57] SigC Tech Committee Meeting No. 198-A. SigC
Hist Sec File, A46-160.

did not pursue it unfairly. Many Air Corps officers recognized Signal Corps difficulties. The more perceptive of them thoroughly understood that radio fabrication was as lengthy a process, demanding as much forenotice, as airplane fabrication.[58] They were also aware that the Signal Corps had cause to object when, without notification to it, Wright Field bought communications equipment outright from the Bendix Corporation for some Hudson bombers, thus directly cutting in upon one of the major facilities for supply. "Now the Signal Corps officer is all mad about it," Wright Field reported. "Yes," responded the executive in the office of the Chief of the Air Corps, "but I agree with Wally Smith that in the future he should be advised so that he can still be on speaking terms with Mike Mitchell." [59]

Most significantly of all, Colonel Marriner intervened for moderation. Hearing from Dr. Karl Compton of the Radiation Laboratory's new experimental 10-centimeter ASV, General Arnold considered procuring it independently of the Signal Corps, then extended that consideration to beginning positive action upon the matter of taking over procurement altogether. He went so far as to have a letter for Assistant Secretary Lovett drafted, requesting that the Air Corps be given authority to procure the AI, ASV, and other disputed items of the year's battle. Marriner, however, suggested that the time was "not opportune for starting another fight with the Signal Corps." He advised rather that the Air Corps ask the Signal Corps to procure the ASV-10 and "see what they can do before we ask General Arnold to take the matter up with Lovett. Otherwise, it may kick back and put the General in an embarrassing spot." [60] Marriner's caution was sensibly

MAJ. GEN. DAWSON OLMSTEAD.
(Photograph taken in 1943.)

conditioned by the fact that the Air Corps could not use the ASV-10 until a major

---

[58] E.g., (1) Msg E-522, Exec to Tech Exec AC Mat Div, 19 Aug 41; (2) Ltr, Maj Alfred H. Johnson, Chief of GFE Br Production Engr Sec, to Chief Production Engr Sec, attn: All Airplane Brs, 20 Dec 41, sub: Radio equip requisitioned for plane contracts. AAG 413.44 Radio Equip, 1940–41, USAF Mat Comd Central Files.

[59] (1) Msg E-495, Exec to Tech Exec AC Mat Div, 18 Aug 41; (2) Record of phone conversation between Lt Col Bennett E. Meyers, Mat Div Office Chief of AC, and Col Kenneth B. Wolfe, Mat Div Wright Field, 18 Aug 41; (3) Msg E-516, Exec to Col Wolfe, 18 Aug 41. In same file.

[60] (1) Ltr, Compton to Gen Arnold, 29 Aug 41; (2) Memo, Col Marriner for Gen Spaatz, CofS Office Chief of AC, 4 Sep 41, sub: Proc of ASV-10 (10-centimeter sea search equip), with Incl Draft Ltr, Arnold to ASWA, same sub; (3) Ltr, "Si" [Marriner] to Lt Col Wallace G. Smith, Radio Liaison Sec, Office Chief of AC, 18 Sep 41, sub: Radio equip—comments on trip to Boston. AAG 413.4-D Coms Equip. (4) Martin P. Claussen, The Development of Radio and Radar Equipment for Air Operations, 1939–1944, pp. 14–16. Photostat in SigC Hist Sec File.

structural change in its bombers could be worked out.

The new Acting Chief Signal Officer meanwhile itemized the status of the new equipment. The radar and related radio program which his predecessor had approved at the end of June for the fiscal year now just begun amounted to nearly a quarter of a billion dollars on the estimate sheets. The amount covered the entire complex for air defense, whether for Coast Artillery Corps sites, the Air Defense Command, the Aircraft Warning Service, or the Air Corps centrally. The two months intervening had made little differ-

ence except the same one: that the more requirements were met, the more there were to be met. The need for 5,400 pipsqueak contactors had become a need for 12,000; for 15,000 airborne IFF's, 30,000.[61] Everywhere through the Office of the Chief Signal Officer there was the effect of a burst of activity. This, or something else, averted the coup which Air Corps policy had contemplated and left the Signal Corps in charge for another three years.

----

[61] (1) Memo, Maj Elder for CSigO, 28 Jun 41; (2) Incl to Memo, Gen Olmstead for Bundy, 5 Sep 41. SigC 676.3 ET 1, 1942.

CHAPTER XI

Signaling the Hemisphere

To the Northwest and the Northeast

In the presence of an undefined, imminent attack, the Army, like the population which maintained it, and the Signal Corps, like any other part of the Army, were sprawlingly but certainly collecting their forces to resist. The scene for this resistance, except for the Philippine Islands, had now become a hemisphere extending from Iceland to the central Pacific. Its bastions, from the point of view of the continental forty-eight states at the center, were the flanking land masses and the islands, large and small, to the northwest, the northeast, and the southeast.

In the continental northwest, Alaskan defense was growing from the lone detachment at Chilkoot Barracks which for many years had been the entire garrison of the Territory. When the infant Alaska Defense Force became the Alaska Defense Command in February 1941, Fort Richardson, the Anchorage headquarters of Brig. Gen. Simon Bolivar Buckner, Jr., was made up of one permanent building, a log hut, and a tent camp.[1] But each of them was a positive mark toward realization of a hemispheric plan. The adjacent Elmendorf Field was emerging. Ladd Field was in process of construction at Fairbanks, and several Ninth Corps Area signalmen were installing telephone lines.

As a result of an authorization to multiply strength to a total of 175 skilled operators throughout Alaska,[2] there were 45 Alaska Communication System men at Anchorage by April, which was almost as many as at the Seattle headquarters. Juneau had 29, Ketchikan 22, and Fairbanks 14. The geographical growth of the system over the mighty subcontinent was even more significant. There were stations at Sitka, Kodiak, Nome, Seward, Kanakanak, Cordova, Bethel, and Wrangell, with from three to six men each; there were one-man and two-man outposts at Skagway, Haines, Petersburg, Annette, Yakutat, Valdez, Kotzebue, Point Barrow, Nulato, Craig, and Flat; and on the list to complete the expansion were Big Delta, Boundary, Cold Bay, Dutch Harbor, Gulkana, McGrath, Naknek, Otter Point, Port Heiden, and Ruby.[3]

This was far more than a tally of place names, although it looked like far less to the men who were assigned to them. The overseas or territorial aircraft warning services were being held up for lack of

---

[1] Ltr, Col Harry L. Vitzthum, Dir Control Div OCSigO, to Sig Officer Alaska Defense Comd, 10 Nov 43, sub: Hist of Sig Sec Hq Alaska Defense Comd. Hq Alaska Defense Comd Files.

[2] Congress had increased the total enlisted strength of the Alaska Communication System to 280. *Hearings Before the Subcommittee of the Committee on Appropriations*, HR, 77th Cong, 1st Sess, On War Department Civil Functions Bill for 1942, 19 Mar 41, pp. 22–23.

[3] (1) O/C Alaska Com System Rpt, Radio Facilities of Alaska Communication System, 25 Apr 41; (2) [OCSigO Com Liaison Div] Revised Frequency Allocations [25 Jul 42]. SigC AC 63.

REMOTE RECEIVER STATION, *Alaska Communication System, at Juneau. (Photograph taken in 1947.)*

housing at the detector sites, and the same thing was true of the transmitter and receiver stations for a communications network flung over empty miles of wilderness.[4] Quarters had to be built. Photographs went to the War Department to picture the tumbled-down shacks which were all that existed at some stations. Even at Anchorage, the radio station was neither at Fort Richardson nor at Elmendorf Field, but eleven miles away by a dangerous road. Many of the stations were so lonely or so rawly new that there was no kind of shelter to rent, at any price, even when the rental allowance was increased to a dollar and a half a day. Furthermore, the Signal Corps had a general policy of sending married men to such duty, in the humane

persuasion that a wife could make a bleak and forsaken spot tolerable. Thus neither barracks some distance away, shacks close by, or more per diem money would do. In order to give the weather reports and communications service required of them, the station operators had to live where they worked. In due time, the War Department approached the Division of Defense Housing Coordination in the Office for Emergency Management for the funds for this humble aspect of grand strategy.[5]

---

[4] Memo, Col Stewart W. Stanley, Exec Officer OCSigO, for Asst Chief of Air Staff Office Chief of AAF, 2 Oct 41, sub: Plan for proc and tng of pers authorized for duty with AAF. SigC 402 Pers—Gen Air, Jul 41–Aug 42. OT 320.2.

[5] SigC File 600.1 Alaska, *passim.*

The department did so in acceding to a full-scale expansion of the Alaska Communication System which ultimately turned the quasi-commercial peacetime organization into a complete army communications service. Believing that the Pacific coast line could not be defended without a considerably more extensive communications system than existed, General Buckner demanded long-line radio to connect, in one large administrative network, all of the outpost garrisons which he planned, the new airfields, the ships on patrol, the coastal stations of artillery and aircraft warning, and his headquarters at Anchorage. It was late in the summer when it became apparent that the most efficient way to provide the network would be to enlarge the Alaska Communication System. The Signal Corps obtained an initial $116,655 to buy more equipment, and permission to plan stations at a dozen remote fastnesses not hitherto reached.

Simultaneously, a survey was made of the whole field of Alaskan and western Canadian communications. Associated with the agreement between Canada and the United States to co-ordinate their air defenses, the survey revealed a considerable diversity and extent of possible communications.[6] Short of the time when the Alaska Defense Command administrative network, the Alaska Defense Command tactical network, and the Army Airways Communications System network for flight control would come into existence, there would be the possibility, if properly integrated, of a radio, telephone, telegraph, and teletype system made up from many private, local, commercial, and governmental facilities. These included the Civil Aeronautics Administration stations, naval air traffic and naval administrative stations, the networks of Northwest Airlines and of Pan American Airways, various other commercial stations operated principally by canneries, the facilities of the Alaska Indian Service, of the Alaska Fisheries Service, of the Alaska Game Commission, and of the Alaska Railroad, the Canadian Pacific and Canadian National Railroad wire facilities, aerological stations, local district defense stations, amateur facilities, Coast Guard radio-equipped shore units, and the unexpanded Alaska Communication System.[7] The degree to which Buckner might be dependent upon all of these facilities was demonstrated by the fact that until Pearl Harbor the Alaska Defense Command's total complement of signalmen was 143. These were the members of a signal aviation construction company, a signal service company, and the long radarless aircraft warning company.

A unique and fortunate decision taken in connection with Northwest defense needs was to recondition and restore to use the Alaska cable. The cable ship *Restorer* sailed from Victoria on October 7, repaired breaks at Resurrection Bay, Trocadero Bay, and the Seward cable landing, sailed into a gale at Ketchikan, the terminal point both for the Seward cable to the northwest and the Seattle cable to the southeast, yet managed to complete the work by the first week of November. Just before Pearl Harbor the

---

[6] (1) Rpt by Wing Comdr C. R. Slemon, Western Air Comd, Victoria, B.C., Aircraft Inspection Corps, RCAF, With Reference to the Coordination of the Defense of the Puget Sound Area, 22 Oct 40. SigC 107 Jt U.S.-Canadian-U.K. Committee on RDF. (2) Memo, CSigO for ACofS WPD, 27 Mar 41. AAG 413.4-B Coms Equip, 1941.

[7] (1) SigC AC-77 Alaska, *passim.* (2) [Hist Sec Alaskan Dept] Official History of the Alaskan Department, Ch. XIV, Communications, pp. 315–37. OCMH.

THE CABLE SHIP *RESTORER*. *Note the cable grapple hanging from the bow of the ship.*

cable took its place as the central link between General Buckner's headquarters and General De Witt's Fourth Army headquarters at the Presidio of San Francisco. A telephone land line was used between Anchorage and Seward, then the cable to Seattle, and then a teletype circuit to San Francisco.[8] The cable restoration was fortunate not only because it provided a secure transmission means when the surprise at Pearl Harbor shook security, but also because it provided almost the only one. For despite promises, the administrative radio network was not ready until mid-1942.

Matters also moved with slowness on the creation of aircraft warning facilities. Buckner had agreed that the Alaska Communication System should handle the communications for the aircraft warning service as well as provide the administrative Alaska Defense Command network, so that when one was delayed, the other was, too. Furthermore, the detector stations at Fairbanks, Kodiak, and Sitka and an information center at Anchorage had

[8] (1) Ltrs, O/C Alaska Com System to CSigO, 6 Nov 41, sub: Monthly progress rpt on expansion of Alaska Com System, and 15 Nov 41, sub: Weekly progress rpt on same. SigC AC-25. (2) Msg, Alaska Com System Seattle to CG Fourth Army Presidio, 3 Dec 41. SigC 413.4 No. 1.

been approved for more than a year before they were finished, and a half-strength aircraft warning company had been waiting for six months. The entire Territory of Alaska was to be one Aircraft Warning Service region, according to plan, and to be subdivided into twelve sectors each with a filter center at its principal airfield or Army establishment. War overtook this proposal, and only five radars altogether were assigned to Alaska until the Dutch Harbor scare.[9]

Radars were being assigned under what seemed a greater urgency to other parts of the defense perimeter. In July the United States moved outward to take Iceland into its military defense zone. On 6 August the Signal Aircraft Warning Company of Task Force 4 arrived to establish itself on the island, especially at the British radio direction-finding stations at Vik, Olfus, and Grotta. Disembarked at Reykjavik with several SCR-268's and SCR-270-B's, the men looked over the situation. A system of coast watching, maintained by the British Navy, was in operation, but long delays in getting information from the observers to the control headquarters had made the system ineffective. The industrial development of Iceland was too limited to provide much power. The island's telephone system could be invoked only in emergencies; to use it would be to lose secrecy, and in any case it was inadequate. The rugged landscape offered numberless commanding sites where warning stations could be set up, but inaccessibility or the extent to which the mountains echoed the pulses ruled out all but a few sites, principally along the coast. As for the weather, although the cold that year proved not to be severe, in midwinter the gales rose high; and the northern lights caused electrostatic disturbances close to the ground.

A temporary fighter-control room began twenty-four-hour operation at the airdrome by the end of August. On duty were an Aircraft Warning Service officer, an Air Corps officer who supervised the traffic control for the interceptor planes, and two enlisted men who plotted on map overlays the information coming in from the spotter craft and stations. On 1 September an SCR-270-B began searching the skies at Grindavik, on a beach forty-seven feet above sea level. As soon as an Engineer platoon had constructed an access road up a mountain two miles to the north, the radar was moved to its permanent site. The men had to take it up the mountainside part by part and reassemble it at the summit in Quonset huts, the generators being 500 yards from the top and the radar actually at the top. From this point of vantage the scope tracked surface vessels at ranges from 80 to 90 miles (although dependably only up to 70 miles), noted echoes as far away as 100 miles, and all in all obtained a clear sweep from approximately 90° true azimuth to 360°.

It had not originally been contemplated that civilians would be sent to overseas defense areas, but the Icelandic radar could never have got into operation so early if they had not been called upon. Signal Corps Laboratories engineers who had studied Signal Corps radar almost from the beginning answered an appeal made a day before sailing time and, reaching Iceland, did at Grindavik what they had been learning to do in New Jersey at Sandy Hook and Twin Lights. For the time being, the Americans were too shorthanded to take over the British CH and

---

[9] AG File 660.2 AA Sec 5 AWS Fourth Army, *passim.*

CHL at Grotta, Olfus, and Vik. But other radar stations came into being soon afterward. An SCR–268 began to be used at Camp Catherine, near Reykjavik, during the middle of October.

By that time, also, signalmen had begun to install a fixed radio station near Reykjavik to provide direct communications with WAR. They completed it in forty days, and opened it slightly less than a month before the United States entered the war. The radio plan had further called for an administrative net of three stations, but on the assumption that the existing communications in the island would be adequate it had been suspended before the material for them had cleared New York. It was revived late in the year, but a tower of other claims had priority over it then. The material was ultimately shipped in February 1942. Because they were dissatisfied with the wire communications which their British predecessors had patched together and made to serve, the Americans also worked out a carrier wire system at a cost of $4,500,000, and, after the war had begun, contracted with the American Telephone and Telegraph Company to build it.[10]

The Danish permission to use Iceland and Greenland, along with the exchange of destroyers for bases in British colonies, led to a general North Atlantic extension of the Army Command and Administrative Network. An American survey party, drawn from the State, Treasury, War, and Navy Departments, set out for Greenland in March, and Army Command and Administrative Networks stations followed the survey at the spots which came to be known as BLUIE WEST 1 (Narsarssuak), BLUIE WEST 3 (Simintak), and, after more than a year, at BLUIE WEST 8 (Sondrestromfjord). These were respectively one-

kilowatt, 350-watt, and 300-watt stations.[11]

Fifteen signalmen established the communications at the Narsarssuak airstrip. Reaching Greenland on 8 July after a succession of changes had delayed their sailing, they had the station installed and in some working order by 17 September. The site was temporary, and a tidal river 800 feet wide repeatedly threatened the control lines. Of the gravest significance were the meteorological interruptions, which, cutting off all contact with the outside world for as long as thirty-six hours, pointed up the inadequacy of these communications for any such project as the Eighth Air Force BOLERO movement put upon them in a few more months.

Nevertheless, its importance to hemispheric defense demanded that Greenland become a major air base. Other units arrived. The I Interceptor Command provided for an officer and twenty-six enlisted men of the 1st Aircraft Warning Company to go to BLUIE WEST, among them being men who, at the Signal Corps School, had been the first American soldiers to be trained in radar. Still more men detached from the 50th Signal Battalion at Fort Sheridan, Illinois, were sent to the New York Port of Embarkation and then held

---

[10] (1) Capt Walter E. Lotz, Jr., Report on the Progress and Future Plans of the AW System, Iceland, for the Period August 6, 1941, to April 23, 1942. SigC AC-76 Atlantic. (2) History of the 556th Signal Aircraft Warning Battalion. AF Archives SIG-556-HI, 10 Jul 41, 5489-2. (3) Harold A. Zahl, "Signal Corps Research and Its Relationships to Educational Institutions," *Signals*, IV, No. 6 (July–August 1950), 23. (4) 1st Lt Charles R. Novick, A Story of Signal Communications in Iceland, 1944, pp. 7 ff. and 28 ff. SigC Hist Sec File.

[11] A site at Angmagsalik for an east coast BLUIE was not found until May 1942, and then found by air. North Atlantic Div CE, Greenland (New York, 1946), Vol. I, p. III-3. OCMH.

there from September to January, because there was no way to take care of them once they got to Greenland.[12]

At St John's, the capital of Newfoundland, signalmen began by using ship's radio in the harbor and, also aboard ship, a 40-line magneto switchboard for telephone service to the local exchange. The first immediate requirement was to extend a wire line north to the site of the new airport, Gander Lake, a name which was to become famous with the establishment of transatlantic air ferrying and passenger service. The next thing was to install a 1-kilowatt transmitter at St. John's, or, rather, at nearby Quidi Vidi Lake, for the use of Fort Pepperell. It was given the call letters WVDN, and 300-watt satellites appeared at Gander, Fort McAndrew, and Harmon Field, the other airfield on the west side of the island. Three SCR-270 sites were to be selected, as well as locations for radio intelligence monitoring. At first, the base command signal officer had so few men that he wrote, "When I get them distributed to their various activities of Supply, Telephony, Radio, Cryptography and Photography I have no men left to operate the switchboard, to operate the message center or to construct any telephone lines." By October, he was much better off, with five officers beside himself and with 143 enlisted men.[13]

To the Southeast

Thus the arc of the great circle route to Europe was arming itself on land and in the air as it already had done at sea. The events which brought this about were tripling the area to be equipped and manned in defense of the United States from attack from the southeast. Beyond

the Panama Canal, now seriously endangered for the first time, lay the island-locked Caribbean Sea. The United States had been fortunate in the arrangement which placed this region at American disposal for development of hemispheric defense; but the newly acquired sites on the irregular string of British islands looked out across the hostile Atlantic as well as in upon the familiar Caribbean. Beyond them, in turn, hemispheric interest now reached into the equatorial Atlantic, two thousand miles beyond Trinidad, the southernmost of the chain, out to the bulge of Brazil.

The build-up of the watery area for which the West Indies make a spine put a fierce pressure upon Trinidad because the three axes of the defense converged there: from Bermuda southward, from the Panama Canal Zone eastward, and from Brazil and the Guianas northwestward. By July the traffic became congested at Trinidad. The 1-kilowatt radio and cryptographic station begun in March by ten

[12] (1) SigC File OT 676 Greenland Reports on Communication 41-42, Summary of Events Relative to Establishment of Garrisons on Bluie West. (2) 1st Lt David R. Guy, Post Sig Officer, Initial Report on Signal Activities, Greenland Base Command, 13 Feb 42. In same file. (3) OCSigO Com Liaison Div Chart, Army Administrative Radio System N. Atlantic, 19 May 42. SigC 676.3 (CC CEB) Canadian Ferry Route. (4) Memo, Brig Gen Leonard T. Gerow for TAG, 28 Jun 41, sub: Site for installation of long-range detector SCR-271. OCS 21001-21110. (5) Memo, Chief of Opns Br OCSigO for CsigO, 23 Oct 41, sub: Rpt on deficiencies in equip, pers, and tng of com units of U.S. Army. SigC OT 322 Gen.

[13] (1) Rpt by Capt Airel B. Cooper, Sig Officer Newfoundland Base Comd, Progress of Signal Communications in Newfoundland Base Command, 17 Feb 41; (2) Reconnaissance of Newfoundland Airport, 10 May 41, extract from Plan for Permanent Signal System—Newfoundland; (3) Newfoundland Base Comd, Quarterly Report on Signal Activities, 10 Oct 41. SigC OT 676 T/E T/BA Gen, Channels, Call Signs, etc., Conferences, Rpts, etc., Newfoundland, 1941–42.

signalmen was endeavoring to handle all of the Engineer Corps traffic created by the far-flung construction activity. Circuits to St. Lucia and British Guiana began to supplement the circuits to Puerto Rico and the Canal Zone, but neither equipment nor manpower was sufficient. Upon strong petition, the War Department authorized a greatly expanded radio project. Trinidad was supposed to be built up to a strength of 17,000, a garrison requiring a considerable maze of wire and radio. Maj. Raymond C. Maude of the Office of the Chief Signal Officer suggested after a personal survey that the Trinidad Telephone Company, Ltd., could provide much of the wire service on a leased-line basis, much as the Bell System would do in the United States, but the fact developed later that the local company's greatest asset was co-operative spirit; its facilities were meager. The effort to provide wire communication among the scattered elements of the garrison was one of the chief communications problems of the whole Caribbean area. And Trinidad's aircraft warning service was nonexistent; as late as the end of August there were no men assigned to it and the sites were still in dispute.[14]

On Jamaica, the 12th Signal Service Company's detachment of 14 men, who had been assembled from so many sources, billeted themselves at Fort Simonds and opened a station for the area administrative net at Spanish Town. The Chief Signal Officer expressed the opinion that the commercial radiotelegraph at Kingston would sufficiently supplement the military station, with no need for anything more at the time. As it turned out in the forthcoming years, this was entirely adequate. The current long-range planning called for the defense of the island to be built up over a period of five years. This intention produced the first accession of strength to the 14-man detachment when the signal complement of Task Force TUNA arrived with 14 more men. Still another detachment of 14 went to Antigua, once Lord Nelson's base in the Leeward Islands, another to St. Lucia, and a third to Atkinson Field, British Guiana. The original aircraft warning complement for Jamaica was to have been an aircraft warning company, frontier—5 officers, 122 enlisted men—to operate an information center and two detector stations. Three officers and 96 men got there during the summer. Permanent and temporary housing for 875 persons was on the books for the immediate future, along with four SCR-271's instead of two.[15]

The swift spread of areas of responsibility, with the need for radar, radiotelegraph, radioteletype, and wire in abundance, focused attention upon existing

[14] (1) AG Ltr, 4 Aug 41, sub: Radio requirements Caribbean Defense Comd. SigC 676.3 Trinidad 2, and also in AG 676.3 MC-E. (2) Ltr, Lt Col John C. Grable to Maj Gen Harry C. Ingles, CofS Caribbean Defense Comd, 14 Feb 42. SigC SIGLO 676.1 Gen (2-14-42) Plant Engr Agency. (3) Ltr, Lt Gen Daniel Van Voorhis, CG Caribbean Defense Comd, to TAG, 15 Jul 41, sub: Sig com Caribbean Defense Comd. SigC OT 381 Puerto Rico Dept (Defense of), 1941. (4) Ltr, CG Caribbean AF to CG Caribbean Defense Comd, 25 Aug 41, sub: Augmentation of SigC troops and Caribbean AF. AAG 320 6th AF.

[15] (1) Incl. Résumé of Installations To Be Made in Jamaica, with Ltr, CSigO to Capt Charles M. Baer, SigC, U.S. Engr Offices, Kingston, 8 Apr 41, same sub; (2) Memo, CSigO for ACofS G-3, 23 Sep 41, sub: Increase of sig sv detachment Jamaica to 28 enlisted men; (3) Memo, ACofS G-1 for TAG, 29 Sep 41, sub: Sig sv detachment for Jamaica Base Comd and Antigua; (4) Incl 1, Jamaica Defense Project, with Ltr, TAG to CG Caribbean Defense Comd, 15 Nov 41, same sub. SigC OT 381 Jamaica Gen. (5) Ltr, CSigO to Sig Officer Caribbean Defense Comd [? Jul 41], sub: Radio station of Tropical Radio Telegraph Co. at Kingston, Jamaica. SigC OT 320.3 AWS.

communications facilities everywhere, just as was the case in the Canada-Alaska region at the opposite corner of hemispheric signaling. Puerto Rico, for example, had four connections with the Panama Canal Zone: a direct Navy radio link; the Army connection, which signaled Washington and thence was relayed; Tropical Radio, a commercial company, which made the link by way of New Orleans; and the All America cable, which ran directly to the Canal Zone. Tropical Radio also joined Puerto Rico and Jamaica; and RCA linked the island possession with two of the destroyers-for-bases sites: Antigua in the Leeward Islands, St. Lucia in the Windwards. The British Cable and Wireless Company had a cable from Puerto Rico to Trinidad and thence to British Guiana. And finally, there were the usual particularized systems of other commercial and governmental enterprises, together with a special American Legion network. Thus a fairly sophisticated level of communications existed on Puerto Rico, associating the island with most of the Gulf-Caribbean region.

Nevertheless, a major military undertaking like the just-established Caribbean Defense Command seemed to require separate systems for its administrative, tactical, and air messages. General Buckner thought Alaska needed them, and Lt. Gen. Daniel Van Voorhis felt the same regarding his command. For the northwest, Anchorage was a somewhat arbitrarily chosen center point; but for the southeast, the vital Canal Zone was the unchallenged center. Actually at the farthest rim of the whole region, it was nonetheless the focus of the entire intercontinental defense. The communications plan accordingly envisaged a huge radio network providing the Quarry Heights headquar-

ters of the command with generally direct (in a few cases, auxiliary) connections with Central America, the Greater and Lesser Antilles, and the entire northern coast of South America: that is to say, with Camaguey, Kingston, Port-au-Prince, Ciudad Trujillo, San Juan, Antigua, Martinique, St. Lucia, Trinidad, British, Dutch, and French Guiana, northern and northeastern Brazil, cities of Venezuela and Colombia, of Panama, Nicaragua, Guatemala, and Mexico, all Army transports, and Washington and San Francisco. An interlocking of 400-watt and 1-kilowatt transmitters forged the system. WVL, the Army Command and Administrative Network's station in the Canal Zone, was at the heart of it all.[16]

Since any number of SCR-188's and SCR-197's would have been inadequate to the task of such long-range communications, commercial equipment was called for. The signal companies of the air and composite wings, however, asked for and got the standard ground radios and used them, as intended, in tactical performance. The 12th Pursuit Wing, for example, preferred the SCR-188's for intercommunicating among its score of locations in the republic of Panama. The wing commanding officer asked for 138 of these radios.

Internally for Panama, as on the various islands, wire communication, with all its flexibility and naturalness, was of course ordinarily to be preferred to radio. Brig. Gen. Harry C. Ingles was the Carib-

---

[16] (1) Maj John M. Baker, Hist Sec Caribbean Comd, Communications and Radar in the Area of the Caribbean Defense Command, 1940–1948, 1948, pp. 31–35. OCMH. (2) Informal Rpt by Joint Committee, A Communications System Between the United States Diplomatic, Military and Naval Agencies in the American Republics, 7 Dec 40. SigC OT 320.3 AWS.

bean Defense Command signal officer, and later the command chief of staff. He argued convincingly that wire was a much better and quicker circuit for the antiaircraft batteries, the end cause of the whole elaborate defense structure. The Canal antiaircraft commander had thought of creating seventy-nine 75-watt stations— still another network in the multinetted area. Ingles showed him that the complications, the delay, and the confusion in communicating during an attack would be enormous, and killed the project.[17]

On a local scale wire telephone and wire teletypewriter links became as significant as the great cross-water radio system. One of these lines, an "open" wire line, strung on wooden poles, ultimately connected Quarry Heights with two small Panamanian towns, Aguadulce and Rio Hato, at a cost of a quarter of a million. Because there were no white construction troops whom he thought capable of cutting through rough and hot country to put up this pole line, Van Voorhis asked for Negro soldiers. Organized at Fort Leonard Wood, Missouri, and designated the 275th Signal Construction Company, they arrived on 8 December. On 7 December General Olmstead was inspecting the route of the line with no pleasure at all in what he saw. Other points were equally lacking in wire facilities: Trinidad, Jamaica, Antigua, St. Lucia, British Guiana, and Puerto Rico, where there had to be wire systems to take care of the projected naval base in Vieques Sound and the aircraft warning and antiaircraft installations steadily expanding from Borinquen Field on the west and Fajardo on the east.

The strategic importance and relative vulnerability of Panama had given it unquestioned priority also for aircraft warn-

ing. The first SCR-271 radar stations to be installed outside the continental United States were the two which had gone into operation in mid-1940.[18] One set was located at Fort Sherman on the Atlantic side, and the second, the Signal Corps Laboratories production model, on the highest point on Taboga Island in the Gulf of Panama on the Pacific side. The natural desire to camouflage them was thwarted when the installing crew found that clearing away the heavy jungle growth left the thirty-six-foot towers nakedly visible. Lt. Col. James A. Code, Jr., proposed installing the detectors in underground bombproofs, and ultimately this was done; but at the time, the Signal Corps had barely got started on the production run of the SCR-271, and did not welcome any change which would interrupt it. Elevating the towers to 100 feet in order to escape the tropical verdure altogether would also have meant changes in design; so until pressure at the Laboratories relaxed enough to permit a new project, the crew was instructed to install the 271's as originally approved.[19]

Other installation teams, made up of a few officers and enlisted men, along with civilian experts, were put ashore thereafter on the jungle-rimmed beaches, with tents and a limited amount of radio equipment, in order to start choosing good SCR-268 radar sites for gun batteries. During the year, such units started work at four locations on the Pacific side, from

[17] Baker hist cited n. 16(1), pp. 43–45.
[18] (1) *Ibid.*, pp. 11–12. (2) Harry M. Davis, The Signal Corps Development of U.S. Army Radar Equipment, Pt. III, 1945, pp. 54, 93. SigC Hist Sec File.
[19] (1) Ltr, CG Panama Canal Dept to TAG, 4 Mar 41, sub: Underground bombproof AWS SCR-271 stations, with inds. (2) Interv, SigC Hist Sec with Maj Gen James A. Code, Jr., Ret., 13 Sep 49, Chicago, Ill.

SCR–271 RADAR STATION IN PANAMA

Costa Rica to Colombia (Burica Point, Coiba Island, Mala Point, and Jaque); at two on the Caribbean side (Almirante and Pito); and at an interior spot, Pinagana.

Operation of the Aircraft Warning Service in the Caribbean was a function of the Air Corps, which controlled the Signal Company, Aircraft Warning, Panama, and the Signal Company, Aircraft Warning, Puerto Rico. The radar stations and the ground observation stations fed information into a temporary filter center in the basement of the headquarters building at Quarry Heights, which relayed it to a control center on the third floor of the base headquarters building at Albrook Field. The assignment of operational responsibility paralleled the assignment of responsibility for theater signals in general, where actual operations were carried out by the signal officers of the Panama Canal and Antilles Departments and the Trinidad Sector and Base Command.[20]

Installation, maintenance, and supply were distinctly Signal Corps duties. "Everyone was more than willing to have a share in selecting locations" for the detectors, filter stations, and information centers, but "content that the responsibilities [for supply and maintenance] should lie elsewhere." [21] Ingles defined the relationship. The Sixth Air Force had the obligation to operate the Aircraft Warning Service and all its equipment, including the radio and wire hookup of its various parts. Everything else was the charge of the Signal Corps, through the local signal officers. This included even arranging with the Engineers for access roads. The responsibility was principally composed of the supply, installation, and heavy maintenance of all the equipment, and the furnishing of all the operators. It was this last point which created so much disgruntle-

ment, for it brought Signal Corps ratings under Air Corps disposal; but as it was a matter of established War Department policy, Ingles was not free to do anything about it.[22] Until 15 July 1941, the General Staff controlled aircraft warning, and after that date the Signal Corps co-ordinated the program within the bounds already set.[23]

From New Jersey

The requirement that the Signal Corps produce the radar operators put a share of the responsibility directly upon the Signal Corps School and the Replacement Center at Fort Monmouth. In mid-June, for instance, the Albrook Field commander made a direct request for seventy-three Monmouth-trained radarmen, and followed it up by outlining an aircraft warning service for the isthmus which would demand many more than that.[24] According to War Department plan, Panama was to have two aircraft warning services, the other overseas possessions one each. Panama, Puerto Rico, Hawaii, and the Philippines were each to have an interceptor command [25] like the four interceptor commands being created for the

---

[20] Caribbean Defense Comd, Operations Plan, Caribbean Theater, Annex 14: Signal Communication, 1 Dec 41. Caribbean Defense Comd File Hq and Staff.

[21] Baker hist cited n. 16(1), p. 60.

[22] E.g., OCSigO R&W Action 1, Air Coms Div to R&D Div, 18 Nov 41, sub: Responsibility for GCI opn. SigC 413.44 British GCI (RB-2330).

[23] Ltr, TAG to Chief of Arms and Svs and Bureaus and Divs of the WDGS, 15 Jul 41, sub: Controlled activities FY 42. AG 112.05 (7-11-41) MD-D-M.

[24] Ltrs, CO 12th Pursuit Wing to CG Caribbean AF, 17 Jun 41, sub: Requisition for qualified men sig co AWS, and 20 Jun 41, sub: T/O's for AWS Orgns. AF Archives Documents 6th AF.

[25] Memo for File, 23 Jul 41, sub: AWS equip. SigC 676.3 AWS ET 1, 1942.

continental United States. Interceptor airplanes and antiaircraft guns completed the aircraft warning mission which radars excited. An aircraft warning service was a regional collaboration of instruments of observation, instruments of communication, and instruments of destruction, in that order: from the "spotter," the sound locator, or the electronic detector to the filter room and information center plotting boards to the gunfire closing with the enemy. Through its equipment, the Signal Corps was a part of this fabric at almost every thread. In its operating assignments, it served two stages of the process. And its training mission was foremost in the first.

Since signalmen sent to the offshore bases were primarily aircraft warning troops, Monmouth communicated very directly with hemispheric defense.[26] In May, the Air Defense Board, which was composed of the Chief Signal Officer, the Chief of Coast Artillery, and the commanding general of the GHQ Air Force, determined that the Air Corps should be strengthened by 1,238 officers and 7,796 enlisted men, to implement its share of the air defense system, while the Signal Corps should be granted an immediate increase of 2,200 officers and 40,200 enlisted men. For the Signal Corps alone, this added up to three times the total number of men actually on aircraft warning duty at the time. Most of the aircraft warning companies in existence were mobile companies. Other units had to be developed for the fixed coastal sector stations. The Fourth Army on the Pacific Coast was to have four aircraft warning companies, frontier; the First and Third were to have three each for the eastern and southern coastlines. The board recommended that the continental aircraft warning person-

nel receive at the minimum military training equivalent to that given by the Signal Corps Replacement Training Center and be activated and organized at stations chosen by the commanding general of the Air Forces one month before the delivery date of their radar equipment. Aircraft warning men destined for overseas stations, the board declared, should receive four months' training before leaving the United States.[27]

Necessity slowed down the rate of this recommended extension, but even the first fraction of it, with the rest to follow, made a sufficiently large impression. The Chief of Coast Artillery proposed a joint school in which his service, the Signal Corps, and the Air Corps would all share, and to which the reception centers would send carefully chosen men to be trained exclusively in aircraft warning. The Air Corps dissented, but the other two went ahead with the plan.[28] Pending anything so ambitious, the Aircraft Warning Department at the Signal Corps School expanded from 100 to 900 students, who would spend four months learning to be radio electricians and three more to be maintenance men or operators. Maj. Gen. Dawson Olmstead asked for and got $1,200,000 more to create the buildings and equipment for this first part of the anticipated

---

[26] Memo, CSigO for Maj Henry I. Hodes, G-3 WDGS, 23 Sep 40, sub: SigC troops required for immediate occupation for bases to be acquired from Great Britain. SigC OT 381 Jamaica Gen.

[27] Air Defense Bd Rpt, WP&T Div OCSigO, 4 Sep 41, pp. 6, 14–18. SigC 334.7 ET (RD).

[28] (1) Ltr, Chief of CAC to TAG, 30 Jul 41, sub: Proc and tng of radio detector pers, and 1st Ind, Actg CSigO to TAG, 14 Aug 41. SigC MT-31 352 Southern SigC School. (2) Ltr, Actg CSigO to CG AF Combat Comd, 30 Aug 41, same sub, and 1st Ind Reply, 20 Sep 41; (3) Memo for File by Maj William P. Pence, 28 Nov 41, sub: Conference on establishment of joint school for tng of radio detection pers. SigC MT-38 353 Gen.

total, and set the Operations Branch of his office to preparing plans for the rest. As these plans developed, providing for courses in a dozen radars beside the original three, they rapidly exceeded the capacity of the Aircraft Warning Department and then the capacity of the School and the Replacement Training Center both. Briefly, while the contemplated total stood at 11,777 aircraft warning men to be trained, a center in Texas was planned; then it was put in Florida instead; and eventually it led to two installations: the Signal Corps' Camp Murphy at Hobe Sound and the Air Corps' Drew Field at Tampa.[29]

As if to flout the planning, reality showed the Aircraft Warning Department amply able to take care of any and all students being sent to it. Through class after class, the Air Corps failed to fill its quotas, and the Coast Artillery Corps also lagged from time to time, although both had as much interest as the Signal Corps in accomplishing the training. Sometimes men failed the basic radio course in the Enlisted Department and had to repeat it, with their intended places in the aircraft warning classes going empty for four more months. And quite often, answering the appeals from the hemispheric outposts, the Office of The Adjutant General pulled men out before they had finished, and formed them into cadres for new AWS units.[30] The shortage or absence of equipment for radar training was equally real. Possibly it was a higher hurdle to training, for there was no substitute for radar. Even with A-1-A or AA priorities, a manufacturer required six or eight months to produce a detector set; and when he had, the Air Corps, determining the use to be made of it, naturally enough assigned it to active duty rather than to the classroom. Yet a tactical assignment at this stage deprived many a radar of its widest use, for only the relatively few men of the operating crew could become familiar with it, whereas large numbers of men would have had access to it at a training center.[31]

Nine tenths of the planning for training radarmen was for training enlisted men. For officers, the planners first assumed that study would be provided at civilian technological schools—an expansion of the peacetime practice, as it were, of sending officers to Sheffield at Yale or to the Massachusetts Institute of Technology. The Canadian aircraft warning school at Clinton, Ontario, also agreed to take officer students. Then arose one of the most interesting of all the training experiments. The National Defense Research Committee stepped to the fore again and suggested an Electronics Training Group.

Upon his return from a trip to England in April, Dr. James B. Conant, president of Harvard University and member of the National Defense Research Committee, saw President Roosevelt and proposed it.[32]

[29] (1) Ltr, OCSigO to TAG, 7 Oct 41, sub: Expansion of aircraft warning course at SigC School, and 1st Ind, AGO to CSigO, 25 Oct 41. SigC School Hq 352 Aircraft Warning Dept 3/31/41–1/12/42, Item 43. (2) Ltr, Col Otis K. Sadtler to Comdt SigC School, 25 Nov 41, sub: Expansion of SigC School. SigC School Hq 352 Aircraft Warning Dept 3/31/41–1/12/42, Item 70. (3) *Hearings Before Subcommittee of Committee on Appropriations,* HR, 77th Cong, 3d Sess, On the 3d Supplemental National Defense Appropriations Bill for 1942, Pt. 2, p. 46. (4) Signal Corps Information Letter, No. 1 (new ser., December, 1941), p. 43. (5) OCSigO R&W Action 1, Air Coms Div to Mil Pers Div, 21 Nov 41. SigC MP 320.22 Requirements Enlisted Men.

[30] Ltr, Brig Gen George L. Van Deusen, Actg Comdt SigC School, to CSigO, 25 Oct 41, sub: Students for Aircraft Warning Dept course. SigC Sch Hq 352 Aircraft Warning Dept 3/31/41–1/12/42.

[31] (1) 1st Ind, TAG to CSigO, 25 Oct 41, on Ltr, CSigO to TAG, 7 Oct 41, sub: Expansion of aircraft warning course at SigC School. In same file. (2) Ltr, Col Sadtler to Comdt SigC School, 4 Dec 41. SigC MT-34 353 AWS Ft. Monmouth.

[32] Baxter, *Scientists Against Time,* p. 123.

In effect, the Electronics Training Group was an application of the principle of lend-lease and of the destroyers-for-bases agreement also. That is to say, it contemplated putting the resources of the United States at the service of those engaged in withstanding the common enemy, just as the nation undertook in the mutual interest to protect Great Britain's colonies in the Western Hemisphere. Conant's proposal and Roosevelt's approval of it were fundamentally more daring; for the resources involved were not property or matériel but men. As worked out and agreed upon by the National Defense Research Committee, the General Staff, representatives of the British, and the Signal and Air Corps, the program undertook to select, as a beginning, from 250 to 500 men with experience in electric communications, commission them as 2d lieutenants in the Reserve, give them three weeks of preliminary training at the Signal Corps School, and send them to England to be student-observers at the radar stations and filter centers there.[33] Three months of a training period of eight months would be spent at one of nearly a dozen British air warning schools, and five months in actual service at defense stations in the British Isles. Great Britain urged a full year rather than eight months, but in America Reserve officers could not yet be kept in service longer than a year, so that it was impracticable to assign the officers of the Electronics Training Group to England for the entire span.

With classes of 50 beginning at frequent intervals, the British, according to forecast, would train 700 men (the ultimate number was greater), between 250 and 300 of whom would remain in England. The rest would return to Aircraft Warning Service operation and training posts in the United States. The details to be considered were dauntingly numerous. There were such matters as National Registration identity cards, ration books, and curfew exemptions for the group, the question whether they should wear uniforms or civilian clothes when on leave, and the difference in the pay scale of British and American officers. Officers assigned to air duty were to be given flight pay. Air Vice-Marshal Sir Philip Joubert was of the opinion that the American officers' advantage in pay would not antagonize the British officers with whom they would serve; and he anticipated no dissension arising from American officers' either having to take orders from British superiors or giving them to British soldiers. Among all, one point which was inadequately discussed was the method to be used for keeping track of American officers scattered through British units after their first three months.[34] Upon this reef in the Electronics Training Group many a fresh career foundered, men who had been the first choice at the time they were commissioned being lost sight of, left unpromoted and, what was far more serious, marooned in outmoded assignments when a thousand needs for their capacities and talents had become pressing.[35]

---

[33] Ltr, CSigO to TAG, 8 May 41, sub: Appointment of 250–500 2d lts Sig Reserve. SigC 210.2 Gen.

[34] (1) Maj Marion Van Voorst, SigC, Notes on Conference Held in [Brig] General [Raymond E.] Lee's Office, 6 P.M., 27 May 41. SigC 352.11 ETG. (2) Ltr, TAG to CSigO, 10 Jun 41, sub: Appointment of 2d lts Sig Sv for AWS. AG 210.1 SigC. (3) Memo, CSigO for ACofS G-2, 30 Jun 41, which is paraphrase of Msg, Mil Attaché, London, to WD, 18 Jul 41. SigC 352.11 ETG. (4) Signal Corps Information Letter, No. 1 (new ser., December, 1941), p. 13.

[35] (1) Interv, SigC Hist Sec with Maj Gen Alfred W. Marriner, USAF Ret., Tech Dir IT&T, N.Y., 13 Feb 50. (2) Incl, Report on Radar Maintenance for Antiaircraft and Coastal Defense in North African Theater, with Ltr, CG AGF to CG's All Major AGF Comds, 18 Aug 43, sub: Observations in North Africa 11 May to 23 Jul 43. SCIA File Misc Observer Rpts, No. 46, Folder 1.

Monmouth established the Electronics Training Group as a branch of the Officers Department at the Signal Corps School, and a campaign began to recruit the candidates. Dr. Vannevar Bush, the National Defense Research Committee chairman, designated George Bailey, the president of the American Radio Relay League, to head the recruiting. To qualify for an appointment as a 2d lieutenant, a candidate had to be single, free of dependents, within the draft age of 21 to 36, a university graduate in electrical engineering or physics, and reasonably well acquainted with radio or electronics. The ROTC was considered the most likely source. Newspapers, magazines, and radio broadcasting stations carried the recruiting announcements, but the response was not overwhelming. The Signal Corps was offering the lowest officer rank to men who could expect more; the prospects in industry were much better even for men of less qualification. First one and then another officer of the Military Personnel Division of the Office of the Chief Signal Officer toured both cities and Army camps, and ultimately turned up 2,000 applications. Four hunderd appeared to warrant consideration, and the recruiting continued.[36]

In July, the first class, thirty-five new 2d lieutenants, reported to Fort Monmouth for their three weeks' basic training: military courtesy, organization of the Army, mission signal communication, administration, property accounting, Signal Corps depot organization, defense against chemical attack, physical training, and drill. At the same time, others began to study at Harvard and the Massachusetts Institute of Technology, NDRC having prevailed upon both to institute courses under a program financed by the United States Office of Education. The successive classes organized at the Signal Corps School and sent to Great Britain comprised the Electronics Training Group proper. Those who went to Boston and Cambridge to do their work were enrolled in the Electronics Training Program. Both projects were administered, with more or less attention, from the New Jersey center. Generally speaking, those new Reserve 2d lieutenants who went to England were either the first and therefore the most urgently needed, whatever their qualifications, or they were the most experienced, because training in the United Kingdom was pressed into little more than half the time allowed for it at Harvard and M. I. T.

For those whose training in radar was to begin at a relatively elementary stage, the Harvard course at the Cruft Laboratory offered the fundamentals of electronics, stressing the operation of the cathode-ray tube and other components. M. I. T.'s, more advanced, organized the components into specific radar systems and included the study of antennas and ultrahigh-frequency circuits. Only a part of the officers taking these courses were Electronics Training Program men. Army, Navy, and Marine officers attended them as well in order to be given the same special and rare knowledge. The Massachusetts Institute of Technology began its first course on June 23 without an SCR-268 until just before the end of the three months' session. Harvard commenced on July 17. Those who did not qualify at Harvard for the M. I. T. course were as-

---

[36] (1) Memo, CSigO for ACofS G-1, 29 May 41, sub: Pers to attend aircraft warning course at M.I.T. SigC 676.3 AWS Gen 1. (2) Memo, Gen Olmstead for Bundy, Special Asst to SW, 15 Aug 41. SigC 352.11 ETG. (3) Ltr, Maj Harrod G. Miller, Hq II Interceptor Comd, to Maj Harold O. Bixby, OCSigO, 21 Aug 41. SigC Hist Sec File.

signed to service schools or to troops.[37]

Delays kept the first Electronics Training Group class at Fort Monmouth until September. On the 12th, the men left for Montreal, and sailed for England three days later aboard the transformed *Empress of Asia*. It had been agreed with the British that they would be listed as military observers. In the recruiting, the press had referred to them variously as electrical experts, electric sentries, and the electronics battalion. Since the United States was in an equivocal position, not being at war with the Axis nations, security officers were therefore understandably wry when the secret aspect of the mission was immediately lost. The King and Queen reviewed the first men soon after their arrival, and New York and hometown newspapers printed the pictures. The commander of the Group, Lt. Col. Willis R. Lansford, had preceded the first detachment. He soon found himself and his three enlisted assistants swamped with administrative details that had been overlooked despite the care in the planning. The worst of them was that by the time 300 American 2d lieutenants had crossed the Atlantic and scattered to a hundred points in the British Isles, keeping in touch with them was an almost impossible task. Lt. Col. Jerry V. Matejka, signal officer with the Special Army Observers Group in London, sent word back to Washington by Brig. Gen. Joseph T. McNarney of the difficulties cropping up in the administrative job, for which he thought additional officers should be provided.[38]

Not all of the men turned out to be satisfactory students; some were poorly qualified in mathematics, and others lacked ability to absorb the intensive courses. For their part, many of the men thought the courses were not well taught, and lacked emphasis on important details.[39] It became apparent, moreover, that an essential part of their training called for flight over the patrol area, and despite a caution from the Signal Corps that any request for flight pay for the men would complicate relationships with the Air Corps, the hazard seemed to warrant it. Both General Chaney and Brig. Gen. Raymond E. Lee, the military attaché to London, recommended that a tenth of them be commissioned in the Air Corps in order to qualify for the extra pay. After first one ETG officer, then a second, lost his life in the course of the air training over England, the recommendation, in somewhat modified form, took effect. But hard fortune followed many of these volunteers. The Air Corps never recognized them; the Signal Corps lost eight of them; and the confusion following Pearl Harbor rolled up such a mountain of other problems that their discontent, however justly prompted, met with little sympathy.[40]

From the Office of the Chief Signal Officer

The first operational assignment of

[37] (1) History of the Massachusetts Institute of Technology Radar School, 23 June 1941 to 30 June 1945; (2) Ruth F. Sadler, History of the Electronics Training Group in the United Kingdom, 1944, pp. 1–10; (3) Capt Frederick Reinstein, Signal Corps Officer Schooling, 1944, p. 18. SigC Hist Sec File.

[38] (1) Ltr, Col Lansford to CSigO, 24 Oct 41, sub: Comments on arrival and processing of ETG officers; (2) Ltr, CSigO to TAG, 16 Sep 41, sub: Property ETG; (3) Memo, by Col Matejka, 5 Dec 41. SigC 352.11 ETG.

[39] Sadler hist cited n. 37(2), Exhibit K, Comments and Observations on the Training at Petersham Command School.

[40] (1) Memo, CSigO for ACofS G-2, 30 Jun 41; (2) Memo, Actg CSigO for TAG, 18 Aug 41, with 1st Ind, TAG to CSigO, 26 Sep 41, sub: Appointment of 2d lts SigC Reserve; (3) Memo, Lt Col Henry L. P. King, P&T Div OCSigO, for Asst Chief of Air Staff, A-3 Office Chief of AC, 25 Nov 41; (4) Ltr, King to Col Matejka, 29 Dec 41, sub: ETG, and 1st Ind, Hq USAFBI to CSigO, 13 Mar 42. SigC 352.11 ETG. (5) Ltr, Exec Officer OCSigO to Comdt SigC School, 18 Aug 41, sub: Transfer of ETG Officers to AC Reserve. SigC 326.21 Transfer 2, 1940–41.

Electronics Training Group men was to TRIGGER, an Air Corps project for a fighter command school at Orlando, Florida. Others were scheduled for SHADOW 82, part of the United States garrisoning of Northern Ireland. The two assignments epitomized the way in which hemispheric action irresistibly translated itself into a larger action. Time grew shorter. The smell of war grew stronger. Ominous incidents occurred on the open seas, and merged hemispheric waters with the Irish Sea and the Bay of Biscay. Even at the heart of the continent, even in the Ozarks, war probed. Everything that was done signaled a steadily widening area. Increase, expansion, intensification in every aspect of military preparedness dropped like a stone into a pool and sent ripples to the outermost banks.

On 1 August the Signal Corps establishment comprised 2,064 officers, 36,762 enlisted men, 6,902 civilians. During the month more officers joined the Corps at the rate of four a day and still more enlisted men at the rate of 112 a day. At the Signal Corps School, the Officer Department was overburdened and an Officer Candidate Department had begun, with 500 men on hand ready to go through the course. With a 30-percent attrition of unfortunates, the first class graduated at the end of September.[41]

In the House of Representatives, a two-vote margin extended the draft act. In Texas, draftees called before the expiration of the first Selective Service act were outfitted in 1918 uniforms and set to learning message center routine in their barracks. ("We would pretend a group around one [foot] locker was one unit and a group around a second locker another unit, and we would practice that way, sending each other messages.")[42]

Congressman Dewey Short of Missouri

sponsored a site for an additional Signal Corps Replacement Training Center in the foothills of the Ozarks near Neosho. The Army acquired it for the use of the Infantry, intending for the Signal Corps center to be established elsewhere, probably at Eastrop, Texas. General Olmstead proposed that expanding Signal Corps training be conducted at three more locations, in the West, South, and Middle West. For the latter, the site at Neosho became available. The first step in organizing it as a Signal Corps installation was taken in October with the appointment of Lt. Col. William S. Rumbough as commanding officer, activation then being scheduled for the first of the year. Rumbough was promoted to be a colonel, and four days afterward became a brigadier general. Camp Crowder, the open field near Neosho, was assigned a capacity of 12,000, then 14,000, then 15,500.[43]

For the first time in its history, the Signal Corps had more than three quarters of a billion dollars to spend. Fortunately skeptical of protestations the Signal Corps had

[41] (1) SigC 352.11 Ft. Monmouth 7, May–Dec 41, *passim.* (2) A History of Fort Monmouth, New Jersey, 1917–1946, pp. 84–85; (3) Capt Frederick Reinstein, Training Study of the Signal Corps Officer Candidate School at Fort Monmouth, N.J., 1944, pp. 5–11. SigC Hist Sec File.

[42] Interv, SigC Hist Sec with Sgts John E. Duffy and Lester Mansfield (formerly assigned 52d Sig Bn, Washington, D.C.), 16 Nov 44.

[43] (1) Interv, SigC Hist Sec with Col Henry L. P. King, Ret., Washington, D.C., 11 Oct 49. (2) Memo for File by Maj Pence, 18 Nov 41, sub: Conference with G-4 relative to additional buildings required at Camp Crowder for SigC tng. SigC MT-38 353 Gen. (3) Memo, SW for President, 27 Nov 41, sub: Temporary promotions. OCS 17336-102. (4) Ltr, Col Rumbough to Gen Olmstead, 22 Nov 41, sub: Reduction in allotment in housing capacity to SigC RTC at Camp Crowder; (5) AG Ltr, 6 Jan 42, same sub. AG 320.2 (12-29-41) MO-C. (6) Ltr, TAG to CSigO, 8 Dec 41, sub: Utilization of RTC Camp Crowder for SigC pers only. AG 320.2 (12-3-41)MR-C.
Camp Crowder was named for Maj. Gen. Enoch H. Crowder, the first world war counterpart of Maj. Gen. Lewis B. Hershey in the second.

made only a few months back that the combat organizations which had demanded $211,492,343 worth of signal equipment in fiscal year 1941 would need only $17,340,522 worth in fiscal year 1942, the Congress had agreed to three big additions to the budget estimate before passing the military appropriations bill.[44] Almost immediately it became clear that none of these was enough.

For the entire defense program, the figure in common use was $100,000,000,-000, and Donald Nelson, then Director of Purchasing for the Office of Production management, awed even the War Department by announcing that defense spending "must reach $35,000,000,000 a year to turn back the threat of Hitlerism."[45] President Roosevelt asked his Secretaries of War and the Navy specifically: how much production would be necessary to defeat the Axis, and could American industry do it? The Secretaries did not have the answer in their files, and turned to their supply services for the information. The Office of the Under Secretary of War began issuing directives asking for complete breakdowns of estimated requirements for 100 raw materials and reports on 350 others. The directives of August 4 and September 5 asked for so much information in such a short time that the Chief Signal Officer brought six engineers into his office from the New York Procurement District for thirty days to help his staff get the estimates out in time. The engineers worked by manual compilation and tabulation methods, using calculating machines for final computations, but there were not enough engineers. To help out, they set up an intensive training program, teaching girls from the clerical staff within the Office of the Chief Signal Officer to read blueprints and to make material estimates.[46] The final reports submitted to the President raised the military sights stupefyingly, but still not enough.

Mobilization plans had taken account of the fact that in time of war the Signal Section of the New York General Depot and the New York Signal Corps Procurement District would be crowded out of their quarters at the Brooklyn Army Base. Plans for occupying the Harborside Terminal Building at Jersey City, New Jersey, were abandoned when city authorities, concerned over the prospective loss of taxes, opposed the condemnation of the building for Army use. Then negotiations began for the use of the big Atwater Kent factory in Philadelphia. A price of $2,000,-000 was agreed upon and the property acquired through condemnation proceedings. Sears, Roebuck & Co., which occupied the plant, was in no hurry to release the space. An appeal to the court granted a brief delay, but by mid-October the Depot and Procurement District moved from Brooklyn to Philadelphia.[47]

---

[44] *Hearings Before Subcommittee of Committee on Appropriations*, HR, 77th Cong, 1st Sess, On the Military Establishment Appropriation Bill for 1942, pp. 457–60.

On June 30, the President signed the regular fiscal year 1942 military appropriations bill, which gave the Signal Corps $320,641,970. On 25 August, he signed the First Supplemental National Appropriation Bill, which provided an additional $347,150,825, all of it for equipment and $339,778,725 of it for combat organizations. André E. Gerard, The Story of Supply in the Signal Corps in World War II, Pt. I, 1945, pp. 28–29. SigC Hist Sec File.

[45] Proc Plng Bulletin, Vol. III, No. 8, 1 Aug 41, pp. 3–4.

[46] W. P. Worrell, Production Div Phila. SigC Proc District, Industrial Summary of Signal Corps Materials and Resources, 31 Jan 46, pp. 7–8. SigC Hist Sec File.

[47] (1) "Hart Protests War Department Plan to Buy Harborside Warehouse," *Washington Bureau, Jersey Journal*, June, 1941. (2) Civil Action 1689 in the District Court of the United States for the Eastern District of Pennsylvania. (3) Ltr, TAG to CSigO, 3 Nov 41, sub: Discontinuance of Sig Sec N.Y. Gen Depot and N.Y. SigC Proc District. AG 681 (10-31-41) MR-M-D.

The new site comprised over a million and a half square feet of space: 37 acres of land in the form of a triangle, bordered on the east by Wissahickon Avenue and on the west by the Pennsylvania Railroad. Four sidings provided space for twenty railroad cars. Buildings containing over 800,000 square feet of floor space covered 12 acres of the tract, leaving 25 acres for outdoor storage and future construction should it be needed. A power plant was available for emergency use, although ordinarily power would be supplied by the Philadelphia Electric Company. The land sloped sharply from east to west, which gave each floor of the buildings access to street levels, the top floor extending over the total size of the building and the floors below shrinking to conform to the natural topography of the land. Because they were supported on separate pillars, the floors were independent of the walls, wherefore expansion and contraction caused by heat and cold would have little effect. On the whole, the plant provided excellent depot facilities, although that part occupied as office space was cold and drafty; the roof leaked when it rained; sun glared through the glass-inclosed spaces by day, and the two night shifts shivered beneath the irritating glare of 500-watt unfrosted lamps fixed to the girders overhead. There was only a makeshift food service in the building and practically no restaurants nearby. The transplanted Brooklyn personnel viewed the site with disfavor, and quit in large numbers.[48]

On October 14 the Signal Corps activated a Procurement District at Wright Field in a pair of two-story barrack buildings. Lt. Col. William J. Daw, assigned to command it, began hiring the 157 civilians he was authorized to employ. Their mission was to handle all new contracts for aircraft communication equipment and

gradually to transfer old contracts, requisitions, back orders, and all radio aircraft material from the Philadelphia District. Within ten weeks the Wright Field Signal Corps Procurement District crowded itself out of its allotted space and far outran its original requirements for personnel.[49] In the Chicago Quartermaster Depot, the Eighth Corps Area Depot at Fort Sam Houston, Texas, and the New Cumberland General Depot at New Cumberland, Pennsylvania, signal sections also were becoming congested. At Avon, Kentucky, buildings were rising for the Lexington Signal Depot, designed especially to store and ship ground radars, and the vehicular equipment necessary to transport them.[50] At Ogden, Utah, Maj. Harry Lynch opened the new Utah General Depot with one civilian clerk-typist as an assistant. The plan was to move part of the Signal Section of the San Francisco General Depot there.[51]

In making him Chief Signal Officer, General Marshall had specifically ordered General Olmstead to do two things: to co-ordinate Army communications and to decrease the number of types of radio sets in use.[52] The second order fitted into the

---

[48] History of the Philadelphia Signal Depot, I, 107. SigC Hist Sec File.

[49] SigC File 314.7 Hist of Proc District—Wright Field Depot, *passim*.

[50] Elizabeth Simpson, Narrative History of Lexington Signal Depot, 1941, Ch. I. SigC Hist Sec File.

[51] History of the [Ogden, Utah] Signal Supply Section, 30 September 1941–1 November 1945. Ogden Gen Depot Sig Supply Sec File.

[52] CSigO, Annual Report, 1942, pp. 25 ff. Marshall's directive to Olmstead was oral, as Olmstead himself said. See also: (1) Services of Supply, *Annual Report, 1942*, p. 70. (2) Memo, CSigO for CofS, 22 Oct 41, sub: Simplification of sig com equip. OCS 16748-19. (3) Office Dir Production WD, Meeting to Review Signal Corps Program, 22 Jan 42. SigC EO 337 Conference, 1942–44. (4) 1st Ind, Gen Olmstead to TAG, 28 Feb 42, on Ltr, TAG to CSigO, 18 Feb 42, sub: Reduction of radio equip. AG 413.44 (2-17-42) MO-D, and also in SigC 413.44 Gen 1, Jan–Feb 42.

first, and the first was trapped in the *status quo.* Long experience had convinced Signal Corps administrators that this was the fact. Under the existing Army regulations, the Chief Signal Officer was responsible for developing, procuring, issuing and maintaining the Army's signal equipment, but the using arm which operated the equipment constituted judge and jury as to what was needed, and when. The Chief Signal Officer could advise, but he could not dictate. Events, world geography, and the advance of electrical science were diversifying signal equipment despite anyone's efforts to keep it simple.

The Laboratories were running hot. Not only was the Aircraft Radio Laboratory busy with the pre-eminent airborne radar projects, but, in addition, it pressed the development of interphone systems, of radio compasses and radio ranges, of electronic landing aids, long-range liaison radios, and adaptations of British command sets in the very high frequency bands. Yet ARL's mission was solely to meet Air Corps demands, and only Air Corps airborne demands, at that. It looked single minded by contrast with the New Jersey laboratories. All of the ground equipment for every part of the Army had to be developed at the Fort Monmouth congeries. The Armored Force required FM tank radios. The Field Artillery wanted them, too, as well as such specialists as sound-ranging and flash-ranging sets. Coast Artillerymen asked for radar, and ahead of them the Air Forces needed it for air defense from the ground. Coast and Field Artillery and Air Forces all sought meteorological equipment. The Infantry wanted more and better and lighter of everything, especially in wire equipment: switchboards, field cable, central office telephone and teletypewriter sets, and, to cap it all, heavy-duty carrier systems which would give even a primitive theater of war something of the easy, swift communications of the homeland.

This multiplication only reflected the evident course of the war abroad, a war which was to be, it plainly appeared, as much a matching of wits as of force. The contribution of science to such a war, the fact that a technological conflict was already in progress which was as real as a campaign, was, however, not yet fully understood. Marshall's order, then, to reduce the variety of communication equipment, to simplify, standardize, and mass-produce, Olmstead was understandably determined to carry out. The difficulty was that although the mission of the Signal Corps specified in the basic law was "all military signal duties,"[53] the regulations had already set unequivocal operating limits, which the General Staff reaffirmed.

The Signal Corps felt that the only way to control the number of radio sets in existence would be to center in a single communications agency all authority to determine what should be provided. Olmstead consequently followed the continuous tradition of his predecessors and contemplated an effort to persuade the General Staff to adopt a plan which would have co-ordinated communications and simplified equipment much more thoroughly than anyone else had in mind. Colonel Rives set forth anew the reasons for a single communications agency for the Army, but warned that in the prevailing climate strong opposition could be expected from the Air Corps and the Coast Artillery Corps. "The strength of the Air Corps case, if they choose to start a counteroffensive to take over their own development, procurement, issue and maintenance," he said, "should not be underesti-

[53] 10 U.S. Code 212.

mated. . . . Should we attempt to encroach on their domain they will set up such a strong defense that we have small chance of gaining our objective. The best 'defense' is an 'attack' and we can ill afford one at this time." [54]

There is no evidence that the memorandum was ever used, although Olmstead did broach the subject informally and found the Chief of Staff cold to it. General Marshall agreed that communications might be technically perfected if placed under single control, but he considered them to be broadly and inescapably an attribute of command not to be detached from tactics. Therefore Olmstead was less the chief of military communications than technical communications adviser to the War Department. That his wings were clipped, however, was not to say that he was not expected to fly. Within the boundaries set upon his power he was charged somehow with persuading much more independent and potent arms to yield some of their independence in the selection of equipment. They would have to reach a common ground in the Signal Corps.

Expressing regret that the "present policy of the War Department does not contemplate a centralization of such power" as would give a single agency full control over signal communications equipment, Olmstead proposed instead an expansion of the Equipment Section of his Office into a Coordination and Equipment Division to which each of the interested arms and services would assign qualified officers. [55] This was approved, and soon the Office of the Chief Signal Officer added liaison officers detailed from the Air and Armored Forces, the Field and Coast Artillery, the Infantry, the Cavalry, and the Navy and Marine Corps. Colonel Mitchell, an old hand in research and development, became the head of the division. If the problems of co-ordinating the equipment needs of the competing branches of the service were not sufficiently underlined by the day-to-day routine, there were signs hung to remind the officers: "Reduce the number of types of radio sets by command of General Marshall." Even so, was apparent that despite the most honest endeavor, there would have to be more, not fewer, types of radio to meet the ever-changing needs of global warfare. Said General Olmstead, "I can't just take an axe and break [radio sets] up." [56]

If Olmstead could not simplify the number of radio sets in signal communications, he thought he could at least simplify the Signal Corps structure, and this he set about to do. The organization that he had inherited had not changed fundamentally since General Gibbs's day. Olmstead sought to find out by inquiry and by personal observation what ought to be done, and how best to organize to do it. [57] He believed in organization; no problem could fail of solution, he thought, if only the proper sort of organization were set up to deal with it. He believed in giving his subordinates wide latitude, and never doubted that they would carry out orders effectively. "I know you have to do it by organization" was to be his approach to every administrative problem. [58]

---

[54] Memo, Col Rives, Opns Br OCSigO, for Chief of Opns Br, 17 Oct 41, sub: Brief on reasons for a single coms agency for Army. SigC ET 322.08 Briefs on Reasons for Single Coms Agency for Army.

[55] Memo, Actg CSigO for CofS, 22 Oct 41, sub: Simplification of sig com equip. OCS 16748-19.

[56] Meeting to Review SigC Program cited n. 52(3).

[57] One of his first acts was to write signal officers throughout the Army, inquiring what their supply problems were, and asking them for suggestions for improvement. Msgs, Actg CSigO to Sig Officers All Army and Corps Hq, 7 Aug 41. SigC 400 Gen 5.

[58] *Hearings Before Committee on Appropriations*, HR, 77th Cong, 2d Sess, On the 5th Supplemental National Defense Appropriations Bill for 1942, Title I—War Department, p. 65.

His first move was to collect some of the Office divisions (a division was then outranked by a branch) into an Administrative Branch, some into an Operations Branch and some into a Materiel Branch.[59] He thus foreshadowed in his office the revolutionary March 1942 reorganization of the Army into a Big Three by bringing a triumvirate of his own into being to replace an eleven-man staff. To do so required just such a breaking and scrambling of eggs as subsequently produced Lt. Gen. Brehon B. Somervell's Services of Supply. Olmstead assigned the Materiel Branch to Col. Roger B. Colton, Operations to Col. Otis K. Sadtler, and the Administrative Branch to Col. Stewart W. Stanley. He moved the Executive Control Section which Mauborgne had added in July down into the new Administrative Branch, but in September detached the unit, raised it to the status of a division, and placed it under his direct supervision, with Lt. Col. James A. Code, Jr., in charge.[60]

The next change emphasized the increasing complexity of training men for service with the Air Corps. It came in October, when Olmstead, making a distinction between air and ground training, withdrew the Aircraft Warning Section from the War Plans and Training Division, raised it to equal status as the Air Communications Division with Lt. Col. Frank C. Meade in charge, and gave it responsibility for training men for signal duty with the Air Corps and for aircraft warning duty.[61] In November he deprived the position of executive officer of much of its prestige and imposed a supervisory level over that officer and over the chiefs of the three branches. By this time Colonel Code was doubling as executive officer until he should be relieved in the control unit by Lt. Col. Charles E. Saltzman. The new

position of assistant to the Chief Signal Officer (renamed assistant chief signal officer, then deputy chief signal officer, then again assistant chief signal officer) to be occupied by Code usurped much of the responsibility formerly lodged in the Executive Office, which became in effect merely a secretariat. Personnel and training functions were divided into three: Military Personnel, Civilian Personnel, and War Plans and Training. General Olmstead selected Lt. Col. Henry L. P. King to head the Military Personnel Division. In the Civilian Personnel Division, Maj. H. C. Taylor became chief when the health of the civilian assistant to the Chief Signal Officer, Edward Barnett, forced him to relinquish his duties just before the onset of war. Lt. Col. Francis H. Lanahan, Jr., was in charge of the War Plans and Training Division. His division soon split down the middle with training removed from it. Lt. Col. Jay D. B. Lattin succeeded him as head of the Training Division.

Undoubtedly Olmstead's motive in his successive reorganizations was to have as few men as possible reporting directly to him. He intended to bring about a decentralization, or at least a redistribution, of control. Actually, the change created the sharpest kind of pyramid. Under Mauborgne, the Office had been a flat pyramid, an administrative structure like that of the executive branch of the government. Division chiefs had direct access to him, as did the chiefs of several field activities. This was like the similar organization of the Army itself, where the several "G's"

[59] CSigO, Annual Report, 1942, p. 25, and orgn chart, 14 Aug 41, opposite p. 29.

The Materiel Branch then embraced only three divisions: for Research and Development, for Supply, and for Plant.

[60] Signal Corps Administrative Log, 1939–1945, OCSigO Orgn Charts No. 2, 14 Aug 41, and No. 2a, 3 Sep 41. SigC Hist Sec File.

[61] Ibid., OCSigO Orgn Chart No. 6, 30 Oct 41.

and the field commanders reported to the Chief of Staff, or like the staff relationship of the Cabinet to the President.

Olmstead's reducing the Office from eleven units to three was an illusory sort of simplification, because the number of parts remained; they were merely one level lower down. As rapid events forced him to set up new divisions and he saw the number of his deputies increasing, he once again combined fundamentally dissimilar functions and managed again to reduce the secondary level of command, the level just below him, to three. This process occurred several times, always with a proliferation of branches on the main stalk, so that what it did was to put upon each of the three principal assistants to the Chief an amount of responsibility which Olmstead himself did not accept. The triumvirate, at first Stanley, Sadtler, and Colton, settled down in a few months to Code, Milliken, and Colton.

General Olmstead climaxed the reorganization on the eve of Pearl Harbor by inviting Secretary Stimson, Under Secretary Patterson, and General Marshall to a conference at which he asked key figures in the communications industry to plan and work with him and his staff in the process of putting the Signal Corps on a war footing. These businessmen constituted the Civilian Advisory Board, which he had established, or were members of the Advisory Council of Reserve officers, which he had revived.

Among them were Dr. Frank B. Jewett, chairman of the board of Bell Laboratories, who had served as an officer in the Signal Corps in World War I and who in 1941 was president of the National Academy of Sciences; Dr. W. R. G. Baker, vice-president of the General Electric Company; Dr. William P. Hilliard, a vice-president of the Bendix Radio Corporation; Walter Evans, manager of the radio division of Westinghouse; J. B. Coleman, chief engineer of the Special Apparatus Engineering Division of RCA Manufacturing Company; Dr. L. M. Hull, president of the Aircraft Radio Corporation; Brig. Gen. William I. Westervelt, Ret., experienced in mail order procedures, who was then a member of the government's Supply Priorities and Allocations Board; C. F. Horle, manager of the Radio Manufacturing Association's matériel bureau and on the board of directors of the Institute of Radio Engineers; Col. David Sarnoff, president of the Radio Corporation of America; Col. Carroll O. Bickelhaupt, assistant vice-president of the American Telephone and Telegraph Company; and Lt. Col. Darryl F. Zanuck, chairman of the Research Council of the Academy of Motion Picture Arts and Sciences.[62]

The interests of these men, brought together for a day in the Office of the Chief Signal Officer, duplicated the interests of a million other men who were as scattered as these were concentrated. Every word had an instant echo. The minutest cause took effect on a wide scale. Office doors had a way of opening right out onto the planet. Papers gained import in the mere course of the journey across the desk from *In* basket to *Out*. The call for signal equipment and signalmen rang every telephone. Olmstead felt that if he were to know which calls deserved the first answer he must trace them to the source. He decided to start at the most nervously alerted of the field exchanges, the Canal Zone. He invited Colonel Bickelhaupt to go with him while he spent two weeks inspecting Caribbean communications, and

[62] Signal Corps Information Letter, No. 2 (January 1, 1942), pp. 9 ff.

scheduled his departure for October 28, his return for November 11. In Panama, General Ingles was resolving upon the same direct action. Almost every mail had brought urgent appeals from him, and he wanted decisive responses with less quibbling over details. Not that he had any complaint to make of the new Chief Signal Officer: he credited the "confusion and side-stepping indorsements" to General Mauborgne's regime. But there was much to settle quickly, and he came up to Washington to settle it at first hand. Olmstead put off his trip for another month.[63]

Ingles wanted a clear-cut division of responsibility for construction of aircraft warning projects; in Jamaica, the Corps of Engineers was in charge, in Panama, mostly the Signal Corps, and in Trinidad the question was unsettled. He sought more skilled personnel, both civilian and military: in particular, two telephone engineers and two radio engineers, one of the latter to be an SCR-271 expert. He inquired about the signal construction company for the Rio Hato pole line, about the 32 officers who were not on a formal table of organization but who had been authorized him, and about bringing the 12th and 21st Signal Service Companies up to strength. He wanted to know why he could not get grades and ratings for the men in these organizations. How and when was the Signal Corps going to augment the Aircraft Warning Company, Puerto Rico? It lacked 5 officers and 100 men of being up to the required 500.

Puerto Rico had three SCR-271's on hand, but the stations were not up, the material not being expected to be shipped from the United States until late in November. One SCR-270 was in operation, and there was a system of ground observers reporting regularly throughout the twenty-four hours. A temporary control board was in operation in San Juan, but the material for the permanent one had not arrived, either. On Trinidad, sites for the radar stations were still in dispute, and nothing else had been done. "The Trinidad situation is going to prove decidedly embarrassing," he warned. The local signal officer had neither the equipment nor the draftsmen to get the proper design and layout work done.

And what of the rest of the equipment? Ten more radars had been granted him. Where were they? The tactical mission of the area also demanded more SCR-188's; above all else, signal and communications officers wanted complete radio sets, provided with enough spare parts to make repairs, and certainly not lacking cords, plugs, and power equipment. Tactical communications were still imperfect. During field exercises, the breakdown of the power supply had interrupted artillery communications for eight hours on two occasions and for forty hours on a third. That was galling; but more painful was the fact that administrative communications, the cerebral system of the whole Panamanian defense, fell silent whenever an air alert cut the master switches at the Canal powerhouses.[64]

To the West

Ingles was not being unreasonable. He

---

[63] (1) Ltr, Gen Olmstead to Col Bickelhaupt, 13 Oct 41. SigC 095 AT&T Co. (2) Bickelhaupt, excerpts from office diary, 6 Oct–26 Nov 41. SigC Hist Sec File. (3) Ltr, Gen Ingles to Gen Olmstead, 4 Mar 42. SigC 320 Augmentation AWS, Feb–Dec 42.

[64] (1) Minutes of Conference in OCSigO Between Sig Officer Caribbean Defense Comd and Officers of OCSigO, 31 Oct 41. SigC OT 320.3 AWS. (2) Gen Ingles, Digest of Conference Notes, 31 Oct 41. SigC EC 337 Conference With Ingles and Associated Papers, 1941–42.

was sizing up an emergency. War was on the way, and a national nerve center was at the mercy of a master switch. He and hundreds of others at home and abroad shared a feeling of waiting and tension. That the Canal might be attacked was quite possible. It seemed particularly vulnerable on the Pacific side, where no chain of island bases screened it. That side opened onto a waste of water too vast for patrol, which swept one third of the span around the world, all the way to the Philippines. The nearest bastion in this ocean was Pearl Harbor, 5,400 statute miles from Panama and 2,400 from San Francisco. A bastion at such distances from the mainland had to be self-sufficient. Both hemispheric defense and the defense of U.S. territorial and economic interests in the Pacific Ocean required it to be.

The defense of the Hawaiian group, especially of Oahu, appeared fairly well set. The islands had a garrison of 43,000. In the eleven months between 1 January and 30 November 1941 Signal strength in the Hawaiian Department jumped from 987 to 1,334. Among these were men drawn from Fort Monmouth and elsewhere to make up the first cadres of an aircraft warning company. More than half the total were assigned to the department signal officer, Lt. Col. Carroll A. Powell. In addition to his own office and an intercept detachment, he controlled the 9th Signal Service Company, consisting of one officer and 327 enlisted men stationed at Fort Shafter, and the Signal Company, Aircraft Warning, Hawaii, of 13 officers and 348 men, whose home base was Schofield Barracks. Not under Powell were various other units, notably the signal companies of the 24th and 25th Divisions and four signal aviation companies at Hickam and Wheeler Fields. Several of

these units had begun to be dispersed beyond Oahu. Platoons of the aircraft warning company were established in the waning months of the year, although without radar, on Kauai, Maui, and Hawaii; and details of the 407th Signal Company, Aviation, had gone to Midway and Wake to set up radio stations extending the Army Airways Communications System toward Australia.[65]

With this sort of strength, either its own or associated to it, the Signal Corps had been able to discharge its responsibilities for wire, radio, and radar in the Hawaiian Islands rather better than at some other points. A perimeter cable ringed Oahu, and from it branched a complex interlacing of communications to serve the island defense. The land cable supported the coastal command and fire control systems; other substantial, fixed wire provided the administrative telephones and teletypewriters to half a dozen old and new posts and airfields; and field wire brought ready communications to others, including the newest locations of all, the sites intended for radars.

The universal expansion going on under the unlimited emergency had approved a number of projects besides. Some, like a new 300-line switchboard for Forts Shafter and Armstrong, had started; others had not. A major construction project, for a long-lines trunk system, was in the hands of an officer and six enlisted

[65] (1) Figures from Machine Records Br AGO, 21 Sep 44. (2) History of the Aircraft Warning System in Hawaii: Signal Company, Aircraft Warning, Hawaii. AF Archives SIG-(Hawaii)-HI, 7896-54. (3) Hist Sub-Sec G-2 HUSAFMIDPAC, United States Army Forces, Middle Pacific and Predecessor Commands, III, 340, and App. Sig Sec, Vol. I. OCMH. (4) History of the 407th Signal Company, Aviation, Seventh Air Force. AF Archives SIG-407-HI, 5074-9. (5) MS File, Pearl Harbor. DRB AGO.

men, who straw-bossed a crew of as many as 450 laborers.[66]

Any longer communications were naturally a matter for radio, where the limitation which held the Army to 10 kilowatts of radiated power was becoming a serious handicap. The Navy could go up to 40 kilowatts, along with the commercial companies. Under certain conditions of the ionosphere, and especially at night, the Signal Corps' 10-kilowatt transmitter at Fort Shafter was strong enough to make direct contact with WAR in Washington; but by day, messages had to be relayed through such intermediate stations as WVY in San Francisco. These were matters that would work themselves out. Telephones, teletypewriters, and radios were familiar, their problems generally predictable.

Radar was the unknown quantity. The establishment of an aircraft warning system in the Hawaiian Islands had proceeded through a number of backings and fillings on the choice of radar sites and the location of an information center.[67] A

board of which Colonel Van Deusen was president had recommended, in April 1940, one fixed and seven mobile radar stations. The War Department did its part to help the project by including a $1,400,-975 request for it in the forthcoming fiscal year appropriations and by advancing $580,000 of that sum without waiting for the appropriation to go through. Up to mid-1940, therefore, things had appeared

other volumes, Parts 1 through 39, comprise the hearings, exhibits, and reports of the eight several investigations to which the Japanese war action gave rise.

The complete description of the series is as follows:
Joint Committee, 79th Cong, 1st and 2d Sess, *Investigation of the Pearl Harbor Attack* (Reports of the Joint Committee), Sen Doc 244 (Washington, 1946), 580 pp.

———, *Pearl Harbor Attack*, Pts. 1–11 (Hearings of the Joint Committee, 15 Nov 45–31 May 46), 5,560 pp.

———, *Ibid.*, Pts. 12–21 (Exhibits of the Joint Committee Hearings), 4,780 pp.

———, *Ibid.*, Pts. 22–25, *Proceedings of Roberts Commission* [Associate Justice Owen J. Roberts, U.S. Supreme Court, Chairman] *to Investigate the Japanese Attack of December 7, 1941, on Hawaii*, 2,173 pp.

———, *Ibid.*, Pt. 26, *Proceedings of* [Admiral Thomas C.] *Hart* [USN, Ret.] *Inquiry*, 565 pp.

———, *Ibid.*, Pts. 27–31, *Proceedings of Army Pearl Harbor Board*, 3,357 pp.

———, *Ibid.*, Pts. 32–33, *Proceedings of Navy Court of Inquiry*, 1,397 pp.

———, *Ibid.*, Pt. 34, *Proceedings of* [Colonel Carter W.] *Clarke* [USA] *Investigation . . . Pursuant to Oral Instructions of the Chief of Staff, U.S. Army, Testimony and Findings Concerning Handling of Certain Top Secret Documents*, 225 pp.

———, *Ibid.*, Pt. 35, *Report of Investigation by Lt Colonel Henry C. Clausen, JAGD* [AUS], *for the Secretary of War, Supplementary to Proceedings of the Army Pearl Harbor Board*, 695 pp.

———, *Ibid.*, Pts. 36–38, *Proceedings of Inquiry . . . Conducted by Admiral Henry Kent Hewitt, U.S. Navy, in Accordance with a Precept Dated 2 May 1945, from the Secretary of the Navy*, 1,341 pp.

———, *Ibid.*, Pt. 39, *Reports, Findings, and Conclusions of Roberts Commission, Army Pearl Harbor Board, Navy Court of Inquiry, and Hewitt Inquiry, with Indorsements*, 527 pp.

Up to within ten years of the events of December 7–8, 1941, no historian had undertaken the major analysis of the *Pearl Harbor Attack* which that enthrallingly inconsistent record invited. However, almost universal interest had produced a multitude of studies on a more restricted scale.

[66] (1) Ltr, Sig Officer Hawaiian Dept to CSigO, 11 Aug 41, sub: Construction and maintenance of tp systems. SigC 676.1 Gen 12. (2) Donald O. Wagner, Army Command and Administrative Network, Part I: The Pacific, 1945, pp. 13–14. SigC Hist Sec File.

[67] Because of the eight investigations of the Pearl Harbor disaster, material on the Aircraft Warning System, Hawaii, is abundant. By far the most comprehensive and convenient source is the MS file (in the AGO Departmental Records Branch) of the Army Pearl Harbor Board exhibit No. 58, Report on the Establishment of an AWS in Hawaii, with 181 inclosures. The account in this section is built upon this bulky file. The printed report of the Joint Committee on the Investigation of the Pearl Harbor Attack (which is printed elsewhere as well and is also included in the MS file) consists of 40 volumes generally known by the short title, *Pearl Harbor Attack*. Of these, the first—unnumbered—volume is devoted to the reports of the Joint [Congressional] Committee on the Investigation of the Pearl Harbor Attack, which brought the whole series to official publication. The

to be well in hand, even allowing for the fact that the plan had altered to envision a chain of three fixed and five mobile stations. The three fixed radars were to be placed on Kauai, Oahu, and Maui, as high as possible. That was the day when every country which had radar endeavored to put it as high as possible: the surface of a curved earth dropped out of scanning range much too close for comfort, as it was. So the site chosen at Kokee on Kauai was a wooded hill 4,220 feet high; on Mount Kaala, Oahu, the location was 4,050 feet up; and for Maui nothing would do but the National Park itself, where Haleakala, the largest extinct crater in the world, rises to 10,032 feet.

Kokee looked easy. An improved motor road led to a point within a mile of the site. The tract, moreover, lay within the confines of a forest reserve, to which the local authorities readily gave access. Yet many months passed before the Corps of Engineers brought it to the stage for signal troops to install the communication cable. These men arrived on 22 November 1941.

On Oahu, the Mount Kaala station, considered the most important link in the chain, proved also to be the most difficult to construct. The location appeared inaccessible for the last mile and a half unless an overhead cableway was built to transport equipment and supplies. According to engineering estimates, the cableway could be completed within five months. Unfortunately, the route selected started near the firebreak trail on the Schofield side, at the very spot which Schofield Barracks used as an artillery range. After taking more aerial photographs and making more surveys, the Engineers agreed to a different approach and began work in February 1941, at about the time when the cableway would have

been finished, had it gone along on schedule. In April they let a contract for cable. In June its priority was slashed to A-1-G. By this time Lt. Gen. Walter C. Short had become the new commander of the Hawaiian Department. He protested the low priority of the cable, and had already expressed to General Marshall his concern over the delays in setting up the aircraft warning system. These were chargeable primarily to the Corps of Engineers. Simultaneously, the Signal Corps, which escaped relatively unscathed in the subsequent recriminations, although individual Signal Corps officers were halted in their careers, was meeting its obligations by shipping the three SCR-271's to be installed as soon as the sites were ready. These were numbers three, four, and five off the production line, Panama having got the first two, and they reached the islands on June 3. The cableway was not completed until 1942, and Kaala, converted by compromise to VHF fighter control operations, was eventually abandoned for radar use.

The Maui site, because it was in Hawaii National Park, required Department of the Interior authorization. Interior officials felt that it was their duty to preserve the natural features of the park as directed by Congress. They were willing to do what was necessary for national defense, but they did feel that there must be other lands equally well suited to whatever purpose the Army had in mind. The spot selected, Red Hill, was on a crater at the very summit of the mountain, where park officials intended to construct a gravity water system, in order to obviate expensive pumping. Would not Kolekole, only five or six feet lower and outside the park, do as well? Radar was so secret that the War Department was hard put to it to explain the uses for which the tract was intended, or to insist that it and it alone would suffice. Van Deusen suggested that the station be made mobile rather than fixed: in that case, the Department of the Interior would have no reason to fear permanent changes, and possible disfigurement, in the location. No one picked up his suggestion; negotiations continued; and the Department of the Interior insisted upon making sure that the use of the area would not ruin the preserve. The National Park Service did issue the permit, however, on 29 April 1941. During the next months, work went forward as far as the point at which the Signal Corps could be invited in to start installing the radar and the Hawaiian Department signal officer could detail the crew to do the job. The Engineers gave him the word on 6 December and he ordered a crew to report on 8 December.[68]

Thus none of the fixed radars—Kokee, Kaala, or Haleakala—was filling the role prescribed for it in the defense of the islands. Nor were three others, which had been added to the first three in a later plan. For them, not only had the sites not been constructed, but the equipment had not been shipped out of San Francisco. The sites had been designated. One was Pahoa on the large island of Hawaii. The other two were both Oahu locations: Manauahua near the small Marine Corps airfield at Ewa, and Opana, at Kahuku Point, the northern tip of the island. Much more was to be heard of Opana, but from a mobile radar which took the place of the proposed fixed radar—in geography and in history.

Denied the use of the six SCR-271's, Hawaiian defense did have the six mobile SCR-270's which one of the latest plans had paired with them. Some of those first

intended for the Hawaiian Department had been diverted to Panama, but others had come from the factory in time to be distributed on Oahu between August and November. If all of the fixed stations had been ready, only three of the mobile would have been assigned to Oahu—two in reserve at Fort Shafter and one at Koko Head; the other three would have been dispersed to Kilauea Point, Kauai; Haleakala Road, Maui; and Kahuku Ranch, Hawaii. But when the SCR-270's came, in August, the aircraft warning company began immediately to install them around the rim of Oahu. The department's new Aircraft Warning Service board sensibly confirmed this action after the fact by observing that Oahu was certainly the heart of Hawaiian defense, since most of the vital installations were located there. Five 270's were in place by September, at Kaaawa, Koko Head, Fort Shafter, Waianae, and Kawailoa. The sixth, replacing the fixed radar planned for the northern tip of the island, was not ready to go into operation until late in November. This was the Opana radar.

The crewmen at each mobile set could report their findings by telephone to the information center. The center, in turn, was supposed to plot the information and if necessary to alert the interceptors and antiaircraft guns against danger. In November the information center was a makeshift, a compromise like the substitution of mobile for fixed detectors, but a perfectly functional compromise if it were manned. It occupied the top floor of a small signal warehouse in the cable yard

---

[68] This Haleakala station did not work out satisfactorily, either. Rain and snow formed ice on the antennas; and the lofty height so laboriously achieved only created a large dead space at a point beginning thirty miles out.

just outside Fort Shafter. The original, more grandiose, project had called for a bombproof within the operations building at Hickam Field. After many shifts, including one to a basement at Wheeler Field, new plans were developed for a bombproof structure to serve the Aircraft Warning Service, the Antiaircraft Group, and the Hawaiian Air Force, while the existing cable warehouse was given a temporary tag in the minds of the persons concerned.

In October a training program of sorts got under way. The Air Corps furnished a few officers to learn the duties of the information center, although their attention to the roster for the assignment was desultory. The Navy sent none, except for a Reserve officer who was detailed in November to be a technical adviser. Neither General Short nor Colonel Powell, who was traveling on the mainland, pressed the matter. On the other hand, it was arranged for fifteen signalmen to go to sea briefly in order to observe the action of Navy radar, and the Navy sent carrier-based aircraft over Oahu in simulated attacks for a predawn exercise of the Army radar. This exercise proved out exactly. With three of the SCR-270's ready to pick them up, the carrier aircraft took off. As they circled over the initial point, waiting until they were all assembled to attack, the airplanes revealed their distance from the radars to be approximately eighty miles. Meanwhile, interceptor aircraft, tuned up and ready to go, waited for the notification that the carrier airplanes had been detected, whereupon they took off and made contact with the Navy planes thirty miles out. There had been a six-minute delay for the word to get to them and thus a six-minute head start for the bombers. At an average air speed of about 190 statute miles an hour, the U.S. airplanes flew toward each other, the incoming doing 50 miles in 16 minutes, the outgoing waiting for 6 minutes and then flying 30 miles in the next 10 minutes. This exercise looked so neat and trig that Powell exclaimed when he heard of it: "When the fixed stations are installed in the higher mountains surrounding Hawaii, we expect to have as good an air warning system available for use as is now operating for the British on their tight little island, as their situation is approximately the same as ours is on Hawaii." [69]

Neat as it was, the interception exercise pulled apart at the seams upon closer inspection. The cloth was cut too close to the pattern. The exercise postulated fully trained personnel operating fully supplied equipment at full alert. These conditions had been artificially created for the test, but did not obtain as a matter of routine.

Informal practice with the pursuits based at Wheeler Field added to the training of the radar crews. They acquired most of their training, or, more exactly, picked up experience on the job, within the hours when their stations were open and operating . Supposedly this meant four hours in the morning and four in the afternoon Monday through Friday, Saturday being a half day and Sunday free. In practice, the scarcity of tubes and the risk of burning out the sets, with no tubes to light them up again, led to closing half the stations for ostensible maintenance during the afternoon while the other sets operated, or to closing them out for the afternoon altogether. In Washington, Powell asked for the money for the expensive vacuum tubes in order to keep longer

---

[69] Memo, Col Powell for Col Colton, 14 Nov 41, initialed as read by "GCM" [Gen George C. Marshall]. SigC EC 337 Conference with Ingles.

operating hours, but received the impression that the Budget Advisory Committee felt that there was too much insistence upon aircraft warning. And indeed, its estimate for the third supplemental appropriation to the fiscal year 1942 funds, planned on October 10 and submitted on November 13, asked for money sufficient only to operate the radars two hours a day, five days a week, fifty weeks a year, for training.

Thus far only the first five of the SCR-270's were operating at any time, but late in November the Opana detector was ready. It joined the others in a new schedule introduced on Thanksgiving Day, November 27. General Short responded that day to secret warnings from Washington by putting his command on alert against sabotage.[70] Inasmuch as the hours just before and just after daybreak were the most dangerous, Lt. Col. William H. Murphy, Powell's assistant and the acting department signal officer in his absence, gave orders to Capt. Wilfred H. Tetley, the commanding officer of the Signal Company, Aircraft Warning, Hawaii, to operate the radars for search every morning, seven days a week, between four and seven, the ensuing hours to be devoted to maintenance and to such training as could be undertaken. After a week end, November 29 and 30, during which nothing occurred to underscore the need to keep the stations open on Saturday afternoon and Sunday, provided the three-hour search were kept up in the dawn hours, a Signal Corps officer in the aircraft warning company sought for and received permission from the Air Corps control officer of the information center to close them on the following Sunday as soon as the 4-to-7 A.M. stint was finished.

The command relationship between these two officers illustrated the odd circumstance of the Aircraft Warning Service, which in Hawaii, as from its very beginnings ten years earlier, was nobody's baby. The Corps of Engineers' responsibility was to prepare and construct the information center and detector sites, the Signal Corps' was to provide and install the equipment and train the men, the Air Corps' was to operate the information center and to take over the detector operation when the men and equipment were ready. At the information center, moreover, the Navy, the Marine Corps, the Antiaircraft Artillery, and both the Bomber and Interceptor Commands of the Hawaiian Air Force were to fill assigned places in the balcony surrounding the plotting board, while the staff were to be Signal men and the Signal Corps was to provide all the communications bringing information in and sending warnings out. Unified action could come out of all this only under unified command.

All of the air and antiair defenses of Oahu, including those of the Navy, were to be made responsive to the information center. That was in prospect. The Navy promised action on assigning a liaison officer for its location at the plotting board. Antiaircraft had already done so; and although the Bomber Command had not, and the Interceptor Command's chief, Brig. Gen. Howard C. Davidson, was absent with Powell, lesser officers of the Air Corps were working many hours a day. The fixed radars had passed the protracted, ugly stage of delay and might be ready before very long. In any case, the six

---

[70] For an account of the confusion caused by G-2's extra sabotage message, see Mark Skinner Watson, *Chief of Staff: Prewar Plans and Preparations*, UNITED STATES ARMY IN WORLD WAR II (Washington, 1950), pp. 505–09 and 518–19.

270's made a highly satisfactory stopgap, as the war exercise had indicated they should. Aside from the fact that they were not permanently located or housed, the only mechanical difficulty still existing was minor trouble with the stand-by generators which were to be used in case commercial power failed.

Short, Powell, and Murphy all wanted to see the training carried a bit further before the detectors were turned over to the Air Corps, for numbers of the men as-signed to the aircraft warning duty had no experience with the work at all. But it was felt that, given enough opportunity, they would learn quickly and that their training as a whole would be sufficiently advanced for the transfer to be made soon. A joint Signal Corps-Air Corps opinion believed that another two weeks ought to do it. If nothing unexpected intervened, aircraft warning could probably be functioning as an integrated service by about the seventh of December.

Appendix

Signal Corps Equipment, World War II

The purpose of this appendix is to present a representative assembly of Signal Corps equipment, not only emphasizing the gear which was known in every wartime theater, but also including some items which, although under development or satisfactorily tested before the end of the war, never reached the field or even the production line. The grouping used is employed for convenience, in an effort to simplify the maze. It points out the principal but not necessarily the sole purpose of the equipment.

Military Communications

I. *Wire communication*
  A. Wire and cable
    1. Assault wire: very lightweight twisted pair (two conductors, each containing seven strands) which could be quickly laid over the ground
      a. W-130: weight 30 pounds a mile, talking range about 5 miles.
      b. WD-1/TT: weight 48 pounds a mile, talking range about 14 miles.
    2. Field wire: heavier and stronger, for use in long lines on the ground or on poles
      a. W-110-B: twisted pair, weight about 130 pounds a mile, talking range 12–20 miles.
      b. W-143: parallel pair, talking range up to 27 miles.
    3. Cable
      a. WC-534 and 535: heavily insulated cable, containing respectively 5 and 10 conductor pairs.
      b. WC-548: spiral-four cable containing two conductor pairs spirally wound about a core. This most popular cable was used wherever possible in carrier systems. It was supplied in various lengths, or cable stubs, chief of which was CC-358, a quarter-mile length complete with snap couplings and built-in loading coils.

c. Coaxial cable: hollow cable, or wave guide, for conducting VHF radio frequencies to and from the short VHF antennas (monopole whips, dipoles, etc.) and the associated transmitters and receivers.

B. Line-laying equipment

  1. Reels for laying or recovering wire or cable

    a. DR-4 and 5: small drums or reels for wire.

    b. DR-7 and 15: larger reels for cable.

    c. CE-11: a reel unit carried by the operator, suspended from his neck, for laying ¼-mile lengths of W-130.

    d. RL-16: a two-wheeled handcart carrying two DR-4 drums; replaced during the war by the somewhat larger handcart, RL-35.

    e. RL-31: a reel cradle for DR-4 and 5, carried by hand or in a vehicle.

    f. RL-26: a heavy reel unit with gasoline engine drive, carried in a vehicle designed in 1932 for slow speed operation. Speedier versions were undertaken in 1945 as RL-108 and 118( )/G.

    g. RL-27: an axle or shaft carried between two men and bearing a wire reel, DR-4.

    h. RL-37: a wire thrower incorporating a small engine to throw wire to a distance from the roadside, carried in a vehicle.

    i. MX-301 and 302: cases holding coils of W-130 and W-110 (wound by special machines) for rapid laying of wire at speeds up to 60 miles per hour.

    j. CY-196/ATC: container holding several MX-301 dispensers fitted beneath a liaison-type aircraft for laying W-130 from the air.

  2. Plow for burying lines (especially spiral-four cable)

    LC-61: towed by a truck; this device could plough wire or cable into the ground at 5 miles per hour to depths up to 18 inches.

C. Telephone equipment

  1. Telephone sets (the telephones themselves are called handsets, *see below under* Accessories, *handsets*)

    a. EE-8: standard field telephone set, hand-carried in a small case which included ringing equipment and batteries.

    b. TP-9: a portable set including the generator and ringing components of EE-8 plus a vacuum-tube amplifier which extended the talking range of the wire line.

    c. TP-3: a sound-powered field set, very lightweight, unencumbered by batteries, utilizing instead the energy of the speaker's voice to produce sufficient current in the wire for ranges of a few miles.

  2. Telephone amplifiers to extend the talking range of wire lines

    a. Loading coils: inserted at intervals in wire lines, they strengthen weak currents by induction

      (1) C-114: used to extend the range of W-110.

      (2) C-426: an improved coil for W-110 and W-143. Spaced at one-mile intervals in W-110, these coils extended its talking range to 20

miles. At ⅝-mile intervals in W-143, they could extend its range to over 80 miles.

b. Repeater sets: containing a power source and vacuum-tube amplifiers, repeater sets could boost wire ranges to scores and hundreds of miles

(1) For noncarrier lines, both two and four wires operating on voice frequencies only

(a) EE-89: a lightweight repeater for two-wire operation, weighing but 13 pounds including a dry battery.

(b) TP-14: also for a two-wire line but much heavier, 75 pounds, powered either by standard a-c or by 12-volt storage battery.

(c) TC-29: a portable repeater for four-wire operation. Its major component was repeater EE-99.

(2) For carrier systems (C-type), four (sometimes two) wires operating both on voice and on higher, or carrier, frequencies

(a) TC-23: a repeater set whose major component was CF-3, generally spaced at 25-mile intervals in spiral-four cable line.

(b) TC-37: a two-wire carrier repeater, whose major component was CF-5. CF-5, used in conjunction with converter CF-4 (part of TC-33) which converted four-wire carrier operation to two-wire, could extend the two-wire range to 150 miles.

(c) AN/TCC-5 and 6: small, lightweight carrier equipment developed for AAF. 5 was a miniature version of the four-wire repeater CF-3; 6 a miniature version of both the four-to-two-wire converter CF-4 and the two-wire repeater CF-5.

3. Telephone terminal sets: for four-wire carrier systems (C-type)

a. TC-21: this carrier terminal, whose major component was CF-1, could handle four telephone circuits on four bands between 200 and 12,000 cycles.

b. AN/TCC-3: a lightweight carrier terminal for AAF, a miniature version of CF-1 for use with either wire or radio relay systems.

4. Telephone switchboards

a. BD-9, 11, and 14: early boards of 4-, 12-, and 40-line capacity respectively.

b. BD-71 and 72: portable switchboards of 6- and 12-line capacity respectively, yet quite heavy, about 45 and 75 pounds.

c. SB-5 and 22( )/PT: lightweight (about 12 pounds) 4- and 8-line field boards to replace BD's-71 and 72.

d. SB-18/GT: vestpocket five-pound 6-line emergency board composed of plastic adaptor plugs U-4/GT.

5. Telephone central office sets (telephone exchanges)

a. TC-1, 10, and 20: Army headquarters sets, TC-1 with a capacity of 100 to 300 lines was based on switchboard BD-80; TC-10 was similar but more rugged and more easily transported. TC-10 was built around

switchboard BD-110 of 90-line capacity, but three to six of these boards could be used in series. TC-20 was built around switchboard BD-120.
    b. TC-2 and 4: sets for corps and division headquarters respectively employing switchboards BD-89 and 96.
    c. TC-12: a small lightweight telephone central office set for AAF, using BD-91 of 20-line capacity.
  6. Interphone equipment, used in tanks, armored cars, and aircraft
    a. For tanks
      (1) RC-53, 61, 99, and 146: for tanks and armored cars.
      (2) AN/VIA-1: an external phone at rear of a tank enabling an infantryman outside to talk with crewmen inside.
    b. For aircraft
      (1) RC-36, 45, and 51: for use in multiplace aircraft.
      (2) AN/AIC-1, 2, and 3: developed for use in rarefied air at great altitudes.
 D. Telegraph and teletype equipment, including radioteletype
  1. Telegraph
    a. TG-5: a portable six-pound field set or buzzer for manual keying and receiving.
    b. Boehme equipment: high-speed keying and recording office equipment for automatically transmitting and receiving Morse code signals over radio circuits.
  2. Teletypewriters and teletypewriter sets
    a. TG-7: a page printer; a tape printer had been developed in the 1930's as TG-6. Late in the war a lightweight page printer suitable for a backpack was under development as AN/PGC-1 to replace TG-7, which weighed over 200 pounds. Several teletypewriter sets were also developed under nomenclature EE-97, 98, and 102. They included teletypewriters TG-7 and 37 and were capable of operation in the field on such portable power sources as PE-77.
    b. TG-15: a heavy office set, 250 pounds, a page receiver and keyboard sender.
    c. TC-16: reperforator teletypewriter set including a reperforator transmitter, TG-26. This set could produce from wire-line signals a perforated tape bearing both the message letter text and corresponding perforations in the five-unit teletype code. If the set were in a relay station, the message could be relayed automatically by running the tape through the reperforator transmitter. TC-17 (with TG-27) was identical with TC-16 and TG-26 except for its special keyboard designed for use in weather communications.
  3. Teletype (and telegraph) repeaters and repeater sets
    a. TG-9: designed to replace TG-4 to extend the wire range of two-way manual or printer telegraph.
    b. TG-28 and 29: portable field repeaters to extend the normal telegraph range (60–90 miles) of W-110.

c. TC-18 and 19: repeater sets, terminal and intermediate respectively, for installation at the terminal or at an intermediate point along the wire line for boosting teletype signals. The chief components were repeaters TG-30 (terminal) and TG-31 (intermediate).

4. Teletype (telegraph) terminals

a. TC-22: a carrier terminal (of which the major component was CF-2) providing four teletypewriter circuits over a single telephone circuit, or twelve such circuits over spiral four since only the three upper voice frequency bands could be used for teletypewriter operation. Often telephone and teletype operation were combined, as one telephone and twelve teletype circuits. Such operation called for both TC-21 (telephone) and TC-22 (telegraph) equipment at the same terminal.

b. CF-6 (originally TC-28): a teletype terminal, used in conjunction with TC-22, to provide additional teletype circuits on two- and four-wire systems.

c. TH-1( )/TCC-1 (originally AN/TCC-1): speech-plus-duplex (S+DX) terminal equipment which provided telegraph transmission over an existing telephone line—allowing a carrier telegraph circuit while retaining the voice circuit.

d. AN/TCC-4: a lightweight carrier terminal developed for AAF, a miniature version of CF-2 providing four telegraph or teletype circuits over a two-wire system or over radio relay equipment.

5. Teletype (and telegraph) switchboards

a. BD-100: providing facilities for 10 telegraph printer lines; a heavy board, weighing about 200 pounds.

b. SB-6( )/GG: a lightweight portable switchboard for four-line telegraph or teletype operation, replacing older telegraph boards, BD-50, 51, 52, and 53.

6. Teletype (and telegraph) central office sets

a. TC-3: a small central office set consisting of teletypewriter TG-7, switchboard BD-100, rectifier, and portable power unit.

b. AN/MRC-2: a mobile teletypewriter station providing two-way (duplex) operation over radio SCR-399, a vehicular long-range set.

7. Radioteletype equipment

Much of the foregoing wire teletype equipment could be, and was, used in radioteletype systems, wherein radio waves substituted for wire lines. Additional equipment designed specifically for radioteletype operation included the following:

a. O-5/FR: a signal shifter which, when attached to a transmitter radiating continuous-wave radioteletype mark and space signals, caused the transmitter to send out two different frequencies or tones—one for mark, the other for space.

b. AN/FRR-3: a frequency-diversity radio receiver (2.5–26 mc) designed to receive both mark and space radioteletype signals on two frequencies or tones.

c. AN/FGC-1: a radioteletype terminal set designed to convert the two-tone (or two-frequency) signals received by AN/FRR-3 into suitable impulses to operate a standard teletypewriter.

d. AN/TGC-1: a semiautomatic tape relay set—a reperforator at the receiver punched a tape, on which it overprinted the letter text for the convenience of personnel unable to read the perforation code. The tape needed only to be manually inserted in the proper transmitter, according to the designation of the message it bore, to be hurried on its way over an outgoing circuit.

II. *Ground radio communication*

A. Short-range: up to 25 miles (usually five miles or less for radiotelephone sets)

  1. Portable sets

a. SCR-131 and 161: two-man pack sets providing continuous-wave Morse code signals up to five miles on 4–5 mc.

b. SCR-194 and 195: one-man pack sets providing voice signals only on 27–65 mc; Army's first walkie-talkies.

c. SCR-284: both portable and vehicular, providing both continuous wave and voice; rather heavy, weighing complete about 250 pounds.

d. SCR-288: a stopgap set for SCR-284.

e. SCR-300: the renowned walkie-talkie, an FM set, manually tuned over 40–48 mc. Signal Corps developed a version of this set for Field Artillery (FA) as SCR-619 (to substitute for SCR's 609 and 610) and a version of the 619 in turn for Armored Force as AN/GRC-12.

f. SCR-509: AF-II, an 80-crystal (any two frequencies preset) push-button FM radio; version SCR-709 had fewer crystals.

g. SCR-511: portable Cavalry guidon set, widely used by Infantry.

h. SCR-609 and 809: FA equivalents of SCR-509 and 709.

i. SCR-536: the handie-talkie, smallest of Signal Corps radio transmitter and receiver sets; a very popular AM set, followed by tropicalized and disguised versions, AN/PRC-4 and 6 respectively.

j. SCR-694: both portable and vehicular, successor to SCR-284 to whose crystal control it added two preset frequencies. Its receiver used alone was SCR-714. A late and improved version with continuous-wave range up to 75 miles was AN/GRC-9.

k. AN/PRC-3: a portable microwave transceiver developed for FA to replace signal lamps.

  2. Vehicular sets

a. SCR-171 and 178: sets carried in a vehicle but operated on the ground; providing a 15-mile range on continuous wave only, 2–3 mc.

b. SCR-179 and 203: cavalry saddle sets. SCR-179 was a saddle version of SCR-178.

c. SCR-209 and 210: continuous-wave, tone, and voice sets for Armored Force.

d. SCR-293 and 294: first FM sets for the Armored Force; crystal-controlled, providing voice communications only on 20–27 mc. A related FM set was SCR-298.

e. SCR-508: AF III, an 80-crystal (any ten frequencies preset) push-button radio (transmitter and two receivers) with variations SCR-528 (transmitter and one receiver) and 538 (one receiver). SCR-708, 728, and 738 were crystal-saving versions. All provided voice only on 20–28 mc, FM.

f. SCR-510: similar to the portable SCR-509 but designed for vehicles only. SCR-710 had fewer crystals.

g. SCR-608, 628, and 610: similar to AF sets 508, 528, and 510 but designed for FA with 120 crystals on 27–39 mc. SCR-808, 828, and 810 were crystal-saving versions.

h. AN/VRC-3: an FM set designed for tanks on the same frequency band as SCR-300 to enable crew men to communicate with ground troops using the walkie-talkie.

B. Medium-range: 25 to 100 miles

1. Portable sets

a. SCR-177: carried in a vehicle but operated on the ground, providing continuous wave, tone, and voice.

b. SCR-543 and 593: vehicular and ground sets for CAC; SCR-593 was portable, being the receiver portion only.

c. AN/TRC-2: a version of SCR-694 designed for eight- to ten-man pack for jungle or mountain use providing a continuous-wave range up to 100 miles.

2. Vehicular sets

a. SCR-193: set which could be operated to provide continuous wave, tone, and voice, while vehicle was in motion.

b. SCR-245: popular mobile set providing four crystal-controlled frequencies, selected by switches.

c. SCR-506: AF II; standard medium-range vehicular set providing continuous wave and voice on four preset crystal frequencies.

d. SCR-583: a saddle or vehicular set designed to replace the short-range saddle set SCR-203.

3. Transportable radio relay equipment, both terminal and relay sets, employing directional beams in VHF, UHF, and SHF; FM or pulse-time modulated

a. AN/TRC-1, 3, and 4: VHF, on 70–100 mc; 1 was a single transmitter-receiver set for simplex operation; 3 and 4 were terminal and relay assemblages respectively for duplex or for four circuits, carrier C operation.

b. AN/TRC-5: UHF, on 1500 mc, designed to provide seven radio circuits, employing pulse-time modulation.

c. AN/TRC-8, 11, and 12: VHF, on 230–250 mc, designed to provide four circuits, FM.

d. AN/TRC-16, 17, and 18: SHF, on 7000–8500 mc, designed as a very lightweight single circuit set for AAF.

e. AN/TRC-6: SHF, on 4300–4900 mc, a heavy duty eight-circuit set, employing pulse-time modulation.

C. Long-range: 100 miles and over

1. Portable sets

a. AN/PRC-1 and 5: suitcase continuous-wave sets designed for Military Intelligence Service (MIS).

b. AN/TRC-10: a larger, yet portable set, also for MIS.

2. Mobile sets: operated in trucks in motion or at rest and powered by large generators carried in trailers

a. SCR-197: powerful set but of poor mobility; on 1–18 mc with five preset crystal frequencies.

b. SCR-505 (AF I) and SCR-597: development of the former was supplanted by designs for the latter to provide 100 miles on voice, 350 on continuous wave (up to 5,000 miles from ground to aircraft) having three crystal pushbutton channels in range 2–20 mc.

c. SCR-299: excellent long-range set mounted in a panel truck and powered by the reliable PE-95 carried in a two-wheel trailer. The 299 replaced SCR-597 and became standard for all the Army. Version SCR-399 was housed in the standard shelter HO-17, mountable in any 2½-ton truck. An air transportable version, SCR-499, became standard for the AAF. These sets radiated about 350 watts of power, yielding dependable 100-mile range on voice while in motion, and many hundreds of miles on continuous wave, in Morse code.

3. Transportable sets

SCR-698: largest of SCR radio sets, a one-kilowatt broadcast transmitter, used (together with receiver and monitor set SCR-696) by MIS (Psychological Warfare Units) for broadcasting to enemy and conquered countries.

D. Radio remote-control devices

1. RM-7 and 14: used respectively with long-range SCR-197 and with short-range 194 and 195, permitting telegraph operation from a distance, or remote-voice operation over telephone set EE-8.

2. RC-47: used with the ground-air liaison set SCR-188 permitting transmission or reception, voice, tone, or continuous wave, over six to ten miles of wire.

3. RM-29 and RC-261, 289, and 290: remote-control units for a number of portable and vehicular short-range sets (SCR-300, 284, 608, etc.) permitting control at distances up to five miles.

4. AN/TRA-2: used with radio-relay sets AN/TRC-1, 3, and 4 permitting control at distances up to two miles.

III. *Air radio communication*
  A. Medium- and long-range command sets
    1. Airborne component
      a. SCR-183 and 283: HF sets (2–7 mc) operating on 12- and 24-volt airplane batteries respectively and providing continuous wave, tone, and voice for 10–45 miles between planes; 10–20 miles plane to ground.
      b. SCR-240 and 261: first airborne crystal-controlled preset radios for 12- and 24-volt batteries respectively. Designed in 1938–39 on 3–8 mc and intended to replace SCR-183 and 283.
      c. SCR-264: first airborne VHF pushbutton set on 100–130 mc initiated by Signal Corps Laboratories in 1939, but use of the set was precluded by adoption of British VHF, SCR-522.
      d. SCR-274: HF, up to 9 mc (VHF later added), 75 miles on voice, 150 miles on continuous wave.
      e. SCR-522: a VHF set (100–156 mc) operating on 24-volt batteries with four preset crystal-controlled pushbutton channels. A version designed to operate on 12-volt batteries was SCR-542.
      f. AN/ARC-3: an improved VHF set providing eight pushbutton channels.
      g. AN/ARC-6: on still higher frequencies (225–285 mc) and especially designed to overcome jamming by the enemy.
      h. AN/ARC-10: a relay set carried by an intermediate plane to extend VHF line-of-sight range from a ground station to combat planes flying beyond the sight of the ground station over the horizon.
    2. Ground component
      a. SCR-562, 563, 567, and 633: VHF transmitters and receivers used with fighter-control system SCS-2, semifixed.
      b. SCR-573, 574, and 643: ditto, used with fighter-control system SCS-3, mobile.
      c. SCR-643 and 644: fixed VHF transmitter and receiver stations.
      d. SCR-624: an adaptation of SCR-522 for ground use, good for 130 miles line of sight ground to plane. A similar adaptation for parachute drop was AN/CRC-1.
      e. AN/VRC-1: a jeep-mounted set combining the HF SCR-193 with the VHF airborne command set SCR-542 to provide both ground and air communication—continuous wave, tone, and voice—up to 60 miles.
  B. Long-range liaison sets
    1. Airborne component
      a. SCR-187 and 287: for 12- and 24-volt operation respectively; manually tuned, continuous wave, tone, and voice on 1–12 mc range up to 2,000 miles.
      b. AN/ARC-8: derived from SCR-287 but incorporating pushbutton tuning; composed of transmitter AN/ART-13 and receiver BC-348 or AN/ARR-11.

2. Ground component
    a. SCR-188: provided continuous wave, tone, and voice on 1–12 mc, the continuous-wave range matching that of the airborne SCR-187 and 287.
    b. SCR-237: developed with 10 preset crystal channels with intent to replace SCR-188.
    c. SCR-499: a version of the long-range SCR-399, packaged for parachute drop in 200-pound bundles. The set became standard for AAF ground liaison. A lighter weight parachute version was developed as AN/CRC-5.
C. Short-range paratroop and glider sets
    1. SCR-585: a modified handie-talkie for use in gliders, talking range up to one mile.
    2. AN/ASC-1: having a range of but 500 feet, for talk between glider and tow plane.
    3. AN/PRC-2: a VHF set for paratroop liaison.
    4. AN/TRC-7: a heavier VHF paratroop liaison set weighing 100 pounds, parachuted in four packages including a hand generator and a 30-foot sectional mast.

IV. *Visual communication*

A. Flags
    1. MC-44: semaphore, 18″ square, divided diagonally into red and white portions.
    2. MC-113: semaphore flag kit containing two MC-44's.
    3. M-238: set of colored flags for signaling between tanks.
B. Panels and panel sets: cotton cloth strips variously colored to identify ground areas and units for friendly planes
    1. AL-119, 120, etc.: square or rectangular, for aerial liaison.
    2. AP-30-A and C: in dark colors, for use on snow or light backgrounds.
    3. AP-30-B and D: in light colors, for use on normal backgrounds.
    4. AP-33 and 34: for signals to high flying planes.
    5. AP-50: large panels (2 x 12 ft) in white, yellow, and red (the last two colors being brilliantly fluorescent).
C. Lamps, to transmit blinker code by night or day
    1. Signal
        a. EE-80-A: heavy (194 pounds) 12-inch lamp and tripod signaling by white, red, or green flashes using commercial 115-volt alternating current or direct current, range up to 12–14 miles.
        b. EE-84: portable searchlight-type set (42 pounds) operating on dry cell batteries with range up to 5,000 yards in sunlight, far greater at night; white or red flashes.
        c. SE-11: highly portable (7–8 pounds), flashlight-type, aimed like a gun with trigger key, daylight range 1,000–2,000 yards using red filter.

2. Identification: enabling planes to identify friendly ground vehicles and installations

    a. AN/VVX-1: delivering intermittent flashes visible in bright sunlight three miles aloft or a mile or more along the ground.

    b. AN/PVX-1: similar to above but portable, operating on self-contained battery to mark front lines, installations, etc. It could also serve as blinker signal lamp.

D. Optiphone (or photophone: *i.e.,* talk by light, by a steady modulated beam, not blinker light)

    AN/TVC-1: formerly SE-10, involving a modulated light-beam transmitter and receiver, portable, with minimum range of 5,000 yards in sunlight and able to link telephone lines so as to span obstacles such as a river.

V. *Pigeon communication*

  A. Lofts, transportable, for housing large numbers of birds

    1. PG-46: prefabricated sectional housing for fixed use.

    2. PG-68/TB: a combat loft, collapsible and easily transported by a truck or trailer.

  B. Pigeon equipment including containers for carrying a few birds

    1. PG-60, 102/CB, 103/CB, and 105/CB: portable, carrying two to four birds, for combat troops.

    2. PG-100/CB and 101/CB: four- and eight-bird containers respectively, with parachutes for dropping to paratroops or isolated ground forces.

  C. Message holders to fasten to the legs of the birds

    1. PG-14: aluminum holders.

    2. PG-52, 53, 54, and 67: plastic substitutes for the PG-14.

  D. Pigeon vest, PG-106/CB, retaining a single bird, to be worn by paratrooper

VI. *Reproduced communication*

  A. Public address sets

    1. PA-1, 2, 3, 4, 5, and 6: sets varying from heavy systems powered by gasoline engine generators to simple portable microphones and amplifiers powered by batteries.

    2. AN/TIQ-1, 4, and 5: powerful outdoor sets with speaking ranges up to 7,000 yards.

    3. AN/PIQ-2, TIQ-2, and UIQ-1: portable battery sets.

  B. Recorders and reproducers of sound

    1. RC-17 and 169: recorders of speech or signals whether telephone, telegraph, or radio. RC-179 and 199 were used in radio intercept work to record any type of signal.

    2. MC-364: record player and amplifier.

    3. AN/ANQ-1 and 2 and GNQ-1 and 2: airborne voice recorders and ground playback equipment developed for air reconnaissance work.

  C. Facsimile

1. RC-58: tape facsimile developed for use in AF vehicles to reproduce hand printed message texts received over vehicular radio sets.

2. RC-120: a page transceiver, to send or receive a seven-inch square page—text, map, picture—transmission or reception requiring seven minutes to complete. A larger version for fixed station use was AN/TXC-1, which could handle a page 12 by 18 inches over voice communication channels.

3. AN/GXR-1 and PXT-1: a portable receiver and transmitter developed for the Office of Strategic Services for continuous-wave transmission of 4-by-5-inch copy in 15 minutes.

4. AN/GXC-2 and 3: transceivers for 4½ by 5¼ and for 8 by 10½ copy respectively.

Military Operations

I. *Radar*

  A. Searchlight control

    1. SCR-268: standard SLC set employing long waves, 1½ meters, on 205 mc.

    2. SCR-668 and 768: experimental SLC sets, the latter patterned after the British "Wigwam" radars enveloped in tents.

    3. AN/TPL-1: lightweight microwave set for use with 60-inch searchlights, developed from SCR-668.

  B. Early warning: for long-range detection of aircraft. EW radars merged into medium-range EW and GCI sets.

    1. SCR-270 and 271: respectively mobile and fixed long wave (3 meters, 109 mc) search sets, giving azimuth and range of aircraft up to 150 miles away. Versions designed to give elevation also were SCR-289, 530, and 531. SCR-539 was a PPI indicator developed for use with the 270 and 271.

    2. SCR-548 and 648: experimental outer harbor aircraft detectors, shipborne.

    3. SCR-602: copy of the British LW, lightweight warning radar, using long wavelengths at 200 mc.

    4. AN/TPS-3: an efficient lightweight radar developed from SCR-548, using medium wavelengths on 600 mc. Other transportable EW radars for use in mobile situations, such as invasions, were AN/TPS-1 and 2, the latter totaling less than 600 pounds.

    5. AN/TPS-10: a height finder and lightweight EW with narrow "beavertail" beam, for Air Forces use in hilly country; dubbed "Little Abner."

    6. AN/CPS-1: the powerful MEW, or microwave early warning radar, a huge set on 3,000 mc, radiating a 10-cm wave with range up to 200 miles.

    7. AN/CPS-2: a medium-range EW developed to employ variable frequencies between 510 and 725 mc in order to evade jamming.

    8. AN/CPS-4: a height finder only, to supplement MEW and SCR-270 and 271.

9. AN/TRS-1: electronic fence, employing continuous-wave radiations; a beat-reflection-type radar developed to detect aircraft flying over hilly terrain where ground reflections handicap pulsed-type radar search sets.

C. Ground-controlled interception

1. SCR-516 and 527: the 516 was developed from the SCR-268; the 527 was copied from the British GCI.

2. SCR-588: American copy, built in Canada, of the huge British CHL/GCI using long wavelengths.

3. SCR-615: a large transportable 10-cm microwave radar with range up to 90 miles.

4. AN/CPS-5 and 6: improved microwave sets for GCI applications.

D. Coastal defense and harbor surveillance: for long-range detection of surface craft.

1. SCR-296: a large fixed radar operating on medium waves, 700 mc.

2. SCR-582: a valuable microwave set, on 10-cm at 3,000 mc. Version SCR-682 was transportable.

E. Gun laying

1. For coast defense, against surface vessels

a. SCR-598: similar to SCR-296 but of shorter range and greater accuracy for fire control purposes, directing gunfire against such small craft as motor torpedo boats.

b. AN/FPG-1 and 2: fixed sets using very short wavelengths, 3-cm, at 10,000 mc which permit great accuracy.

c. AN/MPG-1 and TPG-1: respectively mobile and transportable 3-cm coastal gun layers, long range and very accurate.

2. For air defense and AA batteries, against airborne targets

a. SCR-547: a "radio height finder," replacing optical height finders supplying target range and elevation data. Known as "Mickey Mouse."

b. SCR-545: a gun layer using relatively a long wavelength for search and a microwavelength for tracking or following the target. It was a semiautomatic gun layer, requiring hand tracking.

c. SCR-584: an excellent 10-cm gun layer, completely automatic for fire on unseen targets, very accurate.

3. For aircraft, against airborne and surface targets

a. Aircraft range only, aiding fire on visual targets

(1) AN/APG-5: automatic range finder for turret gunners in B-17's and 24's, developed from experimental SCR-523 and 726.

(2) AN/APG-11: designed for toss bombing, from plane to plane.

(3) AN/APG-14: for B-29 gunners.

b. Aircraft gun sight radars, requiring hand tracking

(1) AN/APG-13: effectively used with the 75-mm nose cannon of B-25's, named "Falcon."

(2) AN/APG-15: an efficient radar gun sight for tail gunners of heavy bombers.

    c. Aircraft gun laying, automatic, for blind firing
       (1) AN/APG-1: (SCR-702) used in the Black Widow night fighter, P-61. Weighed 700 pounds.
       (2) AN/APG-2: (SCR-580) a 10-cm AI and AGL for bomber gun turrets. A 3-cm version for B-32's was AN/APG-16.
       (3) AN/APG-3: a smaller 3-cm AI and AGL for B-29's.

F. Tail warning
    1. AN/APS-13: a small 20-pound radar for fighter planes; it flashed a red light and rang a bell in the cockpit to warn that another plane was approaching from the rear.
    2. AN/APS-16 and 17: similar tail-warning indicators for bombers.

G. Air interception
    1. SCR-540: patterned after the British AI Mark IV, which operated on a long wavelength, 1½ meters, at 200 mc.
    2. SCR-520 and 720: AI-10, superior 10-cm, 3,000 mc, microwave sets, but heavy, 600 and 500 pounds respectively.
    3. AN/APS-4 and 6: smaller improved AI's, operating on 3-cm wavelengths at 10,000 mc, developed in part from SCR-537.

H. Airborne search and bombing: early search types were called air-to-surface-vessel radars, ASV, which developed into low-altitude bombing types, LAB, and bombing-through-overcast, BTO, types.
    1. SCR-521: a long wave (1½ meters) ASV, patterned after the British ASV Mark II.
    2. SCR-517: ASV-10, a microwave 10-cm radar operating in the S-band at 3,000 mc. Weight 500 pounds. A smaller version for LAB, blind bombing at low altitudes, was SCR-717. Other SCR's in these categories were SCR-519, a 10-cm search and tracking set, and SCR-667, a 3-cm, X-band, set.
    3. AN/APQ-5: an auxiliary bombsight much used in combination with the SCR-517 as a LAB set.
    4. AN/APQ-11 and 12: (SCR-626) radar bombsights, designed especially for launching airborne torpedoes.
    5. AN/APQ-13 and APS-15: superior BTO's, 3-cm sets (X-band), known to the Americans as "Mickey," to the British as H2X. They performed well at high altitudes and showed ground features in considerable detail.
    6. AN/APQ-7 and 10: 3-cm BTO's of even greater clarity than "Mickey." APQ-7, dubbed "Eagle," weighed nearly 1,000 pounds.

I. Identification, friend or foe
    1. Mark IV, American sets, involving equipment independent of any associated radars, giving instant response
      a. Ground interrogator-responsor
        SCR-532 and 533: for short and long ranges respectively.
      b. Airborne transponder
        SCR-515: 150-mile range.

2. Mark II, adopted from the British
SCR-535: airborne transponder, which swept the frequency bands of the early EW radars, and caused its plane's echo in their scopes to appear large. No ground interrogator-responsor was needed.
3. Mark III, British IFF, standard for all the Allies; it depended upon associated radars for power and design; response was delayed
   a. Ground interrogator-responsors, differing for each radar type.
   RC-148, 150, 151, 127, 184, etc.: associated with SCR-268, 270, 271, 527, 584, etc.
   b. Airborne transponders
   SCR-595 and 695: on I-band, 157–187 mc. The 695 including also G-band, 200 mc, for benefit of long-wave GCI radars.
   c. Airborne interrogator-responsor
   SCR-729: enabling a plane to challenge the identification of other planes, which could answer if they carried SCR-595 or 695. SCR-729 was also much used in radar beaconry (*see under* Navigation, Radar).
4. Mark V/UNB: a universal identification and beacon system developed by U.S., British, and Canadian services, involving pulse sets in UHF.

J. Bomb proximity fuzing: fuzes operating on radar principles, emitting radio waves whose reflection from a nearby target served to explode the missile carrying such a fuze
1. MC-382: designed for aerial rocket bombs.
2. AN/CPQ-1, 2, 3, 5, and 6: designed to detonate bombs just above ground targets.

K. Glide-bomb control
1. RC-171: radar homing bomb equipment, an S-band radar fitting into a winged bomb designed to seek, or home on, a target illuminated by a radar transmitter in the bombing aircraft.
2. AN/APG-7: send-receive radar bomb, similar to RHB above, but containing its own radar transmitter.

L. Mortar location, enabled by radar tracking of the trajectory of the mortar shells
1. AN/TPQ-2 and 4: microwave radars.
2. AN/TPQ-3: a lighter weight medium-wave version, operating on 600 mc, modified from AN/TPS-3.

M. Personnel detection: radars of the continuous-wave, beat-reflection type
1. AN/PPQ-1: a very short-range, hand-carried set, developed to serve as an aid to night patrols, or as a sensory aid for the blind.
2. AN/PPS-1: a lightweight pack set to detect moving objects (tanks, trucks, men).

II. *Radio*
A. Mine detection: mine detectors bore Signal Corps designations, were produced and distributed by Signal Corps, but their development was a responsibility of the Engineer Corps

   1. Portable: carried and operated by one man
      a. SCR-625: standard detector for metallic mines.
      b. AN/PRS-2, 3, and 4: portable detectors for nonmetallic mines.
   2. Vehicular
      a. AN/VRS-2: detector designed to be mounted on a boom projecting
      ahead of a jeep and to stop the vehicle automatically upon detecting a
      mine ahead.
      b. AN/VRS-3: a similar set designed for use by tanks.
B. Remote mine detonation: remote-control system for detonating mines
   AN/TRT-1 and TRR-2: transmitter and receiver respectively, the latter
   designed to operate under water adjacent to a mine, which it could detonate upon receiving properly coded signals from the transmitter miles
   distant—up to 40 miles when the transmitter was carried by a plane.
C. Bomb control
   1. For glide bombs Azon and Razon
      a. RC-186 and AN/ARW-16: transmitters to control the bombs.
      b. RC-185 and AN/CRW-2 through 5, and 7 through 9: a group of
      receivers designed to fit within the bombs to receive the controlling
      impulses and transfer them to flight-control mechanisms.
   2. For power-driven bombs, such as rocket bombs and War Weary Willies,
   which were jalopy bombing planes loaded with explosives and directed by
   remote control against the enemy
      a. AN/ARW-18: transmitter, carried by the mother craft.
      b. AN/ARW-1: receiver carried by the missile.
   3. Automatic bomb release: whereby the bombardier in lead plane could
   release the bombs of all planes in his squadron simultaneously
      a. AN/ARW-9: controlling transmitter (also used with Azon and
      Razon).
      b. AN/ARW-10: receiver, which actuated bomb release.
   4. Tracking of robot bombs: developed for projected use of American version of the V-1 buzz bomb (JB-2)
      a. AN/ART-19: transmitter carried by JB-2.
      b. AN/CRD-5: a direction finder to track signals from the above trans-
      mitter.
D. Direction finders (DF's) for fighter-control: VHF DF components of
fighter-control (or SCS) systems. The DF's took continuous bearings on aircraft radio emissions, especially airborne pipsqueak (RC-96), which radiated
a signal once a minute. The bearings, laid out on plotting boards at control
centers, served to track the planes in flight and enabled ground-control
officers to guide the planes by radio telephone.
   1. SCR-564, 565, and 566: fixed and mobile DF's, components of SCS-2
   (*see under* Air radio communication, Ground component).
   2. SCR-575 and 634: mobile and air transportable respectively, components of SCS-3.

3. SCR-645: fixed VHF direction finder.

4. AN/CRA-1: a kit embodying an electric goniometer by which VHF sets (SCR-575 and 634) whose H-Adcock antennas had to be rotated by hand, could be converted so as to provide instantaneous indication of direction in a cathode-ray scope.

5. SCR-552: a VHF DF with unique antenna, a conicle or funnel-shaped dipole, which rotated constantly at 75 rpm.

III. *Wire*

A. The operators at SCS control centers and at information, filter, and operation centers for aircraft warning required rapid communication facilities. These were supplied by extensive wire nets, sometimes supplemented by radio also.

1. SCR-561 and 572: not radio sets but assemblies of telephones, switchboards, DF plotting equipment, filter and intercept tables, boards, etc. employed in co-ordinating fighter-control systems SCS-2 and 3.

2. SCS-5: an information center assembly, transported by six 2½-ton trucks.

3. SCS-6 and TC-15: mobile information center and filter center respectively, being successively smaller editions of SCS-5.

4. AN/TTQ-1 and 2: filter and operation centers transportable in two and one trucks respectively for plotting flights of aircraft. Still smaller versions for use with gun and searchlight battalions were AN/TSA-1 and 2.

B. Direction-finding and intercept centrals: transportable sets housed originally in K-35 trailers, later in HO-17 and in HO-27 shelters, and manned by radio intelligence units for locating enemy transmitters and for intercepting and recording their traffic

1. TC-8: a DF central set housed in two shelters and linked to associated DF radio sets by wire (or radio) nets.

2. TC-9: a RI (intercept) central housed in three shelters.

IV. *Sound, thermal, light*

A. Ranging equipment: for determining the range or distance to enemy artillery

1. Sound ranging: utilizing the different arrival times of a muzzle blast received by several spaced microphones to determine the direction and distance to an enemy gun

a. GR-3-C: utilizing a maximum of eight microphone listening posts.

b. GR-8: a lighter weight set using a maximum of six very sensitive microphones; a modified version became AN/TNS-2.

c. GR-6: an extremely accurate set using three microphones; a modification became AN/TND-1.

d. AN/TNS-1: designed to locate enemy mortars by sound ranging up to 5,000 yards.

2. Flash ranging: utilizing the data received by photoelectric cells from muzzle flashes

    a. GR-4: standard set in World War II; but it was too heavy and too
delicate.

    b. AN/GTC-1: a lighter weight, yet more rugged, set.

  3. Sound and flash ranging

    AN/TSS-1: combined both sound and flash reception at a single obser-
vation station. Flash reception was at first accomplished by a photoelectric cell, later by an infrared detector.

  4. Hydrocoustic ranging: equipment utilizing underwater sound, developed for Coast Artillery Corps until it was transferred from the Signal
Corps to the Navy in June, 1942

    GR-5: hydrocoustic tracking set, able to track vessels by their under-
water sound to distances of 100,000 yards; a smaller version was GR-7.

B. Bomb-control (television, for remote control of flying bombs)

  1. AN/AXR-1: television receiver (formerly SCR-550) for installation in
the controlling plane.

  2. AN/AXT-2 and 3: transmitters (formerly SCR-549) for installation in
the controlled craft or flying bomb.

C. Photoelectric bomb fuze

    MC-380: a proximity fuze developed to fit into the nose of a bomb such as
the airborne M8 rocket for use against aircraft. The fuze contained a
photoelectric cell which, on detecting a reduction in light intensity as the
missile came within 60 feet of its target, detonated the bomb.

D. Photoelectric and supersonic detectors, or sensory aids: carried in one
hand, these devices (including the radar sensory aid AN/PPQ-1: under
Operational radar, Personnel Detection), could aid blind men, or night
patrolmen, to detect the direction and distance of nearby objects

  1. AN/PVQ-2: utilizing a pulsed beam of light which, when reflected
from an object, impinged upon a photoelectric cell. This cell in turn modulated an audio signal, which the user detected in an earphone. The aid
was unaffected by nonpulsed light, such as sunlight and ordinary electric
light.

  2. AN/PNQ-1: utilizing a pulsed-supersonic tone (stealing the secret of
the flight control of a bat). The tone, when reflected, was picked up by a
microphone, supersonic like a bat's ear, and reduced to an audible tone in
a hearing aid worn by the user.

E. Thermal detection

    Thermal equipment, utilizing infrared or heat radiations, largely occupied
Signal Corps laboratories in the early 1930's at the beginning of radar
development, which soon displaced infrared research. Yet infrared equipment had proved useful in detection both of ships and aircraft, in searchlight directing and in early forms of the radar SCR-268. It had been tried
in 1941, as the Thermopticon, aboard a B-18 bomber and had detected a
second B-18 up to 1,200 feet away. Late in the war an infrared detector
was incorporated in the sound- and flash-ranging set AN/TSS-1 to detect
muzzle flashes, replacing a photoelectric cell which had first been used in

this set. Also late in the war the Navy desired an infrared ship detector to be used during radar silence, and called upon Signal Corps for
>AN/SSS-1: a shipborne heat-radiation detecting equipment to search for and detect ships up to ranges of 15,000 yards.

V. *Magnetic*

Magnetic airborne detector, or magnetometer
>RC-132: an airborne device which, dangled beneath a low-flying plane, could detect a submerged submarine by its magnetic field, which extends from below the water up into the air. RC-132 became AN/ASQ-1, variations of which were designated ASQ-2 and 3.

Navigation

I. *Radio*

A. Compasses: airborne loop-antenna direction-finding receivers (DF's)
  1. SCR-242: a LF-MF 12-volt set. A 24-volt version was SCR-282.
  2. SCR-246: LF, 12 volts. A 24-volt version was SCR-276. Another version developed to home on much higher frequencies in VHF was SCR-256.
  3. SCR-263, 273, and 280: dual remote-control compasses, operating in LF and MF.
  4. SCR-269 and 279: standard automatic radio compasses for 24 and 12 volts respectively, LF and MF. Later versions of the standard SCR-269 were AN/ARN-6 and 7 (or SCR-599 and 639 respectively).

B. Beacons operating on radio-directional principles
  1. Ground Forces homing equipment
   a. Beacon attachments for radio transmitters
     (1) RC-163: HF directional attachment, 25-mile range, for vehicular radios SCR-508, 510, 608, 610, etc.
     (2) RC-302: attachment converting SCR-284 and 694 into beacons for guiding troops; similar to SCR-277.
     (3) AN/TRA-3: all-directional, rotating antenna set, similar to RC-163 but lighter in weight.
   b. DF attachments for radio receivers
     (1) RC-300 and 303: for SCR-300 (walkie-talkie) and 511 respectively.
     (2) BC-309: similar attachment for SCR-508, 608, and 619.
     (3) MC-619: similar attachment for the handie-talkie SCR-536.
  2. Ground radio range beacons for aircraft guidance
   a. SCR-277: a military version of the commercial A-N quadrant type; fixed LF, 200–400 kc.
   b. SCR-629: an E-T range, omnidirectional with rotating antenna operating in VHF on 100–156 mc.
   c. AN/MRN-2 (formerly SCR-601) and AN/CRN-5: mobile and air transportable respectively, similar to SCR-277 but operating in VHF on 100–156 mc.

   3. Air-sea-rescue beacon and receiver
       a. SCR-578: an emergency transmitter, hand powered, for use by avi-
       ators downed at sea, nicknamed "Gibson Girl"; a modification became
       AN/CRT-3.
       b. AN/ARR-6: an airborne receiver, preset to the frequency of the
       "Gibson Girl" and automatically giving an alarm upon receipt of the
       emergency beacon signal.
   4. Buoy beacons, locator and sonic, parachuted into the sea
       a. AN/CRN-1: a marker beacon, radiating a signal over a 50-mile
       range, received by aircraft radio compasses, SCR-263 or 269.
       b. AN/CRT-1: sonic buoy, picking up submerged submarine sounds
       and transmitting them over a 10-mile range, received by a special air-
       borne receiver AN/ARR-3.
   5. Paratroop beacon
       AN/CRN-4: a portable marker radio beacon supplementing Rebecca-
       Eureka radar types, sending a continuous-wave coded signal every 30
       seconds for two hours over a 30-mile range.
C. Navigational direction finders
   1. SCR-225 and 551: HF sets with H-Adcock antennas; used by RI units
   as well as by AAF to assist plane navigation.
   2. SCR-291: a very large set developed for AAF from the RI set SCR-502
   (see under Intelligence DF's) having fixed U-Adcock monopole antennas.
   3. SCR-292: a smaller set employing rotating vertical-loop antennas.
   4. AN/CRD-2: a transportable set, superior to, and much smaller than,
   SCR-551 and 291.
D. Instrument approach and landing systems: these comprised various
ground and airborne components of SCS-51, formerly SCR-241 and 251 (all
the ground components included SCR-610 for two-way communication with
the airfield control tower)
   1. Marker beacons and receivers (75 mc)
       a. BC-302 and 902: small beacons employed with SCR-241.
       b. AN/MRN-3: a jeep-mounted beacon.
       c. RC-20, 39, 43, and 193: airborne receivers to detect the vertical
       beams from marker beacons up to 16,000 feet; visual indication only
       (flashing light on instrument panel as the plane passed over fan marker,
       CAA beacon, etc.).
       d. AN/ARN-12: an improved lightweight receiver, yielding both visual
       and aural indication.
   2. Localizer and glide-path sets
       a. Localizer VHF transmitter and receiver (110 mc)
           (1) AN/MRN-1: mobile ground transmitter (formerly SCR-591) to
           guide plane to runway. Air-transportable versions were AN/CRN-7
           and 10.
           (2) RC-103: airborne receiver actuating a dial which showed the
           alignment of approaching airplane in relation to the runway.

   b. Glide-path UHF transmitter and receiver (330 mc)
      (1) AN/CRN-2: mobile ground transmitter located along airstrip (formerly SCR-592).
      (2) AN/ARN-5: airborne receiver (formerly SCR-570).
(NOTE: The foregoing development culminated in SCS-51, an automatic instrument-approach radio system, which involved an airborne localizer, ground glide-path receivers, and a robot pilot.)

II. *Radar*

   A. Altimeters (airborne absolute altimeters or terrain clearance indicators)
      1. RC-24: a lightweight continuous-wave beat-reflection radar type (FM), effective only up to 400 feet; renamed AN/ARN-1. An improved version known as AN/APN-1 gave readings up to 4,000 feet.
      2. SCR-518 and 718: pulse-type radar altimeters effective up to about 40,000 feet.
   B. Beacons
      1. Ground
         a. Locators developed for determining ground range and azimuth, used to locate a forward observer for fire control purposes.
            SCR-599: a portable 35-pound short-range set (interrogator and responsor components were later designated AN/PPN-10 and 11 respectively).
         b. Ground "navigation" system, employing fixed base stations which emitted pulsed radiations as in the loran system, providing accurate location for moving tactical units or for mapping purposes: SCR-560.
      2. Ground-to-air
         a. Portable beacons, having a 50-mile line-of-sight range, triggered or interrogated by airborne radars such as AI, ASV, BTO, or IFF types
            (1) AN/UPN-1 and 2: portable S-band sets, operating on 3,000 mc, weighing respectively 115 and 80 pounds.
            (2) AN/UPN-3, 4, and 11: X-band sets, 10,000 mc.
         b. Transportable beacons having a 100-mile line-of-sight range
            (1) SCR-621 and 640: heavy 350-pound sets responding to long wave radars SCR-521 ASV and 540 AI on 170–196 mc.
            (2) SCR-620: responding to microwave AI radar SCR-520 and to other 10-cm S-band sets on 3,000 mc; became AN/CPN-3, a bulky half-ton ground set. A similar set was AN/CPN-1.
            (3) AN/CPN-8: a much smaller S-band beacon.
            (4) AN/CPN-6: an X-band beacon on 10,000 mc responding to airborne X-band radars.
      3. Air-sea-rescue beacon
         AN/CPT-2: designed to transmit a continuous-pulse signal for 12 to 20 hours automatically. Called "Walter," it was of lighter weight than the "Gibson Girl" radio (SCR-578) and could be carried in fighter planes.

4. Paratroop beacons ("Rebecca-Eureka"): portable, 25–100-mile-range sets

    a. AN/APN-2 (developed from SCR-729), 10, and 12: airborne interrogators.

    b. AN/PPN-1 and AN/TPN-1, 2, and 3: ground responders.

C. Loran and shoran

  1. Loran: long-range navigation (LRN)

    a. AN/APN-4 and 9: airborne receivers, originally SCR-622. A variant, SCR-722, derived from a NDRC development.

    b. AN/CPN-11 and 12: (formerly SCR-623) air-transportable slave and master beacon sets.

  2. Shoran: short-range precision navigation, aid in blind bombing (formerly SCR-297)

    a. AN/APN-3: airborne interrogator.

    b. AN/CPN-2: ground transponder station.

D. Blind approach systems

  1. AN/CPN-7: blind approach beacon system.

  2. AN/MPN-1: ground-controlled approach system, involving two mobile short-range microwave radars, in whose scopes the operators watched an approaching aircraft as they coached it to the landing strip, talking over radio telephones SCR-522 or 274. A small air transportable version of GCA was undertaken as AN/CPN-4.

Intelligence, Security, and Countermeasures

I. *Radio intelligence (RI) equipment*

A. Radio monitoring sets

  1. SCR-243 and 244: low-, middle-, and high-frequency intercept receivers—100 kc to 20 mc.

  2. SCR-607, 612, 613, 614, and 616: receivers for frequencies ranging from 15 kc to 600 mc and for continuous-wave, AM and FM types of signals.

B. Direction-finders, DF's: for locating radio transmitters

  1. Short- and medium-range

    a. SCR-206 and 503: small loop-antenna sets for MF and HF (up to 18 mc).

    b. SCR-504: hand-carried, disguised as a suitcase.

    c. SCR-555 and 556: heavy sets with rotatable H-Adcock antennas and extending from HF into VHF (18–145 mc).

    d. SCR-700: set extending into UHF range on 140 to 600 mc; intended for use with RI intercept receiver SCR-616.

    e. AN/TRD-2: an improved version of SCR-503 (incorporating an oscilloscope indicator for instantaneous indication of signal direction).

  2. Long-range, semifixed, and transportable

    a. SCR-255 and 551: HF sets having large rotatable H-Adcock

antennas (dipoles 12 feet long) for taking bearings on sky waves. Also used by AAF for navigational purposes.

b. SCR-501 and 502: very large HF sets having fixed monopole, U-Adcock antennas, and instantaneous oscilloscope indicators. An air-transportable version of 502 was AN/CRD-2.

c. AN/CRD-3: a very large DF, like SCR-502, but designed for LF and MF reception and extremely sensitive to sky waves originating at very great distances.

C. Combined intercept and DF assemblies

1. SCR-558: consisting of DF's SCR-206 and SCR-504, intercept receiver SCR-612, and communication radio SCR-284, the whole assembled in one vehicle.

2. AN/VRD-1: a larger assembly, embracing DF SCR-503, intercept receivers SCR-612 and 613, and radio beacon RC-163, the whole mounted in two vehicles, each carrying an SCR-510 for communication with the other.

3. AN/GRA-2: a loop-antenna DF attachment for any HF or VHF intercept receiver in the range of 18 to 65 mc. A similar attachment was AS-4( )/GR to provide DF for any receiver in the range of 1.5 to 18 mc.

II. *Security equipment, for rendering communications unintelligible, scrambling them at the place of transmission and unscrambling them at the place of reception*

1. Cryptographic machines, enciphering and deciphering message texts mechanically

a. M-209: the Haglin converter, small, portable, hand-operated, converting letter by letter into or from a cipher equivalent, and slow.

b. M-134: automatic cipher machine.

2. RC-62: portable speech scrambler for voice communications by radio or wire.

III. *Countermeasures equipment*

A. Radio

1. Search receivers, airborne equivalents of ground RI sets

a. AN/ARR-5 and 7: receivers covering from .55 to 143 mc. They could be used with radar scope indicators or with panoramic and photographic adapters.

b. AN/ARQ-4 and 5: panoramic receivers for wide and narrow ranges respectively, used in jamming to counter the enemy's efforts to shift his signal from one frequency to another.

2. Jammers, both ground and airborne, often used with search receivers

a. AN/MRQ-1 and 2: powerful mobile ground jammers for LF, MF, and HF bands, modified respectively from SCR-698 and 399.

b. AN/MRT-1: a very powerful 15-kw jammer developed for use against German ground-air communications in the 37–42 mc band, called "Cigar."

c. AN/CRT-2 and PRT-1: small expendable jammers to be placed near enemy radios. CRT-2 was an airborne parachute set. PRT-1 was a portable hand-planted jammer, called "Chick."

d. AN/ARQ-1 ("Sandy"), 7 ("Spotkie"), 8, and 9 (formerly SCR-596) were airborne HF and VHF spot jammers.

e. AN/ARQ-11: a receiver to detect the frequencies of guided missiles and a transmitter to jam them.

f. AN/ART-3, 5 through 11, and 14: a series of high-power barrage jammers called "Jackal," each set able to jam its entire frequency range continuously and unattended; used against enemy VHF and tank communications.

  3. Associated equipment

a. AM-33( )/ART: a wide-band amplifier.

b. AN/ARA-3: a device which converted liaison set SCR-287 into a spot jammer.

c. AN/TRQ-1: a transportable radio-control intercept station developed for monitoring and controlling radio-jamming sets.

B. Radar

  1. Search receivers

a. SCR-587: earliest radar search receiver, 38–3,300 mc.

b. AN/APR-2: autosearch receiver, which could automatically detect and record radar signals.

c. AN/APR-4, 5, 5A, 6, and 7: improved search receivers covering frequencies up to 6,000 mc.

  2. Jammers

a. AN/TPT-1 and 2: ground radar jammers for frequencies from 70 mc to 1,450.

b. AN/APT-1 and 2: low-power radar jammers ("Dina" and "Carpet" respectively) for use in aircraft, able to jam frequencies between 70 mc and 710 mc.

c. AN/APT-3 ("Mandrel") and 5: respectively a spot jammer, 85–135 mc, and a semibarrage jammer, 350–1,400 mc.

d. AN/APT-4, 6, and 8: powerful magnetron jammers, 15–1,100 mc.

e. AN/APQ-2 ("Rug") and 9 ("Carpet III"): powerful barrage jammers.

  3. Deception devices

a. AN/APQ-8 and 15: "Spoofer" sets which could throw back a strong echo, making one aircraft appear to be many.

b. "Chaff" or "Window" aluminum foil strips which, when dropped in quantity, threw back multiple reflections, blinding ground radar scopes. Chaff was also developed for large 60 and 81-mm. mortar shells as reflector RR-7/U, 10/U, 26 and 27 U.

  4. Associated radar countermeasures equipment

a. Panoramic or oscilloscopic devices used with search receivers to enable operators to study and photograph the characteristics of enemy radar signals

(1) AN/APA-6 and 11: panoramic adapters or scopes.

(2) AN/APA-7: movie-camera photo set which provided a permanent record of oscilloscope presentation.

b. Radar DF's (AN/APA-17 and 24) for attachment to radar search receivers, giving instant cathode-ray indication of the direction of radar-beam source.

c. Automatic tape recorder AN/APA-23 developed to make a record of the frequency and reception time of signals picked up by radar search receivers AN/APR-4, 5, and 7.

d. Automatic tuning adapter (AN/APA-27) designed to detect enemy radar beams and to spot jam them without human assistance.

e. Alarm equipment AN/APR-3: warning to ferret-plane crewmen whenever their craft came dangerously within enemy GCI, AI, and GL radar waves. Dubbed "Boozer."

f. Monitor set AN/TPQ-1: assembly of broad-band receivers, 40–4,000 mc, both to analyze enemy radar waves and to direct friendly jammers.

Training, Testing, and Maintenance and Repair

I. *Training equipment*

A. Target control: radio transmitters and receivers for remote control of gun targets

1. Water-target control

SCR-586: receiver and transmitter, the receiver being carried in the target boat to control it on signals from the distant transmitter.

2. Land-target control

a. AN/VRW-1: vehicular receiver controlling motion of target car.

b. AN/TRW-1: transmitter by which a distant operator controlled the receiver and the vehicle in which it was mounted.

3. Air-target control

a. RC-57, 64, and AN/ARW-26: airborne receivers.

b. RC-56 and 65: ground transmitters.

c. AN/ARW-8: airborne transmitter.

B. Firing error indicators

1. For antiaircraft artillery training

a. PH-32: shellburst spotter set including theodolites for observation of shellbursts and a camera to provide a motion-picture record.

b. AN/TVQ-1: shellburst spotter set similar to PH-32.

c. AN/ART-4 and GRR-1: airborne transmitter and ground receiver, the transmitter being carried in a target sleeve aloft, in order to note the projectile's shock waves and radio the extent of error to the receiver on the ground.

2. For aerial gunnery training

AN/ART-16 and ARR-10: airborne transmitter and airborne receiver.

C. Classroom training sets

1. Trainers in the operation of ground and airborne radars

a. BC-968 and BC-1070: trainers for SCR-268, 270, and 271. BC-1070 modified for PPI became AN/UPS-T2.

b. RC-110, 225, and 253: AI trainers for SCR-540, 520, and 720.

c. RC-111, 227, and AN/APS-T1, 1A, and 2: ASV trainers for SCR-517, 717, and 521.

d. AN/APQ-T1: aircraft gun-laying trainer.

2. Trainers in navigational aids

a. RC-242 and 252: for instruction in loran usage.

b. AN/APN-3 T1: for instruction in shoran usage.

3. Countermeasure trainers

a. AN/TPQ-T1 and 2: radar-jamming trainers to teach oscilloscope men to use their radars successfully despite jamming effects.

b. AN/URA-T1: radio-jamming trainer to teach radiomen to copy messages amid jamming effects.

4. Code training sets

a. EE-81, 94, 95, and 96: classroom practice code and tape sets.

b. AN/GGQ-1 and GSC-T1: visual and audible code practice sets.

II. *Testing equipment*

(NOTE: for practically every new radio and radar set and for every new wire system it distributed, the Signal Corps had to provide suitable equipment for testing and maintenance. The items enumerated in categories II and III are selected from huge numbers of test, maintenance, and tool repair sets.)

A. Radio and radar

1. Testing sets for general and specific uses

a. I-56: a universal radio test set.

b. AN/GPM-1 and MPM-1: basic radar test sets.

c. IE-9 and 26: large sets for use by Signal Corps repair and service units.

d. IE-17 and 75: for testing handie-talkie SCR-536.

e. IE-30 and 57: for testing ASV and AI radars, such as SCR-517 and 520.

f. RC-68: for testing the radar SCR-268.

g. TS-20/APN-4: for testing airborne loran receiver.

h. AN/APM-28 and 29: for testing radars in L-band, 50 cm.

i. AN/APM-10, 33, 34, and 37: for testing S-band radars, 10 cm.

j. AN/APM-21, 22, 41, and 42: for testing K-band radars, 1 cm.

2. Frequency meters: for measuring and correcting the frequencies of radio and radar transmitters

a. SCR-211 and BC-221: for LF, MF, and HF to 20 mc.

b. TS-174/U: for VHF extending to 280 mc.

    c. TS-175/U: for VHF and UHF, from 85 to 1,000 mc.

    d. TS-213/U: for UHF and SHF, from 300 to 5,000 mc.

  3. Phantom antennas, used in testing (or in practice sending) to suppress actual radiation and so keep the set "off the air"

    a. A-55, 56, 57, and 58: for SCR-177, 183, 188, and 193.

    b. A-31, 32, 33, 34, and 62: for vehicular radios in the "500" series.

B. Wire

  1. General test sets

    a. IE-10, 29, 53: for testing telegraph and telephone equipment, carrier terminals, repeaters, etc.

    b. TS-2/TG: teletypewriter test set.

  2. Specific test equipment

    a. Telephone and telegraph test boards, to locate and clear wire circuit troubles

      (1) BD-101: 120-circuit board for testing in a central office.

      (2) BD-103: 20-circuit board for roadside testing in the field.

    b. Fault locator, detecting short-circuits along wire lines TS-26 and 27/TSM: volt-ohm meters.

III. *Maintenance and repair equipment*

A. Radio and radar

  1. Maintenance and tool sets

    a. ME-9, 13, 34, and 35: for general radio maintenance.

    b. ME-104, 105, 108, etc.: maintenance and tool sets for specific radars, SCR-584, 545, 268, etc.

    c. ME-53 and 67: for maintenance of walkie-talkie SCR-300.

    d. TE-41, 46, 113, 114: tool sets for radio repair.

  2. Suppression of radio noise (vehicular interference) and static

    a. AN/URM-3: radio-interference meter.

    b. AN/ASA-1 and 3: discharge assemblies to drain static electricity from a plane in flight.

  3. Tropicalization: protecting electrical equipment against moisture and fungus

    a. MK-2 and 1/GSM: kits containing infrared lamps, water-repellent and fungus-proofing varnishes, spray guns, etc.

    b. 68-Q-4 and 5: kits developed to tropicalize radar SCR-268.

  4. Mobile repair stations: mounted in trucks and trailers, for third echelon maintenance

    a. AN/MRM-1: for radio maintenance only.

    b. AN/MSN-1: for both radio and wire.

B. Wire

  1. Construction and maintenance sets

    a. ME-4, 11, and 30: for telephone centrals TC-1, 4, 10, and 12, of which these sets were usually component parts.

b. ME-22: for maintenance of field telephone set EE-8.

c. ME-10: for general maintenance and repair of telephone and tele-graph equipment.

d. ME-7, 18, and 37: for teletypewriter maintenance.

e. TE-16: cable-splicing set.

f. ME-44, 47, 49, 75, 111, 112: tool sets for repair of wire equipment both telephone and telegraph.

g. TE-50: tool set for repair of teletypewriter equipment.

h. TE-27 and 58: for pole line construction.

2. Mobile repair stations

a. AN/MTM-1: mounted in a truck and trailer to provide fourth echelon maintenance.

b. AN/MTM-2 and 3: similar mobile sets designed for third echelon maintenance.

Photography

I. *Cameras*

A. Still pictures

1. General use

a. PH-120, 150, 195, and 205: portrait and view cameras taking large pictures, 8 by 10 inches.

b. PH-47 and 324: taking average pictures, four by five inches, and small 33-mm. pictures respectively.

2. Special use

a. PH-518 ( )/PF: camera especially developed for use in combat areas, stoutly constructed and tropicalized, taking 70-mm. film (pictures 2½ by 2¾ inches).

b. AN/TFQ-6: a photoflash camera developed for recording surgical operations.

B. Moving pictures

1. PH-270 and 274: heavy newsreel-type 35-mm. cameras.

2. PH-330: standard movie camera in World War II, 35-mm.

3. PH-430 and 431: small, 16-mm. movie cameras.

II. *Projectors*

A. PH-131 and 398: 16-mm. sound projectors.

B. PH-331 and 405: 35-mm. sound projectors.

C. PH-526/UF: projector for large audiences (up to 2,000).

D. AN/TFQ-4: projector for small audiences (up to 600); rugged, for use under any conditions from arctic to tropical.

E. PH-420-A: small portable projector screen for use in daylight.

F. PH-222: small projector of film strip and slides.

III. *Other photographic equipment*

   A. Identification sets

      1. PH-385: for field use, including a 35-mm. camera, fingerprint set, lamps, etc.

      2. PH-261 and AN/TFQ-1: field sets including printing and enlarging equipment.

   B. V-mail equipment

      1. PH-512: rapid developer, machine-driven, for developing and drying 100-foot rolls of 16-mm. film or 50-foot rolls of 35-mm. film.

      2. PH-542: enlarger for 16 or 35-mm. film.

   C. Miscellaneous equipment

      1. PH-524/PF: low tripod, permitting the camera man to "shoot" while lying prone.

      2. PH-515/MF: photographic equipment pack for jeep transport, including a tripod for operating a movie camera on the jeep.

      3. PH-253, 298, 406, 413: sets for processing and developing films of various sizes and types.

      4. PH-13, 67, 129, 395: printers.

      5. PH-275, 285, 511: enlargers.

      6. PH-261, 383, 390, and 392: darkroom sets, housed in small tents.

      7. S-11/GF and AN/TFQ-7: darkrooms housed in HO-27, the former a mobile shelter, the latter a transportable laboratory completely equipped for developing still and movie negatives in the field.

Meteorology

I. *Instruments of measurement*

   A. Barometers and barographs

      1. ML-2 and 330/FM: mercury barometers.

      2. ML-9, 102, 331, 332, and 333/TM: aneroid barometers.

      3. ML-3: barograph with clock mechanism and ink-recording equipment.

   B. Thermometers and thermographs

      1. ML-4, 5, and 7: mercury and alcohol thermometers.

      2. ML-352/UM: thallium amalgam for use at temperatures below the minimum of mercury thermometers.

      3. ML-77 and 277: thermographs with ink recorder and clock-regulated mechanism.

   C. Psychrometers: for measuring humidity

      1. ML-24 and 224: relative humidity gauges, rotated by hand.

      2. ML-313/AM: automatic, for upper-air readings.

      3. ML-341/GM: for use in sub-zero temperatures.

   D. Anemometers

1. ML-62 and 80: the former a small hand-carried set; the latter a standard wind speedometer with three cup-shaped wind scoops on a vertical axle.

2. ML-107: portable set, including a wire transmitter, which noted wind direction and velocity as far away as 1,000 feet.

3. AN/GMQ-1: similar to ML-107 but designed to operate with fixed ground or mobile weather stations.

E. Helionephoscope and hygrometer

1. ML-385( )/UM: helionephoscope, an illumination meter to measure intensity of sunlight.

2. ML-342( )/GM: hygrometer to determine dew point at low temperatures.

F. Cloud height indicators

1. ML-121 and 318/TMQ-2: ceiling-light projectors, used only at night with clinometer ML-119.

2. AN/GMQ-2: projector, detector, and recorder; capable of continuous operation unattended.

3. AN/AMQ-4: optical device for use from a moving airplane.

G. Theodolites and plotting equipment: telescopes, plotting boards, etc., for visually tracking ascending pilot balloons to determine wind direction and velocity

1. ML-47 and 247: telescopes mounted on tripods.

2. ML-120 and 122: lightweight wood and plastic plotting boards.

II. *Data-gathering instruments*

A. Radiosonde equipment

1. Airborne radiosondes, transmitters which were carried aloft by balloons or planes

a. ML-141: standard audio-modulated transmitter and associated weather instruments; became AN/AMQ-1.

b. AN/AMT-1, 2, 3, and 4: balloon and parachute sets.

2. Ground receivers and DF's, the function of the latter being to track the emissions of the drifting radiosonde so as to determine wind direction and velocity at all levels through which the transmitter may pass

a. SCR-658: both a DF and a receiver of the radiosonde transmissions; developed from SCR-258, originally designed as a radiosonde DF only.

b. AN/CRD-1: lightweight DF and receiver on UHF developed for postwar radiosondes.

3. Ground receivers and recorders

a. AN/TMR-1 (AN/TMQ-5) and 2: transportable receivers and recorders used in conjunction with SCR-658.

b. AN/FMQ-1: device automatically recording radiosonde data on a printed graph.

B. Wire sonde equipment

AN/UMQ-4: instruments held aloft by a captive balloon and transmitting data to ground over wires running along the balloon cable.

C. Aerographs: automatic weather recorders

1. ML-175 and 195: attached to exterior of airplane and transmitting data to recording equipment inside.

2. AN/AMQ-2 and 3: comparable instruments, but attached to interior of plane and automatically recording pressure, temperature, and relative humidity for four hours to elevations of 23,000 feet.

D. Spherics equipment

AN/GRD-1: semifixed direction finder designed to take bearings on static, or lightning flashes, at distances up to 1,500 miles.

E. Ionospheric equipment

AN/CPQ-7: set developed to measure, by means of radar reflections, the height of the ionosphere and obtain data valuable to HF (sky-wave) radio transmission.

F. Radar trackers: radar sets to track special radar reflectors which were carried either by balloons or by parachutes released from rockets

1. SCR-525: massive radar with large triple antenna array, the whole weighing 15,000 pounds.

2. SCR-825: much lighter set, air transportable.

III. *Weather station sets*

A. Mobile, attended stations

1. SCM-1: mounted on a truck and trailer; designed for the AAF.

2. SCM-9 and 10: respectively, radiosonde and ballistic wind stations, developed for Field Artillery. The sets were subsequently combined and became AN/TMQ-4.

3. SCM-13: radiosonde and wind station developed for Coast Artillery.

4. AN/TMQ-1: air-transportable station with complete meteorological station equipment; for the AAF. AN/TMQ-4 was a meteorological station for the Field Artillery.

B. Automatic unattended stations, including telemetering devices

1. SCM-17: a station developed to transmit, by radio pressure, temperature and relative humidity data up to 300 miles over a month; controlled by clock mechanism and powered by batteries.

2. SCM-18: parachute set designed to begin operation upon reaching ground and to transmit its data up to 100 miles for a week.

3. SCM-19: large semipermanent set powered by a gasoline engine and able to collect pressure, temperature, humidity, wind, rainfall, and sunlight data and to transmit it over distances up to 500 miles for a three-month period.

IV. *Other meteorological equipment*

A. Balloons

1. Pilot balloons: small, for revealing winds aloft

   a. ML-50, 51, 64, 155, 156, 157, 158: of various colors and composition;
all for observing low-level wind conditions.
   b. ML-159, 160, and 161: larger, 100-gram rapid ascent balloons for
observation (by theodolites) of high-level winds.
   2. Sounding balloons: large, for carrying radiosondes to the stratosphere
   a. ML-131: 350-gram balloon (14 feet in diameter when fully inflated).
   b. ML-162: a still larger balloon, 700 grams.
B. Hydrogen generators
   1. ML-165 and 185: heavy generators for field use.
   2. ML-303, 304A, and 305A/TM: one- or two-pound can of calcium
hydride, each capable of inflating a small balloon.
   3. AN/TMQ-3: portable generator for inflating 350-gram balloons.

Accessories

I. *Power equipment*
   A. Electric generators, powered by
      1. Gasoline
         a. SCR-169: a 200-pound unit providing direct current (d-c) to
recharge storage batteries.
         b. PE-49 and 210: lightweight one-cylinder engined d-c generators for
powering SCR-177 and 188 and for charging batteries.
         c. PE-77: a portable 70-pound one-cylinder unit for field teletypewriter
set EE-97.
         d. PE-201: a 300-pound one-cylinder unit which powered telephone
and telegraph carrier equipment.
         e. PE-75 and 95: respectively a 300-pound one-cylinder unit and a
1,500-pound four-cylinder unit both widely used with many Signal
Corps sets to supply standard 120-volt 60-cycle alternating current.
         f. PE-74, 84, and 85: heavy (2½-tons) four-cyclinder-engined generators
used with radars such as SCR-268, 270, and 271.
         g. PU-6/TPS-1: a compact 130-pound unit used with LW radars such
as AN/TPS-1 and 3.
         (NOTE: by 1945 the Signal Corps had many other gasoline engine gen-
erators in the PU category under development to replace the PE types
which served throughout the war.)
      2. Wind
         AN/CSQ-1: an air-transportable generator with a wind-driven propel-
ler mounted atop a 60-foot tower designed to charge storage batteries,
which in turn powered automatic weather stations developed for the
AAF.
      3. Hand: the electric generator, laboriously hand-cranked during the
operation of the radio, yielded sufficient current for small portable sets
         a. GN-35: used with SCR-131, 161, and 171.

b. GN-45 and 58: used respectively with SCR-284 and 694.

4. Heat: thermoelectric power units PP-19, 107, 131–133, were experimental generators of low power (20 watts or less) which converted heat (derived from burning gasoline) to electric current. These generators were not adopted in the field because of the weight of fuel which they required and because of the smoke they produced.

B. Electric power converters

1. Dynamotors and vibrators: devices which draw direct current from storage batteries of low voltages (usually vehicular) and convert it to the various high voltages required by the multiple needs of radio transmitter and receiver components

   a. Dynamotors

      (1) DM-34 and 35: used to power vehicular radios SCR-508 and 608 from 12-volt storage batteries. DM-36 and 37 were similar but operated from 24-volt vehicular batteries.

      (2) PE-55: drawing current from a 12-volt vehicular battery to operate the SCR-245.

      (3) PE-194: used to convert energy from an airplane battery to operate the command VHF radio SCR-522.

   b. Vibrators

      (1) PE-157, which provided power for the SCR-511 when used in vehicles, drawing energy from the storage battery.

      (2) PE-212: power pack developed for use with the walkie-talkie SCR-300. It included a small storage battery and a vibrator to convert the battery energy to the voltage requirements of the radio set.

2. Rectifiers: devices which convert standard commercial alternating current to direct current as required

   a. RA-43 and 120: used to power the teletypewriter central TC-3 and portable radios SCR-510 and 610, drawing on standard power lines, when available.

   b. RA-36 and 87: used to recharge storage batteries.

C. Batteries

1. Dry (primary) batteries

   a. Single and multiple units or cells containing an activating paste, usually sal-ammoniac, and weighing from a few ounces to several pounds

      (1) BA-23, 30, 65: 1½-volt single cells.

      (2) BA-1, 205/U, 209/U: 3-volt cells.

      (3) BA-9, 216/U: 4½-volt cells.

      (4) BA-203/U and 207/U: 6 and 9-volt cells respectively.

      (5) BA-2, 8, 219/U: 22½-volt cells.

      (6) BA-56, 59: 45-volt cells.

      (7) BA-27, 39, 40: multiple-unit batteries consisting of a number of cells and having an increased power output.

(8) BA-102, 127, 130, 140: similar to BA-2, 27, 30, 39, and 40 but especially designed to operate efficiently in cold climates.
  b. Special batteries activated by mercury compounds or by sea water
(1) BA-38, 49, 70, and 80: mercury dry-cell batteries used late in the war in SCR-300, 511, 536, and 694.
(2) BA-229( )/CRN: battery intended to be immersed in sea water, which activated its silver-chloride and magnesium electrodes; developed for use with radio buoy beacon AN/CRN-1.
  2. Wet (storage or secondary) batteries
    a. BB-54, 205/U: 2-volt batteries.
    b. BB-29 and 213/U: 4-volt batteries.
    c. BB-49, 51, 55: 6-volt batteries, similar to automobile 6-volt storage batteries except for the BB-51 which weighed only a few ounces.
    d. BB-46, 50, 201/U: heavy 12- and 14-volt batteries (BB-46 weighed 120 pounds).
    e. BB-52: a 36-volt battery, tiny like the 6-volt BB-51 and the 2-volt BB-54, each of which weighed only about one third of a pound, used to power radiosondes when borne aloft by meteorological balloons.
 II. *Radio antennas and antenna masts*
  (NOTE: in general, antennas were furnished as integral parts of radio sets, such as radio relay antenna AS-19/TRC-1, the 3-element horizontal dipole and 40-foot tube steel mast used with AN/TRC-1, 3, and 4.)
  A. AN-29: fishpole antenna used with the short-range radios SCR-609 and 610.
  B. AN-130 and 131: short and long whip antennas, for walkie-talkie SCR-300.
  C. RC-63: a lightweight 32-foot mast (of fir wood in four sections) and wire providing a vertical half-rhombic (inverted V) antenna for the short-range radios SCR-194, 195, and 609.
  D. RC-291 and 296: special antennas designed to extend the range of the walkie-talkie SCR-300 by elevating its radiations above jungle tree tops. RC-291 consisted of a vertical whip from whose base radiated four horizontal whips, the whole elevated upon a pole or tree top. RC-296 was a single vertical whip mounted upon a lightweight sectional mast 30 feet high.
  E. RC-292: somewhat similar to RC-291 but accompanied by 30-foot mast and designed to extend the short ranges of SCR-608 and 628.
  F. AN/GRA-4: equipment which permitted the construction of several types of antennas for use with short and medium range sets such as SCR-177, 193, 245, and 284.
  G. MS-49 through 56: lightweight tubular steel sections comprising a 25-foot mast for SCR-178, 179, 203, and 284. Some of these sections were also commonly used to form a 15-foot vehicular whip antenna (fishpole), set into mast bases MP-37 or 57. Similar sections MS-116, 117, and 118 were used with mast bases MP-48, and AB-15/GR to provide six- and nine-foot whips.

H. MS-65 through 73: aluminum sections providing a 45-foot mast for the long-range mobile radio SCR-197.

I. MA-6 and 7: heavy sectional masts supporting the antennas of the Air Forces VHF ground radios SCR-573, 574, and 624. MA-6 was a 90-foot mast assembled from 11 three-inch steel tube sections. MA-7 was a 50-foot plywood mast.

III. *Headphones, microphones, handsets, and chest sets*

A. Headphones (or double receiver headsets)

1. P-11, 16, 18, 20: radio headphones.

2. HS-18, 23, 33, 38: headphones used with airplane radio and interphone sets, adapted for use within helmets and at high altitudes.

3. HS-30: very lightweight headset widely used by ground forces, having ear inserts patterned after the phones of hearing aids.

B. Microphones

1. T-17: standard radio microphone, held in the hand, switched on for talking.

2. T-30: throat microphone leaving the user's hands free.

3. T-45: lip microphone, attaching to the upper lip of the speaker and used when the surrounding noise was high, because it does not reproduce "ambient" sound as hand-held microphones usually did.

4. T-49: designed for use amid high ambient noise despite being hand-held.

5. T-34 and ANB-M-C-1: microphones designed for use in an aviator's oxygen mask in rarefied atmosphere.

C. Handsets: both radio and telephone, being the hand-held receiver-transmitter unit only

1. TS-9: standard telephone handset (carbon type), part of the battery-powered telephone set EE-8.

2. TS-10: special telephone handset (magnetic type) used with the sound-powered telephone set TP-3.

3. TS-13: standard radio handset incorporating a switch button which the operator pushed when he wished to transfer from reception to transmission.

4. TS-15: handset which combined parts of TS-9 and 13, and which was used with the walkie-talkie SCR-300.

D. Chest sets: transmitter attached to the speaker's chest, with press-to-talk switch mounted on the chest plate (receivers were of headphone type).

1. TD-1 and 2: radio chest sets replacing HS-19.

2. TD-3: chest set designed for use with a gas mask, employing a lip or throat microphone.

3. TD-4 and 5: improved chest sets for use by vehicular or aircraft radio operators.

IV. *Trucks, trailers, and shelters*

A. Trucks and trailers

1. For wire line construction work

    a. K-43: telephone maintenance and construction truck with a tripod derrick for raising and setting poles.

    b. K-44: truck mounting (1) an earth borer to drill holes and (2) a single derrick mast to set poles.

    c. K-36, 37, and 38: trailers, the first and second for hauling poles, cable reels, etc., the third for transporting cable splicing set TE-56.

2. For transporting and housing large radio and radar sets, communication centrals, meteorological station sets, etc.

    a. K-18 and 19: truck and trailer for transporting and housing the long-range SCR-197. Trailer K-19 was developed into a 4-wheel house trailer, K-35, for mobile telephone, telegraph, RI, DF, and message centrals.

    b. K-51: a panel truck used with the long-range radio SCR-299.

    c. K-53: a special van body mounted on a standard 2½-ton 6 x 6 truck.

    d. K-55: a semitrailer, lighter weight than K-35, used similarly to house central office sets. It was also used for meteorological (SCM) and fighter-control (SCS) components. It was usually hauled by trucks K-53 or K-60.

    e. K-56 and 60: trucks with van bodies to house and transport large radar sets.

    f. K-22, 28, 34, 52, 63, 67, and 72: trailers for radar sets and power units.

    g. K-75 and 78: large van trailers, the former for SCR-545; the latter for SCR-584.

B. Shelters

1. HO-17: a plywood shelter similar to a van truck body but an independent unit. It could be carried by any standard 2½-ton truck and could be removed and placed on the ground. Its plywood walls included built-in wire screening to provide electrical shielding. Its dimensions were approximately 11 by 6 by 5 feet. It was widely used for housing large sets, for wire and message centrals, intercept units, and so on.

2. HO-27: a transportable shelter similar to HO-17 but lacking the wire screen shielding.

Bibliographical Note

The sources for this and the other volumes of the Signal Corps history are as abundant, complex, and massive in most areas as they are critically sparse and incomplete in a few. Let the latter point be explained first. In the age of the telephone, consequential words often die when the receiver is hung up, and leave no trace. In the age of the airplane, face-to-face conferring has become possible for hundreds of matters which formerly would have required an exchange of letters. And in the age of the secret, many of the parts of the whole never find their way into the main stream of record files. For these reasons, the conscientious scholar may feel that he has insufficiently documented a spot here and there through his narrative. If so, later scholars, coming at a point when the material has either emerged from present enclosures or been demonstrated not to exist, will correct the deficiency. As other authors in this series have made clear, the quantity of records has been so vast that a historian wonders at his temerity and good sense in inquiring for more.

The Signal Corps record for the years ending with 1941, covered in this book, is to be found principally in the huge classified and unclassified Signal Corps files in the Departmental Records Branch of the Adjutant General's Office. The major auxiliary sources are the large collections of the Office of the Chief Signal Officer; the National Archives; the Signal Corps Engineering Laboratories; Wright-Patterson Air Force Base; the Alaska Communication System; the Signal Corps Pho-tographic Center and Army Pictorial Service; the Signal Corps School; the Philadelphia Procurement District and related agencies; the Signal Corps Historical Section and the Signal Corps Intelligence Agency; the Office of the Chief of Military History; Air Corps and Army Air Forces files in the Departmental Records Branch of the Adjutant General's Office; the Chief of Staff; the Assistant Chiefs of Staff; and the Services of Supply (Army Service Forces) and its predecessors. The lesser auxiliary sources of the book (although certainly not lesser in themselves) have included the Army Library; the libraries of the National War College and the Industrial College of the Armed Forces; the Library of Congress; the captured German and Japanese document collections; papers, diaries, and recollections of persons concerned; sources in the communications industry, especially the American Telephone and Telegraph Company, Radio Corporation of America, Link Radio, and the late Dr. Edwin H. Armstrong; the Federal Communications Commission; the Civil Aeronautics Administration; the U. S. Navy; the National Security Agency; and documents of the Senate and the House of Representatives.

These and still others have been put together with interviews and direct correspondence, the contemporary historian's boons. Later historians will wish to know which of the sources, particularly which of the file record groups, will best repay research. Probably in a relatively short course of time these records will shake down and consolidate from thousands of file drawers to hundreds, and for the most part will be permanently retired to the care of the National Archives. The most rewarding group of files if the subsequent historian first conquers the difficulty of reading them, will be the detailed records of Signal Corps research and development. Air Corps files are similarly full, and the top administrative files much fuller than those of the Signal Corps. Training and supply files will be improved by the winnowing process, for each of these functions produces blizzards of purely occasional papers whose use melts like the snowflake. As one might expect, files of the Signal Corps' photographic activities are at their best when they are photographic, and the National Archives' collections of still and motion pictures are already increased by them. The most secret files of the Signal Corps, those having to do with cryptography and signal intelligence, will remain inaccessible and, so far as they are concerned with matters at the vital center of security, ought not to be otherwise. Signal intelligence and signal operations reports and records which will have been freed from secrecy will, however, prove extremely interesting. The Alaska Communication System, a remarkable *imperium in imperio,* has a characteristically plain, independent, and useful file record of itself. Among non-Signal Corps collections, and in addition to those of the Army Air Corps, one may single out the files of the Office of the Under Secretary of War.

The principal source for the nineteenth century background of the Signal Corps, upon which the first chapter touches, is Records Group 111 of the National Archives. A small collection chiefly concerned with Brig. Gen. Albert J. Myer is lodged with the Signal Corps Traditions Committee at Fort Monmouth, N. J. The next best source is the Signal Corps Bulletin (which appeared first as the Information Bulletin) from 1920 to 1940. It is also a fundamental source to the two decades in which it was published. Complete files of the Bulletin are to be found in the Library of Congress, the Army Library, and the Office of the Chief Signal Officer. The most convenient quick reference is to the *Historical Sketch of the Signal Corps (1860–1941),* Eastern Signal Corps Schools Pamphlet 32 (Fort Monmouth, N. J., 1942). An earlier version, printed in 1935, was largely prepared by Maj. Donald B. Sanger, S.C. Several manuscript revisions and amplifications of it have also been prepared, among them the following: (1) H. R. Fraser, Early History of the Signal Corps, 1860–1863 (1944); (2) C. R. Hall, Chapter I: Origin and Early Development (1945); (3) several chapters of 1945 and 1947 manuscripts. These are included in the Signal Corps Historical Section File. The standard published work for the Civil War period, a rich secondary source, is J. Willard Brown's history, *The Signal Corps, U. S. A., in the War of the Rebellion* (Boston: U. S. Veteran Signal Corps Association, 1896). See also: (1) William R. Plum, *The Military Telegraph during the Civil War in the United States* (Chicago: Jansen, McClurg & Co., 1882); and (2) F. Stansbury Haydon, *Aeronautics in the Union and Confederate Armies* (Baltimore: The Johns Hopkins Press, 1941). For the Signal Corps in World War I, there is no better record than the fine book-length *Annual Report of the Chief Signal Officer, 1919;* the primary materials already noted as being in the Archives will fully support it. Another good book of the period is A. Lincoln Lavine's *Circuits of Victory* (New York: Doubleday, Page & Company, 1921). The Archives also has title lists to the extraordinary motion pictures and still pictures of that conflict. A disorganized but interesting typescript called the History of the Signal Corps, American Expeditionary Forces, reposes with the Signal Corps Historical Section File. Useful references on the historical origins and development of the arms and services generally are: (1) F. B. Heitman, *Historical Register and Dictionary of the United States Army* (Washington: Government Printing Office, 1903), and (2) W. A. Ganoe, *History of the United States Army* (rev. ed.; New York and London: D. Appleton-Century Company, 1942).

Some description is in order for the often cited file of the Signal Corps Historical Section. The process of developing the historical print of the Signal Corps led from the outset to the collection of reports, memoranda, charts, statistical studies, summaries, photographs, reviews, technical and field manuals, information releases, industrial surveys, special lists, directories, technical glossaries, and everything else of the sort which came to the hands of the Historical Section staff. Through many changes in the staff itself, this file remained relatively intact, then was repeatedly added to. For *The Emergency* and its companion volumes, the most valuable additions to the Signal Corps Historical Section File have been the monographs of the section's wartime staff. Inasmuch as none of these has ever been published, they will interest the future researcher often as much as the raw materials themselves. Among the best is a series on the Signal Corps development of radar, written by the late Harry M. Davis. Others are the training studies of Frederick Reinstein, those on the Army Command and Administrative Network by Pauline M. Oakes, and individual narra-

tives by Donald O. Wagner, Mary-louise Melia, Charles R. Novick, and M. E. Boswell on overseas communications, crystals, and the 17th Signal Service Company. A particularly useful place in the Signal Corps Historical Section File is occupied by a major preliminary work ordered by the Army Service Forces within each of its subordinate technical services. This is the History of Signal Corps Research and Development in World War II, which runs to thousands of pages of typescript and illustration, and which was written in the Engineering and Technical Division of the Office of the Chief Signal Officer, although Dixie R. Harris, Harry M. Davis, and others of the historical staff contributed widely to it. Many other manuscripts enhance the Signal Corps Historical Section File, but the researcher may be especially glad to have the following pointed out: George P. Bush and Martha E. Manning, History of Procurement Planning, 1920–1940; H. D. Hausman, Signal Corps Activity in Procurement Planning and Industrial Mobilization, 1920–1940; Arthur P. Watts, History of the Air Defense Command; Martin P. Claussen, The Development of Radio and Radar Equipment for Air Operations, 1939–1944; Ruth F. Sadler, History of the Electronics Training Group in the United Kingdom; and the Alaska Communication System and Signal Corps Engineering Laboratories histories.

The last-mentioned item naturally deals in part with radar, but the full story of radar, like the full story of any of the other Signal Corps interests, is to be found only in the primary sources, the thousands of file drawers which this note specifies as underlying almost every page of this work. An indication of more amenable sources should nevertheless have some convenience. The radar bibliography grows with every month; anything remarked upon here necessarily dates from the time when research on these three volumes was in progress. Among unpublished accounts, the monographs of Harry M. Davis, History of the Signal Corps Development of U. S. Army Radar Equipment, join the U. S. Navy History of Fire-Control Radar by Lt. Comdr. Marie Frauens and the History of Radar which Dr. Henry E. Guerlac prepared, originally planned as part of the Office of Scientific Research and Development published series "Science in World War II." Published accounts showing civilian, Army, Navy, U. S., British, and enemy participation in radar research began to appear in considerable numbers after security regulations permitted the information to be generally known. They include: (1) John M. Hightower, *The Story of Radar,* U. S. Senate Doc. 89, 78th Cong., 1st Sess. (Washington, 1943); (2) TM 11-466, Radar Electronic Fundamentals (1944); (3) Joint Board on Scientific Information Policy, *Radar: A Report on Science at War* (Washington, 1945 [French translation by Henri Pujade, Paris, 1947]); (4) British Information Series, *Radar: An Official History of the New Science* (New York, 1945); (5) John C. Rogers, *The Story of Radar* (New York, 1945); (6) RCA De-

partment of Information, *Radar, Wartime Miracle of Radio* (New York, 1945); (7) John F. Rider and G. C. Baxter Rowe, *Radar: What It Is* (New York: J. F. Rider Publisher, Inc., 1946); (8) Orrin E. Dunlap, Jr., *Radar: What Radar Is and How It Works* (New York: Harper & Brothers, 1946); (9) A. P. Rowe, *One Story of Radar* (Cambridge, England: Cambridge University Press, 1948). The published sources are so extensive, however, that even shortly after the war several hundred items were listed in Northwestern University Library's *Selected Bibliography on Radar* (Evanston, Ill., 1946). The Northwestern bibliography is the initial checklist for the reader who wishes to investigate the field of radar.

In sum, however eclectic and far-reaching the research for the Signal Corps history has been, the main source has been and always will be the primary materials in the major and minor record groups designated toward the beginning of this note. If the history of that humanly technical organization in a sometimes inhumanly technical age, the Signal Corps, is ever done again, it must be done again from all the files of correspondence, memoranda, and all other kinds of papers in these record groups. In the meantime, let this history indicate that they exist.

List of Abbreviations

AA	Antiaircraft
AAF	Army Air Forces
AAG	Air Adjutant General
AARS	Army Amateur Radio System
AC	Air Corps
a-c	Alternating current
ACAN	Army Command and Administrative Network
ACof S	Assistant Chief of Staff
ACS	Army Communications Service
Actg	Acting
ADC	Air Defense Command
Admin	Administration
AEF	American Expeditionary Forces (World War I)
AF	Air Forces or air force
AFCC	Air Force Combat Command
AG	Adjutant General
AGF	Army Ground Forces
AGO	Adjutant General's Office
AI	Airborne interception (radar)
AM	Amplitude modulation (radio)
AMP	Augmentation Mobilization Plan
APS	Army Pictorial Service
AR	Army regulations
ARL	Aircraft Radio Laboratory
ARRL	American Radio Relay League
ASF	Army Service Forces
ASV	Air-to-surface-vessel (radar)
ASW	Assistant Secretary of War
AT&T	American Telephone and Telegraph (Company)
AWS	Aircraft Warning Service
Bd	Board
Bn	Battalion
Br	Branch
BTO	Bombing-through-overcast (radar)
C&E	Communications (Coordination) and Equipment
CAC	Coast Artillery Corps
CCC	Civilian Conservation Corps

CE	Corps of Engineers
CG	Commanding general
CH	Chain Home
CHL	Chain Home Low
Cir(s)	Circular(s)
CMTC	Citizens' Military Training Corps
CofS	Chief of Staff
CO	Commanding officer
Co(s)	Company(s)
Com(s)	Communication(s)
Comd	Command
Comdt	Commandant
CSigO	Chief Signal Officer
Ctr	Center
CW	Continuous wave
DA	Department of the Army
d-c	Direct current
Dir	Director or directive
Div(s)	Division(s)
DF	Direction finding (radio) or direction finder
DRB	Departmental Records Branch (AGO)
E&T	Engineering and Technical
EFM	Expeditionary Force Message (World War I)
EHF	Extremely high frequency
Engr	Engineer or engineering
Equip	Equipment
ETG	Electronics Training Group
Exec	Executive
FA	Field Artillery (Corps)
FCC	Federal Communications Commission
FM	Field manual or frequency modulation (radio)
FRC	Federal Radio Commission. *See* FCC
FY	Fiscal year
G-1	Personnel section of the War Department General Staff, or of any other headquarters on the division level or higher
G-2	Military Intelligence Section
G-3	Operations and Training Section
G-4	Supply Section
GAO	General Accounting Office
GCA	Ground-controlled approach (radar)
GCI	Ground-controlled interception (radar)
GHQ	General Headquarters
GL	Gun laying (radar)
HF	High frequency

Hist	History or historical
HR	House of Representatives
I&E	Information and Education
ICC	Interstate Commerce Commission
IFF	Identification, friend or foe (radar)
IMP	Industrial Mobilization Plan
Incl(s)	Inclosure(s)
Ind(s)	Indorsement(s)
Inf	Infantry
Kc	Kilocycle (1,000 cycles per second)
LF	Low frequency
M Day	Mobilization Day
Mat	Material or matériel
Mc	Megacycles (1,000,000 cycles per second)
MEW	Microwave early warning (radar)
MF	Medium frequency
MID	Military Intelligence Division
Mil	Military
M.I.T.	Massachusetts Institute of Technology
MS(S)	Manuscript(s)
Msg(s)	Message(s)
MTP	Mobilization Training Program
NBC	National Broadcasting Company
NDRC	National Defense Research Committee
NRL	Naval Research Laboratory
OASW	Office of the Assistant Secretary of War
O/C	Officer in charge
OCMH	Office of the Chief of Military History
OCS	Office of the Chief of Staff
OCSigO	Office of the Chief Signal Officer
OPD	Operations Division (WDGS)
OPM	Office of Production Management
Opn(s)	Operation(s)
Orgn	Organization
OSRD	Office of Scientific Research and Development
OSW	Office of the Secretary of War
OUSW	Office of the Under Secretary of War
P&D	Procurement and Distribution
P&T	Plant and Traffic
Pers	Personnel
Photo	Photographic
PL	Public Law
Plng	Planning
PMP	Protective Mobilization Plan

PPI	Plan position indicator
Proc	Procurement
Prog	Progress
Proj	Project
PWA	Public Works Administration
PWP	Public Works Program
QMG	Quartermaster General
R&D	Research and Development
R&W	Routing and Work (sheet, in SigC office usage)
RCA	Radio Corporation of America
RDF	Radio direction finding *or* radio direction finder
Regtl	Regimental
Reorgn	Reorganization
RI	Radio Intelligence
RL	Radiation Laboratory
ROTC	Reserve Officers' Training Corps
RPF	Radio position finding *or* radio position finder
Rpt	Report
RR	Radio recognition
RTC	Replacement Training Center
SCEL	Signal Corps Engineering Laboratories
SCIA	Signal Corps Intelligence Agency
SCL	Signal Corps Laboratories
SCR	Set complete radio *or* Signal Corps radio
SCRTC	Signal Corps Replacement Training Center
Sec	Section
SHF	Superhigh frequency
Sig	Signal
SigC	Signal Corps
SIS	Signal Intelligence Service
Supp	Supplement
Suppl	Supplemental
Sv	Service
SW	Secretary of War
T/BA	Table of basic allowances
T/E	Table of equipment
T/O	Table of organization
T/O&E	Table of organization and equipment
TAG	The Adjutant General
Tech	Technical
Tg	Telegraph
TM	Technical manual
Tng	Training
Tp	Telephone

T.P.S.	Telegraphie par lc sol (earth telegraphy)
TWX	Teletypewriter exchange
UHF	Ultrahigh frequency
USW	Under Secretary of War
V-1	German buzz bomb
V-2	German long-range rocket
VHF	Very high frequency
VLF	Very low frequency
WAMCATS	Washington-Alaska Military Cable and Telegraph System
WAR	Call letters of the Washington control station of the War Department Radio Net (ACAN), formerly WVA.
WD	War Department
WDGS	War Department General Staff
WP&T	War Plans and Training
WPD	War Plans Division, WDGS
WTJ	Call letters of ACAN radio station, Fort Shafter, Hawaii
WVA	*See* WAR
WVL	Call letters of ACAN radio station, Quarry Heights, Canal Zone
WVY	Call letters of ACAN station, San Francisco

United States Army in World War II

The multivolume series, UNITED STATES ARMY IN WORLD WAR II, consists of a number of subseries which are tentatively planned as follows: The War Department, the Army Air Forces, The Army Ground Forces, The Army Service Forces, the Defense of the Western Hemisphere, The War in the Pacific, The European Theater of Operations, The War in the Mediterranean, The Middle East Theater, The China–Burma–India Theater, Civil Affairs, The Technical Services, Special Studies, and Pictorial Record.

The following volumes have been published or are in press:*

The War Department
>   *Chief of Staff: Prewar Plans and Preparations*
>   *Washington Command Post: The Operations Division*
>   *Strategic Planning for Coalition Warfare: 1941–1942*
>   *Global Logistics and Strategy: 1940–1943*

The Army Ground Forces
>   *The Organization of Ground Combat Troops*
>   *The Procurement and Training of Ground Combat Troops*

The Army Service Forces
>   *The Organization and Role of the Army Service Forces*

The War in the Pacific
>   *Okinawa: The Last Battle*
>   *Guadalcanal: The First Offensive*
>   *The Approach to the Philippines*
>   *The Fall of the Philippines*
>   *Leyte: Return to the Philippines*
>   *Seizure of the Gilberts and Marshalls*
>   *Victory in Papua*

The European Theater of Operations
>   *The Lorraine Campaign*
>   *Cross-Channel Attack*
>   *Logistical Support of the Armies, Volume I*
>   *The Supreme Command*

*The volumes on the Army Air Forces, published by the University of Chicago Press, are not included in this list.

The Middle East Theater
The Persian Corridor and Aid to Russia

The China–Burma–India Theater
Stilwell's Mission to China
Stilwell's Command Problems

The Technical Services
The Transportation Corps: Responsibilities, Organization, and Operations
The Transportation Corps: Movements, Training, and Supply
The Transportation Corps: Operations Overseas
The Quartermaster Corps: Organization, Supply, and Services, Volume I
The Quartermaster Corps: Organization, Supply, and Services, Volume II
The Quartermaster Corps: Operations in the War Against Japan
The Ordnance Department: Planning Munitions for War
The Signal Corps: The Emergency
The Signal Corps: The Test
The Medical Department: Hospitalization and Evacuation, Zone of Interior

Special Studies
Three Battles: Arnaville, Altuzzo, and Schmidt
The Women's Army Corps

Pictorial Record
The War Against Germany and Italy: Mediterranean and Adjacent Areas
The War Against Germany: Europe and Adjacent Areas
The War Against Japan

Index